Charlestown
Southern tip of Peninsula
CHARLES RIVER
Hudson's Pt
Charles
COPPS HILL
Lynn St.
St.
Love Lane
North St.
Princes
Foster Lane
St.
Fleet St.
Ship St.
Mill Pond
Pitts Lane
Leverett
Green Lane
Middle St.
Ward St.
Cross St.
Fish St.
Hancock's Wharf
Cambridge St.
Hawkins St.
Cold Lane
Union St.
Hilliers Lane
Southback St.
Hanover St.
Wings Lane
Ann St.
George St.
Temple St.
Valley
Beacon Hill
Mt. Whoredom
Treamount St.
Brattle St.
Long Wharf
Cornhill
Pudding Lane
Leverett's Lane
Beacon St.
Burying Ground
School St.
The Common
Common St.
Rawson's Lane
Water St.
Milk St.
Winter St.
West St.
Marlborough St.
d'Acosta's Pasture
Summer St.
Pond St.
Long Lane
Atkinson's St.
Hutchinson's St.
Oliver's St.
South Battery
Rowe's Wharf
Cow Lane
Belcher's Lane
Burying Ground
Hog Alley
Sheaff Lane
Rowe's Field
Frog Lane
Essex St.
Coffin's Field
Flounder Lane
Griffin's Wharf
Pleasant St.
Hollis St.
Clough St.
Orange St.
Beach St.
110 220 440 660 880 yards or ½ mile
Dry at Low Tide
Orange St.
Dry at Low Tide
Wharves
Boston Neck
Causeway
British Entrench-ments
1 John Adams's House
2 Court House (or Town House)
+ Boston Massacre
3 Queen Street (Court Street)
4 King Street (State Street)
5 Faneuil Hall
6 Dock Square
7 Old South Church
8 Fort Hill
9 Battery March
A Plan of the Town of Boston
from the Observations of
Lieut. Page
of His Majesty's Corps of Engineers
1775
Drawn by Samuel Bryant from Maps
owned by the Mass. Historical Society

Abigail Adams

By Janet Whitney

Elizabeth Fry, Quaker Heroine
John Woolman, American Quaker
Geraldine S. Cadbury
Abigail Adams

Novels

Jennifer
Judith

ABIGAIL ADAMS AT THE TIME OF HER MARRIAGE
From a pastel drawing by Benjamin Blythe (1764).
By courtesy of Mr Henry Adams

Fr.

Abigail Adams

by

JANET WHITNEY

With seven illustrations in half-tone

GEORGE G. HARRAP AND COMPANY LTD
LONDON SYDNEY TORONTO BOMBAY

To

ABIGAIL ADAMS HOMANS

First published 1949
by GEORGE G. HARRAP & CO. LTD
182 High Holborn, London, W.C.1

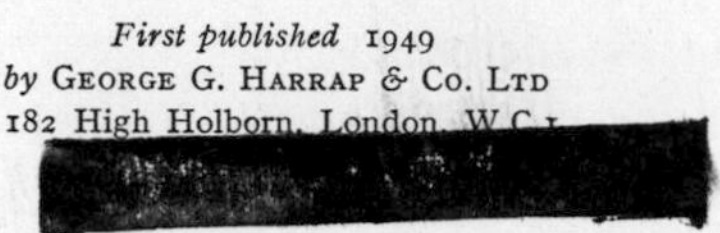

Dewey decimal classification: 923.173

*Composed in Bembo type and printed by Western Printing Services, Ltd
Bristol. Made in Great Britain*

Foreword

THIS IS THE STORY OF THE American Revolution as it seemed to a woman. Hundreds of her letters, carefully preserved by their recipients, bear witness to her close observation of current events and her independent judgment. Members of her family were actors on the great stage. There were cousins in South Carolina, cousins who became pro-British refugees in England, cousins who lived in Boston and were a vital part of its mercantile and political life. All carried on voluminous correspondence, letters written not for the public but for the intimate eyes of relatives. Abigail Adams always had inside and advance information. So her eyes might be as clear as any through which to take a look at the turning-point of American history, her times, and observe their close parallels with our own.

Her husband, John Adams, was the greatest orator, and perhaps the greatest intellect, in the First American Congress, and was called by his fellow-members the Atlas of the Revolution. He was the first shaper of American foreign policy, the chairman of the Peace Commission, the first Ambassador to Great Britain after the peace, the first Vice-President of the new United States of America and the second President. His wife therefore had to play a prominent part in Boston, London, New York, Philadelphia, and, finally, Washington, D.C.

Not only her husband but her eldest son kept her finger on the pulse of public affairs. She lived to see her son John Quincy Adams appointed Ambassador to Russia, Ambassador to Great Britain, and then Secretary of State. Abigail Adams is the only woman so far to be both wife and mother of a President.

She saw, then, a lot more than most women. The great historical figures—George Washington, Thomas Jefferson, Alexander

Hamilton, John Jay, Samuel Adams, Benjamin Franklin—were guests at her table, daily associates and friends. To enter her life is to see the back of the stage, the personal and intimate side of what from the front was the finished dignity of history.

JANET WHITNEY

Westtown, Pennsylvania

Acknowledgments

I OWE A DEEP DEBT OF GRATITUDE to two direct descendants of Abigail Adams without whose help this book would not have been possible. Mr Henry Adams has lent me books, genealogical records, and other manuscript notes compiled by himself, and has allowed me access to relevant portions of the collection of Adams papers known as the Adams Manuscript (Massachusetts Historical Society). In addition he has answered my questions and has taken me personally to the places and houses connected with the Adams, Quincy, and Smith families. Mrs Robert Homans, to whom I have dedicate this book, has also taken me to the family places, has lent me reproductions of pictures, and has accompanied me through long hours of poring over private family manuscripts.

Perhaps this is the place to say that neither Mrs Homans nor Mr Adams nor any other member of the Adams family had any part in the instigation of this book, or read as much as a line of it before it appeared in print. For this generous confidence I am also grateful.

I wish to thank the Massachusetts Historical Society, the Boston Public Library, the American Antiquarian Society, the Philadelphia Library Company, the Boston Athenæum, the Pennsylvania Historical Society, the Westtown School Library, and the Widener and the Houghton Library, Harvard, for every kind of co-operation; and especially Mr Brigham for allowing me access to the, at that time, unused and unpublished collection recently acquired by the American Antiquarian Society, and filed by them as the Adams Letters. (I have referred to this collection throughout my book as the Cranch Manuscript.) This collection has since been published under the title of *New Letters of Abigail Adams*, edited by Stewart Mitchell.

Among numerous others who have given me help of various kinds, I must add my friends Mr and Mrs Arthur Perry, of Boston, Professor and Mrs Henry J. Cadbury, of Harvard, and Mr and Mrs Carroll T. Brown, of Westtown; Mr Zoltan Haraszti, for allowing me the use of the unpublished letters in his care referred to herein as the Thaxter Manuscript; and, for his important co-operation at critical moments, the late Mr Allyn Bailey Forbes.

Dr Thomas S. Drake, Professor of American History of Haverford College, Pennsylvania, and Mrs Helen G. Hole read a large part of the manuscript. And my husband, George Gillett Whitney, gave me, as always, a combined interest and criticism which is truly invaluable.

JANET WHITNEY

Contents

Note

The small superior figures occurring in the text refer to the notes which begin at p. 307.

Illustrations

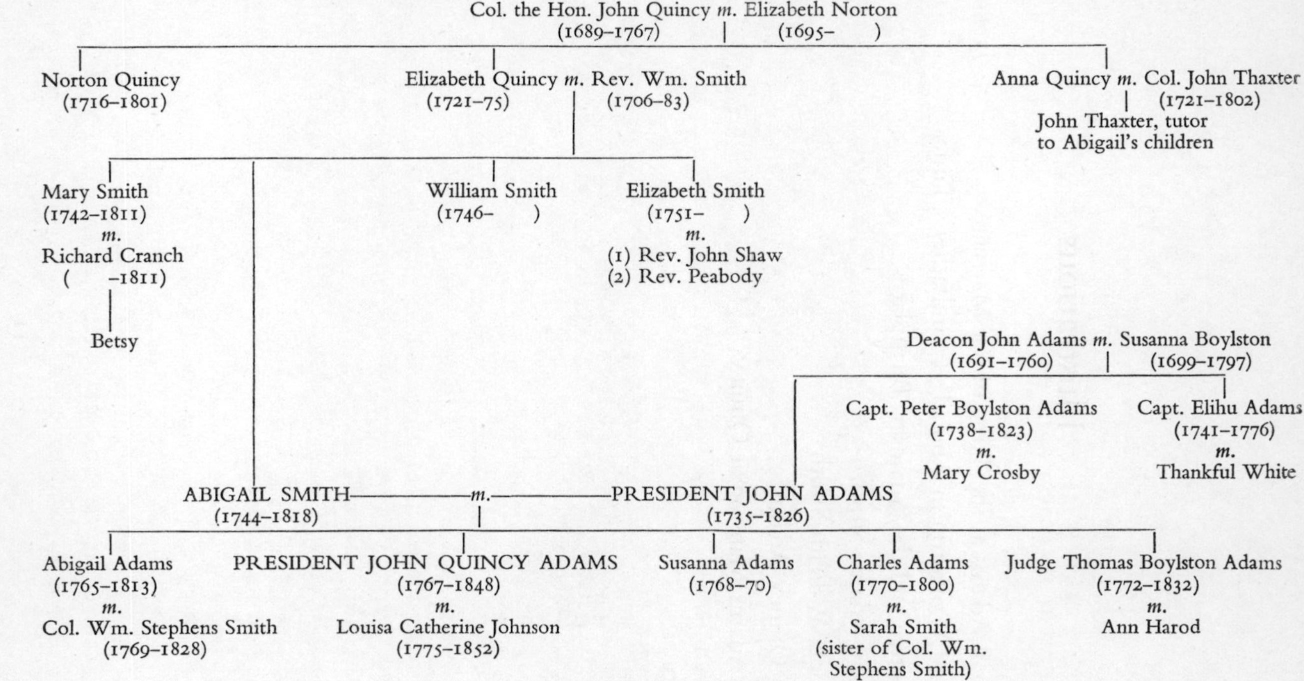

Col. the Hon. John Quincy m. Elizabeth Norton
(1689–1767) (1695–)
Norton Quincy
(1716–1801)
Elizabeth Quincy m. Rev. Wm. Smith
(1721–75) (1706–83)
Anna Quincy m. Col. John Thaxter
(1721–1802)
John Thaxter, tutor
to Abigail's children
Mary Smith
(1742–1811)
m.
Richard Cranch
(–1811)
Betsy
William Smith
(1746–)
Elizabeth Smith
(1751–)
m.
(1) Rev. John Shaw
(2) Rev. Peabody
Deacon John Adams m. Susanna Boylston
(1691–1760) (1699–1797)
Capt. Peter Boylston Adams
(1738–1823)
m.
Mary Crosby
Capt. Elihu Adams
(1741–1776)
m.
Thankful White
ABIGAIL SMITH—m.—PRESIDENT JOHN ADAMS
(1744–1818) (1735–1826)
Abigail Adams
(1765–1813)
m.
Col. Wm. Stephens Smith
(1769–1828)
PRESIDENT JOHN QUINCY ADAMS
(1767–1848)
m.
Louisa Catherine Johnson
(1775–1852)
Susanna Adams
(1768–70)
Charles Adams
(1770–1800)
m.
Sarah Smith
(sister of Col. Wm.
Stephens Smith)
Judge Thomas Boylston Adams
(1772–1832)
m.
Ann Harod

I

Abigail Smith has an Admirer

ABIGAIL SMITH SHARPENED HER quill pen and wrote in her flowing, rapid hand to her new-married dearest friend that she hadn't any sparks—what an idea, were they supposed to be as plenty as herrings? But her sister Mary, whose room she shared, was sitting with her needle at the window, and presently crying "Here they come!" Mary flew down the stairs. Two young men were riding up to the door, their horses' hoof-beats muffled in the thick fallen maple leaves which spread a carpet of gold before the Weymouth parsonage. When they had dismounted and hitched their horses to the post, the elder and taller took Mary in his arms with the privilege of an accepted bridegroom.

The younger man, thick-set, vigorous, said, "Your servant, Mistress Polly—soon to be Mrs Cranch! Is Miss Nabby at home to-day?"

Nabby at the top of the stairs heard him well, and stole softly back into the room again, seized with that unaccountable shyness which John Adams often caused in her. He had been coming to the house a great deal of late, as companion to Richard Cranch during Cranch's courtship of Mary, and of necessity he had been thrown into Abigail's society. For eighteen-year-old* Abigail it had not been unmixed pleasure. This lawyer of twenty-seven, already a rising man of affairs, noted and feared for his sharp tongue as well as respected and loved for his honesty and good nature, made the parson's daughter feel her youth painfully. To be sure he was no stranger. He was the friend and classmate at Harvard College of her cousin Sam Quincy. Sam and he had both been called to the bar in Boston, introduced by the same sponsor, Mr Gridley, on the same day. He was an intimate in the houses

* Abigail Smith was born November 11, 1744. John Adams was born October 19, 1735.

of her mother's cousins, Lawyer Edmund Quincy and Colonel Josiah Quincy, at Braintree, and known well to her grandfather, old Colonel John. Her cousins Esther and Hannah had flirted with him. And Abigail had seen him in company, especially the company of men, talking vigorously, laughing heartily—deep bass gales of laughter—easy and friendly.

But accustomed as she was to queen it in her little circle, to be the liveliest person in the house, admitted by her usual companions to be a clever and brilliant girl, no sooner did John Adams approach her than she was tongue-tied. His keen, appraising glance, catching hers across a room, could make her blush and become confused. Yet—did he *have* to come so regularly with his friend? Did he *have* to pass so much time at Weymouth? Was his asking immediately for Mistress Nabby purely perfunctory?

She admired and feared him. Yet she sometimes thought his interest in her was real and deep. They had had some good talks—about life and philosophy and books, and politics and the place of woman, and education, and the high manners of the Greeks and Romans. . . . She had felt her ignorance beside his erudition. Like Portia, she had confessed that before him she was but an "unlesson'd girl." Yet she had been keenly aware of the unfeigned respect with which he had listened to her opinions, and it had made her talk more brilliantly than ever before. Yes, he had seen her at her best moments. And they were so because of him. But surely he had seen her at her worst as well—gauche, silent, and dull. That, too, because of him. He could create a forbidding silence in which her self-confidence died.

So she hesitated in her room. She looked in the glass, pushed her hair back over her ear, twined a ringlet around her finger. The glass did not reassure her. Her dark eyes, fine complexion, regular features, all lacked that sparkle of animation or the seriousness of thought to give them their true charm. The face in the glass looked blankly back at her, as it was to look blankly back at portrait painters. It was drained of her soul. She went down at last because she must. She greeted John Adams with the stately correctness drilled into her by Grandmother Quincy, and tried to join in the discussion of wedding plans that was going briskly forward between her mother, her sister, and the bridegroom. But it was one of the bad times. Adams was haughty, cold, withdrawn. She felt the pressure of his critical attention to every word, and she felt herself

MOUNT WOLLASTON IN ABIGAIL'S GRANDFATHER'S TIME

From the sketch by Eliza Quincy.

By courtesy of the Massachusetts Historical Society

BRAINTREE AND THE ADAMSES' BIRTHPLACES

From a sketch by Eliza Quincy.

By courtesy of the Massachusetts Historical Society

spent in absolute idleness, or what is worse, gallanting the girls."[2]

And he would swing himself again fiercely towards his mark; reputation, reputation, the bubble reputation. Yet the struggle kept his balance. He compared himself with other young men. Here is Bob Paine* saying, at about Adams's age—twenty-two—"I have ruined myself by a too eager pursuit of wisdom." And Sam Quincy early throwing up the sponge—"We shall never make your great fellows." Depression and lack of courage, diagnosed young Adams; "Quincy's soul is afraid to aim at great acquisition."

Adams's soul had no such fear. Yet, when he rode into Boston to the law court, Bob Paine and Sam Quincy had it all over him. "I felt shy, under awe and concern. The other lawyers present 'looked sour at me,' I had no acquaintance with anybody but Paine and Quincy, and they took but little notice."[3] However, after attending court stubbornly all day, he went in the evening to a party with Sam Quincy—"the most spacious and elegant room, the gayest company of gentlemen and the finest row of ladies that ever I saw." And he learned, he persevered, he made his way.

Shyness might make him awkward, but it did not make him silent. He was quick to make his mark in any company. Men with brains particularly sought his friendship. A letter written by him to one man was shown to another, and the second sought his correspondence.[4] He was provocative, irritating, some said conceited, but he was incurably interesting. He took the trouble to think, and he spoke his real thought, with apparently no reserve. It had the effect of startling originality, and sometimes it was. But it was too honest, too sober to be flashy. He did not deal in the epigram or the paradox. Like his contemporary Dr Johnson in England, he took out and showed you the contents of his mind and heart, and they were genuine and various.

He was very much of a man's man, but women fell for him. They liked his vitality and they liked his susceptibility to their charms. But he always disentangled himself before he had gone too far. His narrowest squeak was with Sam Quincy's sister Hannah. John Adams was often at their house, to drink tea or to spend the evening; and Hannah and her pretty cousin Esther gave him good practice in gallanting. Esther was safe company because she was being courted every week-end by Jonathan Sewall—a friend of

* Robert Treat Paine.

becoming wooden and stiff with constraint. Her father entered, and they all rose to greet him respectfully.

He was as certain of that attention in any room he entered as if he had been born a king, and his confident, authoritative manner showed it. A parson was indeed a king in his little kingdom, anywhere in New England. And since he was seldom rich, his dignity was a counterbalance to the more mundane dignity of wealth. Vehement, salty, the Rev. William Smith was sometimes a rough monarch, but there were none to gainsay it, especially in his own household where his wife was fifteen years his junior.

"And how prospers your career, Mr Adams, now you are in full swing as a Boston lawyer?" he asked, when greetings had been exchanged.

"Oh, finely, sir!" answered John Adams. "Don't you teach 'Woe unto you when all men shall speak well of you'? I am creating enemies in every quarter of the town!"

Their harsh laughter rang out in unison. But Mrs Smith, who had been born a Quincy, turned up her aristocratic nose a little, and looked the other way.

Presently John Adams found himself—by accident or intention—close to Abigail, who sat miserable and paralysed in a corner.

"Well, Miss Nabby, why do you sit and hang down your head like a bulrush, and let the company lose the bright sparkles of those eyes?"*

She lifted her eyes, luminous and wide-open. Her face, young and unguarded, told him much. His eyes answered hers with a sudden glow, an admiring passion. Her constraint melted and she felt freed and gay.

"I've heard, sir," she said, "that two apparitions were seen one evening this week hovering about this house which very much resembled you and a cousin of yours! How it should ever enter into the head of an apparition to assume a form like yours I cannot devise!"

"Come out and stroll around the garden with me," said John, "and I promise to convince you that I am not a ghost!"

That night the Rev. William Smith was asked for permission to court his second daughter. Two daughters of marriageable age; two suitors. All very fine and dandy. Two very different men though, as Mrs Smith was particular to point out. Yet—thought Mr Smith

* Quotations in this chapter are from letters in the Adams Manuscript.

becoming wooden and stiff with constraint. Her father entered, and they all rose to greet him respectfully.

He was as certain of that attention in any room he entered as if he had been born a king, and his confident, authoritative manner showed it. A parson was indeed a king in his little kingdom, anywhere in New England. And since he was seldom rich, his dignity was a counterbalance to the more mundane dignity of wealth. Vehement, salty, the Rev. William Smith was sometimes a rough monarch, but there were none to gainsay it, especially in his own household where his wife was fifteen years his junior.

"And how prospers your career, Mr Adams, now you are in full swing as a Boston lawyer?" he asked, when greetings had been exchanged.

"Oh, finely, sir!" answered John Adams. "Don't you teach 'Woe unto you when all men shall speak well of you'? I am creating enemies in every quarter of the town!"

Their harsh laughter rang out in unison. But Mrs Smith, who had been born a Quincy, turned up her aristocratic nose a little, and looked the other way.

Presently John Adams found himself—by accident or intention—close to Abigail, who sat miserable and paralysed in a corner.

"Well, Miss Nabby, why do you sit and hang down your head like a bulrush, and let the company lose the bright sparkles of those eyes?"*

She lifted her eyes, luminous and wide-open. Her face, young and unguarded, told him much. His eyes answered hers with a sudden glow, an admiring passion. Her constraint melted and she felt freed and gay.

"I've heard, sir," she said, "that two apparitions were seen one evening this week hovering about this house which very much resembled you and a cousin of yours! How it should ever enter into the head of an apparition to assume a form like yours I cannot devise!"

"Come out and stroll around the garden with me," said John, "and I promise to convince you that I am not a ghost!"

That night the Rev. William Smith was asked for permission to court his second daughter. Two daughters of marriageable age; two suitors. All very fine and dandy. Two very different men though, as Mrs Smith was particular to point out. Yet—thought Mr Smith

* Quotations in this chapter are from letters in the Adams Manuscript.

spent in absolute idleness, or what is worse, gallanting the girls."[2]

And he would swing himself again fiercely towards his mark; reputation, reputation, the bubble reputation. Yet the struggle kept his balance. He compared himself with other young men. Here is Bob Paine* saying, at about Adams's age—twenty-two—"I have ruined myself by a too eager pursuit of wisdom." And Sam Quincy early throwing up the sponge—"We shall never make your great fellows." Depression and lack of courage, diagnosed young Adams; "Quincy's soul is afraid to aim at great acquisition."

Adams's soul had no such fear. Yet, when he rode into Boston to the law court, Bob Paine and Sam Quincy had it all over him. "I felt shy, under awe and concern. The other lawyers present 'looked sour at me,' I had no acquaintance with anybody but Paine and Quincy, and they took but little notice."[3] However, after attending court stubbornly all day, he went in the evening to a party with Sam Quincy—"the most spacious and elegant room, the gayest company of gentlemen and the finest row of ladies that ever I saw." And he learned, he persevered, he made his way.

Shyness might make him awkward, but it did not make him silent. He was quick to make his mark in any company. Men with brains particularly sought his friendship. A letter written by him to one man was shown to another, and the second sought his correspondence.[4] He was provocative, irritating, some said conceited, but he was incurably interesting. He took the trouble to think, and he spoke his real thought, with apparently no reserve. It had the effect of startling originality, and sometimes it was. But it was too honest, too sober to be flashy. He did not deal in the epigram or the paradox. Like his contemporary Dr Johnson in England, he took out and showed you the contents of his mind and heart, and they were genuine and various.

He was very much of a man's man, but women fell for him. They liked his vitality and they liked his susceptibility to their charms. But he always disentangled himself before he had gone too far. His narrowest squeak was with Sam Quincy's sister Hannah. John Adams was often at their house, to drink tea or to spend the evening; and Hannah and her pretty cousin Esther gave him good practice in gallanting. Esther was safe company because she was being courted every week-end by Jonathan Sewall—a friend of

* Robert Treat Paine.

spent in absolute idleness, or what is worse, gallanting the girls."[2]

And he would swing himself again fiercely towards his mark; reputation, reputation, the bubble reputation. Yet the struggle kept his balance. He compared himself with other young men. Here is Bob Paine* saying, at about Adams's age—twenty-two—"I have ruined myself by a too eager pursuit of wisdom." And Sam Quincy early throwing up the sponge—"We shall never make your great fellows." Depression and lack of courage, diagnosed young Adams; "Quincy's soul is afraid to aim at great acquisition."

Adams's soul had no such fear. Yet, when he rode into Boston to the law court, Bob Paine and Sam Quincy had it all over him. "I felt shy, under awe and concern. The other lawyers present 'looked sour at me,' I had no acquaintance with anybody but Paine and Quincy, and they took but little notice."[3] However, after attending court stubbornly all day, he went in the evening to a party with Sam Quincy—"the most spacious and elegant room, the gayest company of gentlemen and the finest row of ladies that ever I saw." And he learned, he persevered, he made his way.

Shyness might make him awkward, but it did not make him silent. He was quick to make his mark in any company. Men with brains particularly sought his friendship. A letter written by him to one man was shown to another, and the second sought his correspondence.[4] He was provocative, irritating, some said conceited, but he was incurably interesting. He took the trouble to think, and he spoke his real thought, with apparently no reserve. It had the effect of startling originality, and sometimes it was. But it was too honest, too sober to be flashy. He did not deal in the epigram or the paradox. Like his contemporary Dr Johnson in England, he took out and showed you the contents of his mind and heart, and they were genuine and various.

He was very much of a man's man, but women fell for him. They liked his vitality and they liked his susceptibility to their charms. But he always disentangled himself before he had gone too far. His narrowest squeak was with Sam Quincy's sister Hannah. John Adams was often at their house, to drink tea or to spend the evening; and Hannah and her pretty cousin Esther gave him good practice in gallanting. Esther was safe company because she was being courted every week-end by Jonathan Sewall—a friend of

* Robert Treat Paine.

drew attention to him and got him a job as schoolmaster at Worcester.[1] While at Worcester he had had entrée to the best society the town afforded. There he had qualified himself in the evenings, and in his spare time, for the law—for it had long been clear to him that he could not put his mind into the strait-waistcoat of orthodoxy required by the ministry. At his father's house in Braintree some years before he had witnessed a heresy trial. The boy's sympathy had been with the young minister. If he had not admired Mr Bryant, if Mr Bryant's theology had not been attacked by narrow-minded bigotry,* John Adams might have chosen the ministry, and the course of history have been diverted. But already destiny had marked him for its own.

When Mr Gridley presented Sam Quincy and John Adams to the Boston bar, one or two of the established lawyers h'mmed and ha'd and said, well, of course, they all knew Sam Quincy—he had read law with so and so, he was Josiah Quincy's son and the Honourable John Quincy's grandson and all that—but who was this John Adams? Who was *he*? And Mr Gridley gave his personal guarantee for John Adams, based on a single searching interview.

John Adams was not so and so's son or so and so's pupil, he was himself. He stood on his own merit.

It would not be true to say that he noticed nothing remarkable in himself, because, like every young man of ambition, indeed, he did. He hoped, he feared. But he expected nothing more of himself than to succeed at the law, to make money, and to own land.

These ambitions were enough to take care of his time, because he had to start from scratch. His father, a respectable citizen and a solid farmer, had sent his eldest son to Harvard. From then on his career was his own business.

John's youthful diary is full of exhortations to himself to make better use of his day. To stick to his books and let nothing decoy him—"no girl, no gun, no cards," in descending order of temptation.

But though he would read passionately for days on end—Latin, history, law—he could not make himself a bookworm. His enjoyment of the present, his zest for life, would not be denied. Some girl, some gun, was always getting the better of him. "Friday, Saturday, Sunday, Monday," he would record with disgust, "all

* Bryant won his case, and his liberty of conscience was maintained both by John Adams's father and by the Hon. John Quincy. But the trial had been disagreeable.

—good stuff in both, though Cranch, settled, better balanced, maturer, was obviously the greater catch. He was a partner with Mr Palmer in the glassworks at Braintree. Colonel Josiah Quincy had recently joined the firm.

In November 1762 Mary was married to Richard Cranch. Her father preached the wedding sermon on the text, "And Mary hath chosen that good part." His three remaining children sat in the square white pew and listened to him decorously—Abigail, eighteen; William, sixteen; and little Elizabeth, eleven. The Rev. William Smith did well with daughters, but he was not so skilled with sons.*

But if Abigail, like others present, found a hidden meaning in her father's text, less than complimentary to her suitor, she could afford not to mind. She was certain his future would be distinguished. Her admiration for him was so complete that she could afford to laugh and be saucy.

If parents were to study the secret history of other parents it might diminish their self-confidence even dangerously. For young people rather like their parents to be positive, and would prefer to have them wrong than spinelessly unopinioned. Yet Mrs Elizabeth Quincy Smith, anxiously observing her daughter's girlish infatuation, and setting against it the coolness of her mature experience, her belittling judgment, her knowledge of men and manners, was wrong, and Abigail's young and eager enthusiasm was right beyond compare. There were no indicating circumstances which would make it possible for the Rev. and Mrs Smith to foresee that this stocky, energetic, magnetic man, with his keen mind, his power with words, and his carelessness of making enemies, was to make their little daughter the equal of queens.

And who was John Adams anyway? At Harvard College, where students were still, under the lingering influence of the Old Country, seated in class according to their rank by birth,† Charles Cushing was first, John Adams fourteenth in a class of twenty-four, and he wouldn't have got that high but for his mother's having been a Boylston.

When they were listed academically, however, John Adams was among the first three. His part in the Commencement Day exercises

* Young William, now apprenticed in Boston, was a disappointment to himself and to others and faded out of the family annals.

† Until 1769, when alphabetical order was substituted.

becoming wooden and stiff with constraint. Her father entered, and they all rose to greet him respectfully.

He was as certain of that attention in any room he entered as if he had been born a king, and his confident, authoritative manner showed it. A parson was indeed a king in his little kingdom, anywhere in New England. And since he was seldom rich, his dignity was a counterbalance to the more mundane dignity of wealth. Vehement, salty, the Rev. William Smith was sometimes a rough monarch, but there were none to gainsay it, especially in his own household where his wife was fifteen years his junior.

"And how prospers your career, Mr Adams, now you are in full swing as a Boston lawyer?" he asked, when greetings had been exchanged.

"Oh, finely, sir!" answered John Adams. "Don't you teach 'Woe unto you when all men shall speak well of you'? I am creating enemies in every quarter of the town!"

Their harsh laughter rang out in unison. But Mrs Smith, who had been born a Quincy, turned up her aristocratic nose a little, and looked the other way.

Presently John Adams found himself—by accident or intention—close to Abigail, who sat miserable and paralysed in a corner.

"Well, Miss Nabby, why do you sit and hang down your head like a bulrush, and let the company lose the bright sparkles of those eyes?"*

She lifted her eyes, luminous and wide-open. Her face, young and unguarded, told him much. His eyes answered hers with a sudden glow, an admiring passion. Her constraint melted and she felt freed and gay.

"I've heard, sir," she said, "that two apparitions were seen one evening this week hovering about this house which very much resembled you and a cousin of yours! How it should ever enter into the head of an apparition to assume a form like yours I cannot devise!"

"Come out and stroll around the garden with me," said John, "and I promise to convince you that I am not a ghost!"

That night the Rev. William Smith was asked for permission to court his second daughter. Two daughters of marriageable age; two suitors. All very fine and dandy. Two very different men though, as Mrs Smith was particular to point out. Yet—thought Mr Smith

* Quotations in this chapter are from letters in the Adams Manuscript.

John Adams's from Worcester days. But she combined with Hannah to provoke John to dangerous flirtation. Destiny made haste and interrupted them just in time.

A too early marriage clips a young man's wings. Mr Gridley had impressed this upon his protégé; and John Adams, having to earn his way as he went, could also read the lesson plainly in his circumstances. Unmarried, he could afford to reserve himself time for study, and so lay a foundation for future success. Married, he must give all his time and energy to earning a living, and turn into a pettifogging attorney, grinding along with the small beer of his profession. So he thanked his stars that accident "delivered me from very dangerous shackles, and left me at liberty, if I will but mind my studies, of making a character and a fortune."[5] Hannah quickly consoled herself with another suitor. Adams always boasted that, with all his affairs of the heart, he had never done harm to any woman.

A young man might well be grateful to have experienced such a liberal education as could be provided by women like Hannah Quincy and Esther Quincy; a training in manners, feeling, softer repartee, and in the ups and downs and intricacies of a woman's character. For one thing, it took away his fear of the blue-stocking. A thinking, reading woman was a better companion than another.

But all this time Abigail was present in the background, a delicate, observant girl. She had not yet risen to the surface of his attention, because her elder cousins held the floor. When John Adams graduated from Harvard Abigail Smith—who might have been at the Commencement exercises, a great and popular social occasion for all the good families in and around Boston—was eleven. When he so narrowly escaped getting engaged to her cousin Hannah she was fifteen.

And how did she manage, when she was seventeen, to throw her net over this large and slippery fish?

Abigail was brought up in three homes. First, her own home in Weymouth, eight miles south of Boston, with her father, Parson Smith, and her mother, Elizabeth Quincy, and her two sisters and brother. Then, the house called Mount Wollaston at Braintree, four miles farther along the shore road, the home of her distinguished grandfather the Hon. John Quincy and his wife, Elizabeth Norton; and then the house in Boston of her father's brother,

Isaac Smith, and his wife, Elizabeth Storer. In all of these homes she was exceedingly happy, and the variety of going from one to the other enlivened her mind and polished her manners. Bernard Shaw makes play with a man that had two fathers. Abigail Smith had three fathers, and, what was more to the purpose in her case, three mothers. Outside her own home, which had, after all, her earliest years, it was her Grandmother Quincy and her aunt Elizabeth Smith who meant the most in her development.

Abigail was a delicate child, and for that reason was never sent to school. Change of air was a favourite specific for health, and this, added to care for her education, was the basis of her variety of domicile. But beside that, she was a favourite grandchild and a favourite niece. She was *en rapport* with grandmother and aunt; her childish company and quick response increased their pleasure in life. They invited her for long visits. As she was a welcome guest at Boston and at Braintree, so when she got home again to Weymouth she was like a welcome guest there too.

All three households were well-to-do, and two of them were bookish. Her clergyman father was a reader and lender of books. In his library she browsed through many a volume. Parson Smith's salary was not large in cash, but he got the parsonage rent free with it, and was besides an able farmer. By the time Abigail was nineteen her father had made, saved, or inherited enough to buy an additional farm at Medford.

Parson Smith was not fluent with his pen; he did not run to words, but scratched a hasty line, day by day, of the day's main event on the blank pages of his interleaved almanacs. But these entries in his skeleton diary, scant and curt as they are, reflect the healthy, thrifty rhythm of the home; the easy swing of the parson's mind from the sheep of his congregation to the sheep of his fields. One day (May 16, 1751) "We kept a fast to bewail the burning of our Meeting-house." And another (December 1761), "My winter stock of sheep is 26." A September Sabbath notes "A proclamation for a day of general prayer thro' the province on account of a severe drought. [September 3, 1761.] I prayed from 5 James v. 7." Monday (September 4, 1761) laconically records "A remarkable rain." One day he will kill two hogs, and another he will baptize a baby. The scales swing equal. Life has more than one side. He will pay for his firewood with his hay, but he will hand out cash for a volume of Virgil. He will risk in the lottery

(January 5, 1759)—result, "perdu"—but he will sell a horse (April 11, 1749) for a good price, and will lend half of it to brother Isaac Smith (December 31, 1755). It is a vigorous, prosperous, practical, not narrow, not ungenerous character that emerges as Abigail's father.

It was a great change from country living to be in the Smiths' Boston house. She could feel the exciting stir of the town about her, a town which was the largest city* in the colonies, and the most thriving port. She could go down to the wharf, carefully accompanied, and see the forest of masts, the clean-cut angles of rigging and spars against the blue New England sky, and the bright figureheads and scrollwork of the sea-clean ships. Bran† sometimes flew in the air, from the opening of a bale of perishable goods packed in it, and she could catch a glimpse as she passed of "bran-new" porcelain from Sèvres, or glass from Venice, twinkling in the sun. She could go with dazzled eyes into the pleasant dimness of her uncle's warehouse, which smelt of coffee and wine and spice and sugar from the West Indies and Madeira, tea from the Far East via England, and salted herring and mackerel from the native fisheries. For a special treat she would sometimes be taken by dinghy to one of her uncle's ships, and would see the cabin, with its plush and leather, look out through the dark porthole into the bright water, and feel how the great hollow shell rocked gently in its berth on the tide. The tide of Boston harbour would soon rock the British Empire itself. But now all the ships flew the Union Jack, all owed allegiance to Great Britain, were manned by colonial-born men who called themselves English, and were protected by British men-o'-war.

But it was when Abigail visited Grandmother Quincy that she truly breathed what was to become her native air. There in the township of Braintree‡ by the sea she was to pass the major part of her life. Whatever part of the world she was in, she was to look back, not to Weymouth, not to Boston, but to Braintree as her heart's home. Though not to her grandfather's house, but to another, outwardly more modest.

Her grandfather's homestead was on a spacious scale for those

* Philadelphia was the largest less than forty years later.

† Sawdust was then called bran, and was the chief article used for packing perishables of all kinds.

‡ The New England word was 'town' for the aggregation of community called in other places 'township.' There was no town then at Braintree in the modern sense.

parts, not to be compared with the large mansions of the South, run by slave labour and built for lavish hospitality, but distinctly the great house of the neighbourhood, with grounds that ran down to the sea's edge. It was a good playground for a delicate little girl. Inside the house there was a dignity and order not possible in the bustling Weymouth parsonage. The type of life was the same—the farm life, and abundance from the farm—but there was more time, more leisure to read, discuss, think, and enjoy—because there was more money. The Hon. John Quincy had regarded wealth as an instrument for the public service. For twenty-one years he was annually elected to the Massachusetts House of Representatives from Braintree, and for fourteen of those years he was Speaker of the House. For even longer he had been elected each year Moderator of the Braintree town meeting, succeeding in that office his Uncle Edmund, Judge of the Supreme Court of Massachusetts. John Quincy was also chairman of the Massachusetts committee on currency, and chairman of the legislative committee, with the duty of sending instructions to the agent of the province at the court of Great Britain. At home he did not scorn to accept appointment, at their own request, as guardian of the remnant of Massachusetts Indians, the Ponkapoag Indians, who tramped the twelve miles to his home from their reserve, consumed his beer and cider, told him their troubles and got redress, camped on his land and fished his ocean beaches, broke his fences and burnt his wood; which he bore with patience equal to any Quaker's. As her father's home, then, was pervaded by the air of church and parish matters, so Abigail found her grandfather's home pervaded by the air of the state,* politics, and the law. Sitting quietly on her stool in a shady corner, her chin in her hand, she listened to many a hot conversation among the gentlemen, debates on freedom, the constitution of England, Magna Carta and rights of Englishmen. She heard heated arguments on the right of the Government to search citizens' property for contraband, to break open chests, burst locks; yes, in a man's own store, sir, or worse, his house! And there was sharp comment on the British-appointed Governor of Massachusetts Bay, Sir Thomas Bernard, and his part in the increasing tenseness between the colonies and Parliament.

So Abigail as a girl breathed in the air of liberty and was conscious of the fast-moving current of her times. She also read Shake-

* *I.e.*, the American colonies.

speare, Molière, and "the poets," Locke, and the *Spectator*, learned to cook and sew—both plain and fancy—and was taught the importance of grace and softness to a woman's manner. Grandmother Quincy was as keen as any Southern lady to cultivate the gentle exterior, the controlled movement, the voice without edge.

By the time John Adams noticed Abigail Smith, she was so worthy of his notice that his hesitation, his caution, could be caused only by the fear that she was too good to be true.

John Adams was a warm wooer if he had not been a hasty one. And he found his Abigail, from first to last, the best-educated woman he had ever met. Adams's very first letter to her—or rather aimed at her, for it was addressed to her sister and enclosed in one of Dick Cranch's—referred to some lively political opinions she had been expressing.

> Please give my—I don't know what!—to Mistress Nabby. Tell her I hear she's about commencing a most loyal subject to young George; and although my allegiance has been hitherto inviolate, I shall endeavour all in my power to foment rebellion.[6]

That was 1761, the year that George III was crowned in a blaze of youth and popularity; but it also was the year of the Writs of Assistance in Massachusetts to help enforce the British Acts of Trade. Only a few weeks after writing that ambiguous message to Mistress Nabby John Adams gave a remarkable account, in the Mount Wollaston circle, of his first full-dress day in court, when the test case concerning the Writs of Assistance came up for trial. John Adams's patron and sponsor, Benjamin Gridley, had been counsel for the Crown, and James Otis against him. Young Adams had been deeply, passionately stirred.

"In the noble Council Chamber," he said, "round a great fire were seated five judges, with Lieutenant-Governor Hutchinson at their head as Chief Justice, all arrayed in their new, fresh robes of scarlet English broadcloth, with their large cambric bands and immense judicial wigs. Sam Quincy and I sat there in our new black gowns and bands and wigs, according to Chief Justice Hutchinson's new rules of costume on the model of the English law courts. I was the youngest present, looking, I dare say, like a short, thick Archbishop of Canterbury in that outfit! But I tell you, sir, I sat there at the table, pen in hand, lost in admiration. Mr Otis, as you know, was once Mr Gridley's pupil. Well, Mr Gridley made a learned, well-reasoned speech supporting the right of government to search for contraband. Then Mr Otis demolished it; more than demolished it, blew it all to pieces; not troubling to take it up point by point, but setting principle against principle. And yet, while he refuted all Gridley's arguments and swept on to overwhelming victory, he treated his old master with all the deference of a son to a father!"

"I hope you took notes?" said the Hon. John Quincy.

"Having my pen, I did take some. But my feeling was too great for me to take many. My eyes were constantly on the drama before me. Mr Otis was transformed by speaking. One forgot he was plump, round-faced, short-necked; one saw only that he had the eye of an eagle, a voice and style worthy of antiquity. I can imagine Cicero spoke like him! His view of the attitude of England towards the colonies seemed to me, as he unfolded it, incontrovertibly true. And a contest appeared to me to be opened to which I could foresee no end, and which would render my life a burden, and everything—property, industry, everything!—insecure!"[7]

Abigail, listening to young John Adams, forgot that he also was plump and short-necked; she noticed only that he too had the eye of an eagle.

"As to your life being a burden," said Quincy, "that might depend on which side you take. Mr Hutchinson has shown us the short cut to prosperity!" He glanced keenly at the young man.

"There is no alternative left but to take the side which appears to be just," said Adams, with a downcast look of sombre meditation, "and to trust in Providence for the protection of truth and right."[8]

Preoccupied as John Adams was with thoughts like these, thoughts at war with his private ambition, he found refreshment whenever he came to the Weymouth parsonage with Dick Cranch. He loved to hear that saucy Mistress Nabby talk. His manner to her might at times be forbidding or overbearing, but it was never tainted with patronage. And when he found out at last what he had to give her, there was nothing cold about that.

"Accidents are often more friendly to us than our own prudence,"[9] he wrote to her in February.

I intended to have been at Weymouth yesterday, but a storm prevented—cruel yet perhaps blessed storm! Cruel for detaining me . . . perhaps blessed to you or me or both for keeping me at *my distance.* For every experimental philosopher knows that the steel and magnet or the glass and the platter will not fly together with more celerity than Somebody and Somebody when brought within the striking distance.

And in August:

> Could my horse have helped me to Weymouth, Braintree would not have held me last night. I lay in the well-known chamber and dreamed I saw a Lady tripping it over the hills on the Weymouth Shore and spreading light and beauty and glory all around her.

John Adams had no reason to complain that his ardour was not reciprocated, or that his lady's lively brain had cooled her heart. "My Friend," she wrote, "if I was sure your absence to-day was occasioned by what it generally is, either to wait upon company or promote some good work, I frankly confess my mind would be much more at ease than at present it is." There are bonds of humanity, friendship, and "a type more binding than either. Unite these and there is a three-fold cord—by this I am not ashamed to own myself bound, nor do I perceive that you are wholly free from it." She pressed a flower in there. "Accept this faulty scrawl warm from the heart of Your sincere Diana."[10]

Since they lived only four miles apart, there was not much occasion for love-letters. But the last ordeal of the long period of courtship was a six weeks' separation while John Adams underwent inoculation for smallpox. This practice (introduced into England by Lady Mary Wortley Montagu, who had discovered it among the Turks, and into Philadelphia by Dr Benjamin Rush) had been introduced into Boston by John Adams's uncle, Dr Boylston. It was nothing less than having smallpox on purpose. The theory, supported by a good deal of evidence, was that smallpox induced in a healthy person, well-prepared by diet and drugs, under the constant supervision of a physician, would insure him against a painful, disfiguring, and perhaps fatal attack of smallpox accidentally acquired. The chances of an attack being fatal were so high that inoculation was preferable.* Yet there were risks. Jonathan Edwards's son-in-law, President Burr of Princeton, father of Aaron, died of it.

John Adams, in April 1764, wrote to his lady:

> (Just off to enjoy the Small Pox) Saturday eve. Eight o'clock. My dear Diana—For many years past I have not felt more serenely than I

* The young Jefferson went to Philadelphia to have his under supervision of the famous Dr Rush.

do this evening. My head is clear and my heart is at ease. . . . My room is prepared for a seven days' retirement, and my plan is digested for 4 or 5 weeks. My brother retreats with me to our preparatory hospital and is determined to keep me company through the Small Pox.

He comforts her "tears and anxiety," his hearty confidence sets to work to soothe her fears.

For my part I believe no man ever undertook to prepare himself for the Small Pox with fewer than I have at present. I have considered very thoroughly the diet and medicine prescribed me and am fully satisfied that no durable evil can result from either, and any other fear from the Small Pox or its appurtenances in the modern way of Inoculation I never had in my life. Present my duty and gratitude to Papa. Next Fryday we take our departure for Boston. To Capt. Cunningham's we go. And I have not the least doubt of a pleasant three weeks not withstanding the distemper. Good-night, my Dear, I'm agoing to Bed![11]

A note from Abigail, brought by her brother, cheered his pillow.

Sir—I feel much easier than I did an hour ago, my Uncle having given me a more particular and favourable account of the Small Pox or rather the operation of the preparation, than I have had before. He speaks greatly in favour of Dr Perkins,* who has not lost one patient . . . and knows better what to do in case of any difficulty. He allows his patients greater liberty with regard to their diet than several other physicians. Some of them, such as Lord, forbid their patients a mouthful of bread. My uncle [she means her uncle, Dr Tufts, himself a physician] says they are all agreed that 'tis best to abstain from Butter and Salt—and most of them from meat. Keep your spirits up. Shall I come to see you before you go? No, I won't, for I want not again to experience what I this morning felt when you left.—Your A. Smith.[12]

The Rev. William Smith, already Papa to his intended son-in-law, sent by request all his volumes of Swift, and by personal concern his manservant Tom, to wait on the Adams brothers for the few days until they went into Boston.

The probation week over, John Adams next reported from Captain Cunningham's home in Boston, one of the houses which had been set aside for the smallpox party. Often a group of relations and friends arranged to be "done" together, but John Adams's companions in the adventure were not all under the same doctor. Dr Perkins's patients were well treated. "We have new milk in

* The doctor of Adams's choice.

abundance and as much pudding and rice and indeed anything of a farinacious kind we please, and the medicine we take is not at all nauseous or painful. Five persons in the same room under the care of Dr Lord are starved and medicamented with the greatest severity. No bread, no pudding, no milk (except half-milk, half-water), and powders that keep them sick and weak." Inoculated patients felt pretty uncomfortable "just before the Pock came out . . . some general languor, some fever and shivers," then their aches and pains departed—"Their spirits rise, tongues run and they eat, drink and laugh like prisoners released." Abigail's brother and uncle, who had been done in another house, "have been here to see us this morning. They are charmingly well and cheerful, tho' they are lean and weak." The Quincy brothers, Sam and Josiah, were fellow-patients of Perkins near by. "I asked Dr Perkins how they had it. He answered—'Oh Lord, Sir, infinitely light.' It is extremely pleasing, says he, wherever we go we see everybody passing through this tremendous distemper in the lightest, easiest manner conceivable. The Doctor meant those that have the distemper by inoculation in the new method, for those who have it in the natural way are objects of as much Horror as ever." John Adams was exasperated that with this contrast "before the eyes of the whole Town," as plain as the nose on your face, there were still at least five hundred persons who refused to be inoculated. Clergy and selectmen expostulated in vain. "Is man a rational creature, think you?" he demanded. "Conscience, forsooth, and scruples are the cause. I should think myself a deliberate self-murderer!"[13]

But these charges hit closer home than he remembered. Abigail herself had not been inoculated, and her father could not bring himself to risk her beauty in that way. John converted and thoroughly scared her, and she bewailed her dangerous situation to him. He replied fervently:

> I join with you sincerely in your lamentation that you were not inoculated. I wish to God the Dr wd sett up an Hospital at Germantown* and inoculate you. I will come and nurse you, nay, I will go with you to the Castle or to Point Shirley or anywhere & attend you. You say rightly safety there is not, and I say safety there never will be![14]

He knew that even his letters might carry contagion. And so did Abigail's mother. At the height of his illness John hesitated to obey Abigail's demand for letters—"I am infected myself, & every

* A part of Braintree.

room in the house has infected people in it, so that there is real danger in writing."[15] But his scruples were earnestly set at rest. The letters were fumigated. "Your friendly epistle came like an infernal messenger through fire & brimstone,"[16] Abigail assured him. And she described how her impatience pestered the man-servant at his task.

> Mamma is so fearful I should catch the distemper that she hardly ever thinks the letters are sufficiently purified. Did you never rob a bird's nest? Do you remember how the poor bird would fly round and round fearful to come nigh, yet not know how to leave the place? Just so they say I hover round Tom while he is smoking your letters.

She makes sport with his baby goddaughter, Betsy, one-year-old daughter of Richard and Mary Cranch. "Betsy sends her love to you, says she designed to have kissed you before you went away, but you made no advances & she! . . . know you of any figure in the Mathematics whereby you can convey one to her? Inclining lines that meet in the same centre, will not that figure come as nigh as any?"[17] And she can be as outspoken as himself at times. "Unsociable being" is a charge that has been laid against him. She quotes one of his fellow-sufferers as saying—"I did expect this purgation of Lysander to have set us on a level & have rendered him a sociable creature, but ill-luck, he stands it like an oak and is as haughty as ever!" "I expect you to clear up these matters without being in the least saucy!" she warns him. But before she can offend and wound she hastens to take his part. "As to the charge of haughtiness, I am certain that is a mistake, for if I know Lysander he has as little of that in his disposition as he has of ill-nature. But for saucyness no mortal can match him, no, not even his Diana."[18]

Never does she forget her masculine lover's dictum, commenting on other ladies, that no vivacity or fire or intrepidity or whatever will take the place for him of "the kindness, the softness, the tenderness that constitute the characteristic excellence of your sex, & for the want of which no abilities can atone."[19]

She freely expresses her longing to see him, as the quarantine wears to a close, yet, since "not sight alone would please," it would be advisable to keep at an unseeable distance "till any approach would not endanger." She laughs at cool and prim lovers. The other day she saw a couple meet—

> no danger and no fear—a how-do-ye-do and how-do-ye-do was exchanged between them, a smile and a good-natured look—upon

my word I believe they were glad to see each other. Yet I thought whether Lysander under like circumstances cd thus coldly meet his Diana, and whether Diana cd with no more emotion receive L. What think you? I dare answer for a different meeting on her part were she under no restraint.[20]

But that word "restraint" falls into place like a boulder blocking a torrent. And she is not only thinking of quarantine. How comes it, she inquires, that he can read *Sir Charles Grandison* yet be the very reverse in practice? "Sir Charles called forth every one's excellencies, but never was a thought born in Lysander's presence." This is a heavy charge. She amplifies it in many places. "Sometimes, you know, I think you are too severe, and that you do not make quite so many allowances as human nature requires, but," she is quick to add, "perhaps this may be owing to my unacquaintance with the world. Your Business naturaly leads you to a nearer inspection of Mankind, and to see the corruptions of the heart."

She can bear with it the more easily because he assures her, "my affection for a certain Lady (you know who, my Dear) quickens my affection for every Body else that does not deserve my hatred." And because he is impatient for their marriage and says, "I am, and till then and ever after will be, your Admirer and Friend and Lover,—John Adams." Because he says, after his six weeks' quarantine are over, and they are reunited, and then she goes to Boston for a visit, "My soul and body have both been thrown into disorder by your absence, and a month or two more would make me the most insufferable Cynic in the world. I see nothing but Faults, Follies, Frailties and Defects in anybody lately. People have lost all their good properties. But you who have always softened and warmed my heart shall restore my Benevolence as well as my Health and Tranquillity of mind. You shall polish and refine my Sentiments of Life and Manners, banish all the unsocial and ill-natured Particles in my Composition and restore me to the happy Temper that can nourish a quick Discernment with a perfect Candour."

Yet again he comes to see her and creates "an intolerable forbidding expecting silence which lays such a restraint upon but moderate Modesty that 'tis impossible for a Stranger to be tranquil in your presence. What say you to that charge? Deny it not, for by experience I know it to be true. . . ." And she confesses that she has often examined his countenance to see whether there was anything austere in it. "Indeed . . . when I have been most pained I have thoroughly studied it, but never could discern one trace of the Severe. Must it not then be something in Behaviour, else why shd I not feel as great restraint when I write?"[21]

Sometimes she is half-afraid of the ease with which she pours herself forth in written words, but she lets herself go none the less. "This is a right girl's letter." She suggests that it will serve to light his pipe with!

And yet, deep down, can she not judge of his heart by her own? "When I have often been tempted to believe that they were both cast in the same mould, only with this difference, that yours was made with a harder mettle, and therefore is less liable to an impression. Whether they have both an equal quantity of steel I have not yet been able to discover, but do not imagine they are either of them deficient."[22]

Perhaps the fact that he could daunt her was, to a woman of her strength, a vital part of his charm.

Three years of courting and waiting were too long, and both were irked by it. At last delays were over, his house was ready for her, the Adams cart came to Weymouth in bright October weather to carry away such furniture and goods as the bride would bring to the new home, and she could write, "And—then Sir if you please you may take me."

The autumn was a good time for country weddings, the harvest gathered in and carts and horses and their owners free for other doings. Two years after Mary's wedding, Richard Cranch brought his wife and baby Betsy to John and Abigail's wedding, October 25, 1764. Rumour has it that Abigail's mother was reluctant to the last. Some have written that it was because John Adams was a lawyer; but that will not hold water. Dick Cranch, too, was a lawyer, and Uncle Edmund Quincy, and nephews Sam and Josiah. More likely she felt the difficulty of Jack Adams's temper, without feeling the ameliorations that made up for it. At all events, the Rev. William Smith, with his usual sardonic humour, preached the wedding sermon from the text "For John came neither eating nor drinking, and they say, He hath a devil."

II

Braintree

THE TOWN OF BRAINTREE, CLASSIfied for muster-roll purposes into the North Precinct, Middle Precinct, and South Precinct, numbered about two thousand souls, averaging seven to a family. It was a farming community, and people lived scattered on their farms, with wide fields about them, though all set their houses on the highway.

The small and modest house in Braintree to which John Adams took his bride was just across the garden from his old home. It was his own property, having been left him by his father, along with nine and a half acres of farm and garden land. The homestead and the main farm of one hundred and forty acres had been left to his next brother, Peter Boylston Adams, who had not been given a Harvard education. The youngest brother, Elihu, had been left a little farm in another part of Braintree. Deacon John Adams—or Ensign Adams, according to whether you regarded his rank in the church or in the militia—died three years before John's marriage.

John's house was rented by a Dr and Mrs Savil until the heir should want its use. But all summer the house had stood empty, while John employed what time he could spare from "attending courts and pursuing my studies" in getting house and garden in readiness for his bride. Like the parent homestead its walls were of brick and clay sheathed in wood, built above a deep, stone cellar, round a massive central brick chimney, with enormous fireplaces and deep, brick ovens. It had been built to last. The outside walls had no paint or whitewash, and when John brought home his bride the sturdy wood—more than fifty years old—had weathered to a neutral brownish grey. Before John's father's time a leanter* had been added at the back of each of the Adams houses. This was

* Or lean-to. The New Englanders pronounced and spelled it as above.

a long, sloping roof above a roomy kitchen, with another chimney and additional room, and a tiny crooked stair climbing to the upper floor.

The two houses, similar in appearance and in size, stood near each other, but not side by side upon the highway, nor back to back, nor staring into each other's faces. The father house looked rather towards the son house, as if in not too intent but rather casual oversight, and the son house turned away its shoulder in an independent but not brusque manner. They looked companionable set there in the quiet fields. In front of them, across the Old Shore Road to Boston, rose the steep green slope of Penns Hill, from the top of which one could get a good view of the near-by sea. And behind the farm stretched the long ridge of the Blue Hills. There was something about the region which had made its first settler, Morton of Merrymount*—who had established himself on what was now Abigail's Grandfather Quincy's farm, Mount Wollaston—break into a kind of rough blank verse: "So many goodly groves of trees; dainty, fine, round, rising hillocks; delicate fair large plains, sweet crystal fountains and clear running streams that twine in fine meanders through the meads, making so sweet a murmuring noise to hear." The landscape, now somewhat tamed by the hand of man, was still unspoiled. The weathered houses took their quiet places in the scene, and the lines of farm fields and crops looked calm against the background of wild woods. The main road, a rough track running north to Weymouth and Boston, and south and east to Hingham and beyond, still passed through some virgin forest. Braintree's one industrial enterprise was the glassworks, a large, round building which had been erected upon a peninsula between the river and the sea by newcomers from England, Joseph Palmer and Richard Cranch. Because Palmer had imported German glassworkers, it was called Germantown. Here Mary Cranch, recently Polly Smith, was settled, in close neighbourhood to her sister.

When John Adams ushered Abigail into her new home it is doubtful whether the two of them could stand together in the tiny entry. In front of them rose the precipitous, irregular stairs, roughly curved round the main chimney. On the right of the entry was the parlour, distinctly the room of state; on the left was John's office-study. Behind the office, and opening from it, was

* A renegade Puritan who frivolously set up a maypole, and had it cut down by Endicott.

the dining-room, in the leanter, with the kitchen next to it. The parlour also opened back into the kitchen, so that one could pass freely about the house. The office had an outside door for the use of clients. Upstairs there were two good bedrooms, and a tiny one, for a nurse or a child, opening off the chief room. There was attic space above the leanter on this floor, and the whole of the third floor under the rafters could be used for overflow guests or servants or children. It was simple, solid, and adequate. Abigail was charmed with it.

One of John Adams's last chores in preparation for marriage had been the hunting of a suitable maidservant, and after discussing the merits and demerits of several applicants by letter with his betrothed they had compromised on John's mother's slave-girl, Negress Judah, whom she offered them for the autumn and winter but wished to reclaim in the spring. Abigail did not take to this idea or to Judah, but it was an economical arrangement and she submitted. They would have to count their shillings carefully for the first year or two.

Perhaps it was over Judah that they had a quarrel ten days before their wedding—a dispute in which Abigail had felt really browbeaten. John Adams won his point, whatever it was. But Abigail had afterwards her own dignified and feeling come-back.

> A few things indeed I have met with that have really discomposed me, one was having a corrosive applied when a Semitive would have answered the same good purpose, but I hope I have drawn a lesson from it that will be useful to me in futurity viz. never to say a severe thing because to a feeling heart they wound too deeply to be easily cured—pardon me, this is not said for to recriminate—and I only mentioned it that whenever there is occasion a different method may be taken.*

She makes haste to add:

> 'Tis an old story tho' I hope as pleasing as it is true to tell you that I am
> Unfeignedly your
> DIANA†

But that was ten days ago. They have been reconciled. They are married.

Now the bright October day fades, and she is shut up in the house alone with him—him of the sometimes corrosive tongue, critical glance, forbidding silence—with his widowed mother and his two

*Adams MSS. Abigail from Boston, October 11, 1764. †Adams MSS.

brothers just across the yard, and his mother's old servant at her elbow. Does it promise fair?

Elizabeth Quincy Smith, and many others, would have said "No!"

The night closes down, and Judah has gone to her attic up the tiny back stairs. They take their candle and go up into that simple bedroom, with the windows facing east and south, the scanty, well-made furniture, and the high, canopied bed, and begin their life together, each with a humble heart but with an ardent hope.

And the foreboders turned out wrong. In her first letter after marriage Abigail compared her husband's presence to the sunshine, while John Adams wrote in his diary that his marriage was the source of all his felicity. Yet the strains and tests which lay ahead were beyond anything foreseen.

The first weeks were a kind of true honeymoon, and there is no honeymoon more delightful to a young bride than settling into her own house, feeling herself mistress of all she surveys.

John Adams could be good company, the best in the world;* and that Abigail was good company, with the "saucy spirit" that her friends had admired, no one would deny. They entertained each other well. Then, too, John Adams was not only a man of books, pen, and words; he was also an outdoor man, skilled in the farm. He could mend the fence and clear the spring, cut the firewood, keep an eye on horse and cow, and direct sowing and harvest. It was recreation for him. He loved the land. His hands were as much his servants as what he called "that great gland, the brain." He would come in after a day or an hour of outdoor work, invigorated and glowing, with an appetite as hearty as his laugh. And his young wife could work with her hands. She could cook and bake with the best. And with Judah to do the heavy work, she could sit down to the well-filled table fresh and neat, hair well arranged, eyes bright, bent on sharing her husband's interests, whatever they might be.

The only drawback to her marriage that Abigail noticed was that her husband's law business took him away so much, not only riding circuit but taking cases far afield—even as far as Martha's Vineyard.†

Part of their pleasure the first winter lay in the feeling of grow-

* According to Jonathan Sewall and Thomas Jefferson.

† An island off the coast of Cape Cod.

ing prosperity. Upward-climbing, forward-looking feeling, that is the essence of energy and hope. And from the first the husband, coming home with a wallet full of fees, would empty his leather pouch in his young wife's lap for her to administer the domestic economy. Discontent or argument over money was never known between them. Each was generous and open with the other, and each knew how to "make do" with what they had. They were partners in the building of a life together on a pattern that was agreeable now and promised affluence and larger influence in time to come. John Adams already belonged to a Boston club, and looked forward to a Boston practice. But private ambition and thrift did not begin to quench their public spirit. John Adams gave his time freely where he could to the service of his township, acting as surveyor of highways and selectman, attending town meeting, and serving on committees. And Abigail took it for granted that he should. It was in her family tradition.

Abigail had little time to realize that she was a wife before she had also to realize that she was a mother. Nine months after the wedding a daughter was born, whom the proud father named by the best name he knew, and that only—Abigail. Elizabeth Quincy Smith was at the bedside through the long, hot hours, to aid her daughter in every way that love and experience could devise, to supplement midwife and doctor with comfort and cheer, to welcome the little grandchild with true affection. Parson Smith's diary read, "July 14th, 1765. Mrs Adams deliv[d]. I Bap[d] the Child Abigail—pd from 2 Luke."

But at this crucial time a sharp crisis arose unexpectedly and forced John to make a sudden decision between private and public interest. The Writs of Assistance in Massachusetts had been repealed, the Acts of Trade modified. But the Stamp Act, put on by the British Parliament as an easy way of collecting a uniform tax throughout the colonies to pay for their own defence in time of war, affected all the colonies. The French-Indian, or Seven Years War, just past, had provided an object lesson in the injustice which arose when each colony had to manage its own war financing, for the ones in the front line were forced by circumstances to pay more than their share in both money and men.* This tax, imposed in the form of payment for stamps to be placed upon writs, wills, bills of sale, and other legal documents, had seemed reasonable to

* Braddock and an army also had been sent over at Britain's expense to defend her colonies.

most of the British Parliament. But it proved to be dynamite, and one of those who lit the fuse was John Adams.

The Stamp Act had been discussed for several months before it was passed. Cousin Sam Adams had drawn up a statement against it for the Boston town meeting in the spring of '64. "There is no room for delay!" he said. "Those unexpected proceedings may be preparatory to more taxation. This annihilates our charter right to govern & tax ourselves. We claim British rights, not by charter only; we are born to them!" And he urged the men of Massachusetts, "Use your endeavours that the weight of the other North American colonies may be added to that of this province, that by united application all may happily obtain redress."[1]

These matters were part of the table conversation in the farmhouse below Penns Hill. In the close association of domestic life Abigail was learning to understand her husband's temperament. It was like her own, warm and quick, but never nursing a grudge. It was unlike her own in being instantly expressive, whereas Abigail was more fluent with pen than tongue. John was affectionate, loyal, easily wounded, quick in remorse at wounding others; and, in private or public, always consistent, honest to the core. He had a large heart and a large mind. He fed eagerly on the admiration of other men. But, sharp with himself, he could be sharp with others, and too much of the schoolmaster sometimes lingered in his strictures, rousing resentment in the wounded vanity of others who considered themselves his equals or superiors.

With qualities like these John Adams could easily have become a domestic autocrat, and perhaps that is what Mrs Smith had feared. A meek woman would have been crushed by him, a woman of average intelligence would have been reduced to silence, an assertive woman, like Mercy Otis Warren,* would have found life a misery of continual battle. But Abigail's lively and natural self-confidence, her deep and wide intelligence, and her feminine softness made the ideal combination. Add to these her loving, heartfelt admiration of her husband and one perceived that John Adams, alone among the leaders of his time, had achieved a perfect mating. Familiarity, sickness, all the ups and downs and intimacies of married life in a cottage, never dulled his perception of that fact.

* Brilliant sister of James Otis. She was a poet and playwright much admired by John Adams. Her works were admired by George Washington. She wrote a history of the Revolution.

And as the months passed Abigail became more queenly, more assured, more his true companion in the heart-warming consciousness not only of his ardour but of his increasing respect. He did not scorn to share with her a man's world.

In May 1765 news arrived of the passing of the Stamp Act, to take effect in November. In June James Otis made his great speech in the Boston Assembly proposing the calling of a convention in October of representatives from all the colonies to discuss the Stamp (and Sugar) Acts and arrive at a united policy. The circular letter of invitation had just gone out to the colonies when news arrived in Boston of Patrick Henry's fiery resolutions in the Virginia House of Burgesses. The combination was combustible. A band calling themselves Sons of Liberty immediately formed in Boston, found out that Peter Oliver had been appointed to be stamp distributor for the town, marched his effigy in a roaring mob right through the lower part of the Town Hall while Governor Bernard and Lieutenant-Governor Hutchinson and Council were sitting in conclave in the council room above, hanged Oliver in effigy on a large tree in the main street, and wrecked Oliver's house. The insult was not lessened by the fact that Oliver was Hutchinson's brother-in-law. This demonstration had just shocked the town when John Adams, having seen his wife and child safely through the first month after the birth, left home on a long visit to Martha's Vineyard on legal business.

Abigail's mind, filled with the deep contentment and extraordinary tenderness of new motherhood, had no thought for politics. The Stamp Act would go the way of the Writs, no doubt, in time. It was late in August, and John had been gone about a fortnight, when she drove over to take tea with her Quincy cousins, eager to discuss infant care with her aunt. She had been reading some of the back numbers of *Ames Almanack* on the subject.

"I'm not swaddling my baby," she explained. "When the bodies of tender infants are done up tight in swathing, neither their breasts nor belly can rise so freely as they ought to when the child draws its breath, Dr Hales says."

"Well, my dear, say what you like, it's a great preventive of colic!" said Grandmother Quincy. "I always swathed mine. . . . Why, look who's tying his horse outside! Grandson Josiah!"

In came young Josiah Quincy, now twenty-one, and beginning law in Boston. He was full of agitation and a tale. His father,

Colonel Josiah, met him at the door. His voice was sharp. "Hutchinson! What, Hutchinson mobbed?"

"It was the night before last," said Josiah. "Mr Hutchinson came into court the next morning. I was there. You never saw anything like it! In his shirt and small-clothes! The stripped Chief Justice —such a man!—tears starting from his eyes—destitute of everything—no other shirt even! He was sitting at supper with his children when somebody ran in and said the mob were coming. The evening being warm he had taken off his coat, and put on a thin camlet surtout over his waistcoat. But he had to flee just as he was—got out by the back way and through into another house. His own house was completely broke up with axes and crowbars. Even the trees and garden-house were laid in ruin. The mob looted plate and family pictures, apparel, books, papers—thirty years' collection, he said—and nine hundred pounds in money. The poor gentleman was distraught, and denied he had encouraged the Stamp Act."[2]

"Well, I'm sorry he was treated so," said Abigail, "but I have heard that many a member of both Houses* laboured to obtain a resolution to send home a petition to the King and the Parliament against this Act, and that the Lieutenant-Governor prevented it. And I know, and we all know, that he is greedy of power, holding as he does four of the chief offices of the province. No one man should be Chief Justice *and* Treasurer *and* Lieutenant-Governor all at once, and then appoint his brother-in-law Stamp Collector, if he wishes to be thought disinterested."

"Whatever the provocation, there's no excuse for mob violence!" said the Colonel.

"The weather's partly to blame," said Josiah. "The town's a furnace. People get hot, and then they get thirsty, and then they take too much cider and rum, and their grievances run away with 'em. Good thing the Act isn't to operate until November. Everybody will feel cooler then."

A few days later John Adams came home, and though his young wife had much to tell him about the baby's charms, she had other things to talk of too. How much this Stamp Act and the resistance to it was to affect their personal lives, in ever-widening ripples, they could not guess.

. . .

* The Assembly and Council of Massachusetts.

No map of the American colonies, pored over by a tax-imposing Parliament, was likely to carry the name of Braintree. King George had never heard of its town meeting, or its nine selectmen. And since the King was a man of regular and simple habits, and the clocks of London were five hours ahead of the clocks of Braintree, no doubt George III was sound asleep on that mild autumn evening when Abigail kissed John good-bye as he set off to the town meeting, and she herself stepped across the garden to sit with Mother Adams.

"I doubt Jack is fussing himself too much about this new stamp duty they talk of," grumbled Mrs Adams, as they settled to their knitting. "Peter tells me it's Jack that has stirred up the folk to call this here town meeting. What docs Jack care? It's the lawyers that stand to *benefit* by the stamps, as far as I can see. He's got a wife to support, and now a child. He'd better keep his nose close to his business!"

"John minds his business," said Abigail mildly. And Mrs Adams was silent, uncomfortably remembering a time when she had unwisely and "with cruel reproaches"[3] urged her son to undertake business for which his inexperience was not ready. That was when John had come home to start his law practice, and she had thought it was time he earned his keep. He was then only twenty-three. But now at twenty-nine he was earning well, and had married into the best family in the neighbourhood. His decisions had for a long time been his own.

"John and Grandfather and my Uncle Josiah are all of one mind about this Stamp Act," went on Abigail presently. "They are quite certain that if it is enforced, when it comes due in November, it will mean our ruin. I mean the ruin of the colonies! We all know what the Acts of Trade and the Writs of Assistance were like. This is worse. John has drawn up a paper in which he has clearly stated that the Stamp Tax is 'a burthensome tax because the duties are so numerous and so high, and the embarrassments to business in this infant, sparsely settled country so great that it would be totally impossible for the people to subsist under it even if we had no controversy at all about the right and authority of imposing it.'"[4]

"Why, that last sentence," said the older woman, "is as good as treason. Colonies or none, Jack will ruin himself! Did he take that paper to the meeting?"

"Why, certainly! He's going to try to get it passed as a resolution to instruct the Braintree delegates to the House of Representatives what to do when the Stamp Act becomes law a few months from now."

"Child, he'll be a marked man! And for nothing. What does it matter what we do in a little place like this? Why does Jack have to make himself conspicuous, talking like that in public, when all it will result in will be getting Hutchinson against him? 'Twon't affect the Stamp Act one way or t'other. But a black mark from the Chief Justice can keep a man down!"

Abigail listened to her mother-in-law's words, and she could not deny them. But her mind flew to the town meeting, now in progress. She saw the gathering of the men of Braintree in the meeting-house of the North Precinct, saw the two or three hundred men sitting on the backless benches on the men's side. Most of them she knew, at least by sight. Her mother's cousin, Edmund Quincy, was presiding as Moderator. Dignified in wig and ruffles, he sat in the Deacons' bench below the empty pulpit, his fine figure casting a great shadow on the whitewashed wall, the candles in front of him accentuating the lines deep-graven in his thoughtful face. Jo Cleverly and Major Miller, William Veasey and Jonathan Bass, and Captain Thayer would be sure to be there. And there for sure was Peter Boylston Adams, John's brother, who had accompanied him to the meeting, his loyal supporter and lieutenant in every plan. Now Abigail imagined her husband had the floor. He was addressing the meeting with that fire and vigour, that complete conviction, which she knew so well, and which compelled attention, even from opponents. She could feel the meeting tighten up, she could see them all lean towards him, deeply stirred.

"Oh, Mother," she replied at last to Mrs Adams, "John thinks, and I think too, that this is no time for private interests to come first. He is saying to-night, 'We further recommend the most clear and explicit assertion and vindication of our rights and liberties to be entered on the public records, that the world may know, in the present and all future generations, that we have a clear knowledge and a just sense of them, and, with submission to Divine Providence, that we never can be slaves.'"[6]

There was a long silence. Slow tears gathered and fell, in the candle-light, on the little woollen hood Mrs Adams was knitting for her first grandchild.

"Ay," said John that night, holding Abigail to his heart, "carried unanimously! including the key sentence."[9]

A day or two after the town meeting John Adams rode into Boston to deliver a copy of his Resolutions to Draper the printer, who had asked permission to publish them in his weekly news-sheet, and on the way called on his father's cousin, Samuel Adams. The name of Sam Adams was beginning to be heard in Boston in the way of politics, for, by means of the powerful private caucus created by his father, Sam Adams had been elected this year to the Massachusetts House of Representatives.

He was a graduate of Harvard, but up to this time he had not found his métier. He had dabbled a little in law, a little in trade, and failed at both. But his powerful mind and brilliant conversation had always commanded his younger cousin's admiration. John found him now in his stuffy, dark little office, driving his quill across the paper in clouds of tobacco smoke. Now forty-two, he looked much older. He had a blunt, strong face, but his hair was already grey, and he had fallen prey to an infirmity which kept his head and hands shaking like those of a paralytic. He welcomed John Adams eagerly.

"Now, John, you're just the man I want. I've been appointed by the town of Boston to draw up a set of instructions for their representatives in the House with relation to the coming stamps. And I feel an ambition which is apt to mislead a man—that of doing something extraordinary.[7] Here, cousin, read over what I've put here, and give me your comments. Frank and honest I know they will be. And to the point, I dare swear."

"I read his instructions," said John to Abigail afterwards, "and showed him a copy of mine. I told him I thought his very well as far as they went, but he had not gone far enough."

"And what did he say to that?" said Abigail.

"Well, upon reading mine, he said he was of my opinion, and accordingly took into his some paragraphs from mine."[8]

"But then he will get the credit for them!" said Abigail, jealous for her John.

He laughed out, as surprised as he was amused. He had not yet got used to the odd combination of her clear mind and her woman's point of view.

"My dear," he said, "we are out for bigger things than any man's credit."

John Adams's Resolutions for the town of Braintree, circulated in the press, went through the province like wildfire, and were adopted verbatim by forty towns at their town meetings. They even found their way down to Virginia and rang familiar echoes in the heart of Patrick Henry.

Abigail got early notice from her cousins when the ship bearing the stamps arrived in Boston. But since to unpack and distribute the stamps was obviously to provoke riot, the bundles were dumped in the Castle, three miles out of town. Every province was in the same predicament; no one would unpack and distribute the stamps. Appointed distributors everywhere went in terror. But Lieutenant-Governor Hutchinson of Massachusetts was an astute and obstinate man. He advised Governor Bernard to exercise pressure by closing all law courts and public offices in Massachusetts, on the grounds that all legal documents not bearing the new stamps would be ineffective, and all writers of same would be liable, under the Act, to a fine of ten pounds for each offence. With this encouragement, Peter Oliver quietly took over again the potentially lucrative office of collector of the Stamp Duty.

All the Massachusetts counties except Suffolk County, in which were Weymouth and Braintree and the city of Boston, found ways of getting around the court closure by opening the inferior and probate courts under local judges who defied the stamps and refused to issue fines. But Abigail's husband practised in Suffolk County, where Hutchinson was in complete control of the machinery, and so found himself, with all his fellows at the Boston bar, suddenly deprived of his livelihood. It certainly looked like ruin.

"The bar seem to me to behave like a flock of shot pigeons," he complained bitterly to Abigail.

John was sitting in the quiet house at Braintree, posting his books, regulating his accounts, making himself out a course of reading for the winter, and trying to calm his fretted spirit with Abigail's cheering company, when a deputation suddenly rode up through the December mud to summon him to public action. The Boston town meeting had unanimously voted to appoint him, along with Mr Gridley and James Otis, as counsel to appear before the Governor "in support of their memorial that the courts of law in this province be opened."

John Adams called his wife aside, showed her the letter. "What shall I do? What do you say?"

Abigail's heart throbbed.

"Ah—what an opportunity! How did it happen?"

"Opportunity; not risk." He laughed short, and embraced her.

"The reasons which induced Boston to choose me, at a distance and unknown as I am," he remarked to his Braintree friends, "I am wholly at a loss to conjecture."[9] But it is perhaps not irrelevant that Cousin Sam Adams was chairman of the town committee.

The next day Abigail and baby Nabby waved farewell as John rode off to Boston to discuss with Gridley and Otis and Cousin Sam the line of argument to be taken.

At candle-light the appointed three were summoned before the Governor to present the memorial and to speak for it.

They stood there in the stately council chamber, three men, the wedge of opposition to royal authority, before the King's representative of that authority. But which of them was to be the point of the wedge? Not till that moment did it occur to them that in their consideration of impersonal ideals and high principles they had omitted to arrange the detail of which of them should speak first. Gridley claimed to speak last; Otis claimed to speak second; they laid the difficult opening on their junior, John Adams.

"Then it fell upon me," said John Adams to his wife, when he got home on Sunday, "without one moment's opportunity to consult any authorities, to open an argument upon a question that was never made before, and I wish I could hope it never would be made again! That is, whether the courts of law should be open or not!"[10]

He was not proud of his first appearance upon the stage of history. He gave all credit to Gridley and Otis.[11] And the whole course of the unsuccessful struggle with the Governor stimulated his admiration for his cousin Sam Adams, who with integrity, "an artful pen," genuine piety, and charm of manner, had "the most thorough understanding of liberty."[12]

Sunday he spent at home, "thinking." But what different lively thoughts! And on Monday, back to Boston, to the arena of events, in which he now had a leading part. No more was the winter lean and dull. The lightness of his purse no longer worried him. His mind was keenly bent on studying out the most difficult legal case of his career, making precedents as he went. He worked not in loneliness and solitude but in daily association with the cream of the city of Boston. His companions drew his admiration and pleased him greatly, for it is a delight to a brilliant talker to meet with his peers. Each day he felt more vigorously at the hub of affairs, but deep in his heart, base of his confidence and good humour, was the thought of Abigail, happy at home at Braintree with her baby, sending her thoughts constantly to him, fully understanding the nature of his task. Good humour is the source of moderation. Your happily married man may be a fighter in a good cause, but he is never a sour one. And Sam Adams, chairman of the committee, appreciated this quality in his cousin.

Abigail had no time to be lonely. Friends and relatives were always dropping in to tea. Her precious Grandmother Quincy was an easy walk away; Weymouth was comfortably close; and Boston was not too far for John to come home often. Christmas came on a Wednesday, and John rode home on Christmas Eve to spend the holiday with his family. It was a perfect day. They did not even go to meeting. John took the time "thinking, reading, searching, concerning taxation without consent." They had a cosy dinner at home; and then they walked through the brisk, frosty air to drink tea at Grandfather Quincy's. Old Colonel John had always regarded John Adams as a young man with a future. Grandmother had long since lost her prejudice against him, seeing that he made her beloved granddaughter so happy. Welcome and love and elegance and grace awaited them there. The low winter sun shone on fine china and silver, on polished walnut and maple. The tea-table was drawn to the fire, and the white-haired hostess, erect and dainty in her beautiful striped satin dress and white lace cap, had eyes as bright and dark as Abigail's own. There was good talk, as good as Boston's; "the old gentleman inquisitive about the hearing before the Governor and Council; about the Governor's and Secretary's looks and behaviour, and about the final determination of the board. The old lady as merry and chatty as ever, with her stories out of the newspapers."

But when the candles were brought John and Abigail took their leave, before the country lanes got too dark, and went back to relax by their own fireside and savour their supreme content. "Spent the evening at home with my partner and no other company."[13]

It was good that they took that chance while they had it. It was the last Christmas of their lives of which that might be said.

• • •

In many ways, that winter of the Stamp Act was an extraordinarily happy time for Abigail. Her husband was frequently at home all day. "Mr Hayward dined; Town politics the subject. Doctor Tufts here in the afternoon; American politics the subject." And Abigail, presiding at the table or part of the group on the settle beside the hearth, was a partner in the talk. Modest and discreet, more a listener than a talker, she was learning the arts of politics and feeling under her finger the throbbing pulse of the time. The little cottage at the foot of Penns Hill had become one of the arteries of American opinion.

Severe cold and deep snow shut the house in that winter. The three main fires, kept up day and night, maintained a central triangle of warmth. One bundled up in clothes. Men wore their overcoats to sit down at the table, a few feet from the genial circle of heat, and Abigail had layers of petticoats that made her look like a large rose and feel like a feather-bed. It gave her girlish figure a matronly dignity. She had also a dignity of mind, along with her youthful zest, which struck her husband's visitors forcibly. Not many strangers, however, were likely to find their way to Braintree at that season. The outer world entered by way of the newspaper and the mail. Uncle Tufts and brother Peter Boylston Adams, neighbour Field and Parson Wibird and Mr Cleverly and Cousin Josiah Quincy and Dick Cranch were the ones who came, slamming the door to quickly, stamping off the snow in the little entry.

As they stared into the glowing logs at that simple fireside their eyes ranged over the colonies.

Led by John Adams's bold mind, his wife and brothers and friends lost that strong parochial feeling engendered by close living in one place. Abigail lifted her attention from the cradle, from the flickering shadows of the room, from the small snug house, from the village—nay, from Boston itself, and from the province of Massachusetts. Was she a villager—or a Bostonian—or a colonial? Something much more than, and different from, all these. John had the word.

"Wretched blunders do they make, these British," said her husband, "they know not *the character of Americans*!"[14]

As Abigail's political education proceeded, there was no inner conflict set up in her by difference of opinion among those whom she held dear. Wherever she went, there was the same spirit.

John harnessed the sleigh and drove with Abigail over the smooth surface of the packed, hard snow to Weymouth, a delightful drive in the sharp, glittering air. And there at dinner with Abigail's father and mother and young sister Elizabeth they heard that Parson Smith had recently preached a fiery sermon from the text, "Render therefore unto Cæsar the things that are Cæsar's; and unto God the things that are God's." The tenor of the sermon was to recommend obedience to good rulers and a spirited opposition to bad ones, and its lesson was brought right up to date, in Parson Smith's best manner.[15] The congregation wanted to print it.

Abigail could not even conceive of a contrary opinion. The principal local Tory (as Government supporters soon came to be called), Mr Cleverly, was to her "that unaccountable man, who goes about sowing his seeds of Mischief." Other Tory neighbours were also "poisonous talkers," though not so bad as Cleverly. The "Tories" were trying to divide and disunite the people. That the resisters to the Stamp Act might be regarded as striving to divide people who had all been loyal subjects of the King never entered her head for a moment.

There was a Sunday when Parson Wibird at Braintree warmed her up in the freezing-cold, unheated meeting-house—where the congregation would sit on the uncushioned benches, men to the right, women to the left, boys in the gallery, from ten-thirty to twelve-thirty and from two to four, weekly, regardless of weather—by preaching from the text, "I have nourished and brought up children, and they have rebelled against me." Mr Wibird certainly got attention that day. Nobody went to sleep; all had their ears pricked indignantly for the expected Tory lesson to be drawn. But none was forthcoming. Mr Wibird skilfully skirted round the subject, and let his text speak for itself.

Every week John Adams spent several days in Boston, and always came back full of tales of elegant dinners and political talk.

He described the rich furnishings of his kinsman Nick Boylston's house: "Turkey carpets, painted hangings, marble tables, rich beds with crimson damask curtains and counterpanes, the beautiful chimney clock—the spacious garden." He was struck with unwilling admiration. "It was altogether magnificent. Fit for a nobleman, a prince."[16]

Abigail was intensely curious and felt she would like to see it sometime. It was the nearest she was ever likely to get to any nobleman or prince.

"But tell about the Sons of Liberty. Were they a very wild crew?"

"Not at all. You'd be surprised—as I was! No doubt their methods attract the rowdy element, and give the riff-raff of the town a chance to riot and loot, as we saw in the sad case of Mr Hutchinson. Mob law is no law. But the Sons of Liberty are a very respectable organization. They meet in a counting-room in Chase and Speakman's distillery, in Hanover Square, near the Liberty Tree. A very small room it is. John Avery was chairman —a distiller and merchant, a man of a liberal education—and he invited me. There were present Smith, the brazier, Crafts, the painter, Edes, the printer, Chase, the distiller, Field, the master of a vessel, Trott, the jeweller, and a few other reputable tradesmen. I was very civilly and respectfully treated by all present. We had punch, wine, pipes and tobacco, biscuit and cheese, etc. I heard nothing but what passes at all clubs, among gentlemen, about the times. No plots, no machinations. They were so certain of repeal that they were appointing a committee to be in charge of grand rejoicings when it should occur—such fireworks, bonfires, illuminations and the rest as were never before seen in America! I wish they may not be disappointed."[17]

"Be sure you take me in to see it!" said Abigail.

"Indeed, then, madam, you had better start to make payment in advance for it."

"And how, sir?"

"Why, by paying me back some of those kisses you owe me. I am sure you are in my debt three million at least!"[18]

Abigail perceived that her husband had quite suddenly become an important man, whose influence was sought by many groups, and her pride in it was the greater that it had happened through no one's patronage, but by his own inherent qualities backed by steady self-preparation.

The same outspoken honesty that had made him enemies was now making him friends in every quarter of the town.

Although the Superior Court remained closed, the Gridley, Otis, and Adams committee, backed by the House of Representatives, succeeded in forcing the reopening of the inferior Court of Common Pleas in Boston, and through the late winter and spring John Adams had resumed that part of his law business. Late in March Abigail's uncle, Dr Tufts, came for the night, bearing the newspaper account of Pitt's warm speech for repeal in the House of Commons. And two months later, in the middle of May 1766, the news of the repeal of the Stamp Act reached Boston.

That was the great day for the fireworks, the bells, the bonfires, the cannon, and all the rest, and the well-prepared Sons of Liberty did their part. Boston went mad. The glow of torches and the flare of rockets in the sky could be seen from the top of Penns Hill. But Abigail did not even get that satisfaction, confined to the house, she and her baby both, with whooping-cough. In all this passion of national joy it was not much to light up the house with candles to surprise their quiet cow and dazzle passing owls. For once both she and her husband felt that their country seclusion was almost too complete. "A duller day than last Monday, when the Province was in a rapture for the repeal of the Stamp Act, I do not remember to have passed . . . unable to go to Boston, and the town of Braintree insensible to the common joy."[1]

But the Superior Law Courts were immediately opened everywhere, business was pressing, whooping-cough passed away in the summer sunshine, and Abigail and her child recovered their colour and liveliness. On Sunday, the twenty-fourth of July, appointed as a day of religious thanksgiving for the repeal, they all three drove in the chaise to Weymouth to hear Father Smith preach. His happy knack with texts was once more exemplified. "The Lord reigneth, let the earth rejoice; let the multitude of isles be glad thereof."[20] The application was all that his congregation—and those that came over from Hingham—had hoped for.

At home in Braintree, Parson Wibird, whose political opinions had been suspect but elusive, diddled them again. He chose a text from Genesis, "But as for you, ye thought evil against me; but God meant it unto good, to bring it to pass, as it is this day, to save much people alive."

John Adams, hearing of it, chuckled to Abigail, "Wibird shone, they say!"[21]

There were some rewards to be gleaned in those days for the excessive length of the church services.

A storm had blown over; the colonies had waked out of a nightmare. "The repeal of the Stamp Act had hushed into silence almost every popular clamour, and composed every wave of popular disorder into a smooth and peaceful calm," wrote John Adams in his diary.[22] Every letter and newspaper that came from England breathed benevolence and peace. It was a new era of better understanding and advancing prosperity.

In August Abigail, dressed in her best summer things and radiant with smiles, drove over with John to visit her sister and husband, who had recently moved to Salem. They dined at Boston, drank tea at Dr Tuft's at Medford, lodged for the night, set off next day, oated at Martin's, and reached brother Cranch's at twelve o'clock; dined and drank tea, and then went eagerly about through the flat, level town to see the sights. Next day the two sisters, Mary and Abigail, got into a chaise and drove to Marblehead and back, John Adams escorting them on horseback.[23] It was a delightful holiday.

In November, when John Adams had to attend court in Salem, they repeated the visit. "Arrived at my dear brother Cranch's about eight and drank tea and are all very happy." The sisters had a marvellous gossip, about children, neighbours, all kinds of woman things. It did John good to hear them. "Sat and heard the ladies talk about ribbon, cat-gut and Paris net, riding-hoods, cloth, silk and lace. Brother Cranch came home, and a very happy evening we had."[24] Four people more congenial with each other could hardly have been found.

"My love to Mr Cranch and his lady," said John Adams when he saw his wife writing her letter of thanks; "tell them I love them; I love them better than any mortals who have no other title to my love than friendship gives."[25]

The year that had opened with such serious public thoughts, with events that lifted their eyes to wide and bleak horizons, closed by bringing them back to the snug private circle of their little house at Penns Hill and their nine and a half acres. The unease of change had touched that circle too. Faithful old Tom at Weymouth—he who had smoked the letters—had died, sincerely mourned; Mrs Adams senior was being courted by a Mr Hall, and expected to marry again in December; Abigail herself had entered on what her husband called "all the Qualms that necessarily [are] at end or beginning pregnancy, in all other respects very happy." But in all these changes the land remained, solid and familiar under their feet. In deep serenity, under the blue November sky, Abigail strolled through the wood pasture with John, learning woodcraft from him as she had learned politics. The brilliant sunshine above the arches of red and golden leaves made a rich-coloured gloom in the thick woods. The little stream could be heard struggling with choking rocks and dead leaves.

"We must prune these oaks and buttonwoods and maples," said John Adams, "and fell without mercy all these irregular, misshapen pines. Ay, I'll have them all out. I am desirous of clearing out the rocky gutter—maybe clear out the rocks and make a ditch for the water. But first and foremost we must let in the sun and air to sweeten the grass."[26]

III

Boston

Abigail's second child was born on July 11, 1767. Elizabeth Quincy Smith presided over the agony attendant on the coming of life, all the while holding in her heart the picture of another candlelit room just left, in her father's house by the sea, where life was ebbing out. Parson Smith's diary laconically notes that the Hon. John Quincy died July 13, in the seventy-eighth year of his age. On the day of his death his great-grandson was duly christened John Quincy.

Abigail, lying in the big feather-bed, exhausted, happy, and sad, had no suspicion that the two men who, each in his own way—one so earnestly masculine, one so nuzzling and small—comforted her sorrow were both incipient Presidents of a republic yet unborn.

But fate was busy at the loom. The King was exasperated with his Parliament for repealing the Stamp Act. He regarded the colonies as naughty schoolboys who needed the rod, and resented their triumph. To give in to them was a dangerous precedent. By January 1767 the King and Townshend in England had concocted another act, behind the back of the dying Pitt, setting new duties to raise colonial revenue. William Pitt, Lord Chatham, was not only old and sick; his attention was distracted from colonial affairs. A new object dazzled him. He confessed to Townshend, "I need not tell you how entirely this transcendent object, India, possesses my heart and fixes my thoughts."[1] The House of Commons passed the Townshend Bill to raise revenues in the American colonies by customs duties on glass, paper, painters' colours, and tea, none of which were produced in America, the duties to be spent in maintaining a standing army for defence of the colonies, and providing permanent salaries for colonial governors and judges.

Benjamin Franklin, agent for several colonies in London, had seen nothing wrong with this measure. "The Americans," he said, "think you have no right to levy excise within their country on native products. But the sea is yours; you maintain by your fleets the safety of navigation on it, and keep it clear of pirates. You may have, therefore, a natural and equitable right to some toll or duty on merchandise carried through that part of your dominions, towards defraying the expense you are at in ships to maintain the safety of that carriage."[2]

But the money was not to go for ships. And Franklin missed the main issue—the same as in the Stamp Act. The issue of the right of Parliament to tax the colonies, fairly or unfairly, directly or indirectly.

Paxton, Marshal of the Boston Court of Admiralty, was in London, advising his friend Townshend that "ships of war and a regiment" would be needed "to ensure tranquillity," and then all would go well.

The Sons of Liberty in Boston replied with a campaign to refuse use or purchase of any of the taxed imports. And so did Dickinson in Pennsylvania and Patrick Henry and George Washington in Virginia; the movement was taking hold throughout the colonies. The French naturally had secret agents in America noting and fomenting discontent. Governor Bernard, backed by Hutchinson, was sending home to England for troops to break up resistance and enforce the Townshend Act, when it should go into effect.

At present Abigail Adams's mind was wholly in her home, but what security and warmth she gave her husband! He always kept with him one of her letters from the autumn of '67, telling him that the baby was "better," and that little Nabby, three years old, "rocks him to sleep with the song of 'Come, papa, come, home to brother Johnny.'" And then Abigail adds—though writing during a visit to the parsonage, her old home—

> Sunday seems a more lonely day to me than any other when you are absent; for though I may be compared to those climates which are deprived of the sun half the year, yet upon a Sunday you commonly afford us your benign influence! I am now at Weymouth, my father brought me here last night. To-morrow I return home, where I hope soon to receive the dearest of friends and the tenderest of husbands.[3]

The physical setting of that spiritual entity called "home," however, was soon to change. In the spring of 1768 the demands of a growing law practice induced them to move to Boston, where they rented the White House, Brattle Square.

John had talked things over with Abigail and resolved to avoid further entanglement in public affairs, which brought no grist to the mill. He now had two children, and his family responsibilities must come first. He refused re-election as selectman at Braintree. He would not even attend town meeting in Boston. Indeed, his avoidance of entanglement was so marked, and his determination to get on with his job so openly declared, that Otis accused him of caring for nothing but making money, and Hutchinson, who had successfully limed Sewall by creating for him and placing him in the office of Attorney-General of the Province, thought the time was ripe for catching John Adams also.

One afternoon, near the three o'clock dinner hour, the maid, answering the knocker's clamour, ushered in Jonathan Sewall, dressed ceremoniously in best scarlet coat and fresh ruffles. With an ingratiating bow to Abigail he claimed the privilege of old friendship to invite himself to dinner. Abigail was charmed. She liked company, and Sewall, who had married her cousin Esther Quincy, was a clever and likeable man. John Adams too, coming in from his office, gave hearty welcome. Differences in politics should not dissolve friendship. They sat down together at the family table, happy and easy in talk of people and scenes near and dear to them all. Little Nabby, aged four, comported herself daintily.

Sewall's eye quickly discerned in his hostess's figure the signs of coming motherhood. And here was one child at table, and another upstairs with its nurse. A man who is giving these hostages to fortune is in a conservative—as Hutchinson would say, a reasonable—frame of mind. John Adams had sown his political wild oats and should be ready to settle down, especially if it were made worth his while. His value to the Tory cause could hardly be overestimated. After dinner Sewall made it courteously clear that he had business to discuss—should they perhaps adjourn to the office? But Abigail rose pleasantly and, taking her little girl by the hand, said that she was going upstairs to her chamber, and would bid the gentlemen good evening.

The gentlemen lighted their pipes and drew their chairs to the window, which opened at the back over the green, shady garden, and without further preliminary, and with good hope of success, Sewall broached his errand.

An hour later John Adams came upstairs to his wife.

"Put on your bonnet, my dear. I have ordered the chaise to be at the door in ten minutes. I'm going to take you for a drive in this fine evening air!"

Abigail saw that he was excited and stirred, but she had learned that he would tell her the quicker if she restrained hasty questions. So she put on her light summer bonnet before the glass and pushed her dark curls becomingly into place, while her husband took a turn about the room.

"What do you suppose Sewall came for?" he burst out. "You'd never guess. . . . Why, to ask me, on Governor Bernard's behalf, to take the office of Advocate-General in the Court of Admiralty. To bribe me, in fact, with immediate fortune and a sure career of advancement. . . . Sewall could not bring himself to take my refusal seriously. He said I could not refuse off-hand like that—I must take time to think it over! I reminded him of my political opinions, which were not likely to change overnight. He replied that he was instructed by the Governor to say that I should be at full liberty to hold my opinions—which were well known—and that the Governor *did not wish to influence me* by this office. He had offered it to me merely because he believed I was the best qualified for it and because he relied on my integrity! . . . Well, my dear, what ought I to have said?"

Abigail came to him and put her hands softly on his shoulders.

"Just exactly what I know you did say!" she murmured, as one putting a secret in his ear.

His strong arms came round her waist.

"What? What?"

"Why, that it would put you under obligations and restraints that you could not in honesty accept!"

"Right, right, my lass, my dear girl, my Portia!" He kissed her lips in his eager, ardent way. "And yet Jon Sewall was astounded and vexed! Kept saying 'Why are you so quick and sudden? You'd better consider it and give me an answer another day!' I told him my answer was ready because my mind was clear. But he went away sulky, swearing he would be back in three weeks and would hope I'd changed my mind."[4]

"He can't bear to see another man firm and clear where he himself fell into the toils!" said Abigail.

John was silent and took her down to the waiting chaise. They drove away in a companionable thoughtfulness through the sunny streets. Long evening shadows stretched across the way. There were many trees to spread the refreshment of greenness and shade. Gulls wheeled and floated above their heads against the blue, and an evening breeze, smelling of seaweed and fish, came up from the sea. Abigail remembered a time when her husband had said that he couldn't think in Boston, what with the distractions of the passing traffic, the "rattle-gabble" of the streets. But now the varied sights and sounds fell into place as an undercurrent to their thoughts. Love of the hilly, salty city had taken hold of them. This was the kind of life they wanted: Boston and Braintree, city and country, in a steady re-creating rhythm; a life mainly private, centred in the home, with their children growing up around them and their friends freely passing in and out; and later on, when the basis of secure prosperity was well laid, acceptance of public responsibilities without compromise of principle. The times were restless now but they would settle. Refusal to buy British imports was essential. Townshend himself was dead,* and repeal was only a matter of time, patience, and law-abiding pressure. John Adams, giving his wife her airing, reflected that a man's first duty was to his wife and family. Not riches they wanted, merely security; to have necessaries and comforts and books, to send their sons to college, start them in a respectable profession or business, and keep out of debt.

Men like James Otis, with security established and family grown, or like John Hancock, not yet married and rolling in riches, they were the ones to give their time to the non-remunerative tasks of public reform. While John was expressing this to Abigail they caught sight of Samuel Adams marching along the pavement, a conspicuous figure with his shaking head and occasional involuntary gesture. Now there was a case in point! . . . They drew up beside the curb.

"Come, cousin, drive with us! Come home to supper!"

Sam Adams got in, with his shabby, ill-brushed coat and well-concealed linen contrasting with John's trim suit and ironed ruffles, and at once said:

"John, I want thee to harangue the public meeting I have persuaded the Sons of Liberty to summon next week on the legality of the Townshend Revenue Act. I was walking now to thy house."

* Died September 4, 1767.

"I shall be away on circuit," said John, "and I have told you and my friend Dr Warren I will harangue no meetings. That way madness lies.[5] Even the great Otis is driving himself crazy with constant eloquence to work up public feeling! Tell me, Cousin Sam, did you never, when you were my age, with a young growing family, feel the necessity of laying by and planning for the future?"

"No, I have to confess," said Sam Adams thoughtfully, "I have never in my life looked forward; never made any plan or scheme of laying up anything for myself or others after me."[6]

His discourse that evening on political matters so enthralled John that he almost regretted that he would be absent from the planned town meeting. Dr Warren was most urgent that John Adams should address it, most disappointed that he would not. But before Sam Adams left he drew John aside and quite naturally and simply asked him for a loan. And John Adams, unlocking his desk drawer and taking out the cash with generous readiness, was privately confirmed in his decision to give attention to the necessary task of paying his own way.

So he was away on circuit when the town meeting met, and had nothing to do with the letter it sent out to invite all selectmen of the other towns in Massachusetts to a convention in Boston. The convention was in its closing session when fifteen British men-o'-war sailed into Boston harbour, carrying on board two regiments of soldiers.

Abigail's condition prevented her from being among those who put off in boats to see the ships near to—and who came back with their sight-seeing ardour damped by observation of cannon in readiness upon the decks. But even from Brattle Square she could see in the deep night sky the falling stars of rockets which the soldiers and sailors, in a surprising burst of gaiety, sent up from the ships. And together with every one else who could look from a window or walk to the end of a street she saw the amazing march of the troops into the town a few days later.* They marched through the quiet crowds with their muskets charged and bayonets fixed, drums beating and fifes playing, with a train of artillery and a couple of cannon.[7] But there was a sad fizzle-out at the end of the march when there was nowhere to go but the Common. The citizens of Boston sardonically refused billet. The soldiers, some

* On October 1, 1768. The Townshend duties were to be imposed on November 20.

seven hundred of them,[8] deployed on the Common and pitched tents, and, unable to get firewood except by paying for it, ate cold rations around their cold artillery.

Abigail was startled and indignant at all this martial display. Wherever she went, at Uncle Isaac's or at the Otises', where young Sam Otis was courting her cousin Mary, Isaac Smith's daughter, or at the houses of any of the Quincy connexion save one (the Sewalls), the talk was the same. Why all these guns and fixed bayonets? Are we an enemy town?

It was not more soothing to Abigail that she was wakened every morning early by "the spirit-stirring drum and the ear-piercing fife" when Major Small marched his regiment up to drill in Brattle Square right in front of her house. There they were, the ridiculous lobsters—and the street boys showed their usual uncanny aptitude of phrase in calling them so. In scarlet coats and high pointed caps, with bayonets for antennæ, they turned and wheeled and clanked about, both picturesque and silly in the autumn sunshine. John Adams came back and heard and saw everything, and his comments were caustic. He told her a bitter joke that was running the town: "'Our grievances are red-dressed!' But patience. We must help the town to hold itself steady. Our method of resistance is the lawful, pacific one of passive resistance. Violence in word or act will only weaken our cause. The embargo on all British imports, steadily, unitedly applied, must win. It will hurt us and our trade, but it will hurt the English more. They can't afford to bear it."

"Well, at any rate," said Abigail, "they can't use their bayonets to force me or any other housewife to buy what we don't want to!"

John Hancock's sloop the *Liberty* had been searched for contraband wines by suspicious customs commissioners, who found the cargo had been unloaded at night on Hancock's Wharf to avoid paying the duty. Hancock was prosecuted to the tune of £100,000 sterling. He engaged John Adams as his counsel, and the case greatly inflamed public opinion.

Parson Smith did not step aside from his duties to enter politics, though his opinions were well known, and his laconic diary contains, except by implication, no comment on the times. As the year 1768 rolled to its quiet but storm-laden close Mr Smith impartially notes—"Dec. 1st Thanksgiving Day. 14th brot my sheep from Hingham. 23rd Mrs Adams deliver[d] of a daughter." This third child was christened Susanna.

So this year Parson and Mrs Smith spent the Christmas season with their daughter Abigail in the White House, Brattle Square. And they too could join little Nabby and Johnny at the window to watch the redcoats drilling in the falling snow.

It was hard on a baby to be born in a Boston winter. Little Susanna was a frail child, and her weak cries of discomfort and protest absorbed her mother's attention almost to the exclusion of the sound of drum and fife outside the door. Yet when Abigail passed about the streets on marketing or social affairs the town seemed full of soldiers. Their conspicuous red coats met one at every turn. Four regiments were now in Boston, two from Halifax and two from Ireland, totalling upward of two thousand men. And that number is not easily absorbed by a population of sixteen thousand.[9] The soldiers were under strict orders from General Gage and their officers to behave with circumspection and provoke no incident. But the offences of soldiers everywhere—drunkenness, sex, hectoring—were of constant occurrence.

Their presence, in fact, was a continual provocation and a nuisance rather than a punishment. The Governor found himself unable to administer the Quartering Act requiring free lodging and firewood against the steady passive resistance of intelligent Boston. The Quartering Act provided that if there were a barracks, soldiers could be quartered there instead of in the homes of citizens. Boston pointed out that it *had* a barracks—at the Castle, three miles out. Put the soldiers there; they could live rent free. If in the houses in the town, they must pay. The soldiers paid. The canny Yankees set to work to make money out of them in other ways too—firewood, candles, food. It was exasperating to the high-tempered Governor to see his protecting troops, meant as terrorists, treated as customers.

No one, in fact, was afraid of the soldiers, after the first shock. Street boys booed them—at a safe distance. John Adams had no qualms about leaving his little family unprotected when it was time to go away again on circuit.

Yet the White House on Brattle Square was not unmarked. Leaving her ailing baby with the nurse, Abigail would come downstairs to pour coffee or chocolate (tea being now tabooed) for Cousin

Sam Adams, for handsome John Hancock, for Mr Gridley, Mr Cushing, and many other habitual visitors of note; and would take part in talk which would find its outcome in action. She would listen to constant plans to keep the peace between the population and soldiers. She would see her husband consulted at every turn. John Adams's draft instructions, throughout '68 and '69, though he never attended a town meeting, were adopted without alteration by the town,[10] and no instructions were drawn up unless he had prepared the draft. She felt and approved of the steady moderation and conservatism with which he curbed his fiery, positive energy. And in all the discussions to which she was a part, these keen, farseeing men carefully refused to look farther into the future than to the withdrawal of the troops, the repeal of the Townshend Act.

Often of an evening, especially as the weather grew milder, the sweet plaintive strains of violins and flutes, accompanied by songs, rose under the windows. Nabby and Johnny, preparing for bed, would scramble to the window and look out between the curtains.

"Who are those men, Mama?" asked Nabby the first time.

"They are the Sons of Liberty, your father's friends. At least," said Abigail, looking down too, with a quickening breath, "they think your father is one of *their* friends. . . . Come, Johnny, now the song is done, come say your prayers!"

John Adams, entering the bedroom, hushed the comment he was about to make concerning the serenade. His baby son was kneeling with fat hands pressed together against his mother's knee. The white homespun linen nightshirts made both children look like cherubs. Curly-haired Nabby was earnestly listening to Johnny's performance, her lips silently moving with his.

"Now Ilayme darnter seep . . ."

The drowsy baby lisp of not understood but holy words made something better to listen to than violins.

Abigail presently laid her husband's hand against her cheek.

"You won't let the Sons of Liberty draw you out into their doings?" she murmured.

"No," said the firm, decided voice she trusted. "I'll take no part in public. I've no time, in any case. You and the children come first, and I'm even half sorry I undertook John Hancock's case in regard to the customs' seizure of his sloop *Liberty*. It drags on and on, and is a lot of work for little return. I've far more business than I can handle, even with an office down town and two clerks."

Abigail remembered what Cousin Esther had said yesterday, when she was making a visit at the Sewall house.

"Although you know my Jonathan doesn't hold with your Mr Adams's politics," said Esther, "he said to a group here t'other day that 'John Adams is as honest a lawyer as ever broke bread.' And then another gentleman present spoke up and said, now that James Otis was failing in his mind, it was pretty generally recognized that John Adams was the first lawyer in the province!"

Abigail repeated this now to her husband, and saw the quick gleam in his eye which showed his pleasure at the tribute. But he picked up his little daughter, ruffled her curls, and pressed several warm kisses on her satin cheek as she flung her arms round his neck.

"I will hear Nabby's prayers!" he said.

Though this new struggle over tariffs seemed to Abigail to be taking rather longer than the one over the Stamp Act, there were signs of victory in the air. A circular had come from the British Parliament saying that no more duties should be imposed against the will of the colonists and that the ones on paper, colours, and glass should be removed. That only left the tax on tea. Then Governor Bernard, who had been trying to work the home Government in London up to violent measures of repression, was recalled, to his own surprise and chagrin; and so, less than a year after the troops had sailed into Boston, the Governor sailed out. The city rejoiced. As he drove away he saw flags flaunting on the Liberty Tree, and the last sound he heard over the quiet harbour was the impudent roar of the province-owned cannon fired in good-riddance salute from Hancock's Wharf.

"Well, we are getting on!" said Abigail, delighted as bonfires flared in the July night.

"Ay," said her husband and his friends, sipping their cold beer, "but not fast enough. Hutchinson is as bad as Bernard; maybe worse. And a tax on tea is still a tax."

"Will the non-importation continue, then?" said Abigail.

"Non-importation will continue and will be enforced!" said Sam Adams.

"And Hutchinson's sons are in the tea business!" grunted John Hancock with a wry grin.

"I said 'enforced,'" said Sam Adams, his palsy intensifying with his emotion. "Them Hutchinsons will find themselves a-boiling in their tea if they don't look out!"

Abigail, alert lest John should take fire and commit himself to something, hastened to give the talk a lighter turn.

"My little son is by way of being a Tory!" said she. "He glues his nose to the window when drill is on, and admires the redcoats!"

"So?" said Sam Adams. He did not join the laugh. Next day Abigail was greatly amused to see her son waddling along beside Cousin Sam in the cool of the summer morning. Held fast by Adams's shaky grip, he was being conducted all around the square to watch the drill. She saw the baby's hand eagerly pointing, heard his shrill voice say, "Pitty wedcoats! Pitty sojers!" heard the stern, gruff denial of his companion. As they went out of earshot she could discern by Sam Adams's denunciatory gestures that he was telling the boy, "Naughty redcoats! Wicked redcoats! They must GO AWAY." So Sam Adams gave his tiny distant cousin a lesson in political theory; and the intelligent little boy heard and understood, and was convinced. Sam Adams did not waste his time that morning. To the end of his life John Quincy Adams remembered and told of it.

But as the heat of summer wore on the city tempers grew short. Ugly possibilities raised their heads.

Abigail, having returned with her children from an August spent at Penns Hill and Mount Wollaston, where her uncle Norton Quincy had inherited the big house on the seashore, had a caller early in September. Her friend Mrs James Warren was grief-stricken and indignant. Her brother, James Otis, had been assaulted in the street by a customs officer and badly hurt.

"He's not responsible for what he says, you know!" she said, through her tears. "He's been liable to attacks of wild temper—well, really madness—for some time. Everybody knows it! I suppose this brute said something to vex him, and he roared out, and the next thing the wretch hit him over the head, knocked him down, and struck him repeatedly. He was all bloody before others could run and help him——"

She broke down in Abigail's comforting arms. But a cold chill seized Abigail none the less. This—in Boston—to a man like James Otis? A leading citizen—recently Speaker of the Assembly? The chill returned in even worse form in October. John was away, Nabby and Johnny were in bed and asleep. Abigail and the nurse were in the chief bedroom, tending little Susanna. Several candles made the room bright, and a glow of firelight spread rosily over the walls as the nurse moved to and fro about the hearth stirring a poultice in a little saucepan. Abigail was walking about, rocking the colicky child against her shoulder, patting its back gently, trying to ease its obvious pain, while its little mouth wailed in her ear. But suddenly another sound roused her attention with an uncomfortable start. It was a distant sullen roar, like a herd of beasts, or like storm on the sea, but Abigail knew it at once for what it was —the sound of a mob. It drew slowly nearer, and now there were running feet on the pavement. Men's voices shouted:

"Light up, citizens! Light up! We need the lights of the windows to show up traitors!"

Knockers banged all along the row. Abigail looked out and saw some young men running. One of them glanced up at the lighted window and recognized her. He doffed his cap in a moment.

"Yer servant, Mistress Adams!"

He was gone into the soft autumn darkness. His face was excited, wild. His automatic courtesy to her seemed grotesque, as if a bear should show manners. She believed he was a journeyman rope-walker,* a Son of Liberty named Gray, whose rough bass sometimes joined the serenaders.

And now the roaring of the mob came close, reached the end of the square, came on rolling slowly past the house. Abigail, hugging her baby, looked and shuddered. In the centre, lit by a few torches, were two creatures being carried astride a fence rail. One was shapeless, white, and fluffy, more like a gigantic owl than anything human; the other was a well-dressed man in a dark coat, his face twisted with agony, whom Abigail recognized as a printer who had recently libelled many of the people's leaders in a scurrilous news-sheet violently attacking non-importation. They passed with their tormentors, all too slowly. Abigail put her baby gently into the cradle, then dropped down on the bed, sick and faint.

"Oh, ma'am!" cried the nurse, turning from the window where she had been leaning out to miss no last vestige of the spectacle, "you shouldn't have looked on that in your condition! God help us that it don't mark that which is within your womb!"

She brought vinegar to bathe her mistress's brows, singed a feather and waved it under her nose.

"What was it? What was it?" gasped Abigail.

* A ropemaker.

"A sailor, ma'am—an informer. They'd tarred and feathered him, and serve him right. Forget it, ma'am, don't think of it. . . ."

But when John Adams returned a few days later Abigail was glad to find that in his harder man's way he disliked it as much as she did.

"Mob justice is injustice, even if the man was guilty. Such things mar our cause."

Sam Adams, however, felt differently.

"Action is felt and noticed when words are disregarded. It will be a useful lesson," said he.

He had not been in the mob, but it was rumoured he was among those who high-handedly released eight members of the mob whom Hutchinson had arrested and gaoled. The gaoler could not resist the town pressure. He let them out willingly.

"The troops were in the streets that night, bayonets and all," said Abigail, "I saw several of them, coming along at the rear. Why couldn't they interfere and stop it?"

"The city is not under martial law, my dear!" said John Adams. "Until it is, or unless a civil magistrate gives the order to disperse a riot, the troops are helpless. And well Hutchinson knows it. However, if he don't soon move them out to the Castle, there'll be an incident. There's bound to be. And we shall all be sorry."

"Except me, cousin!" said Sam Adams.

Little Susanna died in February 1770, having managed to pass her first birthday but not to win the struggle against a second Boston winter. Frail as her hold on life had been, her loss brought a peculiar sorrow to her mother's heart through the tenderness aroused by caring for the sickly little creature. But her second mother, Aunt Elizabeth, wise in living, urged philosophy and religious resignation. Children were delicate vessels, her friends said, one could not expect to raise them all. Hardly a mother of their acquaintance had attained middle age without losing one or more children, and was not Abigail expecting another child in May?

John Adams, leaving his wife to Aunt Elizabeth's ministrations, rode himself to Weymouth carrying the tiny coffin on the back of his saddle for burial by Parson Smith. After the service in the church and a night at the Weymouth parsonage it was cheering to ride the familiar road to Braintree, to call on his mother and see her well settled, to call on his brother and see his married state with his prim Puritan wife, and to look over his own house and find it weather-proof and in good condition. So, after visiting the blacksmith to have his horse shod, he rode on back to Boston.

He reached Boston, late that February afternoon, at a critical moment. As he told Abigail over their hot supper, drawn up before the roaring fire:

"When I came into town I saw a vast collection of people near Liberty Tree and found it was the funeral of that boy that was shot in the streets a few days ago.* Sam Adams and others begged my company. So after I had warmed me at the house of a friend, and put up my horse, I walked with them in the procession. We went from Liberty Tree to the town-house and thence to the burial ground. It was a solemn and quiet occasion. I hope it will be marked as a lesson to the practisers of violence on both sides."

"It is the first blood," said Abigail sombrely, "the first death. But I fear me it won't be the last. . . . It is too sad it had to be a child."

"Ay. But that it was a child," said John Adams, "made it appeal to young and old. A vast number of boys walked before the coffin; a vast number of men and women after it, and many carriages. My eyes never beheld such a funeral. The procession stretched away into the distance. . . . It shows the ardour of the people!"[11]

Yes, but where is that procession marching to? What is its real destination? Time alone, sighed Abigail, can show. Fresh from the funeral of his own child, it was no wonder that John had impulsively joined in the funeral of another. But she prayed he would remember his living children, and the ones that were yet unborn. She felt unwell, dispirited, and sad. She would gladly have drawn him back from that procession. Too late. He had taken that fatal step, and what would the next be?

"I'm sorry for James Otis!" said John, his active mind running

* The first incident—that is, the first involving death, as distinguished from the innumerable little clashes involving manhandling and blows—was not a clash between soldiers and citizens but between citizens determined to enforce the embargo and citizens determined to exercise their individual rights and resist it. Stores that ignored the embargo and took the opportunity to sell English imported goods at a high profit—including tea and molasses—to such citizens as would patronize the black market, had their shops picketed by the Sons of Liberty. The neighbour of such a picketed shop, himself a minor customs official, came out and protested to the picket. A mob joined the pickets in no time, the man Richardson was forced to seek refuge in his house, and since even there he thought the enraged mob would storm the door, his terror caused him to bring out a pistol and fire into the crowd. He killed a boy.

on, unsuspecting. "He has often told me that his wife was a high Tory and read him the most unmerciful curtain lectures.[12] It's my guess that friction at home as much as anything has been the cause of the irritability that has broken up his fine mind and got him into trouble. Now that's a thing I could not stand. I thank God for *my* wife!" His vivid, affectionate glance flashed on her and drew its usual response, but she was pale. "Nay, my dear, don't be in the dumps!" He strove to cheer her with all the home gossip that he had collected. But—though she made him think he had succeeded—real cheer was more than she could summon, and she went to bed homesick for Weymouth and Braintree and the old, quiet days. Boston was a vortex. Boston was dangerous.

That was the twenty-sixth of February. Six days later Abigail heard of a rumpus between the journeyman ropewalker Gray and his friends and some men of the 29th Regiment. The soldiers, either outnumbered or afraid to disobey orders, had got the worst of it, and one of them was said to be dangerously wounded. No one had been arrested. Apparently no one could be found to identify the guilty party.

Abigail, well bundled up against the snapping cold, went stepping cautiously about her business in the slippery streets, where cinders and oyster shells had been scattered to make walking safer. She saw the soldiers gathered in sulky groups, their scarlet coats conspicuous against the white snow. And now a snowball whizzed through the air, edgy with cinders, and caught one hard on the ear. No use to turn sharp to see who. All the boys in sight were looking the other way, hands in pockets, or intent on playing an absorbing game with each other. As for pouncing and catching one, as easy catch a fish in the hand. They slid away on the icy gutters, dodged, twisted, disappeared in doorways, up alleys. Chase by the military was undignified and futile. The soldiers resumed their sullen talk, and now a volley of snowballs hit them in the back like stones, melted down their collars, knocked their tall hats sideways. Abigail thought that Providence had been inconsiderate of the soldiers in filling the streets of Boston with piles of snow, the street boys' ammunition. But she was surprised at the youngsters' bold, repeated rudeness.

"They've been intentionally wrought up by designing men!"[13] said her husband when she told her anecdotes at the dinner-table. "There have been some for many months trying to stir up quarrels between the lower sort of people and the soldiers. The night brawls are the worst. I wish Sam Adams would exert himself against it. Some think they have his encouragement. But I can't believe it of him."

The next day was March 5. A lonely sentry, on guard at the customs house in the frosty evening, found himself a target for hard snowballs and lumps of ice, thrown with savage intention and deadly aim by a gang of toughs. These were not boys but men. Their leader was Gray the ropewalker; and his most eager and skilful adjutant showed, in the intermittent light from the customs house window, the dark face and brilliant teeth of a Negro.* The sentry was not only angry and bruised, he was frightened, and shouted for the guard. Half a dozen of his comrades came at the double, headed by a sergeant, and almost at once Captain Preston joined them. He was in command of the guard that night and anxious to prevent any shooting. How did it happen then that there was shooting? Who gave the command to fire? Did anybody? Certainly not Preston. The mob, terrifying and elusive in the half-dark, taunted the soldiers to fire, being certain, from months of experience, that they would not. But suddenly the crack of muskets roused echoes along the Boston streets, and life was snapped in two like a brittle stick. Gray and his Negro follower fell dead, and another young man staggered and died beside them; sixteen others were wounded, two of them mortally. Their blood ran out on the snow, as scarlet as the sleeve of the drummer boy who held up a lantern for the Captain to see by. And the soldiers were appalled and still.

Abigail was sitting alone by the fire, musing and reading. John had gone off to his club, at Mr Henderson Inches's house at the south end of Boston. Of a sudden, about nine o'clock, the bells began to ring. Startled, Abigail went to the window, drawing her shawl about her, thinking it a fire alarm, and looking for the glow of flames in the sky. John, at the other end of town, thought the same, and so did his companions. They snatched up their hats and cloaks and rushed out into the streets. They found a crowd of people all flowing down the street one way; and the word was passed from mouth to mouth that the British had fired on the people, "killed some and wounded others, near the town-house." Abigail's boy ran out of her front door and brought back to his

* Crispus Attucks.

mistress the same news. Now, while Abigail's heart beat wildly, Brattle Square began filling up with soldiers, summoned by the sharp beat of the drums. There, silent except for shouted commands, they formed their ranks, muskets shouldered, bayonets fixed. So they stood ready when John Adams came into the square, hurrying home at a smart pace to take care of his wife. There was just room for him to walk along the whole front of the company in a narrow space they had left for foot passengers. He pursued his way "without taking the least notice of them," as he told Abigail presently, "or they of me, any more than if they had been marble statues."*

His strong arm round her, his reassuring companionship, his first-hand news that all the town was quiet, "in a sombre, tragic, but not violent mood," steadied her racing nerves. She drank a little mulled wine and her colour came back. She was preparing for bed before she heard the soldiers march to their barracks. The commanders had agreed that the first necessity was to get the soldiers off the streets and out of sight.

"We had nothing," said John Adams, "but our reflections to interrupt our repose." But those were disquieting enough.

* John and Abigail Adams were at this time living in "Mr Fayerweather's house" in Cold Lane, just off Brattle Square, to which they had removed in the previous spring. Soon after these events they moved back to "another house in Brattle Square."

IV
The Die is cast

THE DAY AFTER THE MASSACRE* was almost like a Sabbath. No drum and fife broke the morning stillness, no soldiers came to drill in Brattle Square. The forest birds flew undisturbed about the trees, catbird, redwing and scarlet tanager, brown thrush, robin and bluejay, and sea-birds sailed above. The front door opened and shut, and John Adams's breezy presence filled the house.

He entered the room with a quick, hearty greeting to his aunt-in-law, and came directly up to his wife. She, who knew him so well, knew instantly something important had happened. His bright, eager eyes were searching hers, with a serious, intent gaze that yet held a gleam of humour. His firm arm was round her waist.

"What think you, Nabby," said he, "I am about to lay myself open to a charge of Tory!"

Her face lit up, confident even in her question.

"And how do you manage that miracle, sir?"

"Nabby, let me first ask you some questions. Were those soldiers last night monsters of iniquity, or were they stupid men in a tight place who made an error? Which is your opinion?"

"The second is my opinion!" she said thoughtfully.

"And it's mine too. So when a redcoat—an officer, Mr Forrest, whom they call the Irish Infant—came to my office this morning, and with his eyes streaming with tears implored me, in a broken voice, as if he thought I held his friend's life in my hand, to help his friend get justice, what ought I to have said? He came from Captain Preston; and Captain Preston is in the town gaol, having given himself up—he and his eight men—to stand their civil trial according to English law. Are we in Boston to deny them law?

* This event was always afterwards called the Boston Massacre.

Shall we, who are claiming one part of the British Constitution, deny another part? Shall we?"

"Oh, no!" said Abigail fervently.

"So I accepted the charge of the defence of Preston and those eight accused men, and took his guinea. And your cousin Josiah Quincy is my partner in it. I could not wish a better! They went to him first, on their way to me, and he said he would engage if I would. . . . And meanwhile, my dear, while I sat there listening to Forrest, I saw out of the window my friends John Hancock and Sam Adams pass by more than once, going up and down the Court House steps carrying word from the town meeting to the Lieutenant-Governor and his council. From time to time a messenger would slip in to me to tell me how things were going—how the town meeting was standing out for the withdrawal of the regiments to the Castle, and how they were strong for the immediate and condign punishment of Preston and the guard, and were calling in and examining many witnesses of last night's affray. I saw the temper of the town was hot and growing hotter. And but for you and the children, I should have been in there with Hancock and Adams, helping to force the town's demands down Hutchinson's throat. Why then should I find myself compelled to go against the tide? . . . Just because, as I said to Forrest, the law is neutral, and counsel ought to be the very last thing that an accused person should lack in a free country. But I told Forrest plain I would use no tricks, no arts. If I undertook it, my argument would depend only upon facts, evidence and law. Forrest eagerly assured me that Captain Preston desired no more. 'As God Almighty is my judge,' he said, through his tears, 'I believe Preston to be an innocent man.' 'Well, that the trial should show,' said I, 'and if he thinks he can't have a fair trial without my assistance, then without hesitation he shall have it!'"[1]

"You did right!" said Abigail with all her heart. "We will show the world that we are a just and law-abiding people."

Aunt Elizabeth was amazed at her. Not a word of caution or regret—nothing about John's health, or taking on too much, or the risk of losing his popularity, his carefully built-up career, on this quixotic case. Were there no Tory lawyers to undertake it? What about Sewall, for instance? She ventured to say something of this as they all went into the dining-room.

"There are Tory lawyers, yes," said John Adams; "many and

good ones. Why did not Preston choose one of them? I can only answer—he did not. He came to me. And a man on trial for his life is entitled to the counsel of his choice."

The trial would not come on until the autumn assize.

Abigail's fourth child, a son, was born on May 29, 1770. He was christened by his faithful grandfather, Charles. He was from the beginning happy and cheerful, and Nabby and Johnny soon found how delightful a plaything a baby brother can be.

For three months life had been almost normal. Abigail and many others began to believe the worst was over. If a new and more liberal governor were sent across from England to replace Bernard, instead of the crass, though American-born, Hutchinson, there was room for hope. And in the meantime the very fact that John had engaged to defend the soldiers had roused such a clamour in the town that it seemed to Abigail an added safeguard against his being drawn into the vortex of the patriot cause. There were plenty of people now, she was well aware, who were calling John Adams traitor and time-server; and the House of Representatives itself had issued a printed statement of the massacre[2] which pre-judged the case before trial, and condemned the accused out of hand.

So the shock was the greater when John came up to her room on the evening of June 5 with that look of kindled fires within him and of grim resolution which warned her of danger. He told her the worst at once.

"Abigail, what will you say to me? I have accepted election to the House of Representatives!"

"But—John—how is it possible? You were not at town meeting?"

"No. I've never attended town meeting in Boston, as no one knows better than you. I was not there this morning when my election took place. I had no idea of it until a messenger brought the news to my office. Then I went over to Faneuil Hall, where a very large town meeting was assembled, and expressed my sense of the honour of their choice of me, and my own unworthiness and unreadiness, in a very few words."[3] He sat down beside the bed and took his head between his hands. "A few words in which to throw away the hopes of a lifetime."

"But John—when your prospects were so good——" she faltered. "Your future—your children——"

"Ay. I've thrown away to-day as bright prospects as any man

ever had before him." He got up and paced restlessly to the window and back. "In my heart, which I ever show you, I'll confess to you I consider that this step likely condemns my little ones and you to ruin. And myself to worse still!"

"John—*death*?"

"Ay. Hutchinson has already threatened to invoke high treason against patriot leaders. The King may do so in any case, at any time. *May?* Nay, is *certain* to if things go on."

Now the full realization had sunk deep into Abigail's heart, and her numbed feelings woke into agony. She burst into tears.[4]

"Ah, John, John—why must you?"

"For the same foolish reason that I must defend the soldiers, my dear—nothing except a sense of duty. And I can't escape it."

Her tears moved him unbearably. She—"that excellent lady who had always encouraged me"—so broken as this.

"Was I a fool, dear wife? Did I act wrong? . . . When my fellow townsmen turned to me in their need, overlooked more obvious claimants, paid me the high compliment of selecting me, not only without my candidacy but in my absence—should I have said no?"

She sobbed and wept, speechless, but she shook her head. She struggled for control, while he stroked her hair. At last she could trust her voice to speak as firmly as she wished.

"She said she was very sensible of the danger to her and to our children as well as to me," wrote her husband in his diary, "but she thought I had done as I ought; she was very willing to share in all that was to come and to place her trust in Providence."[5]

One of the minor results of this unexpected turn of affairs was to deprive Abigail of her husband's company. The General Court —the full unit of government composed of the Acting-Governor the Council, and the House of Representatives—was in session at Cambridge, where Hutchinson was insisting on its meeting as a punishment to the cantankerous town of Boston. To Cambridge therefore John Adams had to go, and immediately went, next day. Since the village was separated from Boston by the Charles River, and there were no bridges across the Charles, the delegates had to find lodgings in the village. Overcrowding made them uncomfortable. Sessions were held in the halls of Harvard College.

Abigail soon learned, both from her husband's brief letters and from the comments of her friends, that John Adams, on entering the sessions, was at once not only involved in all the arguments, but actually made the leader of them. The anti-Government party, now definitely calling itself the "patriot party," had been in sore need of a first-rate lawyer, one whom they would not be afraid to pit against the highly trained legalism of Hutchinson himself.* John Adams was their man.

As he told his wife, "This was to me a very fatiguing session for they put upon me all the drudgery of managing all the disputes."[6]

When the July recess came he had to be away riding circuit, and catching up a little on his law business. Wherever he went, as he told Abigail on return, he observed how "the spirit of liberty circulated through every minute artery of the province."[7] No one would buy British goods, no one (he boasted ruefully) would offer you a cup of tea; and farmers, innkeepers, country lawyers all over the place proved to be patriotic Sons of Liberty.

In October he had to absent himself from the General Court. The trials of Captain Preston and the soldiers came on. So certain was every one of a verdict of "Guilty" and a sentence of death, that a sermon was preached in Boston anticipating not only the sentence but a reprieve by the Acting-Governor, and arguing against reprieve.

Abigail, present among the spectators in the packed courtroom, was aware of all the prejudice built up around the trial, of the desire for punishment, and the positiveness of guilt. She knew, too, about the illegal circulation of evidence taken down from witnesses who had not been subjected to any responsibility for proof. On the first day of the trial the prosecution seemed to have an overwhelming case. And with the rest of the hushed audience she felt the thrill that ran through the room when, on the second day, after the opening by Quincy, John Adams rose for the defence, and his first words, passionate, unequivocal, human, and sincere, reminded the court at once that they were dealing with no mere affair of party politics or prejudiced opinion, but nothing less than life and death, justice and law.

John Adams's insistent return to fundamental principles, his stirring oratory, and his destructive cross-questioning of witnesses succeeded in getting a verdict of acquittal for Preston and for all of the soldiers but two, the only two who could be positively identified as having fired. Those two were found guilty of man-

* Hutchinson was Chief Justice as well as Lieutenant-Governor and a very able and tricky lawyer.

slaughter and were condemned to be burned in the hand, a light sentence as things were considered.

Abigail felt all the thrill of a girl at her first conquest to have this great man, this public figure, escort her home, and to hear him say with vehement conviction:

"The jury did exactly right—exactly right—and come what may, this was the best action of my life."*

As winter came on John Adams's health began to break. Complicated legal cases, political engagements, a slender diet—the doctor's remedy for nervous indigestion—and especially "constant speaking in public almost every day for many hours,"[8] finally brought on serious illness. At the height of the winter a "complaint in his lungs" threatened his life. To Abigail this seemed a heaven-sent reprieve from duty. Not the King's threat against treason, but Nature itself compelled a halt. The doctor backed her up—good Dr Warren, himself a patriot. It "compelled me," said John Adams, "to throw off a great part of the load of business both public and private, and return to my farm in the country."

Joyful illness that demanded such a convalescence! Little Nabby and Johnny, in their wild delight at going back to the farm, felt nothing like the deep excitement of their mother. "Last Wed. my furniture was all removed to Braintree. Sat. I carried up my wife and youngest child," records John's diary. "The air of my native spot and the fine breezes from the sea on one side and the rocky mountains of pine and savin on the other . . . daily rides on horseback and the amusements of agriculture, always delightful to me, soon restored my health."[9] April was sweet upon the hills.

The plan was that John should ride to and fro to his office in Boston, often lodging for the mid-week with his brother-in-law Richard Cranch, now practising law in Boston. His seat in the legislature was resigned—to its former holder, James Otis, now temporarily sane again. And his mind took rest with his "horses, oxen, cows, swine, walls, fences, etc." That was week-ends, when he returned to Braintree—"still, calm, happy Braintree"—often in time to drink tea with his wife.

Now that the mental conflict between the two loyalties of private and public duty was removed, John Adams flung himself into his private career with zest. Business had piled up, his two pupil-clerks

* It was also the least rewarding financially. John Adams's total fee, including retainer, for his nine clients was fourteen guineas.

were swamped, and there were many arrears to make up. Fatigue fell away from him in the pursuance of straightforward tasks. He boasted eagerly to Abigail that he was in his office by six in the morning and still in it at nine at night, and "I spend but a small space of time in running down to my brother's to breakfast, dinner and tea."[10]

Most evenings he would spend alone in his office, "much more profitably and even pleasantly" than at his club. Sometimes he would drop in for a pipe with brother Cranch before going to bed. And then on Saturday, or sometimes Friday night, he rode back the twelve miles of woods and shore to Braintree, where his young wife, only twenty-eight years old, and Nabby, six, and Johnny, four, and Baby Charles, were as happy and healthy as a man could wish.

Abigail heard, by report at week-ends, all the talk of the town. And though, as John said, "England and America are staring at each other and will continue to stare for a long time to come," America was also staring the other way. There was west on the compass as well as east. Stories were being told of one Daniel Boone.

"Yes, America is a continent, and let us never forget it," said Abigail to her little son Johnny. "It is not just Boston and New York and Philadelphia, nor even just the Northern Colonies and the Southern Colonies. It spreads away so far——"

"How far?" said Johnny. He was so keen and quick and sensible that his mother sometimes forgot how young he was. Now six, he seemed often more mature than Nabby.

"As far—as the sunset!" said Abigail.

Johnny had already learned to read. She was teaching him a lot of her favourite poetry by heart. And John Adams was eager to apply his educational theories to his young son. Copying out, copying out was the thing. "Make my sons copy out the Preceptor's *Elements of Logic* entirely with their own hands in fair characters as soon as they can write in order to imprint it on their memories!"[10]

"And what about your daughter?" said Abigail, lifting her chin.

"Well—'twouldn't hurt my daughter to do the same!"[11]

They all drove over to Weymouth on a summer Sunday, a happy family party, the sweet scent of new-mown hay blowing across the fields. Young Isaac Smith was there with a letter in his pocket from England giving the news. It was from an American, John Adams's relative John Boylston, who wrote:

> Lord T——'s avowed and publicly declared reason for keeping a Military and Naval force at Boston is to corrupt the morals of the inhabitants in order totally to enslave them, and I sincerely hope and wish the principles of the Revolution will have no period but with the Existence of the planet we breathe on.[12]

That word "revolution" seemed to explode and thunder in the room. But John Adams, though he paced up and down restlessly in the ensuing hush, finally stared out of the window and avoided comment.

On September 15, 1772, Abigail's mother and father were at the Penns Hill farm to support their daughter in the agonizing hours of childbirth; and a son was born and promptly christened Thomas Boylston. This was Abigail's fifth child, there were difficulties and complications, and her recovery from the birth was slow.

They had now been back at Braintree two springs, two summers, two autumns, and one winter. They had tried all the possible ways, but the arrangement hadn't worked. John and Abigail Adams were not happy apart. John might think at first how nice to have long undisturbed evenings in his office, "which I never cd do in my family," but presently his spirits sank—"walking about the streets of Boston as hipped as old Father Flynt at ninety," James Otis told him angrily. Abigail alone could make him see the world in pleasant colours. He hungered for sight and sound of her, and he needed her as companion, comforter, and sounding-board for his thoughts.

Abigail too needed the pungent, vitalizing quality of John's presence, the smell of his tobacco, the firm step, the almost rough caress, above all the support of his strong, decided nature. Country life of course was good for the children, but, in Abigail's opinion, their father's company was better for them still.

So when John presently had the offer of a house in Boston that was within his means and situated where he wanted it he purchased it, "having found it very troublesome to hire houses, and be often obliged to remove." In September 1772 he moved his office into it and began to get it ready for his family.

When little Tommy was a month old and Abigail, pale and languid but on the mend, was able to be taken out on to a couch under the trees, they celebrated John Adams's birthday, October

19. A party gathered: Grandmother Elizabeth Quincy and Uncle Norton, Parson Smith and his wife and young Betsey,* brother Peter Boylston Adams and the prim Mrs Peter—whom John could not help pitying Peter for marrying!—Mr Hall and his wife—John Adams's mother—Edmund Quincy and his lovely youngest daughter Dorothy, the flower of the flock (now being courted by John Hancock), and Parson Wibird, the cultured but elusive bachelor, John Adams's old crony. These and others of the neighbourhood gathered to drink John Adams's health and wish him well—and to toast the new baby. And John Adams told them that this was both hail and farewell—that his mother and father-in-law (current for stepfather) were going to occupy his farm, and he and his family were going to return to Boston before winter.

When the guests had taken leave, and the children were in bed and John and Abigail were left alone to watch the sun's last afterglow along the west, reflected in the autumn gold of the maple leaves above them, John fell into a mood of melancholy.

"D'you realize, Nabby, what this day marks? Thirty-seven years of my life are run out, more than half the life of man! The remainder of my days I shall rather decline, in sense—in spirit—and in activity! And yet I still have my own and my children's fortunes to make!"[13]

"Tush!" said she. "Why, your boyish habits and airs aren't yet worn off!"

On Tuesday, November 25, Abigail and the children moved into Boston to take up residence in the house in Queen Street.† Although John Adams spoke of it disparagingly—"inconvenient and contracted as it was"—Abigail was pleased with it because it offered better opportunities of constant companionship than any other they had had. It was just opposite the Court-house. But as the house took order under her hands and cheerful children's voices rang in the halls he insensibly cheered up. A feeling of content and hope began to take possession of him. He did not feel quite so old.

"My father-in-law‡ Mr Hall and my mother are well settled in my farm at Braintree," he wrote in his diary. "The produce of my farm is all collected in; my wood and stores are laid in for the winter. I am disengaged from public affairs—with a fixed resolution to meddle not with them—and I now have nothing to do but mind my office, my clerks and my children."[14]

* Abigail's youngest sister. † Now Court Street. ‡ *I.e.*, stepfather.

As Abigail and Dr Warren both pointed out warningly, though the excursion into the country had partly recovered his health, he was an infirm man yet. The strenuous Boston hours had not agreed with him. They hoped that by this time—and with his wife there to take care of him—he had learned how to live in Boston. If not—if his health should again decline—he must return to Braintree and give up the town entirely. Above all, the doctor reiterated, Mr Adams must remember—no clubs, no meetings, no politics! His recipe for living must be temperance, exercise, and peace of mind! He must ride frequently to Braintree to inspect his farm, and spend evenings in his office or with his family with as little company as possible.[15]

The lion seemed to purr drowsily in complete agreement, blinked mildly at the fire, and appeared quite domesticated.

His wife, peeping into his diary to see what he was putting there, was well satisfied. He had taken the lesson to heart and repeated it verbatim.

Abigail found the resumption of social life in Boston very pleasant. But the British Admiral's wife, Mrs Montague, was giving offence by disdaining the colonial ladies. "Pray, can Mrs So-and-so *afford* the dress and jewels she wears?" And, "Oh, that my son should ever come to dance with a mantua-maker!" The Admiral was more restrained, and therefore, in the presence of ladies, comparatively tolerable. But John Adams's fashionable young clerk, Will Tudor, could cap these stories with anecdotes of the Admiral as a foul-mouthed fellow, with "hoggish, brutal manners," a disgrace to the King's navy.[16]

Such minor annoyances gave outlet to Boston's deep-seated irritation at having the Navy and Army still present; the uniforms of officers might add picturesqueness to a ball, but they were a reminder of the incubus that had only been moved three miles away.

Abigail, anxious to keep the family temperature down, took a good-humoured and tolerant view. She thanked her stars that after safely skirting the reefs and shoals of two evenings running with Sam Adams they were going to see the old year out in the peaceful security of the Cranches' house. A quiet family circle. Just what the doctor ordered.

John was in excellent spirits that evening. "I never was happier in my whole life than I have been since I returned to Boston," he said when Richard and Mary inquired how the move was working out. "The year to come will be a pleasant, cheerful, happy, and prosperous year to me. At least, such are the forebodings of my mind at present."[17]

"John doesn't feel the weight of middle age half so badly as he did a few months ago!" said Abigail.

But it is in Eden that one must look for the serpent. And here it was indeed, in the person of a harmless-looking Englishman, a friendly and courteous fellow—one who was struck, moreover, with admiration for Mrs Adams. A cosmopolitan and a stranger, he was perhaps the first person who ever recognized her quality. He thought her the most accomplished lady he had seen since he came out of England.

All was calm, warmth, and mutual friendship. But some one mentioned the *Gaspee* and court of commission. And Mr Collins, not unnaturally sticking up for his country, ventured to say something mild about the high reputation, after all, of British justice. The resulting explosion astonished everybody—perhaps even Abigail. It certainly astonished in retrospect the remorseful John.

"I found the old warmth, heat, violence, acrimony, bitterness of my temper and expression was not departed. I said there was no more justice in Britain than there was in Hell—and that I wished for war."[18]

So the dream of maintaining a private life went up in smoke.

After such an uprising from the subconscious John felt he must consent when asked to serve the patriot cause again. This time it was to involve a direct challenge to the Crown, and both John and Abigail perceived its full consequences and weighed them well before taking the irrevocable step.

In January '73 Hutchinson opened the General Court with a subtle and carefully prepared speech to the effect "that Parliament was our sovereign legislature and had a right to make laws, lay on taxes, etc., for the colonies."[19] The two Houses appointed a committee to take into consideration the Governor's speech. Their need, they soon saw, was a lawyer, and experience had taught them who. No matter that John Adams was not now a member of the House, they urged and entreated him to meet with them and give them the benefit of his advice, and so he did every evening until the report was finished. The committee had the draft of an answer prepared when he arrived first—the joint production of

Sam Adams and Dr Warren—but it was full of high-sounding phrases about liberty and rights without meeting the legal arguments in the Governor's speech.

John Adams detected the legal flaws in these arguments, saw that the Governor could be hoist with his own petard. But John Adams perceived that he would have to rewrite the answer himself, since he alone had the requisite knowledge and skill. But *if* he rewrote it, he would be personally responsible for it. And his head might be the forfeit.

"I have a wife—and what a wife! I have children—and what children!" he groaned to Abigail.

But this time she was in full health and had two years' more experience behind her, in which she had watched both her husband and the progress of the struggle. No tears now.

"You must not think of us first," she said, "in times like these. The challenge has been made, and I'm proud that you are needed to meet it! You can't be, I know, nor do I wish to see you, an inactive spectator! I will try to be a good Portia to your Brutus!"[20]

He looked at her glowing beauty, illuminated by the leaping fire, and thought of the security that he longed to give her, the bleak dangers and uncertainties that threatened if he took the part his nature—and hers—urged him to.

"I should think myself the happiest man in the world," he said involuntarily, "if I could retire now to my little hut and forty* acres which my father left me in Braintree and live on potatoes and sea-weed for the rest of my life[21]—sooner than expose you and my little ones to what may come! For that which I am to answer the Governor—if I do answer—means revolution, nothing less."

"Dear heart," she said, "you have often read to me that all the misfortunes of Sparta were brought on by their being too anxious for present tranquillity—is it not so? Loving peace so much, clinging to peace, they neglected the means of making it sure and lasting. Ah, peace can only be founded in justice and honour; it can't be purchased at the price of liberty!"[22]

No word now about his health or her children. He was not forcing her, not even persuading her. She was in equal step at his side.

"Then," said he, "I will set friends and enemies at defiance and follow my own best judgment whatever may fall thereon!"[23]

* He had added to his original nine and a half by purchase from time to time.

"Don't fear for me!" said she. "I long impatiently to have you upon the stage of action!"[24]

So John Adams arrived at that main cross-road at which every one arrives some time in life, and chose his path. And his wife chose it with him.

It would not be true to say that they never again looked backward, because they often longed to be able to steer out of the turmoil into the quiet backwater. But since the path of duty led them ever deeper into the thick of affairs, they never after did more than cast a wistful look behind, a mere sigh of relinquishment of a loved pattern of living.

And that this sigh sometimes escaped them only shows the more that John and Abigail Adams were not—as were Patrick Henry and Samuel Adams—the type of people naturally thought of as revolutionary. They belonged to the type of people who valued comfort and culture, who were easy in the established order, successful and at home in it, and normally to be found among its firmest supporters.

Two mortal blows were dealt that winter to Hutchinson's schemes, and both were dealt by John Adams. One was the reply to Hutchinson's address, and the other was the impeachment of the Chief Justice, Peter Oliver of effigy fame, for accepting salary from the Crown when he was an official of the colony.

But the slow transit of mails, in the bottoms of leisurely sailing ships, diverted by winds, delayed by calms, gave plenty of opportunity for the Devil and his servant mischievous Chance to tangle up the skein. Perhaps, too, it was less Chance and the Devil than the familiar human motives of greed and obstinacy that sped catastrophe.

There were quantities of tea stored up, because of the boycott, in British warehouses. Parliament gave attention to the affairs of the East India Company, in which private and national revenue was tied up, and resolved to send some of this tea to America willy-nilly "to habituate the colonies to parliamentary taxes."[25]

Protesting voices were heard in London, from many Englishmen as well as from Americans. But the Prime Minister, Lord North, said publicly, "It is to no purpose making objections, for the King will have it so. The King means to try the question with America."[26]

When news of this reached America the reaction was immediate and violent. The committees of correspondence between the colonies passed round word to form plans for a determined and united stand—as with the stamps ten years before. Philadelphia passed a resolution first this time, not to allow the tea to be put on shore; Boston second. New York followed suit.

Three ships, it was learned, were on the way to Boston, two to New York, one to Philadelphia, one to Charleston, South Carolina. In Boston the consignees to whom the tea was to be delivered included Hutchinson's son. An orderly gathering of the people at the Liberty Tree, under the British flag, headed by Samuel Adams and John Hancock, Dr Warren, and the Town Clerk, William Cooper, summoned the consignees to appear and to agree to send back the tea. The consignees, not unnaturally, refused to appear or to repudiate the tea.

The town meeting met at Faneuil Hall and passed a vote of censure on them.

The three tea ships were expected every hour. Boston grew feverish.

One of the consignees (Clarke) had his windows broken by a mob, and replied by firing out of the window over their heads. It dispersed the crowd, but only added to the anger of the town.

The consignees appealed to the Governor, their silent invested partner, to protect them and their tea.

On the last Sunday of November one of the tea ships arrived and anchored below the Castle. Abigail heard the news given out from the pulpit in meeting, where she sat beside her husband and elder children. Deep and passionate were the prayers. Being Sabbath, there could be no movement on either side.

On Monday morning, when Abigail went out to her early marketing, she saw notices posted on tree trunks and walls, surrounded by rapidly shifting groups of readers. She paused to read one:

> Friends! Brethren! Countrymen! That worst of plagues, the detested tea is now arrived in this harbour.
>
> Every friend to his country is now called upon to meet at Faneuil Hall at nine o'clock this day, at which time the bells will ring, to make an united and successful resistance to this last, worst, and most destructive measure of administration.

Abigail hurried home before the bells should ring. The streets were already filling up with horsemen, chaises, chairs, wagons, people on foot. A crowd predominantly male was flocking into Boston from all villages and towns within a dozen miles. Hancock's partner, John Andrews, wrote to London next day:* "'Twould puzzle any person to purchase a pair of pistols in town, as they are all bought up, with a full determination to repell force to force."[27]

The Governor and council sat in the council chamber opposite Abigail's door, while the body meeting† sat in Faneuil Hall not far off. Watching from the window, she could see John Hancock and another go up the steps, an evident deputation to wait upon the Governor; she saw them return, hats pulled low.

"What will happen?" said Abigail to her husband.

His face was grave and steady.

"We shall continue to the last to try for one of two things: to persuade the consignees to repudiate, as the consignees have done in New York before their ship even reached port; or to obtain a clearance from the Governor to allow this ship to return to England without unloading."

"And if not?"

"You may be sure, my dear, the tea will not be landed in Boston."

Abigail was silent. But at last she found her voice, although it trembled.

"And what consequences will follow such unmitigated resistance?"

"The worst might follow," said John Adams. "The very worst —except one. It might be civil war, no less."

"What can be worse?" said Abigail with trembling lips.

"Why, slavery!" he said vehemently. "If freedom can only be bought at the price of civil war, then I say it is worth the price!"

The days passed without any show of violence. The town resumed its normal life, but under tension, vigilant for a signal. The appointed Committee of Vigilance and Safety met every day. And the tea ship was under armed surveillance, by volunteer shift, day and night.

On December 5 Abigail Adams wrote to her dear friend Mercy Warren at Plymouth:

> The tea, that baneful weed, is arrived. Great and I hope effectual opposition has been made to the landing of it. . . . The flame is kindled

* December 1, 1773. See *John Hancock's Book*, p. 179.

† Body meeting comprising several towns, as distinct from town meeting, representing only one.

and like lightning it catches from soul to soul. Although the mind is shocked at the thought of shedding human blood, more especially the blood of our countrymen, and a civil war is of all wars the most dreadful, such is the present spirit that prevails that if once they are made desperate, many, very many, of our heroes will spend their lives in the cause. I tremble when I think what may be the direful consequences, and in this town must the scene of the action lie. My heart beats at every whistle I hear, and I dare not express half my fears.[26]

The committees of correspondence of all the towns within a radius of twelve miles of Boston sat daily in united session in Faneuil Hall. The Boston Committee of Vigilance and Safety, with Sam Adams and John Hancock leading, had the town in complete control. Two more tea ships arrived, and were ordered by the Committee, along with the first, to move in to Griffin's Wharf, in the heart of maritime Boston. The twenty days of grace ran out, one by one, like a broken string of beads. At their expiration demand for duty must be made by the customs, and if it was not paid, ship and goods must be seized by the fleet. Mr Rotch took an encouraging step when he agreed to order his ship away without unloading.

So quiet was the town, so competent the Committee, that John Adams went on circuit as usual. He had been away a week, and was expected back next day, when Thursday, December 16, 1773, the last day of grace, dawned on Boston. It dawned with the news flying from mouth to mouth that Rotch had withdrawn his promise.

"And why has he so?" said Abigail to her young cousin Will Smith, Isaac's younger brother, who brought the word to her breakfast table.

"Because he finds that to send back the *Dartmouth* without a clearance from the customs house would lose him his ship! The Admiral keeps a ship o' the line in readiness to seize it should it sail under those circumstances. The Governor won't give the ship a clearance to sail away without a clearance from the customs. The Customs won't give a clearance without landing tea and paying duty. You see? It goes round and round. A perfect deadlock. Farewell! I am off to town meeting with my father—or it's more than that! Look at the crowds out of window! It's a muster! Faneuil Hall's too small, we are gathering in the Old South. There go the bells!"

Abigail's heart beat with them. Lessons that morning for Nabby and Johnny were divided between the window and the book, while the cadences of patriotic verse fell on their impressionable ears. What the town does now will be history, and we are in and with the town! An ominous quiet fell on the silent and deserted streets. Abigail, like the other women of Boston, went about her daily domestic tasks with an ear cocked to the outer world for sounds of—what?—while she waited for the returning men to bring some news.

Her loved young cousin Will, her favourite, looked in again. "They've passed a unanimous vote that the tea shall go out of the harbour this afternoon. A committee was sent with Mr Rotch to the customs to demand a clearance, and when 'twas refused unless they would pay the duty on the tea the committee and Mr Rotch set off for the Governor's house at Milton village to beg his clearance for the ship to sail without unloading. There are ten thousand men in the Old South awaiting the Governor's reply!"

Abigail's house boy came in with lighted candles, and replenished the fire; one of the maids followed promptly with the tea-tray. Behind all the lighted windows of Boston the womenfolk and their callers sat down—without their menfolk—to their tea. Will sat down for a cup. But suddenly there fell a sound of distant shouting from a thousand throats. Will ran out and back to the Old South, while Abigail, wrapped in a cloak, stood at her door, straining eyes and ears through the dusk. She heard, indeed, pandemonium.

As she was told afterwards by many witnesses Rotch came back with the not unexpected message that the Governor could not give a pass for the ships without a clearance from the customs. Thus the vicious circle closed completely. The candles had been lit in the church, and threw into chiaroscuro the sea of faces on floor and galleries, and a great black shadow wavered up behind Rotch above the pulpit. As soon as he had spoken "such prodigious shouts were made" that people not in the meeting came running to learn the cause of it. Samuel Adams, Moderator, immediately declared the meeting dissolved, which caused another general shout and three cheers, hip-hip-hooray![29] Then as the thousands poured out and joined the crowds in the streets the noise was as if the infernal regions had broken loose.

Those who knew their parts were fully prepared, and lost no time. They mustered on Fort Hill, a convenient spot not far from

Griffin's Wharf, roughly disguised in soot, paint, and blankets as "Indians from Narragansett." Armed with hatchets and pistols, they marched two by two, in perfect order, to the wharf where the *Dartmouth*, *Eleanor*, and *Beaver* lay, vigilantly guarded by the Committee of Vigilance and Safety, each with 114 chests of tea on board. The first two ships' sole remaining cargo was tea, but "ye latter had arrived at ye wharf only the day before, and was freighted with a large quantity of other goods which the Mohawks took the greatest care not to injure in the least, and before nine o'clock in ye evening, every chest from on board the three vessels was knocked to pieces and flung over ye sides"[30] into the salt water. Almost the entire population of Boston watched along the shore, in the flare of lanterns and torches. Yet in spite of all the witnesses not one of the names of the Mohawks was ever given. Hutchinson, who had taken refuge with his sons in the Castle, said there were fifty Mohawks.[31] Hancock's partner, John Andrews, an eye-witness, said there were two hundred. "Not the least insult was offered to any person," added Andrews, "but a horse-dealer who was discovered to have ript up the lining of his coat and to be stuffing it full of tea was handled pretty roughly. They not only stript him of his clothes but gave him a coat of mud with a severe bruising into the bargain; and nothing but their utter aversion to make any disturbance prevented his being tar'd and feathered."[32]

This modest aversion to making a disturbance would have sounded strange in the Governor's ears, but John and Abigail Adams accepted it at the foot of the letter. John had arrived home from Plymouth early the morning after[33] and was at once informed of everything. He and Abigail watched the Governor drive by their house with the Secretary. "Notwithstanding the forlorn state he was in," wrote the ruined Governor of himself, "he thought it necessary to keep up some show of authority."[34]

"I suppose they're framing a proclamation with reward for names of the ringleaders!" said John Adams. "Take care to mention none in my hearing! I'll likely be called on by some of them to take charge of their defence!"[35]

"What's your opinion of the action, cousin?" said Sam Adams, alert as usual to get John Adams to commit himself. John did not hesitate.

"It was magnificent!" said he. "Sublime!"

It was astonishing how gay every one seemed. Suspense and

tension had been broken by a simple satisfying action. An inextricable tangle, a complete Gordian knot, had been neatly cut. It was an action too that had an element of laughter in it, a saucy and audacious good-humour. It was no child's play, it was the stern action of a man, but of a young man.

"Such is the present calm composure of the people," wrote Andrews to Hancock's business friends in London, "that a stranger would hardly think that ten thousand pounds sterling of the East India Company's tea was destroy'd the evening before last."[36]

But other letters reached the King from his Tory friends in Boston dictated by panic and fury. They said that Boston was full of wild rioters, that there was a terrorist committee to tar and feather people, and that the Governor himself was liable to be its next victim.

Abigail was sent to Weymouth to rest from the prolonged strain, and have a brief holiday from domestic duties and child care. There the eventful year closed for her.

"Alas!" she wrote to John, "how many snow banks divide thee and me and my warmest wishes to see thee will not melt one of them. . . ."

As winter wore into spring John worried increasingly about Abigail. She was far from well. The return to Boston had brought back distressing symptoms. "I cannot get the thought of her state of health out of my mind,"[37] he wrote. Nevertheless they were pleasantly occupied making plans for Braintree. John had purchased from his brother his father's homestead and farm. "How shall I improve it?" he wondered. "Shall I try to introduce fowl-meadow and herds-grass into the meadows? or still better, clover and herds-grass? I must ramble over it and take a view."[38]

V

War comes to Braintree

IN THE MONTH OF MAY 1774, the height of the dazzling, brief New England spring, the season of singing birds and of a thousand flowers, General Gage arrived in Boston as the new governor, straight from England, with the Parliamentary Edict in his pocket. Abigail was not there to see his entry in state, Union Jacks flying, Colonel Hancock and his cadet corps, under British commission, forming an escorting guard of honour, and the citizens of Boston and near-by towns lining the streets in a grave and non-committal mood. John's anxiety for her health—she suffered from a terrible, recurrent migraine—had sent her to Weymouth, where she was basking in country peace under the tender care of her mother and lively young sister Betsey. So she did not watch the inauguration of the last royal governor of Massachusetts. After the pageant before the Court-house General Gage expressed formal regret at his immediate duty, cleared his throat, and read the Parliamentary Edict rescinding the charter of Massachusetts and —as John Adams expressed it to his wife succinctly—"blocking up the Harbour of Boston and annihilating the trade of this town." The audience dispersed in silence. It was, in fact, dangerously quiet.

Abigail, lying very unwell under her father's trees, suffering agonies of headache and a kind of influenza prostration, received John's letters by the manservant next day:

> The Town of Boston, for aught I can see, might suffer martyrdom. Our principal consolation is that it dies in a noble cause. . . . Let me know what is best for us to do.

But while he paid her the compliment of not painting the picture less dark than it really was, he did not expect to depress her or himself.

Don't imagine from all this that I am in the dumps. Far otherwise. I look upon this as the last effort of Lord North's despair.

I am, with great anxiety for your health,

Your

JOHN ADAMS [1]

When Abigail returned to Boston she found it apparently so normal that only in conversation did impending crisis appear. But on the first of June, as the clock in the belfry of the Old South chimed the last heavy stroke of noon, the waiting warships moved in and closed the port. And as the days went by the cruel consequences of the blockade became apparent. Abigail wanted to move her household goods to Braintree by water, on the slow, safe, easy barges; but not a boat could move at Boston—no, not to bring in produce from the harbour islands, nor so much as to make traffic from one wharf to another. All fresh milk, food, and goods coming into the city must travel by wagon along the hot road into the Neck. And there one could see the congested traffic lined up, while milk and butter soured and vegetables wilted.

Taking a drive about the city with Dorothy Quincy that first week, Abigail found it already like a place quarantined for sickness. Ships lay idle at the wharf; warehouses, having sold all their store, lay open to the casual entry of wandering cats and birds. Men thrown out of employment loitered at street corners. The populous traffic of the streets had shrunk to a thin trickle. The poor were in terror of the winter.

Abigail was trying to get ready to move to Braintree, but now more than ever John Adams's office was full, if not with private clients, then with public ones. Said Gridley, "Brother Adams, you keep late hours at your house! As I passed it last night long after midnight I saw your street door vomit forth a crowd of senators!"[2] At last the main part of the furniture was got off. The family only waited conveyance and John Adams's escort.

On June 14 the 4th Regiment landed, marched into Boston, and encamped on the Common, followed the next day by the 43rd. Two companies of artillery and eight pieces of ordnance were unloaded at the Castle. More battalions of infantry were expected hourly.

On the seventeenth the bells rang to call a town meeting in Faneuil Hall, and the male citizens of Boston jammed it to overflowing. John Hancock and Sam Adams were away at Salem, where the Governor had called the General Court. So John Adams, new to Boston town meeting, was elected Moderator. He at once put the question to the meeting: Any in favour of buying off the blockade by paying for the tea now rise and freely argue their case. But the sight of the soldiers again in Boston had put so much iron into Boston blood that not a man stood up.

Abigail, sitting by the window in the dusky, dismantled room, looked anxiously out into the street. The lanterns, hung to walls at intervals—John Hancock's new system of lighting the town—caught the gleam of scarlet and the flash of steel from passing soldiery out to explore their new location. Well she knew that the temper of the city was so much tinder, and the soldiers were the spark. Some hour, hidden in the not far distant future, would inevitably bring the explosion. "Did ever any kingdom or state regain its liberty, when once it was invaded, without bloodshed?"[3] she had said; "yet if the sword be drawn, I bid adieu to all domestic happiness."[4]

Boston had been forbidden "by the King's command" to summon a town meeting, but John had shown a way out of that. The town meeting was not, he said, fresh summoned; it was considered adjourned from the last one.

At last Abigail heard the familiar noise of the crowd issuing into the streets from Faneuil Hall, and presently she discerned her husband's figure coming at a brisk pace. The nearest lantern caught Richard Cranch's long, thin face. His hand was pressing John's shoulder in affection and congratulation as he bade farewell. There was a flourish of hats, a murmur of men's resonant voices, and then John Adams came in alone.

She met him at the door of the room, her pulses throbbing with portent. He gathered her to him in the dusk, and held her to his own hard-beating heart. She felt its strong pulsation more than she felt her own.

"John?"

"Ay, Nabby. Ay, my Portia. . . . A messenger rode hard from Salem to our meeting. . . . There's a new and grand scene opening before me! A Congress![5] Ay, a Continental Congress is to meet on the first day of September at Philadelphia. So well have our Committees of Correspondence functioned, so quick has the word been got from one to t'other. Cushing, Bob Paine, Cousin Sam Adams and myself are appointed delegates from this province. . . .

Ah, this will be an assembly of the wisest men upon the continent. I feel myself unequal to this business!"[6]

Next day John Adams, with coach and chaise and wagon, removed his family to Braintree, "to prepare myself as well as I could for the storm that was coming on. They could not indeed have remained in safety in Boston." After a few days to settle them there he returned to Boston, left three of his clerks in charge of his office in Queen Street, sent two to Braintree to protect his wife, and rode away with Josiah Quincy for the tenth and last time on the eastern circuit.

"My refreshment," Abigail read in one of his treasured letters,

> is a flight to Braintree, to my Cornfields and Grass Plotts, my Gardens and Meadows—my Fancy runs about you perpetually, frequently takes a walk with you and your little prattlings. We walk all together up Penns Hill, over the Bridge to the Plain, down to the Garden. . . .[7]

She loved this simplicity in him. And she loved his earnest attention to the children's training, which urged her "above all Cares of this Life let our ardent Anxiety be to mould the Minds and Manners of our Children, not only to do virtuously but to excel." And, by way of concrete suggestion—tribute also to her culture —"It is time, my dear, for you to begin to teach them French."[8]

But she could not fail most to value in his letters their constant elevation of herself to true equality with him. "My dear Partner" was no empty phrase. "I must intreat you," he said, "to take a part with me in the struggle.[9] . . . I have a Zeal at my heart for my Country and her friends which I cannot smother or conceal. This Zeal will prove fatal to the Fortune and Felicity of my Family."[10] Yet she was willing to take part with him; she encouraged his zeal; she shared it.

Refreshed by the country life, Abigail and the children—Nabby, now nine, and Tommy, the youngest, two—welcomed him home in July for a brief time of rest and preparation for what lay before him. And before the middle of August she drove into Boston with him, where he joined his fellow-delegates. There was a good send-off at Mr Cushing's house, with a dinner and speeches, and the four delegates set out on their journey together in one coach.[11]

It was well organized, open, and dignified, yet Abigail realized, in a sickening stab of panic, that bloody rebellion, wounds, and death might be the end. But what weighed upon her husband, as he had told her in the intimate night watches, was a sense of his own inadequacy. Only she knew his humility, his honest self-criticism, and his often too harsh self-depreciation. He expected to find the representatives from other provinces a dazzling group of superior beings among whom he would be constantly at a disadvantage. He regretted that riding circuit had prevented him from brushing up on his law and history, that "I might appear with less indecency before a variety of gentlemen whose education and experience, family, fortune and everything will give them a vast superiority to me."[12]

A gigantic responsibility rested on this congress, he felt, of which he was only too unworthy. "Should this country submit, what infamy and ruin! Death in any form is less terrible!" But who among his acquaintance were fit for the untried task? That was when his heart sank, for he could see no one.

"We have not men fit for the times!"[13]

Abigail's own duty was clear before her: to administer her household with the utmost thrift, keep a lively oversight of the farm, cherish and educate her children, and keep her husband in touch with home by long and frequent letters. The sad part was she got no letters in return. Hers seemed to be carried off into a void, buried perhaps in the pockets of the friends who, being about to travel, had taken them along. Five weeks dragged slowly by, and she had not had a line.

What, then, about the postal system? It had two drawbacks. It was not considered so safe as private conveyance, and it was ruinously expensive. Said John Adams, in one of the letters she had not yet received, "I have not found a single opportunity to write since I left Boston excepting by the post, and I don't choose to write by that conveyance for fear of foul play. . . . I hope to find some private hand by which I can convey this."[14] And Abigail at last, guessing the cause was lack of "safe conveyance," wrote desperately: "I would rather give a dollar for a letter by the post, though the consequence should be that I ate but one meal a day these three weeks to come."[15]

She laid down her pen and got ready to walk over to Mount Wollaston to spend the day with her uncle Norton Quincy. Little Nabby and Abigail's younger sister Betsey accompanied her. It proved a lively visit. Josiah Quincy and his wife came in, and presently Sam Quincy's wife and a Mr Sumner followed. "A little clashing of parties you may be sure!"[16] said Abigail, "especially as the conversation turned upon the recent speech in the House of Lords by the Bishop of St Asaph, defending the colonies' cause." But there was no ill-will between Quincy and Quincy, differ and argue as they might. All were agreed at last in praise of the Bishop. Abigail and her sister and daughter strolled home, refreshed, in the grape-scented September dusk, with tall goldenrod and purple asters by the wayside catching the light of their lantern, and the new moon shaping a sickle in the sky. The murmur of the sea grew fainter behind them as they turned inland towards Penns Hill. And then, just when expectation was dormant, "Mr Thaxter met me at the door with your letter. . . . It gave me such a flow of spirits that I was not composed enough to sleep until one o'clock."[17]

John Adams had gone to the heart of the political world, for such this modest-looking gathering of fifty-six gentlemen had become. All that then seethed in conscious importance in Moscow, Berlin, London, and even Paris was to weigh lighter, was to mark the future less, than the unpractised deliberations then going on in Philadelphia.

But Abigail had not been left in a backwater. When the family gathered at table there were two young men to contribute news and intelligent discussion, the two law clerks brought out from Boston for protection. They were Nathan Rice, just graduated from Harvard, and John Thaxter, who was Abigail's own cousin,* a grandson of John Quincy. "Never were two persons who gave a family less trouble than they do,"[18] said Abigail. All their time seemed spent in the office, except that Mr Rice was now teaching at the Braintree school and John Thaxter was tutoring young Johnny. Those two liked each other so well and Johnny was getting on so fast, that his mother decided to continue the plan and not send him to school. But though Johnny had graduated to having a tutor, shared also for some lessons by Nabby, he would sit by his mother in the evening and read aloud, stumbling through a page or two of Rollin's *Ancient History*, in which she was passionately interested. Then Abigail would lay down her sewing and finish the chapter. Nabby would get her sewing and listen too while Abigail made the old, far-distant story vivid to her children by relating it to the present time.

Johnny liked to pass by the muster field beside the meeting-house at sunset, for there he could watch the young men, fresh

* Her mother's younger sister, Anna Quincy, married John Thaxter of Hingham.

from the fields, getting to work at their drill, and hear the rattle of old muskets at the loading. "Indeed, yes," said Abigail, "this town appears as high as you can well imagine, and if necessary would soon be in arms."[19]

But in the meeting-house on Sunday the thought of arms was laid aside. Nor was the powder stored, as it was at Weymouth, in the church tower. The Rev. Mr Wibird preached cautious, neutral sermons, expounding obscure texts which had no political undercurrents. But it was a great social occasion, a gathering together of the whole community, and word passed rapidly, with minimum machinery, from man to man, as need arose, at or after meeting, let the pastor be as neutral—or as Tory!—as he liked.

At sunset on a Sabbath the first breath of coming storm came to Braintree. It was right in the middle of the reading of Rollin's *History* that the unmistakable rhythmic beat of marching men broke on their ears in the cool parlour at Penns Hill. Johnny dropped the printed pages and ran to the window. A thousand years vanished in a flash; not Roman legions but American farmers were filing past. "About two hundred men, preceded by a horsecart; they passed without any noise, not a word among them."[20]

"Where are they going, Mother?"

"I don't know!"

"They're fetching the powder from the powder-house," said John Thaxter, buckling on his belt. "A soldier—they suppose a spy—was seen lurking about here this morning. So we expect a redcoat raid to steal the township's store of munitions, such as was made at Charlestown t'other day when the province's store of munitions there was captured by soldiers and carried off in a boat. Now Gage means business; he's mounted a cannon on Beacon Hill; he's fortifying the Neck; what does he mean, anyhow? And if he takes all our munitions, what protection shall we have? . . ." He went out, and joined the rear of the procession. When they came back, with the loaded cart and a captured Tory walking between them—caught with writs to summon juries in his possession—they saw Mrs John Adams and her children at the open casement level with the road.

"Hey, ma'am!" cried one of them jovially. "Are you wanting some powder?"

She laughed, and shook her head. Her dark curls ruffled in the evening breeze, her eyes and cheeks were bright with excitement like their own.

"No, no!" she said. "Not now it's in such good hands!"

And the men laughed softly, passing on.

Soon they halted and asked their Tory to hand over his writs, which he did, and they made a circle round, and burned them. Then they wanted to huzza, but some one objected that it was Sunday; "Those in favour say Ay!—Contrary, contrary sign!" The Nays had it. So after making the Tory swear not to administer the new acts they let him go unhurt, took the powder to a safe hiding-place in the next parish, and dispersed.[21]

This sudden appearance and disappearance of large bodies of men under discipline—summoned how? by whom?—made the country Tories blench, and made Governor Gage prickle nervously in Boston.

Suffolk County, in fact, had a little Congress of its own, organized* and dominated by no less a person than Dr Joseph Warren. It kept up law and order by its own methods now that law courts were 'out.' In fact, wrote Abigail to her absent husband, the people's committees had now taken matters into their own hands in all the places round, and would not permit any of the courts to sit. Last week in Taunton, she had heard in a letter from Robert Treat Paine's sister Eunice that two thousand disciplined men assembled round the Court-house and prevented entry. They waited for two hours to gain their point, keeping ordered rank in the hot sun. The same happened at Springfield, with drums and trumpets and this time a flag—plain black. A flag not yet completely rival to the British flag; not yet affirming another allegiance; a flag that simply said No. . . .

With the first leaf-fall of late September Abigail left home to visit her brother, William Smith, near the town of Salem. William was now married to an attractive and suitable wife, had some children of his own and a commission in the militia, but had fallen into the private difficulties that were to pursue him to his end. Salt meat and salt fish led to cider and to rum. The sin of New England was intemperance. Before other issues claimed him John Adams had inveighed hotly in speeches and in the press against the too numerous taverns and their lack of conscience in pursuing trade. William and his painful affairs were covered by his sister with the charity which is a cloak for all sins and the silence which was the best policy for all parties. The subject of Boston was more

* In consultation, before he left, with Samuel Adams. See Bancroft, IV, p. 379.

interesting to her husband and more urgent. "I called here on my return to see this much injured town."[22] It was the corpse of a city, "the body of a departed friend." The soldiers were now in constant evidence, passing and repassing, the only people who were busy. Many of the principal merchants had moved out of town. Uncle Isaac and Aunt Elizabeth Smith had moved to Salem.

Abigail looked in at her husband's office in Queen Street, and saw that the three young men left in charge there were making the best possible use of their time, and needed the books and papers to study with. By their articles, John Adams was responsible for them, and they wished to avail themselves of the shelter and resources of the office. So she decided against removing the books to Braintree. She went to Judge Quincy's house for rest, a meal, and a family visit. Lovely Dorothy Quincy had a story to tell of an evil undercurrent in the town—a conspiracy of the Negro slaves. It was no idle rumour. The leaders had got an Irishman to draw up a petition for them to Governor Gage, offering their services against the colonists if he would arm them and promise them their liberty. A Negro who was a patriot (like Crispus Attucks) had tried to persuade his brethren against this course, and when he found himself in danger of his life had come secretly to Judge Edmund Quincy for protection and had revealed the plot. "There is but little said," her relatives warned Abigail. "The less this gets about, the better!"

"Well," said Abigail, "I wish most sincerely there was not a slave in the province! It always seemed a most iniquitous scheme to me to fight ourselves for what we are robbing the Negroes of, who have as good a right to freedom as we have! You know my mind upon this subject."[23]

"Yet, cousin, I once heard that your kinsman Thomas Smith, who is so excellent a patriot in the South, had given your Uncle Isaac a figure upon slave cargoes—something about five per cent?"[24] said Dorothy slyly.

"That was at any rate before importing slaves became contraband, like tea!" said Abigail good-humouredly. "The last I heard from Charleston was of a cargo of three hundred slaves being sent back to base by its own consignees, not being allowed to land![25] But all this talk of five per cent. from *you*, lady? It's my guess you've been listening attentively to one John Hancock!"

"There are others!" said Dorothy.

In October John Adams came home to his wife and family after ten weeks' absence. The warmth and *élan* of his presence had not been exaggerated in their hopes and dreams. Wife and children alike felt as if the sun had come out on them. Johnny was praised for reading to his mother so manfully—such a hard book!—and for writing to his father. Nabby was eagerly thanked for her letters, "My dear, they gave me great spirit!"[26] Charley and Tommy were tossed up and hugged. Each child felt its own place secure in its father's heart, without pretence or patronage.

But presently he turned to their mother and spoke of matters they could not understand. "You ask me am I satisfied with the Congress? Tolerably well, tolerably. We should have done more. We were slow! Slow as snails. I have not been used to such ways![27] . . . And yet . . . we have had as great questions to discuss as ever engaged the attention of men. There is a great spirit in the Congress! Above all, there is in the Congress a collection of the greatest men upon this continent. Here are fortunes, abilities, learning, eloquence, acuteness, equal to any I ever met with in my life. There is a magnanimity and public spirit equal to any in ancient history. . . . When we got the false news of the bombardment of Boston every gentleman seemed to consider it as the bombardment of the capital of his own province! I was particularly struck with the Southern gentlemen from Virginia—Mr Peyton Randolph, whom we made our President, and Mr Patrick Henry, and Colonel Washington and Mr Richard Henry Lee. The Virginians have called Lee their Cicero, Henry their Demosthenes."

"Did you accomplish anything definite?" she said.

"Not what I hoped, I confess. I feel—and I urged—that there is a necessity that an American Legislature should be set up without delay.[28] But others thought that that would bar the way finally for reconciliation with the British. Finally, a committee was appointed to draw up an address to the King—Lee, Henry, myself, and two others. The address we prepared was not considered conciliatory enough, by Mr Dickinson especially. And Mr Dickinson —the Philadelphia Quaker whose writings you know well[29]— was added to our committee to help redraft it, which he did— adding softening touches to the document already prepared but not changing its main arguments. This has gone to London, and we must hope for result. It was at least a clear statement and a loyal one. Well, my love, your informative letters have not only cheered me but done us vast service! Tell me about yourself! How have you managed?"

"I've lived a very recluse life since your absence, my dearest!" said Abigail. "Seldom gone anywhere except to my father's! My mother has been exceedingly low, but is a little better. Uncle Quincy often visits me to have an hour of sweet communion upon politicks with me! And Dr Tufts comes in, and Colonel James and Mrs Mercy Warren were here on Monday, and Mrs Warren will spend a day or two on her return with me. I've spent one Sabbath in town since you left—well, I wrote to you from Boston. What struck me was that the city people don't know yet that luxury and fashion are out of date—they haven't the resolution to encourage our own manufactorics* which people in the country have! We must return a little more to the simplicity of our fathers! But, dearest—how do you think I look? My health is much better than it was last fall! Some folks say I grow very fat!"[30]

He had listened to all she said with kindling interest, and now he laughed out. She was always taking him by surprise.

"Down, vanity!" he said. But he showed her what he thought of her looks. Then he set straight the lace on her hair, and taking her arm in his drew her out into the yard. Ankle-deep in the golden leaves, he looked out eagerly over his farm, his walled byre and pasture, his browsing cattle, the well-cut stubble of the sickled corn. Between the fields ran the road, deep in dust.

"And here you saw them pass to get the powder, in armed array!" he said, musing. "Ay, but our people must be peaceable! Let them exercise every day in the week, if they will—the more the better! Let them furnish themselves with artillery and arms and ammunition. Let 'em follow the maxim which you say they have adopted—'In times of peace prepare for war'—but let them avoid war *if possible*, *if possible* I say."[31]

On November 23, with John Adams's assistance, the Provincial Congress of Massachusetts (formed from the dissolved Assembly during his absence) voted to enroll twelve thousand minutemen, who—as the times of the Indian wars—would go about their labour with weapons at hand, ready at a minute's notice to follow the call to arms.

* This alludes to the hand-spinning and weaving, etc., being encouraged to substitute for the finer imported goods. In those days the word "manufactory" clung to its Latin meaning and meant "made by hand."

G

A game of seizing the munitions of the province was on. First the British made a successful coup, then the provincials, in a tremendous hide-and-seek in which the advantages were all on the side of the provincials. They knew the terrain, they knew good hiding-places, and they were almost always informed in time of British intentions. Since minutemen and militia were openly drilling everywhere, three times a week and oftener, it was natural that Gage, who could think of nothing else to do, should try to seize the small local stores of munitions and arms.

Abigail Adams would stroll down to the North Precinct muster field with her husband and son and hear John groan with envy of his youngest brother Elihu, the captain of the local troop. "Oh that I were a soldier! I will be. I'm reading military books!"[32] And he gave thought—and poured it forth to her—on the problems of the organization of an army. Little enough had been done yet, but at least some general officers had been appointed: General Ward, a veteran of the French and Indian War, and two major-generals, of whom Dr Joseph Warren was one. Powder and guns were being assembled in a central spot.

It was five months later that the skirmishes of Lexington and Concord were fought. As soon as the news reached Braintree Captain Elihu Adams and his band of minutemen lit out to join the others. All night minutemen and militia poured into Cambridge. The Penns Hill farm, right on the Old Shore Road, became a scene of bustle and confusion as passing minutemen paused for a drink and a rest. More came and more, and were offered supper—breakfast—a night's lodging. Johnny ran to and fro with big mugs of water from the well. His father brought cider from the cellar. His mother was cutting slices of salt meat and bread on the living-room table, and ordering a large kettle of meat and vegetables to be put on to boil in the kitchen. The good smell of baking bread floated out of the door to the tired and dusty traveller. The barn became full of men bivouacking there for the night, and every corner of the house was full.

John Adams came into the barn, a cordial host to his guests.

"Ye've got a fine little soldier coming along *there*, sir!" said one, pointing to Johnny.

"Ay, and he knows his drill, I'll warrant!" said John Adams. "He's always down at the muster field or playing at drills with his brothers."

The militiaman rose and gravely handed the little boy his musket. "Now then, sir—shoulder *arms*!—right *turn*—slope *arms*!—ground *arms*!——"

The lantern hanging in the barn door shone out across a strip of emerald grass and illuminated the slender boy's figure, gallantly handling the heavy weapon, exactly and smartly performing the manual exercise of the musket at the word of command; while in the shadowy barn, a ruddy cheek, a bright eye, a boot, the gleam of a silver button, a hand playing with the straw, indicated the crowd of intent, resting men.

Abigail had come out to watch, and her hand tightened on her husband's arm. Eight years ago Johnny was born, and the time was short to look back on. Eight years from now he would be as old as some who were present there now in the barn. And what would he be then? A soldier? There were people—Sam Quincy, for instance, Jonathan Sewall—who said that if the war began it would last for twenty years.

Next day John Adams took horse and rode over the route of the battle, collecting information from witnesses of all kinds; visited the camp at Cambridge, and listened to his friends, General Ward, General Heath, and above all General Joseph Warren.[33]

So Abigail presently learned from him the full story.

"This battle of Concord has cost the British more than it cost them to take Quebec!" said John Adams. "And what have they got to show for it?"

"But what have we got to show for it?" stammered the Reverend Isaac, who had ridden back with John from Cambridge. "Their revenge will be terrible."

"Indeed, what I saw and heard yesterday convinced me," said John Adams, "that if we do not defend ourselves, they will kill us!"

"B-but how can we defend ourselves?" said Isaac, despairing.

"What can we do to help?" said Abigail. "Us, I mean—here? How were things at the camp?"

"Confusion and much distress!" said John. "No artillery—little in the way of arms, short of clothing and blankets—short of provisions. But I'll tell you what they're not short of—resolution and spirit!"[34]

He looked fiercely at Isaac, and the gentle young man quailed and glanced appealingly at his beloved cousin Abigail.

"I must say farewell, my dear, dear cousin!" said he. "I am for

England until this trouble is past! I am a man of peace, and out of place here in this distracted province. My mind is full of perplexity and concern! . . . My mother and father agree to my going. . . . I can't be useful here! . . ." His eyes filled with tears. He hated to be the only one of his family of another opinion. He was homesick for return almost before he started. But go he must.

Abigail took his hand.

"You are always," she said, "my dear cousin and friend! You will pray to God for Boston—and for our country!"

Now the Second Continental Congress came on, and John Adams, again a delegate, left his wife and children with reluctance, though he left them in a place as safe as any. He did not anticipate immediate trouble. Had Abigail been inside Boston her situation would have been intolerable. But her farsighted husband had got her out in time—well ahead of time. She tried to feel worthy now of his bracing letters. He was more afraid, it seemed, that she should feel nervous than that she would be unsafe—"surrounded as you are by people who are too timorous. Many fears and imaginary dangers will be suggested to you but I hope you will not be impressed by them! In case of real danger," he added, a bit off-hand, "fly to the woods with our children."

Abigail did not feel heroic. The idea of the woods was not appealing. She had now no men in the house. Her work-people and her neighbours were indeed "timorous." "I feel somewhat lonely. Mr Thaxter is gone home. Mr Rice is going into the army as captain of a company. We have no school. I know not what to do with John." The young men "seem to be discouraged in the study of law and think there will never be any business for them." But she felt they were prematurely discouraged. A pity they didn't talk it over with John Adams before they left.

"As government is assumed," she said with perfect simplicity, "I suppose courts of justice will be established and in that case there may be [law] business to do."[35]

Not "resumed"—"assumed." This tell-tale word reveals that by May 4, 1775, Abigail Adams and her husband—for from him she derived the idea—looked forward to nothing else but complete independence.* And John Adams had driven up to the Congress

* See among many incorrect statements re John Adams and Samuel Adams in *American Statesmen* series this error in particular, that Samuel Adams alone stood for independence at the start of the Second Congress: "Even John Adams and Jefferson were as yet far from being ready for such a step." (P. 333.) The exact contrary is the case.

in his sulky, his manservant on horseback behind him, with a scheme for independence completely formulated in his mind.

Before May was out Braintree discovered that it was not, as John Adams had cheerfully supposed, out of the war zone. In the dark of a Sunday morning the warning drum began to beat, and Abigail wakened to its distant sound. As she came downstairs a farm-hand ran into the kitchen with word that the bell on the meeting-house in Braintree South Precinct was ringing like mad, and beyond to the south-west the bell of Abigail's father's church in Weymouth was heard faintly on the breeze by villagers down that way. The man Isaac came back breathless before they had finished their hasty meal—mistress, maids, and children all sitting down together in the twilit kitchen.

"Three sloops and a cutter have anchored just below Great Hill. Some think they're for Germantown—some say Weymouth. The road's full of folk from Germantown, loaded with their goods, flocking inland this way! And the folk from Weymouth are all going back from the coast into the country, Parson Smith and his family have taken their chaise and gone, and the Parson loaded his wagon with women and children of his parish and took 'em along. Your Aunt Tufts had a bed thrown into a wagon and ordered the boy to drive her to Bridgwater, and your Uncle the Doctor is distracted, whether to go or not. They say three hundred men have landed somewhere, and our minutemen are mustering . . . . Well, mistress, there'll be no church this Sabbath!"

Peter Adams hurried in, his honest face anxious.

"Sister, won't you let me move you and the children and any of your valuables back into the country, to my house? You're in an exposed place here on the highway—if——!"

"I do thank you, Brother Peter! Indeed I will go thankfully, if we're really in danger! But John is always warning me against false fears. Let me wait awhile and see. I can be useful here, I hope."

Thinking of the panic-stricken women all around, Peter gazed at her with admiration as she bundled the children out of the kitchen and directed her work-people to push aside the table, get out the wooden mugs and bowls, and all the spoons—two more buckets of ice-cold well-water——

Elihu Adams appeared at the kitchen door, dressed in his hunting-shirt with his musket slung on his back.

"Good morning, sister! There's a dozen men out here from Weymouth who have packed off their womenfolk and hurried to help us without breakfast. . . ."

"We have some pease-porridge and coffee ready!" said Abigail. "Will they come in?"

A moment or two later Elihu, stepping to the big kettle to ladle out some porridge, exclaimed at the spoon in his hand.

"What, sister, *pewter*? The men in my company have so few bullets that some of them, if they fire once, can't reload. They'd give their ears for pewter this day!"

"Take it, take it!" said Abigail. "Take all my pewter spoons! I've at least two dozen, that we use here in the kitchen." She caught them down from hooks, pulled them out of the dresser. "Look, have you your bullet-moulds? Use that heavy iron kettle!"

Johnny, coming into the kitchen, saw the spoons going into the kettle. The long handles of the bigger ladles stuck up. He squeezed through the people to see more closely.

"Why, Uncle, what are you doing? What funny soup!"

"Bullet soup!" said his uncle. "You've seen your father run shot. We're going to run bullets!"

Johnny understood, and his heart jumped. Danger was close. Why didn't they go all away in the cart to Uncle Peter's? But just as he began to feel that sickening stab of fear he turned round to look for his mother. When he saw her standing so calmly in the doorway between kitchen and living-room, directing things in her quiet voice as if everything were going on just as she expected, his heart, if it did not return to normal, exchanged fear for excitement. He and his mother were sharing in a great day. Her eyes suddenly met his in warm, proud sympathy. She was glad to see him there. "Do you wonder," said John Quincy Adams, sixty-eight years later, "that a boy of seven who witnessed this scene should be a patriot?"*

The road outside was now cloudy with the dust of passing feet. The minutemen came flocking down, even from towns twenty, thirty, and forty miles from Weymouth, till two thousand were collectde.[36]

The look-out men soon reported that the enemy's objective was now apparent. It was a redcoat raid on Grape Island to gather hay. They couldn't be reached there for want of boats; but the formidable array of minutemen on the shore, and the firing of muskets

* Speech delivered in 1843.

which splashed ball into the sea around them, flustered the redcoats and "prevented their getting more than three tons of hay though they had carted much more down to the water. At last a lighter was mustered and a sloop from Hingham which had six port-holes. Our men eagerly jumped on board and put off for the island. Your brother Elihu was one of the first on board,"[37] wrote Abigail to her husband. The British, who had probably intended to get the hay while all the inhabitants were in church, were unprepared for such resistance and hurriedly decamped. "Our people landed upon the island and in an instant set fire to the hay. Both your brothers were there; your younger brother with his company gained honour by their good order that day." Dr Tufts too. "Danger, you know, sometimes makes timid men bold. He stood that day very well, and generously attended, with drink, biscuits, flints, etc., five hundred men without taking any pay. He has since been chosen one of the committee of correspondence for Weymouth, establishing a regular method of alarm from town to town."

The Monday morning sun saw peace restored to Weymouth and Braintree, evacuated families back in their homes, minutemen laying aside the musket for the hoe, and only the look-out men on duty. Nabby and Johnny settled to lessons with their mother, doing some of that "copying out" their father favoured in the delicate, clear handwriting taught them by Mr Thaxter. Charley began to read the primer, and three-year-old Tommy learned his letters from the horn-book. Their little lives were steadied and reassured.

Yet as the days passed it became apparent that not only occasions of critical alarm, and not only soldiers, were now taxing the resources of the Penns Hill farm. "Sometimes refugees from Boston, tired and fatigued, seek an asylum for a day, a night, a week. You can hardly imagine how we live," wrote Abigail to her husband. "Yet,

> "To the houseless child of want
> Our doors are open still;
> And though our portions are but scant
> We give them with good will."[38]

John Adams's passionate love for his wife did not in the least diminish his hardihood. He wrote back cheerily, "Was you frightened when the sheep-stealers got a drubbing at Grape Island? Father Smith prayed for our scow crew I doubt not!" And with a tonic stoicism he acknowledges necessity: "My health and life ought to be hazarded in the cause of my country as well as yours and all my friends. . . . I hope you will maintain your philosophical composure. I think you are in no danger."[39]

But Abigail knew better. Before those letters reached her she had written again, not minimizing for his sake the increasing tenseness of the situation at Braintree.

> We now expect our sea coast ravaged. Perhaps the very next letter I write will inform you that I am driven away from our yet quiet cottage. Necessity will oblige Gage to take some desperate steps. We are told for truth that he is now eight thousand strong. We live in continual expectation of alarms. Courage I know we have in abundance; conduct I hope we shall not want; but powder—where shall we get a sufficient supply?[40]

She added, "I never trust myself long with the terrors which sometimes intrude themselves upon me."

VI

The Battle of Bunker Hill

THE BELL OF THE NORTH PRECINCT meeting-house and the marching drum were silent. But something unusual wakened Abigail at three o'clock that Saturday morning the seventeenth of June. It was thunder. At first, people waking in the dim blue-grey dawn in the peaceful bedrooms of Weymouth and Braintree muttered to themselves, "A storm." But when they leaned out of window, anxious for standing crops, the air was fresh, a few stars hung silver in the pale sky, a light breeze ruffled the leaves; all the farmer's signs pointed towards a fine day. But again that clap of thunder rolled across the sea. . . .

Guns at Boston. It had begun.

The whole house roused; all dressed in haste. As soon as Abigail was ready she set off impatiently to climb Penns Hill, spy-glass in hand. Her eldest son ran after her, and she welcomed his company.

Up through the orchard, and over the coarse turf at the top of the hill where the bare rock made a rough seat facing Boston. Yes, the intermittent flash of cannon and puffs of smoke could be seen clearly even without the glass. Evidently the ships of war lying in the channel between Boston and Charlestown were firing at Charlestown; she could learn no more than that.

"You see, Johnny?"

He saw.

"Is this a battle, Mother?"

"This is a battle. The day is come . . . perhaps the very day on which the fate of America depends!"

The little boy's heart beat hard. He shared her emotion more fully than she would have believed possible. To eight-year-old John Quincy this was like the great battles in the Bible—"the sword of the Lord and of Gideon." Right was marshalled on one side, wrong on the other, and he saw the flash and heard the thunder of their conflict. It was almost more than he could bear. Exalted at being within sight and hearing of such an event, he clasped his mother's hand fervently, and they went down the hill together.

"Is it dangerous, ma'am? What shall we do," cried the servant Patty. "That roar makes me jump so, I don't know what I'm about!"

Baby Tommy was wailing, and Nabby, pale and anxious, was trying to comfort him. Charlie, with a quivering lip, was trying to show off to Tommy that he was *too big* to be scared by that horrid noise. But when their mother appeared they all flung themselves upon her. She did not need to say much to reassure them. Her paleness and over-bright eyes escaped their notice. Here she was, and they were with her. Everything was all right with them.

"Breakfast!" she said. "We must eat all we can. Perhaps we shall go to visit Uncle Peter! No, Patty, it's not dangerous to *us*—yet. But after breakfast we will pack some things in case we think it best to leave the house."

Her brothers-in-law called to see if she was all right, and Peter again offered refuge at his house.

The hot, bright summer day wore on and, duties attended to, she could not restrain her desire to see the distant battle, as she could not fail moment by moment to hear it. And, like a mother of ancient Rome, she believed it was a good thing for her son to see that spectacle, to observe history being hammered out on the anvil before his eyes. So again she took Johnny with her up the hill, and as they climbed the hot slope under the thin, speckled shade of the apple-trees she told him what she thought: in time to come boys in school would learn from their history-books the date of this day, June 17, 1775, and when he was an old man he would be able to tell his grandchildren and his great-grandchildren, "Yes, I *saw* it!"*

* In 1843, when John Quincy Adams was an old man, a granite monument was set up on the site of the battle, and a great day of celebration was appointed for its unveiling. John Quincy Adams refused the invitation to be present, and spent the day solitary in his house writing in his diary: "What a day in the annals of mankind is Bunker Hill! What a day was the 17th of June, 1775; and what a burlesque upon them both is an oration upon them by Daniel Webster! . . . Daniel Webster is a heartless traitor to the cause of human freedom; John Tyler is a slave-monger. What have they to do with the Quincy granite pyramid on the brow of Bunker's Hill? . . . with the ideal association of the thundering cannon which I heard, and the smoke of burning Charlestown which I saw, on that awful day? . . ." This statement will surprise those whose chief impression of Daniel Webster is gathered from Stephen Vincent Benét's imaginative masterpiece of fantasy. J. Q. A. was at loggerheads with Webster on the question of slavery, Adams being an uncompromising abolitionist.

They came out on to the hill-top. The sun beat fiercely down. The rocks were too hot to touch. But what was that which, in mid-afternoon, sent great black clouds of smoke volleying into the blue sky over there beyond Boston and the glittering Charles?

"Good God," said Abigail, "they are burning Charlestown!"

All night and all day Sunday "the constant roar of the cannon is so distressing that we cannot eat, drink or sleep." On Sunday afternoon Peter Adams came back with heavy news. Abigail, stricken, turned in spirit to her distant husband.

> My bursting heart must find vent at my pen. I have just heard that our dear friend Dr Warren is no more, but fell gloriously fighting for his country. . . . Great is our loss . . . his courage and fortitude animating the soldiers. . . . Charlestown lies in ashes. . . . It is expected they will come out over the Neck to-night, and a dreadful battle must ensue. . . . How many have fallen we know not. . . . I shall tarry here till it is thought unsafe and then I have secured myself a retreat at your brother's, who had kindly offered me part of his house.[1]

On Tuesday the guns had been silent for more than twenty-four hours, but authentic news was hard to get. "Ten thousand reports are passing, vague and uncertain as the wind." But Abigail had plucked up heart. Mourning the death of Dr Warren, "those favourite lines of Collins continually sound in my ears—'How sleep the brave——'"[2] She gave her feeling outlet by teaching the verses to Nabby and Johnny, who learned them with fervour, and in the truest sense, by heart.

Companies of colonial soldiers were now stationed at points along the coast in anticipation of raids, for the British held the Boston and Charlestown peninsulas and might strike out against the mainland from either one. "We have two companies [of provincials] stationed in this town—one at Germantown, one at Squantum; in Weymouth one; in Hingham two, etc. I believe I shall remove your books this week to your brother's." Every one whose home was near the shore was securing a retreat farther inland. Colonel Quincy and his family would go to Deacon Holbrook's; Richard Cranch and Mary and their children to Major Bass's. But only in case of necessity.[3] Mr and Mrs Bowdoin, refugees already, decided to seek some less exposed haven, and called on Abigail to take ceremonious and affectionate farewell. "He wished he could have stayed at Braintree," she wrote, "but his lady was fearful."[4]

John Adams must not think that *his* lady was fearful.

> We hear that the [British] troops destined for New York are all expected here: but we have got to that pass that a whole legion of them would not intimidate us! I think I am very brave upon the whole. If danger comes near my dwelling I suppose I shall shudder. We want powder, but with the blessing of heaven we fear them not![5]

Particulars of the battle were now coming in, and the Quincy-Cranch circle at Braintree, pooling information and sorting it out together, got a pretty clear picture of the event.

Dr Warren, the last man out of the redoubt, was killed as he went, by a bullet through the head. The British won Bunker Hill and the Charlestown peninsula. But they paid dear.

Oh, how the hearts at Weymouth and at Braintree kindled at the tale. "Ours" had now been matched in equal fight with the flower of the British Army, and their final withdrawal hardly bore the face of defeat. "Figure to yourself . . ." wrote Abigail eagerly—as if she had been an eyewitness—

> the town in flames all around them, and the heat from the flames so intense as scarcely to be borne—the day one of the hottest we have had this season, and the wind blowing the smoke in their faces—and then consider that we do not count sixty men lost! Every account agrees in fourteen or fifteen hundred slain upon their side.[6]

The final figures were nearer one thousand of the British killed, including seventy officers, against one hundred and forty-five Americans killed, and three hundred wounded and prisoners.[7]

The overwhelming number of wounded and the difficulties of transportation completely upset whatever inadequate preparations had been made. "Our prisoners," wrote Abigail, "were all brought over to the Long Wharf, and there lay all night, without any care of their wounds or any resting place but the pavements until the next day." Then they were carried to the gaol, "since when we hear they are civilly treated." The British wounded were not much better off. Abigail heard that "their wounded men die very fast, so that they have a report that the bullets were poisoned."

John Adams always bitterly blamed Dickinson, and the delay caused by the second petition, for the defeat at Bunker Hill, and for the worst feature of it, the death of Dr Joseph Warren, "a hero," he said passionately, "of more worth than all the town." Abigail's hurt was of like kind.

"Not all the havoc and devastation they have made has wounded me like the death of Warren."[8]

But if the British had taken to burning houses Weymouth was not safe, Braintree might soon be in ashes. The redcoats might come roaring out along both Necks!* "I would not have you distressed about me!" wrote Abigail to her anxious, distraught husband. "Danger, they say, makes people valiant. I have felt distressed but not dismayed."

John Adams was kindled to admiration. "You are really brave, my dear! You are a heroine, and you have reason to be. For the worst that can happen can do you no harm."[9]

It was, however, cold comfort to a husband separated from his wife by four hundred miles to be convinced that she would, if necessary, meet a violent death with courage, and would thereafter go directly to heaven.

Abigail was invited to Cambridge to meet Washington and his companions soon after their arrival. The enthusiasm the new general aroused in her was never after to be dimmed. "I was struck with General Washington," she wrote. "You had prepared me to entertain a favourable opinion of him, but I thought the half was not told me. Dignity with ease—the gentleman and the soldier—" Yes, she flew to poetry, to Dryden, to really describe him:

> Mark his majestic fabric; he's a temple
> Sacred by birth, and built by hands divine;
> His soul's the deity that lodges there,
> Nor is the pile unworthy of the god.

With all that, "modesty marks every line and feature of his face."[10]

As for General Lee, "he," said this surprising provincial lady, "looks like a careless, hardy veteran, and brought to my mind his namesake Charles XII of Sweden." It pleased Abigail that both gentlemen expressed their warm regard for her husband. Washington had not forgotten the debt he owed to John Adams, who had nominated him to lead the Continental Army. Lee was a queer man, with all his dogs. He made one of them climb on a chair and "shake hands" with Mrs Adams. The lady preserved her patience. But the incident seemed to reveal a certain trivialness of mind which she could only hope would not injure Lee's conduct in battle.

* Boston had only one neck, but the British were now also encamped in the Charlestown peninsula (won by the Bunker Hill battle), which was joined to the mainland by the Charlestown Neck.

All Abigail heard convinced her of Washington's supreme excellence for the command. "My brother has a captain's commission and is stationed at Cambridge," she wrote. Many of the young men of her neighbourhood panted to be in the thick of it; not merely minutemen staying on the farm until called by local emergency, but to enlist with General Washington in the Continental Army. Her brother-in-law Elihu confided to Abigail his impatience at being only a local captain of minutemen.

"But why is that not enough for him?" said Mrs Hall.* "Why can't he be content to stay here and mind his farm, and help take care of us? He gets excitement enough here! There's fighting enough here! There was Grape Island. And there was the lighthouse raid. And there was the raid off the Moon with the whaleboats. Why does he want to go off to the army? No, I never will consent to it. Never."

"Your good mother is really violent against it," wrote Abigail to her husband. "I cannot persuade nor reason her into a consent. Neither he nor I dare let her know that he is trying for a place."

So Elihu, encouraged by his sister-in-law, went away without his mother's consent and got his captaincy in the army before the siege of Boston had begun.

It was a peculiar siege. The British had ships and could have got out by sea had there been any friendly place to go. But the coasts north and south bristled with armed men. Nor did their command of the sea bring them any supplies of fresh food, except fish. Yet the besiegers who were trying to starve them out were compelled at the same time to starve thousands of their friends, patriot Americans who were trapped in Boston with the British.† The plight of these besieged citizens roused Abigail's indignant pity; "that of the most abject slaves under the most cruel and despotic of tyrants." The British, however, behaved with moderation. Martial law was proclaimed, and a curfew was imposed.[11] But a ten o'clock curfew was no hardship. The British felt themselves on a live volcano, and lived in constant dread of conspiracy and of spies who were, indeed, all round them. "No man dared now to be seen talking to his friend in the street,"[12] said the angry Abigail. "An order has been given that no person shall be seen to wipe his face with a

* The former Mrs Adams senior, mother of John, Elihu, and Peter.

† "There are about five thous-d Inhabitants still remaining in Town Amongst which is all the Selectmen who are not permitted to come out at all." Isaac Smith senior to Isaac junior, Smith-Carter MSS., June 1775.

white handkerchief. The reason I hear is that it is a signal of mutiny." She was pleased to think that the British reinforcements from York [England] would only increase the food shortage for the enemy. "Every additional man adds to their distress."

But the distress was not all on one side, nor was it to be confined to Boston. A more terrible and undiscriminating foe was about to ravage both sides alike, and range indifferently both city and country. Uncle Isaac Smith got early news, and wrote concerning the hundreds of ill-tended, ill-fed wounded, crowded together in the fly-laden heat—"they begin to have the flux."[13]

Contagion made no bones at all about crossing the guarded Neck. On the tenth of August Abigail wrote in haste to her husband:

> Your brother Elihu lies very dangerously sick with a dysentery. He has been very bad for more than a week. His life is despaired of. We are all in great distress. Your [step]father is with him in great anguish . . . . [Your brother] is sensible of his danger and is calmly resigned to the will of heaven.

Even as she wrote the unexpected word reached her that her husband was on the road and almost home. Congress, unable to bear the humid heat of August in Philadelphia, had adjourned for a brief recess. Abigail's postscript was a tempestuous mixture of joy and grief. "The joy is overclouded and the day is darkened . . . the sympathy I feel for the loss of your brother cut off in the pride of life and the bloom of manhood."[14]

John Adams arrived in time to attend his brother's funeral. But neither he nor anyone else could hope to assuage the bitterness of his mother's grief. Unaware of it, her son's children were perhaps her greatest comfort. She could not mutter to Elihu's three babies, as she was tempted to do to his young widow: "What did I tell you? I told him so. I *told* him!"

John Adams, though he grieved for his brother and cherished every moment with Abigail and their children, yet had public cares heavy on his mind. He attended General Court at Watertown, he conferred with General Washington on the army's needs, and he talked with Ward, Lee, Putnam, Gates, and Mifflin. He looked about him at the growing order of the camp, the regular drilling. "Our Army," he said, with an odd mixture of thoughts, "will be the best military school in the Empire!" He noted exactly the shortage of tents, of shot, of powder, of sick supplies, and in particular of cannon. So, as fully informed as a man could be about matters civil and military at the front, John Adams set off again on the twenty-eighth of August for Philadelphia.

But even as he left home that day—John Hancock's wedding day*—the pestilence arrived there. One of the men, Isaac, was unwell when the master left. His disorder soon showed itself to be a violent dysentery. "There was no resting-place in the house for his terrible groans." Two days later Abigail herself was seized with the same illness "in a violent manner." But hers only lasted, fortunately, three days. The next victim was one of the maids—Susy. She was sent home to be nursed. "Our little Tommy was next, and he lies very ill now," wrote Abigail to her husband. Then another maidservant, Patty, was seized. "Our house is a hospital in every part." Still weak from her own illness, Abigail had to be about nursing the rest. All Braintree was stricken at once. "I can scarce find a well person to assist in looking after the sick." Neighbour after neighbour fell. Family after family had children dying or dead. "Mr Wibird lies bad; Major Miller is dangerous, and Mr Gay is not expected to live. We have been four Sundays without any meeting. So sickly and so mortal a time the oldest man does not remember.[15]

"As to politics," she declared impatiently,

> I know nothing about them. The distresses of my family are so great that I have not thought of them. As to my own health, I mend but very slowly . . . hope it is only with my being fatigued with looking after Tommy, as he is unwilling any one but mamma should do for him. If he was, I could not find anybody that is worth having.

The mother's tender, constant care had its reward. Three-year-old Tommy, so near death, began to mend. His fever abated. His eyes lost their glassy look, and the warm cloths to his stomach assuaged his violent pains. His tense little body relaxed. He smiled tenderly on his faithful guardian. It had happened as he expected. Mamma had driven away his sickness. "But were you to look in on him," she wrote to his father,

> you would not know him. From a hearty, hale, corn-fed boy, he has become pale, lean, and wan . . . entirely stripped of all the flesh he had save what remains for to keep his bones together. Two of the children, John and Charles, I have sent out of the house, finding it difficult to keep them out of the chamber. Nabby continues well.

* To Abigail's cousin, Dorothy Quincy.

Of the remaining domestic or farm staff, "Jonathan is the only one who remains in the family who has not had a turn of the disorder."[16]

Thus does Providence show His power. Not many weeks before Abigail had felt on familiar terms with Deity, hailing Him as a fellow ally, going off eagerly on the Fast Day in July to pray against the wicked British. "I really believe they are more afraid of the Americans' prayers than of their swords!" she had said complacently, getting into the chaise with Mary Cranch. The sisters had driven off together to Dedham to hear some pungent preaching and some really stirring prayers. "I could not bear," said Abigail, "to hear our inanimate old bachelor!"[17] And indeed Mr Wibird was not the man for such a day.

But now providence was less partial. Little Tommy had only just brought forth her humble prayers of thanks for his definite emergence from the dark valley when a message summoned her to the Weymouth parsonage. Her mother was stricken.

> Have pity upon me. Have pity upon me, O thou my beloved, for the hand of God presseth me sore. . . . How can I tell you (O my bursting heart!) that my dear mother has left me? This day, October 1st, about five o'clock, she left this world. . . . After sustaining sixteen days severe conflict nature fainted and she fell asleep. Blessed spirit where art thou? At times I am almost ready to faint under this severe and heavy stroke, separated from *thee* who used to be a comforter to me in affliction; but blessed be God, his ear is not heavy that He cannot hear, but He has bid us call upon Him in time of trouble.
>
> My poor father, like a firm believer and a good Christian, sets before his children the best examples of patience and submission. . . .
>
> Sickness and death are in almost every family in the province.
>
> Almighty God! restrain the pestilence. . . .[18]

Her husband replied:

> If I could write as well as you, my sorrow would be as eloquent as yours, but upon my soul I cannot.[19] I bewail more than I can express the loss of so much purity and unaffected piety and virtue to the world. I know of no better character left in it. . . . But I grieve for nobody more than my children. Her most amiable and discreet example, as well as her kind skill and care, I have ever relied upon in my own mind for the education of these little swarms. I am sure that my children are the better for the forming hand of their grandmother.[20]

But, in his earnest desire to comfort her, John did not forget his wife's impatient protest, in the midst of the epidemic, that she can give no thought to politics. "Your mother," he wrote,

> had a clear and penetrating understanding and a profound judgment, as well as an honest, a friendly, and a charitable heart. There is one thing, however, which you will forgive me if I hint to you. Let me ask you, rather, if you are not of my opinion? Were not her talents and virtues too much confined to private, social, and domestic life?
>
> My opinion of the duties of religion and morality comprehends a very extensive connexion with society at large and the great interests of the public. . . .

A profound natural psychologist, John was well aware that the education of the children was not only his wife's chief duty at present there at home, but was the likeliest avenue out of her crushing sorrow. He referred to Newton and Locke, the intense importance of the earliest years, of habit-formation and the set of the will.

> It should be your care and mine to elevate the minds of our children and exalt their courage; to accelerate and animate their industry and activity; to excite in them contempt of meanness, injustice, and inhumanity, and an ambition to excel. . . . If we allow their minds to grovel and creep in infancy, they will grovel all their lives.[21]

But where's his wife? Where's his companion? Abigail is not only a mother. Her husband needs her too. And he tugs heartily at her attention. "Cheerfulness is not a sin in any times," he says. "I hope that you will resume your wonted cheerfulness and write again upon news and politics. . . .[22] I have nothing now to write but repetitions of respect and affection. . . . Yours, yours, yours —J.A."[23]

She had not waited for the appeal, though no doubt she was glad to have it. It is fine to be needed. Her sorrow had had unrestrained vent through her pen—"I have written many things to you that I suppose I never could have talked"[24]—and now she is back at his side, again alive to the world around her at every pore. But she is maturer. Some of the naïveté of her black-and-white view of the world is gone. Among the news that now and then leaks out of tormented Boston, she remarks not only the distress of the inhabitants, which no language can paint, but "the soldiers [British] are obliged to do very hard duty,"[25] keeping their packs with them everywhere for fear of sudden alarm.

If anyone had ventured to say to her at any time that there are two sides to every question she would probably have replied, yes, indeed, a right side and a wrong side. But she was learning to make allowance for honest error. "My heart," she realized, "is made tender by repeated affliction; it never was a hard heart."[26]

John Adams was pleased with Hancock's recent marriage to Abigail's cousin, Dorothy Quincy, which he had long taken for granted, and saw nothing wrong behind Dorothy's stately front.* He wrote to Abigail that he wished *she* could come to Philadelphia —they would be as happy as John Hancock and his lady.

> Two pair of colours belonging to the Seventh Regiment were brought here last night and hung up in Mrs Hancock's chamber with great splendour and elegance. (That lady sends her compliments and good wishes.) Among a hundred men, almost, at this house, she lives and behaves with modesty, decency, dignity and discretion, I assure you. Her behaviour is easy and genteel. She avoids talking upon politics. In large and mixed companies she is totally silent, as a lady ought to be. But whether her eyes are so penetrating and her attention so quick to the words, looks, gestures, sentiments, etc., of the company as yours would be, saucy as you are this way, I won't say![27]

Abigail might laugh at this sketch of herself, but there was food for reflection there too. Not for the first time it was brought home to her that she had married a man with exacting standards. A woman must be interested in politics, informed, ready to discuss them with her husband in conversation—and in letters!—even to discuss them in small intimate groups, like the Quincy circle, when few if any strangers were present. On such occasions an intelligent woman might even have opinions of her own, and they would be respectfully listened to. Oh, nothing to complain of there! But in a large, mixed company no matter what the talk, no matter what her information and her thoughts—a woman must be totally silent, or forfeit the admiration of John Adams.

Abigail did not dispute the point, but she thought about it. She must have John's approval. And yet . . .? Certainly the brilliant friend of her girlhood, Mercy Otis Warren, did not practise such extreme decorum! And however John might value the softness of a woman's manner, and deplore and hate anything that seemed to tend towards the dominating or the masculine, he had left his wife in a position where softness, perhaps, was not the chief quality needed. She was in sole charge of the farm, giving orders, shouldering

* Dorothy had very nearly eloped with Aaron Burt just before her marriage.

responsibility, paying wages, hiring and dismissing; final court of appeal for every one, directing everybody all day long. Her thoughts began to warm up, like a kettle on the fire, and a little bubble of discontent rose to the surface.

> I wish I could have more of the assistance of my dearest friend. . . . In the twelve years we have been married I believe we have not lived together more than six.[28] But it is my lot. I hope in time to have the reputation of being as good a farmeress as my partner has of being a good statesman.[29]

John Adams, blandly unaware of inconsistency, replied with no idle gallantry: "It gives me concern to think of the many cares you must have upon your mind. Your reputation as a farmer, or anything else you undertake, I dare answer for. Your partner's character as a statesman is much more problematical!"[30]

As for their separation, it is at least a comfort to her that he minds it as much as she does.

> I hope I shall be excused from coming to Philadelphia again, at least until other gentlemen have taken their turns. But I never will come here again without you, if I can persuade you to come with me. Whom God has joined together ought not to be put asunder so long with their own consent.[31]

There was not much hope of his coming home soon, however. "We have so much to do and it is so difficult to do it right."[32] John Adams was busy indeed. During his terms in Congress he served on more than ninety committees and was chairman of twenty-five. This is a record not approached by any other member. Just as in Boston, it was impossible, even for those who would gladly have avoided him, to do without his lucidity, his judgment, his energy, his honesty, his mass of accurate information, and his first-class brain.

Meanwhile the Provincial Congress in Massachusetts, convinced by the logic of circumstances that John Adams was right on the necessity of forming at least a *pro tem.* government in the province, was beginning to make a definite move in that direction. They decided to reopen the law courts, under their own control, and appointed John Adams as Chief Justice. "I wish I knew what mighty things were fabricating," Abigail wrote. "If a form of government is to be established here [in Massachusetts] what one will be assumed." She foresaw all kinds of possible dissensions, ten thousand difficulties. The reins of government had been so long slackened, how could its restraints be voluntarily assumed? "If we separate from Britain," said this lawyer's wife, "what code of laws will be established?" And then again, "How shall we be governed so as to retain our liberties?" No Government could be free which was not administrated by general stated laws. But who would frame the laws? Who would enforce them? People hated new ways, always wanted to go on as before, were jealous of new authority. Yes, "I feel anxious for the fate of our monarchy, or democracy, or whatever is to take place."[33] But that a new independent Government must and would take place, John Adams's wife never doubted.

Economic questions were also to the fore. She suggested the need of a continental excise on spirits,* and of a practice of barter with the West Indies, an exchange of produce, "in order to keep among us our gold and silver." A silver dollar was now so rare that "our traders will give you a hundred pounds of paper for ninety of silver."[34]

Was this a woman who was to hold her tongue when politics were discussed in a mixed company?

From December 9 to February 8, '76, John Adams was back at Braintree, summoned home by his appointment as Chief Justice of Massachusetts. The necessary organization of the law courts was already completely formulated in his mind, and he was at once charged with the duty of drawing up a proclamation to explain and start off the new judicial system. This proclamation was to be read at the opening of every court of justice, and at the town meeting in every town. The Council also recommended that "the several ministers of the gospel" throughout the colony—whose influence had been so fundamental in maintaining public order and morality during the "lawless" year—should read it to their congregations "immediately after divine service on the Sabbath following their receipt of it."

He wrote it during the Christmas recess at home. It was like old times for his wife and family to have him there, driving his busy quill at his desk beside the roaring fire. His presence lifted all their hearts and quickened the vitality of the convalescent house. His warm, hearty approval and comfort shone round on them all; on

* Continental, to be fair to every one; excise, so as to limit the consumption of spirits, as well as raise money.

pretty ten-year-old Nabby, praised for the good help she was to her mother—and also praised for her beginning Latin and French; on pale, thin little Tommy, petted into better appetite and higher spirits; on Johnny, whose letters were respectfully appreciated—"John writes like a hero, glowing with ardour for his country and burning with indignation against her enemies"; and on cheerful little Charles, who must not be forgotten.

But it was to his wife that John Adams's presence meant the most. She loved her children dearly, and spoke to John with pity of "unfruitful women." Yet, in these perilous times, she could understand what Bacon meant when he said that those who had children gave hostages to fortune. Certainly the childless "are freed from the anxiety every parent must feel for their rising offspring."[35]

The only anxiety she ever felt for her husband was in regard to his health or safety. Never once did she, like many other wives, feel anxious lest he should do or say the wrong thing, make mistakes, offend people, be foolish or boorish, or commit himself to a course of which her judgment disapproved. Her confidence in him was not a half-pretence, to boost him up; not the result of a theory of wifely duty, nor a submissive, unintelligent ignorance of what he was about. It was a full, co-operative, entire agreement with the whole of his point of view, and an admiration of his methods and actions.

When Abigail brought in her sewing to the study fire and sat there in her ample, wadded winter clothes and watched his flying pen, he worked twice as well. Reading his document to her, sensing its resonance against her mind, he wrote more clearly and vigorously than in solitude. Her questions clarified his thought. What is government really for? What aim should it have in view? Ay, he had often asked himself that question. Is it order? Is it security? Is it more than these? And from what source does government derive its authority? Nor from the divine right of kings. Then where does power ultimately reside?

As they discussed and meditated in cosy, happy companionship in their snug retreat the old year passed away and the year 1776 took its fateful place in the great procession of time. The January snow whirled outside the window, and hissed down the great chimney on to the leaping flames, while John Adams, in communion with the eager spirit of his wife, wrote down:

As the happiness of the people is the sole end of government, so the consent of the people is the only foundation of it. . . .

It is a maxim that in every government there must exist somewhere a supreme, sovereign, absolute, and uncontrollable power; the body of the people; and it never was, or can be, delegated to one man or a few.[36]

In February, on his way back to Philadelphia, John Adams purchased and sent to Abigail a pamphlet entitled *Common Sense*, by a recent adventurer from England, Tom Paine. It was written in defence of doctrines which, as John Adams remarked, would soon be the common faith. Said Tom Paine: "The design and end of government is freedom and security. In the early ages mankind were equals in the order of creation. . . . Arms must decide the contest. The appeal was the choice of the king, and the continent hath accepted the challenge."

Since the pamphlet was anonymous, and the publication of John Adams's two letters intercepted by the enemy a few months before had made him willy-nilly the first open protagonist of independence in the public press, popular rumour flew over the continent that John Adams was the author of *Common Sense*. "I could not have written anything in so manly and striking a style," said John Adams, with his usual modesty, "but I flatter myself I should have made a more respectable figure as an architect, if I had undertaken such a work! This writer seems to have very inadequate ideas of what is necessary to be done in order to form constitutions for single colonies as well as a great model of union for the whole."[37]

Before returning to Philadelphia John Adams more than once visited the winter camp at Cambridge at Washington's request, to confer with the Commander-in-Chief and to attend councils of war. The question at issue was when and how to attack Boston. The Continental Congress was urgent for it. John Hancock wrote that he stood to lose as much as any man, but never mind about smashing up his property, he was perfectly willing to have Boston bombarded. What am I to bombard Boston with? was Washington's question to John Adams. Where was the artillery, the money, the army? The American Army had then less than ten thousand men; their cause was unformulated; their status uncertain; the support of Congress vague. But over their heads, above the snowy roofs of Harvard College, Abigail saw a new flag flying. On January 1, 1776, the flag had been hoisted for the first time, and its brilliant colour, its new, audacious message, caught the eye from every quarter.*

It was March 1776 and a Saturday night. "Hark! The house this instant shakes with the roar of cannon!" But this time it is "our" cannon—Washington was bombarding Boston. "It has been said to-morrow and to-morrow for this month"; but now the time has come, it is to-day, and General Washington, backed rather by New England than by Congress, short of men, money, and supplies, has felt that inaction itself is a form of dry rot, and has begun the attack.

One of the young farm-hands ran into the house for his gun. "Farewell, mistress! Orders are come for all the remaining militia to repair to the lines before Monday midnight! I must go to my mother's and get ready!"

"No sleep for me to-night!" said Abigail. "Here, take some meat—your mother will give you parched corn . . . and take this blanket for your use in camp. Don't thank me, friend! You are taking your life with you!" The man saw her hands tremble as she made up the bundle. But her eyes were bright in the candle-light. Again and again a heavy cannonade made the dishes on the dresser dance, and the windows rattled as if a huge soft fist had struck the house a heavy blow. But how different to her was the sound of this cannon from the ominous thunder of those others at the start of Bunker Hill! "My hand and heart will tremble," wrote Abigail, as she poured out her immediate feelings to her husband at the close of the Sabbath day, but it was with a deep excitement. "The cannon continued firing, and my heart beat pace with them all night."

On Monday afternoon she and her children and household watched the mustered militia march away to Boston, every man carrying three days' provisions and a blanket if he could get it. "And now we have scarcely a man but our regular guards in Weymouth, Hingham, Braintree or Milton. Can you form an idea of our sensations?"[38] She and her children climbed Penns Hill and sat listening to "the amazing roar" of the twenty-four-pounders, and

* Thirteen alternate red and white stripes in the field, with the cross of St George and St Andrew, red and white respectively, on a blue ground in the corner, was the flag designed and used by the East India Company in 1704; was probably flying at the mast of the tea ships; and was hoisted at Washington's camp at Cambridge in 1776. The number of the stripes at once suggested the number of the colonies, and the star flag was evolved from this base, the first one traditionally being arranged and sewn by Betsy Ross of Philadelphia.

watched the bursting shells in the April dusk. It was terrible! It was sublime! Back to lie down in bed, but not to sleep. The cannonade, no longer intermittent, was an incessant roar. "I could no more sleep than if I had been in the engagement. How many of our dear countrymen must fall." Her pity reaches also to "the unhappy wretches" on the other side.

She endured two nights, with little or no sleep, and on Tuesday the battle still raged. "I sometimes think I cannot stand it. I wish myself out of hearing as I cannot assist them!"

But when, after a mysterious quiet on Wednesday, the militia all came marching back on Thursday and reported that they had taken Dorchester Hill she was disappointed. Is that all? "I would not have suffered all I have for two such hills!" She wrote to her "dearest friend," passionately quoting Shakespeare. "There is a tide in the affairs of men which taken at the flood . . ." Even while she wrote the lines—Sunday evening, March 10—her ears were "again assaulted by the roar of cannon." Trembling with excitement, she hurried with Nabby and Johnny to their look-out post on the hill.

Another week of this strain, till finally, at Saturday dawn, what a sight there was to see! "Between seventy and eighty vessels of various sizes lie in a row in fair sight of this place." They lie low in the water. They are loaded to the gunwales. What can be the meaning of this? They have been plundering the town! Impossible that they could be evacuating it! She can't believe the rumours that she hears when she returns to the house. But "some very important crisis seems at hand." Next morning, Sunday, the news that seemed impossible is confirmed. The enemy are in full flight. Boston is free! "From Penns Hill we have a view of the largest fleet ever seen in America." You could count upwards of a hundred and seventy ships. Their bare masts looked like a forest.[39] "They have not yet come under sail. I cannot help suspecting some design which we do not yet comprehend. No one knows where they are off to, but the rumour is New York." As Abigail said, almost too astonished to give way to rejoicing, it was only lifting the burden from one shoulder to another perhaps less able to support it. Mewed up in Boston, the British had been kept out of mischief. Now they were escaping, to be dangerous elsewhere. Yet is it not a victory? "To what a contemptible situation are the troops of Britain reduced!" She gazed at the white full-sailed ships skimming away before the wind, and felt amazed that they should leave such a harbour, such entrenchments, such fortifications, and the largest city in the colonies, "and that we should be in peaceable possession of a town which we expected would cost a river of blood, without one drop shed! . . . Every foot of ground which they obtain now they must fight for, and may they purchase it at a Bunker Hill price!"[40] Eleven hundred loyalist Tories who had taken refuge in Boston, confident of the triumph of British arms, were struck with sudden ruin. Many of them had been rich people; overnight they became paupers. It was not hard to picture their bewilderment and despair, "crowded in vessels which will scarce contain them," dispatched to Halifax, the nearest British territory. "What will become of them there, God knows. The place is full already."*

It is a hard thing to be on the wrong side in any war, but worst of all to be on the wrong side in a revolution. John Adams wrote to his wife: "Mr Hutchinson, Mr Sewall, and their associates are in great disgrace in England. Persons are ashamed to be seen to speak to them. They look despised and sunk."[41]

Abigail was eager to get in to Boston to see how it looked, but the news that there was an outbreak of smallpox in the city prevented her. A friend, however, went to her house in Queen Street to see what state it was in. It had been occupied by one of the doctors of a regiment and was "very dirty, but no other damage had been done to it." Hancock's mansion too was safe, and the furniture unhurt. The town in general had been left in a better state than most people expected. The chief complaint was of "contempt thrown upon our places of worship" by using them as barracks and hospitals. There had been some vandalism in Boston, of which Sam Quincy's house and furniture was an outstanding example; and Abigail and her neighbours were shocked to see fragments of good furniture, thrown overboard from the ships, washed up on the shores at Weymouth and Braintree by the tide. But on the other hand, she was free to admit that some of the British officers had left behind rent money for the owners of houses they had occupied, and, actually, money to pay for any accidental damage. This was surprising evidence of "honour and justice."[42] And the haste of the evacuation and the shortage of ship space had caused immense stores to be left behind in the town which well might make up for a few

* Abigail heard and reported the details of their plight: "They are much distressed for want of houses at Halifax; provisions scarce and dear. Some of them with six or eight children around them, sitting upon the rocks, crying, not knowing where to lay their heads." *Familiar Letters*, p. 162.

repairs to meeting-houses: "Vast quantities of coal, which the inhabitants have been cruelly denied through the winter, cannon and warlike stores in abundance, horse fodder,"[43] and so on.

Washington made a triumphal entry into Boston on foot. The bells were rung, and prayers of thanksgiving offered. Harvard bestowed on General Washington an honorary degree of LL.D. And then the camp was struck, the army marched away from Cambridge to the southward "where they expect the seat of action to be," and Cambridge sobered itself to become again a scholastic town.

Boston descended from her heights of martyrdom, no longer the cynosure of American attention, and went back to business.

Abigail looked to the spring planting. An access of joy and energy flowed through her. "I feel very differently at the approach of spring from what I did a month ago," she wrote. "We knew not then whether we could plant or sow with safety, whether where we had tilled we could reap . . . or whether we should be driven from the sea-coast to seek shelter in the wilderness."

The refugees who had fled from shore and city were turning homeward like the birds.

What a weight had been lifted, how sweetened was the air! Just to move about freely again was a joy, talk to whom one pleased, go out to a party and come home at midnight or after, take a boat and go fishing without a permit—how the ordinary commonplaces of living sparkled as with a new dew. Every citizen, even the most stolid, experienced a little of the acute, sharp joy of convalescence or childhood, when nothing is commonplace, each thing is seen with clear eyes. But Abigail, in all her joy and energy, did not forget that there might be another "Boston" soon. The long task was not finished; it had not properly begun. She wanted an official beginning, a bugle note to all the world. "I long to hear that you have declared an independency!"

"Your description of your own *gaieté de cœur* charms me," replied her husband.

> Thanks be to God, you have just cause to rejoice. As to declarations of independency, be patient! Read our privateering laws [allowing privateers to prey upon British trade] and our commercial laws. What signifies a word? . . . Yet this is not independency, you know. What is? Why, government in every colony, a confederation among them all, and treaties with foreign nations to acknowledge us a sovereign state, and all that.[44]

So they wrote to each other in March and April 1776.

In the spring of 1776 a sudden acceleration took place. A tide rose, a dam broke, and all John Adams had so long desired and worked for was accomplished. The three months, May, June, and July 1776, were the grand climax of John Adams's life, no matter what greater public recognition the future had in store. And after them John Adams might well write to Abigail and to his friend and former pupil, William Tudor:

> I have had a pretty good trick at the helm. . . . Some of you younger folk [Tudor] must take your turn and let me go to sleep. When a few mighty matters are accomplished here I retreat like Cincinnatus to the plough and like Sir William Temple to his garden, and farewell politics![45]

Abigail heard this with pleasure but with scepticism.

The mighty matters were three interlocked steps which John Adams had continually urged as necessary to American success—that is, government in each colony, confederation of the colonial Governments, and treaties with foreign nations. A statement or declaration of the causes of the revolt of the colonies was also a recognized necessity, although to John Adams it appeared largely a matter of form.

Three committees were formed—one to encourage formation of individual state Governments, one for treaties, and one to draw up a declaration. John Adams was on the latter two of these.

"When I look back to the year 1761," he wrote to Abigail,

> and recollect the argument concerning writs of assistance in the superior court which I have hitherto considered as the commencement of this controversy between Great Britain and America and run through the whole period from that time to this, and recollect the series of political events, the chain of causes and effects, I am surprised at the suddenness as well as greatness of this revolution.[46]

Abigail, reading this letter in Boston, was deeply aware of the ripe mellowness of his mood. The man who wrote was leagues ahead of the man who had been exasperated with Dickinson and his colleagues for their "silly" temporizing, their "piddling" behaviour. In the hour of success John Adams's imperiousness was softened, his impatience disciplined. In a religious mood he saw a wisdom greater than man's in the delay, once so intolerable. It had cost dear. If the Declaration of Independence had been made sooner, even seven months ago, "we might before this have formed alliances with foreign states, have mastered Quebec and been in possession of Canada. On the other hand time has been given for the whole people maturely to consider the great question of independence, and to ripen their judgment, dissipate their fears . . . by discussing it in newspapers and pamphlets, by debating it in assemblies, conventions, committees of safety and inspection, town and country meetings, as well as in private conversations, so that the whole people, in every colony of the thirteen, have now adopted it as their own act. This will cement the union, and avoid those heats and convulsions which might have been occasioned by such a Declaration six months ago. . . . I am well aware of the toil and blood and treasure that it will cost us to maintain this Declaration and support and defend these States. Yet through all the gloom I can see the rays of ravishing light and glory.

"I must submit all my hopes and fears to an overruling Providence, in which, unfashionable as the faith may be, I firmly believe."[47]

Abigail Adams had gone to Boston on Saturday, July 12, with all her children, to be inoculated for the smallpox. The inoculation was performed immediately on their arrival, but they were not considered infectious until some results appeared.* So Abigail was still at large on Thursday, July 18, when the printed Declaration arrived in Boston. "After hearing a very good sermon," she wrote her husband,

> I went with the multitude into King Street to hear the Proclamation for Independence read and proclaimed from the balcony of the State House. The troops appeared under arms . . . bells rang, privateers in the harbour fired—forts—batteries—cannon. . . . The King's Arms were taken down from the State House and every vestige of him burnt in King Street. . . .[48]

It was a thrilling occasion. But even more impressive was the Sunday service a month later. "Last Sunday, after service, the Declaration of Independence was read from the pulpit by order of Council. Dr Chauncy's address pleased me. The good man, after having read it, lifted his eyes and hands to heaven. 'God bless the United States of America, and let all the people say Amen.'"[49]

* All got on well but Charles, who after three inoculations "has to be sure taken the distemper in the natural way. Indeed this smallpox is no triffel [*i.e., trifle*]." A. A., August 20, 1776 (Thaxter MS.). Charles was very ill indeed.

The work on the treaties was not in the limelight, but it was no less vital. As John Adams had urged, the committee had been empowered by Congress to draw up a model for a treaty with France. But in this model treaty he saw clearly that the whole principle of the new United States' relationship with other countries, its commitments and responsibilities, would be laid down. And he knew in his own mind, and had publicly expressed, what that relationship should be. "We ought not," he had said in Congress in September '75, "to enter into any alliance which should entangle us in any future wars in Europe. We ought to lay it down as a first principle and a maxim never to be forgotten, to maintain an entire neutrality in all future European wars. Therefore, in preparing treaties to be proposed to foreign powers, and in the instructions to be given to our ministers, we ought to confine ourselves strictly to a treaty of commerce. Such a treaty would be an ample compensation to France for all the aid we should want from her." The speech had created a great effect.

When the treaty* came before Congress it occasioned great surprise, because it did not offer complete alliance.

Most members expected, and were ready for, a complete merging of interests with France. Because France was at the moment the enemy of Britain she was erroneously regarded as the friend of liberty. John Adams stuck to the facts. Not for America's sake but for her own, France must jump at the chance to help the American colonies to split off from the British Empire. But if America should go into common cause with France to subjugate Britain, or be involved by France's policy in any future war: "We should be little better than puppets, danced on the wires of the cabinets of Europe, the sport of European intrigues and politics." His arguments prevailed, "the treaty passed without one particle of alliance, exclusive privilege or warranty,"[50] and Adams saw the foreign policy of the new sovereign power shaped by his hand.

Well might Abigail, sharing intensely in the struggle from afar, write to her husband of her pride and joy that "a person so nearly connected with me has had the honour of being a principal actor in laying a foundation for our country's future greatness."[51]

His letters were her meat and drink. From her Uncle Isaac's house in Boston, where she was convalescing from smallpox, she wrote:

I have spent the three days past almost entirely with you. The

* Drafted by John Adams.

> weather has been stormy. I have had little company and I have amused myself in my closet, reading over the letters I have received from you since I have been here.
>
> I have possession of my aunt's chamber, in which, you know, is a very convenient, pretty closet, with a window which looks into her flower garden, and bookshelves . . . and a pretty little desk, where I write all my letters and keep my papers, unmolested by any one. I don't covet my neighbour's goods, but I should like to be the owner of such conveniences! I always had a fancy for a closet with a window which I could more particularly call my own.[52]

But in case the expression of this modest wish should seem like a complaint, she hastened to assure her husband that their poverty does not rouse in her any discontent. She has a suit of homespun ready for him when he comes back, she has been busy making clothes for the children. Colonel Warren has borne witness to her husband that the farm is flourishing under her care. They have all they need, she does not hanker for riches or great position or a fashionable life like Cousin Dorothy Hancock's. If John could be at home with her, she would ask no more. No ambition of hers need ever distract him from the fascinating, exacting, unrewarding leadership which he has achieved in the poorly paid public affairs of a new and poor country. No, no. Let him indeed even give up the Massachusetts Chief Judgeship which brings in regular income, but which will involve giving up more important tasks in the large world! "All my desire and all my ambition," she earnestly assures him, "is to be esteemed and loved by my partner, to join with him in the education and instruction of our little ones, to sit under our own vines in peace, liberty and safety."

The main tide of war had now swept away from Boston, but the seafaring men of Boston, Braintree, Weymouth, Hingham, Salem, and Marblehead were all taking to privateering, an exciting and rewarding sport. There would soon be no men left, Abigail said, half-laughing. Women would have to work the farms as well as direct them. "I am willing to do my part!" she told her husband. "I believe I could gather corn and husk it! But I should make a poor figure at digging potatoes!"[53]

On June 14, 1777, the Stars and Stripes was adopted as the flag of the American Army—thirteen red and white stripes to mark the thirteen independent states, thirteen stars in the corner on a blue ground to mark "the new constellation" of the Union. The Union Jack was a foreign flag now, for ever. But among the Americans who now joyfully celebrated the first anniversary of their freedom there were some who were not free. There were still Negro slaves. Samuel Johnson, paid publicity agent of the British Government, had sourly commented in London that "the loudest yelps for liberty came from the slave-drivers of the south." And Abigail told her husband: "I have sometimes been ready to think that the passion for liberty cannot be equally strong in the breasts of those who have been accustomed to deprive their fellow-creatures of theirs."[54]

There were other thousands of American patriots who had ungranted rights to claim—the very rights which the Declaration held to be "unalienable." Well in advance, before any declarations had been irrevocably crystallized, Abigail Adams had clearly and audaciously pointed out this neglected multitude, of whom she was one, and had broken a lance for their liberty. "By the way," she wrote to her husband in March 1776,

> in the new code of laws which I suppose it will be necessary for you to make, I desire you would remember the ladies and be more generous and favourable to them than your ancestors! Do not put such unlimited power into the hands of the husbands. Remember all men would be tyrants if they could. If particular care and attention is not paid to the ladies, we are determined to foment a rebellion, and will not hold ourselves bound by any laws in which we have no voice or representation.
>
> That your sex are naturally tyrannical is a truth so thoroughly established as to admit of no dispute, but such of you as wish to be happy give up the harsh title of master for the more tender and endearing one of friend. Why then not put it out of the power of the vicious and the lawless to use us with cruelty and indignity with impunity?

But her masculine husband, clear-minded and generous though he was, found this simply funny. What next?

> As to your extraordinary code of laws, I cannot but laugh! We have been told that our struggle has loosened the bonds of government everywhere—children and apprentices . . . schools and colleges . . . Indians, Negroes grow insolent. But your letter was the first intimation that another tribe, more numerous and powerful than all the rest, were grown discontented. This is rather too coarse a compliment, but you are so saucy I won't blot it out! Depend upon it, we know better than to repeal our masculine systems. Although they are in full

force, you know they are little more than theory. We dare not exert our power in its full latitude. We are obliged to go fair and softly, and in practice you know we are the subjects. We have only the name of masters, and rather than give up this, which would completely subject us to the despotism of the petticoat, I hope General Washington and all our brave heroes would fight! . . . A fine story indeed! I begin to think the ministry as deep as they are wicked. After stirring up Tories . . . bigots . . . Canadians, Indians, Negroes, Hanoverians, Hessians, Russians . . . at last they have stimulated the women to demand new privileges and threaten to rebel!

Abigail did not quarrel about it. He was thoroughly wrong-headed, but perhaps she expected what she got. She replied gaily and charmingly—concealing the iron hand of good sense in the velvet glove of her soft manners:

> I cannot say that I think you are very generous to the ladies; for whilst you are . . . emancipating all nations, you insist upon retaining an absolute power over your wives. But . . . we have it in our power not only to free ourselves but to subdue our masters, and without violence throw both your natural and legal authority at our feet—
>
> Charm by accepting, by submitting sway,
> Yet have our humour most when we obey.

Such questions after all were purely academic to Mrs John Adams. Except when challenged on the equality of the sexes, John Adams never failed to honour his wife as his equal.

One day she added a postscript: "I wish you would burn my letters!" He was deeply stirred. "Is there no way for two friendly souls to converse together although the bodies are four hundred miles off? Yes, by letter. But I want a better communication. I want to hear you think or see your thoughts. The conclusion of your letter makes my heart throb more than a cannonade would. You bid me burn your letters! But I must forget you first![55]

"In one or two of your letters you remind me to think of you as I ought. Be assured there is not an hour of the day in which I don't think of you as I ought, that is, with tenderness, esteem, and admiration."[56]

VII

John Adams returns Home "for Good"

ABIGAIL WAS LEADING TWO LIVES. All day she was active directing house and farm, but: "It is true I never close my eyes at night till I have been to Philadelphia, and my first visit in the morning is there."[1]

Through John's eyes she watched history in the making. He had resigned the post of Chief Justice of Massachusetts—now that the courts were functioning another could do it as well—and had become President of the Board of War. He was, in fact, what might be called War Minister, and his responsibilities and labour were the greater because the government was immature and he and his board had all to make. Thomas Jefferson was his favourite fellow-member on that board. "Jefferson in those days," he said later, "never failed to agree with me in everything of a political nature."[2] And though John Adams did not bother his wife with dry or technical details, he cleared his mind by discussing with her the basic principles.

"We have at last agreed upon a plan for forming a regular army," wrote the President of the Board to his wife. "We have offered twenty dollars and a hundred acres of land to every man who will enlist during the war" (that is, for the duration).[3] It was not a waste of his time to discuss such matters with her. Even Mr Lovell sent Mrs Adams "a map to show the present theatre of war." So she felt drawn close to her husband, still his full comrade and partner. "Is there," she said, "a dearer name than friend? If there is, teach it to me."[4]

Philadelphia was now in danger from the armies of General Howe marching up from the south, whither they had gone by water from Boston. Adams's confidence in Washington, however, was complete. "Howe will make but a pitiful figure." And as to the possibility of Howe's taking Philadelphia, he tells Abigail cheerfully: "I almost wish he had Philadelphia, for then he could not get away. I really think it would be the best policy to retreat before him and let him into this snare, where his army must be ruined."[5]

Washington, after losing the Battle of the Brandywine on September 11, 1777, pursued this very strategy. He abandoned Philadelphia to the British, thereby saving the military stores at Reading. Congress hastily left the city before the enemy's advance and reassembled finally at York, Pennsylvania. Howe complacently encamped at Germantown,* and prepared to make Philadelphia his winter quarters.

It was a low moment for the American cause. Friends all round Abigail thought the occupation of Philadelphia was a major defeat, the beginning of the end. Tories lifted up their heads. There were several to tell Mrs Adams that she would never see her husband again. All communication would be cut off, he never would be able to return! Many prisoners, she knew, had already been shipped to England. If John Adams was taken he would certainly suffer a like fate, and once in England his execution for high treason was certain. "It is a plan your enemies would rejoice to see," she wrote him guardedly, "and will effect if it lies in their power." But she refused them the satisfaction of frightening her. Her bright eyes would meet theirs disconcertingly, her colour did not change. "I am not apt to be intimidated, you know. I have given as little heed to bugbear reports as possible. I have slept as soundly since my return† not withstanding all the ghosts and hobgoblins as ever I did in my life." Nor was she the only one to ride high the tides of rumour. Mary Cranch and the Quincy and Palmer women, and Mrs Peter Adams, prim but loyal, and many another neighbour responded to her cheering leadership.

"We are in no wise dispirited here," she wrote. "If our men are all drawn off and we should be attacked, you would find a race of Amazons in America." And when Mr Wibird came, "in the horrors," moaning that General Howe's taking of Philadelphia "would immediately negotiate a peace," she could not help replying warmly that, "I did not believe it, and that if General Washington and his whole army should be cut off I hoped that an army of women would oppose him."

* The Philadelphia suburb. † From a visit to the Warrens at Plymouth.

But when provocative visitors had gone her mind contemplated clearly the reality of battle, and her heart recoiled. "Why is man called *humane* when he delights so much in blood and slaughter and devastation? Even civilized nations!"[6] . . . But nothing short of victory or defeat could now stop the war. And good news was drifting down from the northward that even as Washington and his Virginians were being beaten on the Brandywine the New England troops under Gates and Herkimer were giving a dose of the same medicine to General Burgoyne.

The news of the final, complete capitulation of Burgoyne reached Boston before it reached York, and Abigail, on October 22, wrote joyfully: "I believe I may venture to congratulate my love upon the completion of his wishes with regard to Burgoyne! Tis reported to-day from many ways that he has with his whole army fallen into our hands." And three days later, on her wedding anniversary, she drove into Boston with daughter Nabby, "to join to-morrow with my friends" in the services of thanksgiving for the victory. "The vapouring Burgoyne" and the rest of the prisoners were expected to be brought into Boston later in the week.

On November 11, believing that his trick at the helm was done, John Adams shrugged public burdens from his shoulders and became again, in his mind, a private citizen. "A slavery it has been to me," he wrote Abigail, "whatever the world may think." He would not have his wife send a servant or horse. "The expense is so enormous that I cannot bear the thought of it. I will crawl home upon my little pony and wait upon myself as well as I can." He even added, as he weighed his empty purse, "I think you'd better sell my horse." But as he mounted at last, and turned his way to the north, he was in chuckling good spirits. The bright autumn weather was the best riding weather in the world. Cousin Sam, riding with him, was an excellent companion. And when, after ten or eleven days of travel, he arrived home to an exhilarating welcome at Braintree he was in a contented mood.

Abigail, clinging to him that evening, said, "Ah, Jack—Jack—I have you home safe at last! But are you home to stay?" and he answered her with hearty reassurance.

"Indeed I am! From this moment I become a private gentleman, the respectful husband of Mrs A. of B. and the affectionate father of her children—two characters which I've scarcely supported for these three years past, having done the duties of neither!"[7]

"You talk about three years?" said Abigail, half laughing but equally near tears. "It may be true the last three have been the worst. But look you, sir, we have been married now thirteen years, and scarcely half of that time—if you add everything up—have we spent together. And the children—they are missing you at just that impressionable time when they need their father most!"[8]

It was, in fact, delightful to see the children making friends again with their father. Nabby and Jack, twelve and ten, and responsible for their years; Charlie, irrepressibly jolly; and five-year-old Tommy, bound and determined to keep his end up, and assert his equality with Charlie. They were all handsome. They were all gifted.

John had frequently complained, "If I live much longer in banishment I shall scarcely know my own children.[9] I've often wanted to send each of my little pretty flock some present or other. . . . I've walked over the city twenty times and gaped at every shop like a countryman to find something, but could not. I wish, my dears, you would have written me what you wanted!"[10]

But he had brought gifts for them all. Now how rapidly he broke down barriers, established contact; with what respect he listened to their remarks! It was always better than Abigail had dreamed. The house hummed with his presence.

Abigail heard her husband assuring all his relatives, friends, and clients that he was home to stay. They must elect a new representative to Congress in his place. Mr Adams must now attend to his wife and family, and—faith—his own income! Yes, he was open for law business! Cases poured in. An immense and lucrative practice was open to him.

"My heart is as light as a feather!" said Abigail, "and my spirits are dancing! We are starting a new life!"

"Ay, this is what I mean by domestic felicity!" said John. He drew her to the window, beside Dick Cranch, and looked out over the lion-coloured winter fields. "I've had to leave this rural kind of life for too long, and reconcile myself to the smoke and noise of a city![11] To give up my private peace for the vexation of worming out the deep intrigues of politicians! . . . I've panted for domestic life and the duties of the farm, like yours, brother Cranch![12] And now we shall all four be together again, as in the old days—you and your Polly, and my bright-eyed mistress Nabby and me!"

Abigail's heart was almost more full of happiness than she could bear. How much more had *she* wanted to lay down her heavy burdens, to relinquish responsibility, to rest in the guidance and protection which she had always found in her husband, and in his warm, enveloping love. Instead of "solitary hours spent ruminating upon the past and anticipating the future," she could now share her hopes and fears with him.

Bar the door now against the world. Out with the candle. War may still rage, but we have "our private peace."

Abigail had three weeks of entire content. Then young Johnny, now weekly mail-carrier between Boston and Braintree, rode home carrying a large packet from Congress, with portentous seals. Abigail's heart leapt into her mouth when she saw it.

A day and a night its presence threatened her while she waited for John to return from handling a lawsuit at Portsmouth, New Hampshire. He came home suddenly, forewarned by a returned Congress member, and lost not an instant in breaking the seals and sharing the contents with her.

"Ay—here it is! Mr Deane is recalled from Paris. . . . I am appointed in his place. . . . Here, see, are new commissions to Franklin, Arthur Lee, and myself, as plenipotentiaries from the United States to the King of France . . . !"

They sat down together on the settle. Indeed her legs would no longer support her. Her trembling hand could hardly hold the letter he handed her. There was a roaring in her ears.

"The question is," said his strong voice from a great distance, "shall I accept the commission or return it to Congress?"[13]

One of the letters, that from her friend Elbridge Gerry, contained a direct appeal to her. "I hope to have the concurrence of your lady when I urge the necessity of your accepting your appointment. It is the earnest wish of Congress and every friend to America. . . . Chagrin and disappointment will result from a refusal."[14]

So '77 passed into '78 in a haze of preparations, farewells, visits, delays, and Abigail, numbed by activity in the daytime, tried to conceal from her husband the sleeplessness which threatened her nights.

On February 14, 1778, the wind blew sharp around a lonely figure on Penns Hill. The American frigate *Boston* lay at anchor out in the sea-lane. At about noon a rowing-boat could be seen to put out from Uncle Norton's beach and to make its tedious, rocking way, up and down on the waves, towards the ship. Well Mrs Adams knew that, wrapped in heavy watch coats with their feet buried in straw in the boat bottom, her husband and son were the cause and burden of the boat's labour. One week before that day the American treaty with France had actually been signed in Paris. But as far as America was concerned that event was still concealed in the womb of the future, and John Adams's fate was leading him blindly forward, ostensibly to accomplish something that was already done. The dark spot of the boat was hard to see in the surf, and was soon out of sight; useless to stand and stare. Abigail, shivering, drew her cloak tighter and went down to the warm house.

Uncle Norton Quincy came in later to bring her all the details of the departure, and her husband's last note. "Johnny behaves like a man!" Over the teacups by the fire Norton described how Captain Tucker and a young midshipman, not so much older than Johnny, had arrived promptly from the beach, and a pleasant noon lunch they had had together as planned, before all walked down to the water's edge. There the sailors launched the ship's barge, and carried their passengers pick-a-back to it through the surf. Johnny waved gallantly to the last, his round young cheeks wet with spray. "Give my love to Mamma——" came back in the wind. Yes, she had judged herself aright. She could not have borne it had she been there on the shore, she could not have borne to see them go.

Next day Abigail, searching for distraction, snatched her quill and wrote to her young cousin John Thaxter, now in York:

Dear Sir—My hands and my heart have both been full, my whole time has been taken up in prepareing my dearest Friend, and Master John, for their voyage, and yesterday they embarked. . . .

And now cannot you immagine me seated by my fireside bereft of my better Half and added to that a Limb lopt off to heighten the anguish . . . in vain have I summoned philosophy, come then religion. . . .

The world may talk of honour, but sure I am no consideration weigh'd with me but the belief that the abilities and good integrity of your Friend might be more extensively usefull to his country in this department at this particular time than in any other. . . .

My desire was you know to have run all hazards and accompanied him, but I could not prevail upon him to consent—the danger from Enemies was so great . . . in case of capture my sufferings would enhance his misery . . . these arguments prevailed upon me to give up the favourite wish of my heart. Master John was very happy in his pappa's consent to accompany him, but young as he is a mother's heart will feel a thousand fears and anxieties. . . .[15]

The decision to send Johnny had arisen out of a variety of considerations, in which the immediate problems of the boy's education, the responsibility of his extraordinary promise, and the need of establishing his father's influence in his life, all played their part. Against his youth were set the advantages of foreign travel, the example of Benjamin Franklin's little grandson, Benjamin Franklin Bache, already over in France, and the value and safeguard of his father's company. So the son went with the father.

The mother's heart, however, hardly woke up to its full burden, fears, and anxieties until Johnny was well away. The wife's feelings eclipsed the mother's. "Tender as maternal affection is, it was swallowed up in what I found a stronger."[16] "Whence shall I gather firmness of mind, bereft of the prop upon which it used to rest?"[17] she wrote her husband. The long, free-written letters which were her only relief were stored in ships which idled weeks in dock, sailed at last without warning—missing perhaps some last important packet by an hour—and, driven by contrary winds, chased by privateers, as like as not finally gave up all their papers to the grim safekeeping of the sea. Her husband, on his side, wrote her frequent letters, but sodden and unread, one after the other, they drifted in the ocean with the seaweed as if he had but thrown them, like waste paper, overboard. For six months Abigail did not receive a line. Husband and son might have dropped over the edge of the world when they set off on that winter sea.

Meanwhile Abigail heard rumours that Franklin had been assassinated, that the *Boston* had been taken by British men-o'-war, that her husband was in the Tower, and if in the Tower most certainly condemned to death. These were not the kind of idle tales which could be flung off swiftly by the stout of heart. British frigates had been cruising on the coast for weeks watching for the *Boston*, and twice, early on in her voyage, she was sighted and chased and fought off her pursuers.

With official news of their landing in France her sensations of relief were only temporary. "I promised myself a negative kind of happiness whenever I cd hear of your safe arrival, but alas," said Abigail, "I find myself some days more unhappy than I would ever wish an enemy to be, in vain do I strive to divert my attention, my heart, like a poor bird hunted from her nest, is still returning to the place of its affections."[18] And to John Thaxter she wrote: "No news from the far country—no letters, no vessels—heigh ho ten times in an hour."[19] Her usual active life went forward, but not her heart. The summer set in hot and enervating, "the hottest summer I ever remember," and she was all the lonelier because she had put Nabby in school in Boston, where she boarded as her mother had done before her as guest of Uncle Isaac and Aunt Elizabeth.

In late August and early September war came their way again:

> Poor Boston is again distressed. . . . Howe's fleet is hovering about this coast 20 sail of them and I own my spirits not a little agitated. As I sit writing to you [John Thaxter], I hear the alarm guns fired. . . . More guns—I believe I shall not sleep very soundly to-night. You inquire after my dearest Friend. O sir, I know not how to curb my impatience . . . only twice have I heard . . . dated in April. I wish a thousand times I had gone with him.[20]

But Abigail knew she must not give way to this brooding misery. She taught Charlie—who was almost beyond her now, but no good school was handy—and she taught Tommy his hornbook, she directed house and farm, she pursued her usual social activities, she read, and with her account books of an evening she concentrated on how to circumvent the rising inflation. "A Regulating Bill is still kept off . . ." she wrote to John Thaxter, "how does it go down with you? There is no reformation with regard to prices here, though money grows scarcer.[21] A hundred pounds lawful money is reduced to thirteen pounds six and eightpence."[22] The price of labour was steeply rising, "the most indifferent farmer is not to be procured under 10 or 12 pounds per month." She curtailed her simple style of living still further—only two maids now, and two industrious young fellows whom she engaged to work the farm on shares. "You know my situation and that a ridged economy is necessary for me if I am to preserve independancy. . . . I mean that I might always have it in my power to answer the first demand of a creditor, a dun was always my abhorrence."

But how deadly dull was this economy, this paring of pence. Was this the way for an Ambassador's wife to live? "My frugality will be termed meanness." But "to those who reflect upon me for not living any ways answerable to the character my partner sustains in publick life, I would make the same reply which one of Queen Elizabeth's ministers did to her, when upon visiting him she took notice of the meanness of his habitation, 'the house may it please your majesty is big enough for the man, but you have made the man too big for the house.'"[23]

One sunny September morning a couple of chaises drove up, and out stepped eight or nine French officers of the new-arrived fleet, come to fight in the American cause. Mrs Adams's composure was unshaken—except, indeed, by delight. Tangible result of the new treaty, the French fleet had just come to Boston, after various minor encounters with the British in American waters, and the well-bred French officers hastened to pay their respects to the wife of the gentleman who was an American Envoy to France. Her little room was filled with them, their glittering uniforms, their fast, fluent speech, their Gallic grace. Some of them had already met her husband in Paris. The strain on Abigail's French was not severe. Monsieur Rivière, the leader of the party, spoke English well. And when the others politely withdrew Monsieur Rivière accepted an invitation to dine and spend the day.

If these gentlemen, many of them of noble blood and born in great houses, were surprised at the setting from which an Ambassador to the Court of France had gone out, their perfect manners gave no sign. And in Mrs Adams they found the ease of an equal. She spoke gracefully and with unmistakable sincerity of sharing her husband's joy "in finding the great interest of our country so generously espoused and nobly aided by so powerful a monarch." They discovered she had read Molière, and could discuss his plays in a lively way.[24]

"The gentlemen officers have made me several visits," Abigail wrote, "and I have dined twice on board . . . sumptuously entertained with every delicacy that this country produces," and a lot of foreign ones. The Count d'Estaing invited her and her family to a party on board the fleet with any friends she chose to bring, and sent his barge to fetch her. It was a gay feast, with music and dancing on deck for the young folk. Abigail immensely enjoyed all this attention, took most warmly to the French, and wished she had it in her power "to entertain every officer in the fleet."[25]

But none of this could really restore her morale. Six months without any word from John, and then two or three letters which rasped on her taut nerves as dry and cold, had filled her with a bitterness of repressed reproach. Neither she nor John were accustomed to repress themselves for long. In the reaction from the excitement of Count d'Estaing's party, she seized her pen and let down the sluices on her anxiety, her misery, and her sense of neglect. Had her husband, her lover and friend, "changed hearts with some frozen Laplander, or gone to a region which had chilled every drop of his blood? If he could not take the trouble to notice and acknowledge her letters with his own hand, perhaps he would direct his secretary . . ."

She dared not finish the sarcasm.

> My heart denies the justice of the accusation . . . but my soul is wounded at a separation from you and my fortitude is all dissolved in weakness when I cast my thoughts across the Atlantick and view the distance, the dangers and hazards which you have already past through . . . the time of your absence unlimited, all, all conspire to cast a gloom over my solitary hours. In vain do I strive to throw off in the company of my friends some of the anxiety of my heart. [. . . And that heart, she added] so wounded by the idea of inattention that the very name of my dearest Friend would draw tears from me.[26]

Then a fresh batch of letters from John Adams arrived, crossing hers, saying that he had not received a line from her up to June 6, nor heard a word about her, directly or indirectly, since his departure; but by no means reproaching her about it. Going on cheerfully to tell her how delightful France was—"It is one great garden." And the manners of the French had such politeness, elegance, and charm. "In short, stern and haughty republican as I am, I cannot help loving these people for their earnest desire and assiduity to please." Religion and government needed improvement, but that did not worry him. "I have well fixed it in my mind as a principle that every nation has a right to that religion and government which it chooses." The French seemed content with theirs. He was greatly struck by the popularity of the young King and Queen,* and Johnny was writing her about the marvellous—and, truth to tell, extravagant—illuminations in Paris on the occasion of the birth of their first child, the little Princess Royal. "The nation is very happy," said John Adams, "to have discovered a way by which a dauphin may come to them next year or the year after."[27]

This direct contact with her husband's own spirit was the only antidote to Abigail's poison, and of a sudden she was healed. "Your letters of April 12th, June 3rd, and 16th, calmed my soul to peace," she hastened to write. "I cannot describe the effect they had upon

* Louis XVI and Marie Antoinette.

me. Cheerfulness and tranquillity took place of grief and anxiety. I placed them next my heart and soothed myself to rest with the tender assurances of a heart all my own."[28]

But again a long silence sapped the letters of their power, the antidote wore off, the poison again worked in blood and nerves. Although John Thaxter rejoined her household as tutor, in return for his board and the use of the office (a little private law practice), he was not much company. Too quiet and too busy. The dismal and lonely winter shut Abigail up from her father, her sisters, her friends. And she gave way wholeheartedly to depression. "How lonely are my days, how solitary my nights." There was no one in the house with her at Christmas-time but Charlie and Tommy and the two domestics. Even Nabby, now her mother's best companion, is away visiting the Warrens. "By the mountains of snow which surround me I could almost fancy myself in Greenland." It is bitter cold, the wind is blowing a hurricane, the roads are impassable. And Charlie, who has developed one of those poignantly sweet treble boy voices that make a boy's choir so like the imagined songs of angels—unearthly, ethereal—had learned to sing a Scotch song which went:

His very foot has music in't
As he comes up the stairs.

"How often," she wrote, "has my heart danced to the sound of that music."[29]

Yes, Charlie was certainly the one to see his mother's tears.

Perhaps afterwards she wished that those letters about the Laplander and so on had been among the many sunk; but no, by the usual perversity of circumstance, those were the very ones that got through. And her husband, cut to the quick, turned on her his thunder.

"The joy which the receipt of these packets afforded me," he wrote from Passy,

> was damped by the symptoms of grief and complaint which appeared in the letters. For Heaven's sake, my dear, don't indulge a thought that it is possible for me to neglect or forget all that is dear to me in this world! If I were to tell you all the tenderness of my heart, I should do nothing but write to you. It is impossible for me to write as I did in America! It is not safe to write anything that one is not willing should go into all the newspapers of the world. . . . I have written to you not much less than fifty letters. I am astonished that

you have received no more. But almost every vessel has been taken. . . . It would be an easy thing for me to ruin you and your children by an indiscreet letter, and what is more it would be easy to throw our country into convulsions. For God's sake never reproach me again with not writing or with writing scrips. Your wounds are too deep. . . . Millions would not tempt me to write you as I used. There are spies upon every word I utter and every syllable I write. Be upon your guard. I must be upon mine, and I will.[30]

Abigail was shaken to her feet, and her tears were roughly dried for good and all. Between the lines, in half-writ, guarded sentences, she felt that her husband was grappling with large affairs and with hidden dangers of a different kind from those she had been troubled by. He was careful, too, not to send a letter that was all reproach. He knew the note to strike to bring back sunshine to her downcast face. "Your son," he wrote,

is the joy of my heart, without abating in the least degree my affection for the young rogue* that did not seem as if he had a father, or for his brother and sister. Tell Abby her papa likes her the better for what she tells her brother—viz. "that she don't talk much,"—because I know she thinks and feels the more.[31]

Abby was indeed feeling too much for her years, stifling back into her reserved little heart a terrible grief, a quite devastating loneliness. The separation from her favourite brother and close companion was a sort of death. To suffer so much, and to control her suffering, matured her early. And Johnny, out in the world with no mother or substitute mother near, at a strict school at Passy, where he was taken out to dine by his father only at week-ends, continued to keep a stiff upper-lip and behave like a man. Both these elder children had somehow imbibed with their Latin lessons —was it from their tutor John Thaxter?—some of the Stoic philosophy, and both exemplified it to the end of their days.

Their mother was not of that school. But even at her most depressed moments Abigail was not entirely unworthy of her dignified children and her robust husband! Just after a bitter outburst she would remark that she had decided to avoid instilling into her children a narrow nationalism (this was after the French visits when the charm of other nations was to the fore). One should look for merit wherever it was to be found. But, oh, this America, this New England. She looked out at the dazzling whiteness of the

* Charles.

drifts, which hard frost had now made not a barrier but a bridge. The music of sleigh bells rang out cheerfully in the snapping air. "The sublimist winter I ever saw! The Bay has froze so hard that people have walked, rode, and sledded over it to Boston. . . . Difficult as the day is," exulted Abigail—"cruel as the war has been—separated as I am—I would not be any other than an American!"[32]

So she took up the daily burden—dull as her part of it often seemed—the wearisome struggle to make ends meet. If her husband had been left at home to pursue his law business, instead of being elevated to an expensive, precarious, ill-paid, and thankless public office, she "need not have had a care of this kind."[33] Yet farewell repining, carping, and complaint.

"It is true, says one," she wrote to John Thaxter,

> that mankind in general are a worthless and ungrateful set of beings for a man to wear out himself in serving, but if we do not lay out ourselves in the service of mankind whom should we serve? Our own insignificant selves? That would be sordid, indeed.
>
> Thus I hush all my murmurings by considering we are all embarked upon the same bottom and if our country sinks we must sink with it.[34]

Abigail was alone this time for eighteen months. On August 2, 1779 the French frigate *Sensible* put in to Boston harbour, and John Adams and his young son Johnny Q. disembarked. Abigail's precarious happiness was all the greater because her friends in Congress, especially Mr Gerry and Mr Lovell, who kept her informed, had told her there was every likelihood of her husband's being sent straight from Paris to Holland.

John Adams had come back of his own accord, in the absence of directions from Congress to do anything else. When letters had arrived confirming Franklin as Ambassador to Versailles, appointing Arthur Lee to Madrid, but containing no advices for John Adams, nor even mentioning him, he had said, with outward cheerfulness, that he was now no more than a private citizen, and as a private citizen he had but one duty—to go home as soon as possible to his family. So here he was; and however they felt in Philadelphia about his return, here at Boston and Braintree it was unmixed joy.

John Adams was not sorry he had come back; nor was he sorry, as he told Abigail, that he had been to France. He understood now many things that he could not have understood had he not gone.

"I found plenty to do!" he said, "as I will tell you later! What do you think of Johnny? Has he not grown? Our company on board the *Sensible* was the new French Ambassador to the United States, the Chevalier de la Luzerne, and Monsieur Marbois, the Secretary. They were in raptures with our son! They used Johnny to teach them English! He gave them lessons every day. Ay, he was strict with them, too! They said he made them no compliments, he had '*point de grâce, point d'éloges.*' *I* would not do! They must have Master John! Luzerne was greatly struck with Johnny's precocity. 'He is master of his own language like a professor!' he said.[35] And of course Johnny speaks French now, not in my clumsy manner, but like a Frenchman!"

"And can you speak it?" cried Abigail.

"Well enough to make shift to conduct a conversation on any subject!" said John Adams. "Not well, but adequately. I can read it, write it, listen to and understand it, and make myself understood. Dr Franklin can do no more. Franklin's recommendations for learning to speak French quickly were to take a mistress or to go to the play! He took the first method, I the second. But on the boat going over I had a phonetic Grammar, and I was constantly associating in France with friendly people who knew no English. Coming back I read French history on the voyage, as easily, almost, as my native tongue.[36] But to learn a foreign language in youth, to learn it idiomatically, is a great advantage, and that's one thing we can give to our children!"

So thoughtful parents plan, and no doubt it was an advantage for John Quincy Adams to learn French perfectly and to become early polished in cosmopolitan manners. Yet the greatest advantages his parents gave him were unconscious ones, first their own selves; second, lack of wealth; and, third, a sister. Charles Lamb once said of his sister that he didn't know what kind of wife such a reading woman would make, but she certainly was an incomparable old maid; so John Quincy might have said that he didn't know what kind of wife fate had in store for him but he surely had had a nonpareil of a sister.

The two eagerly resumed their old comradeship and the roses came back to Abby's cheeks and the sparkle to her eyes. Those months were one of the happy seasons of her life, and happiness was to be with her rather a rare plant, seldom in full bloom.

Her mother's more ardent temperament needed happiness

for daily bread. And every hour now she tasted its good substance.

John Adams supplemented his abundant talk with his journal, where, when he had gone to Philadelphia to make his report, or when he sat writing in his office, she could go backward in time and see his life pass. He hid nothing from her.

"I lost many of your letters which are invaluable to me," he said, "and you have lost a vast number of mine. But not a word to you about politics because you are a woman!" He roared with laughter at her face. "What an offence have I committed! A woman! I shall soon make it up." He was serious. "I think women better than men in general, and I know you can keep a secret as well as any man whatever. But the world don't know this. Therefore if I were to write my sentiments to you, and the letter should be caught and hitched into a newspaper, the world would say I was not to be trusted with a secret."[37]

"So I must be the loser!" said Abigail. "I've always thought that in separations the one left behind was the greatest sufferer."[38]

"God knows how much I suffer from want of writing to you!" he said. "It used to be a cordial to my spirits! But the falsest thing the English Press said of me was that I am disgusted with the Parisians. The very opposite is true! I admire the Parisians. They are the happiest people in the world, I think, and the best inclined to make others so. If I had had your ladyship and our little folks over there in Paris with me, and no politics to plague me, I could have been the happiest being on earth!"[39]

John Adams had had to straighten out many errors in the Commissioners' handling of affairs in France but he had nothing but praise of the treaty. And John Adams had a talent for praise.

"Ah, the excitement here was tremendous when the news of the signing of the treaty with France arrived!" said Abigail. "It came on the first of May, and the soldiers in Valley Forge, after their hard, terrible winter, went wild with joy. The dogwood was in bloom, and was abundant there, and they picked it and put it in their hats and paraded. Surely for that treaty we owe Mr Franklin much!"

"Yes," said John Adams, "but the treaty was inevitable. France wanted it, as I surmised, as much as we did. The victory of Gates over Burgoyne brought the treaty to a head, it was not a victory of diplomacy. The longer I stayed in France the more I was aware of the supreme importance to the French of their struggle with England. The Count de Vergennes—the foreign Minister—only hesitated to make alliance with us in our fight with England until he had good assurance that he was not linking France to a losing cause."

"I remember meeting Dr Franklin when he was in Cambridge in November of '75," said Abigail. "I dined with him—I wrote you about it. How I admired him! I couldn't very well help it. I'd been brought up to venerate him from my infancy. I found him social though not talkative, and when he spoke, something useful dropped from his tongue. He was grave, yet pleasant and affable. You know I pride myself on reading faces, and I thought I could read in his the virtues of his heart—patriotism in its full lustre; and with that is blended, isn't it, every virtue of a Christian? A true patriot must be a religious man!"[40]

John Adams would not harm her innocence by denying it.

"There has been nothing in any of your letters, to me or anyone else," she went on, "to change this first impression. When you wrote to Cousin Sam that important letter about the system of American embassies which he showed to so many members of Congress, there was no criticism of Mr Franklin in it. You said there that three commissioners to France were too many, there should be only one. And every one supposed you meant Mr Franklin to be the one."

"And so I did," said John Adams. "Before I wrote that letter I considered carefully what would be the consequences to—myself, for instance—if my plan should be adopted. Dr Franklin's reputation was so high in America, in France, and all over Europe, that he would undoubtedly—as he ought—be left alone at the Court of Versailles. Mr Arthur Lee held two commissions, one to the Court of France and one to the Court of Spain. The one to Versailles should be annulled, but that would leave the one to Spain in force. I alone would be left without commission—because Holland is not yet ready to receive a Minister! Well, I was glad enough to come home! I did expect Congress would arrange for my passage back however, and pay my expenses. That was my only disappointment!"[41]

"And now what?" said Abigail, between hope and fear.

"Now—when I've written my report for Congress—as they have no business for me in Europe, I must contrive to get some at home! Prepare yourself for removing to Boston, into the old house, for there you shall go, and there I will draw writs and deeds, and harangue juries and be happy!"[42]

Abigail had three months with John, bright pageant of summer's end and early autumn. Her husband sent in his report to Congress. It was no pettifogging report of details, nor a backbiting of the absent, but a statesmanlike survey of the whole European situation as it affected the new United States of America. And then he settled down in his pleasant office at Penns Hill to draft a constitution and a Bill of Rights for the State of Massachusetts.

Congress, in the meantime, disconcerted by John Adams's uncalled-for return, deeply impressed by his report, had at last decided what office they needed him for. They commissioned him to return to Europe as Minister Plenipotentiary with powers first to negotiate a peace with Great Britain and second to negotiate a treaty of commerce with Great Britain, Mr Dana being appointed Secretary to both commissions.

John Adams took leave of his wife on November 13, 1779, rode to Boston with his nine-year-old son Charles, and went on board the *Sensible*. Johnny Q., now twelve, and Mr Thaxter, and the manservant Joseph Stevens, had ridden ahead and were already on board; Thaxter was going as private secretary to John Adams.

The decision to take Charles was a natural result of the proved success of taking Johnny. It seemed only fair. Why should Johnny have all the advantages? Abigail had made another passionate plea to go herself and take all the family—or perhaps to leave little Tommy with one of his aunts. But she had been crushed by overwhelming arguments: uncertainty of domicile, necessity of being foot-loose for emergency, the likelihood of quick return, the financial strain, and—to her, clinching—"my dear, a lady is an odious creature at sea!"

So, in the bright Sabbath hush of the next day, she sat at home in an agony of weeping. "My habitation, how disconsolate it looks! My table, I sit down to it but cannot swallow my food. . . . Were I sure you would not be gone, I could not withstand the temptation of coming to town, though my heart would suffer again the cruel torture of separation. Does your heart indeed forebode that we shall again be happy? My hopes and fears rise alternately. I cannot resign more than I do, unless life itself were called for. I had a faith and reliance that supported me before, but now my heart so misgives me that I cannot find that confidence which I wish for. My dear sons! Little do they know how many veins of their mother's heart bled when she parted from them. My delicate Charles! How will he endure the fatigue of the voyage? John is a hardy sailor, seasoned before, I do not feel so much for him. I will not wish myself with you because you say a lady cannot help being an odious creature at sea; and I will not wish myself in any situation that should make me so to you. God Almighty bless and protect my dearest friend."[43]

Fortunately, she had two other children, fourteen-year-old Nabby and seven-year-old Tommy, to distract her with their daily problems and charms. Nabby, indeed, needed comforting herself, but her reserve prevented the healing overflow of her stricken heart. It was just as well that they could not follow the voyage. Their dearest ones were crossing the stormy Atlantic in a leaky, overcrowded ship, "with perhaps four hundred men on board, who were scarcely able, with two large pumps going all the twenty-four hours, to keep water from filling the hold, in hourly danger, for twenty days together, of foundering at sea."[44]

Letters arrived in February, telling of safe landing. But the ship had limped into harbour at Ferrol, Spain, three or four hundred leagues from John Adams's destination, and the rest of the way must be covered by land. No joke this, to cross the Pyrenees in the dead of winter, "bad roads, bad taverns, and very dear. I must get some kind of carriage for the children if possible," wrote her husband. "They are very well. Charles has sustained the voyage, and behaves as well as ever his brother did. He is much pleased with what he sees. Sammy Cooper, too." (Another youngster in Mr Adams's care.) But Mr Adams fervently confesses: "These young gentlemen give me a vast deal of trouble in this unexpected journey. What could we do if you and all the family were with me?" He was amazed at the spectacle of the poverty and wretchedness of Spain: poor people standing about barefoot in the frozen mud, no business, no traffic. "Nobody appears rich but the churches."

Later letters described the miseries of the journey: wretched taverns, cold, verminous, filled with smoke because there were no chimneys, dark because there were no windows; poor food and bad beds. A thousand times John Adams regretted bringing his sons. "I have undergone the greatest anxiety for the children. . . .

I hope their travels will be of service to them, but those at home are best off."[45] And though he suppressed any word of little Charles's miserable homesickness—which, indeed, the sweet-natured Charles did his best to keep under cover himself—John Adams let fly candidly with his own. "If I return again safe to America, I shall be happy the remainder of my days because I shall *stay at home*, and at home I must be to be happy."[46]

The party arrived in Paris at last on February 5, 1780, and settled at the Hôtel de Valois. By the sixteenth John Adams could write his wife: "The children are happy in their academy, of which I send you the plan enclosed."

And those at home? Abigail wrote:

> I am rejoiced to hear my Charles behaves so well, but he always had the faculty of gaining hearts and is more mourned for in this neighbourhood than I could have believed if I had not heard it. All your letters from Spain [overland route to France] I have traced and followed you on the maps through your peregrinations, it has been a pilgrimage indeed, and the care of the children! . . . I cannot wish to have shared with you, it would have been an additional burden to you.

But all the while, above the deep current of her warm emotional life, she was conducting practical affairs with the most composed efficiency. Congress, inexperienced in European expenses and short of cash, consistently underpaid its early Ministers, and more than one, unsustained by a private fortune, was to return bankrupt. That John Adams escaped this fate was almost entirely due to the ability of his wife.

At the very start of his ambassadorship expenses had exceeded income. Paris was dear. The unexpected journey through Spain had already made hay of the budget allotted by Congress. None the less, said John to his wife, "I must and will send you something for your use by every opportunity."

Abigail had already decided that she did not want money in face of the rising inflation, she wanted goods. Some she could apply directly to the family's needs, and others she could barter at advantageous rates for groceries, furnishings, and farm tools. Cousin Will handled all this business for her, either by direct exchange of his own merchandise or by bartering for her with others, all on a strictly commercial basis—except that young Will Smith, though an admirable business-man, was also incurably generous, and was bound to make the most liberal terms.

Immediately on his arrival at Paris John Adams wrote to Abigail that he had made arrangements for her with a French house of exporters so that she could order direct from them, "anything you want by any vessel belonging to your uncle or M. J., or Mr T., provided you don't exceed one hundred dollars by any one vessel. Mr Gardoqui will readily send them and draw upon me for the money." As a beginning, he had at once dispatched to her a first consignment of "necessaries for the family."

So Abigail became a business-woman, and showed that she could do it well. She kept the farm running, her family well clothed and fed, domestic and other equipment and buildings in good repair, paid her bills and taxes and kept out of debt; yet touchingly and gracefully assured her absent husband that she was "lost without her pilot"!

Meditating on the mysterious closeness, the absorption of identity which she had experienced in married life, she wrote to John Thaxter about marriage. Her ostensible reason was to rally her young cousin about the possibility of losing his heart to some gay Parisian and to urge on him the claims of "some worthy girl in my own country—some fair American," for Thaxter had a heart "unhackneyed by gallantries—a *rara avis* in these days of modern refinement and Chesterfieldian politeness." She condemned getting married for worldly reasons without love or indulging in sensuality outside of marriage—vice, she roundly calls it. She could make allowance for individuals, and neither she nor her husband, though they commented at times on Dr Franklin's extra-marital affairs and illegitimate children, ever passed judgment on him for it. Yet such a habit, she advises her young man, with eighteenth-century candour,

> excludes all that refined and tender friendship, that sweet consent of souls, that harmony of minds congenial to each other, without which it is in vain to look for happiness in that indissoluble union which naught but death dissolves. The heart must be engaged to reap the genuine fruits of tenderness; contemptibly low must that commerce be in which the mind has no share. . . . Even the senses will be weakly affected where the heart does not participate.[47]

As she reflected on the fascinations of the French ladies, and their very free manners—her husband had described how they petted and caressed Dr Franklin, and had jocosely commented that Franklin's seventy years made him enjoy privileges "that were much to be envied"—the thought crossed her mind as to whether her warm-blooded husband could remain "loyal" to her during such long separation in face of such temptations. Visitors from France brought fresh anecdotes of Franklin "embracing and being embraced by" the dazzling fair. But no, she is sure of her husband as of herself. That is never one of her worries.

> Mrs Dana made me a visit. We talked as much as we pleased of our dear *absents*, compared notes, sympathized, and mingled no little pride that no country could boast two worthier hearts than *we* had *permitted* to go abroad—and then they were such honest souls too, and so entirely satisfied with their American dames that we had not an apprehension of their roving. We mean not however to defy the charms of the parisian ladies, but to admire the constancy and fidelity with which they are resisted.[48]

And again: "Much must be allowed for forms and customs," she remarks easily.

> I can even consent that they should practise their *forms* upon your Lordship considering your natural fondness for the practice whilst I hold possession of that I think they cannot rob me of—'tis mine by a free gift, mine by exchange, mine by a long possession, mine by merit, and mine by every law human and divine.[49]

When election time came on Massachusetts Abigail was heart and soul in the campaign. Richard Cranch was elected Representative from Braintree by a unanimous vote; Dr Tufts was chosen Senator. But in the state election the votes went against her views, as indeed she had feared they would. She wanted Bowdoin for governor, but the showy John Hancock, with his clever political tricks and wider publicity, was elected by a large majority; "low, mean arts," said Abigail, in the fierceness of political contest, "I could tell you many, yet nothing that would surprise you, for you know every avenue of his vain heart!"[50] And now John may well remember her appeals about the position of women. Well, "if I cannot be a Voter upon this occasion," she wrote with good-humoured irony, "I will be a writer of votes. I can do something in that way!" And since he might think even this unwomanly, she turned it sharply back upon himself—"What a politician you have made me—?"[51]

"What a fine affair it would be," wrote John Adams to his wife, "if we could flit across the Atlantic as they say the angels do from planet to planet! I would dart to Penns Hill and bring you over on my wings."[52]

At the end of 1782 John Adams sent his wife, by careful conveyance, the volumes of his private journal and the letter books containing copies of correspondence. "I dare say there is not a lady in America," he wrote, "treated with a more curious dish of politics than is contained in the enclosed papers. You may show them to discreet friends, but by no means let them go out of your hands or be copied. Preserve them in safety against accidents."[53]

John Adams had arrived in Paris armed with powers which made him the most important American Ambassador in the world. True, there were only three American Ambassadors; but one of the three was Benjamin Franklin. Until this time Franklin had been in reputation, influence, and prestige the leading American representative abroad. The most important negotiation afoot had been the treaty with France. Now that was accomplished, and Franklin, though showered with praise, and given sole and full powers at the Court of Versailles, felt himself suddenly shorn of his glory and shifted from the centre of the limelight. For another negotiation was now to be begun, the treaty with Britain, beside which the one with France would look pale. And in this great, this crucial diplomatic effort, Franklin found himself allotted, not merely not the leading part, but no part at all.

Franklin's shock and mortification, though intense, were slight, had he but known it, compared with the consternation of Gerard, Luzerne, and above all de Vergennes. The position of France in the world was precarious in the extreme. De Vergennes, the most skilled diplomat of his time, was treading on egg-shells, a secret here, a secret there, this item balanced against that, in order to gain for France a day or two more of safety. The forces of revolution and bankruptcy were gathering underneath. A victory against England was, to the mind of de Vergennes, France's only hope. For this he had needed the United States as a tool against England, and for this he had bought the help of Spain with the secret promise of Gibraltar and of some of the American fisheries and wilderness boundaries. A premature peace between England and the United States would free British troops and ships for use in Europe. Mr Adams was also empowered to make a treaty of commerce. De Vergennes did not want England to have a treaty on terms of trade reciprocity. He wanted, and was determined to have, French priority. And, further, Mr Adams was going to be stubborn about the fisheries and boundaries; and he knew what Mr Adams would think about that prickly burr that was tickling up his sleeve, the question of Gibraltar.

He therefore blocked the diplomatic channels and refused to allow Adams to publicize his commission. Franklin, instead of helping Adams, was blinded to the real situation by jealousy of Adams and by the flattery of the French diplomats, and sided with de Vergennes, even to the extent of trying to provoke Congress to recall John Adams. And John Adams immediately left Paris for Holland, July 1780. A Dutch loan would free America from uneasy dependence on France.

Arriving without any portfolio for Holland, he took up residence as a private gentleman, put his two sons in school, and proceeded to make social contacts—one introduction leading to another—with the leading bankers and statesmen of the country. "This country where I am," he wrote his wife, "is the greatest curiosity in the world. This nation is not known anywhere, not even by its neighbours. The Dutch language is spoken by none but themselves. Therefore they converse with nobody, and nobody converses with them!"[54]

Difference of language, however, never daunted John Adams. He had gone to France in the first place not knowing any French (though he had at the time protested his unsuitability on that score). And now he was in Holland not knowing any Dutch. Were there no interpreters? Why, certainly! His French at least (in which he was now fluent) could obtain them. "A man must have something in his head to say . . . he will never fail to find a way of communicating to good purpose."[55] He got on excellently. And there is no greater tribute to John Adams's social gifts and his power to make himself interesting than the two years he spent among the Dutch. He invented an entirely new form of diplomacy —the personal, gradual approach—promoting the cause of his new country first by explaining it and then by seeking to build up confidence in it. Some questions asked by an intelligent Dutch banker and statesman in the early stages of his visit gave Mr Adams the idea to write and publish a series of articles in the Dutch papers about the causes of the American Revolution, and the resources of the United States, which just hit the spot.

John Adams did not expect to be in Holland very long, because Henry Laurens had been commissioned as American representative there and would presumably take over. But Laurens was captured by a British frigate on the voyage and somehow did not manage to throw his papers overboard. The capture gave the game away. Holland hastily denied all interest in the United States, and panic seized the Dutch merchants as to any American connexions. It looked as if all Adams's work would be undone. But in the nick of time the inept British monarch goaded his slavish ministry into a declaration of war against Holland for her detected unfriendliness in being about to receive an American ambassador. In January John Adams received from Congress a commission appointing him, in Laurens's place, as Minister Plenipotentiary to the United Provinces of Holland, with power to negotiate a treaty of alliance whenever practicable. This was not only staggering power for one man to carry—in addition to his other unique powers to treat with Britain—but was in the nature of a vote of confidence in him, in answer to Franklin's and Vergennes's innuendoes against him. A letter and resolution of Congress in approbation of John Adams's work accompanied and underlined it, and Abigail, informed of both by her friends, wrote him her joy. She added her pleasure in noting that error of the wicked British.

> The United Provinces are at last obliged to declare themselves! . . . Britain will rue the day that in breach of the Laws of Nations* she fell upon their defenceless dominions and drew upon her, as it is thought she must, the combined force of all the Neutral powers![56]

Congress was encouraged to take advantage of the anti-British feeling now evident in Russia and in December appointed Mr Dana as Minister to St Petersburg.

So Mr Dana moved off to St Petersburg, and though John Adams missed him he was fully in favour of the move. It was decided between them that it would be a good opportunity for young Johnny Q. to see more of the world, so Johnny, now fourteen, joined Mr Dana's party. They made a very strenuous journey of fifty-one days to the Russian capital via Leipsig and Berlin. After leaving Leipsig Dana pushed on day and night, and but for the frequent accidents which forced them to pause, Johnny might have died of exhaustion. In Berlin the carriage broke up entirely,

* It is interesting to observe this idea of the "law of nations" and of the method of enforcing it, quite taken for granted in 1781, without any recognized body of international law. Abigail was talking of the Armed Neutrality Pact, initiated by Catherine of Russia, between the neutral northern powers of Europe to protect their shipping against interference by the British Navy on the high seas.

and they had to stay nine days. They found St Petersburg, said Dana, "the finest city I have seen in Europe," and since by this time they had seen most of them, that was no idle tribute. They settled down in the Hotel de Paris, and Johnny prepared to get on with his education. His mother heard of his adventure in due course, and wrote cheerfully, "I learn by Mr Brush that Mr Dana is gone to Petersburg with Master John—for this I am not sorry. Mr Dana's care and attention shd well satisfy him—and Russia is an Empire I shd be very fond of his visiting."[57]

Johnny's departure left Charles alone. The flat, foggy air of Holland was unwholesome both to him and to his father, and the delicate boy was passionately homesick for his mother and the happy life at Penns Hill. John Adams found that the duties of a father, especially a tender and anxious father, did not fit well with the increasingly exacting duties of an ambassador. He was sorry to admit to himself that it had been a mistake to bring Charles at all. And he at last decided that the lesser of two evils was to send the boy home again. So to Charles's rapturous joy he was placed in the care of Commodore Gillon and set sail for Boston. His mother heard of it indirectly, by the unwise publishing of a passenger list including the name of "a son of Mr Adams," and by later word from Mr Brush. Her restraint gave way and she reproached her husband, "Why did you not write me about it?" She became a prey to all the horror of suspense;

> 3 frigates of the enemy and a 50-ton ship the *Chatham* are cruising upon our coast for the vessels which are expected from Holland. I tremble if he should not speedily arrive. His homesickness must have been great indeed to induce the poor fellow to cross the Atlantick without Father or Mother.

On the voyage there was trouble with Gillon, and the passengers —Charles and a friendly protector among them—were put off at Bilbao, and stranded there for many weeks. The distracted mother, with two such young sons adrift in the world, ceased to try to be brave, or to disguise her feelings from herself. The well-known dangers of the Boston winter coast, and the added peril of British frigates seeking a hostage, threatened the one; the unknown rigours of the far-off frozen city threatened the other.

> Ah, my dear John!* Where are you? in so remote a part of the globe that I fear I shall not hear a syllable from you. Pray . . . send

* A. A. is writing to her husband about her sons, and exclaims here regarding Johnny Q.

> me his letters to you. Do you know that I have not had a line from him for a year and a half? Alas! my dear, I am much afflicted with a disorder called the *heartache*, nor can any remedy be found in America. It must be collected from Holland, Petersburg, and Bilboa.[58]

So she wrote and felt on December 9, 1781, and not until January 19 did Charles safely arrive at last, and change some of her heartache into joy. By the middle of March she could write that Charles was in good health and "going to school" to a temporary tutor, getting on with his Latin, and happy in his return to his native land. But the problem of education was getting serious again. "I know not what to do with my children. We have no Grammar School in the town, nor have we had for 5 years." It would be expensive to board them out, and, besides, "I know not how to think of their leaving home, I could not live in the house were it so deserted, if they are gone only for a day it is as silent as a tomb."[59]

Charles had brought with him, too, another worry and heartache for the one his coming relieved. He brought the story of a severe illness his father had had at The Hague. Abigail had often dreamed, when silences stretched long, of her husband lying ill, without her to tend him, too ill even to write to her. Now her fears were seen to be no more than the truth, and she felt she had been too little anxious rather than too much.

John Adams was well again months before she heard of his sickness, had spent most of the summer (1781) in exciting work, and was writing to her regularly and vigorously, if guardedly. But her husband's letters, most of them, did not reach her, and hers to him were long delayed. The state of war between England and Holland made the passage of mails still more precarious. In August, after dreaming of his return, she awoke to write: "the next month will complete a whole year since a single line from your hand has reached my longing eyes. Congress have no dispatches from you since October." Almost as bad as her personal deprivation is the advantage such cutting off gives to his enemies.

> I cannot protect you from the slanderous arrow that flieth in secret, a specimen of which you will find enclosed in a letter from Mr Gerry. My indignation is too big for utterance. I will not comment upon this low, this dirty, this infamous, this diabolical piece of envy and malice![60]

Undisturbed by slander of which he did not hear, John Adams was getting on well with the Dutch. The loan was in sight when he was suddenly summoned to Paris by de Vergennes in July 1781. Now Mr Adams heard for the first time of the peace treaty, or rather armistice, which de Vergennes and Franklin had been concocting behind his back.* They had now gone so far that they had got preliminary articles for registration ready for signature. But alas! John Adams had such powers that without *his* signature it would be invalid. They were forced to summon him and show it to him. But they hoped—especially de Vergennes—that haste would be in their favour. There was a time-limit on the document. They reckoned on hurry to push it through. Surely, when Franklin was ready to sign, Mr Adams would not dare—especially when flustered! —to take upon his shoulders the whole responsibility of continuing a bloody fight which could be called to a halt that very day; or as soon as the fastest sailing-ships could carry the winged word!

But the worst of it was, Mr Adams was not flustered. He did not even waste time in giving way to anger. He simply took the document and shut himself up alone with it to go over it closely with a lawyer's eye. He was a past master at the quick digesting of complicated arguments and phrases. Although he was taken completely by surprise, and had no background to go on but de Vergennes's scanty communication of the secret diplomacy of the past twelve months, Mr Adams was ready with his answer in two days.

John Adams refused categorically to be a party to any agreement which allowed British forces to remain on American soil, and also declined to enter into any negotiation which treated the United States otherwise than as an equal sovereign power.

Vergennes's disappointment could only vent itself in fury. He sent a diplomatic insult to Mr Adams, addressing him as the *agent* of the United States, instead of as the Minister empowered to negotiate a treaty of peace. And he let fly privately to Mr Franklin as to what wonders they could have accomplished together—and so nearly had!—but for this obstinate madman.

Mr Adams at once packed up and returned to his task in Holland, having single-handed saved his country from disaster.

But the cold anger of Franklin was worse than the almost impersonal anger of the Frenchman. If John Adams was wrong, as Franklin was determined to believe, then he, Franklin—accustomed to think of himself for long years past as *the* American diplomat in

* As part of a suggested pact between France and England, to be arranged by a congress of powers at Vienna.

Europe—had been completely thwarted by a stronger man. But if John Adams was right, he had been shown up for a fool. Either way, he was determined to ruin John Adams. Perhaps, as a professed philosopher, he did not confess it baldly to himself—though he was cool-headed and cynical enough to do so. But he acted as if it were true. And he passed on the feud to his son-in-law and grandson, the Baches, father and son, who were to have their innings in later years as poison pens in the Press.

French diplomacy was having better luck in America. In the autumn of 1781, the first full-rank Secretary for Foreign Affairs was elected by Congress. The winner of the ballot was Robert Livingston. "*He is not ignorant*," wrote Luzerne to Vergennes on November 1, "*of the part I took in his election*."[61]

Despite the French activities, the worst John Adams's enemies could obtain against him was a modification of his powers. His commission to make a treaty of commerce was taken away, without explanation, and four colleagues were given him to help in negotiating a peace with Britain. They were John Jay, Franklin, Henry Laurens, and Jefferson. Of these gentlemen, Franklin, Laurens, and Jay were already abroad. Jefferson was prevented from sailing by private affairs. John Jay, now representing the United States in Spain, was regarded by Luzerne as the cream of the collection, a strong pro-French, pro-Franklin man. Gerard and Luzerne lobbied for him! But that was not John Jay's fault, nor did he know it.

Abigail was highly incensed by the new commission, and wrote her husband in October: "You will see with whom and what you are colleagued! Some you can have little hope of assistance from, considering their present situation"—Laurens a prisoner in the Tower, and Jefferson with his dying wife—"and some will have no inclination but to obstruct your measures."[62]

In vain John wrote her, in a mood of determined humility and philosophy: "It is more honourable than before and much more easy, I assure you it has been a great comfort to me. The measure is right. It is more respectful to the powers of Europe concerned, and more likely to give satisfaction in America." Abigail was too painfully conscious of the slanders, public and private, marshalled against her husband, the attempts to belittle his service, which were being promoted by the French agents in America as the inevitable crisis of the peace treaty approached. But Abigail took the slanders too personally, without knowing what lay behind them, and unconsciously she played straight into the hands of the enemy. She wrote to her husband, Why not give up this thankless task? Retire, come home!

But no sooner was the letter out of her hands than she hastily followed it with a change of mood. Not really retire, though. No, she could not believe her husband would "retire unnoticed nameless to a rustick cottage. . . . I need not much examination of my heart to say I would not willingly consent to it." Not riches but service is her aim. "Ardently as I long for the return of my dearest friend, I cannot feel the least inclination to a peace but upon the most liberal foundation."

Her husband received her ups and downs—all out of date by the time he got them—calmly, though tenderly. He was himself in good heart as the summer of 1782 moved through to the fateful autumn. His spirits always rose before a fight. And this fight he was immensely ready for, armed at all points, knowing now intimately the policy of his opponents, and resting secure in the knowledge that no treaty could be made without his signature. So he gave himself unreservedly to pushing through the business in Holland, so as to have that in the bag before he moved on to Paris.

"I am going to dinner with a Duke and a Duchess and a number of Ambassadors and Senators in all the luxury of this luxurious world," he wrote his wife cheerfully from The Hague,

> but how much more luxurious it would be to me to dine upon roast beef with Parson Smith, Dr Tufts, or Norton Quincy! or upon rusticoat potatoes with Portia! . . . I hope to sign the Treaty [with Holland] this week or next, or the week after. All points are agreed on and nothing remains but to transcribe the copies.[63]

Done at last, with that notable achievement in his pocket, he travelled quickly to Paris to join the quorum of commissioners with Jay and Franklin. And as if she felt the mood of serenity and triumph in which her husband now, in that October, approached his major task, Abigail, in far-off Braintree, filled the night of their wedding anniversary (never forgotten) with a sober digestion of experience. Quarrel as she might with a fate which had cut her off "in the midst of my days from the only society I delighted in," yet she could rejoice too that the same supreme Being who "blessed us in each other, endowed my friend with powers and talents for the benefit of mankind," and gave him a willing mind to improve them for the service of his country. "You have obtained," she now realized, slanders or none, "honour and reputation at home and abroad. Oh, may not an inglorious peace wither the laurels you have won!"[64]

Abigail did not know that the treaty had been signed six weeks before she wrote these words, but her satisfaction was complete when she learned the news. She wrote:

> Peace! . . . The garb of the favourite of America is woven of an admirable texture, and proved the great skill, wisdom and abilities of the master workmen. It was not fabricated in the loom of France, nor are the materials English, but they are the product of our own American soil.
>
> May you, my dearest friend, return to your much-loved solitude with the pleasing reflection of having contributed to the happiness of millions.[65]

VIII

Abigail and Nabby in Europe

NOW SURELY THE TIME OF separation was over.

"If you had known Mr Adams would be away so long," asked one of those friends who so add to the joy of life, "would you have consented to let him go?"

Abigail paused a moment to collect herself, then answered with some of her husband's own fullness and emphasis. "If I had known, sir, that Mr Adams would have been able to accomplish what he has done, I would not only have submitted to the absence I've already endured, but would if necessary, endure three years more!"[1] (But God forbid, she inwardly groaned.) "You must be proud, of course, of your husband's great honour and distinction," said the friend. "Oh, I can't refrain," confessed Mrs Adams, "from considering his honours as badges of my unhappiness." Yes, she did not acquire indifference, nor reconcile herself to the habit of absence.

"You write so wise, so like a minister of state," she complained to him. And further—she aged thirty-eight, he forty-seven—"The age of romance has long ago past but the affection of almost infant years has matured and strengthened until it has become a vital principle.[2] Should I draw you the picture of my heart . . . the early possession you obtained there, and the absolute power you have always maintained over it, leave not the smallest space unoccupied. I look back to the early days of our acquaintance and friendship; nor have the dreary years of absence in the smallest degree effaced from my mind the image of the dear, untitled man to whom I gave my heart."[3]

John Adams was tired and cross and homesick. He sent in his resignation as soon as the provisional articles were signed. He was writing to all his friends about going home and had been trying to get away. With his extraordinary indifference to the record, so characteristic and so damaging, he chafed at remaining to put his name on the parchment of the Peace. The work is done. Why worry over a trifle? But the daily duty—just this more, and then just this—continued to hold him fast.

Mr Dana was resigning from Petersburg, and wrote his friend that they would soon serve in Congress together. And John Adams wrote back: "I shall be happy to sit alongside of you upon one of those seats and rise up now and then and tell stories of our peregrinations and the robbers we met upon the highway!"[4]

So far was he from any ambition for further service in Europe that he wrote to Congress in praise of Mr Jay and Mr Dana, and "Would heartily recommend Mr Jay for the now necessary and most important post of Minister to Great Britain."

Yes, there was no mistaking his desire. But as usual it was to his wife that he showed his heart fully.

> Whether there should be peace or war, I shall come home in the summer. Our son is now on his journey from Petersburg through Sweden, Denmark and Germany . . . he shall come with me, and I pray we may all meet once more, you and I never to separate again. You may depend upon a good domestic husband for the remainder of my life. My children, I hope, will once at length discover that they have a father who is not unmindful of their welfare. They have too much reason to think themselves forgotten, although I know that an anxiety for their happiness has corroded me every day of my life. With a tenderness which words cannot express, I am yours for ever. . . .

And again:

> I am determined not to wait for an acceptance of my resignation, but to come home without it, provided it does not arrive within a reasonable time. Don't think therefore of coming to Europe. If you do we shall cross each other. . . . I shall certainly return home in the spring. . . . With or without leave, resignation accepted or not, home I will come.[5]

So in a passion of restlessness, Abigail awaited him. "One month of daily expectation is more tedious than a year of uncertainty." She filled her heart and her time with the affairs of her children.

Charley and Tommy, thirteen and eleven, must begin to prepare for Harvard. She tried to put them in Andover, but it was full. That delightful sister Betsy, however, married to an impecunious parson, and having a boy and a girl of her own, was ready to open her roomy house at Haverhill to nephews who wished to tutor with her husband. And the Rev. Mr Shaw was both a scholar and an excellent educator. This solved the school problem very satisfactorily. Charles and Tommy and their cousin Billy Cranch all went together. But though no care could be better than Aunt Shaw's, Charles was too delicate. His mother had to go from time to time and fetch him home to get stronger. And then he caught the measles epidemic in the heats of August—"it was very mortal in Boston—three hundred children buried since March."[6] A long holiday on the farm at Penns Hill put him on his feet again, and he resumed his studies in the autumn, but Abigail was called to Haverhill early in November, for Tommy had rheumatic fever a second time. He lost the use of his limbs for a fortnight, with "fever and a stricture across his breast," but it was not so bad as his mother first feared.

They were eager, attractive boys, earning praise from Mr Shaw, encouraged to think of college life as not more than a year and a half away. Charles was determined to be ready at fifteen. "I have a thousand fears for my dear boys as they rise into life," their mother wrote their father.

> The most critical period is the University. I hope before either of our children are prepared for college you will be able to return. I have hitherto been able to obtain their love, their confidence and obedience, but I feel unequal to the task of guiding them along.[7]

But Abigail's daughter's problems were not those of health or education, they were affairs of the heart. Mistress Nabby—second of the name—had a serious suitor. A dashing young lawyer, Royall Tyler, handsome, moneyed, well-connected, with elegant scarlet coat and a gift for poetry, had come to take up practice in Braintree, and instantly turned the heads of all the girls in the place except one. And to that one—accustomed as he was to easy conquest—he assiduously paid his court.

"Indeed my dear Sir, you would be proud of her," wrote her mother.

> She is not like her Mamma—she has a stateliness in her manners which some misunderstand as pride and haughtiness, but which is really only a too great reserve. She needs more affability, more of the charm of softness, but she has prudence and discretion beyond her

years. In person she is tall, large and majestic. Her manners forbid intimacy. Indeed she is not like her Mamma. Had not her Mamma at her age too much sensibility to be very prudent? It however won a heart of as much sensibility—but how my pen runs—I never can write you a short letter.[8]

Mrs Adams received the young man at first with some suspicion. Though charming and promising, he seemed too gay and dissipated, and Nabby, of course, was stand-offish as a cover to her intense shyness. "Yet I see a growing attachment in him stimulated by that very reserve."[9] Indeed, if Nabby had thought out a definite plan of fascination, she could not have done better. Her Palmer cousins at Germantown, where the young man lodged, were hardly on speaking terms, setting their caps at Tyler. And little eight-year-old Mary, Joe's daughter,* was giving Royall Tyler a child's worship. He rode away from a very hothouse of adulation to the refreshing indifference of Miss Adams, who at seventeen had the grave dignity of a princess. He made more obvious headway with the mother, who looked on with sympathy and wrote vivid accounts to the absent father which might enlist his approval better than the young man could do for himself.

In the Christmas season, when John Adams in Paris was resting on his oars after the accomplishment of the provisional treaty, Abigail wrote:

> Let me draw you from the depths of politics to endearing family scenes. I don't know any young man whose natural disposition is more agreeable—his days are devoted to his office, his evenings of late to my fireside. His attachment is too obvious to escape notice. I do not think the lady wholly indifferent, yet her reserve and apparent coldness is such that I know he is in miserable doubt.[10]

And in the spring she wrote confidently that, yes, "I daily see that he will win the affections of your image, your superscription." And John Adams need not fear that the daughter had been attracted by the superficial charms of her suitor, "his dancing, singing and playing. He has given those things up since his residence in this town. The gay volatile youth appears to become the studious lawyer."[11] Falling in love would be good for Nabby, just what she needed; a little laughter, a little warmth. "Should she be caught by the tender passion sufficient to remove a little of her natural

* Granddaughter of General Joseph Palmer.

reserve and soften her form and manners, she will be a still more pleasing character." While Mr Tyler, himself an eager reader of books, cherishing a secret ambition (very dismaying to John Adams when he sniffed it out) to be a writer of poems and plays, was developing his lady's taste in literature, Abigail, in obedience to John's anxious remonstrance, refused to encourage an engagement she would have allowed. But she wrote earnestly that

> to extirpate the idea from the hearts and minds of either is not in my power, violent opposition never yet served a course of this nature. Whilst they believe me their best friend and see that their interest is near my heart, they submit to my prohibition, earnestly wishing for your return and for more prosperous days. What ought I to say? I feel too powerful a pleader within my own heart and too well recollect the love I bore to the object of my early affections.

But the father could not see his reserved daughter warming to life under the influence of a deep and slow passion. He did not think the match good enough and sent strong protests home across the sea. He had met Tyler in earlier days when Tyler was reading law with Mr Dana, and thought him a lightweight, a frivolous youth. Perhaps, living in a man's world, he had heard more details about Tyler's early dissipations. He reproached Abigail for being impressed by that young man's attentions, and urged that the affair be broken off for a while.

So Nabby was packed off to Boston.

> What you wish has taken place, it is done with. Not that any of those qualities you justly dread have appeared in this gentleman since his residence in this town—I say this in justification of my having had a partiality in his favour. The world looked back to the days in which I knew him not.

She added firmly that she had never heard any vices ascribed to him, and, though she agreed that a longer period of probation was necessary to establish a "contrary character," she wrote again, in June 1783,[12] that Tyler's business was increasing and that "if he has been the gay, thoughtless young fellow, he has at least practiced one year of reformation." He had even purchased a house, and that one of the best houses in the neighbourhood. It was the Vassall House, vacated by its wealthy Tory owners during the Revolution, and in 1780 leased by the court to Richard Cranch. Now, 1783, the heir returned from exile and claimed her house under the terms of the new treaty,* obtained it, and put it up for sale. "Mr Tyler has made the purchase," wrote Abigail. "There are 108 acres in the whole, 50 of which is fine woodland. The garden contains the best collection of fruit in town."[13]

Did not this look steady, look serious?

Mrs Adams clearly suffered for both the young people. But far from being a stoic herself, she did not know a stoic when she saw one. Young Nabby's self-control was too perfect, had been practised too long. "I cannot affirm," wrote the mother, "that it is wholly eradicated from their minds but time will do it," she reassured her husband. He can count confidently on his daughter's filial affection. She will never marry anyone against his consent. "That she has a partiality I know and believe, but she has submitted her opinion, and relinquished the idea of a connexion." But the young girl's awakened and hungry heart could not resign itself to complete banishment from the man who had become the very sun around which her little planet revolved.

> It was her request that she might be permitted to see and treat the gentleman as an acquaintance whom she valued. "Why," said she, "should I treat a gentleman who has done nothing to forfeit my esteem with neglect or contempt merely because the world have said he entertained a regard for me? If his foibles are to be treated with more severity than the vices of others, and I submit my judgment and opinion to the disapprobation of others in a point which so nearly concerns me, I wish to be left at liberty to act in other respects with becoming decency." And she does,

said her mother, rendering those bitter sentences to the father verbatim to let him judge for himself what repressed feeling lay behind them—"she does, and has conducted herself so as to meet the approbation of all her friends. She has conquered herself."[14]

Unfortunately Abigail bolstered up her plea with a "poetick piece" of Tyler's which had moved her own heart. She was in haste to add, "You will tell me you do not want a poet, but if there is a mind otherways well furnished, you would have no objection to its being a mere amusement?"[15] But John Adams could not stomach marrying his daughter to an obscure country attorney of shady past who was so much of a popinjay as to commit the indiscretion of verse! It is to be feared that finally cooked Tyler's goose.

* The treaty with England specified that Tory refugees might reclaim their property under certain conditions.

Yet both parents, great lovers as they were, would have given way to the young people's passion had it been on the girl's side more articulate, and on the young man's side had it stood the test of time. But the test the parents set was too severe. John Adams had courted his Abigail for four years—and not without preliminary opposition. But they had seen each other frequently throughout the time; they had comforted and sustained each other's affection with the small change of love. Tyler, a more inflammable character and much courted by women, was asked to stand first discouragement and then absence with the slenderest thread of hope. It is not surprising that he should have given way under the strain—and it is still not quite certain that he did. At first he stood up to it well, better than could possibly have been expected from a man of his type. His endurance is eloquent witness to the powerful fascination of Abby's grave, sincere beauty. In the autumn of '83 Abigail replied again to the anxious father's questions that:

> tho the connexion is broken off and nothing particular has since passed, yet it is evident to me, as well as to the family where he lives, that his attachment is not lessened. He conducts prudently, and tho nothing is said upon the subject I do not imagine that he has given up the hope that in some future day he may obtain your approbation. Your daughter (tho fully obedient)—her sentiments she says are not to be changed but upon a conviction of his demerit, I most sincerely wish you was at home to judge for yourself, I shall never feel safe or happy until you are.[16]

That brings her to her own feelings. For more than a year past she has been entreating him at intervals to allow her to come to him:

> but you must give me full assurance of your entire approbation of my request. I cannot accept a halfway invitation. Permit me, my dearest friend, to renew that companionship—my heart sighs for it, I cannot, oh I cannot be reconciled to living as I have done for three years past. . . . But I resolve with myself to do as you wish . . . waking or sleeping I am ever with you. If you do not consent, so much is my heart intent upon it that your refusal must be couched in very soft terms—and you must pledge yourself to return speedily to me.

And so he did pledge himself, and so he hoped and intended, and she lost a good chance to go in June 1783 with her favourite cousin, young Will Smith, as escort. Will was then setting off in his turn on the grand tour, but he sailed without her, taking only her letters, and she took her husband's word that Cousin Will would probably pass him on the high seas. Autumn would surely bring him who had been due in the spring. Often in her desperate restlessness she "wandered from room to room without a heart and soul at home, and felt myself deserted, unprotected, unassisted, uncounselled! . . . oh there is a moral evil in this separation!"[17]

When she took Nabby into Boston in December, for another long visit to Uncle Isaac and Aunt Elizabeth, Uncle Isaac came in, stamping the snow off his boots, and called from the hall that whom should he just meet in State Street but Mr Dana, arrived that hour from shipboard. He was coming in to dine with them right now—"particularly on your account, my dear niece, when he heard you were here!" Abigail, stricken and speechless—Dana back and Adams not!—had to go to her room to weep passionately, so as not to give way to "childish emotion" when she greeted him.

No, Mr Adams was absolutely necessary over there, Mr Dana explained, to work on the new commission for the treaties of commerce with Mr Franklin and Mr Jefferson. Dana's vivid word-pictures of her husband and son increased her longing but roused her pride. He at once delivered a letter from her husband informing her of his "determination to pass another winter abroad," and urging her to come to him with the least possible delay. She resolved irrevocably on the great adventure.

Difficulties loomed up mountain high. She must arrange for the care of her sons, the care of the farm and all the business that had been under her hands, must break the ties and the habits of a lifetime to take up a kind of life which she did not know about and did not want.

> You invite me to you, you call me to follow you, the most earnest wish of my soul is to be with you—but you can scarcely form an idea of the conflict of my mind, it appears to me such an enterprise—the ocean so formidable—leaving my children and friends with the idea that perhaps I may never see them again, without my husband to console and comfort me under these apprehensions—indeed dear friend, there are hours when I feel unequal to the trial. If you were abroad in a private capacity I should not hesitate so much at coming to you. But a mere American as I am, unacquainted with the etiquette of courts, taught to say the thing I mean, and to wear my heart in my countenance, I am sure I should make an awkward figure; and it would mortify my pride if I should be thought to disgrace you.

She thinks wistfully of her life, "sequestered in this humble cottage, content with rural life and my domestic employment, in the midst of which I have sometimes smiled upon recollecting that I had the honour of being allied to an ambassador." Her longing for him cannot be denied, no monsters can keep her from him now, but, as she candidly says, "the difficulty is my fears and anxieties are present, my hopes and expectations distant!"[18]

But she went to work in her orderly, seemingly casual way. Her uncle Isaac Smith and cousin Tufts would take care of her business. Sister Betsy Shaw would continue the care of her sons. One strong tie had been broken by the death of her father, Parson Smith, in September. He had often begged Abigail not to go abroad while he lived. Now he was gone, dying in great pain of a "stranguery" with Christian fortitude, surrounded by his three daughters, his son's dear wife, and two of his sons-in-law. Sons indeed they were to him, taking the place of his only son William, who had sunk by this time completely out of sight and touch with the family circle. William's children and patient wife were parcelled out among the family. Abigail had had one, a loving little niece, living with her for some years.*

As well as a legacy from her father of half the Medford farm and some money, Abigail inherited a caretaker. The faithful and well-loved slave-woman Phœbe was left her freedom in Parson Smith's will and a generous legacy of a hundred pounds a year for life. This made her a matrimonial catch, and she soon took a husband—"Mr Abdee, whom you know." Abigail had the wedding at her house, and afterwards it occurred to her that Phœbe and her husband would be the ideal caretakers of house and furniture in her absence. The Abdees accepted the trust with enthusiasm and simple pride. Mrs Adams was certain of their care and faithfulness.

Then she needed servants for the journey. The death of Colonel Quincy in February 1784 put a good manservant out of a job, one John Briesler, who had originally been brought up as a bound boy in the family of General Palmer. Both families recommended him to their relative as "a virtuous, steady, frugal fellow, with a mind much above the vulgar, very handy and attentive." And so began a happy association of many years. For a maidservant she had a pleasant woman named Esther, who later became Briesler's wife.

* She grew up to be happily married, in her early 'teens.

At last the tedious arrangements were all made, the farewells, for years or for ever, said. The sensitive and delicate Charles, still everybody's favourite, again lost his mother, and Mrs John Adams, with her daughter and two servants, went on board the ship *Active* on June 20, 1784.

She had told her cousin Isaac, twenty years before, that she longed to see the world. Now her wish was to be granted, with fate's perverseness, at a time when she least desired it. At forty, she saw her children's childhood fast departing, and longed to have round her a united family for at least the holiday seasons of the last precious years.

"Patriotism in the female sex," she had written her husband a year ago,

> is the most disinterested of all virtues—excluded from honours and from offices we cannot attach ourselves to the state or government from having held a place of eminence—even in the freest countrys our property is subject to the control and disposal of our partners, to whom the laws have given sovereign authority—deprived of a voice in legislation, obliged to submit to those laws which are imposed upon us, is it not sufficient to make us indifferent to the public welfare?

Yet that strange passion was in her blood. For its sake she had submitted to a lot the most trying of any to her temperament. "Hope and fear have been the two ruling passions of a large portion of my life, and I have been bandied from one to the other like a tennis ball."[19] Above all she had mourned, "Life is too short to have the dearest of its enjoyments curtailed. The social feelings grow callous by disuse. The blossom falls and the fruit withers and decays. Could we live to the age of antediluvians we might better support this separation. Give me the man I love! I know I have a right to your whole heart, because my own never knew another lord."[20]

Well, that sacrifice at least is over. The dripping anchor is weighed, the sails belly out, dazzling, in the brisk breeze. Soon they have left Boston harbour, with its green fertile islands, they are out in the sea-lane opposite Mount Wollaston. She strains her eyes to see the loved home of her childhood. Good-bye, dear Braintree; good-bye, old duties. As when she was a bride, she is leaving behind the lesser loves to give herself completely to her husband. But self-deception was never one of her gifts, and there is an agony that she can't hide—an eye or a limb lost in battle. Go forward to her new life gallantly as she may, "Who shall give me back time? Who shall compensate to me those years I cannot recall?"[21]

But, ah, what a hideous motion as the dancing ship meets the full roll of the Atlantic.

Mrs Adams went precipitately below.

These were not the days of the fast clipper ships. The boat was a trader of about three hundred tons, with clumsy equipment and the usual large crew to work it. Heavy-laden as she was, she none the less bobbed like a cockle-shell on even a moderate sea. The cargo was oil and potash. The oil leaked, the potash smoked and fermented. "All adds to the *flavour*." The passengers all succumbed to the rolling of the ship.

The ladies slept two by two in little cabins without windows, curtained off from the main cabin. Several of the gentlemen slept in the latter, and it was the lounge and dining-room by day. For the first sixteen days Abigail Adams was unable to undress—or at any rate no more than New England "bundlers," as she said—owing partly to the prostration of seasickness and partly to her exposed situation. Her servants were as sick as herself, and she and her daughter were tenderly cared for by a sailor named Job. John Adams had been perfectly right—a lady was an odious creature at sea; and she was only too thankful he was not with her.

After that, however, she got her sea-legs, struggled up to the deck—assisted by two of the gentlemen—to be bound into her chair and get some fresh air. After that her progress was rapid. Oil and potash could not be helped, but poor housekeeping could. Why put up with bad and irregular meals, dirty decks, and a slovenly steward ("be thankful the pen is not in the hands of Swift or Smollett," she wrote to Mary Cranch). Mrs Adams

> made a bustle among the waiters and demanded a cleaner abode. By this time Briesler was upon his feet, and as I found I might reign mistress on board without any offence, I soon exerted my authority with mops, brushes, infusions of vinegar, etc., and in a few hours you would have thought yourself in a different ship. Since when our abode is much more tolerable, and the gentlemen all thank me for my care.[22]

The captain, too, was grateful. He was, she thought, a good captain, an admirable seaman, kind and humane to his men. There was nothing cross or dictatorial in his manners, yet the men were all "as still and quiet as any private family." As for the passengers, there were six gentlemen and one lady, besides Mrs Adams's party. The other lady was also named Mrs Adams—no relation—a quiet, pretty woman, who politely shared her cabin with Esther so that mother and daughter could be together.

It was a good passage, averaging a hundred miles a day. The *Active* made it in thirty days. But it was tedious. "O dear variety! How pleasing to the human mind is change." Abigail Adams had books and needlework and her neighbours to entertain her, but her best amusement was writing. "Reading tires one; work I do sometimes, but when there is no writing there is less pleasure in working." But, ah me, a ship is little better than a prison! "I cannot find such a fund of entertainment within myself as not to require outward subjects for my amusement. 'Tis a vast tract of ocean we have to traverse." She tried to remind herself that the ocean was a secret world of wonders, but the changeless, round horizon brought yawns. One longed for "the varieties of landscape." Already she was secretly consoling herself with dreams of returning to her native land.

Yet rest and sea-air wrought its magic in the blood. By July 20, when they landed at Deal, her spirit of adventure was fully awake. She had learned all about the rigging. Her pen dripped with nautical terms. "We made land on the 18th," she wrote her sister Mary, "expected to put in at Portsmouth, but a sudden squall and fog prevented, we carry double-reefed topsails only, the captain couldn't leave the deck for forty-eight hours, but suppose there was no danger as we had plenty of sea-room." Then the fog lifted, they saw the cliffs of Dover through driving rain, and the ship anchored in the Downs "and the little town of Deal was before us." Some of the gentlemen, impatient to land, talked of going on shore in the pilot boat, which came out in the morning. There was a high surf, but Mrs Adams, encouraged by the pilots, decided to go with them. Captain Lyde had told her so many dismal stories of coming up the Channel (which would take another week), of the bad weather, cross-tides, and colliers who took pleasure in running foul of other vessels, that Abigail was determined to land if she could. The ladies were wrapped up and lowered from the ship into the boat,

> the whole ship's crew eager to assist us, the gentlemen attentive and kind as though we were all brothers and sisters. We have spent a month together and were as happy as the sea would permit us to be. We

set off from the vessel, now mounting upon the top of a wave as high as a steeple, and then so low that the boat was not to be seen.

One of the gentlemen, braced against the boat, held Mrs Adams firm, and she had both her arms round him. The other ladies were held in the same manner. Every wave gave them a broadside, and finally a wave "landed us with the utmost force broadside upon the beach." The roar of the surf was terrifying, so "out we sprang as fast as possible sinking every step into the sand and looking like a parcel of naiads just rising from the sea." But a warm inn was at hand, with rest, change of clothing, hot tea, every attention. And they engaged carriages for next day, and settled down there for the night; five gentlemen, three ladies, and assorted servants. All, in fact, but Mr Green, the Scotsman, who set off at once for London. "Nobody mourned."[23]

But Mr Green, the unpopular passenger, the pest and bore on board ship, had played a useful part in Mrs Adams's education. He was the first full-blown specimen of a species she was to encounter more of, the snob. She could pin him down and examine him under the magnifying glass of ocean travel, the daily life in the large general cabin, or on the limited deck. "He was always inquiring, 'Who was such a general? What was his origin and rank in life?'" Mrs Adams restrained herself, and only answered mildly that "merit, not birth or title," gave a man eminence in her country. But she finally roused herself, and to the delight of the rest of the company gave the gentleman his deserts once and for all by saying in her gentle voice, with her royal Quincy manner, that "no doubt it was a mortification to the British nobility to find themselves so often conquered by mechanics and mere husbandmen, but that Americans esteemed it their glory to draw such characters not only into the field but into the Senate," and that she believed no one could deny that they had shone in both. That finished Mr Green. "Such men," wrote Mrs Adams to her sister, "have no music in their souls."[24]

At six in the morning the four post-chaises were at the door. The party distributed themselves among them and drove away on the London road. Eighteen miles to Canterbury and breakfast, first stop. Mrs Adams, looking out eagerly as they drove, exclaimed that the country was cultivated like a garden down to the very edge of the road, "and what surprised me was that very little was enclosed within fences. Hedge fences are almost the only kind you see. And the cows and sheep were very large, such as I never saw before." Canterbury proved to be a larger town than Boston. It seemed to contain a number of old Gothic cathedrals which looked to Mrs Adams, gazing at their heavy stone, more like gaols for criminals than places of worship, "as if," she said, "they thought devotion might be stolen."[25] The houses, too, had a "heavy" look with their thatched or tiled roofs.

But the inns filled her with praise. Such efficiency, such food, such service, "with your powdered waiters"; and a fresh carriage ready for you as soon as you had finished your meal. They dined at Chatham and then hurried on their way so as to cross Blackheath before dark. Stories of highwaymen flew about. A man could ride the lonely forests from Boston to Philadelphia and never meet a robber, or think of one, but the great moor was not safe after nightfall in civilized England. As the carriages (two now) drove along at a spanking pace they were passed by a lighter conveyance, a gentleman alone in a chaise. And not long after they came upon the empty chaise and a mail coach stationary upon the highway. An excited group of passengers were crying, "A robbery! a robbery!" The man in the chaise was the person robbed, and this in open day, with carriages constantly passing! Every one in Abigail's party at once took pains to hide his money. Now every place they passed and every person they met was crying out "A robbery! a robbery!" Abigail Adams was surprised, "if the thing was so common, to see such a fuss." The robber was pursued and taken in about two miles, "and we saw the poor wretch, ghastly and horrible, brought along on foot, his horse ridden by the person who took him, who also had his pistol. He looked like a youth of twenty only, attempted to lift his hat and looked despair." Mrs Adams could not help pitying him, especially when she heard them telling him, "Ay! You have but a short time. The assize sits next month, and then my lad you swing."[26] Not that she thought the penalty too severe, it was the bad taste of the taunts. In *her* country they might hang thieves but they did it more kindly! She was already making the inevitable contrast between *Our* country and this, with the scales already loaded in "our" favour.

About eight o'clock in the evening Mrs Adams and her daughter and servants were set down at Low's Hotel in Covent Garden. This was Mr Adams's usual hotel, and here she learned for certain that neither her husband nor her son was in London. But the disappointment was not unexpected, and she was still surrounded with friends. Dr Clark and Mr Spear, fellow-passengers, took lodgings at the same inn, and when they learned that her cousin Will Smith was in town good-natured Mr Spear set out at once in search of him. He had, however, to call first at the customs house, and outside it Will Smith and young Storer were lying in wait to catch new arrivals. Spotting an American* descending from a coach, they pounced on him for news. As soon as they heard of Abigail Adams's arrival they set off at a run, and ran almost the full mile to her lodging. Now she had a real welcome. They told her that her son had waited for her in London a full month, expecting her on another ship, but when that ship came in with letters only, he returned to his father at The Hague. Will Smith had had a letter from *his* father† three days before, informing him of Abigail Adams's passage on the *Active*. He had forwarded it to The Hague at once, and hourly he expected either Mr Adams or Master John.

Meanwhile the two young men took affectionate care of their cousins (Charles Storer was the young son of Mrs Isaac Smith's brother, and the same relation to Abigail that Will Smith was—that is, first cousin) and next morning conducted Mrs Adams and her daughter to the lodgings they had already taken for them at Osborne's, in the Adelphi, "well-situated on the Thames. In sight of the terrace is Westminster Bridge one way and Blackfriars the other." This was where John Adams had stayed most recently, and where John Quincy Adams had awaited her arrival for a month. Abigail and Nabby had a handsome drawing-room and a large bedroom at their private disposal, and they had hardly settled in and looked about them before they were overwhelmed with visitors. The news of their arrival spread, and all the Americans in town flocked to welcome them, Tories or not. Here was old acquaintance from the happy past; a breath of home. "I hardly know how to think myself out of my own country," said Abigail, "I see so many Americans about me."[27]

She had more invitations than she could accept—or wanted to. Young Will Smith and Charles Storer escorted her and Abby everywhere. London was rather like Boston, she thought, but when you started to drive about in it you found its sprawling extent. It was a *monstrous* great city.

* How did they know he was an American? Well, it can still be done!
† Abigail's Uncle Isaac.

They took her to see Mr Copley's pictures, where she saw his full-length portrait of her husband, "very large and a very good likeness." It was owned by Copley. They visited Mrs Wright's Waxworks, and the Foundling Hospital on Sunday. ("Really glad I was that I could, after so long an absence, tread again the courts of the Most High.") The little orphans all in uniform looked very neat, a touching sight. The Magdalen Hospital, again a divine service; she began to think the English more serious and religious than she had thought they were. The Magdalens were behind a screen, which saved them from being stared at. Mrs Adams was even persuaded to go for a walk with young Storer; one could see the effect of the city so much better on foot. But his enthusiasm took her too far. Though "the walking is very easy here, the sides of the street being wholly of flat stones" (not like the Boston cobbles), four miles was too much. "I shall not get the better of it for a week," she laughed ruefully.

It was a glorious holiday, the only one Abigail Adams had had since her marriage. Nothing to do but enjoy every day, and something new every day to enjoy. Even the pageant of the streets held endless variety, and the items of dress, manners, and food. Abigail Adams was surprised to find all three on a lower standard than at home in Boston. Gentlemen seemed to give little attention to dress, and the ladies "much less so than with us." "True you must put a hoop on, and have your hair dressed, but a common straw hat with only a ribbon upon the crown is thought sufficient to go into company." Muslins are the taste. Or if you were very fashionable you might have a dress of the new calico, perhaps blue and white.

English ladies seemed to Abigail Adams to lack the stylish trimness of American ladies, and their manners were "masculine," they despised the softness that was so attractive in females and went in for being "Amazons." She was told that American ladies in London were much admired by the gentlemen, and she confessed you couldn't wonder at it. Having taken up this very natural point of view, based on her first callers, any English lady who did not fit the pattern, being agreeable and well turned out, was classified as not typically English—"she looks like one of us."[28]

As to dinners—why, our country is extravagant, she must confess, compared to this. Smith and Storer regaled her with anecdotes to add to her scanty experience. You would not find at a gentleman's table more than two dishes of meat though invited several days beforehand. She got nothing but "a turbot, a soup, and a roast leg of lamb with cherry pie" at the Atkinsons' dinner party, but it was such a jolly time that she hardly noticed the frugal fare. She really enjoyed it more "than if a sumptuous feast had been set before me."

But the gardens—Kew and Hampton Court and Ranelagh—ah, there the English climate came into its own! They were beyond praise. In the height of summer they were a riot of flowers, a miracle of green. "To walk in some of these places you would think yourself in a land of enchantment."

Full days ensured fatigue, and fatigue should ensure sleep. She summoned the mental picture of the flowers to soothe her in the night watches.

Suspense was the thorn in her roses.

She tried to keep her suspense under control by having worked out the earliest possible day for son or husband to return from The Hague. That would be Friday, July 30. Abigail Adams and Nabby stayed home that day, refusing all engagements. They had not long to bear that unendurable tension. Briesler ran puffing in —"as if he were really interested in the matter."

"Ma'am, young Mr Adams is come!"

"Where, where is he?"

"In the other house, madam. He stopped to get his hair dressed." Considering the journey, and the requirements of powdered hair, he was well justified.

"Impatient enough I was. Yet, when he entered, I drew back. Was this just another fashionable caller? Not really believing my eyes till he cried out, 'Oh, my mamma, and my dear sister!'

"His appearance is that of a man, and in his countenance the most perfect good-humour."[29]

Because he was an easy and well-bred man, there was no constraint, no stiffness in his greeting. At once they were all talking together, trying to bridge the unbridgeable years. It was a big gap, from twelve to seventeen, with not even frequent letters to diminish spiritual distance. But if they could not renew the old contact, they could make a new one, and they made it fast. Fortunately for their happiness there was a kinship of mind between them. And the woman who was a loved and attractive companion to young Will Smith and Charles Storer could also be an attractive companion to young John Quincy Adams.

If Abigail offers one of the most striking examples in history of equal friendship between husband and wife she also presents an outstanding example of friendship between mother and son. As for Abigail Adams junior, John Quincy Adams was better loved by his sister than perhaps any man she ever met. She had not forgotten him, nor he her. "His sister he says he should have known in any part of the world."[30]

He brought messages and letters from his father, whose ardent impatience throbbed in the cold ink. "Your letter has made me the happiest man upon earth. I am twenty years younger than I was yesterday. It is a cruel mortification to me that I cannot go to meet you in London." He urged her to provide such clothes as she needed for herself and daughter—"do what is proper, let the expense be what it may." Above all she must not get overtired. "Every hour to me will be a day, but don't you hurry or disquiet yourself. Be careful of your health." After a few weeks in Holland with him while he winds things up, she will have to set out with him to France, but there are no seas between—a good road, a fine season. He eagerly planned short daily stages, and much sight-seeing on the way. "It is the first time in Europe I looked forward to a journey with pleasure." He looked forward with special delight to showing her Paris, and imagined her enjoyment of it, language and all. (John Adams still suffered the illusion that his wife knew French.) For his own part, he felt himself *made* for the world of Paris. He signed himself, "Yours with more ardour than ever, John Adams."

Yes, that was a letter to comfort and quiet secret heartache; full of meat for reading and rereading. Meanwhile, she had her son to get acquainted with all over again, to take care of her and plan for her, and make the preparations and the journey easy.

She saw at once that young John was executive. It would be ten days, he told her, before they could get off. He was commissioned by his father to buy a carriage, and had various other duties to carry out. But the time would fly. They could fill the days with entertainment and sight-seeing.

Abigail Adams remarked that *she* did not feel twenty years younger, with a grown-up son on one hand and daughter upon the other, "and were I not your mother I would say a likelier pair you will seldom see in a summer's day!" Yet, though the brother and sister were like each other, it took time to get used to young

M

John. "I look upon him scarce recognizing that he belongs to me. Yet I should be very loth anyone else should lay claim to him."[31]

Will Smith sailed for home the day after John Quincy arrived, having admirably filled the interval for his cousins. He carried with him a large batch of letters, especially the shipboard diary which both Abigail Adams and Abby had kept, the one for Mary Cranch, the other for Mary's daughter, Abby's bosom friend Betsy—who had once been John Adams's baby goddaughter.

Well, first Holland and then France it had to be. But Abigail Adams looked forward a bit ruefully. "As you know, I am fond of sociability"; and how was she going to satisfy that "in a country the language of which I am a stranger to"?

They expected to get off for The Hague on August the 8th. On the evening of the seventh John Quincy took his sister to the theatre for a last treat. Abigail chose to stay home alone, in preparation for the journey on the morrow. Suddenly the door opened, and there was her husband.

Sharp joy went through her like a sword. Never afterwards could she speak of that moment. She gave a vivid description of her reunion with her son, but she drew a veil, she could not help it, over her reunion with her husband. Ah, he could not hold himself on the continent of Europe, he could not wait for her to come to him. With a young man's ardour he had hurried to her side the very instant he could drag his business to a conclusion. How different now the morrow's journey looked! It turned into a kind of honeymoon.

So they were together again "after a separation of 4½ years, indeed ten years except for a few visits."[32]

Next day, as planned, the happy party set off together in the sturdy English carriage so well purchased by young John, the servants following in a hired chaise. But the destination had changed. Holland was no longer necessary. John Adams was taking them direct to Dover and Paris.

IX

Abigail in France

Abigail went to England prepared to criticize. She went to France prepared to praise. But there was shock after shock.

When they disembarked at Calais, after twelve hours of misery buffeting about in the narrow seas, the best inn was a wretched affair. And when their stout English carriage was ready to take them on by road, the French postilions presented themselves in rags and huge jack-boots, with a harness for the horses of ropes and chains instead of the shining steel and leather of English harness. Seven clumsy cart-horses took the place of the smart English team of four which had brought them to Dover. Seven horses were none too many for the state of the roads, which under the French system of peasant forced labour were as bad as could be. The landscape through which they lumbered along was depressing. "The villages," wrote young Abby, "are the most wretched of all the habitations of man,"[1] streets narrow and dirty, houses mean and mostly windowless, apparently made of some kind of clay and covered with thatch. Flocks of men, women, and children were at work in the fields, yet the forced serf labour had poor results in agriculture. Crops and animals appeared thin and poor, "nor have they ornamented their fields with the hedge," which made England so pretty.

The manners of postilions, innkeepers, and peasants were a match for the rest of the country. "The English have a sprightliness and alertness, but in the French there is a heaviness, dirtiness, and no elasticity."[2]

The honeycomb of irksome laws which had resulted in these conditions lay behind the scenes, invisible to the passing traveller's eye. But there were out-thrusts of the system which became sharply apparent. "Custom house officers in almost every town demanded a search of your baggage, even though it consisted only of your own private clothes."[3] One found they could be bribed to leave the bags unopened, but it cluttered up movement, and made one long again for the free travel in England.

Even Paris was a disappointment at first. They paused there briefly before going on to Auteuil, and John Adams anxiously urged his obviously unimpressed wife to reserve judgment—she hadn't really *seen* Paris yet! "One thing I know," she said somewhat tartly, "and that is that I have *smelt* it! It is the very dirtiest place I ever saw." Apart from a few of the public buildings, she thought "Boston as superior to Paris as London is to Boston."[4]

John Adams had leased a house at Auteuil, to which he had moved from Paris during a serious illness the year before, and there they went in August 1784. Auteuil was a pretty place, four miles from Paris and one from Passy. It was on the edge of the Bois de Boulogne. This forest, laid out in straight avenues, was ideal for long walks and drives, and John Adams kept them up vigorously.

The house was a stately one, with white stone columns and a beautiful garden. It was fully furnished in the French style, but so large that housekeeping was a heavy task. There were about fifty little rooms upstairs, so small, said Nabby, as to make inconvenient bedrooms.[5] The reception rooms downstairs were spacious, but the French taste was not altogether to their liking. "No carpets" gave a chilly look to the rooms. Some had floors of red tiles and others, including the great salon, had floors of shining parquet. All were cleaned the same way—swept, waxed, and polished. Never scrubbed. "Water is an article very sparingly used in this place."[6] A man called a *frotteur* did the polishing, with brushes fixed to his feet, on which he did a kind of roller-skating,[7] very jauntily, with arms akimbo.

Mrs Adams found that no servant would do any work out of what he considered his province, even if it meant hours of idleness, so that she was forced to keep eight servants, counting coachman and gardener, and even then suffered for want of a ninth. But with the help of Briesler and Esther she managed to keep even French servants up to the mark. And they turned out to be very human. When American Esther fell ill French Pauline nursed her like a sister.

Pauline was the lady's maid. Yes, though one blushed to tell it, one had to have a lady's maid—to dress one's hair. This tedious elaborate hairdressing was an absolute necessity. A lady could go into company scantily washed, and with a dirty chemise and soiled ribbons, Mrs Adams observed, but with undressed hair never! The very servants went to the coiffeur to have their hair dressed and powdered. So Abigail and young Abby shared a lady's maid. John Adams and his son, by the same necessity, shared a *valet de chambre*.

But the garden was her comfort and joy. There were five acres of it, "so sweetly arranged."[8] Near the house were beds laid out in the formal French fashion with a profusion of summer bloom. In the middle of the garden was a fountain with two small stone images. There were rows of orange-trees in tubs, and spacious walks, and grape arbours terminating in green alcoves in which were statues; large china vases dripped with growing flowers, trees were clipped to form arbours to sit in; there was no end to the delights; even the vegetable garden, hidden by a neat fence and a surrounding row of orange-trees, was a pleasure. Every room had a view. Now, in August, the long French windows stood open, and the scents of the garden blew through the house. "This is a beautiful climate, soft, serene and temperate."

As soon as Mrs Adams had got her house in order, she began to go visiting, for it was the etiquette in France for the newcomer to call first. If she had had any illusions about her French she had lost them in the struggle with her servants. To them she must speak willy-nilly, "bad grammar and all!"[9] But it was a different matter with her social equals. "Not speaking the language lays me under embarrassment. To visit a lady merely to bow to her is painful"[10]—especially as the ladies were very voluble and Mrs Adams loved conversation. She struggled with it. She read Voltaire, Racine, Molière, dictionary at elbow, to beguile the tedium while her hair was dressed. In reading French, and understanding it when spoken, she became proficient, but her ability in speaking lagged. However, almost any visits were better than none, and she felt forlorn when winter mud made intercourse with Paris more difficult. But for her garden, she would rather have lived in Paris —the gaiety of Paris gradually magnetized her—but John's health could not stand the smells and lack of hygiene in the city.

No barrier of language prevented her from admiring the cultivated grace of the French ladies. "There is an ease and softness in their manners that is not found in any other country perhaps in the world." And the gentlemen were a fine sight, wearing their swords and carrying their tiny *chapeaux de bras*. But there were some odd points in this society of the "haut monde." There were no general introductions at a party. People seemed to do as they pleased, stroll about the room, speak to this one and that. At dinner, instead of the American arrangement in which the ladies all sat on one side of the table and gentlemen on the other, the ladies and gentlemen were mixed, and you conversed with the one who sat next to you. "Conversation is never general as with us," said Abigail rashly. She was not acquainted with the French salon, where brilliant general conversation was dominated and guided by a woman, and what she heard of Madame de Staël did not move her to admiration. As far as she could make out, the lady had done what no wife should: dimmed the lustre of her husband, and she well deserved the loss of his affection.

On a chilly evening gentlemen tended to stand about round the hearth, and "it shuts out all the fire from the ladies. I know," said Abigail Adams feelingly, "I have suffered from it many times." A curious inconsiderateness among a nation "who really do deserve the appellation of polite." Ladies would sit all night playing cards for high stakes and would then receive company at noon in bed, their hair carefully dressed in high powdered coiffeur, but otherwise in deshabille. These French ladies were obliged to put their daughters into convents to keep them out of bad home influence!

The Marquise de Lafayette, who spoke some English, became her friend; and Mrs Barclay, the American Consul's wife, and the lovely Mrs Bingham. That lady's behaviour was a bit scandalous by Boston standards, but she was very handsome and so lovable one must forgive her. Come to that, Mrs and Miss Adams were often at Passy visiting Franklin and his frequent companion, Madame Helvetius. She was a queer one: rich, a "grande dame" (or so Franklin said), but with wild manners, always shouting and flinging her arms round people. She was slovenly dressed, too—"a chemise made of tiffany over a blue lute-string, which looked as much upon the decay as her beauty," wrote Abigail dryly. "A small straw hat with a dirty gauze half-handkerchief round it, and a bit of dirtier gauze than ever my maids wore was bowed on behind." When her little dog (whom she was kissing almost as often as she kissed Franklin) wet the floor, she wiped it up with her chemise.

Abigail's best friend in France was the high-bred Marquise de Lafayette. The product of an old and fine aristocracy met the New England parson's daughter, and each found in the other a lack of affectation, a love of the real things of life, and that serene simplicity of behaviour which is the cream of good manners.

When the American lady visited the Marquise the pretty pageant of etiquette was laid aside. The Marquise received her in her bedroom, where they could chat over their knitting with Madame de Lafayette's mother and sister, while the two children, Virginia and George Washington, played around them. And when the Marquise came to see her American friend it was with the same pleasant informality: "As we were sitting round the fire the door opened and this lady entered with all the freedom of a familiar friend, how much more agreeable than any other manner possible."

Only once did Abigail Adams see the Paris mob, which, like a clumsy giant roused, was soon to take up the glittering toy of the court and break it in pieces. The occasion was the *Te Deum* in Notre Dame for the birth of a second prince, who seemed to make the succession doubly secure. Madame de Lafayette invited Mrs Adams and her son and daughter to drive with her to the ceremony. Jefferson also drove with them. It was a bright April day, and Paris was at its best. A holiday had been proclaimed, and crowds were in the streets. "I believe I may say with truth there were millions of people," wrote Mrs Adams. And her bright eyes noted another fact, surprising at the time and later full of significance and sullen threat. "There were as many police as there were people."

The mob, apparently gay and good-humoured that day, had peculiar rights, young John Quincy Adams told his mother. It could squeeze in to watch the King have his dinner when he held a routine *couvert-à-roi*. And when the Queen had a baby—well, take this very Duke of Normandy whose birth they were now celebrating; it was lucky for the Queen, said sophisticated John Quincy, that she was taken ill only an hour before her delivery. "For a few minutes before she is delivered, the doors of the apartment are always opened and everybody that pleases is admitted to see the child come into the world, and if there had been time enough all Paris would have gone *pour accoucher la Reine*." Yes, the mob knew its rights, and let none of them grow rusty by disuse. They were the safety-valves to its immense oppression. But the safety-valves were too few and too small, and explosion was very near at hand.

If Mrs Adams was tempted to think she had been transformed by fairy spells into a princess, she was quickly weaned from her enchantment by the familiar, gruelling worry about money. Expenses were like weeds in a garden too large for the gardener. Watch and keep them down all she could, they would mount. "Mr Jay went home because he could not support his family here with the whole salary. What then can be done, curtailed as it now is?"[11]

Congress had just docked five hundred dollars from Mr Adams's pay. Well, Congress was hard up and in a spasm of frantic economy; but they docked without a due perspective on expenses of Ministers abroad, and they did it to a man who had just almost killed himself by a hideous winter journey,* in ill-health, raising a large loan for them in Holland.

Mr Adams alone among the Ministers then abroad was without private means, and lack of funds seriously curtailed the natural social instincts of himself and his wife during their time in France. They had to reduce entertaining to a minimum, when the dinners they did give cost them fifty or sixty guineas at a time. Yet, as Mrs Adams said, "More is to be performed by way of negotiation many times at one of these entertainments than at twenty serious conversations." She called the policy of her Government "penny wise and pound foolish." And the very man who was so forced to pinch was the man, as she justly observed, who had been the means "in great measure of procuring such extensive territories to his country and saved their fisheries."†

The social obligations of rank multiplied. A dinner once a week was a necessary minimum. "As your uncle had been invited to dine at the tables of many of the foreign ministers it became necessary to return the civility." Fifteen or twenty persons was the average for these formal dinners. They had lustre. The Swedish Ambassador, Baron de Staël, was a favourite from the first. He was tall and graceful, a very handsome man and much attracted by Miss Adams. He managed to talk to her in French, and complimented her to her brother, saying that one could not find in France a complexion

* For description, see John Adams's account in his journal, *Works*, I, pp. 408–412. The company and help of his son probably saved his life.

† By his clauses in the Peace Treaty relative to boundaries and fisheries.

to equal hers. Blanchard, who flew the Channel in a balloon on a crisp January day, was fêted by every one. He and his flight companion, Dr Jefferies, had come on to Paris to enjoy their glory. After that letters from John and Abigail wishing that friends in America could join them no longer said "if I had wings," but "if I had a balloon to bring you."[12]

Every American who passed through Paris came out to pay his respects. Frenchmen, Spaniards, Hollanders might turn up with letters of introduction which must be honoured. Dr Franklin would drive over for dinner, though oftener to tea, with Madame Helvetius* or Madame Hewston. Mr Jefferson was like one of the family.

The theatre and the ballet had put their spells on Abigail. As for the opera ballet! "The first dance which I saw upon the stage shocked me. The dresses and beauty of the performers were enchanting; but no sooner did the dance commence than I felt my delicacy wounded and I was ashamed to be seen to look at them. Girls clothed in the thinnest silk and gauze, with their petticoats short, springing two feet from the floor, poising themselves in the air with their feet flying and as perfectly showing their garters and drawers as if no petticoats had been worn, was a sight altogether new to me." But shock passed into delight. "Their motions are as light as air, and as quick as lightning. They balance themselves to astonishment. No description can equal the reality. They are trained to it from early infancy at a royal academy instituted for this purpose. You will very often see little creatures not more than seven or eight years old, as undauntedly performing their parts as the eldest among them."[13]

Yet she admits moral objections, "the tendency of these things, the passions they must excite. . . ." And the girls, fairies in their fairy world, hadn't a chance in real life. "As soon as a girl sets her foot upon the floor of the opera, she is excommunicated by the Church, and denied burial in holy ground. She conceives nothing worse can happen to her. All restraint is thrown off and she delivers herself to the first who bids high enough for her."

Such girls are a danger to young men in a monogamous society. And a young man the dearest in the world to Abigail Adams was observing them with a lively eye. But off the stage they were invisible to John Quincy. He left no part of his heart in France.

· · ·

* The house of Madame Helvetius was at Auteuil. A. A. says "she is my near neighbour."

John Quincy Adams was working hard at his Latin in preparation for Harvard. Yet he dreaded the wrench of parting again, and he foresaw clearly the irksomeness of tutelage. "After having been travelling for these seven years almost all over Europe, and having been in the world and among company for three, to return to spend one or two years in the pale of a college, subjected to all the rules which I have so long been freed from: then to plunge into the dry and tedious study of the law for three years . . . it is really a prospect somewhat discouraging for a youth of my ambition. But still I am determined that so long as I shall be able to get my living in an honourable manner I will depend upon no one . . . which I shall never be able to do if I loiter away my precious time in Europe and shun going home until I am forced to it." He never regretted this iron decision. At the age of seventy-seven, looking backward at his youth, he wrote in his Journal: "It is almost surprising to me now that I escaped from the fascination of Europe's attractions. My return home from Auteuil decided the fate and fortunes of my after-life. It was my own choice and the most judicious I ever made."

His mother's influence had coloured his thought. With that unswerving strength and objectivity which made her private wishes nothing against a son's or a husband's welfare, she had made him see things plain. "I feel very loth to part with my son," she wrote,

> I shall miss him more than I can express, but I am convinced that it will be very much to his advantage to spend one year at Harvard. . . . He will find there companions and associates. Besides, America is the theatre for a young fellow who has any ambition to distinguish himself. So that if his father consents, I think it not unlikely that you will see him in the course of next summer.

There is also the all-important American girl. The mother is looking forward to a suitable wife. It's only teasing, but . . .

> Where is Miss Nancy Quincy? Well, I hope. We often laugh at your cousin John about her. He says her stature would be a great recommendation to him, as he is determined never to marry a tall woman, lest her height should give her a superiority over him. He is generally thought older than your cousin Nabby; and partly I believe because his company is with those much older than himself.[14]

John Quincy Adams had been driven by circumstances into an early maturity, but he had much of his father's warmth and of his mother's charm—"A great flow of spirits and quick passions."[15] Yet with a more austere behaviour than his father had been able to boast at his age, he was learning of woman from his mother and his sister. For exercise he took his sister to walk in the Bois. For amusement he took her to the opera and theatre in Paris. No other young lady was in his eye.

Young Miss Adams, suffering from the dying love-affair with the inconstant Tyler,* and from the anticipation of a new separation from her beloved brother, was said by French society to be handsome but *triste*. But Madame de Lafayette said, no, not *triste* but *grave*. This comforted Nabby, who knew that by *triste* the French meant mopy.

In fact Miss Adams aroused a lot of admiration for her fine figure and clear, bright complexion, in which Jefferson liked to see the ready blushes come and go. And she naturally enjoyed admiration, Mr Jefferson's particularly. Although Jefferson had followed the fashion in placing his own daughter in a convent school, which was very contrary to Boston standards, he was so dear to the whole Adams circle that he could do no wrong. When the Marquis de Lafayette arrived in January with the news of the death of one of the two younger daughters whom Jefferson had left behind in America all the Adamses felt it like a death in the family. Jefferson's habitual depression sank into a low melancholy. Mrs Adams's motherly cheer, and Miss Adams's grave and quiet solicitude, were very soothing.

Meanwhile, during the winter of '84 '85, John Adams remained the chief and, for weeks at a time, the only conductor of American diplomatic business with the French Court. Franklin's infirmities kept him immobile, and Jefferson was constantly ill. But the business was straightforward and uncomplicated.† Mr Adams and de Vergennes, having long taken each other's measure, worked together harmoniously, and a serene content possessed John Adams's mind. Now, instead of solitary lodgings, he had a beautiful and well-ordered home to return to, warmed by the lively presence of his wife and of a son and daughter who gave him every satisfaction a father could have.

* At least letters from the Cranch cousins so reported him, and his own letters were infrequent and unsatisfactory. Probably hers were more so.

† Chiefly regarding the Barbary pirates and the vexed questions of tribute to the Emperor of Morocco, to prevent piracy on the high seas. One of the chief uses of the British Navy had been to police the seas, but the war situation had kept it busy with French and American ships.

Yes, during those months at Auteuil the happiness of all of them was all but complete. As complete as mortals mostly know. A time to look back on as under a charm.

It rushed to a close. On May 4, 1785, letters arrived from America bearing a commission from Congress which appointed John Adams the first American Ambassador at the Court of St James's. It was a climax neither unforeseen nor yet quite expected. Farewell, then, to Auteuil, and to all the foreign things and people which had become so familiar and even liked. Farewell to the cold mirrored rooms and the tiled floors; farewell to Pauline, now so well trained, and to the statues and the pet bird. "Delightful and blooming garden," sighed Abigail, "how much shall I regret your loss. The fishpond and the fountain are just put in order; the trees are in blossom, the flowers are coming on . . . and the forest-trees, several beautiful rows of which form arched bowers at the bottom of our garden! It will not be easy to find in the midst of a city so charming a scene."[16]

And she will miss her friend the Marquise. And there's Jefferson. Yes, almost most of all, "I shall really regret to leave Mr Jefferson. He is one of the choice ones of the earth."[17] But emotion lost its breath and was drowned in a tidal wave of packing and preparations. "May 10th. My son takes his departure for America tomorrow morning, and we go next week to England."[18]

X

Ambassador's Wife in London

"You will be well stared at!" said the Duke of Dorset, the friendly British Ambassador in France.

But their sanguine temperaments could already foresee compensations in their bed of thorns. Back they went from ill-kept France to well-kept England, from a sullen peasantry to a cheerful one, from customs barriers in every town to untrammelled movement—except indeed for thieves on lonely stretches of highway. Above all, rejoiced Abigail Adams, from a country in which talking was so difficult to "a country the language of which I shall be able to speak without an interpreter—or so much twisting and twirling of my tongue, and then pronouncing badly at last!"[1]

The drive up the Dover Road to London had a home-coming feeling, and it was in good spirits and good-humour that they prepared themselves for the ordeal of presentation at court.

Foreign ministers, according to custom, were presented in a private audience with the King. Four days after arrival, therefore, on Wednesday, June 1, John Adams, standing in the King's antechamber at St James's Palace, found that Dorset's words had expressed an exact truth. The room was very full. His escort, the Foreign Secretary, Lord Carmarthen, had gone in to announce his arrival to the King, and the American, first official representative of the seceded colonies, became the inevitable centre of haughty curiosity and attention. He stood it with sturdy dignity. But before he could feel uncomfortably embarrassed, the Ambassadors from Sweden and Holland came up together and engaged him in conversation. Some English noblemen whom he had met before joined the group. Thanks to these gentlemen, John Adams went on into the King's closet warmed and eased. The moment could be freed for the great emotions which alone rightly belonged to it.

The inhibitions of false shame, the frozen voice of shyness, the truculent self-assertion which is the visible top of the iceberg of self-distrust, were absent. John Adams was himself.

Now at last the Atlas of the American Revolution, whose powerful emotion, marshalled argument, and extraordinary command of language had literally lifted the members from their seats time and again in the Revolution Congress, stood face to face, as symbol of his people, with the King who had for long been symbol of their oppression. John Adams's magnetic power, his dignity, his feeling, were turned full on to that one man, the King. No wonder that under that great electric discharge the King became greater than himself.

Mulling it over afterwards with Abigail, savouring the full flavour of that meeting, it seemed to John most amazing of all that the King had behaved so well.

John Adams addressed George III in words which he had carefully prepared. "The appointment of a Minister from the United States to your Majesty's Court will form an epoch in the history of England and America. I think myself more fortunate than all my fellow-subjects in having the distinguished honour to be the first to stand in your Majesty's royal presence in a diplomatic character. I shall esteem myself the happiest of men if I can be instrumental in recommending my country more and more to your Majesty's royal benevolence, and of restoring an entire esteem, confidence, and affection, or in better words, the old good-nature and the old good-humour, between people who, though separated by an ocean, and under different governments, have the same language, a similar religion, and kindred blood.[2] . . .

"The King listened to every word I said with dignity, but with obvious emotion," said John Adams. "I felt more than I could express. Whether it was my visible agitation that touched him, or whether it was the nature of the interview, I cannot say. But he was much affected. Presently he answered me with more tremor than I had spoken with, and said—'Sir, the circumstances of this audience are so extraordinary, the language you have just used is so extremely proper—your feelings so justly adapted to the occasion—that I must say I not only receive with pleasure the assurance of the friendly disposition of the United States, but that I am very glad the choice has fallen upon you to be their minister. I wish you, sir, to believe—and I wish it to be understood in America—that

I have done nothing in the late contest but what I thought myself indispensably bound to do by the duty which I owed to my people. I will be very frank with you. I was the last to consent to the separation. But the separation having been made, and having become inevitable, I have always said, as I say now, that I would be the first to meet the friendship of the United States as an independent power. The moment I see such sentiments and language as yours prevail, and a disposition to give this country the preference, that moment I shall say—let the circumstances of language, religion and blood have their natural and full effect.' These were the King's exact words as nearly as I can remember them."

"He talks of blood and language," said Abigail, "but he's a German. Did he speak with a thick German accent?"

"No. His pronunciation is as distinct as ever I heard. Emotion made him speak slowly, and he hesitated some time between his periods. I was no less moved than he. When he had done, we waited to recollect ourselves. Then the King asked me if I came last from France, and when I said I did then he put on a change of manner and an air of familiarity and jest, and said—'There's an opinion among some people that you are not the most attached of all your countrymen to the manners of France!' I didn't quite like it!" said John Adams to Abigail. "Between ourselves, I thought it an indiscretion. It was out of keeping with the dignity of the rest. I was a little embarrassed. Trying to reply in a light enough tone to match his, I none the less said, 'That opinion, Sir, is not mistaken. I must avow to your Majesty that I have no attachment but to my own country.' The King replied as quick as lightning, 'An honest man will never have any other!'"[3]

The King then murmured a word or two to the Secretary of State, and bowed dismissal. Mr Adams retreated backward according to etiquette, and went his way.

The Master of Ceremonies joined him as he issued from the door of the King's closet, and escorted him through the crowded apartments to his carriage, servants roaring out before them "like thunder," "Mr Adams's servants! Mr Adams's carriage!"

The great hour had come and gone, and was folded up into time past. But it had not been inauspicious.

Three days later John Adams very much enjoyed his first full day at court, at the King's Birthday Levee, June 4. At that levee it was the King's custom to speak first to the foreign ministers, and he had made himself not only pleasant but human. "My father observed," said Nabby, "that he had never heard anything like conversation at Court before. One of the Ambassadors who had attended at the French Court for thirty years said Monsieur the King's brother had asked every time he had been to Court, which was generally every Tuesday, 'Have you come from Paris to-day?' and no other question. But George III conversed a quarter of an hour with the Spanish Minister upon music, of which he said he was passionately fond, especially Handel's music. He respected the memory of Handel, for he owed to him the greatest happiness of his life, and observed that Handel had said of him when young, 'that young man will preserve my music.'"[4]

There was every reason to reflect with a certain deep satisfaction on the parting compliment of the Count de Vergennes when Mr Adams took leave at Versailles: "It is a great thing to be the first ambassador from your country to the country you spring from! It is a mark!"[5]

On June 9 John Adams was presented in private audience to the Queen, and made her a noble speech, recommending to her attention "a rising empire and an infant virgin world. Another Europe, madam, is rising in America. . . . It will in future ages be the glory of these kingdoms to have peopled that country." He begged her indulgence to "a person who is indeed unqualified for courts and who owes his elevation to the distinguished honour of standing before your Majesty, not to any circumstances of illustrious birth, fortune or abilities, but merely to an ardent devotion to his native country, and some little industry and perseverance in her service."[6]

But the Queen of England was no Abigail Adams. Neither her mastery of the English language nor her mental equipment was equal to comprehending Mr Adams's majestic periods. She replied with the formula she had learned by rote for all foreign ambassadors. "Sir, I thank you for your civility to me and my family, and I am glad to see you in this country." Then she "very politely" inquired whether he had got a house yet. John Adams might have replied that that was a matter he was leaving to his wife.

Two days later it was Abigail's turn to be stared at, not in private presentation, but when the Queen held a Circle. That happened on Thursdays. "Last Thursday Colonel Smith was presented at Court," she wrote to her sister, "and to-morrow my ladyship and your niece make our compliments. There is no other presentation in Europe in which I shall feel so much as in this."

The Queen's drawing-room really was a circle. The day Abigail went two hundred people, ladies and gentlemen, were arranged around the walls of a large reception room in St James's Palace. There was no order of precedence, people stood as they came. At two o'clock a bugle announced the approach of royalty, and the King and Queen and their entourage entered the door. At the door they divided, the King and his gentlemen going round the room to the right, and the Queen and her ladies going round to the left. "Only think of the task!" said Abigail with sympathy, "the royal family have to go round to every person, and find small talk enough to speak to all of them!" She noticed that they very prudently spoke in a whisper, so that "only the person next you can hear what is said." But the effect of this slow, whispering progress was anything but lively. Who spoke of the gaiety of courts? The only entertainment to be found was watching the main actors as they came round, and—if a court habitué—the comparative length and graciousness of their pauses. "The King is a personable man," said Abigail, although she did not like the effect of his red face and white eyebrows. George III was this year forty-seven years old, three years younger than John Adams.

Mrs Adams came off very well. When the King got to her, Lord Onslow, the gentleman-in-waiting, presented her, saying simply, "Mrs Adams." "Upon which I drew off my right-hand glove, and his Majesty saluted my left cheek. He then asked me if I had taken a walk to-day. I could have told His Majesty," remarked Mrs Adams, "that I had been all the morning preparing to wait upon him; but I replied, 'No, Sire.' The answer seemed to surprise the King, 'Why, don't you love walking?' says he. I answered that I was rather indolent in that respect. He then bowed and passed on." More than two hours after this it came to her turn to be presented to the Queen. Standing in silent tedium and increasing fatigue on aching feet, Mrs Adams had long exhausted every detail of the Queen's appearance. Her dress was purple and silver. She resembled the King in having a red face and light eyebrows, but "she is not well-shaped nor handsome." Charlotte was in fact a dumpy figure, made worse by excessive childbearing. She had at this time borne fourteen of her ultimate fifteen children. Even royal-portrait painters, Benjamin West for one, trying their best to flatter, could not disguise her wide, frog-like mouth, though they did refine her pug-nose out of knowledge. Perhaps there was something in Mrs Adams's appraising gaze which was uncourtier-like. Perhaps Charlotte was uncomfortably conscious of being looked at as a woman rather than a queen. Or perhaps—product as she was of an insignificant German court—her snobbishness resented having to receive among duchesses the daughter of a mere "dissenting parson." Whatever it was, the two women disliked each other at sight. "The Queen was evidently embarrassed when I was presented to her. I had disagreeable feelings too. She however said, 'Mrs Adams, have you got into your house? Pray, how do you like the situation?'"[7] As far as we know, her duty thus accomplished, the Queen never spoke to Mrs Adams again.

"The drawing-room at St James's!" exclaimed Mrs Adams in an exasperated moment. "Never again would I set my foot there if the etiquette of my country did not require it! I know I am looked down on with a sovereign pride. The smile of royalty is bestowed as a mighty boon. As such, however, I cannot receive it. I know it is due to my country, and I consider myself as complimenting the power before which I appear as much as I am complimented by being noticed by it."[8]

And at a later day, when England was in imminent danger of invasion by Napoleon, Mrs Adams, though warmly for England, reflected that there would be one compensation in England's disaster. It would bring the Queen down to the dust. "Humiliation for Charlotte is no sorrow for me. She richly deserves her full portion for the contempt and scorn which she took pains to discover."

Others, however, were more pleasant. Mrs Adams liked the Princesses. Even at the presentation circle, the Princess Royal and Princess Augusta, who followed behind their mother, dressed in black and silver, paused to speak to the attractive American ladies with real friendliness. The Princess Royal, who was probably tired to death herself—not only of that particular circle, but of the whole tiresome routine of her life—"looked compassionate, and asked me if I was not much fatigued, and observed that it was a very full Drawing-room." The Prince of Wales, seen at later drawing-rooms, was admired by the American ladies as a handsome man, if, Mrs Adams modified, he had not sacrificed so much to Bacchus! The Prince's manners were graceful and ingratiating, and he took pains to pay due attention to the foreign ministers and their appendages. But he did not think it his duty to speak to every one in the room. He followed his pleasure. Nabby got fun out of the dullness of one drawing-room watching the vain efforts of a lady near her, "Lady C," who made herself conspicuous by extreme anxiety to have her daughter spoken to by the Prince. It was no good. The Prince stood and conversed an hour next to her with the lovely and well-bred Lady Stormont,* but walked away at last serenely blind to the existence of Miss C. Of such small poisoned darts were the tragedies of court life made. Abigail despised it from beginning to end. "I own I never felt myself in a more contemptible situation than when I stood four hours together for a gracious smile from majesty, a witness to the anxious solicitude of those around me for the same . . . I however had a more dignified honour for his Majesty *deigned to salute me*."[9]

The King's compliment was partly one to her appearance. Mrs Adams in her wide-hooped white gown with lilac bows could bear being stared at. Her mirror had assured her of it. "My head is dressed for St James's and it looks, in my opinion, very tasty."[10] But an independent and sympathetic witness was alongside, a young American, former aide to Washington, named Colonel William Smith (no relation). "Mrs Adams and Miss were presented at Court this day and behaved to a charm," he wrote back to America.

> Mr Adams fully answers your and Mr Jay's account of him. The ladies of his family do honour to this country. . . . I attended them to the Queen's Drawing-Room and free from partiality assert that they were fully equal to any there. As for the young lady—she is more than painters can express or youthful poets fancy when they love.[11]

Abigail Adams might have answered the Queen—probably did—that she had found a house, and that she did indeed like the situation of it. It was in Grosvenor Square, "one of the finest squares in London." At Auteuil they had the Bois; here they had Hyde Park—which they thought resembled Boston Common, only larger, with more trees about. It would be very nice and handy for walking or, preferably, driving. And when they drove farther afield, there were fresh delights. The flowery pageant of

* Wife of Lord Stormont.

England in summer overwhelmed sight and scent. "All the villages that I have seen round London are just gardens!"[12] Not only was it beyond compare lovelier than France, but even America—even Braintree—had to take a back seat. "But give us time!"

Most of the gentry had retired to their country seats for the hot weather, and, fashionably speaking, London was now a desert. The King and Queen were at Kew, or Windsor, whence they came in to St James's every fortnight for levees or drawing-rooms. Most of these affairs were very thinly attended during the summer, but the King seemed unable to disentangle himself from the habit. Sometimes the royal family could be encountered riding in the Park with retinue—the King in his Windsor uniform of blue and gold, the Queen in black hat and cloak, the Princess Royal, Princess Augusta, Princess Elizabeth, Princess Mary, Princess Sophia, all on horseback in white muslin polonaises and white chip hats with white feathers, all flowing, floating, blowing—surely their magical appearance expressed a temporary happiness!

But, however bravely they might ride by, back in the seclusion of their dull palace life they were not a happy family. Abigail was called on by the foreign Ministers and their ladies, by the Countess of Effingham, one of the Queen's ladies, by Miss this and Lady that, and soon learned the current talk. The Prince of Wales was dissipated. Reckless extravagance. Debts. The King behaved harshly. And the Prince, even before he was twenty-one, had publicly appeared in the Opposition. The Prince said his father had hated him ever since he was seven years old.[13] The Princesses thought their mother hated them.

George III would have been shocked at the charge that he hated his son, or that he and the Queen were dominating their children, taking the life out of them. Why, he loved children, all and any children! And indeed it was a charming sight at the Children's Ball at Buckingham Palace to see the King fussing over his little guests—charmed with their dancing—warning them against chilling their little stomachs with cold drinks. . . .

Yes, it was not until the Prince was seven years old that he had noticed a horrid change in his father's feeling. Not until he grew up that he named it. Domestic miseries such as these soured Charlotte's expression and coarsened her manners to those whom she had no reason to conciliate. This Queen, knowing so well what pregnancy meant, could keep Mrs Siddons standing to read a play, when far gone with child, until she fainted, sooner than allow an actress to be seated in her royal presence.

Mrs Siddons was pregnant when Abigail first saw her act. This prevented her from "exerting that force of passion and energy of action which have rendered her so justly celebrated," but she had contrived her dress very neatly to disguise her situation, and "chose only those tragedies where little exertion was necessary such as Shakespeare's *Othello*." Although already the mother of several children, Mrs Siddons did not look more than twenty-five. Tall, commanding, majestic, she was supreme in tragedy. Her greatest part by public acclaim was Lady Macbeth. But Shakespeare, brought to overpowering life by the genius of Mrs Siddons, was rather a dose. "Much of Shakespeare's language is so uncouth that it sounds rash," Abigail confided to her sisters. "He has beauties which are not equalled. But I should suppose that they might be rendered much more agreeable for the stage by alterations. I saw Mrs Siddons a few evenings ago in *Macbeth*, a play, you recollect, full of horror. She supported her part with great propriety, but she is too great to be put in so detestable a character."[14] Abigail Adams preferred her as Matilda in *The Carmelite*, and looked forward to seeing her in "her most pathetic characters in *Venice Preserved* and *The Fatal Marriage*."

The second of the great Handel festivals instituted annually by the King took place soon after the Adamses' arrival in June, before the summer migration of society.

"The most powerful effect of music I ever experienced," said Mrs Adams, "was at Westminster Abbey, the celebration of Handel's music . . . five days set apart for the different performances. I was at the piece called *The Messiah*. When it came to that part the Hallelujah, the whole audience rose and all the musicians, every person uncovered. . . . I could scarcely believe myself an inhabitant of earth. I was one continued shudder from the beginning to the end of the performance."[15]

With society again in full swing, Mrs Adams found herself saddled with the difficult job of maintaining the dignity of the new American embassy on insufficient funds. And she succeeded in doing it. Her first dinner, a *sine qua non* to the Diplomatic Corps, was graced by a timely present from an American captain of a gigantic turtle, considered a great luxury, which provided an ample and thoroughly American repast. Mrs Adams's standards of a good dinner were far from stingy. And her occasional at-home days, on the London pattern, were conducted with quiet elegance. Mrs Adams, however, despised the London pattern.

Almost everybody held receiving days and routs, some on the weekly at-home day, some by special invitation for an evening. "Card-tables were the chief occupation." It bored Abigail Adams. Rooms were so crowded that not half the company could sit at once. The only agreeable thing, she thought, was that you might go away when you chose without disturbing anybody. You might not start conversation with anyone, even if you met them three times a week, without being specially introduced. "Yet this," said Abigail, fresh from conversable France, "is called *society* and *polite life*!"[16]

"I was at a stupid rout at the Swedish Minister's last evening," she described to her sister, "got home about twelve. There were about two hundred persons. Three large rooms full of card-tables. The moment the ceremony of courtseying is past the lady of the house asks you, 'Pray, what is your game? Whist, cribbage, or commerce?'—and then to hunt a set! The lady and her daughter last evening were almost fatigued to death . . . toiling at pleasure for seven hours, in which time they scarcely sat down. I went with a determination not to play but could not get off. So I was set down to a table with three perfect strangers, and the lady against me stated the game at half-a-guinea apiece. I thought it full high; but I knew she designed to win so I said no more, but expected to lose. It happened otherwise however," said Mrs Adams with dry satisfaction; "I won four games of her. Luck rather than skill, though I have usually been fortunate."

A ball at the French Ambassador's was more fun, more the kind of real gaiety Mrs Adams would have liked to provide, though her good taste warned her that such display would have been out of key for the representatives of a new country—and a democracy at that—even if they could have afforded it. This Ambassador, Abigail observed, had twenty thousand guineas allowed him to furnish his house, and an annual salary of ten thousand more. With such resources he could attract the very cream of smart society. "The Prince of Wales came about eleven o'clock. Mrs Fitzherbert was also present. She appears with him in all public parties, and he avows his marriage wherever he dares." The light from the lustres was more favourable to beauty than daylight, and the dresses were much prettier than the huge-hooped regulation court dress which took up such a lot of room in dancing. Here one small hoop was all, or even no hoops. And "the prettiest girls in England" looked like Dresden china shepherdesses come to life, hats and all. Abigail's prevailing colour this time was sapphire blue, Nabby's was rose pink. But poor Nabby had the London cold, and couldn't have any fun, so her mother—who was enjoying herself immensely—had to take her away at one o'clock and miss supper.

Was Nabby's heart really broken by an inconstant lover? Would she return anon to Boston and marry him, and find him—God forbid—inconstant still? Stately and handsome, more like a princess than the King's dumpy daughters, she moved through the minuets and the country dances, indifferent to her partners and surroundings.

Seeing Mrs Fitzherbert was the high point of the evening. "It seems this amorous Prince," Abigail Adams eagerly narrated to Mary, "has been for two years violently in love with a widow lady near forty years of age. As she is said to be a lady of virtuous character she avoided him . . . and finding that he could not bring her to his terms, it is said and believed, that he has married the lady. . . . She now appears with him at the opera, rides in his carriage with her servants behind it. He is three times a day at her house. . . . In the eye of heaven the marriage may be valid, but the law of the land annuls it, she can never be Queen or the children legitimate. . . . They say his toast is 'fat, fair and forty'!"[17]

The rumour of this secret marriage had just got about, and Abigail Adams, after a visit to Court, noted gleefully, "The Royal family appeared much out of spirits yesterday; . . . the nation are all in a ferment, though they hardly dare speak loud."[18]

When in April a new play, *The School for Scandal*, appeared at Covent Garden Theatre, Mrs Adams remarked that "tho it is one of the best modern plays that has appeared upon the stage," the title was really almost too appropriate. "Scandal is the forte of this nation, and a school in which they have arrived at great experience, that and lying make the greater part of their daily publications, as their numerous Gazettes fully testify!"[19]

Mrs Adams was not merely referring to society gossip, but to the more dangerous and more personal scandal which daily attacked her husband and her country.

Underneath the glittering surface of society's correct behaviour to the American Minister and his wife, strong anti-American currents were flowing. All the soreness of a proud country defeated was in them. More dangerous still was the determination of a certain section of the public not to accept the defeat. Both feelings were heated up and fanned on by the refugees from America—the Tories, as Abigail continued to call them—who had confidently expected to go home again in triumph. These people, who included old friends and connexions like Jonathan Sewall, bitterly resented the creation of an American legation. They hoped the American Minister would not be received at Court, or, if received, at least on some less honourable footing than that of a "real" foreign Power. And the full honours accorded John Adams caused the refugees at once to "spit forth their venom," as Abigail made no bones about expressing it. The news-sheets of an exceedingly scurrilous period continued to pour forth attack after attack. Mrs Adams shared to the full her husband's difficulties, and understood them well.

Mr Adams's task was twofold. One part of it was to obtain a treaty of commerce with Great Britain, in conjunction with Mr Jefferson (the new Minister at Versailles). The second, and more delicate negotiation, was to obtain the implementing of the peace treaty. "The civil and polite reception given to the American Minister and his family from the Court does not ensure to America justice in other respects," Abigail wrote to her Uncle Isaac.[20] And to her sister she explained clearly: "The immense debt, due from the mercantile part of America to this country sours this people beyond measure, and greatly distresses thousands who never were nor ever will be politicians—the manufacturers who supplied the merchants. I think our countrymen greatly to blame. . . . It makes the path very difficult for negotiation.[21] The Marquis of Carmarthen and Mr Pitt appear to possess the most liberal ideas with respect to us of any part of the ministry."

Progress was extremely slow, but not all their business was abortive. The Ambassador from Portugal was already a friend of Mr Adams, and had been closeted with him frequently to some purpose. Abigail wrote to her son John Quincy:

> Your sister has written you so many pages that I suppose she has not left me anything to write to you, but as I am very rarely honoured with a sight of any of them I shall venture to inform you that Mr Jefferson is here from Paris and that the Treaty with Portugal will be completed in a few days.[22]

After a stay of seven weeks, enjoyed in spite of his dislike for the Court,* Mr Jefferson returned to Paris, to his house on the Champs-Elysées, his daughter in her aristocratic convent, his debt-ridden grandeur, and Monsieur de Vergennes's insinuating "but."

Mrs Adams was getting a good stiff training as a public character. Certainly she had read attacks on her husband before. There had been plenty in America, but then she herself had been living a retired and private life. She had not had to go to a party or royal drawing-room or fashionable rout and know that every one there had just read the paper that morning, and that the sizzling criticism was very likely present in the mind of her neighbour.

But if Grandmother Quincy's training had given her a fine start in social poise and correct behaviour, and Boston society provided good practice, France had furnished a superlative finishing course.

Fulfilling her duties as ambassador's wife, Mrs Adams presented several American ladies at court, among them the magnificent Mrs Bingham, "and I own I felt not a little proud of her." She had got her dress in Paris, and her loveliness was really stunning. "The various whispers which I heard around me, and the pressing of the ladies to get a sight of her, must have added an atom to the old score, for [the Queen] could not but see how attractive she was. 'Is she an American, is she an American?' buzzed everywhere. 'You have,' said an English lord to me, 'one of the finest ladies to present that I ever saw.'" And, again, there was the lovely Miss Hamilton of Philadelphia, "an heiress, with sweet and modest manners." "The Emperor's Ambassador whispered your Pappa, 'Sir, your country produces exceeding fine women!'"[23]

Indeed, Mr Jefferson's presentation was the only failure. One might compare English and French manners, as he did, to the disadvantage of the English. Yet, Abigail Adams confessed to Aunt Elizabeth, "on many accounts I like this Country best and have in my heart a greater fondness for it."[24] That is the statement of a happy and confident woman, one who found herself in command of the situation, neither uneasy nor at a loss. And she gave her husband, in Grosvenor Square as in Boston, the continual refreshment of a happy home.

Abigail's children were a great source of her happiness. The two eldest seemed perfection itself, and their uncommon devotion to

* When John Adams presented Jefferson to George III, there was mutual dislike on sight, which the King displayed.

each other was one of their charms. The brother and sister exchanged a regular journal of their thoughts and doings. John Quincy was absorbed in his readjustment to American ways in the simple household of Uncle and Aunt Shaw at Haverhill, where he was tutoring for Harvard under Uncle Shaw, and making reacquaintance with his brothers and cousins. Bent on doing a year's study in a few months, he had no time for his father's old pastime of gallanting the girls.

Nabby's many, many pages contained painfully intellectual comment on the passing scene, the ridiculous habits of courts, and the elaborate elegance of English country houses, her own activities of various kinds, the compliments of Mr Jefferson; but hints of something else crept in more and more frequently between the lines.

The hour soon came when some subtle thawing in Miss Adams's manner gave Colonel Smith a welcome signal; he made some direct questions and received satisfactory answers. "I perceived all at once upon a day," wrote Abigail to her son, "a dejection dispelled, a brightness of countenance and a lightness of heart" in your sister, "and in the evening a gentleman asked permission to attend us to the theatre." The request was in itself a declaration of successful suit, and when they returned late the Colonel placed in Mrs Adams's hands, "with much emotion," a bunch of testimonials to himself as to character, courage, and so on, obtained from the generals under whom he had served—documents which the Colonel repeatedly relied on through life with naïve and unshaken faith to get him out of scrapes or to make his fortune. In this case they were to be presented to John Adams in lieu of statements of income, real estate, and expectations.

The engagement was cheerfully accepted by both Mr and Mrs Adams. After all, the chief thing was a daughter's happiness. And she did seem happy. "I think she must feel a calmness and serenity in her present connexion which she never before experienced. I am sure it has relieved my mind from a weight which has hung heavy upon it for more than two years."[25]

Abigail Adams wrote to her son:

> When I used to visit your chamber at Auteuil and converse with you and mutually express our anxiety with respect to future events, neither of us dreamt of what has now taken place. You was then frequently witness to a regard and attachment which repeated proofs of neglect, finally dissolved. Instability of conduct first produced

> doubt and apprehension which in silence she suffered. Time and reflection dispelled the mist and illusion and has united her to a gentleman of a very different character. . . . And so, my dear son, your sister is really and bona fide married, as fast as the Bishop and a Clerk could tie them, in the ceremony of the Church of England with all its absurdities about it—that through necessity,

added the New England parson's daughter acidly, "for you know that such is the liberality of this enlightened country that the dissenting clergy are not permitted to perform marriages!"[26]

It was a consolation to Mrs Adams, however, that the ceremony was performed by the Bishop of St Asaph. This distinguished divine had been an outspoken supporter of the cause of American independence, and had gone out of his way to welcome the American Minister. He had introduced his wife and daughter to Mrs Adams, with the happiest results. "Truly well-bred," said Mrs Adams, measuring them by her yardstick of Grandma Quincy and the Marquise; "a friendship and acquaintance which I should like to cultivate." They wore well. Above all, the Bishop—whose very office made him suspect to a New England nonconformist—"justly deserves the character of a liberal man."[27] Such conclusions were in themselves broadening to the mind.

But the disabilities which in England followed dissent from the Established Church could not fail to rankle in Abigail's mind. "The dissenting clergy in this country," she wrote to her Aunt Elizabeth,

> appear a very different set of men from those which inhabit ours. They are cramped, condemned and degraded. They have not that independent appearance and that consciousness of their own worth which gives an air of dignity to the whole deportment. Dr Price (for instance) notwithstanding his literary fame and his great abilities, appears like a man who has been browbeaten.[28]

So with all the mumbo-jumbo—to Abigail's mind—of the Established Church, and the consoling dignity of the Bishop of St Asaph there took place a reversal of the system by which an Abigail Smith had become an Abigail Adams. Now an Abigail Adams became an Abigail Smith.

After a short honeymoon Colonel and Mrs William Stephens Smith set up housekeeping in Wimpole Street. Aunt Betsy Shaw, whose charm was of the heart and deepened with the years,* wrote

* Presently, on the very day of the funeral of one husband, she was to be asked in marriage by another, in a country teeming with maiden aunts.

to her niece from Haverhill, "I would wish you, for your own comfort, to be a most obliging wife," and "Mr Shaw joins me in wishing you 'health, long life, long youth, long pleasure, and a friend.'"

On April 30, 1787, Abigail Adams, herself only forty-three years old, became a grandmother. Nabby's little son was christened William Steuben, after his father and his father's friend. The proud grandmother wrote to her son John Quincy: "You became an Uncle on the end day of April. Your nephew has the brow of his grandpappa and the shape and form of his father. Colonel Smith set off for Lisbon (on a mission to Spain and Portugal) as soon as he thought it safe to leave your sister." And so excellently had Abigail entered into the relationship of mother-in-law that she unaffectedly added, "We felt his absence not a little, he was not only the sensible rational companion but the enlivener of all our scenes and the soul of our little parties."[29]

The marriage seemed in every way satisfactory. True, Nabby had never given William Smith the shy ardour she had offered Royall Tyler. But there are many natures in which, if that first love is thwarted, something in them is for ever frozen. Nabby, cooled and tutored in self-possession by the time she met her husband, could never again give herself without reserve. But he took it for granted that she loved him to capacity, and that no woman could have loved him more. Her mother was pleased to see how she lived on his letters while he was abroad, and what good long lively affectionate letters they were. As they sat one warm day together in Hyde Park the daughter said to the mother, "This is our first separation, and I pray it may be the last!" The baby filled up full the cup of joy, put the final lid on old sorrow.

Abigail Adams, enchanted with her first grandchild, found room in her heart that summer to adopt another. "I have had for a fortnight a little daughter of Mr Jefferson's," she wrote in July,

> who arrived here with a young Negro girl, her servant, from Virginia. Mr Jefferson wrote me some months ago that he expected them, and desired me to receive them. I did so and was amply repaid for my trouble. A finer child of her age I never saw. So mature and understanding, so much sensibility, united, are rarely met with. I grew so fond of her, and she was so much attached to me, that when Mr Jefferson sent for her, they were obliged to force the little creature away.

She is but eight years old. She would sit sometimes and describe to me the parting with her aunt who brought her up and the love she had for her little cousins, till the tears would stream down her cheeks; and how I had been her friend and she loved me. Her papa would break her heart by making her go again. She clung round me so that I could not help shedding a tear at parting with her. She was the favourite of every one in the house. I regret that such fine spirits must be spent in the walls of a convent. She is a beautiful girl, too.[30]

Abigail looked again at the date of her letter—July 16. Why surely that must be Commencement Day! In Harvard Yard the gay crowds would be gathering. The Doctors would march in procession in their scarlet gowns, and the graduates, perhaps thirty of them, in their black gowns, carrying their mortar-boards until the great moment when they were capped. John Quincy Adams would be one of them. His name would be read out in the assembly, as his father's had been before him. And like his father, he would deliver an oration. The mother's heart trembled. To see and hear her son on his great day was her right and his. Ah, these separations were unnatural, not to be borne.

"God willing, once I set my foot on American ground," she wrote to her son,

> not all the embassies in Europe consolidated into one shall tempt me again to quit it. I do not wonder at your longing to return, and I have many inducements which you had not—not one single one to remain here.
>
> My dear lads, you know that we shall return poor, but at the same time you know what have been the services your father has rendered his country . . . his honour and his integrity shall be your inheritance. If we can get you all through college the world is all before you and providence your guide.[31]

Well, John Quincy was through college, and all the concern he had caused his parents so far was that he worked too hard. His health suffered from his incessant drive. But he felt especially obligated not only to his parents, but to the college authorities, who, in recognition of his father's public services, refused to accept any fee for his tuition. He graduated Phi Beta Kappa. His oration was obtained by the newspapers and printed in the public Press. And at the same time he had avoided the high-hat manners which his father and mother had rather dreaded for him. He was well liked by his fellow-students.

And now what next? That was a constant subject of discussion between John and Abigail.

John Adams had written to their cousin and agent, Cotton Tufts:

> A year will soon be about, and what are we to do with John? What lawyer shall we desire to take him, in town or country? (expenses, etc.). Shall I come home and take all my boys into my own office? I was once thought to have a tolerable knack at making lawyers.[32]

Johnny wrote promptly to his father:

> Should you return home next spring, and be yourself at leisure to instruct me, I would certainly prefer it to studying elsewhere. But if you are still detained in Europe, I should wish to live in some place where there might be society sufficient for relaxation at times, but not enough to encourage dissipation.

Yes, to go home in the spring was their other chief concern. In December John Adams at last received permission from Congress to go home any time after February 24. It was accompanied by a resolution of praise. "Resolved, that Congress entertain a high sense of the services which Mr Adams has rendered to the United States in the various important trusts which they have from time to time committed to him; and that the thanks of Congress be presented to him for the patriotism, perseverance, integrity, and diligence with which he hath ably and faithfully served his country."[33]

Foreign Secretary John Jay's personal word of heartfelt sincerity was almost equally valued: "You have been in a situation that required much circumspection. I think you have acquitted yourself in a manner that does you honour."[34]

Coming in from his last conference at Whitehall, the February sleet sweeping along the square and making the bare trees in the centre garden almost invisible from the windows, he said to his wife: "Guess what Lord Carmarthen's parting words were, my dear!"

Abigail poured his tea, while he hitched his chair a little nearer to the glowing coal fire.

"Something non-committal, cold and polite!" she guessed.

"Well, I thought I knew him," said John, "but he surprised even me. His Lordship thought it proper to express a wish *that this country had some sort of a treaty of commerce with the United States of America*!"*

Abigail threw up her hands. "Is it possible?"

* John Adams had been working in vain for exactly this, but the absence of a constitution and a central government to deal with in the loosely federated United States had effectively blocked his effort.

"So!" said John Adams. "I remained for the moment speechless, and he immediately very quickly said, 'I presume, Mr Adams, that the States will all immediately adopt the new Constitution. I have read it with pleasure. It is very well drawn up.' So all this oracular utterance was to signify to me what has all along been insinuated, that there is not as yet any national government, but that as soon as there shall be one, the British Court will treat with it."[35]

Delegates from nearly half the states had assembled in Philadelphia the previous May, and had elected George Washington President of the Constitution Convention. A majority of the delegates resolved to form a national Government consisting of a supreme judicial, legislative, and executive branch. Two rival plans for working this out were submitted. A compromise plan was evolved. Congress then forwarded it to the several states legislatures for ratification. No Government was ever formed on so thorough, so dignified, and so democratic a method.

News of ratification by Delaware, Pennsylvania, and New Jersey had already reached England.

Abigail's public spirit was not dormant. Up to the last John Adams was pressing John Jay, even with exasperation, for formal letters of recall, never did obtain them (not Jay's fault), and for the want of them was forced to make a last-moment trip to Holland to take ceremonious leave in person, still acting as American Minister to the Dutch Court.

"What sins I've done that I must pay for by this winter journey I know not!" he grumbled.

But Mr Jefferson welcomed his necessity, and urged on him a job of retrieving American credit from some more private difficulties created by an American agent. Bankruptcy was again threatening the new U.S. currency. And when her husband had gone Abigail thought to herself, Why not get a new loan for the United States from Holland while he was about it? It was a good chance. No harm in trying. John Adams had already proved over and over again his unique skill in dealing with the Dutch financiers. She wrote to Thomas Jefferson in Paris urging her idea that John try to obtain a new loan for the United States from Holland, and asking his co-operation. Jefferson was convinced by her plea, and met John Adams at The Hague and they went together to Amsterdam.

John wrote thence to Abigail Adams:

> Well, ma'am, you have put off your own journey! If you should meet souwesters on the coast of America and have your voyage prolonged three weeks by it, *remember it is all your own intrigue which has forced me to this loan.* I suppose you will boast of it as a great public service. . . . I think I shall be forced, to open an additional loan. At least, that is Mr Jefferson's opinion.[36]

Money enough was obtained in this new loan to meet the United States' debts and preserve credit for two years at least, till the new Government should have time to collect revenue from taxes.

John Adams's farewell interview with the King of England was as friendly as their personal intercourse had always been. A bluff honesty and an honest patriotism were two qualities which John Adams and George III had in common. The official sentences interchanged, the King fell into chit-chat about Mr Adams's family—how many children were left behind in America, what were they doing, and what was the form of education in Massachusetts? Domestic details were always dear to the King's heart. It was no pretence. And if his friendly talk became at times a little garrulous, it was appreciated by his hearer. The King was at all times a great gentleman. The Queen, as Mrs Adams would dryly comment in her private circle only, was never a great lady.

John Adams, bent on the courteous, made three attempts to do his official duty by the Queen, but she detested them both as proud colonial upstarts; he had overwhelmed her at their first meeting. "The Queen was indisposed." Yet such an excuse could always be valid with a lady for ever in the family way.

As preparations to depart went briskly forward in Grosvenor Square the British Parliament seemed to be making preparations for a war. But what war? With whom? "The world can find no enemy nor object."[37] Habit suggested France.

"In the general flame which threatens Europe," wrote Abigail Adams, "I hope and pray our own country may have wisdom sufficient to keep out of the fire. I am sure she has been sufficiently a burnt child."[38]

Mr and Mrs Adams embarked on April 20, 1788, from Cowes for Boston. Colonel and Mrs Smith embarked a few days later from Falmouth for New York, but they got home first.

This, Abigail's last voyage, was horrid. She missed her little grandson acutely—why couldn't they sail on the same vessel? "O what a relief would his sportive little pranks have been to me in

ABIGAIL ADAMS SMITH
From a portrait by Mather Brown.
By courtesy of Mrs Robert Homans

COLONEL WILLIAM SMITH
From a portrait by Mather Brown.
By courtesy of Mrs Robert Homans

the tedious hours! I took only a few books and a little sewing, all of which were exhausted in one week."

As for her servants, they kept her busy taking care of them. "Briesler has been much the sickest person on board ship. I expected him to have been half nurse, instead of which he has needed constant nursing." While as for Esther—"yesterday at five she had a daughter, a poor little starveling, but with special lungs. I had for the first time in my life to dress the little animal, who looked buried in its clothes. I hope and pray I may never again go to sea!"[39]

So ends ambassadorship.

But in her heart there is a deep contentment. She and her husband have been together, are still together, never more to be parted—he has sworn—by anything but Death. And the ship is turned homeward; every tossing, tedious day is one day nearer.

But nearer what, my dear? Does she realize how far away she has travelled in spirit from the narrow walls of her cottage? She rose easily to her high place. But how will she step down again? Will she not feel the jar?

Her husband, with worldly wisdom, tried to prepare her mind, in anxious tenderness and candour. But she reassured him.

"I have learned to know the world and its value. I have seen high life. I have witnessed the luxury and pomp of state, the power of riches and the influence of titles. Notwithstanding this I feel that I can return to my little cottage and be happier than here; and if we have not wealth, we have what is better—integrity."[40]

XI

America Again

ABIGAIL WAS NOT ACTUALLY returning to her cottage. She was going to live in the Vassall House, the very house which might have been her daughter's married home. Royall Tyler had not fully completed the purchase when the news of Nabby's marriage to another set all his plans awry. So the Vassall House came again into the market, and John Adams instructed his agent, Dr Tufts, to purchase it for him in the autumn of '87.

The Vassall House was the most impressive in Braintree after Colonel Quincy's, and its land was equally extensive. Abigail was pleased at the purchase, and plunged into house decorating at long distance with zest. "Painting both within and without I shd be glad to have completed as soon as possible in the spring, the East lower room to be painted what is called a French grey and as the furniture is red [the Louis XVth chairs, always called "the Lafayette chairs," bought and used at Auteuil, were upholstered in red damask], a paper conformable will look best. The chamber over it will have green furniture and may be in the same manner made uniform by a paper green and white."

The original John Vassall had been a sugar-planter in the West Indies, and, permanently dazzled by the tropic sun, had wanted a dim house of soothing shadows. It was to seem at first sight to Mrs Adams dark and cramped. "It feels like a wren's house!"[1] It was, however, a sturdy, well-built house, with a dignified entry and fine staircase, definitely a gentleman's mansion and not a farmer's cottage as Penns Hill had been. They set to work to think of a suitable name for it. John Adams's favourite was "Peacefield," and so he called it during his lifetime. But neighbours and subsequent generations simply called it the Adams Mansion.

The *Lucretia* made port on the anniversary of the battle of Bunker

Hill. When John Quincy got word that the ship was in he hurried from Newburyport to meet them.

The arrival home, so long dreamed of by Abigail, fulfilled her expectations in full measure; pressed down and running over. The bright New England air, the breezy joyousness of Boston with its steep streets and white-painted houses, the high honour of their welcome, and, more than all else, the eager warmth of friends and family. There was great competition for Abigail's loved presence. "The Governor* was for escorting us to Braintree in his coach-and-four, attended by his light horse; and even Braintree was for coming out to Milton Bridge to meet us, but this we could by no means assent to! Accordingly we quitted town privately, your Pappa one day and I the next," wrote Abigail to daughter Nabby on July 7, "and we went to our worthy brother's† where we remained until the next week, when our furniture came up."

The furniture came by water, was hastily lightered from the ship to the beach at Norton Quincy's farm, hauled by farm wagons to the mansion, and piled up anywhere. So there was litter and confusion all round the Vassall House when Abigail Adams arrived to survey her new home. When she got out of the chaise and had her first good look at the house, she sat down on the horse block and shed tears of disappointment. "We have come into a house not half repaired," she candidly complained to her daughter, "such a swarm of carpenters, masons, farmers, as have almost distracted me——"[2]

John Adams did not help matters by his eager attention to the outdoors and his determination to stock the farm. Says Abigail with rueful humour, "We have for my comfort six cows without a single convenience for a dairy. But you know there is no saying nay. (Sweetly do the birds sing!)"‡

John Quincy Adams remained five weeks, gave his parents yeoman service in settling in, and had a wonderful time himself. It was the first glimpse he had caught of the kind of young manhood he might have had. But manhood had begun, and those lost years of home life were part of the price John Quincy had to pay for his exceptional education in foreign affairs.

Charles, aged eighteen, and Thomas, sixteen, were part of the restored circle. Only Nabby was absent, away on Long Island with her husband, and prevented by pregnancy from arduous travel.

* John Hancock. † Richard Cranch. ‡ Summer 1788.

She would certainly have come if she could for her brother's twenty-first birthday. On July 11 John Quincy wrote in his diary: "This day completes my twenty-first year. It emancipates me from the yoke of parental authority, which I never felt, and places me upon my own feet, which have not strength enough to support me. I continue therefore in a state of dependence."

He had two more years to run of his three-year articles* with Theophilus Parsons of Newburyport.

It had been twelve years since Abigail had been so near to all her children. At least one child, if not two, and at the last three, had been divided from her by a waste of waters. Nabby, who had always been under her wing, was three hundred miles distant, and approaching, far too soon after the first, the crisis of her second childbed. Well, at least there was no sea to cross. John Adams wrote to his daughter, "Our anxiety for you has prevailed upon me to make a great sacrifice, in consenting to your mother's journey to Long Island."[3]

On November 24, 1788, Abigail wrote to Mary, "Mrs Smith safely abed before I reached her, she and my young grandson as well as usual at this period." This second son was christened John Adams. The young grandmother was delighted to see her other grandson again, not yet two years old and already with a younger brother to push him out of babyhood. "Master William is the very image of his Mama at the same age, except that he has a greater share of vivacity and sprightliness—the merest little trunchion that you ever saw, very pleasant and good-humoured." And she added, towards the end of her visit, "The little boy grows finely, but I don't feel so fond of him yet as I do of William. Whether it is because he was born in our own house, or the first or the best tempered child I cannot determine."[4]

Nabby's married circumstances seemed all one could wish. Her husband and she had taken a house on Long Island at Jamaica, with a good garden and fifty acres of land. Mrs Adams liked it. "I find this place a very retired one, rural and delightful. I am eleven miles from New York with a great ferry between." Colonel Smith's mother and numerous brothers and sisters were friendly and well-bred people, and seemed very fond of their new sister-in-law. One

* J. Q. A. was an "articled clerk" in the law office of Theophilus Parsons, the regulation way of studying law until very recently in both Britain and America.

of them, Belinda, with the admired "softness of manner," was in charge in Nabby's house when Mrs Adams arrived, taking care of her sister-in-law "with much ease and tender sisterly affection." And a lot of neighbours came to call, very genteel people, "but all of the ceremonious kind." Indeed, Nabby confided to her mother that that was the way in New York.

"When we arrived in this country," she said, plaintively, "I found myself in a land of strangers. Not one I had any friendship for! I was visited in New York by fifty or sixty ladies. I returned their visits, and there the acquaintance ceases."

"What, no repeat calls? No invitations?" said her mother incredulously.

"Oh, yes, I've visited frequently with some," admitted Nabby, "but with no one shall I ever become intimate." She explained further: "There is no family where I can make a home and go with freedom and unreserve."

She saw her mother concerned on her behalf, and braced herself to be cheerful, or at least philosophical. "My home is satisfying!" she said. "It's enough for me. I have as much society as I wish in our own family."[5] That might have been true enough. There were six daughters in the family and four sons, not to mention many cousins.

Among the charming Smiths the fourth daughter, Sally, about seventeen, was graver than the rest. She was tall, had a fine figure and pretty face, "unaffected and artless, modest and composed. She wants only a little more animation to render her truly interesting." But Sally certainly made herself interesting to Mrs Adams, for the latter goes out of her way to make excuses for her not being as lively as Belinda. "She has dignity, and that you know is inconsistent with a gay playful humour!"[6]

Little did Mrs Adams suspect that she was favouring the good points in a future daughter-in-law.

When the time came for Mrs Adams to make her wintry journey homeward she carried in her heart some hidden causes of disquiet. They chased themselves round in a circle, like three blind mice. Bundled up in the stage, with her feet deep in straw, she brooded on them as the springless wagon bounced in a seasick manner over the ruts and stones of the Boston Post Road. One was that Nabby's second pregnancy had followed too close upon her first, and her strength was depleted in spite of her elastic youth. And one was that Nabby was lonely. Well, so are we all; but Nabby was lonelier than most. She had clung touchingly to her mother at parting, so reserved as she usually was.

"I wish I lived nearer you, Mama!"

"I wish so too, dear. But you will get used to it."

"No," Nabby had said, with the quiet conviction of experience. "I do not find that time lessens the painfulness of a separation!"[7]

And the last and greatest was something Abigail did not like to put into clear words to herself; not to call it dissatisfaction with her son-in-law. But why did not Colonel Smith take up an independent career?

When they had all been together in London, John and she had talked this over together, and John had there urged the young man to go on with his preliminary studies in the law; why not enter one of the Inns of Court and qualify himself for the bar? Mr Adams had offered him time for study. But Colonel Smith had set the idea rather haughtily aside. Now John Adams had written and again ventured through his daughter to influence his son-in-law to a career of his own. "My desire would be to hear from him at the bar, which in my opinion is the most independent place on earth. A seeker of the public employment is the most unhappy of men. Mr Smith's merit and services entitle him. . . . But I would not be dependent; I would have a resource. There can be none better than the bar."[8]

But nothing so humdrum was on the programme of William Stephens Smith. He had a high opinion of his merits and capacities. He had hoped to be left behind as Minister Plenipotentiary to the court of Great Britain. But since that had not materialized—though he had persuaded John Adams to suggest it, or at least to leave him as *chargé d'affaires*—well, something as good or better probably would. Had he not been aide to George Washington, who was certain to be President?

Washington for President was the phrase that was buzzing about wherever men met together. The new Constitution was about to be tested. The first Federal election was not far off and it was an apprehensive hour. The timbers of the ship of state had appeared all right in dry-dock, well and truly fashioned. But when launched on the great ocean of affairs, would she float?

The name of Washington gave assurance. To him as a person,

rather than to an untried and not perfectly understood system, the ordinary people clung.

The machinery went into motion. The individual states appointed electors to the first Electoral College, and the Electoral College, numbering this time sixty-nine members from ten states,* met in February 1789.

The Constitution required that the votes of the Electoral College should determine who should be the two Chief Executives. The largest number of votes should determine the President, the second largest number should automatically determine the Vice-President. The idea was that two men should be elected who would be equally capable of acting as the Chief Executive in case of accident to the first.

Washington received a unanimous vote, the only man in history whom everybody wanted for President. John Adams had no competitor for second place. His wife had said and thought that he was not popular—too outspoken to be popular. But what is it to be popular? Certainly he was not, like Washington, worshipped as a demigod and a hero, but John Adams was universally trusted. Even his enemies believed in his integrity. And when it came to voting for the highest office in the State, this public trust might give a man a power rivalling that of the chief. This enormous confidence had many facets. Men relied on John Adams as a lawyer, as a framer of treaties and laws, as a dealer with foreign dynasties, and as a man who understood as well as anyone alive the principles which lay behind government itself.

Yet John Adams got only thirty-four of the sixty-nine votes, the other thirty-five having been deliberately scattered among ten politically impossible candidates, no one of whom got more than nine votes. This vote scattering, which reduced John Adams's majority in a humiliating degree, was due to the secret intrigue of Alexander Hamilton, who here showed the innate duplicity and love of pulling secret wires which became increasingly dangerous, and ended in his own complete disaster.

It was not that Hamilton did not want John Adams. He rather admired him, and believed that "to a sound understanding Mr Adams joined an ardent love for the public good." But he wanted him in with as little power as possible. So he set to work to clip his

* Rhode Island and North Carolina had not yet joined the Union by ratifying the Constitution, and New York had trouble with her elections. They came in later.

majority. His plan was a clever one, deceiving many of John Adams's supporters. He sent riders dispatch to the state elections to warn candidates that there was serious risk that John Adams would win the first place over Washington, or at least tie him, unless measures were taken to prevent it by casting away some of Mr Adams's natural votes. "He had made an exact calculation on the subject—New Jersey were to throw away three votes and Connecticut two, and all would be well," as a Connecticut friend told John Adams. "So our electors threw away two votes where they were sure they would do no harm."[9] And Mr Gerry bore independent witness that others of the "States which were not unanimous for you" had thrown away votes "apprehensive that this was a necessary step to prevent your election to the chair."[10] Without understanding Hamilton's real reason for the policy, John Adams perceived the fact and resented it.

Still, the fact remains that Adams was elected safely to the second most honourable position in the new Federal State and he was happy at the unsought honour and the national recognition. He accepted his position with determination to pull his weight to make the new machinery of government work smoothly and fulfil the ideals which he had often expressed—"the formation of a national government which may bind us together." John Adams never nursed a grudge. And Hamilton had not at present any grudge against John Adams. His intrigue had been largely impersonal; and it had been successful. He was ready to welcome the Vice-President.

New York was to be the first seat of the Federal Government. Abigail was delighted at the prospect of living near her daughter. The date set for the launching of the new Government was the first Wednesday in March, which happened to be March 4. But to John's chagrin she could not set out with him. A farm cannot be suddenly left; some one must supervise the spring planting, the finishing of the new dairy, the mending of fences; some one must disband the numerous household, arrange the care of the house and farm for an indefinite time. There was Tom at Harvard, and Charles in a scrape. Not to mention Abigail's pet lark and puppy. At least John could get a house in New York ready for her. So they bid each other reluctant farewell, and he drove off in the spring weather. Abigail heard afterwards of the reception he met on the road all the way along. Crowds turned out to greet him, "most affectionate and respectful." In one place they would present him with specimens of local manufactures, cloth, buttons; at another with the freedom of their city. Surprisingly enough at New York, stronghold of the anti-federalists under Governor Clinton, both Federalists and Antis emulated each other in their testimonials of respect and affection to John Adams.[11]

The Vice-President's main duty was to preside over the meetings of the Senate. As soon as a quorum had arrived John Adams was solemnly inducted into this duty and, on April 21, he assumed the chair he was to occupy for eight years. The heart of his speech of acceptance was an eloquent tribute to George Washington.

But as the profound emotions stirred up by the great day of Washington's inauguration sank down again to their place at the bottom of his heart John Adams turned with reproach and loneliness and exasperation to the empty pillow at his side. Why could not Abigail be here to share them?

> My dearest Friend,
>
> If you think it best, leave Thomas at college, but I pray you to come on with Charles, as soon as possible. As to the place, let my brother* plough and plant as he will, as much as he will. He may send me my half of the butter, cheese, etc., here. As to money to bear your expenses, you must, if you can, borrow of some friend enough to bring you here. If you cannot borrow enough, you must sell horses, oxen, sheep, cows, any thing at any rate rather than not come on. If no one will take the place, leave it to the birds of the air and beasts of the field, but at all events break up that establishment and that household. . . .

"Ah?" said Mrs Adams. "Well, well. Sweetly do the birds sing!"

Leave the farm to the birds of the air and the beasts of the field, and depend on what in our old age? She could not escape the penalty of her foresight and her competence.

But her arrangements with Richard Cranch were almost completed. Impatience and thoroughness struggled within her as the days grew warmer, the flowers came out, the cows calved, the first crop of hay matured. . . . In high June with a great send-off from friends and relations, with her luggage and furniture, her son Charles to escort her and her young nieces,† and her maid Polly, she embarked on the packet, and set out for New York by water.

* Richard Cranch. † Her brother's children, Matilda and Louisa.

XII

New York

THIS TIME MRS ADAMS TRAVELLED like a queen. Wherever the boat put in to take up goods or passengers the news of her being on board flew about. At Providence, Rhode Island, where the packet docked for the night, Mrs Adams went to an inn. Within an hour of her arrival local notables and friends came calling on her, reproaching her for not sending them word, inviting her to dine or drive. Rhode Island was Anti-federalist, but the people admired John Adams personally, and no bitter party feeling had yet arisen. "Mr Brown (a Quaker) sent his carriage and son to conduct me to his house which is one of the grandest I have seen in this country . . . magnificence and taste. Mrs Brown met me at the door. . . . 'Friend, I am glad to see thee here.' The simplicity of her manners and dress with the openness of her countenance and the friendlyness of her behaviour charmed me beyond all the studied politeness of European manners. 22 persons to dine with me tho the notice was so short . . . elegant entertainment upon a service of plate. Towards evening I made a tour around the town, and drunk tea and spent the evening with Mr and Mrs Francis . . . large company to be presented. About eleven I returned to my lodgings and next morning went on board the packet. . . ."

The exhilaration of these affairs was short, but oh! how long the miseries of the sea! The captain of the packet, who was also called Brown, had "very civilly taken his wife to attend upon me during my passage . . . but neither civility, attention nor politeness could remedy the sea-sickness or give me a fair wind or dispel the thunder-gusts. In short I resolved upon what I have frequently before, that I would never again embark upon the water, but this resolution I presume will be kept as my former ones have been.

We were five days upon the water. Heat, want of rest, sea-sickness and terror (for I had my share of that!), all contributed to fatigue me, and I felt upon my arrival quite tame and spiritless. Louisa was very sick, but behaved like a heroine. Matilda had her share, but when she was a little recovered she was the life of us all. Polly was half-dead.... Charles ate and slept without any inconvenience."[1]

The Captain was her willing slave, and on docking at New York he went himself to the Hall of Congress to announce her arrival. John Adams, of course, could not leave his place without automatically dismissing the Senate, but Sam Otis, her cousin by marriage,* Secretary to the Congress, quit his taking of minutes, met her at the water's edge with a carriage, and drove her to Richmond Hill, the house John Adams had taken. There she found her daughter and Colonel Smith waiting to welcome her, "to my no small joy," with baby John, "grown out of knowledge." They had everything "so well arranged that beds and a few other articles seem only necessary towards keeping house with comfort, and I begin to think my furniture will be troublesome to me, while Mrs Smith remains with me." Her "tame and spiritless" feelings soon vanished. It was noon of a bright June day. The house was lovely. It stood on rising ground. In front lay the "noble Hudson," on the left the city, screened by trees, on the right an open expanse of fields and pastures, and at the back a grove of trees and a flower garden enclosed with a hawthorn hedge. When John came home to dinner from the Senate nothing seemed wanting to complete her joy, except the riddance of those troublesome little heartaches below the threshold, about Nabby's being obviously expecting again, about Colonel Smith's lack of prospects, and about Charles's peccadilloes.

Charles had accompanied her to New York to start working in an office there, studying law. The trouble with Charles was that he was simply too charming, too fond of the popularity he came by so easily. He could not say no, could not turn the cold shoulder even on an undesirable companion. So he fell a prey to bad company. There were men at Harvard who drank too much, who played too high. Abigail knew of such, before her own sons went to college. But you didn't have to keep their company. John Quincy Adams did not, nor Will Cranch. She had written from England asking John Quincy to be sure to look after his younger brother. But Charles wasn't going to be bossed by Johnny. . . .

* His wife was a daughter of Uncle Isaac Smith.

Had there always been something a little soft about Charles? Soft here, obstinate there? So difficult to deal with, because he did not hold his shape. As long as he was with you he seemed so sweetly reasonable, he went into the mould you made. But, away from you, the mould would not stay, and without the home pressure his shape altered, became—like his uncle, Abigail's lost brother. But his mother would not give up, she struggled valiantly.

Well, now she was to have Charles under her wing for a time, and she could see how pleased he was to see his sister again. Nabby and he made fast friends, and Charles was soon introduced to the lively bevy of young Miss Smiths on Long Island. Charles was repentant, reformed, bent on behaving circumspectly, and as always, bad or good, possessing the art of winning love and giving happiness. When he came in from his office day after day he greeted his mother with warm affection. He knew that the painful subject would never again be raised between them, unless by his own fault. Abigail had never been a nagging parent. That too she had learned from Grandma Quincy.

"Amongst the many good rules and maxims of my worthy Grandmother with whom I chiefly lived during the early period of my life, I recollect with pleasure that one of them was never to bring a painfull subject twice into recollection. If a poor culprit had transgressed she reprimanded with justice and dignity, but never lessened her authority by reproaches. The consequence was that love towards her and respect for her opinion prevented a repetition of the offence."[2] It was a good habit and sound psychology, even if the perfect consequence did not always follow. There is no doubt that Charles to the end of his wasted life maintained a great love towards his mother and respect for her opinion, even though it was to him a source of pain. But in the sunny house at Richmond Hill they were a happy family group and all was set fair.

Mrs Adams must now assume her social duties, and she took them up with eager pleasure. "I took the earliest opportunity (the morning after my arrival) to go and pay my respects to Mrs Washington. Mrs Smith accompanied me. She received me with great ease and politeness. She is plain in her dress, but that plainness is the best of every article. She is in mourning. Her hair is white, her teeth beautiful, her person rather short than otherways, hardly so tall as myself, and if I was to speak sincerely I think she is a much better figure! Her manners are modest and unassuming, dignified and feminine, not the tincture of ha'ture about her. *His Majesty* was ill and confined to his room. I had not the pleasure of a presentation to him.

"Mrs Washington is one of those unassuming characters which create esteem. A most becoming pleasantness sits upon her countenance, and an unaffected deportment which renders her the object of veneration and respect. With all these feelings and sensations I found myself much more deeply impressed than I ever did before their Majesties of Britain."[3]

Apart from the President and his wife, Mrs Adams, as the newcomer, must of course receive callers, and they crowded upon her. Before June ended she had been called on by "the lady and daughter of the Governor, Lady Temple, the Countess de Brehin, Mrs Knox, and twenty-five other ladies, many of the Senators, all their ladies, all the foreign Ministers, and some of the representatives." In all this whirl she longed for her competent servants the Brieslers, who were following her and arrived a week or two after. Briesler could take full charge of the domestic staff and affairs, and Esther, among other things, could dress her mistress's hair. New York took almost as much hairdressing as Paris.

The Washingtons' cordiality manifested a wish for closer friendship. Mrs Washington promptly returned Mrs Adams's call, and invited her back. And Washington, having missed her first visit through illness, would not make that an excuse a second time lest he should seem not sufficiently anxious to see her. "The fever which he had, terminated in an abscess, so that he cannot sit up. Upon my second visit to Mrs Washington he sent for me into his chamber. He was laying upon a settee, and half raising himself up, begged me to excuse his receiving me in that posture, congratulated me upon my arrival in New York and asked me how I could relish the simple manners of America after having been accustomed to those of Europe."[4] Mrs Adams replied that she esteemed the simple manners of her countrymen, but she had noticed many had some taste and fondness for luxury and the manners of Europe. It certainly never entered her head that Washington himself, still less that she and her husband, would ever be accused by their enemies of being among the latter.

Abigail had met Washington in Boston years before. The impression he made upon her then was not weakened, it was only deepened and amplified when she came to know him better. "Our august President is a singular example of modesty and diffidence. He has a dignity which forbids familiarity mixed with an easy affability which creates love and reverence."[5]

Weak from his fever and tortured by his abscess, the President crawled downstairs and had a bed put into his carriage and "rides out in the way with six horses in his carriage and four attendants. Mrs Washington accompanies him. I requested him to make Richmond Hill his resting place, and the next day he did so, but he found walking up the stairs so difficult [Mrs Adams's drawing-room was on the second floor] that he has done it but once."

Indiscriminate calling, long continued, in such a society would soon leave every one with no spare time, no peace. In self-defence it was necessary for leading hostesses to adopt the English plan of an "At Home" day, let Senator Maclay and his ilk carp as they might. "I have waited for Mrs W. to begin," wrote Mrs Adams in August,

> and she has fixed on every fryday 8 o'clock. I attended upon the last, with Mrs Smith and Charles. I found it quite a crowded room. The form of reception is this—The servants announce, and Col. Humphries and Mr Lear (the secretary) receives every lady at the door and hands her up to Mrs Washington to whom she makes a most respectful courtsey and then is seated without noticing any of the rest of the company. The President then comes up and speaks to the lady, which he does with a grace and dignity and ease that leaves Royal George far behind him. . . . Ice-cream and lemonade . . . and the company retire at their pleasure, performing the same ceremony when they quit the room. Now on Monday evenings Mrs Adams receives company. That is, her rooms are lighted and put in order. Servants and Gentlemen and Ladies, as many as inclination, curiosity or fashion tempts, come out to make their bow and curtzy, take coffee and tea, chat half an hour or longer, and then return to town again. On Tuesday the same ceremony is performed at Mrs Jay's.[6]

It was not too tedious. No one felt it necessary to go every time to all the receptions. But dissipation? Heavens above! "I cannot help smiling when I read the Boston press, that the President is rumoured amidst all the 'dissipations' of the city of New York. . . . Not a single public amusement is there in the whole city, no, not even a public walk, and as to dinners, there are six made in Boston to one here. There are six Senators who have their ladies and families with them, but they are in lodgings the chief of them, and not in a situation to give dinners. . . . The weather is so warm we can give only one dinner a week, 24 persons at a time." Mrs Adams, by August 9, had got through the Senators and begun with the House; though she couldn't find a cook who would not get drunk. In the meantime, while she had already returned sixty calls, the intense summer, the busy flies, no screens, no ice, played their usual havoc. "My family all sick, Mrs Smith's two children with hooping-cough, Charles with dysentery, Louisa and Polly with summer complaint. . . . It is very sickly in the city." Yet she immediately adds: "I am every day more and more pleased with this place. Should they go to Philadelphia I do not know how I could possibly live through the violent heats."

Another rumour against Washington comes to her in the mail from New England, and she hastens to his defence. "The President uses no more state than is perfectly consistent with his station. I do not love to see the news writers fib it so." And then John Adams is libelled for putting on dog, and she categorically contradicts it. "The Vice-President ten times to one goes to Senate in a one-horse chaise, and *levees* we have had none. The President only has his powdered lackies waiting at the door."

It is envy which gives rise to such rumours. And Abigail provided her sister with an answer to give to any envious neighbours.

> It has been my lot in life to spend a large portion of it in publick life, but I can truly say the pleasantest part of it was spent at the foot of Penns Hill in the humble cottage when my good man was a practitioner at the Bar, earnt his money during the week and at the end of it pourd it all into my lap to use or what could be spaired to lay by. Nobody then grudged us our living, and 25 years such practice would have given us a very different property from what we now possess.[7]

The relationship of President's wife and Vice-President's wife was new to history. The first two made it a very intimate one. Mrs Washington, once the wealthy young widow Custis, inheritor of great estates, mistress of hundreds of slaves, and entirely a product and flower of the Southern culture, curiously enough found most congenial company in the New England lady. Mrs Washington was a quiet woman, not lively-minded nor with much to talk about. She was not much of a reader, and the theatre rather bewildered her. The pitfalls of her new position hedged her round. "I live a very dull life here, and know nothing that passes in the town . . . more like a state prisoner than anything else," she complained. The new friend fascinated her. She knew so much, she had seen so much, she knew reams of poetry by heart, she had such interesting opinions. Her presence enlivened any ladies' tea-party, kept one entertained on the dullest of drives and calls. Mrs Washington continually asked for her company, and she had what she wanted. "We live in a most friendly intercourse," wrote Mrs Adams, "and Madam makes very few visits but those of ceremony when she does not request my ladyship to accompany her, and I have several appointments of that kind on hand now."[8]

While Mrs Washington wrote to her niece that she was sending her a present of a watch and chain: "I hope it is such a one as will please you—it is of the newest fashion . . . such as Mrs Adams the Vice-President's lady and those in the polite circle wares."[9]

In October, when Congress rose for recess, John Adams felt he must have a journey for relaxation, and was eager to see his new farm and how all that livestock was doing. So he determined on a short visit to Braintree. Abigail decided not to accompany him—too strenuous, and Nabby was still weak after the birth of her third son in September; and there was Charles, and her household.

"The President sets out this week for a like excursion. He wd have had Mr Adams accept a seat in his coach but he excused himself from motives of delicacy.

"We yesterday had a very pleasant party together," wrote Abigail to Mary.

> The whole family of us dined with the President on Thursday, and he then proposed an excursion to Long Island by water to visit Princes Gardens, but as Mrs W. does not love the water [nor in fact did Mrs A.] we agreed that the gentlemen should go by water and the ladies should meet them at a halfway house and dine together, and yesterday we had a most beautiful day for the purpose. The President, Col. Smith, Major Jackson, Mr Izard, etc., went on board the barge at 8 o'clock. At eleven the ladies, namely Mrs W., Mrs A., Mrs Smith, Miss Custis [Mrs Washington's attendant granddaughter] set out in Mrs W.'s coach-and-six and met the gentlemen at Harlem, where we all dined together and returned in the same manner. Whilst the gentlemen are absent we propose seeing one another on terms of much sociability. Mrs Washington is a most friendly good lady, always pleasant and easy.[10]

Although Mrs Washington, at fifty-eight, was considered quite an old lady by every one, and seemed so to Mrs Adams at a lively forty-five, they were both grandmothers, and could find there an

JOHN QUINCY ADAMS
From a portrait by John Singleton Copley.
Museum of Fine Arts, Boston

THE ADAMS MANSION AT QUINCY

Sketched in 1822 by Sarah Apthorp.

By courtesy of the Adams Memorial Society

inexhaustible subject. "A grandchild," said Abigail, "is almost as near to your heart as your own children; my little boys delight me and I should feel quite melancholy without them. William came from his Grandmamma Smith an almost ruined child, but I have brought him to be a fine boy by now."[11]

It became the custom, on public occasions, for Mrs Adams to have her station "always at the right hand of Mrs Washington." And if, when Mrs Adams entered, some one else had taken that place and showed no signs of giving way, the "President never fails of seeing that it is relinquished for me."[12]

Even more than the heroes of antiquity such as David, Julius Cæsar, Alexander, who all one day or other were moved by whims of vanity, selfishness, or eroticism, George Washington, having relinquished personal hope, fulfilled the classic ideal of the heroic. Common soldiers, fellow-officers, aristocracy of the South, rough-cornered intelligentsia of Boston, merchants of New York, students of Harvard College, all were moved to hero-worship. On the Eastern tour, made in October and November by advice of John Adams, he was greeted with wild enthusiasm, serenaded with "the Hero comes." "He was much gratified with the attention shown him," wrote Abigail to her son John Quincy, "I have it from his own mouth. Is it human nature to be otherways?" And she added her own heartfelt comment: "*He ought to be immortal, for who can ever fill his place?*"[13]

Indeed, Washington's tact and power were so great, it gave one pause. A close observer, valuing democratic government, almost trembled at it. Washington's very existence created an aristocracy, even if only of one individual. John Adams, who saw him at his daily work, was aware of him in a man's world, often discussed it with Abigail, and it is his thoughts as well as hers that she expressed in the balanced judgment which constitutes one of the finest tributes to Washington: "This same President has so happy a faculty of appearing to accommodate and yet carrying his point that if he was not really one of the best intentioned men in the world he might be a very dangerous one. He is polite with dignity, affable without familiarity, distant without haughtiness, grave without austerity, modest, wise and good. These are traits in his character which peculiarly fit him for the exalted station he holds, and God grant that he may hold it with the same applause and universal satisfaction for many years, as it is my firm opinion that no other man could rule over this great people and consolidate them into one mighty Empire but he who is set over us."[14]

However, it could not be denied, the air around him was a little rare, a little chill. Dinner with the President was more formidable than festive. Mr Maclay's vinegar hero-worship cannot stand the strain. "At a little after four we went to the President's to dinner. President and Mrs, Vice-President and Mrs, Gov. and wife, Mr Jay and wife, seven other guests and the President's two secretaries. The President and Mrs Washington sat opposite each other in the middle of the table; the two secretaries one at each end. It was a great dinner and the best of the kind I ever was at. The room however was disagreeably warm. The middle of the table was garnished in the usual tasty way with small images, artificial flowers, etc. The dessert was first pies, then iced creams, jellies, etc., then water melon, musk melon and other fruit. It was the most solemn dinner I ever sat at. Not a health drunk; scarce a word said. When the cloth was taken away the President, filling a glass of wine, with great formality, drank to the health of every individual round the table. Everybody imitated him, charged glasses, and such a buzz of 'Health, sir!' and 'Health, madam,' and 'thank you, sir,' and 'thank you, madam,' never had I heard before. The ladies sat a good while, and the bottles passed about; but there was a dead silence almost. Mrs Washington at last withdrew with the ladies. The President is a cold formal man. I often looked around the company to find the happiest faces. The President seemed to bear in his countenance a settled aspect of melancholy. No cheering ray of convivial sunshine broke through the cloudy gloom of settled seriousness. At every interval of eating or drinking he played on the table with a fork or knife like a drumstick."[15]

But tame-cat affairs in ladies' drawing-rooms or the stately formalities of dining with the President were by no means Mrs Adams's chief interest. Every morning at ten o'clock John Adams drove down to the Senate, and every afternoon he returned to four o'clock dinner—unless they were dining out—with a budget of news. Mrs Adams could not say that *she* did not know what was going on in the town. A husband could be a wall between his wife and the world, like Mr Washington, or he could be a channel like Mr Adams. Pacing the gravel walk under the trees, sitting on the piazza and watching the innumerable boats flitting by like huge white butterflies on the Hudson, Mr and Mrs Adams zestfully shared each other's lives. And since his affairs went along in a great public tide, it was his life that they mostly shared. Going over the day in the Senate with her sharpened his perceptions, refreshed his memory, often—looking at a matter through her eyes—gave him a new insight.

The Senate numbered twenty-two members; seldom more than twenty in attendance. The Government was experimental, feeling its way, forming itself as it went. Those in favour of giving it a good deal of power, the Federalists, were scarcely in a majority over those who favoured restricting it (in favour of local States' rights)—the Anti-federalists. Consequently on important points the presiding officer often had to give the casting vote. John Adams had to do so twenty times in the First Congress.

"If the United States had chosen for the V-P's chair a man wavering in his opinions," Abigail justly commented,

> or one who sought the popular applause . . . this very constitution wd have had its death wound during the first six months of its existence. On several of the most trying occasions it has fallen to this dangerous Vice to give the casting vote for its life.[16]

In January the well informed Abigail wrote to her sister: "The next question I presume that will occupy Congress will be the assumption of the State debts, and here I apprehend warm work and much opposition but I firmly believe it will terminate for the general good."

On February 20 Abigail speaks of going to the House for the first time "to-morrow" to hear the debate, with Mrs Dalton, Mrs Jay and Mrs Cushing. "I hope," she says fervently, "some method will be adopted speedily for the relief of those who have so long been the sufferers by the instability of Government."[17]

The debate was a revelation in verbal fireworks. And so it continued day after day. John Adams reported that in the Senate—to which the public were not admitted—things were just as hot. The controversy had risen to a passionate height, and a dangerous deadlock had been reached, when Jefferson arrived in New York in March to join Washington's Cabinet as Foreign Secretary or Minister of State.

No one welcomed Mr Jefferson more warmly or more sincerely than his old friends John and Abigail Adams. "Mr Jefferson is here," wrote Mrs Adams joyfully, "and adds much to the social circle."[18]

They had no idea that Mr Jefferson was going to act as a catalyst to the situation, and that some very curious and poisonous crystals were to be formed as a result.

The assumption by the Federal Government of all the debts incurred by all the states as a result of the war—which in some states were very heavy, in others negligible—was part of Hamilton's astute finance to restore United States credit and put the new nation on its feet. John Adams supported Hamilton in this, Jefferson (no economic expert) was against it. But Hamilton succeeded in making a private deal with Jefferson.

To quote Jefferson himself:

> It was observed that this pill (assumption) would be peculiarly bitter to the southern states, and that some concomitant measure should be adopted to sweeten it a little to them. There had before been propositions to fix the seat of government either at Philadelphia or at Georgetown on the Potomac; and it was thought that by giving it to Philadelphia for ten years and to Georgetown permanently afterwards, this might, as an anodyne, calm in some degree the ferment which might be excited by the other measure alone. So two of the Potomac members (but with a revulsion of stomach almost convulsive) agreed to change their votes, and Hamilton undertook to carry the other point, . . . and so the Assumption was passed.[19]

The bile and gall and sulphur and brimstone stirred up in people's blood and viscera by this hot political fight over assumption seemed to take form in actual fever. At all events, a great distraction from debates in Congress hit New York at the end of May 1790, put many of the main actors out of commission, and almost cost the President his life. "The disorder termed the influenze has prevailed with much violence," wrote Abigail,

> and in many places been very mortal, particularly upon Long Island. Not a creature has escaped in our family except its head, and I compounded to have a double dose myself. Hitherto he has escaped, not so the President. He has been in a most dangerous state, and for 2 or 3 days I assure you I was most unhappy.

It was not only on Washington's account that she worried. It seemed to her that the very union of the states and the permanency of the Government depended upon Washington's life.

"Most assuredly I do not wish for the highest post! I never before realized what I might be call'd to."

As for her own household, her remedy for influenza did not encourage malingerers. "I keep a bottle of tartar emetic and administer it as soon as they complain." (She gave herself several "pukes.")[20]

After all that worry and sickness, personal and vicarious, Mrs Washington and Mrs Adams both felt the need of a holiday. Just to get a complete change, to wash their hands of all domestic duties, and of the repercussions of politics on husbands. And it is evidence of their real affection for each other that they took it together. In June, "I last week accompanied Mrs Washington to the Jersies to visit the Falls of Passaic. We were absent three days and had a very agreeable tour."

They returned from their holiday to an atmosphere of impending change, the pulling up of new-formed roots, the breaking of ties. When Congress rose in August for the summer recess it would be the end of business in New York. The Washingtons prepared to go to Mount Vernon for the recess, and Abigail wrote, "I shall part with her, tho I hope only for a short time, with much regret. No lady can be more deservedly beloved and esteemed than she is and we have lived in habits of intimacy and friendship."[21]

One of the last important acts of Congress at New York was to sign a treaty with the Indians in July. Abigail was much interested in the Indian delegation. They lodged at an inn near Richmond Hill, and she had never seen anything like them before. "They are very fine looking men, placid countenance and fine shape. Mr Trumble says they are many of them perfect models. . . . They are very fond of visiting us. We entertain them kindly and they behave with much civility. Yesterday they signed the Treaty and last night they had a great bonfire, dancing round it like so many spirits, hopping, singing, yelling, and expressing their pleasure in true savage style. These are the very first savages I ever saw."[21]

Their chief, MacGillvery, dressed in the white man's fashion, spoke English like a white man, and was not particularly dark-skinned. "He is grave and solid, intelligent and much of a gentleman."

So the Indians went away content, and Mrs Adams, whom they had called "Mammea" (she professed herself at a loss to know what that implied), turned her attention to preparations for departure.

Charles was going to board with his sister. It was a wrench to have to leave those two behind, Nabby in "unsatisfactory circumstances," Charles in—what? It was hard to explain her uneasiness about Charles. He "is quite fat. He is very steady and studious. There is no fault to be found with his conduct. He has no company or companions but known and approved ones, nor does he appear to wish for any other."[23] Indeed, he seemed to have made it a rule not to go into company except with his father or his brother-in-law. Every morning for a year past he had driven into the city with his father, and gone to his office as his father went to the Senate. In the evening he had returned in the same manner. It was a little too careful, too perfect, too circumspect. It wasn't, in fact, like Charles! The mother missed in him something gay, resilient, and debonair. He was too sober, too self-repressed, too eaten by inward shame and remorse and a desperate determination to make amends. But what could one do? She had urged all these things on him, and now she was distressed at seeing them. "I sometimes think his application too intense, but better so than too remiss."[24]

John Quincy's application was also too intense, but up to now the only worry was on account of his stomach. John Q. had now completed his three years' articles with Mr Parsons, and in July had been admitted to the Boston bar. In August he moved into Boston, opened his father's old office in Court Street. Instead of showing pleasure at starting out in life, however, he seemed depressed. The prospect of a young barrister's tedious waiting for briefs caused him to fret. His mother had tried to cheer him, turning away from her Indians. "You must expect to advance slowly at first . . . but it must be some dire misfortune or calamity, if I judge not amiss, that will ever place you in the shallows."[25]

What was behind all this chafing at dependence, this excessive impatience to be making an income and standing on his own feet? Was it what one would naturally suspect? Yes; indeed it was; rumour brought her word, and Thomas confirmed it.

A lovely girl named Mary Frazier had captured John Q.'s heart two years before in Newburyport. And at her touch the bright young man had come alive. The seasons flew; the melon parties, the water parties, the picnics, the snow parties, the dances; the walking home after Meeting; the sitting on verandah steps in the dusk. All the glorious iridescent days and nights of joy and pain. And then, the dreaded end. Then, Boston. Sitting in the old office, hour after hour, among his father's books. Then the sudden first case, a hasty call, which he was sure he muffed—though Charles wrote him a most kind, encouraging, brotherly letter about it. The intolerable vista that swam before his sleepless eyes of years of this—his clothes, his food, his books, his rent, his pocket-money, all provided for him by his parents; nothing, not a cent, not a crust of bread, of his own.

Abigail approached the delicate subject with a mother's nervousness. A nervous touch is always wrong. "Your Father sets out for Philadelphia to-morrow to see a house belonging to Mr Hamilton, the uncle of my favourite Nancy" (whom she had presented at court). "Perhaps you may one day come and see her but you must get a great deal of money first, 'tis said this uncle has already wounded her by preventing a connexion with a gentleman who was not great and noble and rich enough for him." She sets out ostensibly to comfort and reassure her son because he can't support himself yet. But what is it but to point out his lack of riches, his ineligibility, his necessarily prolonged dependence? "I will prophesy for you that you will be able by the close of one year to pay your own board, and if you do that it's as much as you ought to expect, and if you do not, why don't worry your face into wrinkles about it, we will help you all we can, and when you are better off than those who assist you, you shall help them again if they want it, so make yourself easy and keep free from entanglements of all kinds. Thomas says you are in love. So far as it will serve to make you more attentive to your person—for you are a little inclined to be negligent—so far it may be of service to you."[26]

Parents work against serious handicaps. Abigail had in some ways come off very well, notably well, in adjustment to a grown son. There were many directions in which she had approached him as an equal, even looked up to him. And a great many parents can never say as much. But, though she herself had married at twenty, perfectly convinced, at the time and ever since, that hers was a mature passion, she could not give her son credit for equal dignity and maturity at twenty-three.

With some irony and some bitterness he read her letter, missing none of its implications. Thwarted, miserable, and rebellious, he yet felt he had no case. She hardly needed to rub it in. But that fierce maternal anxiety that wants to guard the young from every pitfall, small and great—and how great a one could this be!—made her write again in November concerning rumours of his attentions which are passing her way. "Do you not know that the most cruel of situations to a young lady is to feel herself attach'd to a Gentleman when he can testify it in no other way than by his actions, I mean when his situation will not permit him to speak?"[27] The best of mothers can be diabolically clever when setting themselves to break off such an affair. That was precisely the line to take, the very one which kept John Quincy awake in anguish night after night, which was slowly impaling him on its inescapable point. He could not afford to marry unless his parents helped him. He could not bring himself to ask them to help him—more than they were doing, which was too much already—and if he should ask them, the warnings against too early marriage which had been so valid with his father, and which were repeated in his mother's letters, proved that they would refuse, or would at best do it unwillingly. No. There was no way out but one. The takings of his first year in Boston showed all too clearly what that way must be. And John Quincy Adams was not the man to hug illusion, and deny the logic of fact. He made a clean cut. He said good-bye to Mary Frazier, for her own sake; he wrenched himself away from a false, an untenable situation; and he broke his heart. He was never the same man after.

So little did his mother understand his deep, repressed, mature suffering, that when he paid them a visit in Philadelphia in the new year, feeling his way on this subject for the last time, her sympathetic concern was curiously beside the point. She wrote to her sister that J. Q. A. was "depressed owing to want of business in his profession and the dismal prospect for practitioners of the law in Massachusetts. Being still dependent on his parents irks him. He appears to have lost much of his sprightliness and vivacity." Although these feelings are "proof of a good mind and sensible [sensitive] heart, I cd wish they did not oppress him so much. He wishes sometimes he had been bred a farmer, a merchant or anything by which he could earn his bread, but we all preach patience to him."[28]

So these good and excellent parents, with the best of intentions and great self-confidence, interfered with the first choice of both their elder children. In neither case had the choice been really intrinsically unsuitable; in neither had it been a mere passing fancy. But as Abigail herself would say, useless to look backward; let us look forward.

XIII

Philadelphia

From 1790 till 1800 the city of Philadelphia was the seat of government and the official home of John and Abigail Adams. These ten years had brought for the Adamses growth and fulfilment in every respect save one—Abigail's health. The climate of Philadelphia, as she had foreseen, never suited her, and she was obliged to spend long periods away from it.

The house they first settled into was the Hamilton (no relation to Alexander) property, Bush Hill. It was a large brick house, well outside the city. There were no bushes left on the hill—the British troops had cut them all for firewood when using the house during Howe's occupation of Philadelphia. But it made a good sheep pasture, and a shepherd and his flock came every day, to the delight of any resident grandchildren. There were open fields in front, and the views were rather beautiful, though "the country round has too much of the level to be my style," said Mrs Adams, "and as to the river—the Schuylkill is no more like the Hudson than I to Hercules!" Behind the house was the usual shady grove with a spacious gravel walk winding through it, and this time (reminiscent of Auteuil) it was ornamented by a number of marble statues.

Everything promised well except that nothing was ready. The furniture arrived by water just at the same time as Mrs Adams arrived by chaise—although she had travelled very slowly, not more than twenty miles a day. She drove up to the house, expecting to find everything got in order by the Brieslers, and there were the painters rushing about with wet brushes finishing up, and the rooms all empty, dank, and chill not only with wet paint but with four years of disuse. But this time Mrs Adams did not sit down and cry. This sort of thing was becoming quite a habit. So, murmuring that it was no more than she expected, she ordered fires in every room, and retired to the inn for the night.

At that, "the furniture must come in and we must inhabit it unfit as it was, for to go with 14 or 16 to lodgings was much beyond my revenue." Sickness naturally followed within a day or two. First niece Louisa was ill, then the maid Polly; then son Thomas, liable to rheumatism, was helpless for eighteen days, and "had to be carried from his bed to the settee, and fed like an infant," in spite of pukings and bleedings. "Dr Rush has attended them, and I have found him a kind friend as well as physician."

Mrs Adams had been very ill herself just before leaving New York, and while still convalescent had further taxed herself by helping to nurse Nabby's baby, who nearly died of inoculated small-pox. But she managed to get through the journey and the subsequent difficulties without a relapse, thanks to her resilient vitality.

Cordial Philadelphia, hearing of Mrs Adams's arrival, could not wait, never thought of waiting; the quicker the warmer. Visits and calls of welcome "took place none the less every day from 12 to 3 o'clock in the midst of rooms heaped with Boxes trunks, cases, etc." Poor Abigail Adams lost weight. But all was done at last. And it was lovely to see old friends again. Mrs Adams summed up early impressions in her journal letter to her sister—"Inhabitants most courteous, servants terrible."[1] (The new cook was put to bed drunk.)

And now the social whirl of Philadelphia, the gayest city in the United States, sucked her in. All those calls to return—invitations to tea and cards, to routs, pouring on her. "I will spend a very dissipated winter if I accept half!" she said to John. Mrs Washington arrived—also to a house not ready—and invited them to dinner; and presently started her drawing-room. Charles arrived for a long Christmas holiday, and escorted his mother to the drawing-room—"the circle very brilliant. How could it be otherwise, when the dazzling Mrs Bingham and her beautiful sisters were there, the Misses Allen and the Misses Chew—in short a constellation of beauties?"[2] Mrs Bingham with her Paris gowns was evidently the arbiter of fashion, and under her leadership the society of Philadelphia scintillated. The visiting Duke de la Rochefoucauld himself admitted, "I have seen balls where the splendour of the room, and richness of the dresses, did not suffer by comparison with Europe." And the beauty of the ladies he thought surpassing. "It would be no exaggeration to say that in the numerous assemblies of Philadelphia it would be impossible to meet a plain woman." This enormous butterfly of compliment inevitably carried a sting in the tail. "The young men for the most part seem to belong to another species."

Philadelphia boasted a theatre, and a box was provided by the actors for the President and Vice-President. Abigail was delighted. "It did not equal the French theatre, but the house was very neat and prettily fitted up." She saw *The School for Scandal* played by American actors, and enjoyed it, but missed "the divine Farren."[3] Curiously enough, too, she missed the English weather. "The climate of Old England for me! People do not grow old half so fast there. Two-thirds of the year here we must either freeze or melt. The weather now is winter in all respects." She looked out of her windows on the glittering surface of the January whiteness and turned away blinking. "Such a plain of snow as puts out my eyes!"[4]

Never has she been such a prisoner of weather. The two-mile drive to town was over an unpaved road of miry clay. In open weather "you must wallow to the city," the mud up to the horses' knees. If dry or frozen, "the holes and the roughnesses are intolerable."

Not only weather kept her tied down that winter. Thomas, just after entering Mr Ingersoll's office in Philadelphia as an articled clerk to study the family trade of law, had a sharp return of rheumatic fever, and was ill for two months. His mother nursed him tenderly. For the first four weeks he was again entirely helpless. And he was greatly depressed. Charles's coming was as good as medicine for him. Charles "cheered his spirits." That was Charles's great and universal gift.

Tom, just out of Harvard and now taking his turn as the son at home, had not particularly wanted to study law. His mother, with her prosperous merchant relatives, rather wished Tom could have gone into merchandise, "as I am sure he has more of a turn for an active life." Yet after all, as she said to Mary, "Let us look into our national legislature. Scarcely a man there makes any figure in debate who has not been bred to the law." And though the accents of John Adams are plain in the remark, she made it with full conviction. She has herself glanced over the men of note in the legislature—all of whom came from time to time to her house—and George Washington was the only notable exception.

Tom found it heavy going at first, however. And his health made it all the harder. His mother was certainly no mollycoddle. "Tom is not strong yet," she remarked, when he was back at work again after his illness. "I fear an attendance upon two offices through the day and studying through the evening at home is not calculated to mend it. But it is a maxim here that he who dies with studying dies in a good cause, and may go to another world much better calculated to improve his talents than if he had died a blockhead. Well, knowledge is a fine thing, and Mother Eve thought so; but she smarted so severely for hers that most of her daughters have been afraid of it since!"[5]

"Come, now!" said John Adams, "you are always complaining that women are not better educated—that fathers give their boys all the advantages!"

"Yes, education," said Abigail, musing. "Nothing's more important, yet how incalculable it is! Here I've had little grandson John more under my eye than ever I had my own children, and yet—look at the naughty things that he will sometimes say and do! Where does he learn them? . . . That reminds me I must write to Nabby and recommend her Dr Watts' *Moral Songs for Children*. They can learn them as easy as they can learn 'Jack and Jill' and 'Little Jack Horner,' that John can now say so glib. One must keep in mind the great importance of instilling precepts of morality early into their minds. I'm sometimes led to think that human nature is a very perverse thing, and much more given to evil than to good."[6]

Her son-in-law, for instance, she sadly reflected, was not evil, but he surely was perverse. Abigail had hardly taken leave of her daughter and got to Philadelphia and settled in Bush Hill before the Colonel had up and sailed for England, just like that. What a time to go, anyway, early in December, with all the winter before you! The worst possible sailing-weather. "His going was sudden and unexpected to us, but some private family debts which were due in England to his Father's estate was one motive, and some prospects of assisting his family by his voyage was a still further motive. I do not know why he has been so poorly provided for in the distribution of offices. The President has always said that he was sensible to his merit and meant to provide for him, but has not yet seen the way open to it. She, poor Girl, is call'd to quite a different trial from any she has before experienced, for tho the

Colonel was once before absent she was in her Father's house (in London). Now she writes that she feels as if unprotected, as if alone in the wide world. One of his brothers and sisters remain with her during the Col's absence. I have Johnny here with me, and a fine boy he is and the enlivener of the whole family."[7]

When Congress reopened in October 1791, Philadelphia hostesses presently became aware that they could not comfortably invite Mr Hamilton and Mr Jefferson to the same party. This perhaps was especially evident to Mrs Adams, whose husband was a close personal friend of Mr Jefferson and a political ally of Mr Hamilton. This latter alliance was the effect of John Adams's long contact abroad with the problems of commerce and credit, and his reluctant approval of Hamilton's schemes for national finance. Funding the public debt, assumption of the States' debts, creation of a Bank of America, and a system of revenue from taxation and excise, the four main points, each in turn aroused a storm. The Vice-President was not a member of the Cabinet. As presiding officer of the Senate he had no opportunity to debate. His splendid talents as debater and orator were all wasted. But he could exercise influence. He was not a man given to sit silent in groups of his peers who were discussing hot subjects as the wine bottle passed around the table. This influence was steadily exercised, in Senate and out, for the measures of Hamilton. And Jefferson could not bear it. Old friendship suffered schism.

In April 1792 Abigail wrote to her sister:

> The Southern members are determined if possible to ruin the Secretary of the Treasury, destroy all his well-built systems if possible, and give a fatal stab to the funding system. The V. President they have permitted to sleep in peace this winter. . . . The Secretary of State and even the President have not escaped. I firmly believe if I live ten years longer I shall see a division of the Southern and Northern states, unless more candour and less intrigue—shd prevail.[8]

The climate of Philadelphia had roused the dormant tendency to rheumatic fever which Abigail had had as a child, and which reappeared as inflammatory rheumatism. Remedies were not soothing. Blisters were applied to her wrists. Her daughter came from New York to nurse her, but in the midst of it was fetched away by her husband. Then Betsy Smith, who was visiting Mary Otis, took charge, and wrote to her sister-in-law, Will's wife:

I am now with Mrs Adams, she has been very ill and confined to her room for seven weeks, but is now better and intends leaving here by the middle of next month. I shall very much regret the loss of her society from which is to be derived both pleasure and improvement. She has few superiors and not many equals. Whoever knows must esteem her, for she adorns every situation with peculiar dignity.[9]

The last thing Mrs Adams noticed as she got into her chaise in Philadelphia for the journey to Braintree was the new coinage. "The coin is not permitted to wear the stamp of the President," she remarks, "because it would savour too much of royalty."[10]

The first thing she noticed on arrival—after the lovely greeting of delicate sweet scents and opal colours—was that her home-town had changed its name. The long, straggling township, which for many years past had recognized a North Precinct and a South Precinct, had at last agreed on division into two "towns." The South Precinct retained the name Braintree; the North Precinct, in which the Adams Mansion stood, had taken the name Quincy, after its most distinguished resident of old time, Abigail's grandfather.

Abigail, basking in this honour to her grandfather, found Boston ringing with praises of her son. Jefferson had recently sponsored the American printing of Tom Paine's new book, *The Rights of Man*. He had meant to do it secretly, as he promoted Freneau, but, bad luck, his signed letter to Paine appeared on the title-page of the first Philadelphia edition. This book seemed to George Washington and John Adams and others of their way of thinking to be urging the American Revolution along the downward path of the French, to the overthrow of stable government. Both President and Government party were therefore greatly satisfied when a series of articles signed "Publicola" began to appear in the Boston Press, which most ably answered the specious arguments of Tom Paine.

Jefferson at first thought they were written by John Adams—in England that was confidently stated to be so—but Madison perspicaciously pointed out to Jefferson that Publicola had an easier, less ponderous style. Publicola was, in fact, John Quincy Adams. Thus, by his own initiative, John Quincy unconsciously laid the foundation stone of his future career. For the articles gave Washington just what he needed, when he needed it.

John Adams sat down in a glow of fatherly pride to write to his absent wife with that warm appreciation of others and humble opinion of himself which he felt in his heart: "They get all that's good from their mother! Family and all! Look at Abigail's letters, for instance! Why, they were fit to print themselves, every one.

"You apologize for the length of your letters," he wrote,

> and I ought to excuse the shortness and emptyness of mine. Yours give me more entertainment than all the speeches I hear. There are more good thoughts, fine strokes, and mother wit in them than I hear in the whole week. . . . And I rejoice that one of my children, at least, has an abundance of not only mother wit but his mother's wit. It is one of the most amiable and striking traits in his composition! . . . If the rogue has any family pride, it is all derived from the same source. His Pa renounces and abjures every trace of it!

Abigail was left behind at Quincy when John Adams went back to Philadelphia after the second Presidential election. Washington again carried a unanimous vote which gave him first place. Although the Vice-President was not voted for as such, it was an understood thing that any rival candidates voted for by the Electoral College in 1793 were put up against John Adams, Washington being quite unassailable. Clinton of New York, a prominent stand-pat Anti, was the man campaigned for by the Anti-federalists, and for the first time party strife and political methods, including lies and misrepresentations, were seen in full blast. Abigail was much disgusted. The influence of the "Jacobins"* was very patent, and their democracy cry most irritating. John Adams got in, with seventy-seven votes against Clinton's fifty, but:

"Few old countries have exhibited more intrigue and falsehood than the Anti-federal party has done in the late election," wrote Abigail to her daughter.

> The cry of rights of man, liberty and equality were popular themes. Their object was to represent the Vice-President as inimical to them, and as a man whose object was to introduce a government of King, Lords and Commons and a hereditary nobility. They made unfair extracts from his writings. . . . They said in Virginia that he has recommended to Congress to make a son of George III King of America!

Another line of attack was to say "that he was opposed to the President. This Washington himself contradicted."

But though her feelings as a wife were hurt, she was fair enough and keen enough to realize that all this row and rumpus was not

* Jefferson's party of extreme Antis, nicknamed Jacobins because of their admiration of the French Revolution. They more than once had the new United States on the verge of war with Britain, in support of France.

directed personally against John Adams. It was really against Hamilton. "They despaired of destroying Hamilton unless they could remove the present Vice-President and place in his stead an enemy of Hamilton. Their object was to destroy his funding system and destroy the government."[11]

In fact the opposition was hard put to it to find a popular cry to use against two such men as George Washington and John Adams. If it had been Hamilton—why, he was wide open to attack. His *affaires* with women alone would have been a godsend for innuendo. But Hamilton was not up for election. Washington and Adams were in every important way above reproach. Both commanded unshakable public confidence. Yet the opposition had a case—as an opposition always has—if it could only put it into terms that would appeal to the mass. It was very clever to raise the cry of monarchy. Although it is hard to believe that any thinking man could possibly have taken it literally, it none the less put into picturesque and concrete form a dangerous tendency which did exist.

"Since the last election the President has been openly abused in the *National Gazette*," wrote Abigail, hardly able to believe it. But there were the sheets in front of her, sent on to her by her husband:

> . . . abused for his levees as an ape of royalty; Mrs Washington abused for her drawing-rooms; their celebration of birthdays sneered at; himself insulted because he has not come forward and exerted his influence in favour of a further compensation to the army. They even tell him that a greater misfortune cannot befall a people than for their President to have no competitor; that it infuses into him a supercilious spirit, renders him self-important, and creates an idea that one man only is competent to govern. They compare him to a hyena and a crocodile; charge him with duplicity and deception. The President has not been accustomed to such language and his feelings will be wounded I presume![12]

John Adams, spending the summer at Quincy with Abigail, learned of the fearful yellow-fever epidemic in Philadelphia which had almost depopulated the city and was more certain than ever that city was an unwholesome place for her. When he returned to his duties in the autumn he left her behind, though he missed her desperately. He was not the only one who missed her. Mrs Washington had sent her love, and Mrs Knox and Mrs Bingham —many of the ladies, and even of the men! Mr Jefferson for one. Another male admirer had said that Mrs Adams was needed in

Philadelphia, that she ought to be Autocratrix of the United States! In Abigail's absence from the Washingtons' levees, Mrs Knox often took her place at Mrs Washington's right hand. But it was not the same. A life-giving element was gone.

There were times when John Adams could hardly bear it. "I for my part," he wrote to her,

> am wearied to death with ennui. Obliged to be punctual by my habits, confined to my seat as in a prison, to see nothing done, hear nothing said, and to say and do nothing. O that my rocks were within a mile or two, and my habitation and pretty little wife above all. Ah, I fear some fault unknown has brought upon me such punishments, to be separated both when we were too young and when we are too old.[13]

Mrs Adams saw her house taking shape pleasantly according to her plans; her garden planted, the roses she had brought from the garden at Auteuil weathering the winters well, her dairy coming on, and butter going regularly by sea to her husband in Philadelphia. There was pleasant social intercourse with friends and neighbours, and above all it was heart-warming to have her eldest son coming out for week-ends from Boston. A quiet, restful, healthful life, yet one fully occupied.

England, at war with the Jacobin party in control of France, and trying to restore the House of Bourbon, was attempting to apply the weapon of blockade. This involved interference on the high seas with neutral vessels bound for French ports, and American ships thus interfered with were in a mood to resent it. The situation was on a hair-trigger, and Washington, after consulting privately with John Adams, decided to send a special envoy to England to arrange the treaty of commerce, which still waited completion.

"He made me a very friendly visit yesterday," wrote John Adams to Abigail,

> which I returned to-day, and had two hours' conversation with him alone in his cabinet. The conversation, which was extremely interesting, and equally affectionate, I cannot explain even by a hint. But his earnest desire to do right, his deliberate and comprehensive view of our affairs with all the world, appeared in a very respectable and amiable light.[14]

Washington could not spare John Adams to go to England—in fact, the Constitution would hardly allow it; if Washington died suddenly the Government, so new and raw, would fall apart without the sturdy Vice-President to summon public confidence and go ahead without a break. The next best choice as envoy was John Jay, both gifted and experienced. He was Chief Justice, but he at once made the self-sacrifice of resigning that post, at Washington's request, in order to accept the thankless and difficult errand. Before his appointment could be ratified by Congress a (Jefferson-Madison) Bill had passed the House, pushed on by Madison,* prohibiting the admission of any commodities from Great Britain until the grievances complained of by American seamen should be redressed.

This Bill came up before the Senate and was debated, and the Senate was equally divided on it, thirteen to thirteen. If it had passed, Jay's mission would have been abortive, there would have been no use his going, and war with England would have been inevitable. But Vice-President John Adams had the casting vote. He alone conspicuously stood between the country and the disaster of then falling into Jefferson's plan (though Adams did not know it as Jefferson's). John Adams exercised his casting vote, and the measure was thrown out.

Yet such dramatic emergencies did not console John Adams for the paralysis of his great powers which the speakership of the Senate entailed. With his oratory all banked up within him, he had to listen to the inept and feeble speeches of others on subjects near his heart. With his incisive skill in debate, he had to see others missing points and letting their opponents get away with victory when they, at his hands, would have been utterly demolished. He could give the casting vote, yes; but had he been able to speak from the floor, the question probably never would have got to such a close call. It was a sort of daily purgatory.

He wrote to his wife: "My country has in its wisdom contrived for me the most insignificant office that ever the mind of man contrived or his imagination conceived."

John Jay went to England and came back a year later† with a treaty of commerce. Abigail said: "It is well the Senate only have the discussion of it, if it was to go to the House for ratification and was a Treaty from the Kingdom of Heaven proclaiming peace on Earth and Good Will to Men there would not be wanting Characters to defame and abuse it!" However, even in the Senate, Jay's Treaty was considered so unfavourable that it was difficult to get the two-thirds vote necessary to ratify it.

* Jefferson, without office, was living in retirement at his Virginia estate, Monticello, pulling his wires from afar. † March 1795.

Abigail, who, wherever she was, always heard from husband or son or cousin or admiring male the inside story of whatever was going on, knew of French secret-service money circulating in America against the Jay Treaty. "Hireling orators and printers . . . Bache's paper and the noted *Chronicle* have become the infamous vehicles of insolent and perfidious defamation. . . . Floodgates of scurrility and abuse upon the President and Mr Jay." Particularly Washington. She can only compare it with the ostracism the ancient Greeks inflicted on their best: ". . . these observations will occur to every one who read the attacks upon one of the Fairest Characters who ever gave fame to a Nation."[15]

The discovery of a secret correspondence between the French envoy Fauchet and Edmund Randolph, who had succeeded Jefferson as Secretary of State, gave a severe setback to the Jacobin Antis. Randolph retired in disgrace. Congress rallied in indignation to the support of the Government and passed the Jay Treaty.

"In the course of a few weeks," wrote Abigail to John Quincy,

> the table of Congress was covered with petitions from all parts of the Union requesting them to make the necessary appropriations to carry the Treaty into effect, that the faith and honour of the United States might be preserved, even those who did not like the treaty united in this wish, considering the faith of the nation pledged.
>
> The triumph of the friends of government in Boston was such as to astonish the Anarchists,* for a Town Meeting was call'd by them to oppose a memorial from the merchants in favour of the treaty, when behold they were out-voted by an hundred to one.
>
> All through the towns and villages the voice was, we will support the Government, we will not have war. Even the little village of Quincy presented more than a hundred petitions,[16]

added Abigail Adams modestly. And no doubt Mrs Adams had done her part in getting them.

John Adams's influence, backed by his years abroad, was strong behind the scenes—closeted for long, intimate hours with Jay; dining with the new Secretary of State Pickering; dining with the President. He wrote to Abigail—then visiting Nabby in New York —and warned her to be careful what she said in that *milieu*. There was much he would like to tell her—"but mum-mum-mum." When they were together for the summer at Quincy she would hear it all.

* *I.e.*, the Jacobins.

Abigail had been horrified and moved at the guillotining of Marie Antoinette and at the cruelties of the Reign of Terror now setting in. She suffered for her friends the Lafayettes, now suspect and in danger as aristocrats. But her point of view was like Washington's. She wanted every one to let France alone. "I wish most ardently that every arm extended against that unhappy country might be withdrawn, and they left to themselves to form whatever constitution they choose; and whether it is republican or monarchical is not of any consequence to us provided it is a regular government of some form or other which may secure the faith of treaties."[17]

Mrs Adams sympathized with Washington's unending troubles, in such excessive variety, in the Cabinet and out of it. Threat of war abroad need not be added to by rebellion and treachery at home. Why could not people settle down quietly and let the Government they had themselves created get along with governing? The French people had had something to complain of, she had seen it for herself. It was not surprising they had lost their tempers. But "even in one of the freest and happiest governments in the world, restless spirits will aim at disturbing it."[18]

Colonel Smith had come back unexpectedly at the height of Abigail's illness in February '92 and carried his wife and children off with him to England. They remained a year, then back they came again, in time for Nabby to give birth to another baby, this time a little girl. Every one was delighted, and the new Caroline grew up to be everybody's favourite. She had the charm and lovableness of her Uncle Charles without his weaknesses. As for Colonel Smith, he was suddenly rolling in money. Successful speculations in land, the sale of large tracts of upstate New York to some English nobleman, had apparently made him a millionaire. He bought a coach-and-six like General Washington's. He began to build a huge and elaborate house in New York, which he named Mount Vernon. But even from the beginning it was looked at askance by the canny descendants of the Dutch patroons, and the common people called it "Smith's Folly." All this display was another kind of torture to Nabby's grave and sensitive spirit. However, at first Mr and Mrs Adams were rather impressed. They had been accustomed to excuse their son-in-law's restlessness by saying to their friends: "The Colonel is very active!" Now—"I wish my boys had a little more of his activity!" said John Adams.[19]

XIV

John Adams becomes President

HE DID NOT WISH THAT LONG. A most important event took place in the Adams family in the spring of 1794. Washington appointed a resident Minister to Holland, and the Minister he chose was the young Boston lawyer, John Quincy Adams. This was the reward for Publicola and other spirited articles in the Boston Press—articles which, like his father's before him, were not aimed at stirring up the passions of the uneducated mob but at appealing to the reason of the intelligent. They had done good service to President Washington, and they showed a mind of uncommon calibre. Washington had only waited for a suitable task to present itself to make use of both.

John Quincy, receiving the startling summons, saw the door of opportunity opening, not where he had been vainly looking for it, in the street door of his office, but in a dark corner where he had assumed a blank wall. He might well curse himself for his too great reasonableness in the matter of marriage. Life was not logical. In trying to safeguard against bad chance, one forgot to allow for good.

After a visit to Quincy to talk things over with his mother and his father—just returned from Congress in Philadelphia—he must wind up his business. Then the stage for Providence, and the packet to New York, and on by stage again to Philadelphia to receive his instructions, and study the situation a while in the State Department (reading there, chiefly, the six folio volumes of his father's masterly correspondence when Minister to Holland himself). He returned to Quincy for final farewells, and embarked from Boston on September 17, just as he had done as a boy. He took his brother Tom with him as secretary. His mother was glad for Thomas to have some experience abroad—the only member of the family who had not had any.

In October John Quincy Adams was in London, bearer of urgent dispatches for John Jay. He received Jay's advice as to how to conduct himself in Holland, conferred with him on the draft of Jay's treaty, and enjoyed a little relaxation showing his brother Tom about London.

Now that Abigail's son was American Ambassador at The Hague, there began one of the most remarkable correspondences between mother and son ever penned. "I wrote to my mother and to the Secretary of State," became a frequent entry in John Quincy's journal. Comment on scenes, persons, books, politics, international problems, and the philosophy of life passed freely between the gifted man in the early flower of his manhood and the lady at Quincy. No need for this mother to beg this son to write. He wrote because he wanted to. And though he had for her a large amount of that particular affection which is known as filial, he often called her "friend." The letters are more such as would pass from friend to friend. He valued her mind. He felt a sauce in her personal comments, quite her own. Her news and information from home were better than he could get from any newspaper, and from most dispatches; her keen, critical interest in his affairs at the Dutch court were not just maternal. She enlarged his horizon and sharpened his wits. She kept him interested and warmed. And her thoughts were a woman's thoughts. She was, above all else, a fully completed woman, and as such she showed him all the time a slightly different world.

As for her, she appreciated to the full, with none of a parent's patronage, the different world which this intelligent man, her son, so freely showed to her. "Your letters," she told him, "always possess one good quality beyond many others, they have an intrinsic value which age does not impair."[1]

And now John Quincy was very much upset by hearing from his mother the surprising news that his brother Charles was married! The bride was impeccable, Sally Smith, one of the Colonel's charming sisters. But here was Charles beginning the practice of law in New York, no better off than John Quincy had been in Boston; just as dependent on the help of parents; a bride with no more money in her own right than lovely Mary Frazier; and Charles was the younger brother! The elder brother suffered a burning sense of injustice, and did not conceal it.

The pen which was writing able reports of public affairs with such "valuable information and political foresight" that President Washington prophesied to his father that the writer would ere long be found "at the head of the Diplomatic Corps" dipped into a little personal gall. John Quincy informed his mother that the strangling of a first love often induced a premature state of frigidity, which he was conscious was beginning within himself. A cold ambition would replace the natural warm impulses of the heart. . . .

Abigail wrote back as best she could.

> It was natural, my dear son, for you to make the reflections you did upon your Father's wish, & at the same time learning that your Brother was united to the choice of his Heart, I do not wonder that it awakens the dormant feelings of your soul & uncovers the fire which tho smothered gleam'd up again upon the recollection of the sacrifice you had made. . . . Sincere Friendships are more generally form'd at an early age when the Heart is tender soft & unsuspicious before we have been jostled by the tumults of life & put out of humour & conceit of the world or the paltry competitions of Ambition & avarice freeze up the generous current of the soul. But it must be longer than I hope you will remain single before you reach that frigid state, therefore do not despair of one day feeling a similar regard for a kindred soul yet in reserve for you.
>
> Your Brother Charles writes me that he is very happy. Sally is an amiable virtuous girl, with every disposition to make him a good wife & it will be his fault if he is not in future what he now is . . . happy, his business increasing and like to do well. When I was in New York I had much conversation with her, & tho I advised them to continue longer single, I did not wish to shake their determination to be for none other.[8]

But a few weeks later she is acknowledging some cloaks sent from London which John Quincy Adams had got "a young lady of great taste" to choose for him.

"Oh," says his mother, "I perceive some fair one has . . . taught you to admire! Youth & beauty have penetrated through your fancied apathy. . . . As you tell me that the enthusiasm of youth has subsided, I will presume that reason & judgment have taken its place."

She hears of the repeated sickness of poor Thomas.

> He must return home when you take to yourself this lady whom you still leave in the clouds to me. Yes, you plainly tell me in your last letter that you are betrothed, but you leave me to the wide field of conjecture where to fix. My own imagination has carried me to the

family of Mr Johnson as I have before related to you. I approve of the young lady's discretion in sending you to the Hague without her, and shd learn to accumulate some solid property before you take upon you the charge of a family.[3]

In thus getting hastily engaged and announcing it to his parents, without giving the lady's name, John Quincy relieved his feelings by violently asserting his independence, and remarked that he was "old enough to get married." His mother insists on pretending not to read the bitterness, refusing to show hurt, maintaining a calm sensible tone which must have been galling to her son. "You are certainly old enough," she says mildly. "Your father was married nine days younger than you now are."

But what she can't tell him is the reason behind Charles's marriage. All is not well with Charles. He needs an anchor. The responsibility of a wife and home of his own may be his salvation. No great career will be placed in jeopardy by Charles's early marriage. All one can hope for there, she has sadly learned, is that the liquor habit may be controlled and a decent respectability maintained. What lies before Charles is no steep climb up the slopes of fame but a dreadful possibility of disaster. It is Sally to the rescue. Signals are set for quiet in the laboratory while the experiment proceeds.

With Charles safely married to Sally, and apparently steadied and happy, and John Quincy consoling himself with Louisa Johnson, a suitable American girl, Abigail gave way in this spring of 1796 to a halcyon interval. "If Envy owes me a grudge now is her time whilst I am in the peaceful enjoyment of domestic quiet free from the anxious cares which are always attendant upon the most elevated stations."[4]

The possibility of the most elevated station loomed. Washington had firmly announced his intention to retire at the end of his term. As it affected John Quincy, this looked to Abigail like an inevitable signal for her son's withdrawal to private life, whichever way the new election turned. But Washington did not leave this subject to embarrass his successor. His last act at the close of Congress was to appoint John Quincy Adams Minister to Portugal.

When Abigail heard presently that both the brothers had regretfully decided that Tom's health forbade his further service abroad, and that he was making plans to come home, she had a change of heart. It would never do for John Quincy to go to a place like

Portugal with no one to keep him company or do for him! She wrote hurriedly; he must not misunderstand her about Louisa. She is in favour of the marriage! In fact:

> I think you ought not to go to Portugal alone. Your brother means to return to us, you whose chief delight is in domestic life must feel yourself in a desert without a companion. I advise you to marry the lady before you go to Portugal, give my love to her and tell her I consider her already as my daughter, and as she made England delightful to you I hope she will every other country.[5]

For a young man engaged to be married and thus encouraged, John Quincy Adams closed the year 1796 in his diary at The Hague with a rather singular entry: "The situation of two objects the nearest to my heart, my country and my father, press continually upon my reflections. They engross every thought and almost every power, every faculty."

The ship bearing the mail arrived at last. It was the eldest son of the President of the United States who called, at nine o'clock of a summer morning, at Mr Johnson's house on Tower Hill and became part of a wedding cortège to the Church of All Hallows Barking. There he was married to Louisa Catherine Johnson, the second daughter of Mr and Mrs Joshua Johnson, in the presence of her family and one or two friends, Tom Adams acting as best man. The slanting sun made coloured patches on the dim stone, and touched the bride's bright golden hair where her blue-ribboned hat turned up at the side. The snowy powder of the groom made his eyes look the darker. The hum of London's traffic rattled outside, the cries of the cockney street-hawkers were musically audible, coming and going, heard and not heard, as the two young Americans plighted their troth. Their low voices echoed among the ancient shadows as he vowed to love and to cherish, she to love, honour, and obey, until death do us part. Then—for neither of them came to this marriage in a romantic mood, each knew the other had parted with the unrecapturable first ardour before they met—they filled in the day prosaically with a drive to "Tilney House, one of the splendid country seats for which this country is distinguished."

Louisa Adams's soft, yielding grace and charming face concealed unexpected resources of strength and intelligence. In a mood of self-revelation years later she wrote:

> I set out in life with the most elevated notions of honour and principle;

> ere I had entered it fully my hopes were blasted, and my ideas ot mankind, that is all the favourable ones, almost, were suddenly chilled, and I was very near forming the horrid and erroneous opinion that no such thing as virtue existed. This was a dreadful doctrine at the age of little more than twenty.

She was in this mood of heartbreak and disillusionment when she first met John Quincy, whom she married at twenty-two. The wedding day was July 26, 1797. And, sober as it was, it was a fortunate day.

Abigail had foreseen that her husband would be elected to the Presidency, though not without a struggle. In November 1796 she had written her son: "No man can expect a unanimous choice; there were such a combination of circumstances united in Washington as no age or country have produced." And she sadly reflects, "It requires courage and firmness, wisdom and temperance, patience and forbearance to stand in such a conspicuous, such an elevated station."

But however clearly one might foresee a tussle, and however accurately one might list the qualities requisite for one who would aspire to be President, the dust and confusion of the arena were something else again. It was all the worse because it was the very first time there had been a contested Presidential election. No onc had before seen a Presidential campaign. Abigail described it to her son as she saw it.

"All the arts of the Jacobins are in practice, united with the pride of the Old Dominion* and foreign influence. . . . The democratic Societies circulating Hand Bills containing libels on Mr Adams, attacking him as attached to monarchy and titles." (They were even stuck on gateposts, doors of houses and posts, which she considers "a right Gallic measure.") "The *Chronical* [Bache's paper] has been teeming for this month past on the old story of Monarchy and Aristocracy, quoting detached sentences and ringing all the Changes and Chimes."

However, John Adams and his supporters did not let libels pass in complete silence, nor were they without any counter-offensive. As Abigail remarked, they too were "not without something of the joy of battle. . . . They have dropped all candidates but the Vice-President and Mr Jefferson,† who on the other side has his principles

* Virginia. † That is, it was a straight fight for the Presidency between Adams and his party (Federals) and Jefferson and his party (Anti-Federal Jacobin Democrats).

and practices thoroughly dissected. . . . You will readily suppose that a fiery ordeal is preparing."

The two friends were now in open fight. But to John Adams it was purely a political fight. It should not affect private friendship. He did not blame Jefferson for the mud-slinging campaign in the papers against himself. He blamed Bache and such small fry. Jefferson was above all that. So when the returns were in, and John Adams was at the top of the poll with seventy-one votes, Jefferson second with sixty-eight, a position which automatically gave Jefferson the post of Vice-President, John Adams concurred in his wife's opinion as expressed to her son; Abigail wrote:

> I consider the Vice-Presidency as a conciliatory union of the States, and on that account a fortunate event. I have always entertained friendship for Mr Jefferson, from a personal knowledge and long acquaintance with him; tho I cannot altogether accord with him in politics I believe him to be a man of strict honour and of rare integrity of heart.

She added, a little puzzled as she reflected on it, but unsuspicious, "The most reprehensible part of his conduct was countenancing that Frenner [Freneau] when he was continually libelling the government."[9]

To have the opposing candidate for President elected to the Vice-Presidency was a difficult circumstance. However, John Adams prepared himself to meet the future in a composed, confident, and tolerant mood.

The first action he had to take was, on February 8, to announce to the Senate, as their presiding officer, the results of the election. His wife, in far-off Quincy, looking out of her window on the sunny winter day, shared with him the greatness of the moment, and met it with him in loftiness of spirit. Not pride but prayer filled her heart.

She wrote to him:

> You have this day to declare yourself head of a nation. "And now, O Lord my God, Thou hast made Thy servant ruler over the people. Give unto him an understanding heart, that he may know how to go out and come in before this great people; that he may discern between good and bad. For who is able to judge this thy so great a people?" were the words of a royal sovereign; and not less applicable to him who is invested with the chief magistracy of a nation, though he wear not a crown, nor the robes of royalty. My thoughts and meditations

are with you, though personally absent; and my petitions to Heaven are that "the things which make for peace may not be hidden from your eyes. . . ."[7]

A week later John Adams formally laid down his job of presiding over the Senate, with a parting address; tribute to eight years of "perfect and uninterrupted harmony" with Washington, "without envy in the one or jealousy in the other," and "on the other hand, have never had the smallest misunderstanding with any member of the Senate." He thanked them that in sharp difference of opinion there had been no resentment of his casting vote but that he had received "uniform politeness and respect from every quarter of the house."

Then he drove home to Quincy for a few days—he liked journeys, they rested his active mind—saw his Abigail, shared his experiences and thoughts with her; sat in quiet by the bedside of his dying mother, whose life had been slowly ebbing for many months; and went back to Philadelphia alone for his inauguration. He had hoped to take his wife with him, but his mother's condition forbade it.

So Abigail was not there to see her husband at his moment of greatest triumph, the public peak and summit of his career, the climax which could never, humanly speaking, be surpassed. She did not hear the fanfare, the cheers of the great crowd, nor the thrilling chiming of the bells. She did not share the hush which fell over the assembly at the solemn taking of the oath; nor the emotion stirred in the House by the noble, rolling periods in the inaugural address of one of the greatest orators of his time.*

Nor did Abigail see the sight which had never been seen before, nor has ever been seen again, of a departing President assisting in the inaugural ceremonies of another.

From some points of view it might seem a lack of tact for Washington to be present on this occasion. Public farewells and floods of adulation had swept the country at the recent celebration of his birthday on February 22. To reappear at Mr Adams's inauguration was to invite a repetition of that emotion, to blend a powerful element of sadness at the obvious end of an era with the joyful welcome due to the new elected leader. But Washington set such considerations aside for others which seemed more important. He wanted to show personal friendship and honour to Mr Adams. He

* Mason, the treaty publisher, said he had never heard such a speech in public in his life.

wanted also to show that he was behind the new administration, and give it publicly any prestige which his support might gain for it.

John Adams wrote from his heart to his wife the next day, with great simplicity:

> Your dearest friend never had a more trying day than yesterday. A solemn scene it was indeed; and it was made more affecting to me by the presence of the General, whose countenance was as serene and unclouded as the day. He seemed to me to enjoy a triumph over me. Methought I heard him say—"Ay, I am fairly out, and you fairly in! See which of us will be happiest."*
>
> When the ceremony was over he came and made me a call and cordially congratulated me, and wished my administration might be happy, successful and honourable.
>
> In the chamber of the House of Representatives was a multitude as great as the space could contain, and I believe scarcely a dry eye but Washington's. The sight of the sun setting full-orbed, and another rising, though less splendid, was a novelty.[8]

But Abigail was not there. The letter came to her where she was tied to the tedious duties of a sickroom, easing the lingering final hours of an aged woman. And her eyes rained to read it.

But when she was free at last to go to join her husband, to assume her place as First Lady of the United States, it was with a sober mind. Death came in April, and struck twice. In a single week, the death of John Adams's mother, eighty-eight years old, and Abigail's niece Mary Cranch, aged twenty-one, gathered the same group of relatives for funeral rites. "I have asked was all this necessary to wean me from the world?" mourned Abigail. "Was there danger of my fixing too strong an attachment upon it . . . forget that here I have no abiding place? . . . I have received your letters of April 16th and 19th. I want no courting to come. I am ready and willing to follow my husband wherever he chooses; but the hand of Heaven has arrested me. . . . I prepare to set out on the morrow."[9]

* Bache's farewell to Washington when he retired, March 1797: "If ever there was a period for rejoicing, this is the moment—every heart in unison with the freedom and happiness of the people ought to beat high with exultation that the name of *Washington* from this day ceases to give a currency to political iniquity and to legalize corruption."

XV

When Yellow Leaves . . .

As she got into the chaise, however, her attention was very much upon the world and the immediate part she and her husband were to play there. Among the letters which she could reread to entertain her on the long journey there was one which gave her a glimpse of the arena and of her champion's readiness at all points.

"John Adams must be an intrepid," he wrote, "to encounter the open assaults of French, and the secret plots of England, in concert with all his treacherous friends and open enemies in his own country. Yet, I assure you, he never felt more serene in his life!"[1]

But her own heart trembled. As the chaise jogged southward at a steady pace over the best road in America, the Boston Post Road, travelling through forest and moorland with frequent glimpses of the sea, Abigail took out her pen and inkhorn and wrote to her sister. She quoted from her well-stored memory:

> Is Heaven tremendous in its frowns? Most sure,
> And in its favours formidable too . . .

"Such appears to me the situation in which I am placed, enviable no doubt in the eyes of some, but never envyd or coveted by me." Brooding on it, she looked out of the window, and her gardener's eye caught sight of something. She dipped into the ink briskly. "I forget to mention to Mr Porter to attend to the first caterpillar webb and take them off as soon as they appear," she wrote with restored cheerfulness. "Pray send me word! I see they are beginning along the road."[2]

She paused a day or two in New York and its environs to visit her daughter Mrs Smith and her son Charles and his wife and baby. May was well in when "on Wednesday morning, about 25 miles from Philadelphia I was met by my friend, who claiming his own, I quitted my own carriage and took my seat by his side. We rode on to Bristol where I had previously engaged a dinner, and there upon the banks of the Delaware we spent the day, getting into the city at sunset."[3]

Abigail was fifty-three and John was sixty-two. They had reached an age when, in the average marriage, mutual interest is at a low ebb. The lover period is long past, the mutual care of young or growing children is finished, the man's widening interests have few points of contact with the narrowing field of the domestic woman. But seldom had Mr and Mrs Adams had a better day than this. His heart, when apart from her, yearned for her continually. When he was with her his mind sought after hers. And she brought to him at all times quick response, eager interest, grave judgment and apt comment. Above all, never did she exacerbate his irritation or add to his fret, either by fanning the flame of his resentment, however just, or by opposing him with disagreement. Each was to each still the favourite, the wanted companion. John Adams, President of the United States, had just summoned a special first session of Congress to hear his report of the French Directory's bad treatment of the American envoys and what he proposed to do about it. Issues of peace and war loomed on the horizon, and the weighty responsibility that rested on him was the heavier because it was new. But he took a day off to drive to meet his wife and honeymoon with her among the peach and dogwood blossoms on the banks of the Delaware.

They talked about France; and about Mr Jefferson and Mr Hamilton; and about daughter Mrs Smith, and son Charles.

"I found Mrs Smith and her children in good health," reported Abigail, "but Mrs Smith grows very fleshy! However, being older and more moulded into the form of a woman, she doesn't look so burdened. The Colonel had been gone for a fortnight up to his new lands, leaving her solitary and forlorn indeed, but for the youngsters. This house they now have at East Chester is miles from the nearest neighbour! It's a poor, wild place, but they must retrench! That gambling in land has got hold of him. Buying one property and selling another, losing so much here, gaining so much there, huge sums passing—his accounts get very confusing. Nabby hardly knows how they stand. My thoughts about their prospects took away all my appetite. I could not discuss them with her. I saw her heart too full. Such is the madness of speculation and extravagance. *She* is not to blame in the least!"

"No. To her no blame is due," said John. He knew remonstrance with his son-in-law was useless. But yet the man had good abilities and some excellent qualities. If he would just get himself a sound steady job. . . . The cardinal's song whistled in poignant sweetness above their silence. John threw some fretful pebbles into the Delaware. *Splash! Splash!* "Well, how was Charles getting on?"

"Charles seems well-settled in New York. He lives prettily but frugally. He has a lovely babe and a discreet woman I think for his wife." Abigail could not help adding, "Quite different from many of the family!"[4]

"I will tell you a secret," said her husband, "knowing that you are one of the few women who can keep one! Your son John Quincy is going to be sent, if Congress agrees, to Berlin instead of Portugal. The political situation now demands that we have a minister there, one has been asked for, and Portugal must wait."

The sun lowered from the meridian too quickly, the holiday was too soon over. Yet it did not much matter. They were not to part. They got into the chaise and drove together through the flowery afternoon into the sunset city.

The house they were now in was the same one on Market Street which had been occupied by Washington. A larger house had been especially built as a Presidential mansion on Ninth and Market, and was just ready, but Adams refused it. The financial strain would be too great on a President who wanted to live on his salary. Washington had been in command of great private wealth, but even he had used little ostentation. The most showy item had been his cream-coloured coach with the painted panels, drawn by six horses with postilions and outriders.

Relations between Mr Jefferson and Mr Adams, as Mr Adams assumed office, were friendly. Mr Jefferson made a graceful opening speech when he took his seat in the Senate as Presiding Officer, saying that "the high functions of the first office had been justly confided" to Mr Adams. And Mr Adams privately asked Mr Jefferson whether he would consider placing his experience of France at the service of the Government and accepting appointment on a new French Commission which Mr Adams proposed sending to try to untangle the deadlock over there. Mr Jefferson, however, refused this service very decidedly, not only for himself but for Mr Madison or for any of his party.

June saw the routine of Presidential life for Mr and Mrs Adams fully under way. John felt the harness of office already easy on his shoulders, and, as always when Abigail was with him, his eagerness was tempered by a steady serenity.

Abigail had made up her mind to "bear her honours meekly." In fact, the road up had been so gradual, so natural in all its steps from the obscure parsonage of her birth, that there was no shock of transition. From the days when Grandmother Quincy had taught her lady's manners, and Grandfather Quincy had taught her public spirit, she had been unconsciously preparing for this station—the highest a woman could hold in her country, the First Lady of the United States. The hand of destiny that had shaped her put her now into the place, and she fitted it exactly.

Not many months had passed before an observer could say of her, "She is very much respected by everybody. Notwithstanding she comes from the Eastward many acknowledge her to be superior to her sex."[5]

Abigail wrote to her sister Mary an account of her day.

> I keep up my old habit of rising at an early hour. If I did not I should have little command of my time. At 5 I rise. From that time till 8 I have a few leisure hours. At 8 I breakfast, after which till 11 I attend to my family arrangements. At that hour I dress for the day. From 12 until 2 I receive company, sometimes until 3. We dine at that hour unless on company days, which are Tuesdays and Thursdays. After dinner I usually ride out until 7. I begin to feel a little more at home, and less anxiety about the ceremonious part of my duty, tho by not having a drawing-room for the summer I am obliged every day to devote two hours for the purpose of seeing company.

The chief trial of that summer for Abigail was the keeping of the Fourth of July as established by Washington.

> We must then have all the gentlemen of the city, the Governor and officers and companies, all of whom the late President used to treat with cake, punch and wine. . . . As we are here we cannot avoid the trouble nor the expense. I have been informed the day used to cost the late President 500 dollars. . . . More than 200 wt of cake and 2 quarter casks of wine besides spirit. You will not wonder that I dread it, or think President Washington to blame for introducing the custom if he could have avoided it. Congress never were present on

that day,* so that I shall have a hundred and fifty of them in addition. . . . Long tables are set in the house and yard.[6]

To make it worse—this trying to live up to a standard set by a wealthier man and yet keep within one's income—Bache's paper started its long-continued personal abuse of President Adams by an attack on his salary. This made Abigail very angry. "The President's salary is $14,000—the same granted to President Washington without half its value. . . ."[7]

Congress rose late in July, to avoid the "season of the pestilence," now annually looked for. The members scattered. Jefferson went to Monticello, and John and Abigail went back to refreshing Quincy.

On the way to Boston through New York they paused to pick up their grandsons, to take them away from the squalor and loneliness of Colonel Smith's farm at East Chester. They were put to school at an academy in Atkinson, to board in the family of Aunt Peabody (sister Betsy, formerly Aunt Shaw). This was a fine chance for young William and John, now ten and nine. "It will be the making of them, the father's misfortunes will prove the salvation of the children, as their grandfather sometimes observed to me."[8]

Returning in October, Mr and Mrs Adams went round by East Chester to get Nabby and her baby girl, who were going to spend the winter with them in Philadelphia. They were held up at East Chester by news of the raging epidemic of yellow fever in the city. Congress had to extend its recess an extra month on account of it. "The deadly disease . . . but for the fleeing of the inhabitants to the number of thirty thousand, wd have made as great ravages as in the year 1793. The frost only puts a stop to it."[9]

During the month of enforced holiday at Nabby's farm, Abigail received a packet of letters from her sons abroad. John Quincy Adams, to his parents' astonishment, was grumbling heartily at having to go to Berlin. His disgruntlement gave his mother "real pain." She confided to him to console him, "If Washington had been in office I can tell you where you wd have been employed—as one of the Envoys to France. This was the desire and opinion of all the Ministers."[10]

As for Thomas, he was not keen about Berlin either. He dreaded

* Always before absent for the summer recess. The critical situation with France kept Congress in session this year until after the Fourth.

making that winter journey, to such a climate, with his rheumatism. But go he must, he could not leave his beloved brother in the lurch. He implored his mother to start things moving to send out a substitute. Nothing else would release him. But he was greatly taken with his new sister-in-law. He reported that Louisa was beautiful and intelligent, would be a true helpmeet for her husband, and that "she loves him as she ought."

He added, "He is very happy and doubtless will remain so, for the young lady has much sweetness of temper. . . . She is indeed a most lovely woman, and in my opinion worthy in every respect of the man for whom she has with so much apparent cheerfulness renounced father and mother, kindred and country, to unite her destinies with his."[11]

Abigail knew that Tom's standards as to what was fit for his brother were exacting indeed. She was impressed. "This," she ruminated, "is a great deal for Thomas to say."

Relations with France steadily deteriorated, and on March 5, 1798, Abigail wrote to Will Smith:

> I see not but war is inevitable. This morning for the first time dispatches have arrived from our Envoys. The latest is of January 8th, informing that they had not been received nor was there the least probability that they should be. . . . The French papers are full of abuse against them. In one they call Mr Pinckney "a Wretch sold to England." Every deception is made use of to exasperate the publick mind against America and to prepare them for hostilities. Every paper being under the despotism of the Directory not a line can be published to undeceive them.[12]

This passage is evidence of how completely Abigail was in her husband's secret counsels. The dispatches, though they inspired John Adams's address to Congress in March, were not published to Congress and the nation until April 5. But his wife had read them on the day of their arrival.

Bache's Press never knew that, but the uncommonly close relationship between the President and his wife was plain to the naked eye, and the Jacobin newspapers were already sneering at Darby and Joan. (Who were "Darby and Joan"? Abigail wanted to know. She could not place the reference. Oh, well—she philosophically decided to take it as a compliment!)[13]

John Adams's March message contained a paragraph, written in by himself, permitting merchantmen to arm. Jefferson, fastening on this single gesture of self-defence, called this dignified and temperate document "*an insane message.*" Hamilton set in motion through a member of the House a demand for the dispatches to be read in full. A resolution was adopted, and the President with some satisfaction released them. He had only hesitated for fear of the safety of the envoys.

The French Revolutionary Government, misled by Jefferson's support of the French Revolution, had supposed they had the United States—also a revolutionary government!—in their pocket. Had not the American Revolution been won by the aid of French arms? They supposed that Britain would always be regarded as an enemy of America, and expected American help in the war now waging with Britain as Britain attempted to restore the Bourbon dynasty. The Jay Treaty of Commerce was a horrid shock, and in resentment of it the French Government attempted openly to take sides in American politics, refusing to accept the envoys of the John Adams Federalist Government (which they labelled pro-British), and accepting only the one envoy, Gerry, who belonged to the Jefferson party.

The publication of the dispatches caused an uproar throughout the United States. Jefferson's national pride was deeply touched. He saw that he had been misled, and had misled others. There was an almost universal demand for war with France to avenge this insolence. John Adams rode on a tremendous tide of national popularity. Addresses poured in on him, praising his stand. Young men formed volunteer corps, drilled; marched two and two—eleven hundred of them—wearing the black cockade, through the streets of Philadelphia to offer the President their loyal services. A song, "Hail, Columbia," was made up to the music of the "President's March" (composed for Washington) and was sung to the President in theatres and other public places. Mrs Adams was saluted and cheered in the streets.[14]

"In short, we are now wonderfully popular except with Bache and Co who in his paper calls the President" (a hale and vigorous man of sixty-three) "old, querilous, bald, blind, crippled, toothless Adams!"

In fact, Bache's peculiar brand of personal invective, often pointless, obviously false, but for ever harping, did for that very reason in the end get under people's skins. He observed Mrs Adams in the theatre, for instance, moved to very natural tears by an immense ovation to the President with the "new song," and sneered at it in his paper the next day. No one likes to be caught crying, still less to have it rudely publicized. Mrs Adams lost her temper. A wife's pain lies behind the bitter tone, unlike her own, at "the vile incendiaries who keep up in Bache's paper the most daring and base, violent and calumniating abuse. . . . But nothing will have an effect until Congress pass a Sedition Bill, which I presume they will do before they rise. Not a paper from Bache's press issues nor from Adams Chronical but what might have been prosecuted as libels upon the President and Congress."[15]

And on May 26, in a calmer mood, she repeats her opinion more firmly. "I wish the laws of our country were competent to punish the stirrer up of sedition, the writer or printer of loose and unfounded calumny. This would contribute as much to the peace and harmony of our country as any measure, and in times like the present a more careful and attentive watch ought to be kept over foreigners. This will be done in future if the Alien Bill passes without being curtailed and clipt until it is made useless."

The Alien and Sedition Bills were passed in the summer session of 1798, as in times of war fever such measures always have been, to be repealed when the national temperature returns to normal. Whether or not John Adams really approved them, at least he signed them. What his wife thought, we see.

But it is only fair to say that the bills were passed under John Adams in the heat of immediate expectation of war, and they were repealed under Jefferson in the calmness of the peace which had been maintained singlehanded—one might almost say forcefully created—by John Adams.

The expectation of war was so serious that in July Abigail wrote, "The commander-in-chief of our Armies raised and to be raised is the great, the immortal Washington. . . . 'His name is a host, and the knowledge that he lives a bulwark.' His commission . . . on 4th July is a new edition of our Declaration of Independence."

Meanwhile national indignation was intensified by the return of John Marshall in June, with first-hand accounts of his ignominious treatment by the French. One of the most dignified and able men in the United States, a rising leader in the Federal party, and a brilliant lawyer, his character and appearance gave sharper point to his story, for in his person his Government had been belittled. The fact that Gerry (an Anti-federalist, or Democrat) was being received politely made things no better.

Deeply stirred, Mr Adams sent another message to Congress in June, in which he included this pungent sentence:

"*I will never send another minister to France without assurances that he will be received, respected, and honoured as the representative of a great, free, powerful and independent nation.*"

It was known now that Bache and his like had powerful backing. The year had taught John Adams that there was a deep gulf between himself and Thomas Jefferson. Their friendship could have survived disagreement, but it could not survive distrust. It was no longer possible for them to talk to each other. The externals of politeness and quick avoidance were all that could be endured if by chance or necessity they met. John Adams was incapable of pretence.

"How different," Abigail bursts out, "is the situation of the President from that of Washington! The Vice-President never combined with a party against him and his administration, he never intrigued with foreign Ministers or foreign courts against his own government and country! He never made Bache his companion and counsellor, on the contrary he aided and strengthened every measure in support of the Executive and went hand in hand with him."[16]

It stung all the more because she had liked and trusted Jefferson so much, as had John Adams also. These two great men were bound together with a strong chain of mutual work, aims, interests, experiences, memories . . . yes, mutual admiration and respect. They could not move apart without pain.

Who could ever have convinced John Adams that in 1783, on his appointment to the Peace Commission, Jefferson had written of his "friend," "He has a sound head on substantial points and I think he has integrity. . . . His dislike of all parties and all men, by balancing his prejudices, may give the same fair play to his reason as would a general benevolence of temper."[17]

And yet four years later, after close association with Adams in Europe, Jefferson wrote, in spite of himself, "He is so amiable that I pronounce you will love him if ever you become acquainted with him."

These things at least John Adams never knew. No cynicism cut, as it might have done, at the very roots of his friendship. As far as he ever knew, all that was bad began with the rise of the Anti-federal, or Democrat-Jacobin, party, and with Jefferson's leadership of the same.

Now the Jacobins appeared guilty of real sedition, in any language. Abigail wrote fiercely to Cousin Will (who had lost several of his ships to French privateers), "I believe it impossible for honesty and truth to reside in the breast of a Jacobin. . . . Talleyrand is in close communication with his friend Bache. . . . He was furnished with Talleyrand's letter. . . . Bache sent out his handbills on Saturday by the thousand."[18] Bache and another printer, Burke, who had recently been driven out of Boston for sedition, presently went too far. Each published statements

> in the most positive language that the letters sent to Congress by the President as from Mr Gerry were altogether a forgery. Bache . . . was arrested* in consequence as Burke will be. . . . Yet the Bill to punish sedition sent down from the Senate will be hard fought in the House, and will have the old French faction opposed to it.[19]

Abigail Adams had enjoyed France in her way and in her briefer time almost as much as Mr Jefferson had done in his. But her contacts had been almost entirely with the aristocracy, and of a kind which merely showed the social charm which whitened a decadent and heartless régime. The beginnings of the French Revolution had none the less roused her sympathy. An oppressed people were claiming the inalienable right to life, liberty, and the pursuit of happiness, which every American theoretically believed to be the right of all mankind.

But the Reign of Terror and the execution in particular of Marie Antoinette had filled her with horror. The rise of Napoleon to the leadership of the armies, and the change from a defensive war to protect France from invading armies which sought to restore the Bourbon dynasty to an offensive, aggressive war designed to spread the doctrines of revolution everywhere in the world—that was as intolerable and horrifying to her as to the King of England himself.

Abigail reflected a feeling very general in the United States in 1798 when she wrote to Cousin Will in March and June:

* Benjamin Franklin Bache was arrested on June 26, 1798, on charge of libelling the President and Executive, and released on parole. It is interesting to see the change of tone in the *Aurora* after Bache's arrest. On June 28 one reads: "France already possesses the most valuable commercial parts of Europe. Let the British navy be removed and her empire is complete. The moment France has the ocean under her control she will dictate to us, as she does to the small powers of Europe, all the regulations of trade."

> France!—so unprincipled, so depraved, so bloodthirsty, so tyrannical a power never before existed. There are no established laws or customs or treaties which they regard, all barriers are broken down and levelled to their necessities and ambition, the people are no more in their estimation than mites upon a cheese.
>
> . . . the astonishing success of the French in overturning every country into which they have carried their arms . . . gives new stimulus to their greedy ambition of becoming masters of the world. England alone appears capable of making a stand against them! Ireland appears to be in a state of actual rebellion. Martial law is proclaimed [there] and rendered necessary by the fermented state of the country. It appears to me that England is the only barrier remaining between France and America and that their attempts upon us will be measured by their success or defeat upon her.[20]

Change the name of a single country, and Abigail Adams's letters to William Smith of Boston in March and June 1798 could be lifted almost entire to the years 1939–41.

The conversation of her intimate circle emphasized the aggressive intentions of the French towards the United States. Cousin Will and other merchants were suffering heavy losses at sea. Sam Otis came in one day with another tale to tell, of perhaps even heavier import. *Invasion*? "Indeed, yes. I fear the French have opened their plan," he said, "by taking possession of Louisiana, whence they have easy access to Georgia and the other southern states. In this or some other way they will, in my opinion, compel us to war."[21]

"Indeed we are all but at war," said Abigail, her dark eyes glowing. "Intercourse with France forbidden, the Treaties declared void and no longer obligatory—navy building, and three frigates already at sea—a capture made![22] All we need is a declaration of war. And—though the President must not hear me say this!—one undoubtedly would have been made—*ought* to have been made—but for Mr Gerry's unaccountable stay in France! What can he be doing?"

"The President certainly appointed Mr Gerry against the opinion of many of his friends," said Sam Otis. "Gerry's behaviour is an unpleasant surprise—most improper!"

"That vile intriguer Talleyrand has trapped him!" said Abigail, flashing. "But who would have thought it? I should have supposed him the most wary. Like the serpent he has charmed him! But what a fine answer was made to 'X. Y. Z.' by Mr Charles Pinckney! 'Millions for defence but not a cent for tribute'—this is the toast from Georgia to Maine!"[23]

Hamilton saw everything coming his way. Washington had been juggled into making him second-in-command of the new-formed army. General Knox, with experience both in battle and in the War Department during the Revolution, had been the far more suitable nomination of John Adams, but the President yielded to Washington.

A worse hurt, a very sharp one, was in connexion with his son-in-law. Colonel Smith was by profession a soldier, and here was a chance for professional soldiers.

The President accordingly proposed Colonel Smith on his list of officers as Adjutant-General, and it was approved by Washington. The nominations then had to be confirmed by the Senate. Taking advantage of his confidential knowledge of the list of recommendations, Secretary of State Pickering hurried from the President's study to the Senate House to work up feeling against Colonel Smith. He also wrote a letter to Hamilton on the subject. He put, in fact, the machinery of the Hamilton party in motion against Colonel Smith before the President's list reached the floor. The betrayal was highlighted by the fact that the Senate confirmed all the nominations except that of the President's son-in-law. Confirmation of the nominations was looked upon as more or less perfunctory, and the personal insult was marked.

"It was the last day of the session," wrote Abigail to Cousin Will,

> & there were many secret springs at work, some were made the tools of they knew not whom . . . others glad to do anything which they thought would wound the President. . . . I cannot however say but what much of the unpopularity in which Colonel Smith is placed is owing to his own folly & indiscretion which has ever been condemned by the Pres. and by me as fully as by others. Yet as an officer he was beloved . . . I think it will wound and hurt the Col. more than anything he ever met with.[24]

Sam Otis, as a member of the family, felt it too. "I had the mortification to hear Col. Smith negatived on Thursday by the Senate. . . . The poor fellow has now no prospect."[25]

But this incident gave John Adams a great light. He detected leakage.

When Congress rose, immediately after the Smith incident, in the third week in July, members scattered hastily to escape the yellow fever, and the Adams's, with their household, drove up to Quincy.

XVI

Abigail Adams's Last Winter in Philadelphia

Two mosquitoes now took their place upon the national stage. Both were natives of Philadelphia. They have remained anonymous and unsuspected until the present day, but the combined searchlights of history and science have spied them out, and fidgeting bashfully they take their bow. The first bit Mrs Adams on or about July 25, perhaps at the very moment when she was getting into the coach to leave the city. It set the germs of malaria in her blood. The second, working later in the summer with hosts of its sisters spreading yellow fever about the town, bit Franklin Bache, the printer, Franklin's grandson, and silenced him for ever.

Neither Mrs Adams nor Mr Bache even noticed or thought of the familiar short-lived irritation of the bite as the origin of their ills. Mrs Adams found explanation enough in the weather and the travel. "The season of my journey was the hottest I ever knew."[1] She reached Quincy at last, in her husband's anxious care, and for eleven weeks she was confined to her chamber and expected to die. "A bilious disease and an intermitting fever" made her days and nights miserable. Even after she was up and about again, restored to life, the fever still hung on in a low, recurring way, right into November, "depressing my spirits and depriving me of my sleep in a manner which I never before experienced."[2]

She longed for frost, the blessed, healthy frost. And indeed the first frost, by killing off all the mosquitoes, did check plagues of malaria and yellow fever like magic. No one knew why, but they observed the fact, and drew the conclusion that cold itself was healthy.

Abigail's mosquito kept her from going to Philadelphia again until November 1799. But the hideous ravages of yellow fever in the late summers of '98 and '99 compelled long recesses for Congress. In '99 Abigail told John Quincy Adams, "Your father spent six months at Quincy in as much tranquillity as the public business of his station would permit."

Throughout the whole of this period from the summer of '98 to the autumn of '99, in Quincy, in Philadelphia, and in the final climax at Trenton, John Adams was engaged in a singular struggle with the members of his Cabinet. Or rather not so much with the members of his Cabinet as with the unseen foe behind them, for whom they were the cat's-paws and stalking-horses.

When Mr and Mrs Adams drove away from Philadelphia in the heavy, choking dust that hot July Mrs Adams expected—and so did everybody else—that once Mr Gerry got safely home the administration next session would make a declaration of war against France.

But Mr Adams had something else that he wanted to think about in the quiet. Colonel Smith's rejection was like a tiny leak in a dike. A torrent of ideas poured after. He looked backward. During the tussle over the generalship something had gone on that he did not understand. Washington was away at Mount Vernon, out of sight, out of touch, dimmed to the mental vision by distance, like a man muffled in a cloak. John Adams, recommending Knox, had stretched out a confident hand towards the muffled figure, sure of a reciprocal handclasp, as of old—and had met beneath the folds of the cloak the blow of a mailed fist. It was not Washington. What was it?

The answer became clear, carrying many implications in its train. It was Hamilton.

What, then, was Hamilton working for, if this accumulating evidence was correct and he was exercising secret dominance in the Cabinet through Pickering, and—yes—through McHenry? He was working indubitably for war.

Abigail, who saw so much with those bright eyes of hers, who heard so many cross-currents of talk, had struck out one of her illuminating sentences when Hamilton had been made a general. "I am surprised," she said, "at the want of knowledge of human nature! That man would in my opinion become a second Buonaparty if he was possessed of equal power!"[3]

That surely was the clue. Hamilton wanted to become a second Bonaparte. Therefore, everything suggested by his henchmen,

Pickering and McHenry, became suspect. John Adams's candid nature did not even yet suspect the extent of the treachery of those two, and he never suspected Wolcott—in some ways the arch-traitor—at all.*

There might have to be war—it looked very much that way. But if so, it should be in spite of Hamilton's pressure, not because of it.

In the quiet of Quincy, going about his farm tasks, sitting beside the sickbed of his wife, John Adams gathered his soul. In the presence of the threat of death and sorrow human affairs took on a different proportion. It was easy to see that, in whatever difficulties lay before him as President of a disloyal Cabinet, he could steer his way correctly if he maintained clearness, steadiness, integrity. Did not allow personal resentment to cloud his vision, nor obstinacy to distort his just opinion.

The urge towards war on every side was tremendous. Even Abigail had shared it. Surely if she had been President of the United States instead of her husband war would have been declared before Congress rose. How touched she had been by the young men. The youth of all the great cities from eighteen to twenty-three offering themselves; the students of Harvard sending in an address which she had learned by heart, so noble, so Roman, she thought it.

> We solemnly offer the unarrested ardour and unimpaired energies of our youth to the services of our country, our lives are our only property and we were not the sons of those who seal'd our liberties with their blood if we wd not defend with those lives that soil which now affords a peaceful grave to the mouldering bones of our forefathers.

And as for her ardent pro-Britishness, Hamilton himself could not do better! The French thought they would invade England, did they? Ha, let 'em just try! "They will find that they have not Italians and Dutchmen to deal with."[4]

But now all her fire was quenched in sickness. She lay with a different, pathetic charm, her cheeks flushed almost with her girlhood-bright complexion, her eyes large with fever, holding her

* It is quite touching to see him giving the suave Wolcott a justiceship for life as a parting present in 1800, when Wolcott had just been providing Hamilton with copies of papers from the State Department to provide ammunition for Hamilton's great attempt to blast John Adams's reputation. And Wolcott was touched at last by the man's simple greatness, and shedding tears of gratitude (and secret remorse) promised to be grateful as he ought. His reform was negative, and too late, but it was something.

husband's hand, being read to in his sonorous voice—Shakespeare and Milton and sister Peabody's[5] letters, who "knew as well as ever Shakespeare did every avenue to the heart." If left alone too long she grew depressed. She, who had taken care of every one, now had every one taking care of her. And it endeared her to them all the more. Husband, nieces, friends, domestics, they took their willing turns. Her pet birds and puppies were brought in to amuse her. In her low state the tears were all too ready if she brooded long: about Nabby and her difficulties; about parents and friends long dead; and about Charles. In the night-time, about Charles.

Charles was going downhill. And it was not all his fault. Charles was unlucky. He had fallen into complicated financial difficulties, all of which he did not confess to his mother until the end of this year. But in June, a friend and connexion, Dr Welch, with whom all of the family had from time to time invested money, went suddenly bankrupt. He and Charles were in charge of the small remittance which John Quincy Adams squeezed out of his meagre salary, with an eye to the future when he should return home out of a job. Abigail got early word of Dr Welch's failure, and wrote at once to Charles to stop making any remittances to him on John Quincy's account, but got no reply. "Indeed, my dear son," she wrote John Quincy, "I am not without fears that you will lose all you have been so prudently and carefully saving."

Charles's stubborn silence had painful reasons. In fact, Charles was the worst person in the world to bear financial trouble and when remorse and mortification at mishandling his brother's funds was added it drove him into just the course bound to increase his distresses. Luck at cards could turn a man's fortunes overnight. Liquor could help a too sensitive heart to forget a misery it could not endure.

In November the distressed mother, frail from her long sickness, wrote to one son about the other. "In several of your late letters," she said to John Quincy,

> you have mentioned a subject which has been a source of distress to me for a long time; it is hard upon you. . . . I have written again upon the subject and expostulated in such terms as must procure an explanation and reply. I will write you whatever I can collect, but the poor child is unhappy, I am sure; he is not at peace with himself; and his conduct does not meet my wishes. He has an amiable wife, prudent and discreet, who has every wish and disposition to render *Home*

the most delightful spot; two lovely children—I hope my letters will in time have their effect, I have discharged my duty I hope faithfully, but my dying bed was embittered (as I then thought it) with distress for the only child whose conduct ever gave me pain.[6]

In December Charles braced himself at last to the painful task of coming clean with what he had done with that part of his brother's money that had not sunk with Dr Welch. He wrote explaining that, to save Colonel Smith from immediate imprisonment for debt, he had exchanged John Quincy Adams's mortgage for a note drawn by Colonel Smith's young brother Justice, but the fall of the price of land had prevented him from paying the interest.

Justice Smith lives upon his lands and has a large tract in possession, but what he owes I know not. Charles you know never had the power of resistance. I dare say his own property has gone the same way. Charles said, "I have not enjoyed one moment's comfort for upwards of two years on this account, my sleep has been disturbed and my waking hours embittered."

Justice Smith, it might be said, was a most attractive character, a genial bachelor, on whose large frontier tracts up in the Lebanon Valley of New York State Colonel Smith took refuge after his final ruin by his rash part in the Miranda expedition to South America in 1806.

Colonel Smith's foolishness was always getting him into trouble, his sweetness and good faith were always involving other persons to get him out. This time he unfortunately involved Charles Adams, whose sweetness and good faith certainly were not less than his brother-in-law's, but whose sensitiveness was painfully greater. The family disapproval on this matter—and they could not help it—added one more weight to Charles's sinking self-respect. A weight all the heavier because he knew how much they loved him.

Troops were drilling, camps were forming.

Colonel Smith by this time had a modest commission and was happy, doing wonders at camp. Preparations were going forward as if war were imminent. But the international crisis held off, marking time, while the President of the United States waited the return of the fully informed envoy, Mr Gerry.

On October 1 Mr Gerry arrived, coming straight to Quincy to make his peace with the President. John and Abigail welcomed him, and heard his detailed reasons for staying. Sufficient or not, at least he now had definite news to give. Talleyrand desired to begin a new negotiation.

War was an essential part of Hamilton's plan and ambition. His cabal in the Cabinet set themselves to prepare a form of words for the President's adoption at the opening of Congress which, holding him rigidly to his former statement that he would never again send an envoy uncertain of full reception, would leave no loophole of retreat, no alternative but war. Hamilton called a secret council and composed a careful draft.

Late in November 1798 John Adams arrived at Philadelphia for Congress—ignorant of this council and its project. He called his Cabinet, examined their draft, his keen lawyer's eye sharpened by his inward knowledge that two of them at least were Hamilton's men, and calmly rewrote the key sentences. With this revised speech he opened Congress. "Vigorous preparations for war would be continued since those alone will give us an equal treaty . . . further negotiations would depend upon evidence of return of good faith in France."

The more Hamilton's policy was resisted, the more Hamilton had to declare that policy in order to fight for it. Moreover John Adams now had evidence that not only was Hamilton dictating policy to members of the Cabinet, but, far worse—there was a regular leakage of private information from the Cabinet to Hamilton. However, as he had said when he first entered on his stormy Presidency, he had never felt more serene. His inward compass pointed steadily to the north. The change in French policy was continually borne witness to by William Vans Murray, the American Minister to Holland. Encouraged by Mr Adams, that excellent diplomat had incited the Dutch to make an offer of mediation, in order that a regular channel might be opened between the French and the American Government. On January 21 a French message reached the President. It declared that "the disposition of the French to reconciliation had been already unmistakeably made known at Philadelphia—it was the responsibility of the United States if they persisted in misconstruing or repulsing it."[7] This was followed in a few weeks by a letter from Talleyrand himself through the same channel, in which the experienced French diplomat introduced the very form of words which John Adams had used in his speech to Congress as his condition for sending an envoy to France.

On receiving Talleyrand's letter, so full and complete, John Adams determined on action. Useless to consult his Cabinet again—to do so was to invite not only obstruction but leakage. He must exercise the hitherto unused prerogatives granted by the Constitution to the President of the United States. On February 18, 1799, the members of the Senate, not one of whom knew what was coming, received a message from the President enclosing Talleyrand's letter, and announcing the President's appointment of William Vans Murray as special envoy of the United States to France. Always provided further unequivocal assurances of his right reception should be given the United States Government by the French.

This announcement was equally astounding to all parties. Jefferson averred that John Adams had held back Talleyrand's letter for months to jack up the war party, and only produced it now and made this nomination in order to get the mission rejected by the Senate! (It is hard to believe that Jefferson could really think that outright John Adams was capable of such a devious policy. Mr Jefferson was always being tripped up by his own subtlety.) Hamilton's party felt the ground ripped out from under them.

Mr Adams met protests by joining two other delegates with Mr Murray on the Commission. He nominated Chief Justice Oliver Ellsworth and Patrick Henry. Hamilton warned his adherents they must submit. The Senate ratified. Now Hamilton and his faithful henchmen in the Cabinet settled down to a silent policy of stultifying delay.

John Adams wrote to his wife:

> I have instituted a new mission, which is kept in the dark, but when it comes to be understood it will be approved. O, how they lament Mrs Adams's absence! She is a good counsellor! If she had been here, Murray would never have been named nor his mission instituted! This ought to gratify your vanity enough to cure you![18]

And again he expresses the inward quiet, the sense of proportion, engendered in him by the profound experiences of the summer. Party strife is in abeyance (in his heart). Ambition has no more to ask.

> I have no idea that I shall be chosen President a second time; though this is not to be talked of. The business of the office is so oppressive that I shall hardly support it two years longer. . . . I do not remember that I was ever vindictive in my life, though I have often been very

wroth. I am not very angry now, nor much vexed or fretted. The mission came across the views of many, and stirred the passions of more. This I knew was unavoidable. The reasons which determined me are too long to be written. . . .

Your sickness last summer, fall and winter has been to me the severest trial I ever endured.

Not that I am at this moment without other trials, enough for one man.[9]

The Hamiltonians might well regret the absence of Mrs Adams! As her health grew stronger her old mood of Hurrah for Britain, 'ware Jefferson and the wicked French, returned. Nelson was her hero.

"Great Britain is fighting for all the other powers!"[10] she said to Cousin Will. But she did not claim—not really—to dispute with her husband on affairs of state.

"Government of States and Kingdoms, tho God knows badly enough managed, I am willing should be solely administered by the lords of the creation. I should only contend for Domestic government, and think that best administered by the female."[11]

John was taking care of France. Her mind was more concerned with her sons. Thomas got back from Berlin in February. He went straight to Philadelphia, to give dispatches and report to the President and Secretary of State, but in a week or two he came to Quincy to his mother. "His father needs him," she wrote eagerly to John Quincy, "he wants that comfort and relief, encompassed as he is with public cares and perplexities as well as a share of private anxiety for the health of your Mother, which is still feeble." Tom's visit in the early spring was like a tonic. It was health-giving happiness just when she needed it. After all, she had four children. Why should her mind brood so incessantly over the one? . . . But like the shepherd in the story, so it did. The lost one took more of her thoughts than any other. Tom left Quincy in April to return to Philadelphia, where he had taken lodgings and an office to set up as a lawyer. There was nothing wrong with Tom except his delicate health. But Charles . . .

Your brother Charles is—what shall I say that will not pain us both? Wd to God that I might kill the fatted calf and put upon him the robe of rejoicing. He has formed good resolutions, cd he keep them how it would rejoice us all. But the heart, the principles must co-operate. How sharper than a serpent's tooth it is to have a graceless child, may you, my dear son, never experience. Blessed be God, I have those in whom I can rejoice.[12]

She tried to dissuade Thomas from settling in Philadelphia.

> The dreaded Yellow Fever must drive him annually from it . . . unless some measures are speedily discovered to stop its progress. It becomes every year more destructive and horrible. There is no doubt of its being still in the city, though the winter checks its baneful influence. New York and Boston both suffered the last season. Much pains is taken to investigate the causes, I hope the researches may prove successful, and God grant the remedy may be found.[13]

Congress rose early, to escape the hot weather and the plague, the ravages of the previous summer ('93 and '98 were the two worst epidemics known to history) being vivid in their minds. Husband and son joined Abigail at Quincy. In the long, hot peace of July, filled with the hum of insects and the sound of the everlasting surf, refreshing to an exile's ears, dispatches arrived with Talleyrand's reply. It bore a categorical acceptance of John Adams's terms, which itself was assurance of a disposition to peace. John Adams sat down in his study, with the scent of the roses of Auteuil blowing in through the windows, and wrote to Colonel Pickering. He directed immediate action, the prompt preparation of the commission papers and departure of the envoys. But Pickering delayed.

Late in August the raging yellow fever in Philadelphia compelled the moving of the Government offices to Trenton. The very day they settled in, August 26, Pickering received a private letter from Mr Murray that another revolution had happened in the Directory, and Talleyrand himself was out. There were rumours of returning the French Jacobins to power. This was a stroke of luck for the Cabinet cabal. On consultation, it was resolved to send Mr Adams the correctly prepared papers for the envoys—to show the work done—but to enclose a remonstrance against the Commission's going at this time. John Adams examined the papers, acquiesced in a short period of delay, set the latter part of October as its term, and promised to be himself in Trenton by October 15. Hamilton came to Newark, to be within call.

John Adams arrived in Trenton on October 10, rather unwell with a cold taken on the journey, but filled with that deep calm engendered in him by a sense of crisis, and fortified by the healthy, quiet months at Quincy with his wife. He met the members of the Cabinet politely, yet one* of them soon perceived a difference in his treatment of them. Mr Hamilton was soon on the spot too, to support his henchmen strongly in the background. All awaited the moment for a trial of strength. They expected a violent altercation. In such a scene Mr Adams could easily be provoked to put himself in the wrong—or so they conjectured. News from Europe, of British and Russian successes, made Hamilton believe the Bourbons were almost as good as back on the throne of France. A treaty made with any section of the revolutionists would be no treaty! They talked with passion. Mr Adams watched their vehemence, and wrote a letter to his wife of calm surprise. He read their motives clearly. He saw it was not delay, it was final defeat of the mission they were after.

On the evening of October 15 he summoned the Cabinet to a meeting. They came, all armed for battle. But things did not go as they expected. He laid before them the draft of instructions to the Commission which had been sent to him at Quincy, and requested their advice on some technical points. The draft was discussed, amended, finally approved unanimously. But time was passing, it was eleven o'clock; too late to start a new discussion. The President stated no new propositions, and after a thoughtful pause it seemed good manners to go. The Cabinet members took their leave, suppressing yawns, feeling vaguely flat and punctured, but expecting to be summoned in the morning for the real showdown.

Instead, before breakfast in the morning two of them—the Secretary of State and the Secretary of the Navy—received a laconic order from the President, in writing, that the instructions finally agreed on for the Commissioners should be at once made out, and the frigate *United States* should be put in readiness for their use, and the Commission should set sail for France on or before the first of the coming month.

So the President used to the full the powers of his office as no one had supposed he would dare to do. So he defeated the schemes of Hamilton, who had the mind and will of a dictator, and who saw himself left without a generalship and without an army. So—accused by Jefferson of warmongering—John Adams by his single will carried America to peace. The averted war would have been

* Adams's only appointee so far, the new Secretary of the Navy.

as popular with the country at large as it would have been disastrous. John Adams lost some popular support, earned at one stroke the undying jealousy of Jefferson and the malicious hatred of Hamilton, and launched the United States on an era of peace and prosperity, for which his successor in office, who had only to reap the harvest, got most of the credit.

The Commission* sailed on November 5. Napoleon Bonaparte was now in power.

They were received with all honour by Napoleon, a clear-sighted statesman who regarded war with America as preposterous. He concluded with them a peace which has remained unbroken to this day.

All John Adams cared was that that great end was accomplished; far greater than party strife or party victory.

And if tombstones were being designed, what John Adams wanted on his was just one line—"Here lies John Adams, who took upon himself the responsibility of peace with France."

The winter of 1799 was the last winter the Government was to spend in Philadelphia. When Congress rose in the spring for the hot season—the fever season—it would be farewell. They would reassemble in the autumn in the new headquarters so long building on the banks of the Potomac.

Abigail enjoyed that winter. Her health was good, she was able to be with her husband and perform her social duties as First Lady; and two of her children were with her. Tom, who was a great comfort, and Nabby, with that darling little Caroline, who "had soft and tender manners and yet was as lively as a bird." Colonel Smith had a commission as Lieutenant-Colonel and was in camp with his regiment in the Jerseys. Poor Nabby, when peace was declared in the spring of 1800, her first thought was that her husband was out of a job again!

The President and his wife, though both had a great deal of natural dignity, put on no ostentation. The routine of drawing-rooms, levees, and dinners was much as in Washington's time, but something had happened to thaw the etiquette. Talk flowed freely. John Adams, said a youth who knew him, "had not the smallest chip of

* Chief Justice Ellsworth and Governor Davie, of North Carolina. The first appointees, John Marshall and Patrick Henry, were unable to serve. The head of the Commission, William Vans Murray, was of course already abroad, in Holland, and had only a short overland journey to meet the others in Paris.

an ice-berg in his composition."[14] While Mrs Adams "continues the same pleasant attentive person as at Quincy."[15]

The last drawing-room took place on May 2. But for many weeks before social festivity had been overshadowed, bright scarves and trimmings of the fashionable transparent muslins gave way to black and white. "I wish some one would persuade them that muslin is not suitable for winter dress!" Mrs Adams had sighed. It was a French fashion too. But mourning was a dismal change. And the reason for it sank through to the heart. George Washington was dead.

He died in the dead of winter at the close of the year. He had only had three years to enjoy his retirement, to call himself Farmer Washington; and the latter part of those had been disturbed by his technical generalship of the new-forming army.

Abigail's sister's son, William Shaw, rode to Mount Vernon with the official letter of condolence from the President and Congress to Mrs Washington, and the official request to bury Washington's body in a national monument, perhaps at the new city. He came back with Mrs Washington's reply, and with details of the last illness.

"It was due to the General's eagerness to get on with some improvements on his farm that he caught his death," he told his aunt and uncle as they sat together in a firelit family circle in mutual sorrow.

"I can understand that," said John Adams. "But what in winter? In December?"

"He had in contemplation a gravel walk on the banks of the Potomac," said Shaw. "Between the walk and the river there was to be a fish-pond. Some trees were to be cut down, and others preserved. On Friday—the day before he died—he spent some time by the side of the river marking the trees. There came a fall of snow, but he still continued till his neck and hair were covered with snow. He spent the evening with Mrs Washington, reading the newspapers, which came by the mail of that evening; went to bed as usual about nine o'clock—waked up in the night—found himself extremely unwell, but would not allow Mrs Washington to get up or the servant to be waked. In the morning he was worse. Dr Craik of Alexandria was sent for. He saw it was serious, and asked for more help. Two consulting physicians were called in, but all would not avail. On Saturday evening he died. Mrs

Washington was in the room but he took no particular leave of anyone."[16]

There was a silence. The older ones were busy with memories.

"He was writing a history of the Revolution, I understood?" said Tom.

"No," said his cousin. "But he left a minute journal of his daily life—at least his public life!—which will contain material for a history. This journal, and his library of 1500 volumes, and Mount Vernon with 4000 acres of land he has left to his nephew the Judge, after Mrs Washington has had them for life. All his negroes are to be made free on Mrs Washington's decease."[17]

"May I read her letter?" said Mrs Adams. And she wept upon it. Later she wrote to Hannah Smith:

> You will have seen and admired Mrs Washington's answer to the letter of the President, so expressive, so dignified, so pathetic. Yet there are persons who will not allow her the merit of having penned it. I know the contrary. Not only her last letter to me, but many others which upon different occasions I have received from her show her to be not only a good, a virtuous, a religious woman, but of a dignified mind.

No one certainly was a better judge of that than Abigail Adams.

The Presidential election was coming on apace. Mr Adams had no organized party behind him as did Jefferson and Hamilton. His mind did not run on those lines. He did no campaigning, spending the summer quietly at Quincy organizing his new Cabinet*—now for the first time all his own appointees—and attending to current business. The election was not even run on a straight party issue, owing to the queer three-cornered turn given to it by Hamilton. He started a strange campaign introducing another Federalist candidate against John Adams. And worse, a pamphlet written by him, virulently attacking both Adams and his administration, and openly betraying the secret knowledge of State documents, fell into the hands of the Anti-Federalists and was published by them on the eve of the election. And yet John Adams came near getting in for a second term. The defection of South Carolina was the chief and final weight which loaded the scale against the Federalists.

The defection of South Carolina and other waverers was due less to loss of confidence in Mr Adams than to the extraordinary split

* He had, in any case, several months more to run. The Presidential election takes place in November; the new government does not take over till March.

in the Federal ranks made by Hamilton's complicated intrigues.

Hamilton had the mortification of not only ruining himself, but of seeing his two most hated enemies, Jefferson and Aaron Burr, tied for first place with seventy-three votes apiece. The House of Representatives, forced to exercise its constitutional right of choice in case of a tied election, appointed Jefferson as President with Burr as Vice-President.

Braintree's answer to Hamilton's malignant attack was to give John Adams a big public birthday celebration on October 19, to toast and praise him. People came in from Weymouth and Hingham and Boston. There were fireworks in the clear autumn evening over the sea. Abigail had already left, to break her journey to the new capital, Washington, with a visit in New York with Nabby. But she read of it in the Boston newspapers with joy and comfort. In fact, she was so proud of it that she became quite stiff and Biblical with pride.

"It was truly gratifying to find in a world of calumny and falsehood that a prophet cd meet with honour in his own native soil."[18]

XVII

Retirement to Quincy

ABIGAIL NEEDED SOMETHING TO be proud of. She needed to gather up all the good things she could and press them like fragrant, healing herbs against that bruise in her mind which was the thought of Charles. When her fevers came on now the doctor bled her, and she was quickly well. But Shakespeare knew too much when he adjured the wise physician, "Canst thou not minister to a mind diseased? Pluck from the memory a rooted sorrow?" What had she done that was so wrong with Charles? Or was it her fault, when John Quincy, surely brought up much the same—and Nabby and Tom, too—had turned out so well? "Seeing you a wise and virtuous man," she wrote to John in September 1800,

> is a cordial to my heart and mitigates in some measure the weight of sorrow which weighs it down from another source by one from which I have not a hope of change, habits are so rooted, the temper so soured, the whole man so changed that ruin and destruction have swallowed him up and his affairs are become desperate. Sally and her infant daughter are gone to her mother, Susan [the other little girl] I brought home with me—all is lost—poor, poor, unhappy wretched man—all remonstrances have been lost upon him. God knows what is to become of him. His Father has renounced him—but I will not.
>
> Your sister and her little girl have passed the summer with me. The Colonel has been appointed Supervisor and inspector of the port of New York since the disbandment of the Army. As he has suffered in the school of adversity I hope he will consider and make a proper estimate of life.[1]

But the Colonel no more than Charles could make a proper estimate of life. With Charles the disease of alcoholism had fastened on his being, as on the being of his mother's brother before him. Moral suasion tormented but could not cure. The Colonel, on the other hand, was afflicted with an incurable ailment of another kind, a romantic megalomania, which always saw himself four times as large as life, performing an admired part on a stage. A little Hamilton, a pocket Napoleon, even an imitation Washington. So he would make a big splash with money when he had it, and then run into debt, to the ruin of his friends. Just the man to be caught by Miranda,* as he was a few years later. But Jefferson too was caught —even Napoleon said of Miranda, "He has fire in his heart." And Jefferson, resentful at the Colonel's public statement implicating him, when on trial in 1806, and trying to subpœna his Secretary of State, exercised one of those gestures of petty spite which marred his career, and removed the little man from his little post at the Port of New York. So he and John Adams's delicate daughter (Jefferson's once admired young friend) had to go and live in the wilderness, on the farm broken out by Justice Smith in the Colonel's frontier land in upstate New York, and wring from that rough life as much comfort as they could.

John Adams had written to his son-in-law in December 1798:

> I will be plain with you. Your pride and ostentation, which I have seen with inexpressible grief for many years, have excited among your neighbours so much envy and resentment that if they have to allege against you any instance of dishonourable conduct, as it is pretended they have, you may depend upon it, it will never be forgiven or forgotten.[2]

But something more bitterly deserving the name of grief than Colonel Smith's efforts to assume greatness awaited Abigail in New York. She found her son Charles deserted and alone in the last stages of sickness and squalor. And the news of his death followed her to Washington three weeks after her arrival there. Her letters to her sister and to her son John Quincy in December, from Washington, D.C., give vivid detail of the end of his sad days.

> Weep with me over the grave of a poor unhappy child who cannot now add another pang to those which have pierced my heart for several years past. Cut off in the midst of his days, his years are numbered and finished. . . .
>
> I knew not that he was sick. When I arrived at New York on my way to this city [Washington] I went to see him. He had been ill a week. But you may judge my feelings when I saw that his case was

* A Spaniard infected with the Napoleon virus who conceived a project of alliance between England and America for the conquest of the entire South American continent.

desperate. He was at lodgings. Your sister, who had spent the summer with me, returned to New York when I did. She removed him immediately to her home and every kind care and sisterly attention was shown him. The removal of him was all the release, all the consolation I could derive. I came to this city with a heavy heart in daily expectation of his death, which took place on the first of December.

His constitution was so shaken that his disease was rapid. His sufferings were severe, his patience under them was great. Food has not been his sustenance, yet he did not look like an intemperate man. He was bloated, but not red. He was no man's enemy but his own. He was beloved in spite of his error, and all spoke with grief and sorrow of his habits.

He appeared most tender and affectionate. His mind was constantly running upon doing justice and making reparation. Early principles, though stifled, now discovered themselves; and Mercy I hope was extended to him. The tender remembrance of what he once was rises before me. Think of him, my son, with the compassion of a brother.[3]

All this was on Abigail's heart during the journey, with the added pang that she could not wait with her dying son, for her public duties inexorably claimed her.

The execution of L'Enfant's beautiful designs for the city of Washington—the first American city to be designed from the start on a great basic plan—had been constantly held up for lack of funds from an unimaginative Congress. But the ten years allotted to Philadelphia were up, and the seat of government must be moved, ready or not. So it moved.

On November 21, 1800, Abigail sat down in the unfinished President's House,* in the smallest room she could find, by the biggest fire she could get, and took up her eager pen to tell her sister all about her adventures on the journey, and what she had come to.

I arrived in this city on Sunday (the 16th ult.). Having lost my way in the woods on Saturday in going from Baltimore, we took the road to Frederick and got nine miles out of our road. You find nothing but a forest and woods on the way, for 16 or 18 miles not a village. Here and there a thatched cottage without a single pane of glass, inhabited by Blacks. My intention was to have reached Washington on Saturday.

Last winter there was a Gentleman and Lady in Phila. by the Name of Snowden. . . . They visited me and were invited to dine . . . but did not as they left the city . . . they . . . live on the road to this place

* Not yet called the White House.

21 miles distant. I was advised at Baltimore to make their House my stage for the night, the only Inn at which I could put up being 36 miles ride from Baltimore . . . but I, who have never been accustomed to quarter myself and servants upon private houses, could not think of it, particularly as I expected the chariot and 5 more Horses with two servants to meet me. I set out early intending to make my 36 miles if possible: no travelling however but by daylight. We took a direction as we supposed right, but in the first turn went wrong, and were wandering more than two hours in the woods in different paths, holding down and breaking boughs of trees which we could not pass, until we met a solitary black fellow with a horse and cart. We inquired of him our way, and he kindly offered to conduct us, which he did two miles, and then gave us such a clue as led us out to the post road and the Inn where we got some dinner. Soon after we left it we met the chariot, then 30 miles from Washington, and 20 from our destination. We rode as fast as the roads would allow of, but the sun was near set when we came in sight of the Major's. I halted, but could not get the courage to go to his House with ten Horses and nine persons. I therefore ordered the coach man to proceed, and we drove rapidly on. We had got about a mile when we were stopped by the Major in full speed, who had learnt that I was comeing on, and had kept watch for me, with his Horse at the door, as he was at a distance from the road. In the kindest and politest manner he urged my return to his House, represented the danger of the road, and the impossibility of my being accommodated at any Inn I cd reach. A mere hovel was all I shd find. I pled my numbers. That was no objection. He cd accommodate double the number. There was no saying nay, and I returned to a large Handsome, Elegant House, where I was received with my Family with what we might term true English Hospitality, friendship without ostentation, and kindness without painfull ceremony. Mrs Snowden is a charming woman of about 45. She has a lovely daughter of 16, and one of 6, a son whom I had seen often in Philadelphia and who had several times dined with us. I need not add that they are all true federal characters. Every attention possible was shown me and the next morning I took my departure, having shared in the common bounty of Major Snowden's hospitality for which he is universally celebrated.

I arrived about one o'clock at this place known by the name of "the city," and the Name is all that you can call so! As I expected to find it a new country, with Houses scattered over a space of ten miles, and trees and stumps in plenty, with a castle of a House, so I found it.

The President's House is in a beautiful situation, in front of which is the Potomac, with a view of Alexandria. The country round is romantic, but a wild wilderness at present.

But surrounded with forests can you believe that wood is not to be had, because people cannot be found to cut and cart it! Breisler entered into a contract with a man to supply him with wood . . . but a few cords only has he been able to get. We have had some very cold weather and we feel it keenly. This House is twice as large as our meeting House. I believe the great Hall is as Bigg. I am sure 'tis twice as long. Cut your coat according to your cloth. But this House is built for ages to come. The establishment necessary is a task which cannot be born by the present sallery. Nobody can form an idea of it but those who come into it. . . . Not one room or chamber is finished of the whole. It is habitable by fires in every part, thirteen of which we are obliged to keep daily, or sleep in wet and damp places. To assist us in this great castle, and render less attendance necessary, bells are wholly wanting, not one single one being hung through the whole house, and promises are all you can obtain. This is so great an inconvenience that I know not what to do! . . .

The ladies from Georgetown and in the "city" have many of them visited me. Yesterday I returned fifteen visits—but such a place as Georgetown! I felt all that Mrs Cranch described when she was a resident there. It is the very dirtyest Hole I ever saw for a place of any trade or respectability of inhabitants. It is only one mile from me, but a quagmire after every rain. Here we are obliged to send daily for marketing. The capitol is near two miles from us. As to roads, we shall make them by the frequent passing before winter! But I am determined to be satisfied and content, to say nothing of inconvenience, etc. That must be a worse place than even George Town that I could not reside in for three months! If they will put me up some bells and let me have wood enough to keep fires, I design to be pleased. We have not the least fence-yard or other convenience without, and the great unfinished audience-room I make a drying-room of, to hang the clothes in. The principal stairs are not up, and will not be this winter.

But as the forlorn picture of the unfinished house takes shape, and the smell of the wet plaster is in our nostrils, she hastens to ameliorate it.

Look, there are six chambers made comfortable. And two lower rooms, one for a common parlour, and one for a levee room. And upstairs there is the oval room, which is designed for the drawing-room, and has the crimson furniture in it. It is a very handsome room now; but when completed it will be beautiful.

Now, she warns her correspondent, "Keep all this to yourself, and when asked how I like it, say that I wrote you the situation is beautiful, which is true!"

She had a nephew to welcome her, the attractive Will Cranch, who had gone through Harvard with John Quincy Adams. There are other dear friends too, one especially—not too far off, though a difficult drive in present weather. "Since I sat down to write I have been called down to a servant from Mount Vernon, with a billet from Major Custis, and a haunch of venison, with Mrs Washington's love, inviting me to Mount Vernon, where health permitting, I will go before I leave this place."

"Before I leave this place." It won't be long now before she has to lay down the rank of First Lady, and become again merely Mrs John Adams of Quincy. This "castle" will before long be made comfortable, but it will not be for her. It will perhaps be for Martha Jefferson, now Mrs Randolph. And for a long succession of other ladies unknown who will queen it here. They will have bells and fires, and a drying-yard. Their husbands will be rich enough to support the place in style. Even the great "audience-chamber," the East Room, will be in glittering use. Yes, but we want to preserve our simple democracy, thought Mrs Adams. We don't want an aristocracy of wealth. . . .

She could not foresee that Jefferson and Monroe would both die bankrupt through trying to keep up style in their great office on inadequate pay and lavish use of private funds.

Well, Aunt Tufts had not been altogether wrong when she had said that Abigail, off to Philadelphia to assume her duties four years ago, was going to "splendid misery." And she hadn't been altogether right either. On the whole it had been tremendous fun.

But now, the sooner over the better. Abigail's heart was heavy with her private sorrow. She longed for the simple duties, the healing quiet and orderly beauty of Quincy.

". . . If my future peace and tranquillity were all that I considered, a release from public life wd be the most desirable event of it. I feel perfectly tranquil upon the subject, hoping and trusting that the Being in whose Hands are the Hearts of all Men will guide and direct our national counsels for the peace and prosperity of this great people.

". . . We are all at present well, tho the news papers very kindly gave the President the Ague and fever. I am rejoiced that it was only in the paper that he had it."

. . .

When Mr Jefferson assumed the Presidency, he was to make an experiment of new "American" manners: no levees, no drawing-rooms, no order of precedence; dinners for fourteen guests at a round table, self-service through a hatch in the wall; careless personal dress, down-at-heel slippers. It was good and enlivening to break up the old patterns and try to make some new ones. But Mr Jefferson could not have done it in New York or Philadelphia. Mere pressure of numbers would have driven him to order and organization, tedious and stiff as it might be, as it drove Washington and Adams. When Mrs Adams tried to live one short spring in Philadelphia without formal drawing-rooms, in order to save every one exertion, the populous and social city flooded in on her, and she had to work overtime receiving callers all day long. The emptiness of Washington—a handful of houses in a muddy wilderness carved out of the dense forest—was what made Jefferson's go-as-you-please ways temporarily possible. And ladies were scarce. Congressmen were forced to live in boarding-houses, and many left their wives at home.

Such ladies as were extant, however, besieged Mrs Adams to start her drawing-rooms, and she did. In January 1801 the first New Year reception was held in the President's House. Many candles and roaring fires did their best to make a festive air. The President and his wife received their guests in the beautiful oval room, with their red furniture from Auteuil, and gave Washington its first sensation of being a society. Foreign ministers wore their orders, gentlemen their snowy powder, their bags, and swords. Ladies decorated the scene with their elaborate dresses. Washington, D.C., took a definite step from looking like a trading outpost to looking like the capital of a great nation. But it still had a very long way to go.

John Adams had not anticipated subjecting his wife to the rigorous life of the frontier when he brought her to Washington. He was alarmed when he saw what she would have to put up with, and he dared risk it no further when he saw her attacks of rheumatism return. The severe lesson of the near loss of her in the summer of '98 had left its mark. February was a bad season to travel, but worse yet to remain in a house so poorly heated. He packed her off to Quincy.

To Thomas she had written earlier her final salutation to public life:

> I feel not any resentment against those who are coming into power, and only wish the future administration of the government may be as productive of the peace, prosperity and happiness of the nation as the two former ones have been.
>
> I leave to time the unfolding of a drama. I leave to posterity to reflect upon the times past; and I leave them characters to contemplate.[4]

"I have commenced my operations of dairy-woman," said Abigail joyfully in May. "Tell Nabby she might see me, at five o'clock in the morning skimming my milk! And in July, you will find your father in his fields attending to his haymakers"; she demands:

> Who that has reason and his smell
> Would not among roses and jasmine dwell?[5]

A letter from John Quincy, concerned at a remark in her last letter from Washington that they would have to economize, offered earnestly to help them, and gave them exquisite pleasure. "Your father and I were both much affected with the filial and affectionate tender of what, thank God, we have not any occasion for! You know our habits . . . many curtailments necessary, and have made them but we have many comforts and enjoyments; and we can adopt the words of Shakespeare—'Hath not old custom made this life more sweet?'"[6]

In September when the apples were ripe, John Quincy Adams came home from Berlin. First he took his wife direct to her parents at Washington,* and with her the little boy George Washington Adams, who had been safely born, after one or two miscarriages had made hopes of a family faint. Then John Quincy left his wife in Washington for a week, and himself hurried to Quincy. His mother's joy was full.

When Louisa came on to them at last, they loved her. She and her husband's dear friend and sister Nabby (there to welcome her brother) became fast friends. John Quincy opened again the old law office in Boston, remaining there until, in 1803, he was elected to the Senate over the head of his father's old enemy, the traitorous politician Pickering. To be beaten by a younger man was bad enough; to be beaten by John Adams's son was unspeakable. So when Pickering got into the Senate a little later he laid himself out for John Quincy Adams. And such was the cabal against the latter,

* Mr Johnson had been given a post in connexion with the Post Office organization.

that he found it better, to get any measure across, to have it proposed by some one other than himself. These were embittering experiences for a man new to the political arena. But that is another story.

Abigail shared an extraordinary amount of her son's life and thought. When he came out to Quincy from Boston on a Sunday she "picked a political bone" with her old verve and more than her old wisdom. She eagerly watched his career when he went to Washington, and rejoiced in his wife, who was such a charming hostess in that forlorn spot. But she did not need to know, her son rightly thought, all that got under a man's skin.

There was one bitter stab, however, dealt by Jefferson's hand, which rankled like a poisoned thorn in Abigail's mind. The Judge of the District Court of Massachusetts had immediately appointed John Quincy Adams one of the new commissioners in bankruptcy, a job which would ensure him a sound income. But John Quincy Adams had held the post for only a short time when a new ruling, giving these appointments directly into the control of the President of the United States, came into force, and Jefferson instantly crossed from the list the name of John Quincy Adams. It was the only name the President deleted, and it was a marked gesture. Despite this, the next year young Mr Adams was elected to the Senate. Jefferson, at any rate, had done his best to slap him down.

The thorn was accidentally probed out of its festering position in the mother's heart by the only possible surgery—free and frank expression—in an exchange of letters between herself and President Jefferson in 1804.

The occasion was the death in early womanhood of Jefferson's daughter Mary,* whom Abigail Adams had so dearly loved. And after hesitation she wrote him a letter in which her desire to offer comfort could not conceal the wounds of old friendship.

Quincy, May 20th, 1804

SIR,

Had you been no other than the private inhabitant of Monticello, I should, ere this time, have addressed you with that sympathy which a recent event has awakened in my bosom; powerful feelings of my heart burst through the restraint, and called upon me to shed the tear of sorrow over the [death] of your beloved and deserving daughter, which I most sincerely mourn.

* Mrs Francis Eppes. The elder sister, Martha, who had wanted to be a nun, was Mrs Randolph.

The attachment which I formed for her, when you committed her to my care upon her arrival in a foreign land, has remained with me to this hour; and the account of her death, which I read in a late paper, recalled to my recollection the tender scene of her separation from me, when she clung around my neck and wet my bosom with her tears, saying, "Oh! now I have learned to love you, why will they take me from you?"

It has been some time since I conceived that any event in this life could call forth feelings of mutual sympathy. But I know how closely entwined around a parent's heart are those cords and when snapped asunder, how agonizing the pangs! I have tasted of the bitter cup. That you may derive comfort and consolation from that only source calculated to heal the wounded heart, a firm belief in the being, perfections and attributes of God, is the sincere and ardent wish of her, who once took pleasure in subscribing herself your friend.[7]

ABIGAIL ADAMS

Jefferson's own heart carried festering wounds. Her candour released his, as her loving sympathy reached his fatherly grief. He replied:

Washington, June 13th, 1804

DEAR MADAM,

The affectionate sentiments towards my dear departed daughter . . . have recalled your kindnesses to her. . . . They had made an indelible impression on her mind, and to the last, on our meetings after long separations, whether I had heard lately of you, and how you did, were among the earliest of her inquiries.

I . . . am thankful for the occasion furnished me of expressing my regret that circumstances should have arisen which have seemed to draw a line of separation between us. The friendship with which you honoured me has ever been valued, and fully reciprocated; and although events have been passing which might be trying to some minds, I never believed yours to be of that kind, nor felt that my own was. Neither my estimate of your character, nor the esteem founded in that, has ever been lessened for a single moment. . .

Mr Adams friendship and mine began at an earlier date. It accompanied us through long and important scenes. The different conclusions we had drawn from our political reading and reflections were not permitted to lessen personal esteem . . . conscious they were the result of honest conviction.

Like differences of opinion existing among our fellow citizens attached them to one or the other of us, and produced a rivalship in their minds which did not exist in ours. We never stood in each other's way; for if either had been withdrawn . . . his favourers would not have gone over to the other but would have sought for some one of the homogeneous opinions. This consideration was sufficient to keep down all jealousy between us and to guard our friendship from any disturbance by sentiments of rivalship; and I can say with truth that one act of Mr Adams' life and one only, ever gave me a moment's personal displeasure. I did consider his last appointments to office as personally unkind. They were from among my most ardent political enemies, from which no faithful co-operation could ever be expected; and laid me under the embarrassment of acting through men whose views were to defeat mine, or to encounter the odium of putting others in their places. It seems but common justice to leave a successor free to act by instruments of his own choice.

If my respect for him did not permit me to ascribe the whole blame to the influence of others, it left something for friendship to forgive, and after brooding over it for some time, and not always resisting the expression of it, I forgave it cordially, and returned to the same state of esteem and respect for him which had so long subsisted. Having come into life a little later than Mr Adams, his career has preceded mine, as mine is followed by some other; and it will probably be closed at the same distance after him which time originally placed between us. I maintain for him, and shall carry into private life, an uniform and high measure of respect and good will, and for yourself a sincere attachment.

I have thus, my dear madam, opened myself to you without reserve, which I have long wished an opportunity of doing; and without knowing how it will be received, I feel relief from being unbosomed.

. . . though connected with political events, it has been viewed by me most strongly in its unfortunate bearings on my private friendships. The injury these have sustained has been a heavy price for what has never given me equal pleasure.[8]

This gave Abigail a wide opening, a challenge even, to defend the appointments her husband had made in the last few months of his Presidency. She well knew the appointment of John Marshall as Chief Justice of the Supreme Court had been deeply resented by Jefferson, and, she thought, most unreasonably so. At all events, the slander of "the midnight appointments" could be scotched—a slander which had made it seem as if John Adams had sat up late on the last night of his Presidency in Washington making appointments definitely and on purpose to wound and thwart the incoming President. She replied:

Your letter of June 13th, came duly to hand. If it had contained no other sentiments and opinions than those which my letter of condolence could have excited, and which are expressed in the first page of your reply, our correspondence would have terminated here. But you have been pleased to enter upon some subjects which call for a reply. . . .

"One act of Mr Adams's life, and *one* only (you repeat) ever gave me a moment's personal displeasure. I did consider his last appointments to office as personally unkind; they were from my most ardent political enemies."

As this act, I am certain, was not intended to give any personal pain or offence, I think it a duty to explain it, so far as I then knew his views and designs. The Constitution empowers the President to fill up offices as they become vacant. It was in the exercise of this power, that appointments were made, and characters selected, whom Mr Adams considered as men faithful to the constitution, and where he personally knew them, such as were capable of fulfilling their duty to their country. This was done equally by General Washington in the last days of his administration, so that not an office remained vacant for his successor to fill upon his coming into office. No offence was given by it and no personal unkindness thought of.

But the different political opinions, which have so unhappily divided our country, must have given rise to the idea that personal unkindness was intended. You will please to recollect, Sir, that at the time these appointments were made, there was not any certainty that the Presidency would devolve upon you,* which is another circumstances to prove that no personal unkindness was intended. . . . I know it was his opinion that if the Presidency devolved upon you, except in the appointment of Secretaries,† no material change‡ would be made. I perfectly agree with you in opinion that these cabinet members should be men in whom the President can repose confidence, possessing opinions and sentiments corresponding with his own; or if differing with him, that they ought rather to resign their offices than to cabal against measures which he may consider essential to the honour, safety and peace of the country. Neither ought they to unite with any bold and daringly ambitious character to overrule the Cabinet or to betray the secrets of it to friends or enemies.§ The two gentlemen who held the offices of secretaries, when you became President, were not of this character. They were persons appointed by your predecessor nearly two years previous to his retirement. They had cordially co-operated with him, and were gentlemen who enjoyed the public confidence. Possessing, however, different political sentiments from those which

* The House of Representatives not having yet given their decision between the tied candidates.

† The Cabinet. ‡ Change in policy.

§ Showing here her full information as to the Hamilton cabal in her husband's Cabinet.

you were known to have embraced, it was expected that they would, as they did, resign.

I have never felt any enmity towards you, Sir, for being elected President of the United States. But the instruments made use of and the means which were practised to effect a change have my utter abhorrence and detestation, for they were the blackest calumny and the foulest falsehoods. . . . I can truly say, that at the time of election, I considered your pretensions much superior to his who shared an equal vote with you. . . . I must rely upon the friendship you still profess to entertain for me (and I am conscious I have done nothing to forfeit it) to excuse the freedom of this discussion, to which you have led with an unreserve which has taken off the shackles I should, otherwise, have found myself embarrassed with. And now, Sir, I will freely disclose to you what has severed the bonds of former friendship, and placed you in a light very different from what some viewed you in.

One of the first acts of your administration was to liberate a wretch, who was suffering the just punishment of his crimes for publishing the basest libel, the lowest and vilest slander which malice could invent or calumny exhibit, against the character and reputation of your predecessor; of him, for whom you professed a friendship and esteem. . . . The remission of Callender's fine was a public approbation of his conduct. . . .

Until I read Callender's seventh letter containing your compliment to him as a writer and your reward of fifty dollars, I could not be made to believe that such measures could have been resorted to, to stab the fair fame and upright intentions of one who, to use your own language, "was acting from an honest conviction in his own mind that he was right." This, Sir, I considered as a personal injury; this was the sword that cut asunder the Gordian knot, which could not be untied by all the efforts of party spirit, by rivalry, by jealousy, or any other malignant fiend.

There is one other act of your administration which I considered as personally unkind, and which your own mind will easily suggest to you; but as it neither affected character nor reputation, I forbear to state it.

This letter is written in confidence. Faithful are the wounds of a friend. Often have I wished to have seen a different course pursued by you. . . .[9]

Jefferson found himself hit too shrewdly. He had to reply, to clear himself to his inward self, as well as to Mrs Adams. His answer is one of the best examples of his specious, twisted thought, his need to have it both ways—to be a man of stainless, chivalric honour and to be a secret slanderer at the same time. He had, he said, to rectify certain facts which seem not to have been presented to you under their true aspect. As early as 1796 I was told in Philadelphia that Callender, the author of the *Political Progress of Britain*, was in that city, a fugitive from persecution for having written that book, and in distress. I had read and approved the book: I considered him as a man of genius, unjustly persecuted. . . . I expressed my readiness to contribute to his relief. . . . It was a considerable time after that I contributed to his relief, and afterwards repeated the contribution. Himself I did not see till long after, nor ever more than two or three times. When he first began to write, he told some useful truths in his coarse way; but nobody sooner disapproved of his writing than I did, or wished more that he would be silent. My charities to him were no more meant as encouragements to his scurrilities than those I give to the beggar at my door are meant as rewards for the vices of his life.

With respect to the calumnies and falsehoods which writers and printers at large published against Mr Adams, I was as far from stooping to any concern of approbation of them as Mr Adams was respecting those of Porcupine, Femmo or Mussell, who published volumes against me for every sentence vended by their opponents against Mr Adams. . . . I knew myself incapable of that base warfare, and believed him to be so.

. . . whatever I may have thought of the acts of the administration of that day, I have ever borne testimony to Mr Adams's personal worth; nor was it ever impeached in my presence without a just vindication of it on my part. I never supposed that any person who knew either of us could believe that either of us meddled in that dirty work.

But another fact is that I "liberated a wretch who was suffering for a libel against Mr Adams." I do not know who was the particular wretch alluded to; but I discharged every person under punishment or prosecution under the sedition law, because I considered, and now consider, that law to be a nullity, as absolute and as palpable as if Congress had ordered us to fall down and worship a golden image; and that it was as much my duty to arrest its execution in every stage as it would have been my duty to rescue from the fiery furnace. . . . It was done in every instance, without asking what the offenders had done, or against whom they had offended.

He then became very high-flown about his motives and the tenor of his character, appealed to the country, posterity, and that Being, and so on, and continued:

You observe there has been one other act of my administration personally unkind, and suppose that it will readily suggest itself to me. I declare on my honour, Madam, I have not the least conception what act was alluded to. I never did a single one with an unkind intention. My sole object in this letter being to place before your attention that the acts imputed to me are either such as are falsely imputed or as might flow from good as well as bad motives, I shall make no other addition than the assurance of my continued wishes for the health and happiness of yourself and Mr Adams.[10]

Abigail does not let him get away with this. She states her case without mincing matters:

Candour requires of me a reply. Your statement respecting Callender, and your motives for liberating him, wear a different aspect as explained by you, from the impression which the act had made, not only upon my mind, but upon the minds of all those whom I have heard speak upon the subject. With regard to the law under which he was punished, different persons entertain different opinions respecting it. It lies not with me to determine its validity or constitutionality. That devolved upon the Supreme Judges of the nation. . . . If a Chief Magistrate can by his will annul it, where is the difference between a republican and a despotic government?

. . . If there is no check to be resorted to in the laws of the land, and no reparation to be made to the injured, will not man become the Judge and avenger of his own wrongs, and, as in a late instance,* the sword and pistol decide the contest? . . . Party spirit is blind, malevolent, uncandid, ungenerous, unjust and unforgiving. It is equally so under federal as under democratic banners. . . . Upon both sides are characters who possess honest views and act from honourable motives; characters who abhor calumny and evil speaking, and who will never descend to newspaper reviling. You have done Mr Adams justice in believing him incapable of such conduct. He has never written a line in any newspaper to which his signature has not been affixed since he was first elected President of the United States.

You exculpate yourself from any intentional act of unkindness towards any one. I will, however, freely state that which I considered as such. Soon after my eldest son's return from Europe, he was appointed by the District Judge to an office in which no political concerns entered. Personally known to you, and possessing all the qualifications, you yourself being judge, which you had designed for office, as soon as Congress gave the appointments to the President, you removed him. This looked so particularly pointed, that some of your best friends in Boston at that time expressed their regret that you had done so. I must do him the justice to say that I never heard an expression from him of censure or disrespect towards you in consequence of it.

* The duel between Aaron Burr and Hamilton, in which Hamilton was shot dead.

I have written to you with a freedom which only former friendship would warrant; and to which I would gladly return, could all causes but mere difference of opinion be removed . . . desirous of seeing my children and grandchildren heirs to that freedom and independence which you and your predecessor united your efforts to obtain.[11]

Jefferson's reply to this broadside was very remarkable Candour was the last and least of its ingredients. He was driven to the conclusion—painful but surprising—that Mrs Adams was citing

the removal of your eldest son from some office to which the judges had appointed him. I conclude then he must have been a commissioner of bankruptcy. But I declare to you on my honour that this is the first knowledge I have ever had that he was so.

It may be thought, perhaps, that I ought to have inquired who were such before I appointed others. But it is to be observed that the former law permitted the judges to name commissioners occasionally, only for every case as it arose, and not to make them permanent officers. Nobody therefore being in office there could be no removal. The judges, you well know, have been considered as highly federal; and it was noted that they confined their nominations exclusively to federalists.

The Legislature, dissatisfied with this, transferred the nomination to the President, and made the office permanent. The very object in passing the law was that he should correct, not confirm, what was deemed the partiality of the judges. I thought it therefore proper to inquire not whom they had employed but whom I ought to appoint to fulfill the intentions of the law. In making these appointments I put in a proportion of federalists. . . . Had I known that your son had acted, it would have been a real pleasure to me to have preferred him to some who were named in Boston in what was deemed the same line of politics. To this I should have been led by my knowledge of his integrity, as well as my sincere disposition towards yourself and Mr Adams.

He reverted to the easier case of Callender, and tries to lift that awkward subject from the particular to the general. He was in fact out against the Sedition Law itself.

You seem to think it devolved on the judges to decide on the validity of the sedition law. But nothing in the Constitution has given them a right to decide for the Executive, more than to the Executive to decide for them. Both magistrates are equally independent in the sphere of action assigned to them. The judges, believing the law constitutional, had a right to pass a sentence of fine and imprisonment. . . . But the executive, believing the law to be unconstitutional, were bound to remit the execution of it. . . . That instrument [the Constitution] meant that its co-ordinate branches should be checks on each other. But the opinion which gives to the judges the right to decide what laws are constitutional and what not . . . would make the judiciary a despotic branch.

And he winds up with a good smoke-screen on the freedom of the press, the similar aims of the two political parties, and his own impeccable loftiness of character. His longing for real loftiness, his right conception of the generous and the fine, are self-confessed.

While we deny that Congress have a right to control the freedom of the press, we have ever asserted the right of the States, and their exclusive right, to do so. . . . In general the State laws appear to have made the presses responsible for slander as far as is consistent with its useful freedom. In those States where they do not admit even the truth of allegations to protect the printer, they have gone too far.

The candour manifested in your letter and which I ever believed you to possess has alone inspired the desire of calling to your attention those circumstances of fact and motive by which I claim to be judged. I hope you will see these intrusions on your time to be, what they really are, proofs of my great respect for you.

Both of our political parties, at least the honest part of them, agree conscientiously in the same object—the public good; but they differ essentially in what they deem the means of promoting that good. . . . One fears most the ignorance of the people; the other the selfishness of rulers independent of them. Which is right, time and experience will prove. We think that one side of this experiment has been long enough tried and proved not to promote the good of the many; and that the other has not been fairly and sufficiently tried. Our opponents think the reverse. With whichever opinion the body of the nation concurs, that must prevail.

My anxieties on this subject will never carry me beyond the use of fair and honourable means, of truth and reason; nor . . . alienated my affections from a single friend who did not first withdraw himself.[12]

Abigail was not a lawyer's wife for nothing. She points out his begging of the question concerning John Quincy Adams, with equal firmness, candour, and courtesy, corrects him as to the powers of the Executive with regard to the law, and politely closes the correspondence.

SIR,

When I first addressed you, I little thought of entering into a correspondence with you upon subjects of a political nature. I will not regret it, as it has led to some elucidations, and brought on some explanations, which place in a more favourable light occurrences which had wounded me.

Having once entertained for you a respect and esteem . . . I could not suffer different political opinions to obliterate them from my mind. . . . It was not until circumstances concurred to place you in the light of a rewarder and encourager of a libeller, whom you could but not detest and despise, that I withdrew the esteem I had long entertained for you. Nor can you wonder, Sir, that I should consider as a personal unkindness the instances I have mentioned. I am pleased to find that which respected my son altogether unfounded. He was, as you conjecture, appointed a Commissioner of Bankruptcy, together with Judge Dawes, and continued to serve in it with perfect satisfaction to all parties (at least I never heard the contrary) until superseded by the appointment of others. The idea suggested that no one was in office, and consequently no removal could take place, I cannot consider in any other light than what the gentlemen of the law would term a quibble—as such I pass it. Judge Dawes was continued or reappointed, which placed Mr Adams in a more conspicuous light as the object of personal resentment. Nor could I, upon this occasion, refrain calling to mind the last visit you made me at Washington, when in the course of conversation you assured me that if it should lay in your power at any time to serve me or my family, nothing would give you more pleasure. With respect to the office, it was a small object, but the disposition of the remover was considered by me as the barbed arrow. This, however, by your declaration, is withdrawn from my mind. With the public it will remain.

I will not any further intrude upon your time; but close this correspondence by my wishes that you may be directed to that path which may terminate in the prosperity and happiness of the people over whom you are placed, by administering the government with justice and impartiality.[13]

This correspondence had been carried on without her husband's knowledge. A month later she handed him the whole—seven letters in all, three of Mr Jefferson's and four of hers. Her astonished husband read it with care, and laid it away with no comment but this: "Quincy, Nov. 19th, 1804. The whole of this correspondence was begun and conducted without my knowledge or suspicion. Last evening and this morning, at the desire of Mrs Adams, I read the whole. I have no remarks to make upon it, at this time and in this place."[14]

It was probably a relief to Mr Jefferson that Mrs Adams claimed a woman's last word, and saved him the embarrassment of further reply. Protestation of sincere friendship and of high dispassionate behaviour against the evidence of facts wears thin. Five years passed, and Mr Jefferson had another chance to prove his noble words by action. The Court of Russia sent a request for an Ambassador from the United States. What candidate was more obviously, patently, glaringly suitable than John Quincy Adams? Even that he belonged to the other party, Federalist-Republican, could hardly count against him, since he was notoriously far from being a party man. He had offended the Federalist party the year before by putting his weight on the side of Jefferson and the Democrats in the struggle over the embargo. But Mr Jefferson none the less did not appoint John Quincy Adams. Mr Jefferson nominated instead an obscure professional diplomat by the name of Mr Short. What Mr Short's qualifications were to represent America in Russia are lost in the mist of history. Before his name could be confirmed Mr Jefferson's second term as President ended in the new elections which placed Mr Madison in the President's office. When Congress opened in the spring of 1809 Mr Madison dutifully presented Mr Jefferson's nominee for the important diplomatic mission to St Petersburg, and the Senate promptly voted it down, saying candidly that they did not object to the mission but to the man. It was Mr Madison who then presented hastily (and successfully) the name of John Quincy Adams.

Does one hear Mr Jefferson's thwarted second self busily muttering in an undertone, excusing himself to Abigail, "Had I known that your son would have acted, it would have been a real pleasure to me to have preferred him! To this I should have been led by my knowledge of his integrity" (and he might have added, "my knowledge of his exceptional experience and education, qualifying him so uniquely for this especial post, as none knows better than myself")? But no. Jefferson's deep-lying jealousy of John Adams went too far down into his subconsicous for his intelligence to overcome it. He could not bring his will to give preferment and opportunity to John Adams's son.

Yet the avenue opened by Abigail between her husband and his former friend was still unclosed. Weeds and poison ivy perhaps made a thick tangle over its untrodden path, but a way had been cut through the timber of misunderstanding. It would not be hard to stroll down that avenue some day—if one did not have to go all the way, if one were sure of being met at the half-way mark. With one part of his divided heart, Jefferson longed to take those steps, to feel again the sturdy warmth of the warmest friend he had ever known.

In 1812 Dr Benjamin Rush, friend of both men, negotiated with each one to bring about a reconciliation. John Adams, guiltless of underhand action and unsuspicious of any, bore no grudge. To Rush's overtures he said, "His administration and mine are passed away into the dark backwards. I have always loved him as a friend."[15] Jefferson told Rush he had forgotten all the bitterness he once felt. So John Adams, in his hearty go-all-the-way-if-need-to manner, then wrote to Jefferson a simple letter sending him some specimens of homespun.

Jefferson was deeply moved. "A letter from you . . . carries me back to the time when we were fellow-labourers in the same cause, struggling for what is most valuable to man, his right of self-government." He dramatically threw to the winds what he chose to assume to be the old bone of contention: "As for France and England," said Jefferson largely, "the one is a den of robbers, the other of pirates." He passed quickly to domestic and personal detail of daily habits and family. "I salute you with unchanged affection and respect. . . ."[16] So the correspondence began.

Adams wrote oftener than Jefferson, saying with his habitual generosity, "Never mind if I write four letters to your one, your one is worth more than four of mine."

So the old friendship, nipped for a while by the frosts of party, put forth a green shoot. Adams was seventy-seven in 1812, Jefferson sixty-nine. The two elderly men found pleasure in exploring each other's minds, not along the dangerously divergent lines of politics, but in the wide field of the history of mankind, and of the theories and philosophies that lie behind all government and all human life. Not many could discuss these things as they could. It was a recreation, a distraction, an entertainment in their declining years. John Adams gave himself to it with all good faith; Jefferson, as usual, with reservation. Following the mysterious adjuration of Abigail's "Ancient Author," "let not thy left hand know what thy right hand doeth," Thomas Jefferson, writing to John Adams with his right hand in candid friendship, concealed from that right hand what he was about, so to speak, with the left—writing a memoir, an autobiography, which, with specious half-truths, loaded witness, unverified assertions, was preparing after his death to wound John Adams's reputation with a wound only short of mortal.

But their ghosts are not uneasy. America has taken them both to her bosom. Both of them ministered to her greatness, both fertilized her living growth with their vitality. Both were needed. A great country is nourished by more than one or two great men. In the story of America, the separate genius of each—yes, and their titan struggle, too—has its right and necessary place. It is part of the democratic method, in which we still believe. But the lying and deception, the false witness, is no right part of that, and its results were evil and lasting. The division of South and North which led at last to the war between the states had its roots in this early distrust. And we have not seen the finish.

The immediate results left their mark on the austere, upright, sensitive spirit of John Quincy Adams. But he shared with his mother only his success, his work, and his uncompromising reasoning, not his suffering. Let her remain in peace!

XVIII

Hath not Old Custom made this Life more Sweet?

YES, PEACE. THAT WAS THE CHIEF pattern of her days, her years. The seasons were their lovely frame, the sea and the bees and birds their constant soothing music. John was with her; never more would they separate until the great parting came which no man can avoid. The present was all-sufficient, and in the future there was nothing to strive for, except to make it as much like the present as possible.

Rural social life gave variety to their pleasant monotony: the Saturday Fish club of eight families, the visits of Mary and Richard Cranch—now Judge Cranch—of one or another of John's brothers, of Quincy cousins, and Smiths. Thomas is married and has come to live near by in the old homestead at Penns Hill. There is always a little "Chinese chatterer" darting about from one family to another, enjoying the "daffies" and the "puppy children" with Grandmamma.

Mrs Adams in her silks and laces is a bit awe-inspiring to the little daughters of Josiah Quincy the third when they come to Sunday dinner, but she is a most engaging grandparent, and a busy supervisor of dairy and baking on weekdays. And John Adams, jovial and easy, makes the table lively, carving the liberal roast after a course of corn-meal pudding has clogged the too sharp appetite.

A little storm began blowing up on the international sky in 1808. The immediate cause was the impressment of seamen, the old grievance. Abigail's pro-British mood, fanned by Napoleon, is past. The British are now "insolent and haughty."

John Quincy Adams, to his father's indignation, backed Jefferson's embargo.* How strange. But John Quincy explained it

* Trying to force redress of American grievances by trade pressure instead of war.

carefully to his mother, earnestly anxious for her approval. And his mother in turn explained it to his sister Nabby. Well, his motives, anyway, were above reproach. And Abigail was proud of his complete independence of judgment, his strength to hold his own. He and Louisa now have three sons—John Adams and Charles Francis, as well as little George Washington.

John Quincy Adams's career was moving on and up. When in 1809 he was made Minister to Russia by President Madison at half an hour's notice, Abigail's heart stopped for a second, beat on heavily. John Quincy noted in his journal, "I received yesterday a letter from my mother which would have melted the heart of a Stoic." She never expected to see him again in this life. But it was the price one must pay for greatness, for public service. Separation. Exile. She has paid it over and over again. It was a comfort to her to have his two little sons, George and John, left behind in her care.

In the autumn of 1811 Judge Richard Cranch died. Mary too lay dying. They told her of her husband's death. She said, "He has only stepped behind the scene; I shall know where to find him."

Abigail through her tears wrote it all to Mary's absent son, her favourite nephew, Will Cranch, in Washington.

"I hope, my dear nephew, while I live, that you will consider me as a parent, although I can never supply her place to you."[1]

The loss of Richard and Mary was the worst break possible in their circle. Abigail's earliest childhood memories clung to Mary, her youth and maturity had found in her sister her best and closest friend. The bond between John Adams and Dick Cranch had drawn the sisters ever closer.

It did not seem so very long ago that two young men rode together to the Weymouth parsonage in the bright October weather. And now it was a funeral cortège which ruffled the golden leaves, the years had all gone by, and that close quadruple relationship was ended. Almost fifty years of unbroken sweetness. "Such friends grow not thick on every bough." But like a fine piece of music, there was a triumph in the sorrow.

Thanksgiving Day, 1812, again at war with Britain. Abigail made a typical note:

> In our own way, and with tempers suited to the occasion, we gave thanks. . . . We were in health. We had good news from a far country. We had food and raiment, and we still enjoyed liberty, and our rulers were men of our own election and removable by the people.

Your uncle and aunt with their three children [Mr and Mrs Thomas Boylston Adams and Abigail, six, Elizabeth, four, and Thomas B., three], your Aunt Smith [brother William's widow, resident with Abigail Adams], George and John Adams with our own family, made the joyful group.

Letters are handed over the garden wall, from horsemen, carriages, sleighs. . . . The currents of the world flow in through the veins of the Adams breed.

In 1813 Nabby came home to die. Her husband in Congress now, representing his far-away outpost,* herself fatally ill with cancer and knowing it—she never told!—she "had the courage and resolution to have a bed placed in a carriage, and after a journey of fifteen days and three hundred miles she arrived in her father's house, attended by her dutiful children and her affectionate sister-in-law. . . . Emaciated, worn with pain, still she appeared delighted to embrace her parents, and feel herself surrounded with all that love, respect, and affection could afford." Immediately the best medical aid and advice was obtained, but opium was the only palliative, the only relief she could obtain.[2] She died three weeks after her arrival, on Sunday morning, August 30, 1813. The Colonel hurried from Washington to see her, and got there just in time. She had all her wishes fulfilled except her desire to see her son. Her eldest son, William Steuben (who had missed his senior year at Harvard to go on the Miranda adventure, but had graduated later from Columbia University, New York), was away in Petersburg as secretary to his uncle, John Quincy Adams.

"My only source of satisfaction," wrote the grief-stricken Abigail Adams to her son, whom she knew would so sorely feel his sister's loss, "and it is a never-failing one, is my firm persuasion that everything—and our oversights and mistakes among the rest—are parts of the great plan."[3]

Eighteen-fourteen flared up with the burning of the President's house, Capitol, and Library of Congress in Washington by the British, in that queer sporadic war in which Boston and Baltimore alike expected siege. "Useless," wrote John Quincy grimly, "to discuss now the policy, the justice or the necessity of our late war with Great Britain."

But Abigail was looking at the arson. "Modern Goths and vandals! All Europe blush at the deed. . . . The city a wilderness

* Lebanon Valley, New York.

thinly inhabited . . . the great part of the population slaves! We have heard that private property was respected, but a general destruction of the public."

No one regretted that rash act more sincerely than the British home Government, who were negotiating a peace treaty with John Quincy Adams when it occurred. Few English people were aware of it. All America resented it.

And now there is a ship of the Navy called the *John Adams.* Honour is given "the President," as all the neighbours called him, at all times and places. The lane before the house is called the President's Lane, and the rise is the President's Hill.*

Eighteen-sixteen rolled up, bearing with it a last sorrow for Abigail's loving heart. Her cousin Will Smith died in April. A warm and generous person, the finest type of open-handed, square-dealing American merchant.

"My friend and relative," Abigail mourned, "who from his earliest years I have loved as a brother, whose father's house in youth was a home to me, as my father's was to him. Although it can be but a short time before I shall follow him, I feel a limb lop'd from the body."[4]

But there was also in store a last joy. John Quincy Adams, eight years abroad, Ambassador to the Court of Russia, and then negotiator of the Peace Treaty and Ambassador to the Court of Great Britain (like his father before him), was coming home.

On the bright day of August 18, 1817, "about ten this morning a carriage and four were seen coming down the hill." Yes, it was John Quincy Adams, a mature man, a polished diplomat, her little son of the Bunker Hill morning—coming home. "I ran to the door." His sons, George and John† and Charles, poured out of the carriage—"John, who with his former ardour was round my neck in a moment. George followed half crazy, crying out 'O Grandmother, O Grandmother'; Charles more shy. . . ."[5]

"The inexpressible happiness," said John Quincy Adams, "of that moment." All the family gathered from far and near. Within half an hour "my Uncle Peter Adams. . . . My son John went immediately to my brother's house, and he—Tom—came with

* Not to be confused with Penns Hill (much more of a hill) at the other farm, a mile or two down the village.

† Their father had sent for his sons when his removal to England from Russia made it possible to have them with him, and their grandmother had parted with them regretfully in May 1814.

his wife to dinner. . . . My brother's five children came immediately after. . . ."[6]

That was a Thanksgiving Day indeed, out of season, or with a whole season of its own. A day worth living for through a long life. Abigail looked round on her husband, her two excellent sons, her grandchildren, and her great-grandchildren. John Quincy Adams had just accepted appointment from President Monroe as Secretary of State. The August sunshine poured down upon the hot road; the great trees gave friendly shade; the house was now dignified and ample. Plenty and comfort, freedom, and love, and not an enemy ship on all the sea.

Now, Lord, lettest thou thy servant depart in peace, for mine eyes have seen thy salvation.

Abigail's room was the west bedroom, sunny and warm. Here her little grandson, Charles Francis, watched on a summer's day "the yellow and green brilliancy of the garden beneath the windows," and in the autumn he saw the yellowing leaves of the maples making an extra sunshine. Over the north wall, the oak beams, hardened by time to the consistency of iron, showed the adze marks of the hewing when they were green wood. Around the fireplace were the picture tiles brought home by John Quincy Adams in 1801, when he returned from Berlin and gave them to his mother.

Here is Abigail's armchair, which she used all day when rheumatism occasionally lamed her, and in the increasing lethargy of her last slow illness. And here is John Adams's high-backed armchair where he sat to be with her. Never tired of her company. Always wanting her most and best.

There Abigail was remembered by her grandchildren and her great-grandchildren, sitting enthroned with her little dog Satan beside her, talking in her lively way to visitors* who sat on the long sofa near by.

Here in the fourpost bed, on October 28, 1818, of typhoid fever, she died. Yes, as she lay and dreamed into a sleep, with that dear hand to hold to to the last, it had been a long way to come. Much farther than she had fancied when she left the Weymouth parsonage on that autumn day, October too, fifty-four years ago. The road had taken her through war and pestilence, over great oceans, into

* One of the last of whom was Daniel Webster.

foreign places; it had given her scorn and honour, but much more honour; it had given her pain and joy, but much more joy. And, most of all, she had found upon it a comradeship rare on earth.

Her husband survived her by eight years, dying in the second year of their eldest son's Presidency, and on the fiftieth anniversary of the Revolution, July 4, 1826. Thomas Jefferson died the same day.

Let Abigail Adams's son, John Quincy Adams, speak her epitaph.

"Last Wednesday, the 28th of October, between eleven and one o'clock of that day, my mother, beloved and lamented more than language can express, yielded up her pure and gentle spirit to its Creator. She was born on the 11th of November, 1744, and had completed within less than a month of her seventy-fourth year. Had she lived to the age of the Patriarchs, every day of her life would have been filled with clouds of goodness and of love. There is not a virtue that can abide in the female heart but it was the ornament of hers. She had been fifty-four years the delight of my father's heart, the sweetener of all his toils, the comforter of all his sorrows, the sharer and heightener of all his joys. It was but the last time when I saw my father that he told me, with an ejaculation of gratitude to the Giver of every good and every perfect gift, that in all the vicissitudes of his fortunes, through all the good report and evil report of the world, in all his struggles and in all his sorrows, the affectionate participation and cheering encouragement of his wife had been his never-failing support, without which he was sure he should never have lived through them. She was the daughter of William Smith, minister at Weymouth, and of Elizabeth Quincy, his wife. Oh, God! may I die the death of the righteous, and may my last end be like hers!"

Notes

CHAPTER I

1. *Works of John Adams* (8 vols.), ed. Charles Francis Adams (Boston, 1856), II, p. 88.
2. *Ibid.*, p. 48.
3. *Ibid.*, p. 45.
4. *Ibid.*, p. 78. John Adams's letter to Sam Quincy shown to Jonathan Sewall, and Sewall writes to J. A. to ask his friendship and correspondence.
5. *Ibid.*, p. 70.
6. *Ibid.*, p. 133 *n*.
7. *Ibid.*, p. 145.
8. *Ibid.*, p. 145.
9. Adams MS. "Mis Nabby Smith, Weymouth. These. In favour Dr Tufts. from John Adams, Braintree. Feb. 14th, 1763."
10. *Ibid.*, April 20. "Miss Nabby Smith ('Diana') to Mr John Adams, Braintree. Aug. 11th, 1763."
11. *Ibid.*, April 1764. The *Dictionary of American Biography* incorrectly states that it was Dr Joseph Warren who inoculated John Adams. John Adams's letters to his betrothed make it clear that his physician was Dr Perkins. There is no evidence in these early letters that Dr Warren was taking part in this anti-smallpox campaign or was an acquaintance—no mention of him at all.
12. *Ibid.*, April 1764.
13. *Ibid.*, April 1764.
14. *Ibid.* Abigail was inoculated in 1776 as we shall see. Parson Smith himself suffered a late conversion, and June 3, 1778, his diary notes: "Was inoculated by Dr Wales in the 72nd year of my age at Col. Quincy's. Tarried at the Col. 3 weeks wanting a day."
15. *Ibid.* April 1764.
16. *Ibid.*, April 1764.
17. *Ibid.*, April 1764.

18. Adams MS., April 30, 1764. This Diana-Lysander business was a popular convention of the period, and implied no more affectation than our Buddy and Ginger type of nickname to-day.
19. *Ibid.*, April–May 1764.
20. *Ibid.*, April–May 1764.
21. *Ibid.*, spring and summer, 1764.
22. *Ibid.*, spring and summer, 1764.

CHAPTER II

1. *Samuel Adams*, James K. Hosmer (Boston, 1893); and *History of the United States* (6 vols.), George Bancroft (Boston, 1876), III, p. 420.
2. *Memoir of the Life of Josiah Quincy*, by his son (Boston, 1874). (Entry of August 28, 1765.)
3. *Works*, II, p. 53.
4. *Ibid.*, III, p. 465.
5. *Ibid.*, III, p. 467.
6. *Ibid.*, III, p. 467.
7. *Ibid.* Sam Adams had had a similar duty the year before, May 1764. See Bancroft, III, p. 418.
8. *Ibid.*, II, p. 154.
9. *Ibid.*, II, p. 157.
10. *Ibid.*, p. 157.
11. *Ibid.*, p. 158*n*.
12. *Ibid.*, p. 163.
13. December 25, 1765. On December 29 they "dined at Weymouth, at Father Smith's." See *Works*, II, pp. 165, 167.
14. *Works*, II, p. 170.
15. *Ibid.*, p. 168.
16. *Ibid.*, p. 179.
17. *Ibid.*, p. 179.
18. Adams MS. From an undated love-letter between 1761 and 1764.
19. *Works*, II, p. 195.
20. *Ibid.*, p. 197.
21. *Ibid.*, p. 197.
22. *Ibid.*, p. 203.
23. *Ibid.*, p. 198.
24. *Ibid.*, p. 199.
25. Adams MS. November 1766.
26. *Works*, II, p. 201.

CHAPTER III

1. *Correspondence of William Pitt, Earl of Chatham* (4 vols.), edited by W. S. Taylor and J. H. Pringle (London, 1838–1840), III, p. 153.
2. *Memoirs & Writings of Franklin*, Parsons (London, 1793), II, p. 371.
3. *Letters of Mrs Adams*, ed. Charles Francis Adams (Boston, 1848), p. 9.
4. *Works*, II, pp. 210, 212. 1768.
5. *Ibid.*, p. 214.
6. *Ibid.*, p. 238.
7. *The History of the Rise, Progress and Establishment of America* (3 vols.), William Gordon (New York, 1789), I, p. 247.
8. *Ibid.*, p. 247.
9. *A History of Boston, the Metropolis of Massachusetts, from its Origin to the Present Period*, 2nd ed., A. Bowen (Boston, 1828), p. 254.
10. *Works*, II, p. 215.
11. *Ibid.*, pp. 227–228.
12. *Ibid.*, p. 227.
13. *Ibid.*, p. 230.

CHAPTER IV

1. *Works*, II, pp. 230–231. 1770.
2. *Ibid.*, I, p. 110.
3. *Ibid.*, II, p. 232.
4. *Ibid.*, p. 232.
5. *Ibid.*, p. 233.
6. *Ibid.*, p. 233. 1770.
7. *Ibid.*, p. 243.
8. *Ibid.*, p. 255. 1771.
9. *Ibid.*, p. 255.
10. *Ibid.*, p. 256.
11. *Ibid.*, p. 269.
12. *Ibid.*, p. 269.
13. Smith-Carter MS. April 3, 1772
14. *Works*, II, p. 299.
15. *Ibid.*, p. 304.
16. *Ibid.*, p. 302.
17. *Ibid.*, p. 306.
18. *Ibid.*, p. 314.
19. *Ibid.*, p. 308.
20. *Ibid.*, p. 310.
21. *Letters of Mrs Adams*, p. 21.
22. *Works*, II, p. 312.

23. *Letters of Mrs Adams*, p. 12.
24. *Works*, II, p. 312.
25. *Letters of Mrs Adams*, p. 12.
26. Bancroft, IV, p. 266.
27. *Ibid.*, IV, p. 266.
28. *John Hancock his Book*, ed. Abram English Brown (Boston, 1898), p. 179.
29. *Letters of Mrs Adams*, p. 10. 1773.
30. Hancock, p. 180. Letter of John Andrews, eye-witness.
31. *Ibid.*, p. 180.
32. *The History of the Province of Massachusetts Bay* (3 vols.), Hutchinson (London, 1828), III, p. 438.
33. Hancock, p. 180.
34. *Works*, II, p. 334 *n*.
35. Hutchinson, III, p. 438.
36. *Works*, II, p. 324. They decided against proclamation. Hutchinson says, "So many of the actors and abettors were universally known that a proclamation for discovery would have been ridiculed." Hutchinson, III, p. 438.
37. Hancock, p. 179.
38. *Works*, II, p. 337.
39. *Ibid.*, p. 326. February 1774.

CHAPTER V

1. *Familiar Letters of John Adams and his Wife Abigail Adams during the Revolution*, ed. Charles Francis Adams, p. 2.
2. *Works*, II, p. 331. 1774.
3. *Familiar Letters*, p. 12.
4. *Ibid.*, p. 21.
5. *Works*, II, p. 338.
6. *Ibid.*, II, p. 338.
7. Adams MS. June 1774.
8. *Familiar Letters*, p. 28.
9. Adams MS. June 30, 1774.
10. *Ibid.*, July 7, 1774.
11. *Works*, II, p. 340.
12. *Familiar Letters*, p. 5.
13. *Works*, II, p. 338.
14. *Familiar Letters*, p. 26
15. *Ibid.*, p. 33.
16. *Ibid.*, p. 35.
17. *Ibid.*, p. 35.

18. *Familiar Letters*, p. 35.
19. *Ibid.*, p. 34.
20. *Ibid.*, p. 51.
21. *Ibid.*, pp. 33–34.
22. *Ibid.*, p. 41. September 24, 1774. Abigail Adams dates this letter bitterly from "Boston Garrison."
23. *Ibid.*, pp. 41–42.
24. Smith-Carter MS. March 29, 1773. Thomas Smith of South Carolina to Isaac Smith of Boston.
25. *Ibid.*, March 29, 1773.
26. *Familiar Letters*, p. 40.
27. Adams MS.
28. *Works*, II, p. 319.
29. *Letters from a Farmer in Pennsylvania to the Inhabitants of the British Colonies*, John Dickinson (Boston, 1768).
30. *Familiar Letters*, p. 49, and Adams MS. September 14, 1774.
31. Adams MS. September 16, 1774.
32. *Familiar Letters*, p. 59.
33. *Works*, II, pp. 405–406.
34. *Ibid.*, p. 406.
35. *Familiar Letters*, p. 52.
36. *Ibid.*, p. 56.
37. *Ibid.*, pp. 56–57, 69.
38. *Ibid.*, pp. 55–57.
39. *Ibid.*, pp. 60–62.
40. *Ibid.*, pp. 63, 64. June 15, 1775.

CHAPTER VI

1. *Familiar Letters*, pp. 67–68.
2. *Ibid.*, p. 68.
3. *Ibid.*, p. 69.
4. *Ibid.*, p. 73.
5. *Ibid.*, p. 69.
6. *Ibid.*, p. 71.
7. Bancroft, IV, p. 612.
8. *Familiar Letters*, p. 74.
9. *Ibid.*, p. 77.
10. *Ibid.*, pp. 78–79.
11. *Ibid.*, p. 73.
12. *Ibid.*, p. 80.
13. Smith-Carter MS. June 30, 1775.
14. *Familiar Letters*, p. 94.

15. *Familiar Letters*, p. 95.
16. *Ibid.*, p. 97.
17. *Ibid.*, p. 89.
18. *Ibid.*, p. 102.
19. *Ibid.*, p. 117.
20. *Ibid.*, p. 109.
21. *Ibid.*, p. 119.
22. *Ibid.*, p. 117.
23. *Ibid.*, p. 110.
24. *Ibid.*, p. 115.
25. *Ibid.*, p. 112.
26. *Ibid.*, p. 115.
27. *Ibid.*, pp. 121–122.
28. *Ibid.*, pp. 114–115.
29. *Ibid.*, p. 152.
30. *Ibid.*, p. 165.
31. *Ibid.*, p. 127.
32. *Ibid.*, p. 110.
33. *Ibid.*, p. 126.
34. *Ibid.*, p. 130.
35. *Ibid.*, pp. 128–129.
36. *Works*, I, p. 193.
37. *Familiar Letters*, p. 146
38. *Ibid.*, pp. 137–138.
39. *Ibid.*, p. 142.
40. *Ibid.*, p. 144.
41. *Ibid.*, p. 145.
42. *Ibid.*, p. 149.
43. Smith-Carter MS. Letter of Andrew Eliot, Boston, to Mr Isaac Smith, London, April 9, 1776.
44. *Familiar Letters*, pp. 149–155.
45. Tudor MS. June 1776.
46. *Familiar Letters*, p. 191.
47. *Ibid.*, pp. 192–193.
48. *Ibid.*, p. 204. 1776.
49. *Ibid.*, p. 212. August 14, 1776.
50. *Works*, II, pp. 505–506, 516–517.
51. *Familiar Letters*, p. 201. July 1776.
52. *Ibid.*, p. 221. August 1776. Uncle Isaac and Aunt Elizabeth Smith were still at Salem.
53. *Ibid.*, p. 230. October 1776.
54. *Ibid.*, p. 148.
55. *Ibid.*, p. 166.
56. *Ibid.*, p. 175.

CHAPTER VII

1. *Familiar Letters*, p. 309.
2. *Works*, III, pp. 68, 82–83.
3. *Ibid.*, p. 83.
4. *Familiar Letters*, p. 228. September 22, 1776.
5. *Ibid.*, p. 301.
6. *Ibid.*, pp. 309–312.
7. *Ibid.*, p. 273.
8. *Ibid.*, p. 288.
9. *Ibid.*, p. 321.
10. *Ibid.*, p. 159.
11. *Ibid.*, p. 165.
12. *Ibid.*, p. 281.
13. *Works*, III, pp. 90–91.
14. *Ibid.*, I, p. 276.
15. Thaxter MS. Letter of A. A. to John Thaxter, February 15, 1778.
16. *Familiar Letters*, p. 328.
17. Adams MS. July 1778.
18. *Ibid.*, 1778.
19. Thaxter MS. July 23, 1778.
20. *Ibid.*, September 1778.
21. *Ibid.*, April 9, 1778.
22. *Ibid.*, September 2, 1778.
23. *Ibid.*, April 1778.
24. *Familiar Letters*, p. 339.
25. *Ibid.*, p. 342.
26. Adams MS. November 1778.
27. *Ibid.*, p. 350.
28. *Ibid.*, Autumn 1778.
29. *Familiar Letters*, p. 351.
30. *Ibid.*, December 1778, February 1779, pp. 347, 358, 357.
31. *Ibid.*, p. 348.
32. Thaxter MS. September 1778.
33. *Ibid.*, September 1778.
34. *Ibid.*, September 1778.
35. *Works*, III, p. 214.
36. *Ibid.*, pp. 211–213, 216, 223, 226.
37. *Familiar Letters*, p. 355.
38. Thaxter MS. March 2, 1780.
39. *Familiar Letters*, pp. 354–455.
40. *Ibid.*, p. 122.
41. *Works*, III, p. 162.

42. *Familiar Letters*, p. 356.
43. *Ibid.*, pp. 368–369.
44. *Works*, I, p. 412.
45. *Familiar Letters*, pp. 370, 374, and *Works*, III, pp. 231, 240.
46. *Ibid.*, pp. 376–377.
47. Thaxter MS. July 21, 1780.
48. Adams MS. September 1780.
49. *Familiar Letters*, p. 375.
50. Adams MS. July 1780.
51. *Ibid.*, September 1780.
52. *Familiar Letters*, p. 398.
53. *Ibid.*, p. 412.
54. *Ibid.*, p. 386, September 1780.
55. *Works*, VIII, p. 39.
56. Adams MS. January 1781.
57. *Ibid.*, September 20, 1781.
58. *Letters of Mrs Adams*, p. 129. December 9, 1781. "Bilboa" was the old spelling for Bilbao, the capital of Biscay province in Spain.
59. Adams MS. March and April 1782.
60. *Ibid.*, August 1781.
61. *Ibid.*
62. Adams MS. October 21, 1781.
63. *Familiar Letters*, pp. 404–405. 1782.
64. *Ibid.*, p. 406.
65. *Letters of Mrs Adams*, p. 139.

CHAPTER VIII

1. *Letters of Mrs Adams*, pp. 133, 137.
2. Adams MS. April 10, 1782.
3. *Letters of Mrs Adams*, p. 137.
4. *Works*, VIII, p. 57.
5. *Familiar Letters*, pp. 410, 412, 413.
6. Adams MS. August 1783.
7. *Ibid.*, November 1783.
8. *Ibid.*, October 8, 1782.
9. *Ibid.*, October 1782.
10. *Ibid.*, December 1782.
11. *Ibid.*, April 7, 1783.
12. *Ibid.*, June 1783.
13. *Ibid.*, December 27, 1783.
14. *Ibid.*, April 28, 1783.
15. *Ibid.*, April 28, 1783.

16. Adams MS. June 20, 1783.
17. *Ibid.*, August 5, 1782.
18. *Ibid.*, August 1782.
19. *Ibid.*, July 21, 1783.
20. Letters, pp. 135–136.
21. *Familiar Letters*, p. 406.
22. *Letters of Mrs Adams*, pp. 161–170.
23. *Ibid.*, p. 170.
24. *Ibid.*, p. 167.
25. *Ibid.*, p. 171.
26. *Ibid.*, p. 172.
27. *Ibid.*, p. 173.
28. *Ibid.*, pp. 174–184.
29. *Ibid.*, p. 185.
30. *Ibid.*, p. 185.
31. *Ibid.*, p. 186.
32. *Works*, III, p. 389. (John Adams's Diary, August 7, 1784.)

CHAPTER IX

1. *Journal and Correspondence of Miss Adams*, edited by her daughter (New York, 1841).
2. *Ibid.*, p. 10.
3. *Ibid.*, p. 11.
4. *Letters of Mrs Adams*, p. 198.
5. *Journal and Correspondence of Miss Adams*, p. 14.
6. *Letters of Mrs Adams*, p. 195.
7. *Ibid.*, p. 189. Of course Mrs Adams had never seen roller-skating. She said "dancing like a Merry Andrew."
8. *Ibid.*, p. 195.
9. *Ibid.*, p. 193.
10. *Ibid.*, pp. 203, 211.
11. *Ibid.*, p. 192.
12. *Ibid.*, p. 211.
13. *Ibid.*, p. 234.
14. *Ibid.*, p. 231.
15. Abigail Adams, 1783. The Adams MS.
16. *Letters of Mrs Adams*, p. 242.
17. Adams MS.
18. *Ibid.*, May 10, 1785.

CHAPTER X

1. *Letters of Mrs Adams*, p. 243.
2. *Works*, VIII, pp. 255–259. Letter to Jay.
3. *Ibid.*
4. *Journal and Correspondence of Miss Adams*, p. 79.
5. *Works*, III, p. 391.
6. *Ibid.*, VIII, p. 265.
7. *Letters of Mrs Adams*, pp. 257, 270.
8. *Ibid.*, p. 270.
9. *Ibid.*, p. 260.
10. *Ibid.*, p. 255.
11. Letters of Col. Wm. Smith to Baron Steuben and to Rufus King
12. *Letters of Mrs Adams*, p. 264, September 2, 1785.
13. *Memoirs of the Life and Reign of King George III*, J. Heneage Jesse (London, 1867), II, p. 495 *ff.*
14. *Letters of Mrs Adams*, pp. 275–276.
15. *Ibid.*, p. 266.
16. *Ibid.*
17. Adams MS. April 1785.
18. *Ibid.*
19. *Ibid.*, April 24, 1786.
20. Smith-Carter MS. June 1783.
21. *Letters of Mrs Adams*, p. 275.
22. Adams MS. 1786.
23. *Ibid.*, February 18, 1786. Letter of John Quincy Adams.
24. Smith-Carter MS. August 1785.
25. Adams MS. Spring 1786. Abigail Adams to John Quincy Adams.
26. *Ibid.*, June 13, 1786.
27. *Ibid.*
28. Smith-Carter MS. August 29, 1785. Letter to Uncle Isaac and Aunt Elizabeth.
29. Adams MS. May 1787.
30. *Letters of Mrs Adams*, p. 328, July 1787.
31. Adams MS. 1787.
32. *Ibid.*, June 2, 1787.
33. *Works*, VIII, p. 466.
34. *Ibid.*, p. 310.
35. *Ibid.*, pp. 475–476.
36. Adams MS. February 1788.
37. *Works*, VIII, p. 458.
38. *Letters of Mrs Adams*, p. 343.
39. Adams MS. April and May 1788.
40. *Letters of Mrs Adams*, p. 319.

CHAPTER XI

1. Adams MS.
2. *Ibid.*
3. *Ibid.*, November 10, 1788.
4. Cranch MS. Jamaica, Long Island, November 24, 1788.
5. Bobbé, pp. 202–203.
6. Cranch MS. December 15, 1788.
7. Bobbé, p. 200.
8. *Ibid.*, p. 204.
9. *Ibid.*, p. 484. Gerry to John Adams.
10. Tudor MS. Letter from John Adams to William Tudor, May 3, 1789.
11. Adams MS. May 1789.

CHAPTER XII

1. Cranch MS. June 1789.
2. Adams MS. Letter to John Quincy Adams, December 1790.
3. Cranch MS. June 1789.
4. *Ibid.*, July 12, 1789.
5. *Ibid.*, July 12, 1789.
6. *Ibid.*, July 1789.
7. *Ibid.*, summer, 1789.
8. Adams MS. Letter to John Quincy Adams, November 1789.
9. Frank M. Etting Autograph Collection, *Washingtonia.* Oct. 22, 1789.
10. Cranch MS. October 1789.
11. *Ibid.*, August 1789.
12. *Ibid.*, January 1790.
13. Adams MS. November 22, 1789.
14. Cranch MS. January 5, 1790.
15. *Journal of William Maclay*, William Maclay (New York, 1890), pp. 138, 177, 206.
16. Cranch MS. Autumn 1789.
17. *Ibid.*, March 1790.
18. *Ibid.*, March 1790.
19. *Selected Writings of Thomas Jefferson*, pp. 125–129.
20. Cranch MS. New York, 1790.
21. *Ibid.*, summer, 1790.
22. *Ibid.*, July 4, 1790.
23. *Ibid.*, January 5, 1790.
24. *Ibid.*, January 5, 1790.
25. Adams MS. August 1790.
26. *Ibid.*, New York, September 1790.

27. Adams MS. November 1790.
28. Cranch MS. March 12, 1791.

CHAPTER XIII

1. Cranch MS. September 1790.
2. *Ibid.*, December 26, 1790.
3. *Letters of Mrs Adams*, p. 352.
4. *Ibid.*, p. 353.
5. *Ibid.*, p. 358
6. *Ibid.*, p. 356
7. Cranch MS. December 12, 1790, January 1791.
8. *Ibid.*, April 1792.
9. Smith-Carter MS.
10. *Ibid.*, March 1792.
11. *Letters of Mrs Adams*, pp. 360–361.
12. *Ibid.*, p. 361.
13. Adams MS. Autumn, 1793.
14. *Works*, I, p. 462, January 9, 1794.
15. Adams MS. November 1795.
16. *Ibid.*, 1796.
17. Cranch MS.
18. *Ibid.*
19. Adams MS. February 1793.

CHAPTER XIV

1. Adams MS. February 1798.
2. *Ibid.*, May 1796.
3. *Ibid.*, Spring, 1796.
4. *Ibid.*, Spring, 1796.
5. *Ibid.*, Spring, 1796.
6. *Ibid.*, February 1797.
7. *Letters of Mrs Adams*, p. 374.
8. Adams MS. March 5, 1797.
9. *Letters of Mrs Adams*, p. 377.

CHAPTER XV

1. *Works*, I, p. 494.
2. Cranch MS. April 1797.

3. Cranch MS. May 5, 1797, and later.
4. *Ibid.*, May 1797.
5. Smith-Carter MS. Mrs Sam Otis to Mrs Wm Smith, March 30, 1798.
6. Cranch MS. June 23, 1797.
7. *Ibid.*, June 1797.
8. Adams MS. November 3, 1797.
9. *Ibid.*, Abigail Adams to John Quincy Adams, November 23, 1797, Philadelphia.
10. *Ibid.*, November 3, 1797.
11. Cranch MS. October 31, 1797.
12. Smith-Carter MS. March 5, 1798.
13. Cranch MS. December 1797.
14. *Ibid.*, April 26 and 28, and May 7, 1798.
15. *Ibid.*, April 26, 1798.
16. Smith-Carter MS.
17. *Autobiography of Thomas Jefferson*, ed. Paul L. Ford (New York, 1914), III, pp. 309–310.
18. Smith-Carter MS. June 19, 1798.
19. *Ibid.*, July 1798.
20. *Ibid.*, March and June 1798.
21. *Ibid.*, Letter from Sam Otis, April 3, 1798.
22. Adams MS. Letter to John Quincy Adams, July 14, 1798. Also, "Capt. Decatur has captured a 12 gun French privateer and brought her into this port." July 20, 1798.
23. *Ibid.*, July 14, 1798. Letter to John Quincy Adams.
24. Smith-Carter MS. July 1798.
25. *Ibid.*, Sam Otis to W. S. July 21, 1798.

CHAPTER XVI

1. Adams MS. July 1798.
2. *Ibid.*, Letter to John Quincy Adams.
3. Smith-Carter MS. July 1798.
4. Adams MS. April 1798.
5. *Ibid.*, July 14, 1798. Abigail's youngest sister, Betsey
6. *Ibid.*, 1798.
7. *Works*, I, p. 541.
8. *Ibid.*, p. 547.
9. *Ibid.*, p. 545.
10. Smith-Carter MS. January 2, 1799.
11. Adams MS. 1796.
12. *Ibid.*, June 12, 1799. To John Quincy Adams.
13. *Ibid.*, February 1799.

14. *Figures of the Past*, Josiah Quincy (Roberts Brothers, Boston, 1892).
15. Smith-Carter MS. April 30, 1800. Hannah Smith.
16. Smith-Townsend MS. Letter of William Shaw to William Smith, January 1800.
17. *Ibid.*, January 1800.
18. *Ibid.*, March 1800.

CHAPTER XVII

1. Adams MS.
2. Bobbé, p. 238.
3. Cranch MS. December 8, 1800, and Adams MS. Letters to John Quincy Adams, January 29 and May 30, 1801.
4. *Letters of Mrs Adams*, p. 380.
5. *Ibid.*, p. 386.
6. Adams MS. May 30, 1801.
7. *Letters of Mrs Adams*, pp. 389–390.
8. *Jefferson's Letters*, pp. 143–144.
9. *Letters of Mrs Adams*, pp. 390–394.
10. *Jefferson's Letters*, pp. 147–149.
11. *Letters of Mrs Adams*, pp. 394–396.
12. *Jefferson's Letters*, pp. 150–151. September 11, 1804.
13. *Letters of Mrs Adams*, pp. 396–398.
14. *Ibid.*, p. 398.
15. *Jefferson*, Saul K. Padover (New York, 1942), p. 367.
16. *Ibid.*, p. 367.

CHAPTER XVIII

1. *Letters of Mrs Adams*, p. 408.
2. Adams MS. August 1813.
3. *Ibid.*, July 1813.
4. Smith-Carter MS. August 7, 1816.
5. Adams MS. Letter from Abigail Adams to Harriet Welch, August 18, 1817.
6. *Ibid.*, John Quincy Adams's MS. Diary, August 18, 1817.

A Comment on Sources

TWO VALUABLE COLLECTIONS OF Abigail Adams Letters have been published (and edited) by her grandson, Charles Francis Adams, and have long been known to the public. The Smith-Carter, the Smith-Townsend, and the de Windt manuscript collections, in the care of the Massachusetts Historical Society in Boston, furnish others, as well as valuable correspondence of many family connexions.

In addition to these, and the printed *Diary*, letters, and public papers of John Adams, I have been privileged to use three new sources of material, hitherto untapped.

The first and most important of these is the great collection known as the Adams Manuscript, privately owned by the Adams family.

The second is the recently discovered Adams collection of several hundred letters, including some two hundred written by Abigail Adams to her favourite sister, Mary Cranch, during the twelve years of John Adams's Vice-Presidency and Presidency. This collection is owned by the American Antiquarian Society, and I am gratefully indebted to them for their generous treatment. To avoid confusion with the Adams Manuscript and Adams Letters referred to by me, I have referred to this as the Cranch Manuscript. They have since been published under the editorship of Mr Stewart Mitchell, under the title of *New Letters of Abigail Adams*.

The third is the Thaxter Manuscript, a small collection of (twenty-five) letters written by Abigail Adams to John Thaxter, a young cousin who was a law pupil of John Adams, and who was for a time tutor to the Adams children, and went abroad as John Adams's secretary when he went to negotiate the peace. This interesting group of letters has been recently acquired by the Boston Public Library.

John Adams was often a centre of controversy. His wife was always on his side. Though this in itself is a tribute to him, there is a risk in it to one who wishes to practise fair play.

I have taken pains to let Mr Adams's outstanding opponents—Mr Hutchinson, Dr Franklin, Mr Hamilton, and Mr Jefferson—state their own case, and have read such histories, autobiographies, diaries, or letters as they may have left behind, with, I hope, an open mind.

In the pages of this book, when they speak, they at least speak for themselves.

. . . and on form

Professor Trevelyan has said, "The poetry of History does not consist of imagination roaming at large, but of imagination pursuing the fact and fastening upon it." But in using imagination as a hunting dog or as a tool, how avoid the pitfalls of that horrid hybrid, 'fictionized biography'?

My own method is to feel free to express the abstract by the concrete (a girl is feeling shy, then let her go through the motions of a shy girl) and to express 'indirect speech' reported in a letter or journal by 'direct speech' in dramatic form. But I do not feel free to make up an emotion which I am not *certain* was experienced by my subject, or to make up anything supposedly said or thought (no matter how appropriate).

Every sentence of dialogue in these pages attributed to any historical character is taken with little or no change from an authentic written source.

J. W.

Principal Manuscript Sources

The Adams Manuscript, in the care of the trustees of the Adams Trust, Mr Charles Francis Adams and Mr Henry Adams.

The Cranch Manuscript (the Adams Letters), owned by the American Antiquarian Society.

The Thaxter Manuscript, owned by the Boston Public Library.

The Smith-Townsend Manuscript collection, owned by the Massachusetts Historical Society.

The Smith-Carter Manuscript collection, owned by the Massachusetts Historical Society.

The de Windt Manuscript collection, owned by the Massachusetts Historical Society.

The Manuscript Diary of Parson Smith, owned by the Massachusetts Historical Society.

The Sparkes Manuscript, owned by the Houghton Library, Harvard University.

The Tudor Manuscript, owned by the Massachusetts Historical Society.

Principal Books and Publications read and consulted

Adams, Charles Francis: *Three Episodes of Massachusetts History* (2 vols.) (Boston, 1893).

Adams, Henry: *History of the United States* (9 vols.) (New York, 1903, I–IV).

Adams, James Truslow: *The Living Jefferson* (Boston, 1936).

Adams, John Quincy: *The Diary of John Quincy Adams 1794–1845*, edited by Allan Nevins (New York, 1929).

Adams, John Quincy and Charles Francis: *Life of John Adams* (2 vols.) (Philadelphia, 1871).

Bancroft, George: *History of the United States* (6 vols.) (Boston, 1876).

Beard, Charles A. and Mary R.: *A Basic History of the United States* (New York, 1944).

Bobbé, Dorothie: *Mr and Mrs John Quincy Adams* (New York, 1930).

Bolton, Charles Knowles: *The Private Soldier under Washington* (New York, 1902).

Boston under Military Rule (1768–1769). A Journal of the Times compiled by Oliver Morton Dickerson (Boston).

Bowen, A.: *A History of Boston, the Metropolis of Massachusetts, from its Origin to the Present Period*, 2nd ed. (Boston, 1828).

Bowers, Claude G.: *Jefferson in Power* (Boston, 1936).

The Young Jefferson (Boston, 1945).

Bridenbaugh, Carl: *Cities in the Wilderness* (New York, 1938).

Burney: *Journal of Fanny Burney—See* D'Arblay.

Correspondence of William Pitt, Earl of Chatham (4 vols.), edited by W. S. Taylor and J. H. Pringle (London, 1838–1840).

Craik and Macfarlane: *The Pictorial History of England* (8 vols.) (London, 1849).

D'Arblay: *Diary and Letters of Madame D'Arblay* (7 vols.), edited by her niece (London, 1842).

Dickinson, John *Letters from a Farmer in Pennsylvania to the Inhabitants of the British Colonies* (Boston, 1768).

Familiar Letters of John Adams and his Wife Abigail Adams during the Revolution, edited by Charles Francis Adams (Boston, 1876).

Fitzgerald, Percy: *The Good Queen Charlotte* (London, 1899).

Franklin, Benjamin: *The Autobiography of Benjamin Franklin* (New York, 1939).

Memoirs and Writings of Benjamin Franklin (London, 1793).

Gordon, William: *The History of the Rise, Progress and Establishment of Independence of the United States of America* (3 vols.) (New York, 1789).

Hancock: *John Hancock his Book*, edited by Abram English Brown (Boston, 1898).

Hicks, Frederick C.: *The Flag of the United States* (Washington, 1926).

Hosmer, James K.: *Life of Thomas Hutchinson* (Boston, 1896).

Samuel Adams (Boston, 1893).

Hutchinson: *The History of the Province of Massachusetts Bay* (3 vols.) (London, 1828).

Jefferson, Thomas: *Autobiography of Thomas Jefferson*, edited by Paul L. Ford (New York, 1914).

Life and Selected Writings of Thomas Jefferson, edited by Adrienne Koch and William Peden (New York, 1944).

Jesse, J. Heneage: *Memoirs of the Life and Reign of King George III* (London, 1867).

Journal and Correspondence of Miss Adams, edited by her daughter (New York, 1841).

Letters of Mrs Adams the Wife of John Adams, edited by Charles Francis Adams (Boston, 1848).

Maclay, William: *Journal of William Maclay* (New York, 1890)

Miller, John C.: *Origins of the American Revolution* (Boston, 1943).

Monaghan, Frank: *John Jay, Defender of Liberty* (New York, 1935).

Morse, John T.: *Benjamin Franklin* (Boston, 1896).

Muzzey, David Saville: *Thomas Jefferson* (New York, 1918).

Padover, Saul K.: *Jefferson* (New York, 1942).

Pattee, William S.: *History of Old Braintree and Quincy* (1878).

Pellew, George: *John Jay*, edited by John T. Morse (Boston, 1890).

Prussing, Eugene E.: *George Washington in Love and Otherwise* (Chicago, 1925).

Quincy, Josiah: *Memoir of the Life of Josiah Quincy*, by his son (Boston, 1874).

Quincy, Josiah: *Figures of the Past* (Boston, 1892).

Roof, Katherine Metcalf: *Colonel William Smith and Lady* (Boston, 1929).

Sparkes, Jared: *The Life and Treason of Benedict Arnold* (Boston, 1839).

Statesman and Friend, Correspondence of John Adams with Benjamin Waterhouse, edited by Worthington Chauncey Ford (Boston, 1927).

Sumner, William Graham: *Alexander Hamilton* (New York, 1890).
The Works of John Adams, edited by Charles Francis Adams (8 vols.) (Boston, 1856).
Tudor, William: *Life of James Otis* (Boston, 1823).
Tyler, Mary Palmer: *Grandmother Tyler's Book*, edited by Frederick Tupper and Helen Tyler Brown (New York, 1925).
Van Doren, Carl: *Benjamin Franklin* (New York, 1938).
Warren, Charles: *Adams Letters 1743–1814* (2 vols.) (Massachusetts Historical Society, 1917).
Odd Byways in American History (Cambridge, 1942).
Wharton, Anne Hollingsworth: *Martha Washington* (New York, 1897).
Whitlock, Brand: *LaFayette* (2 vols.) (New York, 1929).
Wilson, Daniel M.: *Colonel John Quincy* (1908).
Three Hundred Years of Quincy (Boston, 1926).
Where American Independence was Born (Boston, 1902).

Index

The Early Works of John Dewey

1882–1898

John Dewey

The Early Works, 1882–1898

3: 1889–1892

Early Essays and Outlines of a Critical Theory of Ethics

Carbondale and Edwardsville
SOUTHERN ILLINOIS UNIVERSITY PRESS
FEFFER & SIMONS, INC.
London and Amsterdam

The Early Works of John Dewey, 1882–1898, *is the result of a co-operative research project at Southern Illinois University.*

Jo Ann Boydston is the General Editor. Fredson Bowers is Consulting Textual Editor.

Standard Book Number 8093–0402–3
Library of Congress Catalog Card Number 67–13938
Printed in the United States of America
Designed by Andor Braun
Frontispiece drawing of John Dewey by Herbert L. Fink

Contents

Early Essays

Outlines of a Critical Theory of Ethics

Preface

WITH THE ASSISTANCE of many scholars and friends we began, in 1961, to collect and prepare for publication all of the extant published works of John Dewey. During the six years between 1961 and the issuance of the first volume in the series, the magnitude and difficulty of the undertaking confirmed the need for ready access by the public to this important philosopher's forty books and nearly eight hundred articles published in some one hundred fifty journals. Students had found it increasingly difficult to examine Dewey's thought, both because of the inaccessibility of materials and the size of the corpus of Dewey's writings. As work on the texts progressed and news of our project spread, we received numerous requests for copies of hard-to-locate materials, for identification of items, and for information about revisions. The varied sources of these requests indicated that the collected works will be useful to students in a number of specialized disciplines; and, of course, many readers will be interested in the reactions of a great mind to seventy years of tumultuous events. Americans will be able to follow Dewey's interpretation of and his growing concern with the global scene. Readers in other countries will have a basis for estimating the extent to which Dewey's thought transcends national boundaries and is viable for the twentieth century.

We decided that the extraordinary effort and expense of publishing the collected works would be best justified if we developed definitive texts. Therefore, in this edition we have applied the principles and techniques of modern textual criticism. This approach, developed primarily in connection with editing the works of such American literary figures as Hawthorne, has been used here for the first time in editing the writings of an American philosopher.

Those familiar with Dewey's essays will appreciate the reasons for our decision to print most of his works in approximately chronological order. (The exceptions are those in which Dewey's participation was limited or questionable—*The Psychology of Number* [1895], the Chinese lectures, and a few other items—all scheduled for late volumes in the series.) Many of

Dewey's insights were reflections upon the interrelations of such fields as philosophy, education, law, and the social sciences. To have identified a book or an article with only one particular discipline would have been to ignore its relevance to both the history and the continuing inquiries in other disciplines. It was decided that the disadvantages of a chronological order would be offset by two special features of the edition: (1) a complete analytical index; and (2) a guide to the works of John Dewey, presenting, in one volume, surveys by outstanding scholars of Dewey's contributions to such subjects as logic, psychology, and æsthetics. Included in that volume will be a listing of the works classified in each of the selected fields, with cross-references to major works in other fields.

The first five volumes, *The Early Works*, present most of the writings published in Dewey's "formative period," beginning in the year 1882 and ending in 1898. In addition to the articles, reviews, and other short pieces, the five volumes of *The Early Works* include the *Psychology*, *Leibniz's New Essays Concerning the Human Understanding*, *Outlines of a Critical Theory of Ethics*, and *The Study of Ethics*.

Each volume has the following parts: Preface, Table of Contents, Introduction to the Volume, Texts, Checklist of References, various kinds of textual apparatus—Textual Principles and Procedures, A Note on the Texts, Emendations in the Copy-Texts, Textual Notes, Correction of Quotations, special emendations lists—and an Index.

We are grateful to all those, and there were many, who helped in the work of preparing and publishing these volumes. Some of them are mentioned in the paragraphs that follow.

The administrative officers of Southern Illinois University most directly involved in our work were: Delyte W. Morris, President; Charles D. Tenney, Vice-President for Planning and Review; John E. Grinnell, formerly Vice-President for Operations, now retired; Robert W. MacVicar, formerly Vice-President for Academic Affairs, now Chancellor of the Carbondale Campus; John S. Rendleman, formerly Vice-President for Business Affairs, now Chancellor of the Edwardsville Campus; William J. McKeefery, formerly Dean of Academic Affairs; Elmer J. Clark, Dean, College of Education; Arthur E. Lean, former Dean of the College of Education; Ronald G. Hansen, Associate Dean of the Graduate School and Co-ordinator of Research and Projects; John O. Anderson, former Co-ordinator of Research and Projects; C. Richard Gruny, Legal Counsel; William E. Simeone, former Dean, Graduate School; Jacob O. Bach, former Chairman of the Department of Educational Administration.

The Chairman of the Advisory Committee throughout the history of this undertaking was Willis Moore, Chairman of the Department of Philosophy, who deserves special thanks for his perceptive and able leadership. Members of the Advisory Committee not mentioned in other connections were: Henry Dan Piper, former Dean of the College of Liberal Arts and Sciences; Roger E. Beyler, Dean of the College of Liberal Arts and Sciences; and the late Robert D. Faner, former Chairman of the Department of English. In the Office of Research and Projects, Webster Ballance, Wayne Stumph, and Larry Hawse were of special help.

Many persons consulted with the Editorial Board on a variety of aspects of the work. We are indebted to all of them. Among those who helped with the design and advancement of the Project were: John L. Childs, George S. Counts, George Dykhuizen, George R. Geiger, James H. Hall, Harry W. Laidler, Corliss Lamont, Charles A. Madison, Richard P. McKeon, Charles Morris, Donald A. Piatt, George Kimball Plochmann, Paul A. Schilpp, and Horace Kallen. In addition, the scholars involved in preparing a guide to the works of John Dewey have made outstanding contributions: William W. Brickman, Max H. Fisch, Horace L. Friess, Gail Kennedy, Bertram Morris, Tsuin-Chen Ou, Darnell Rucker, and Herbert W. Schneider. Professor Schneider contributed to almost every aspect of our work.

We are profoundly indebted to M. Halsey Thomas, whose excellent bibliography[1] saved us years of work. For suggestions about materials and where to find them, we owe thanks to many of the persons mentioned in other connections as well as to Karl Andrén, James W. Merritt, Sidney Ratner, Paul G. Kuntz, R. D. Archambault, William S. Minor, Robert L. McCaul, Lewis S. Feuer, Charles A. Lee, the late Archibald W. Anderson, Erwin V. Johanningmeier, Burton Raimer, Hensley C. Woodbridge, James Collins, and Francis Sparshott. For invaluable help on the Chinese materials, we thank Robert W. Clopton, Cho-Yee To, and Barry Keenan.

For the specialized help that only experienced and enthusiastic library personnel can give, we thank: Ralph W. McCoy, Director of Southern Illinois University Libraries; Ferris S. Randall, Director, Morris Library; Elizabeth O. Stone, former Assistant Director, Morris Library, now retired; Harold J. Rath and Maxine E. Walker in the Special Services Division; Thomas

1 M. H. Thomas, *John Dewey: A Centennial Bibliography* (Chicago: University of Chicago Press, 1962).

J. Jackson, Rare Book Librarian. Bill V. Isom and Thomas L. Kilpatrick, former and present staff members of the Education Library, and the Humanities Librarian, Alan M. Cohn, gave assistance far beyond the call of duty. Kenneth Duckett, University Archivist, contributed valuable insights and materials in the course of his work on the oral history aspect of this project.

We are grateful to Peter Draz, Robert H. Land, Joseph E. Hall, and Waldo H. Moore of the Library of Congress; Alice Bonnell, Carole Carlson, the late Roland Baughman, and Kenneth A. Lohf of Columbia University Library; and Hilmar A. Sieving, Education Librarian, University of Chicago. Although we cannot acknowledge them by name, many other librarians in the United States, Formosa, Germany, England, and Hawaii co-operated in helping us obtain materials.

The continuing support and co-operation of the College of Education of the University of Illinois, Champaign-Urbana, have played an important role in numerous aspects of this work.

We are indebted in several ways to the textual consultants who worked with us in the initial stages to suggest procedures for our work: Matthew J. Bruccoli, Neal Smith, and Bruce Harkness.

For the outstanding role he played in this work in its beginning and for his continued interest, our gratitude goes to Harold Taylor. Ernest Nagel, Mason W. Gross, and Agnes E. Meyer were also very helpful.

We acknowledge gratefully the contribution made by a grant from the National Endowment for the Humanities which helped us to produce the volume on schedule.

The following, who were members of the Project staff at various times, were instrumental in the successful launching of this publishing venture: Aldona Johnson, Alimae Persons, Marilee Kuehn, Joan Lash, Kathleen Poulos, Helen Wilfinger, David L. Miller, Edward F. McClain, Robert Andresen, and Deems Brooks.

The Editors

A note on *Applied Psychology*

ALTHOUGH John Dewey was a prolific writer, he was not in fact the co-author of one book widely and consistently attributed to him—*Applied Psychology* (Toronto: Copp, Clark and Company, 1889). The evidence is now clear on this point and is of three kinds: archival, in the copyright registration records and in the biography of the book's sole author, James A. McLellan; textual, developed from a study of seventeen copies of the book on the Hinman Collating Machine; and peripheral, in inferences that can be drawn from related facts.

Dr. James A. McLellan was Director of Normal Schools for Ontario from 1875 to 1885, when he became Director of Teachers' Institutes. In 1890 he was appointed Head of the School of Pedagogy (later Ontario Normal College) and in 1897, as well as Principal of the College, he was Professor of Psychology and History of Education. In a letter of 1896[1] listing this information for a biographical sketch (later published in *Canadian Men and Women of the Time*), he mentioned among his "works on arithmetic and algebra," his book *Applied Psychology* (1889). W. Stewart Wallace gives McLellan's publications in detail in the Macmillan *Dictionary of Canadian Biography*, including *Applied Psychology* (Toronto, 1889). In this sketch McLellan is noted as co-author of only two works: with A. F. Ames, *The Public School Arithmetic*, and with John Dewey, *The Psychology of Number.*

McLellan acknowledged in the Preface to the first printing of *Applied Psychology* his indebtedness to Dewey's *Psychology* for many ideas he had used. That acknowledgement appeared even after Dewey's name had been added to the title page as co-author. The listing of Dewey on the title page of several later printings has been, of course, the most misleading and confusing bibliographical fact about *Applied Psychology.* Inasmuch as the theoretical content of *Applied Psychology* stemmed from Dewey's *Psychology*, philosophers have assumed that the title-page listing of Dewey as co-author was reflected in the sub-

1 Public Archives of Canada, File No. 68–2946/1436.

stance of the work. Statements from *Applied Psychology* have been noted frequently in support of interpretations of Dewey's early philosophy. Though McLellan drew freely on Dewey's material, he was almost certainly the only author of *Applied Psychology.*

The exact details of the publishing history of *Applied Psychology* cannot now be established, but the available facts lend themselves to extrapolation. For the purposes of the present discussion the basic consideration is that Dewey's name as co-author was added to the title page of *Applied Psychology* after the book had been through at least three printings.

Applied Psychology was set in type, electroplated, and printed by Copp, Clark and Company in Toronto, Canada, in 1889. On 23 March 1889, Mr. W. W. Copp, President of the Copp, Clark Company, wrote to the Copyright Branch of the Ministry of Agriculture in Ottawa, "we are the proprietors of the book called *Applied Psychology* by J. A. McLellan L.L.D., . . . published in Canada by The Copp Clark Company Limited in the City of Toronto."[2] With the letter, Mr. Copp forwarded two copies of the book as required for registration of copyright. The book was registered on 26 March 1889, Register No. 20, Folio 4792.

Although the book was apparently printed only once by Copp, Clark and Company,[3] the publisher maintained it in stock for a number of years. The earliest record now extant, the publisher's stock-list for 4 January 1895, includes a notation on *Applied Psychology.* For 27 April 1904 the stock-list entry reads, "Still in Catalogue but no sale. Do not reprint, some in stock." Finally, on 13 January 1920 in the same records, there is the note, "112 copies—to be destroyed."[4] It now seems likely that *Applied Psychology* was discovered to be a slow seller as early as 1892, and that since enough copies were on hand for normal expectations, Copp, Clark and Company sold the plates to an American publisher, Willard Small.

The book was first listed in the United States in *Publishers'*

2 Certified copies of this letter and other relevant documents from the Canadian Copyright Office are preserved at the Dewey Project Offices, Southern Illinois University, Carbondale, Illinois.

3 One copy of the Copp, Clark and Co. printing of *Applied Psychology* (listed as I[1][b]) was used as the basis for all collations on the Hinman Machine. Three copies of this printing (including the copyright deposit copy) were compared and found to be identical. Copies of the books examined are described at the end of this Note.

4 R. J. Williams, College Department Manager, wrote on 17 May 1968 that a fire in 1910 had destroyed many of the company's nineteenth-century records. The references cited are the only ones extant.

Weekly on 12 March 1892,[5] the author being given as J. A. McLellan and the publisher as Willard Small, Boston. In the *American Catalogue* for 1 July 1890 to 30 June 1895, the Willard Small printing also appears. Willard Small, a bookdealer in Boston who engaged in the publishing business, was, according to one obituary, interested in "rare scientific works, in editions of the classics and particularly in text-books used in higher educational institutions."[6] *Applied Psychology* would fit the last classification. No copy of this printing of the book has been located; hence its order in the publishing history is necessarily inferential.

With McLellan listed in the title as sole author, *Applied Psychology* was also published in the United States by the Educational Publishing Company, Boston and New York, the company responsible for all remaining printings from the original plates. All printings of the book show only McLellan's name on the spine and cover. However, starting with the second Educational printing, both Dewey's and McLellan's names appeared on the title page. On the assumption that the Educational Publishing Company printings—first with McLellan only and later with McLellan and Dewey as authors—were continuous rather than interrupted by the Willard Small issue, the Small has been labeled the first American printing.[7] There is no record of copyright registration of the book in the United States either by Willard Small or by the Educational Publishing Company.

If the Willard Small printing was the first in this country, the dates of those subsequent, all by the Educational Publishing Company, were post-1892. Examination of the first Educational Publishing Company printing yields no physical evidence to establish the date of impression: The title page is identical with that of the Copp, Clark and Company printing except for the last three lines, which have been reset to show the change of publisher. The date 1889 on the title page was not reset, nor was "March, 1889" at the end of the Preface, although "Toronto" just before the date was deleted. Internally, type has been reset with changes in accidentals at x.1, 35.17, 37.33, 259.1, pre-

5 No. 1050, p. 418.

6 From the Growell Collection, R. R. Bowker and Co., New York. The clippings in these scrapbooks are dated but not identified as to source.

7 It appears that Small bought the plates from Copp and ran off a printing which, on the evidence, was still on sale three years after publication. His interest in out-of-the-way books having been satisfied, he then sold the plates to Educational Publishing, which issued several printings. That Educational would lease its plates to another publisher between the first and second impressions is less probable than that the firm acquired the plates from Small and retained possession of them thereafter.

sumably to repair plate damage. In the Preface two lines were revised and reset for American readers at viii.14–15, and several lines with references for the Canadian reader were omitted at 311.38–40, 313.36–38, and 317.16–26.

Whatever may have been the earlier acquaintance between Dewey and McLellan, the two became collaborators at least by late 1893 or early 1894, possibly through the good offices of William Torrey Harris, then U.S. Commissioner of Education. Harris edited the books in D. Appleton and Company's International Education Series—including *The Psychology of Number* by Dewey and McLellan. Dewey and McLellan were surely acquainted before signing their contract with Daniel Appleton and Company on 2 July 1894.[8]

It can be conjectured that the Dewey-McLellan collaboration on *The Psychology of Number*, though not published until September 1895, in some manner led the Educational Publishing Company to issue *Applied Psychology* with Dewey as co-author and Chicago among the places of publication. The company undoubtedly wanted to take advantage of Dewey's prestige in America, but whether McLellan added Dewey's name as a courtesy because of his indebtedness, or whether the company inserted it without authorization, remains in question.

The second Educational Publishing Company printing, which listed both men as authors, appeared before or at most shortly after September 1894, when Dewey left the University of Michigan to take a position at the University of Chicago, since he is identified on the title page as "Prof. John Dewey | Of Michigan University." The title page for this printing was reset and the date deleted. It seems unlikely that the publisher would reset the title page and incorrectly name Dewey's institutional affiliation—especially a publisher located in Chicago. The title page was not reset or corrected for later printings.

Other changes for the second printing were the deletion of the date at the end of the Preface and the addition of five pages of Educational Publishing Company advertising at the rear. The first page of advertising is on the verso of the last page of the text, p. [318], and the remaining four on the successive pages of the gathering, which were blank in earlier impressions. The remainder of the text shows no change from the first Educational Publishing Company issue under McLellan's name, but from collation this first Dewey-McLellan run shows sufficient evidence of wear to indicate that it followed the McLellan printing.

8 Contract preserved in D. Appleton and Co. Collection, Lilly Library, Indiana University.

Educational Publishing Company reprinted the book four more times, although it has not been possible to ascertain the dates of issue. The chief distinguishing factor among the last four impressions is the deterioration of the type, increasingly heavy inking, and blurring characteristic of wear. The third Educational printing (I^5), differs from the second (I^4) in the omission of the advertising pages at the end and in that all of page 197 has been reset, with three changes in accidentals[9] and in the type-face used for symbols. The newly set page 197 appeared in all subsequent printings. The next two printings (I^6 and I^7) are characterized by further wear. Three copies of the last printing (I^8) were examined on the Hinman Machine. All showed examples of continued batter and deterioration of the type, even to the complete omission of the last two lines of type at 179.33–34.

One additional fact in the *Applied Psychology* story lends support, however inferentially, to the thesis that Dewey's "authorship" was spurious. The book was not reviewed in the United States or, in fact, in any English language journal—in contrast with Dewey's two earlier books and, particularly, in contrast with Dewey's and McLellan's *Psychology of Number*. On the other hand, Dewey's first book, *Psychology*, was reviewed by four journals in the United States, one in England, and two in France; his second book, *Leibniz's New Essays Concerning the Human Understanding* was reviewed by two American journals and one British; the *Psychology of Number* was reviewed by four journals here and one in England.

Jo Ann Boydston

15 April 1969

PRINTINGS OF *Applied Psychology* AND COPIES EXAMINED

Copp, Clark and Company
James A. McLellan

I^1 *a.* National Library of Canada. Copyright deposit copy. Copy deposited No. 4792 handwritten on front binder's paste-down.

9 197.18 comma deleted; 197.24 period moved outside parentheses; 197.30, colon changed to semicolon.

I[1] *b.* University of Illinois Library. Acquisition number 1017737 stamped on p. [v]. Handwritten on p. [v], 21 je '38, ex. U. of West. Ont. lib. 30 Nov. 38.

c. Oberlin College Library. Label glued to front paste-down, Oberlin College Library, The Gift of Univ. Minn. Accession No. 95930.

Willard Small
James A. McLellan

I[2] No copies discovered

Educational Publishing Company
James A. McLellan

I[3] *a.* University of Vermont Library. Label glued to front paste-down, Library of the University of Vermont, The Gift of Frederick Billings.

b. University of Chicago. Label glued to front paste-down, University of Chicago Libraries, Gift of Chicago Institute. 484480 and 178190 stamped on p. [v].

Educational Publishing Company
James A. McLellan and John Dewey

I[4] *a.* Harvard University. Harvard College, Gift of the Graduate School of Education, 5358, 50–223, 11, handwritten on p. [iv].

b. University of Michigan. 121622 handwritten on p. [iii].

I[5] *a.* Yale University. Label glued to front paste-down, Yale Library, Gift of the Yale Divinity School. Lbb14/890m handwritten on p. [iv].

b. University of Southern California. Acquisition number 74682 stamped on p. [v].

I[6] *a.* University of Chicago. Label glued to front paste-down, The University of Chicago Libraries, Gift of Chicago Institute. Acquisition numbers 207823, 484513 on p. [v].

b. Ohio State University. Acquisition number 46754 handwritten on p. [v].

I[7] *a.* Southern Illinois University, Morris Library. Label glued to front paste-down, Library of Southern Illinois State Normal University. On first binder's end-paper, M. M. Steagall, Golconda, Ill., hand-printed.

I[7] *b.* University of California. Library of the University of California stamped on front paste-down. Acquisition number 62059 handwritten on p. [iv].

c. University of Chicago. Label glued to front paste-down, The University of Chicago Libraries, Gift of the Publisher. Stamped on p. [v] 81630, 197913.

I[8] *a.* Northwestern University Library. Label glued to front paste-down, The Gift of Louisiana State University Library. Acquisition number 315755, Northwestern University Library, Feb. 15, 1938, stamped on p. [v].

b. University of Illinois. Label glued to front paste-down, Library of the University of Illinois, 370.15 M 21a 1892. Acquisition number 35646 stamped on p. [v].

c. University of Pennsylvania. Label glued to front paste-down with seal, Library of the University of Pennsylvania, 179.4 M 223 handwritten. Acquisition number 112734 handwritten on p. [v].

Introduction

THE CONTENTS of this volume range from an intellectual portrait and memorial appreciation of Dewey's beloved teacher and colleague, George Sylvester Morris, to the technical treatments of theory of knowledge, ethical theory, and psychology. The volume also contains observations on educational theory and practice, including detailed accounts of the teaching of philosophy at the University of Michigan. Along with commentary on men and literature, Dewey wrote reviews of current books, and in some his own philosophy weaves its way into what he writes. During this period he also revised his *Psychology* (1887) in 1889 and 1891. These revisions are not included in this volume because they are incorporated in the definitive edition of *Psychology*, Volume II of *The Early Works of John Dewey, 1882–1898*.

Dewey was brought to the University of Michigan in 1884 by Professor Morris, and the two men enjoyed a rich personal and intellectual friendship. In 1888 Dewey went to the University of Minnesota, but the death of Professor Morris in March 1889 created a crisis in the Michigan department and Dewey was brought back as Professor of Philosophy and Head of the Department. The death of Morris was a deep personal loss to Dewey, and he wrote of Morris that his was a life great "in spirit, and in the quality of its achievements" (p. 3). One of Dewey's first acts as Head of the Department was to employ James H. Tufts, a recent graduate of Yale, to be his assistant. Tufts remained at Michigan for only two years, 1889–1891, leaving to continue his studies toward the doctor of philosophy degree in Germany. Dewey then employed George Herbert Mead to fill the vacancy. Tufts, Mead, and Dewey had important influence on each other. In 1894, when Dewey and Mead joined Tufts at the University of Chicago, the three composed the nucleus of what came to be called the "Chicago School" in philosophy.

During this second period at Michigan, Dewey's thinking underwent significant changes. One of his biographers writes: "During these years Dewey's thinking veered away from traditional Hegelianism and toward the instrumentalism for which he later became famous."[1] The term "instrumentalism" is ambiguous, and toward the end of Dewey's career he abandoned its use. Originally, the term meant that conceptions and theories are instruments which produce future facts. William James applies the theory to the moral aspects of certain concepts and to the sentimental value of various philosophical systems. For Dewey, instrumentalism means a logical theory of concepts, judgments, and inferences, and "it attempts to establish universally recognized distinctions and rules of logic by deriving them from the reconstructive or mediative function ascribed to reason."[2] Dewey was compelled to restate, amplify, and defend this notion of a logical theory of concepts against a host of misinterpretations which developed later, the most notorious being that ideas and concepts are instrumental to the knower or instrumental to what brings emotional and psychological satisfaction to him. If one keeps in mind the logical nature of the theory, then one can see that Dewey's writings contained in this volume on theory of knowledge or logical theory (as he conceived the broad scope of logical theory) reveal definite trends in the direction of an instrumentalist or functional theory of concepts in the context of reflective thinking and decision.

During this period Dewey published six articles and reviews in the field of logical theory,[3] and some of these show the slowly developing, perhaps unconscious, influence of Charles Sanders Peirce, with whom Dewey had studied logic at Johns Hopkins. When Dewey lists the advocates of the new logic, he does not mention Peirce; however, he admitted in later years that the influence of Peirce on his thought was gradual in developing. Ideas put forth in these early articles have affinities with those of Peirce, for Peirce had maintained that logic had made no progress for two hundred years, and that scientific developments during these centuries could be explained by the fact that scientists were motivated by inquiry rather than logical theory. Peirce had argued for the union of logic and science so that this integration could effect a more fruitful method of inquiry. Dewey appears conscious of Peirce's emphasis on experimental inquiry when he writes: "The Newer Logic may be

1 George Dykhuizen, "John Dewey and the University of Michigan," *Journal of the History of Ideas*, XXIII (Oct.–Dec. 1962), 513.

2 "The Development of American Pragmatism," in *Studies in the History of Ideas*, II (New York: Columbia University Press, 1925), Supplement, 367.

3 "Galton's Statistical Methods" (1889); "Is Logic a Dualistic Science?" (1890); "The Logic of Verification" (1890); "The Present Position of Logical Theory" (1891); "How Do Concepts Arise from Percepts?" (1891); "Two Phases of Renan's Life" (1892).

roughly described as an attempt to take account of the methods of thinking employed by science, that is, of the methods the aim of which is truth, and which deal with a material of fact" (p. 75). These early essays set a problem for Dewey on which he worked until the end of his life, the problem of overcoming the dualism which had developed between logic and science. His proposal in these early writings is similar to that of Peirce: Logical forms must be set inside a general pattern of scientific inquiry where a working harmony and unity of all procedures can be effected, and logic must be concerned with the pursuit of truth, which is the goal of all scientific inquiry.

In these essays the themes are current ones, dealing with contemporary writings and contemporary logical theory. They refer to formal logic as if this were traditional Aristotelian logic; they speak of Mill as the defender of empirical logic; and the third alternative is taken to be transcendental logic referred to as that of Wundt, Sigwart, Lotze, Jevons, Bradley, and Bosanquet. They contain a critical review of Venn's *The Principles of Empirical or Inductive Logic* and an essay on Renan's *The Future of Science.* From the topical nature of the themes discussed, from the apparent allegiance of Dewey to the transcendental logic which he refers to as Hegelian (and which, in the case of Lotze, he later criticizes severely[4]), and from the neglect of contemporary early work in modern symbolic logic, one might think that these essays are of little positive value. But there are vital themes developed in these essays which are important later in Dewey's development of a mature logical theory.

The first major theme developed at length in "The Present Position of Logical Theory" is the needed integration of scientific inquiry and logical theory. In this essay Dewey attacks the sterility of formal logic, that is, logic which disclaims any concern with content, with subject-matter, with facts, and insists that a logical theory can be adequate only if it deals with the way inquiry is actually being carried out in its own time. He finds in Mill's kind of logic an appreciation of this necessity, but thinks Mill has accepted the restriction of the old logic as dealing with the form of thought, and this in isolation from the matter of thought. In the "transcendental logic" of the Hegelian tradition he finds a promise of this interrelatedness of logical theory and science, but he thinks that transcendental logic has been rejected by scientists as speculative and metaphysical because

4 Dewey *et al.*, *Studies in Logical Theory* (The Decennial Publications, Second Series, XI [Chicago: University of Chicago Press, 1903]). See Essays II, III, IV for Dewey's criticism of Lotze.

they have not yet appreciated the fact that this logic is not Kantian (metaphysical) but Hegelian, and that it is at least an attempt to analyze the very movement of thought in the real world. He hopes to see a rapprochement of transcendental logic and scientific theory in the future.

The similar theme of the required integration of logic and scientific inquiry recurs in his review of Venn's *Empirical Logic*. He finds Venn is correct in refusing to restrict logic to the formal and in finding that logic is concerned both with ideas and concepts, like psychology, and with the observation of external phenomena, like the observational sciences. His objection is that this dualism should not be made, as in Venn, between an inner, subjective, mentalistic realm of ideas and an outer, objective realm of fact, with logic considered as a third thing intermediate between the two. He shows what he thinks to be the difficulties to which this leads and quotes Venn against himself, as both overtly and tacitly recognizing that there can be no such thing as the bare occurrence of observational facts without the influence of the mind in ordering, selecting, and interpreting them. Dewey interprets the division of ideas and facts as internal to inquiry rather than external.

This theme is further developed in the essay, "The Logic of Verification," in which he considers a possible objection against the position he had taken in the Venn review, that it overlooks the importance to science of verification, that is, the confrontation of the internal concept with the external fact. Dewey's answer is to show the difficulties of interpreting the verification of hypotheses on such dualistic terms, and to reinterpret verification as it occurs in science in terms of his own logical theory.

All of these early essays on logic are concerned with very important themes which recur in Dewey's later writings, the relation of idea to fact, of theory to matter, of concept to percept in inquiry. In these essays all the ideas in his later discussion of this "conjunctive" relation of ideas to facts are foreshadowed. Although the context is what he himself calls "transcendental logic," the way in which these two elements of inquiry are shown to be related is itself pragmatic. In working this out, he refers also to the parallelism of what happens in commonsense knowing with what is done self-consciously in scientific inquiry. He says,

> Methods of thought are simply the various active attitudes into which intelligence puts itself in order to detect and grasp the fact. Instead of rigid moulds, they are flexible adaptations. Methods of thought fit fact more closely and responsively than a worn glove fits the hand. They are only the ideal evolution of the fact,—and by

"ideal" is here meant simply the evolution of fact into meaning (p. 133).

Dewey says that ordinary perception does unconsciously what science does self-consciously; it follows out a hypothesis by methods of induction and deduction, of analysis and synthesis, and so on, to guide the recognition of facts and the formulation of theories. The difference between ordinary perception and scientific observation is that it is easier for ordinary perception to go astray because its method is unconscious. But "it is one and the same world which offers itself in perception and in scientific treatment" (p. 80), and the method of dealing with it is the same—that of logical method.

The discussion of the relation of method and subject-matter, of idea and fact, is further developed in the discussion of verification. Dewey says that ideas and facts are the same in the innocent experience of the baby, but what happens is that, in developing science, some idea-facts are followed by disappointed expectation, whereas others are supported by new experience and found reliable. The former are distinguished as "ideas" (mere ideas) whereas the latter are accepted as facts. A fact is an idea for which there is no longer tentative status but an accepted one; an idea is a fact about which difficulties are felt. In inquiry, ideas need extension, transformation, and verification; facts need enlargement, alteration, and significance. The process of verification is the "process of transforming the hypothesis, or idea entertained tentatively, into a fact, or idea held definitely" (p. 86). The distinction of universal and particular is set in the same context. The mind "picks out" some one aspect of "facts" and isolates it, and forms a hypothesis or idea which is then set over against the facts from which it has been isolated. The facts are the observed particulars; the isolated idea-hypothesis is the universal. This has a dialectical quality, but it is also in line with the later treatment of the interrelation of concepts and percepts in *Logic: The Theory of Inquiry* (1938). This is especially true of the concluding passage of the essay on verification in which Dewey says that there is no other test of theory than its ability to *work*, to organize facts into itself as specifications of its own nature.

The short essay on Ernest Renan, "Two Phases of Renan's Life,"[5] is important for those looking into the intellectual in-

5 Dewey published a later article, "Renan's Loss of Faith in Science," *Open Court*, VII (Jan. 1893), 3512–15. This essay appears in Vol. IV of *The Early Works of John Dewey, 1882–1898*.

fluences on Dewey's life. In 1848 Renan wrote *The Future of Science*, which Dewey thought was "far from having received the attention, or exercised the influence, it deserves" (p. 174). What interests Dewey is the way the old comprehensiveness of Hegelianism (Absolutism) is transformed by Renan into a science of philology or language in which the history of man's development is described as "the law of historic growth, not as the dialectic unfolding of the absolute" (p. 175). Renan replaces the category of Being with the category of evolution, and he proposes that inquiry start with an undifferentiated, homogeneous whole, and through analysis produce the multiplicity, and through synthesis produce comprehension, a comprehension, however, which does not destroy the multiplicity. These ideas alone are enough to merit the attention of scholars interested in Dewey's development. Renan advocates a genetic approach to the study of the individual and of the human race, believing that consciousness has *evolved* in man. Furthermore, he believes that the direction of study should be toward "the psychology of humanity," or what we call today "social psychology." Dewey also appreciates in Renan his ideas on the problem of the specialization and the generalization of knowledge; minute studies in monographic form are necessary in the on-going of science, but Renan thought there was needed an organizational machinery for the dispersion of the conclusions of these studies. In 1848 Renan was enthusiastic about the social and religious significance of science; by 1890 this enthusiasm had waned, and he had lost faith in science. On the other hand, it was about 1890 that Dewey was beginning to see the promise of science as a means of creating in human life a deeper and richer quality.

During this period Dewey published two very important articles on T. H. Green, one on his general philosophy and one on his ethical theory. A third article on Green was published in 1893, and since these three essays are related, they should be read as a unit.[6] The extent and depth of Dewey's concern with Green's philosophy reveal both the positive influence which it had upon him and the difficulties he finds in Green's position. In the first of these articles, "The Philosophy of Thomas Hill Green," Dewey assumes the role of expositor more than that of critic. He claims that "the theoretic difficulties and the practical

6 "The Philosophy of Thomas Hill Green" (1889); "Green's Theory of the Moral Motive" (1892); the third article, "Self-Realization as the Moral Ideal," *Philosophical Review*, II (Nov. 1893), 652–64, appears in Vol. IV of *The Early Works of John Dewey, 1882–1898.*

aspirations of this last half century are voiced by Green" (p. 16). Dewey's analysis starts with the speculative side of Green and explains that Green's philosophy is an attempt to reconcile science and religion. Green is shown to hold that there is a principle, spiritual in nature, at the root of ordinary experience and science which is also the basis of ethics and religion. It appears that Green was led to this consideration by way of "a certain conflict between poetry and natural science" (p. 17). The failure of contemporary philosophers to deal adequately with poetry sets the problem, for no one seemed to want to relegate poetry to the realm of feeling or mere illusion, yet poetry could not be assimilated to the realm of science. Green shows that if the validity of poetry and religion cannot be shown, then this applies to ethics as well. Green lays the blame for this conflict between science and religion upon the empiricists, particularly those from Locke through Hume, for these philosophers did not have an adequate view of the role of intelligence. He goes further than this, however, and maintains that "a consistent interpretation of Empiricism sapped the roots of knowledge as well as of faith" (p. 18).

The crux of the issue as Green sees it is that intelligence is a spiritual principle uniting science and religion, as well as making possible poetry and ethics. The empiricists, he thinks, had an inadequate view of the constructive function of intelligence; thus, if one followed the implications of their contentions, one would be compelled to deny even that science is possible. This criticism applies to Herbert Spencer as well, for Green does not find in Spencer any notion that intelligence has a constructive, synthetic function. There is a connected whole of experience, Green believes, and the unity of the world implies "a single, permanent, and all-inclusive system of relations" (p. 22), and this, in turn, implies "a permanent single consciousness which forms the bond of relations,—'an eternal intelligence realized in the related facts of the world'" (p. 22). Divine intelligence is not human intelligence, yet there is a relation between them, for "eternal intelligence reproduces itself in us, partially and gradually" (p. 22). Scientific order, relations, and laws are grounded in eternal intelligence, and this spiritual principle of science also reveals that man is not a mere child of nature, but is capable of a consciousness of a moral ideal and of actions which flow from it.

Green's analysis of human nature shows that sensations are transformed into theoretic experience and science, a point with which Dewey is in general agreement. Furthermore, Green thinks that impulses and wants are "transformed into practical experience, into moral action" (p. 24). Dewey claims that Green develops the moral ideal in the following way: "The reproduction in man of the consciousness which is an end-in-itself makes man an end in himself, and gives his actions, therefore, both an absolute law and an absolute ideal or good" (p. 24). Green makes much of the point that animals do not have consciousness of an ideal, but man "must know that something ought to be" because "the divine has supervened" (p. 25). Dewey agrees that animals do not seem to have consciousness of ideals, but he does not agree that man's ideals must be lodged in an Absolute. On the contrary, ideals, principles, concepts which direct action are generic; that is, they have developed out of past experience. Ideals are more empirical in their genesis and in their directive functions than Green thinks. Green's ideal is too abstract, too devoid of content, and the unrealized self and the realized self are set in a dualistic opposition to each other. These issues lead to a difference in the meaning which Green and Dewey give to self-realization. For Dewey, self-realization is not a filling-up process of an undetermined self as it is for Green; rather, it is the self acting *as* self and not *for* the self. Dewey agrees with Green up to the point where moral experience involves a process in which the self in becoming conscious of its want, objectifies that want. But the objectified want is not set over against the self; for Dewey this distinguishing process means the method by which the self specifies and defines its own activity, its own satisfaction. Particular desires and ends are simply the systematic content into which the self differentiates itself in its progressive expansion. The ends are not particular and isolated from the self, for each is a member of the self's activity, and each particular becomes universalized in the total activity of the self (p. 161). There is thus a unity of the self, and no opposition of the self to particular and specific desires; in fact, "the unity of the self and the manifold of definite desires" (p. 161) are the synthetic and analytic aspects of one and the same reality. Thus, for Dewey, there is a principle of continuity which runs through his treatment of fact and theory, of form and content, of ideal and real, of ideal self and actual self, and this principle of continuity he later called one of the leading ideas of his view of experience.

One of the ways to characterize the difference between Green and Dewey on their moral theories is to say that Green holds to an *abstract* self-realization theory, whereas Dewey holds to an *empirical* self-realization theory. This becomes more evident when consideration is given to how Dewey develops a functional and empirical view of "capacity" in the article on "Self-Realization as a Moral Ideal" of 1893. Here he takes a suggestion from William James and shows that when we speak of capacity, we are speaking of some activities which can be observed here and now; and because of the connections of these activities with goals achieved in past experience, we can use these observed behaviors as conditions for the formulation of present goals. The moral ideal thus grows out of past experience; it is not a duplication of that experience, to be sure, but its content and its potentiality as an ideal are continuous with the actual experiences which precede it.

There is a further point which should be explored in Dewey's treatment of Green. Both Green and Dewey agree on the constructive and synthesizing role of intelligence in experience; but Green projects this function into an Absolute, whereas Dewey is concerned with human intelligence. Green seeks to find the basis for unity of science, religion, poetry, and ethics in Absolute intelligence, since all these parts of the universe flow from one source and that source has an interrelated character. It is interesting to note that in his later writings, Dewey, like Green, is faced with this problem of the unity of these various activities, and his solution is to ground them in the continuity of an individual life; and since these activities flow from a single source, they are interrelated at least in the manner of their genesis.[7] There remains the difficulty, however, of how an individual human intelligence can relate the various activities of his life to one another; such a harmony requires not only a common source but a functioning interaction of the activities themselves. For instance, the relations of scientific endeavors and moral practices in a single individual life posed a problem on which Dewey worked for many years.

Most of the book reviews written by Dewey during this period are short and descriptive, for example, the reviews of Caird's *The Critical Philosophy of Immanuel Kant* and Erdmann's *A History of Philosophy*. One critical review merits care-

7 Dewey writes: "I lay no claim to inventing an environment that is marked by both discreteness and continuity. Nor can I even make the more modest claim that I discovered it. What I have done is to interpret this duality of traits in terms of the identity of experience with life-functions." At the same place, Dewey goes on to say: "There can be no genuine continuity unless an experience, no matter how unique or individualized in its own pervasive quality, contains within itself something that points to other experiences—or, . . . unless experiences '*overlap*' with respect to their subject-matters." "Experience, Knowledge and Value: A Rejoinder," in *The Philosophy of John Dewey*, 2d ed., ed. Paul Arthur Schilpp (The Library of Living Philosophers, 1 [New York: Tudor Publishing Co., 1951]), 545.

ful study, for it is a treatment of some conceptions of the self, and it ends with a statement of Dewey's analysis of Green's problem, part of which is related to the above discussion on the self. Professor Andrew Seth (also known as A. Seth Pringle-Pattison) published two books, *Scottish Philosophy* (1885) and *Hegelianism and Personality* (1887), and these, along with his "Discussion" comment in *Mind* (IV, 117), afford the stimulus for Dewey's essay, "On Some Current Conceptions of the Term 'Self.' " In this treatment, Dewey limits his analysis to the meanings of the transcendental self, and the language of philosophical idealism in which the discussion is couched is sometimes difficult to follow.[8]

In Seth's treatment of the transcendental self in *Hegelianism and Personality*, Dewey finds essentially three views: (1) "the self is the correlative of the intelligible world" (p. 57); (2) "the transcendental Ego represents *merely* the *formal* unity of the universe" (p. 58); (3) "self is the 'ultimate category of thought' " (p. 59). Dewey finds difficulties with all of Seth's descriptions, and he uses the occasion to make his own analysis of the treatment of "the historical origin of these various meanings, chiefly as found in Kant, incidentally in Hegel as related to Kant" (p. 62). He shows that Kant could not have held any of the three views put forth by Seth, and, in his own reconstruction of Kant, he comes to the following conclusion:

> . . . the self cannot be thought of as equivalent, on the one hand, to the world, because this world, as knowable by us, is always subject to certain forms, namely, space and time, which condition sense; nor, on the other hand, as equivalent to the highest category of thought, because the self is more than thought, more than a category, namely, the activity of synthesis of sense through thought. It is, I think, this twofold character of time and space, as at once forms of knowledge conditioned by the self, and yet conditioning self as it works in us, that is the genesis of Green's notion (p. 74).

Dewey thinks that some such reasoning is assumed in Green's adoption of the completely realized self (the Absolute) which makes the animal organism the vehicle of its own reproduction through time. This completely realized self and the unrealized

8 John Herman Randall, Jr., makes this observation about Dewey's language: "Dewey formed his own instrument of language in the midst of nineteenth-century idealism, in a world eager to talk the new tongue of evolutionary thinking. As our colleague Herbert Schneider has acutely pointed out, Dewey used the language of philosophical idealism to direct evolutionary thought against its conclusions. This proved a most effective technique for undermining and reconstructing idealism." "The Future of John Dewey's Philosophy," *Journal of Philosophy*, LVI (Dec. 1959), 1007.

selves of human beings form the dualism in Green's notion of the self which was the target of Dewey's criticism of Green in the articles discussed above.

The major work in the present volume is *Outlines of a Critical Theory of Ethics*, which grew out of classroom work, but was intended to have a wide circulation. The organization and treatment of subject-matter in this work are an innovation, for ethics texts during this period in American universities were predominantly religious in orientation. Thus some attention should be given to the topics treated and to the sequence of their arrangement. The first part is organized around the concepts of good, obligation, and freedom; the second part treats of the social nature of morality and of moral institutions; the third part deals with the moral life of the individual. It may be noted that Dewey's literary expression in this work is uneven, often ambiguous, and sometimes vague. Some ideas are not thoroughly worked out; some are put forth as mere suggestions. Perhaps Dewey's style can be explained by the fact that he not only is adapting an academic syllabus to a coherent exposition, but is groping his way into a new theory in this field; thus his language is cryptic and his ideas are not always clear. There is little wonder that the reviewers had some rather severe remarks to make about the work, about the ideas put forth, about their organization, and about Dewey's expression. But the work must not be ignored because of these shortcomings. The germinal ideas of much of Dewey's later philosophy are put forth in this work, and this alone gives it significance. Dewey acknowledges Green, Bradley, Caird, and Alexander as men influencing his views, and though he mentions Herbert Spencer and Leslie Stephen, he says that he cannot adopt their standpoint. A student of Dewey's philosophy will detect, however, that he has been influenced by men other than those he mentions.

A significant note appears in the "Preface" which is pertinent to the understanding of the approach to philosophy which persisted throughout Dewey's life work. He says that "comparing opposite one-sided views with the aim of discovering a theory apparently more adequate" (p. 240) is the method he has adopted. Later in his career he called these one-sided views "selective emphases" or "biases" and once said that philosophy is "a critique of prejudices."[9] His effort is to discover a more adequate theory by working through the various one-sided accounts. Dewey's way of philosophizing, whether the field be theory of knowl-

9 *Experience and Nature*, 2d ed. (New York: W. W. Norton and Co., [c1929]), p. 37.

edge or theory of ethics, is to show that all philosophers, from Plato to the present, are of value, for all have laid hold of some important constituent of experience, but each has "failed to place it in the context in which it actually functions."[10] Approaching the history of thought in this manner, Dewey appears to have ambivalent attitudes toward the men whose theories he analyzes. At one time he may lash out with critical severity at one aspect of a philosopher's thought; at another time he may praise the same philosopher for another of his ideas. Furthermore, this philosophic method is vulnerable to a critic who, with a selective bias of his own, can choose a certain passage and interpret it out of context, attributing to Dewey one or another of the positions he is criticizing or treating "dialectically."

The use of the word "critical" in the title of the book obviously means "evaluative." It means that the theories selected are to be compared and analyzed and put into the context of a new theory, in much the same way that Dewey thinks Leibniz critically analyzed and absorbed into his own philosophy the ideas of previous theories. Thus theories as far apart as hedonism and Kant's formalism both have some truth in them, yet each has objectionable parts, and Dewey's "functional" reorganization yields his own theory. Dewey's later writings on ethics, particularly the text he wrote with James H. Tufts in 1908 and revised in 1932, follow this same pattern of analysis and reconstruction. Attention must be given also to the concise "Introduction" to the *Outlines*, for here the definitions and meanings set the stage for the development of the *Outlines*, as well as for Dewey's subsequent ethical thought. The habit of tracing basic terms to their root meanings and early usage pervades much of Dewey's method of thinking; for instance, in this work the term "ethics" is traced to its Greek origin and the term "morals" to the Latin. The distinction between branches of knowledge which describe and those which judge (*de facto* and *de jure*) remains important throughout his career. Dewey did not hold in 1891 or later that it is the business of ethics "to prescribe what man ought to do"; rather, it is the business of ethics "to examine conduct to see what gives it its *worth*" (p. 241). In "Moral Theory and Practice," an article written during the year the *Outlines* was published, Dewey says: "Theory is the cross-section of the given state of action in order to know the conduct that should be; practice is the realization of the idea thus gained: it is theory in action" (p. 109). Thus moral theory is both descriptive and normative.

10 Dewey, "Experience, Knowledge and Value," p. 561.

Another important concept put forth in the *Outlines* which figures prominently in later writings is the notion of conduct. For Dewey conduct means the whole of action; conduct is the whole self in activity in contrast to the special social sciences, which deal with partial and segmented aspects of human behavior. Conduct implies more than action in general; it "implies purpose, motive, intention; that the agent knows what he is about, that he has something which he is aiming at" (p. 242). It is the end or ideal "which gives action its moral value" and which gives us "a standard by which we judge particular acts" (p. 243). It should be recalled that the end of conduct for Dewey is not an abstract ideal or an unchanging form as it is for Green; it is an end or ideal which has been constructed out of past experience of an individual's life and the life of men in general. Although the ideal has some stability and persists through time, it is subject to change and modification as experience refines its meaning.

In the first part of the work Dewey takes up four main theories concerning the good: hedonism, utilitarianism, evolutionary utilitarianism, and Kantianism. His detailed criticisms of these theories should not be ignored, especially those of utilitarianism and of Kantianism, for they are pertinent to the careful appraisal of Dewey as borrowing from each theory, although he is neither a full-fledged utilitarian nor a full-fledged Kantian. After critically evaluating their various themes, he selects and rejects certain aspects and uses the selected parts to construct his own theory. An adequate theory is not the "getting of a lot of pleasures through the satisfaction of desires just as they happen to arise," as hedonism claims, and Kantianism fails in the way in which it demands "obedience to law simply because it is law" (p. 300). He says that the satisfied self "is found in *satisfaction of desires according to law*" (p. 300), a law not external to the desires but generic to them. Dewey holds that moral experience results in building up generic universals, rules, and principles which apply to specific kinds of moral situations; it is in this sense that laws are not imposed upon desires from without but are generic.

Some critics claim that over his long life of philosophizing Dewey failed to develop an adequate account of moral duty and obligation.[11] There is little doubt that in his early writings, the

11 Morton G. White says: "Evidently pragmatism is united on the subject of value but not on obligation or justice. Dewey, in spite of a valiant attempt, has not given us a naturalistic account of obligation." "Value and Obligation in Dewey and Lewis," *Philosophical Review*, LVIII (July 1949), 329.

Outlines included, the concern is primarily with the concept of good rather than with those of duty, right, and obligation. Furthermore, Dewey is not clear in the *Outlines* on the relation of duty to the good. When he sets forth his preliminary definitions in the "Introduction," he says: "The end or good decides what should be or *ought* to be. Any act necessary to fulfill the end is a *duty*" (p. 243). Dewey's notion of the end of conduct is linked to desires, the empirical touchstone of his naturalistic theory, and in this sense he can be classified as an axiologist. He criticizes Kant for not taking account of desires and appetites, and claims that the Kantian theory leaves these "untouched or would abolish them—in either case destroying morality" (p. 334).

On the other hand, Dewey cannot accept the views of Bain and Spencer on obligation, although both take desires into account, for their views do not give a clear distinction between the moral control of desires and the coercion of desires by a superior physical force. Dewey holds that the concept of duty limits and transforms a desire, but that the proper context in which to put the relation of duty to desire is one in which a specific desire is related to other desires and interests of the individual, and to the specific needs and demands of the community in which the desire must be fulfilled. Confusion enters Dewey's theory when he seems to say that an act is done from duty if it achieves the end or the good, and when he tries to explain the meaning of the phrase "duty for duty's sake" in a non-Kantian sense. He rejects the notion of doing one's duty in order to conform to an abstract idea, for such an idea leads to a morality which is "at once hard and barren, and weak and sentimental" (p. 339). Then he goes on to say that to be moral an act must be performed for duty's sake, and must not be degraded "into a means for some ulterior end" (p. 339).

It has been mentioned that desires and interests of an individual involve a social context for their fulfillment. The metaphysical dualism of individual and social is avoided by showing that an individual's existence, functioning, and fulfillment cannot be separated from his social environment. The position taken here, reminiscent of Aristotle, is that ethics is concerned with individual conduct, goals, and decisions. It is within this individual-social continuum that Dewey develops his views of individuality and freedom. Freedom of choice depends upon many conditions, such as an individual's emancipation from particular appetites and desires so that he can fashion his conduct in terms of conscious ends, ends many and varied, some of which may even be contrary to one another. Without a plurality of consciously formed ends, there is no freedom of choice. Freedom is not mere random activity, nor is it mere freedom from the restrictions which the social environment places upon it (negative freedom), nor is man endowed with it as a kind of innate gift. Freedom is an achievement of the individual living in society, where the individual-social continuum contains the conditions required for its function.

Dewey's self-realization theory in ethics means that the individual develops within society. He develops by projecting an ideal forged out of his concrete experiences and his particular function in his social setting. Dewey writes: "The exercise of function by an agent serves, then, both to define and to unite him. It makes him a *distinct* social member at the same time that it makes him a *member*" (p. 326). Every individual is marked off from every other individual by his peculiar capacities and the special surroundings in which he functions. The adjustment of individual capacity to environment in the exercise of function effects the realization of individuality, and this accomplishment marks off each individual from others.

One idea in the *Outlines* tends to drop out of the later writings, or to be implicit rather than explicit. This is Dewey's notion of the ethical postulate. It is not an arbitrary postulate, and Dewey qualifies it in many ways. He says: "The basis, in a word, of moral conduct, with respect to the exercise of function, is a faith that moral self-satisfaction . . . means social satisfaction—or the faith that self and others make a true community" (p. 320). The presupposition which Dewey thinks underlies all moral conduct is put again in another way: "In the realization of individuality there is found also the needed realization of some community of persons of which the individual is a member; and, conversely, the agent who duly satisfies the community in which he shares, by that same conduct satisfies himself" (p. 322).

It will be recalled that T. H. Green was led to the consideration of the relation of ethics to science by way of the problem of the relation of poetry to science. The advance of scientific understanding of the world during the nineteenth century was taking place with such rapidity that religious beliefs were being challenged, and it appeared to some thinkers that the whole of man's non-scientific culture would collapse. Most intellectuals outside of science did not want to relegate non-scientific endeavors, such as poetry, to the realm of mere feeling or illusion. Ethics and religion, as well as philosophy, were felt to be threatened by this scientific advance. Some remarks by Matthew Arnold concerning the place of poetry in this intellectual situation were the occasion for Dewey's essay on "Poetry and Philosophy." Arnold gave expression to the intellectual crisis by showing that the old Christian faiths were perishing, and that contemporary man was isolated from nature and from his fellow man. This condition gives man a sense of loss, and a pessimistic view of life ensues. Arnold accepts the authority of science concerning the world, and he contends that "most of what now passes for religion and philosophy will be replaced by poetry" (p. 110). He appears to be a precursor of the positivistic view of science and culture in which the world is denuded of value, and thus value is compelled to take refuge in the realm of art. Dewey was deeply disturbed by Arnold's view, and he sought in this essay to put forth his own views on the relations of science, poetry, and philosophy.

In order to understand the basis for Dewey's views on the roles of these three endeavors in human life, one must first grasp his general theory of meaning. The realm of meanings is wider than that of science. Scientific meanings have relations and implications which go beyond science itself; thus they are not inaccessible to the poet and the philosopher. Furthermore, since meanings are wider in their range than those which science describes, the poet and the philosopher have other meanings at their disposal. Thus, Dewey writes, "As it comes to the poet, life is already a universe of meanings, of interpretations, which indeed the poet may fill out, but not dispense with" (p. 113). Philosophy and poetry have a common root, the meanings found in experience. Dewey then shows that some of these common meanings have been used by both philosophers and poets as their material. Philosophers have written about the pessimistic phases of life, for instance, and so have the poets. At times poets have been exuberant, like Robert Browning with his optimism and faith in life, and so have philosophers. Dewey admits that at some times, including the present period, philosophers lag behind the poets in their sensitivities to the problems of human life, but at other times the poets have built upon the meanings of the philosophers.

If philosophy and poetry have a common source of meanings, what is the difference between them? The difference, according to Dewey, is in their expressions and purposes. Dewey says that the goal of science is knowledge, that the goal of philosophy is wisdom, and that "poetry may deliver truth with a personal and a passionate force which is beyond the reach of theory painting in gray on gray" (p. 112). It appears that Dewey thinks that poetry and art generally make emotional meanings uppermost, while philosophy using the "cold, reflective way of critical system" attempts to justify and organize what poetry "with its quick, naïve contacts, has already felt and reported" (p. 123). Philosophy is concerned with the truths and meanings of experience as they relate to human conduct (morals) and to values generally, or to "the ideals and aspirations of life" (p. 112). Dewey admits that poets may at times be concerned with morals, with the relation of scientific beliefs about the world to beliefs about values, but this is not their chief concern. Both poetry and philosophy are kinds of commentary on life, but their language is different and their functions, although overlapping in some respects, are different also.

Dewey is appreciative of many of the insights of Matthew Arnold, and in later years he turns again and again to ideas he attributed to this poet and critic. Arnold once wrote that "poetry is a criticism of life," and while Dewey thinks that poetry is more than this, he was influenced by Arnold's view in transferring it into philosophy, for he later writes that philosophy "is inherently criticism," and in his own method makes philosophy "a criticism of criticisms."[12]

During this early period Dewey was impressed by another writer, Paul Bourget, who wrote a two-volume work, *Essais de psychologie contemporaine* and *Nouveaux essais de psychologie contemporaine*. This is not a work on psychology, as its title suggests, but a criticism of French literary writers. Dewey's essay on "The Lesson of Contemporary French Literature" reveals that it is the critical method of Bourget, as well as the conclusions which the method produces, which interests him. Dewey thinks that Bourget penetrates into the deeper meanings of French consciousness, tracing "thoughts back to their germ" and indicating how these thoughts are "connected with the contemporary movements of life" (p. 37). This is what criticism should do. It should show the ideas which cause men to feel and to think the way they do; it should reveal how their literary works are expressions of the deeper meanings of their lives. Criticism is thus "the dissection of their thoughts, their emotions, their attitude toward the problems of life" (p. 37). This is what Bourget had done in his work, and the lesson to be learned from him is that "the problem of the nineteenth century reduces itself to a choice between faith and pessimism" (p. 42).

The four years from 1889 through 1892 represented by the writings in this volume were active and fruitful ones for John Dewey; he was directing the department at Michigan; he was

12 *Experience and Nature*, p. 398.

lecturing, teaching, writing, and taking part in community activities. He worked out a syllabus for the introductory philosophy course, wrote numerous comments on educational practice, and published short philosophical commentaries in *Inlander.* His philosophical views were taking on definite form, and his mind was moving toward the more mature statements of many of the germinal ideas developed during this period. Dewey's two dominant interests at that time were logical theory and ethics, and in these fields he continued to make notable contributions throughout his life.

S. Morris Eames

15 March 1969

EARLY ESSAYS

The Late Professor Morris

The story of the outward life of the departed teacher and scholar, George Sylvester Morris, may be briefly told. It was a life great, not in outward circumstance, but in spirit, and in the quality of its achievement.

George S. Morris was born November 15th, 1840, at Norwich, Vermont. After pursuing the courses in the district schools and village academy, usual to the New Englanders of that period, he entered Dartmouth College. He was graduated, with high standing in his class, as Bachelor of Arts in 1861. Three years afterwards, he received the degree of Master of Arts in course from the same institution. The same year he entered Union Theological Seminary in New York City. Here he studied for two years. Doctor H. B. Smith, whose own philosophical ability placed him high among the theologians of our country, discerned the unusual strain of Mr. Morris's mind, and advised him to continue his studies in Germany. This he did, carrying on, as is usual, his studies at more than one University, but chiefly with Trendelenburg in Berlin, and Erdmann and Ulrici in Halle. In 1868, he returned, having acquired a command of the German and French languages, and considerable acquaintance with Italian. He then spent some time teaching in a private family in New York City.

Meantime Doctors Smith and Schaff had projected a "Theological and Philosophical Library." This they desired to open with a history of philosophy. That of Ueberweg was selected, and none was found more fitted to do the work of translating than the scholar fresh from philosophical and

[*First published in the* Palladium, *An Annual Edited by the College Fraternities at the University of Michigan, XXXI (1889), 110–18. Reprinted in part in* The Life and Work of George Sylvester Morris (*New York: The Macmillan Co., 1917), 308–13.*]

language studies in Germany. The translating was performed in such a way that excellent judges, German as well as English, have pronounced the translation superior to the original. All the numerous references to Greek and Latin authorities were verified and translated, ambiguities in style and statement were corrected; the bibliographical references were increased from the ready and ample store of the translator; numerous accounts of the more noted contemporary German philosophers were added. The translation is a monument not only to the breadth and accuracy of Professor Morris's scholarship, but to his entire fidelity and thoroughness in executing whatever was committed to him.

At about this time there was a vacancy in the chair of modern languages at the University of Michigan. Professor Frieze was then acting president, and upon his invitation, an invitation delivered, I believe, in person, Mr. Morris accepted the position. For eleven years the department of modern languages had the benefit of his wide learning, his native love of thoroughness, his culture of mind. During these years, however, he continued to cherish above his other intellectual interests, the study of philosophy, and when in 1878 the opportunity opened for him to give instruction as a lecturer in philosophy in the recently opened Johns Hopkins University, at Baltimore, he gladly responded. For three years he joined this lectureship to his teaching in Ann Arbor. In 1881 the scope of his lectureship in Baltimore was broadened, and he resigned his chair in Michigan University. Only for a year, however, was the University deprived of his inspiring service. Arrangements were made, whereby, as the colleague of Doctor Cocker, he gave one-half of each year to instruction in philosophy in this institution. In 1883, upon the death of Doctor Cocker, Mr. Morris was made professor of philosophy, retaining this position up to the time of his untimely death, upon the 23rd of March, 1889.

Professor Morris was married at Ann Arbor, June 29th, 1876, to Miss Victoria Celle. She, with two children, remain to mourn him who is departed. It would not be possible becomingly to speak of the family-life thus disrupted by death. Its beautiful character is so well known to the students who so often shared in its graceful hospitality, as well as to those to whom this home was a continuation of their own earlier home, that the thought of it is a grateful memory. The tenderness and depth with which Professor Morris, in his lectures upon political philosophy, dwelt upon the institution of the family are more than explained by the natural and close companionships of his own life.

We cannot cease to regret that the entire unconsciousness of Professor Morris that his own experiences could be of interest to others should have deprived us of any more adequate record of his intellectual development, especially in the growth of his philosophic thought. In the opening of his lectures upon *British Thought and Thinkers*, there is an allusion to himself, which is worth quoting, both because of its rarity and because it reveals how early his mind sought the philosophic channel. "I can remember," he says, "how as a mere boy, more than once, in an evening reverie, an experience somewhat in this vein came to me. All my boyish ideas of things seemed, as pure creations of my own fancy, to melt away, and there remained, as the whole sum and substance of the universe, only the empty and inexplicable necessity of being, plus a dull, confused and indescribable sensation as of a chaos of shapeless elements. Then came the return to the world such as it had actually shaped itself in my imagination—the earth, with its green fields and forest-covered mountains, the world-inhabited heavens, the changing seasons, man and his past history and unrevealed earthly destiny, not to mention the myriad little and familiar things which would necessarily crowd the foreground of such a picture in a boy's mind. The view which a moment before had demonstrated so signally its capacity of dissolving again became a slowly changing panorama of a world. It was into such a conception of a world that I, following unwillingly a bent common to the universal mind of man, was more or less blindly seeking to introduce order and permanence. What must be? Why must anything be? Why must all things be? I need not say that the immediate result of my reflections was tolerably negative!" We cannot but wish as we read this that we had more autobiographical fragments to draw upon.

The instruction Professor Morris received in college

does not appear to have appealed to him particularly. Indeed, it seems rather to have impelled him, with a dislike which never left him, from what is often miscalled metaphysics, the partly verbal, partly arbitrary [ ] of various recondite notions. At one period, he was a disciple of the English Empirical School, of the Mills, and of Bain and Spencer. He went so far as to consider himself a materialist. In later years, it was something more than a logical conviction of the purely theoretical short-coming of these forms of philosophy that made him so strong, though so fair and appreciative, an opponent of them. It was also, if we may make use of some remarks of his upon one occasion when materialism was under discussion, the conviction, which personal experience had brought home to him, of their ethical deficiencies, of their failure to support and inspire life. It was in Germany, and immediately under the influence of Trendelenburg, in the main, that his trend of thinking was changed to a manner which he never ceased to regard as more catholic, more profound, more truly experimental. The change seems to have been due to a more adequate acquaintance with the history of philosophy, especially in its classic Greek types. Trendelenburg was among the first of a class of university teachers now numerous in Germany. He based his thinking and teaching mainly upon the history of philosophy, taken in connection with the leading results of modern science. Professor Morris was brought, seemingly, into a position somewhat similar to that of his teacher. At least, he never surrendered the belief that genuine personal philosophic conviction must be based upon a knowledge of philosophy in its historic development. This belief was the basis of his opinion that what American thought needed above all else as a condition of getting out of its somewhat provincial state, was an adequate acquaintance with the great thought of the past. While he held a definite philosophical position of his own, and held it firmly, his instruction was based upon the idea that the main thing after all is to get the individual out of his restricted ways of thinking and in contact with the stream of reflective thought that has been flowing on well nigh twenty-five hundred years. For a time his own philosophic conviction was probably an Aristotelianism modified and developed by the results of science. While Professor Morris never abandoned the positive features of his conviction, later and independent study convinced him that there were wider and deeper truths with which it must be conjoined. Although Trendelenburg had incorporated within his own teaching the substantial achievements of that great philosophical movement which began with Kant and closed with Hegel—the ideas, for example, of the correlation of thought and being, the idea of man as a self-realizing personality, the notion of organized society as the objective reality of man—he had taken a hostile attitude to these positions as stated by Hegel and to the method by which they were taught. While Professor Morris was never simply an adherent of Trendelenburg, he probably followed him also in this respect. At least, he used sometimes in later years to point out pages in his copy of Hegel which were marked "nonsense," etc., remarks made while he was a student in Germany. It thus was not any discipleship which finally led Mr. Morris to find in Hegel (in his own words) "the most profound and comprehensive of modern thinkers." He found in a better and fuller statement of what he had already accepted as true, a more ample and far-reaching method, a goal of his studies in the history of thought.

This is not the place, of course, to attempt any *resumé* of Professor Morris's philosophical thought. That fortunately stands for itself in the writings which he has left; it advances in the "living epistles" which he has written in the hearts and brains of scores of students. But since Professor Morris never held his philosophy by a merely intellectual grasp, since it was fused with his personal character, and gained its color and tone from his own deeper interests, it seems worth while to speak of his thought in relation to his other characteristic qualities,—his love of beauty and his strong religious nature.

All who knew Professor Morris knew how genuine and deep was his appreciation of the beautiful, especially as manifested in poetry and music. In music, indeed, he had not only a theoretical appreciation, but a practical and loving knowledge. This love of the beautiful found an abiding home in the very heart of his philosophy. It gave to his thought a peculiar elevated tone. It brought him into congenial sympathy with some of the greatest spirits of the race, notably Plato. While he did not draw his essential intellectual nutriment from Plato, he did derive from him, in large measure, intellectual inspiration. He never spoke of Plato without a kindling enthusiasm, a warmth of sympathy which no other philosopher ever aroused in quite the same degree. It was this genuine kinship of spirit which led Professor Morris to write in the following words, of Plato: "He is the intelligent poet of philosophy rapt with the moral power and fascination of philosophic truth, and in his wonderful dialogues bringing its resistless spell nearer home to the mind and heart of humanity than any other one whom the earth has been privileged to see. Reason in him is all aflame with feeling, but not mastered by it. He has not simply the acute perception, but the warm impression of eternal and essential being—of truth, beauty, goodness—and he is consequently enabled with the electrical effectiveness of a poetic touch to deliver this impression to mankind." The further tie which bound Professor Morris to the thought of Plato is in the fact that Plato dwells on the ideal character of beauty, not upon its sensuous quality; the ethical factor in beauty is what attracts. It was the beauty of spirit, the beauty of the eternal idea manifesting itself in outward form that drew Mr. Morris. The delight in this factor made his idealism poetic as well as philosophic. There was a prayer of Socrates which Professor Morris was wont to refer to and which he could not quote without his very countenance revealing how much it had been already realized in him: "Beloved Pan and all ye other gods who haunt this spot, give me beauty in the inward soul and may the outward and the inward man be at one."

It was characteristic of Professor Morris that the two writings from which he most often quoted were the *Dialogues* of Plato and the Gospel of St. John. In the fundamental principle of Christianity, he found manifested the truth which he was convinced of as the fundamental truth in philosophy—the unity of God and man so that the spirit which is in man, rather which is man, is the spirit of God.

"The very sense of philosophical idealism," he says in one of his works, "is to put and represent man in direct relation with the Absolute Mind so that its light is his light and its strength is made his." The firmness with which he held this truth is the key to all of his thinking. It is also the key to his attitude towards current religious beliefs. In the ordinary antithesis between the supernatural and the natural, he saw concealed the deeper truth of the antithesis of the spiritual and the natural—an antithesis involving, however, a unity; the natural being only the partial and dependent manifestation of the spiritual of such a position, he found all history to be the demonstration, the showing forth. The philosophy of art, of the state, of religion, as well as of knowledge, was to him inexplicable upon any theory. It was because he found in Hegel not merely the general recognition of this idea, but the attempt to work it out in its bearings upon concrete fact, that he was in later life so attracted to Hegel. The result of this conviction was that his philosophical knowledge gave body and masculine vigor to his religious faith, and his faith stimulated and quickened his theoretical convictions. But we do him wrong to speak of his religious faith and his philosophic knowledge as if they were two separate things capable of reacting upon each other. They were one—vitally and indistinguishably one. In this union, that union of his, his intellectual and moral nature had its roots—a union which made him so complete a man and his life so integral. He was preëminently a man in whom those internal divisions, which eat into the heart of so much of contemporary spiritual life, and which rob the intellect of its faith in truth, and the will of its belief in the value of life, had been overcome. In the philosophical and religious conviction of the unity of man's spirit with the divine he had that rest which is energy. This wholeness of intelligence and will was the source of the power, the inspiring power, of his life. It was the source of the definiteness, the positiveness of his teaching, which, free from all personal dogmatism, yet made the pupil instinctively realize that there was something real called truth, and this truth was not only capable of being known by man but was the very life of man.

The other personal quality which gave color to Professor Morris's thought was his profound feeling of the organic relationships of life—of the family and the state. At one with himself, having no conflicts of his own nature to absorb him, he found the substance of his being in his vital connections with others; in the home, in his friendships, in the political organization of society, in his church relations. It was his thorough realization in himself of the meaning of these relationships that gave substance and body to his theory of the organic unity of man with nature and with God. This theory, like any theory, may be held in an empty formalism of thought, but in Professor Morris's teaching, it was quickened and made real by his own practical realization of such relations in actual life.

Of Professor Morris's writings, nothing can be here said, excepting to give an incomplete list. Among his earlier writings are two essays, written for the Victoria Institute of London, of which he was an associate member, and published by them. The titles of these are: *The Theory of Unconscious Intelligence as Opposed to Theism* and *The Final Cause as Principle of Cognition in Nature*. About this time should be placed an account of the philosophy of Trendelenburg, published in the *New Englander*. Here should be mentioned also the translation of Ueberweg's *History of Philosophy*. There was published in the *Journal of Speculative Philosophy*, while Professor Morris was still professor of modern languages, a lecture, which he had delivered before a class reading Taine, upon the theory of Art, a lecture which contains in germ, the ideas later developed in his lectures upon Æsthetics. Marking his connection with Johns Hopkins University are *British Thought and Thinkers*, and later the *Exposition of Kant's Critique of Pure Reason*. The latter was the initial volume of a series of works, called German Philosophical Classics, and published by S. C. Griggs & Co. Of this series, Professor Morris was the proposer and editor, and at the time of his death it included seven volumes, one of which besides the Kant, that upon *Hegel's Philosophy of History and State*, was by Professor Morris's own hand. This was his last work. Between it and the Kant comes an article in the *Princeton Review* entitled, "Philosophy and its Specific Problems," the book upon *Philosophy and Christianity*, made up of lectures delivered upon the Ely Foundation before the Union Theological Seminary. He published also, as the first of a series of Philosophical Papers of the University of Michigan, an address which he had delivered before the philosophical society of the University upon *University Education*. About the time when he was seeing through the press his exposition of Hegel, the scheme of a "Library of Philosophy" was under discussion in England. Professor Morris was asked by its editor, Mr. J. H. Muirhead, to write the volume upon the history of logic. Professor Morris was even then thinking of what he should turn to next, and he welcomed with great pleasure the opportunity thus afforded him. Nothing could have been suggested which would have awakened so ready a response. When he spoke of it, he said that for some time back, it had been his desire to give the next years of his work to the study of Real Logic with a view to preparing something that might last. This history of logic gave him in an unexpected way, the chance to make thorough preparation for this treatise upon logic itself. For a year and more before his death he had been busy reading for the history. It is to be feared, however, that nothing was left in shape for publication. Professor Morris's death has brought a loss no less deep, in its way, to the philosophical world at large, than that which has come upon the University, and his circle of personal friends. He was, indeed, in the prime of his work. His own feeling, as expressed in one of those rare moments when he broke through his accustomed reserve in such matters, was that in past work he had been serving an apprenticeship for what he hoped to do.

It remains to speak of Professor Morris as a teacher. There is, indeed, nothing to be said of him as a class-room instructor that is not to be said of him as a man. Nothing could have been more foreign to his character than to assume in any respect an attitude or quality in the class-room different from that which marked him elsewhere. There was the same sincerity, the same simplicity, the same force of enthusiasm in him in one place as in another. No "officialism" such as sometimes gathers about the work of teaching ever touched him. He was everywhere simply and only a man. But Professor Morris had unusual gifts as a philosophic instructor. He was, among other things, a commentator of the first order. That is, he had the selective eye which made at once for the heart of an author under discussion; he had the pregnant phrase that lays bare this heart to the eye of the student. He had the gift of inspiring in his pupils the same disinterested devotion to truth that marked himself. He conveyed in large measure what, in his essay upon *University Education* already alluded to, he himself calls "the power to detect and the will to condemn all essential shams and falsehoods." Scholarship never lost itself in pedantry; culture never masqueraded as mere intellectualism, with ethical inspiration and backing. He was especially successful in arousing pupils with any particular aptitude for philosophy to advanced and independent work. The spirit of his work was that which he declared should be the spirit of all truly University work—a free teacher face to face with a free student. He once defined idealism as faith in the human spirit; this faith he had, and his voice and his influence were always for broadening and freeing the scope and methods of college work, without in any way relaxing the solidity and thoroughness of mental discipline.

Of the place and function of philosophy in University training he had a high conception—not because he in any way would magnify his own office at the expense of others, but because he saw in philosophy the organic bond of all special sciences, "the coördination of all knowledge." The University, to quote again from Professor Morris, "is the institution devoted to the fullest and freest cultivation of the universal condition of human freedom—knowledge of the truth." This end is humane, is ethical; and it is only because philosophy tended to knowledge of the truth, that he made high claims for it. So far was he from desiring any exclusive treatment of philosophy that he writes that "her praises will never be rightfully and effectively sung until they are sung by others than adepts." I can find no better expression of the spirit in which Professor Morris himself taught philosophy than is voiced in one of his own earlier writings. He speaks there of "the noblest common-sense which seeks reform, not simply protest and the demand for change, but by fitly feeding the fountains of intelligence, through which alone a true and authentic reform can be maintained." To feed the fountains of intelligence was precisely, it seems to me, the work of Professor Morris in philosophy. While we cannot estimate the loss to thought in the sudden death of Professor Morris, we cannot be sufficiently grateful that there are so many scattered over the whole land who have felt the quickening touch of his divine love of truth, and who have felt the "fountains of intelligence" within their own breast, called into life and energy by the truth as he bore witness to it.

No attempt can here be made to appreciate the intimate and personal qualities of Mr. Morris. Were I to attempt it, the flood of personal memories and affections would prevent. To those who did not know him, no use of adjectives would convey an idea of the beauty, the sweetness, the wholeness of his character. To those who did know him, it is not necessary to speak of these things. His gentle courtesy in which respect for others and for himself were so exquisitely blended, his delicate chivalry of thought and feeling; his unusual union of intellectual freedom and personal simplicity—who shall speak adequately of these traits? The words of one who knew Mr. Morris only by his outward presence, and through the report of others, comes to my lips: "There was nothing which he held as his own; he had made the great renunciation."

The Philosophy of Thomas Hill Green

It is no secret that the Professor Grey of Mrs. Ward's *Robert Elsmere* is the *umbra*, if not the *nomen*, of the late Professor Green of Oxford. Professor Green is known in this country, where he is known at all, as the author of certain philosophical treatises and criticisms which the uninitiated, if not the expert, would class as decidedly hard reading. Indeed, it suggests the irony of fate that one whose writings are anything but popular, in the ordinary sense of the term, should become part of the intellectual background —Grey is hardly a living character—of the most popular novel of the day. For Green's writings lack popularity both of style and of aim. Clear they are, but only because they are the adequate expression of thought which is remarkably exact and painstaking, as well as conscientious to a degree that will allow no possible qualification to go unmade, no possible objection to remain unanswered, no possible limitations to be passed over. And they were not written *ad populum*, but for philosophical students, one might say for philosophical specialists. Green's intellectual conscience was so sensitive that he very obviously refrains from any attempt to win assent by any adventitious appeals. He is scrupulous to a fault, it sometimes seems, in refusing any alliance with outside movements or parties that might make for his advantage. In form and in substance he will have his thoughts gain the influence that the truth embodied in them can command, and only that influence.

While Green's influence has been growing year by

[*First published in the* Andover Review, *XI* (*Apr. 1889*), *337–55. Not previously reprinted.*]

year, and while those whom it has touched, it has touched profoundly, even radically, I do not think that it can be said to have extended beyond the circle of his personal pupils and of philosophical teachers and students. In this country, at least, hundreds must know Professor Grey to whom the "Introductions" to Hume, the *Prolegomena to Ethics*, and the *Lectures on the Principles of Political Obligation* of Professor Green are unknown.

But the remoteness of his philosophy from life is, after all, more apparent than real. There is even a more specific connection of his thought with a novel that pretends to touch life seriously than the general tendency of our times to get the imagination and the understanding upon common ground. The connection is in the character and philosophy of Green; for his character was practical in the highest degree, and it is impossible to hold his philosophy as a mere speculative theory apart from its applications to life. It would be profitless, it might seem impertinent, had not Mrs. Ward set an example, to compare the living Green and the fictitious Grey. But common report, brief sketches by some of his contemporaries, and by some of his pupils, the brief but authoritative biographical account, all speak for the intensely practical bent of his nature, and his philosophy is there to speak for itself. Both theoretically and personally, the deepest interests of his times were the deepest interests of Professor Green. The most abstruse and critical of his writings are, after all, only attempts to solve the problems of his times—the problems which meet us in current magazine discussions, in social and political theory, in poetry, in religion, and in the interpretation of the higher results of science. Professor Caird gives us the clue to the connection of Professor Green's philosophy with the actual life of his times, in saying that one of the main features of Green's character was the distinctness with which he lived by conviction, not by impulse. It was the belief, the profound belief, that all action should spring from conviction, not any love of abstract and abstruse speculations, that made him a philosopher. He saw in what is called philosophy only a systematic search for and justification of the conviction by which man should live. We are not surprised, therefore, when Professor Caird goes on to say that the other main trait of Green's character was the intensity of his intellectual and political interests. His philosophic theory was in the service of these interests, and his political thought and activity was the application of his philosophic conviction. He was (to quote Caird again) "a democrat of the democrats. From a somewhat exclusive interest in the essentials of humanity —in the spiritual experiences in which all men are alike—his sympathies were always with the many rather than with the few."

Upon both sides, the side of philosophic conviction, and the side of political and social life, Green is in closest contact with the deepest interests of his times. In the true sense, his philosophy, however strictly logical and impersonal in form, is vital and concrete. The theoretic difficulties and the practical aspirations of this last half century are voiced by Green. He is in a more real and, I cannot but think, more lasting way the prophet of our times than many hailed as prophets who have addressed themselves to the public in more direct and popular ways. In this article I wish, so far as I may, considering the technical character of the subject-matter and the limits of space, to give an account of the burden of this prophecy. I wish to point out the theoretic conviction by which he met the doubts and questionings of the intellectual life of these times, and the practical conviction in which he articulated the best political desire and conduct of to-day.

Beginning with the speculative side, I may say that Green's object was to reconcile science and religion. But this phrase needs to be carefully interpreted. If it means a forced exegesis of Scripture on the one hand, and a somewhat questionable use of somewhat doubtful facts on the other, nothing was more remote from the intention of Green. Nor did he work in the more legitimate field of showing that the main doctrines of theology find no contradiction in the general theories of science. Indeed, he carefully refrains from the introduction of specifically religious ideas,—almost of the word religion. By the reconciliation of science and religion, I mean the attempt to show that science, as the fundamental, theoretical interest of man, and religion as his fundamental, emotional, and practical interest have a common source and a common guaranty. It was the main work of Green's speculative philosophy to show that there is a spiritual principle at the root of ordinary experience and science, as well as at the basis of ethics and religion; to show, negatively, that whatever weakens the supremacy and primacy of the spiritual principle makes science impossible, and, positively, to show that any fair analysis of the conditions of science will show certain ideas, principles, or categories—call them what you will—that are not physical and sensible, but intellectual and metaphysical.

Professor Green has himself given a statement of his general intention at the beginning of his *Prolegomena to Ethics*. He there points out that there is a certain conflict between poetry and natural science. The ideas contained in the best poetry of our times, the ideas that recommend it to select and serious spirits, are not verifiable by sense. These ideas, if outside the domain of dogmatic theology, are as surely outside the domain of natural science. And yet the most intelligent critics are not willing, says Professor Green, that any justification should be sought for the ideas of poetry. While they cherish these ideas as their own deepest personal convictions, yet they are not willing that their systematic analysis should be attempted. Natural science alone gives certainty and truth; compared with science these ideas are illusions. Yet they are illusions which interest the imagination, and which have power over the heart. Better leave them as they are, these critics say, than attempt a philosophy of them which would be equally an illusion, and which, dull and pretentious, would not touch even the feelings. And yet Professor Green says, in substance, he must insist that fundamental ideas of life and conduct cannot be left to the domain of individual feeling, of poetry, but have an independent justification in the shape of philosophy. This justification he finds to be the more necessary, because, unless the validity of the deeper ideas of poetry and religion can be shown, the conception of a man as a moral being must also vanish. If the underlying ideas of poetry are incompatible with natural science, ethics must also be eliminated. Yet we cannot deny physical science. What shall we do? Analyze the conditions of science, or connected knowledge of matters of fact, and see if it does not presuppose a principle which is not scientific, that is, a principle which is not a matter of fact. If we find embedded in the heart of knowledge of nature a principle not natural, we may then ask whether this same principle is not active in moral experience, if it does not have an expression in the consciousness of a moral ideal and in action in accordance with this ideal.

Professor Green begins accordingly with the complete acceptance of physical science,—not merely of its details, but of its methods and principles. Not in spite of, but through these principles he expects to justify the reality of spiritual and moral ideas. A right examination of science will show it to be not an enemy of poetry and religion, but a most helpful ally. But these phrases should not be misunderstood. It is not science as a body of knowledge of matters of sensible facts, nor science in its characteristic physical methods, that points to an ideal principle which morals may employ. On the contrary, there is an antithesis between the natural and the moral. But a *metaphysical* analysis of science will reveal, as the basis of natural science, a principle which transcends nature, a principle which is spiritual.

If this is true, one may well ask why the belief should be almost universally current that there is something hostile to religion in the principles of science. Green found the reason for this seeming contradiction in the current interpretation of the characteristic empirical philosophy of Great Britain. This interpretation seemed to make spiritual ideas an outlaw, while it amply justified the methods and categories of "experience" and of the science of nature. If this interpretation were correct, if it were possible for a philosophy at once to guarantee a knowledge of the sensible, and render invalid any knowledge of that which lies beyond the sensible, the position that from the fortress of science turns its guns upon religion would be impregnable. Green's first efforts were directed, naturally, to an investigation of this empirical philosophy. He wished to show that it was no more compatible with science than it was with religion; that a consistent interpretation of Empiricism sapped the roots of knowledge as well as of faith. Empiricism cannot be worked in two opposite directions at once. It cannot bless science and curse religion. Green believed that Hume was the historic proof of this statement,—that his skepticism was the legitimate outcome of Locke's empiricism. It was because contemporary thought failed to recognize this that it trusted science as natural and positive, while rejecting philosophy and religion as fanciful and arbitrary. It retained Hume's negation as to theology, but not as to knowledge. It adopted just enough of his skepticism to cling to science and to reject philosophy. Green's first work was, therefore, in a sense, negative and polemic; it was to go over the movement from Locke to Hume, and to show how completely and inevitably it led to a skepticism which meted out to science the same measure that the anachronistic empiricism of to-day would mete out only to religion. This once accomplished, a truly constructive movement might occur. Modern consciousness might be trusted not to deny science, and having once realized that an empirical philosophy made it impossible, would turn to a spiritual philosophy which would justify it. This done, the application of the spiritual principle to ethics and theology would follow as matter of course. This represents fairly, I think, the underlying motive and the general character of Green's first important philosophic work,—the "Introductions" to Hume's *Treatise of Human Nature*.

To give a synopsis of almost four hundred closely printed octavo pages in a magazine article would be neither possible nor edifying. The mode in which the examination is carried on is, however, highly characteristic of Green. The criticism is exhaustive and laborious to the last degree. It contains a minute and thorough analysis of Locke, Berkeley, and Hume, which does not content itself with general views and theories, but takes up every detail of doctrine that in any way bears upon their underlying principles. Nor is it an external criticism. The examination is of Locke himself, and not of Locke as tested by some other thinker. The criticism is directed towards discovering his own self-consistency, and the reasons which made it practically impossible for him to be self-consistent.

The general result may be stated apart from all detail. The contention of Green is that while empiricism must either make intelligence a mere product or deny to it all constructive function, as matter of fact it cannot get along without ascribing certain powers to intelligence. Stated in another way, empiricism must always base its explanations upon the reality of certain relations, but these relations, according to its own theory, must be products. The *basis* of empiricism is the reality of some relation, whether with Locke that of substance, or with Hume that of succession. But the result of empiricism is that every relation is a mere product of sensations. This contradiction is essential to the very method of empiricism. It is, to use illustrations of Professor Green, as if a geologist were to teach that the first formation of rocks was the product of all layers built upon it, or as if a physiologist were to teach that a certain digestive act, exercised by some organism, was the cause of that organism. If the minimum of relation due to intelligence and not to external causes be allowed, constructive function is allowed to intelligence, and we have a spiritual principle at the basis of experience, a principle which may be the source of morals and of religion as well as of experience and science. But if all relation is eliminated, then experience as well as science must be eliminated. "A consistent sensationalism would be speechless."

Three years afterward, in 1877, Green returned to the charge,—but this time it was the philosophy of Herbert Spencer and of G. H. Lewes that received his criticism. His object was the same as in his earlier work: to show the incompatibility of an empirical philosophy with science, and to show the necessity for English-speaking people of a new departure in philosophy. Professor Green had learned, he tells us in the introductory paragraph of his new work, that "each generation requires the questions of philosophy to be put to it in its own language, and, unless they are so put, will not be at the pains to understand them." As Spencer and Lewes were the typical representatives of the same kind of thought as that of Locke and Hume, the philosophy that separated reality from intelligence, Professor Green thought he could best justify a philosophy which made reality depend upon intelligence, by an examination of these writers. It was characteristic of Spencer's philosophy that using the same empirical method as the earlier empiricists, framing the same theory of knowledge, as built up of impressions forced upon the mind from without, it had tried to unite with this theory of knowledge a positive, constructive philosophy which should rest upon the certainty of particular scientific facts and laws, and upon the certainty of the fundamental conceptions of science, such as the relation of cause and effect, the principle of the persistence of force, etc. Spencer, like Hume, regards knowledge as built up out of sensations; he moves a more extensive, a more cumbrous machinery, but, after all, his encyclopædic marshalling of facts, his broad deploying of scientific forces, comes to the sensational theory of knowledge that possessed the earlier empiricists. And yet Spencer frames a theory of the development of the universe, of life, of mind, and of society. Here, without going into details, is where Green finds the vulnerable point of Spencer. He unites a theory of knowledge which makes science impossible with a theory of the construction of the universe built up at every point upon science. Spencer denies all constructive, all synthetic function to intelligence; he makes intelligence a product of events and forces which are not intelligent. All knowledge is thus a product, an effect of something wholly unrelated to intelligence, hence unknowable. Between knowledge and reality there is thus a great gap fixed. And yet Spencer tells what the laws and forces of the universe are, and how they have produced life and mind. Science, as a body of facts, is to be implicitly relied upon; science, as the process and product of human intelligence, has no objective value. On this contradiction the philosophy of Spencer is based.

Spencer, in a word, only tells us, taking a longer, more roundabout road than the earlier empiricists followed, using the life of the race instead of that of an individual, that experience is the source of knowledge, while he has a theory of experience which would not allow it to be the source of anything. The question, the real question of philosophy, is thus left unanswered: What is experience? How is it constituted? In his *Prolegomena to Ethics* Green takes up this question at first hand. It is impossible even to give the successive steps of the argument, much less the reasonings upon which the conclusions depend. We may, however, summarize some of the leading results. If we ask what is implied in saying that any experience is real instead of illusory, or if we ask how it is that we can distinguish between being and seeming, between fact and fancy, the answer is, because there is a connected whole of experience, "a nature of things." What is mere seeming or unreal is not capable of becoming a member of this unified world. In this unity of the world there is further implied the existence of a single, permanent, and all-inclusive system of relations. But even now we have not found an ultimate fact in which intelligence may rest. We have to ask what is implied in the existence of this system of relations. And the answer is, that its existence has meaning only upon the supposition of a permanent single consciousness which forms the bond of relations,—"an eternal intelligence realized in the related facts of the world."

If it seems to be a far cry from our ability to distinguish fact from fancy to the proof of an eternal self-consciousness, the reader must attribute the gaps to our summary, and not to the argument of Professor Green. The reader must also avoid confusing the argument of Green with the so-called causal proof of the existence of God. The argument does not attempt to show that God is necessary as a cause of the world, but that in the existence of knowable fact, in the existence of that which we call reality, there is necessarily implied an intelligence which is one, self-distinguishing and not subject to conditions of space and time. This intelligence cannot be identified with *our* intelligence, that is, with an intelligence which has a succession of experiences in time, because *our* intelligence is only "a part of the partial world"; it is part of that experience which is to be accounted for. What, then, is the relation of our intelligence to this eternal divine intelligence? Just this, according to Green: the eternal intelligence reproduces itself in us, partially and gradually; it communicates to us piecemeal, but in inseparable correlation, experience, and the world of which we have experience, understanding, and the facts understood.

These are the two fundamental positions of Green's

constructive work: on one side an eternal self-consciousness, as involved in the reality of experience; on the other side, human consciousness as a progressive reproduction of this divine consciousness. Since there is a tendency in some minds to call every philosophic theory pantheistic which does not offer itself as the baldest deism, it may be well to call attention to the two traits which distinguish Green's philosophy from pantheism. One of these traits is found in the relation of God to the world. God may, indeed, be thought as the unity of the world, but only as its *spiritual* unity. God and the world are not facts of the same order, as they must be according to pantheism. God is *self*-consciousness; that is, a consciousness which distinguishes itself from every fact of nature, and from the sum total of such facts, although *apart* from nature this consciousness would not be what it is. In the second place, while pantheism would make the relation of human consciousness to the world and to God one of bare identity and absorption, the relation, according to Green, is one of spiritual, personal unity, and this implies that there be really spirit, personality on *both* sides of the relation.

It may be well to give a statement substantially in Green's own language of what is meant by the human self or man. Our consciousness may mean, he says, either of two things: either a function of the animal organism, which is being made, gradually and with interruptions, a vehicle of the eternal consciousness, or that eternal consciousness itself, as making the animal organism its vehicle. In this process, by which the divine self-consciousness makes the animal operations organic to its own reproduction, it is subject to the limitations and qualifications of the physical conditions to which it subjects itself; and yet, in itself, it retains its essential characteristic, that of being self-consciousness. And so, too, the product, the human consciousness, carries with it under all its limitations and qualifications the characteristic of being an object to itself. Of both the divine and the human consciousness, in other words, it may be said that it is spirit, for each is an object to itself; and of both it may be said that it is person, for each is an end in itself. Of self-consciousness, or spiritual personality, whether in God or in man, it may be said that it is "the only thing that is real in its own right; the only thing of which the reality is not relative and derived."

Experience thus means the continual reproduction in man of an eternal consciousness. This reproduction is limited by physical conditions, by the fact that it takes place in what is otherwise an animal organism, and thus the resulting experience is sensible and not merely rational. Yet this experience, so far as it has any meaning, retains the marks of its spiritual, its rational source; experience comes to us in successive moments, but that which is brought by experience neither comes nor goes,—it is the permanent divine intelligence. Science is simply *orderly* experience. It is the working out of the relations, the laws, implied in experience, but not visible upon its surface. It is a more adequate reproduction of the relations by which the eternal self-consciousness constitutes both nature and our understandings. It is clear how such a doctrine prepares the way for a moral theory,—indeed, in his *Prolegomena*, Green introduces it simply for the sake of getting a philosophical basis for ethics. Having found that in respect to his knowledge man is not a child of nature, but holds from a spiritual source, there is reason to apprehend that this spiritual principle may find expression in action: in consciousness of a moral ideal, and in the determination of action by it.

In truth, we find that man's organism makes him not only a being of sensations, but of impulses and of wants. And just as the sensations, by becoming the organs of a divine spirit, are transformed into theoretic experience and science, so the impulses and wants, as *media* of the same divine spirit, are transformed into practical experience, into moral action. The reproduction in man of the consciousness which is an end-in-itself makes man an end in himself, and gives his actions, therefore, both an absolute law and an absolute ideal or good. As the action of the divine consciousness upon passing sensations makes them into an experience of what *is*, so the same consciousness acting upon transitory impulses creates our practical world, our conception of what is not, but *should* be, *ought* to be. The reproduction of the divine intelligence in us is, therefore, as much a condition of moral as of scientific experience. Indeed, it is more than a condition: the reproduction of the divine intelligence through the organism of our needs and our impulses to satisfy them *constitutes* our moral experience. A purely animal intelligence, one whose life was constituted by sensations and impulses alone, has no conception of any ideal world, of anything that ought to be, of any good, or of any duty. The wholly divine intelligence knows no distinction of real and ideal; the *ought* and the *is* are one to God. But a being like man, in whom the divine has supervened upon the animal, must know that something ought to be, the divine intelligence, the divine will, which for him is not. Hence the constant conflict of the moral life; hence the necessity of living it by faith, not by sight; living, that is, by the conception of something which absolutely ought to be, rather than by the perception of what can be sensibly verified as already in existence.

But this general outline of Green's moral views must be made somewhat more specific. We may, perhaps, best accomplish this by analyzing into four stages our moral experience; that is, the relation of our actions arising from animal wants to the divine practical reason or will. (1) The mere presence of the divine consciousness to our wants constitutes an ideal self, which is both an absolute good and an absolute obligation. And if we ask concerning the nature of this absolute good, *what* it is as distinct from the mere fact *that* it is, the answer is (2), that it can be found only in some development of *persons*, and in that relation of persons to one another which we call *society*; and (3), if this answer is still vague, we may know that the consciousness of an ideal of this nature has been the parent of the institutions and usages and of the social judgments and aspirations through which human life has hitherto been bettered. Hence from these institutions and aspirations we may judge more concretely as to the nature of the ideal. (4) Man's *actual* achievements in morality, his virtue, is decided by the degree in which he is habitually responsive to the demands made upon him by the various institutions and customs in which the ideal good has already embodied itself, and to the spirit which is their source.

The first point is, in substance, that the presence of the permanent self-distinguishing consciousness in man determines man's real good. His good cannot be found in the satisfaction of this and that want, in the enjoyment of this and that pleasure, or in any possible series of pleasures. For the satisfaction of such wants does not satisfy the man, the person. His personality *is*, and is *what* it is only through the activity in him of the divine reason, and only that can really satisfy him which satisfies this reason. This can be found only in its own complete reproduction. What man wants is not satisfaction of any given impulse, but satisfaction of self, and this can be found only in God, because God is man's true self. In other words, by virtue of the supervention of God upon man's animal wants and impulses, man has certain capabilities and aspirations which can be adequately named only by calling them divine. In the realization of these capabilities, human because more than animal, is man's good to be found. This good, the ideal self, is also a law to man. It is absolutely obligatory, that is, obligatory without qualification or exception. It is obligatory because it is man's own real self. Were it a law or a goodness merely external to him, man might be forced or constrained to it, but he could never be obliged to it. But because it is the reality of his own being, man recognizes it as a law binding upon him. It is man's own duty to strive for perfection, because this striving is the expression of his own nature.

The statement that God is the ideal, or even the true self of man, is liable to interpretation from the wrong side, and, indeed, has often been so interpreted. It is taken to mean that God is only a projection of man; that he is an ideal that man forms of what man would be were he perfect, and that, therefore, God has no reality excepting as a conception of man's ideal, and that God becomes real in the degree in which man realizes his ideal. But this is a complete inversion of Green's thought. The reality of God in himself is a condition of our having the notion of Him as our own ideal self, of our attempts, our striving to make this ideal real, and of our measure of success. Human nature is rather the projection of God, that is, the reproduction of Him, through physical conditions, than God the projection of man's ideal. Man forms the conception of what he may possibly be, only because in itself this possibility is more than possible, because it is forever actual. "God *is* all which the human spirit is capable of becoming."

It is hardly a satisfactory explanation of moral experience, however, to say *that* there is an absolute good and an absolute duty constituted by the presence in us of a divine intelligence. We want to know *what* this good is; *what* we shall do in order to do our duty. In part, it must be confessed that this question cannot be answered. We cannot say what in fullness the ideal is until we have realized it. What our capabilities are we shall never know until we have manifested them. Yet every manifestation must conform to the nature of the ideal self which it manifests, and must be a partial revelation of its nature. From these two facts we shall be able to define somewhat more adequately the nature of the ideal.

Secondly, then, since the principle which is reproducing itself in us is a self-conscious personality, we may know that its reproduction must also be a self-conscious personality. Of one thing we may be sure: "Our ultimate standard of worth is an ideal of *personal* worth. All other values are relative to value for, of, or in a person." This ideal cannot be found, then, in impersonal humanity, in some national or world consciousness, in some organization of society, nor in some far-off event, however divine, towards which the world is supposed to be making. "The spiritual progress of mankind is an unmeaning phrase unless it means a progress *of* personal character, and *to* personal character, – a progress of which feeling, thinking, and willing subjects are the agents and substainers." But, on the other hand, this progress can be realized only in society. While its beginning, its process, and its end is in an individual, yet without society, and the conditions afforded by it, there can be no individual, no person. "Society is the condition of development of a personality." "Social life is to personality what language is to thought. Human society presupposes persons in *capacity*, but it is only in the intercourse of men, each recognized by each as an end, not merely a means, and thus as having reciprocal claims, that the capacity is actualized, and that we really live as persons." And not to speak of society at large, from a historical point of view, we know that we now "learn to regard ourselves as persons among other persons, because we are treated as such. It is through the action of society that the individual comes practically to conceive his own personality and to conceive the same personality as belonging to others; it is society, also, that supplies all the higher content to this conception, all those objects of a man's personal interest, in living for which he lives for his own satisfaction, except such as are derived from the merely animal nature." This much at least, then, we know of the end of moral conduct: it is to be found only in the perfection of persons living together as persons, that is, living in society.

But, thirdly, the divine consciousness not only presents itself to man as an ideal in which the capacities of all persons are realized, but it has communicated itself to some degree already in man's experience; man's wants and desires and choices have already, to some degree, become the vehicles or organs of the realization of the divine practical reason or will. This communication, piecemeal, interrupted, has constituted the moral experience of the life of the individual and of society in history. History, indeed, cannot be defined, excepting as the process by which a divine will, determined by reason, has articulated wants, desires, and ideas, by making them organic to its own reproduction. The idea that there is an absolute good, an ideal personality living in ideal relations to other persons, has been the moving spring, the vital source of all history, while the attempts to realize it have been the parent of all that makes history more than a mere succession of events; of its institutions, of the family, the state, and the church, and of all the customs, laws, and aspirations of society.

The progress thus made in history in giving the inchoate idea of the good, definite articulation may be considered under two aspects. One is the extension of the area of the common good, the practical widening of the range of those who are considered members of society or interested in the same good. The other is the fuller determination of the content of this good. For in either case, it must be noticed that the good can be conceived only as a *common* good. This was implied when it was said that personality could be realized only in a society of persons. It is implied in the fact that the very idea of a divine consciousness reproducing itself in humanity does away with "all respect of persons." Each being in whom God so communicates himself is a person, an end in himself, and has the rights of personality. An ideal so constituted cannot be exclusive, cannot be other than common. If we put it in a more psychological way, the person who is to realize his capacities has interests in persons; not merely interests in them so far as they are *means* to his own gratification, but interest in them as in himself—interest in their good as in his own. Man cannot be thought as man without this fundamental social interest. This social interest cannot by any possibility be developed or evolved from forms of life which do not already in germ possess it. It is an ultimate fact in human history; a fact without which there would not be human history; a fact not deducible from any other history. A unity of interest, a conception of well-being common to a number of persons, however small the number, the idea of community is the necessary presupposition of all human history. Once given this community, this number of persons who conceive themselves and one another as persons, as ends in themselves, and any conceivable development of morality is possible. Without it, morality has no existence.

Progress in knowledge of and realization of the moral ideal has consisted largely just in the widening of the number of persons among whom there is conceived to be a common good, and between whom there is a common duty. So far as we can discover, in what we call the early periods, the area of those conceived to have common ends was limited to the family, or, at most, to the grouping of families of common birth in the tribe. And even in these limited areas, the grasp of the idea of community of welfare was feeble and incomplete. The woman, the child, were theoretically, and in large manner practically, outside society,—society being defined as the group of persons recognizing themselves and each other as persons. To-day, theoretically at least, it is a belief, almost an axiom, that there is a potential duty of every man to every other man,—a duty which becomes actual so soon as one has dealings with the other. The Stoic philosopher, the Roman jurist, the Christian teacher, have all contributed to the development of the idea of human equality; the idea that every man and woman is a sharer in the common good, and hence has the rights and claims of personality.

If we interrupt the exposition a moment, it is worth while to notice the extent to which this idea of the value of personality, of the potentialities contained in the lowest and the worst of mankind, was a governing motive in the life of Green. His conscience was developed to a point in which it became a public and political force as well as a private and "moral" monitor. His political and historical writings, as well as his purely philosophical ones, show that he realized the idea of the personality embodied in every individual, not merely as a theoretic proposition, but as a claim, even as a burden upon himself; and his life, as a teacher and as a citizen, is full of evidence that the "enthusiasm of humanity" was not a vague phrase, an abstract formula, nor an emotional indulgence with him, but the ruling motive of his life. To him as to Aristotle the virtues of a good man are identical with those of the good citizen, and citizenship was widened from the Greek *polis* to a kingdom "as wide as the Humanity for which Christ died."

But this extension of the area of the sharers in the common good is not the only sign of growing correctness in the moral ideal. Progress is also marked in the fuller content given to the conception of the common good. In one sense, indeed, there cannot be said to have been any growth in the conception. To the Greek philosophers who first articulated the conception as to the most reflective moralist of to-day, goodness consisted in "purity of heart," that is, in a character controlled by interest in the good for its own sake, in conscious direction of the will to human perfection. But as habits and institutions have arisen in answer to this demand for perfection, our conception of what this perfection is has become richer and fuller, and the demands it makes upon us more comprehensive. "Faculties, dispositions, occupations, persons, of which a Greek citizen would have taken no account, or taken account only to despise, are now recognized as having their place in the realization of the powers of the human soul." And "where the Greek saw a supply of possibly serviceable labor, having no end or function but to be made really serviceable to the privileged few, the Christian citizen sees a multitude of persons, who in their actual condition may have no advantage over the slaves of an ancient state, but who, in undeveloped possibility, and in the claims which arise out of that possibility, are all that he himself is. Seeing this, he finds a necessity laid upon him." If we apply this principle to virtues like fortitude and temperance, we find that in idea, in underlying motive, these virtues were the same to the Greek as they are to us. Bravery, then as now meant willingness to do and to bear, to any extreme, in the service of the highest public cause that the agent can conceive,—in one case the cause of the state, in the other, of the kingdom of God,—because it is the more excellent way so to do. But because man has realized his possibilities now so much more than in Greece, because he has revealed so much more his possibilities, the application of bravery is so much wider, so much more exacting, that it hardly seems like the same virtue. Aristotle found it only in the citizen-soldier willing to die for the state. Now the will to endure even unto death finds objects worthy to call forth this will where the Greek saw nothing but ugliness and meanness. It finds expression in the obscure laver of love, as well as in the splendid heroism at which a world wonders. So temperance to the Greek meant only control of the appetites of hunger, thirst, and sex, in the interests of the higher life. That was the sole conception of self-denial open to the Greek. But now interest in the problem of social deliverance, in the development of the "mass of men whom we call brethren, and whom we declare to be meant with us for eternal destinies," forbids a surrender to enjoyments, however innocent, however valuable in themselves, which do not aid in this social deliverance. But we should not allow any self-gratulation over the greater fullness of our moral ideal to hide from us the failures in its realizations. In large degree, the ideal is negative. "It makes itself felt in certain prohibitions, as of slavery, but it has no such effect on the ordering of life as to secure for those whom we admit not to be slaves much real opportunity of self-development. So far as negative rights go,—rights to be let alone,—they are admitted to membership in civil society, but the good things to which the pursuits of society are in fact directed turn out to be no good things for them. Civil society is founded on the idea of there being a common good, but that idea in relation to the less favored members of society is unrealized, and it is unrealized because the good is being sought in objects which admit of being competed for."

And this brings us to the fourth point under discussion. The first point was, the reader will recall, our consciousness of absolute obligation and good; the second, the fact that this good consists in the perfections of persons in society; the third, that the search for this perfection has been the source of the institutions, habits, and aspirations of society, and has found expression and got meaning in them; and the fourth, that the moral character of the individual is based upon the extent to which he is loyal to the good embodied in these institutions, in the family, the realm of social relations, and in the kingdom of God on earth, and upon the degree in which he endeavors to react upon these institutions so as to embody in them more fully the freedom of humanity. It is not enough that man should conform faithfully to the ideals already articulated in the social relations about him; he must remember the infinite nature of this ideal; the infinite capacities yet unrealized. And thus the temper of the individual—so far as he is what he should be—is a spiritual act which may be described either as self-abasement or self-exaltation. "Towards an infinite spirit, which is really the only ideal, the attitude of man, at his highest and completest, could still be only that of self-abasement before an ideal of holiness," and yet this attitude must be "one in which the heart is lifted up to God, in which the whole inner man goes forth after an ideal of personal holiness." Awe and aspiration, the sources of all achievements in history, of all advance in individual life, must be, when all is said and done, the final form of human endeavor,—awe, marking the individual's sense of the petty achievements of himself and of humanity before the realities and requirements of the Infinite Spirit; aspiration, as the realization that this Infinite Spirit is still one in principle with man's spirit, and is, therefore, to be forever aimed at. The most perfect expressions of the moral life may be said to be found in the spirit of the expressions of St. Paul to the Philippians: "I count not myself to have apprehended: but this one thing I do, forgetting those things which are behind and reaching forth unto those things which are before, I press towards the mark for the prize of the high calling of God in Christ Jesus,"—the lowest humility as to self, conjoined with the highest aspiration for self.

This, then, is the sum of the matter. The Spirit of God, of the eternal Reason and Will, which is one with our spirit, because it is one, presents itself to man as the perfect good, and as the source of unconditional duty. As so presenting itself, it has moved man to action, and this action has found expression in history, in the institutions, the laws, the customs, and the expectations, the rights and duties that make our life what it is. The individual introduced into the circle of these complex relations finds this social order, this embodiment of divine Reason, confronting him and demanding of him allegiance and loyalty. This social order is thus the source of obligations to the individual; he is bound to loyal service and self-devotion in courage, temperance, wisdom, self-denial, justice. He is bound, not because this order confronts him externally, but because it is the expression of the Spirit that is in him; because it expresses in reality his own being, which is as yet only in capacity. But in fulfilling these duties man learns of other duties and of other goods. He finds that his highest achievements come short of answering even to the demands which actual institutions and laws make upon him, and he finds that these actual institutions are, after all, but feeble and imperfect expressions of the Spirit which makes him and them what they are in possibility as well as in fact. And thus he finds his highest good in what are sometimes called the "religious virtues," in faith, in humility, in awe, in aspiration, in longing for the union of man's will with God's. But these virtues are one in source and principle with the commonest virtues of everyday life. The attitude of will that finds expression in them finds expression in every recognition of duty, in every attempt by which man sets himself to better himself and others, in every service which the father does in the family, which the citizen performs in the state in the interest of the good of the family and of the state.

What has just been said gives an opportunity for a brief statement of Green's religious views. Religious, it is evident, his whole theory is. Science and the moral life—both are based on the communication to us of a divine, perfect Spirit. Science is inexplicable except upon the supposition of an eternal, all-inclusive Intelligence which reproduces itself in us; the life of duty and of the good is this communication in us of the divine Reason and Will. It would be to be false to the memory of Green to attempt to identify his theories with extraneous creeds, or to attempt to win favor for his philosophy by claiming its agreement with any form of orthodoxy, or by relieving it of any kinship with views that are unpopular. The intellectual sincerity of Green, perfect to human eye, would rebuke any such effort. But since Mrs. Ward so evidently means Grey for Professor Green, and since the two are being popularly identified, it is but historic justice to say that Green's religious teaching goes farther than the position just laid down. Green undoubtedly held that in Jesus Christ this communication of God, which in us, at best, is partial and hindered by seeking of the private self, was perfect and pure. Christ was to Green, in actuality, what every man is in capacity; He was in reality what we are in idea. Undoubtedly he held that Christ was subject to the same physical conditions and possessed of the same physical powers as all men; he would allow neither a miraculous birth nor miraculous, that is, supernatural power; but morally and spiritually, he held Christ to have embodied in his personality perfect union with the Spirit of God. Furthermore, the self-abasement and the self-exaltation which are the highest attainments of the moral life find their adequate expression in language when termed sharing in the death and resurrection of Christ. For it is the death and resurrection of Jesus as eternal facts, as the fundamental expressions of the true life of the Spirit, that are of avail to us. We share in the death of Christ when we share in his spirit of absolute sacrifice of all self-seeking and selfish interest and will; we share in his resurrection when we share in the unity of his Spirit and Will with God's. For the resurrection is the other side of the crucifixion; it is the life of the Spirit, as the crucifixion is the death of the flesh. The desire of St. Paul that he may forget the things that are behind, and reach forth unto the things that are before, also finds expression in his aspiration to know the fellowship of Christ's suffering, to be made comformable unto his death, if by any means he may attain unto the resurrection of the dead. And this is the highest expression of the ethics of Professor Green. We are saved, to use the theological formula, so far as there really is in us interrupted, imperfect, partial though it be, union with that death and resurrection which in Christ was eternal, perfect, and entire.

The Lesson of Contemporary French Literature

Among the youngest French critics it is Bourget, perhaps, who wears the mantle of Sainte-Beuve. The older writer did not live in the stress of modern science, and his work is more personal and genial, while the abstract and philosophic tendencies often master Bourget. But the latter is yet the inheritor of the spirit of the former. They both understand the word "critic" in the same sense. With each it means putting one's self at the standpoint of the author and seeing what he sees, but with the additional advantage of knowing why he sees as he does. While it is still a rarity to find an English critic who will sympathize enough with a writer to comprehend him, Sainte-Beuve founded a school whose first word is that sympathy is the sole condition of comprehension. And while the English critic who does sympathize and understand usually becomes an enthusiast, a partisan, the French critic remembers that the function of criticism is not exhausted when the meaning of an author is penetrated and exhibited; we must know also the forces which led him, the causes which influenced him in his thought. Criticism, in a word, as understood by the French, is the ability to stand with and outside of an author at the same time. Sympathy and detachment are its mottoes.

Bourget's *Essais de Psychologie Contemporaine* suggests by its very title the characteristics of the essays contained in it. It is not the psychology of the schools; as the word is ordinarily used, it is not psychology at all. But it is criticism of the souls of the writers passed in review. Its aim

[*First published in the* Christian Union, *XL* (*11 July 1889*), 38–39. *Not previously reprinted.*]

is not external description, but internal penetration. It is psychological analysis of the French spirit as revealed in its representative authors; it is the dissection of their thoughts, their emotions, their attitude toward the problems of life. These volumes, then, are something more than endeavors to give various poets and essayists their relative standings. In the thoroughness and subtlety with which they track thoughts back to their germ, in the grasp in which they hold these thoughts connected with the contemporary movements of life, they become intellectual history—a picture of the French consciousness. And it is as such a record that I wish to present them here. Bourget is a critic, not a moralist; and yet there is more textual matter for the moralist in these two small volumes than in many bulky ethical dissertations. They show us the spiritual bankruptcy of the current thinking of a great nation; and they show its origin. Bourget is not a preacher; but his volumes are a comment on one small text: "Without faith ye can do nothing."

But Bourget shall speak for himself. What does he find to be the characteristic note of contemporary French emotion and thought? Hear him. His first volume closes with the words: "I have examined a poet, Baudelaire; a historian, Renan; a novelist, Flaubert; a philosopher, Taine; I have just finished examining one of these composite artists in whom the critic and the creative writer are closely united [Stendhal]; and I have found in all five the same creed of the thoroughgoing emptiness of the universe. These magnificent minds are completely nauseated with the vain strivings of life." His second volume begins: "From all the works passed in review in these ten essays there seems to breathe the same uneasy influence—an influence profoundly and continuously pessimistic." Everywhere, he concludes, is there to be found the gradual enfeebling and paralysis of the will; the decay of hope, courage, and endeavor; the growing belief that the world is a bankrupt, passing paper notes which it cannot redeem.

But the interest does not center in this general conclusion. It gathers about the analysis of the various influences which have shaped this pessimism, and the various forms which it takes. Of the many which Bourget signalizes, we shall select three: dilettanteism, the influence of physical science, and (very briefly) romanticism. It is Renan who affords the occasion for the study of dilettanteism—a term, as Bourget remarks, difficult to define, for it represents rather an attitude of mind than a formulated doctrine. The term, in his use of it, however, means something more than a mere playing at everything. Its significance may be understood when we find that, according to him, Goethe is the great dilettante. It is love of culture for itself. It is capacity for emotional and intellectual metamorphosis, and a capacity which finds constant exercise. It is not far different from the brutal definition by an English writer of liberalism: the feeling that so many things in general are true that nothing in particular is very true. It is, more delicately expressed, a disposition which induces a thinker to lend himself to all points of view without giving himself to any. Its favorite expression is of "shades" of truth. There is no white light; there is an infinite number of shades.

It is not, then, to be confounded with skepticism. It is not inability to discover truth; it is a surfeit of truths. It is not the weariness of mind which says that there is so much to be said on every side of a question that no good comes of investigation; it is the very height of mental agility which plays about all these sides and successively realizes them. It can assert nothing absolutely; there must be the reservation in favor of the contrary also—also, mark you, and not instead. Life, truth, and reality are complex. They cannot be grasped as wholes. Nay, how shall dogmatism go so far as to say that they are wholes? They must be grasped here and there. We get at fragments, and each shift of the kaleidoscope is as true as any other. Hence the true dilettante must refuse to give himself up to any creed, for decisions imply a fixity of mind not consistent with the ability of the soul to vibrate with every note of truth. Every conclusion is an exclusion. Experience is composite, flexile, many-sided. Decisions are hard, fast, and rigorously limited.

If this is not skepticism, it comes to the same result. The part of the wise man is to take no part. His business is to comprehend the dreams of others—nay, more, to let them play through his soul, that he may realize all there is in life, and yet to remember that as one goes another comes which may contradict it. When there are so many values in the world, who shall assert an absolute value? Thus dilettanteism leads to pessimism. It is not the wild pessimism of the nihilist; it is not the soured pessimism of Schopenhauer; it is the mild and tender consciousness that the doom of transitoriness is upon all aspects of life, upon all forms of what we call truth. The sentiment that all shades of belief have their own relative justification, that from its own standpoint each is as true as any other, is, in reality, the sentiment that no belief has justification. Such a feeling is pessimistic, for it finds that the universe takes no sides; it is more than impartial—it is indifferent. The world of the lover of culture has no bias in favor of anything—not even of truth and goodness. It teaches but one thing—the hopelessness of action which is more than playing with various forms of experience in order to obtain from them some self-development. Its imperative is only: Do not give yourself to any; use them only for your own rounded development. And since men have never been able long to persuade themselves that their value is more than that of the universe, the result is pessimism. One cannot but wish that he could follow in detail the application by Bourget of these thoughts to the *credo* of Renan, but we must content ourselves with this impersonal exposition.

This love of many-sided personal development is not the only tendency working for pessimism. Flaubert, De Lisle, Taine, exemplify, if we trust Bourget, a pessimism resulting from the effect of physical science upon the imagination and the emotions. Realism and naturalism are, as he shows, the outcome of the application of scientific methods to human life. The procedure of realism is to start from the exact representation of a group of facts, and then analyze these till we discover their causes. Such a method has no place for personality or character. Such words are only terms which point out a particular set of effects. They are products of antecedent and surrounding forces. Literature becomes a study of heredity and environment. Human nature is simply one part of physical nature. Reason and health are, in Taine's words, happy accidents. Physical nature is a series of ceaseless changes, every change having its cause, and every change having its justification in this cause. From the standpoint of physical science (that is, leaving out purposes or ends), disease is as natural as health, insanity as sanity. Each has its antecedent cause, and what more can you ask for? To quote Taine again: "Moral beings as well as physical are a series of events of which nothing is permanent except the law of change. Nature is one vast aurora borealis." Necessity and change—these are the two conceptions of physical science, and, applied to the treatment of human life in literature, they resolve all human aspirations, loves, and ideals into the insignificant outcome of petty changes. All hope is vain, all effort is fruitless, all aspiration unavailing. Thus there arises from another instrument the swelling tone of the worthlessness of life—the tone of a saddened pessimism. Nature responds to the simulacrum of personality with the ruthless ongoing of blind changes; we can but yield ourselves, and in yielding give up the possibility of moral action and of religious faith. Life is shorn and empty.

Romanticism, again, has proved a tributary to pessimism. Romanticism is the attempt to find the satisfaction of life in the enjoyment of intense emotions; in the constant renewal of feeling; in the production of remote and unwonted forms of sentiment. If the dilettante would put himself in all modes of looking at experience, the romanticist would revel in all moods and ranges of emotion. A varied play of passion is his aim. A succession of vast and ever-changing feelings gives life its value. If the traditions and environment of human life do not admit such a succession, flee to far-away times, to the mediæval age, to lands of chivalry, to fairy countries, or, planting yourself in the present epoch, rebel. As it is law which keeps men in grooves, which forbids them the sought-for stream of emotions, disregard law. As it is especially family life which restricts the display of feeling to the channel, away with family life, and in with the freedom of feeling! In all ways and at hazards, fresh, vivid, and continual emotion! Such was the cry of the romanticists in the instances analyzed by Bourget.

But such a banner could lead its adherents to but one field, that of pessimism. The world is not in harmony with such an ideal. The school staked its belief in the worth of life upon the one point whether life affords the desired abundance and intensity of passions; and it found every passion a pathway to a grave. Lord Byron will serve the English reader as an example both of romanticism and of the pessimism which is its inevitable outcome. Flight and rebellion are both in vain. The every-day world is too much for us, and brings us back to a hard routine. Even escape and rebellion leave us with emotions jaded and with no capacity for renewal.

So much, in substance, we may gather from Bourget as he pursues his studies into the influences which made the style and thought of the representatives of the best French literature of the last fifty years. Hugo is almost the only name of the first rank which does not come within his scope. And everywhere—again in his own words—a nausea of these splendid minds at the emptiness of life. Such a tale tells its own moral without the added index finger of *Hæc fabula docet*. Without faith ye can do nothing, ye are nothing. It is something more than decay of faith in this or that doctrine of Christianity, of this or that dogma of the Church, of this or that school of ecclesiasticism. It is lack of faith in the supremacy of spiritual things; nay, in their reality. It is bankruptcy of idealism; it is apotheosis of the things that can be seen and handled. It tells in modern tones and in strange garb the tale of old, that if hope be confined to the things grasped of the senses, and by the culture of the intellect, and in the play of emotions, then is life indeed most miserable. In the moral determination of the will lie peace, hope, and courage; and the moral determination of the will comes not from the culture of the intellect, from the methods of physical science, nor the abundance of pleasure. It is born of faith in unseen ideals. The intellect may set up a multitude of ideals, and find some value in each. It may set off each against the other. Pure intellectualism is dilettanteism. But choice, moral choice, breaks the equilibrium, and asserts the absolute value of one. Such an act of faith declares that even if the universe seems to the intellect indifferent to all ideals, it at least *will* have an ideal of life by which it will measure all, and for which it will stake all. Leave out faith, and you have in human life level plains of equal richness, each bounded with the horizon of ignorance, and with paths leading everywhere and therefore nowhere. Put in faith, and there is perspective; there is background and foreground; there is goal and way. So, too, the methods of physical science, pure naturalism, lead to pessimism simply because they do not allow that free movement of personality called choice. The sole method of manifesting the reality of personality is for personality to manifest itself in the act which chooses the ideal of absolute value. Back of this choice must lie faith in the supreme reality of such an ideal. Faith involves the determination that personality shall not be the playground of natural forces, but shall itself be a moving force counting for something in the universe. Given faith, the pessimism which results from the conclusions of natural science becomes a buoyant faith that the very natural processes are the tributary mechanisms of an end, a purpose, an ideal which does not manifest itself to the eye of sense. Romanticism, again, is the attempt to state the value of life in terms of that which can be immediately experienced, of feeling. It is denial of a criterion which, though unseen, shall serve to measure all that is seen and felt. Each of these three influences reduces itself, then, to lack of faith, to denial of the power of man to lay hold on spiritual reality. This study of French literature but gives an added testimony to the fact that the problem of the nineteenth century reduces itself to a choice between faith and pessimism. In the things which are seen and temporal lies no permanent satisfaction; in the things which are unseen and eternal lies the value of that which passes away.

Galton's Statistical Methods

Natural Inheritance, by Francis Galton, F.R.S. London and New York: Macmillan and Co., 1889. ix, 259 pp.

This work is of double interest. Its primary purpose is biological, being to subject the question of heredity to accurate quantitative and mechanical treatment. As such it is doubtless the ablest work on the subject extant. But in the course of his investigation Galton has collected a large mass of statistical information, and, what is more important, has developed some new and interesting statistical methods. The key-note to the statistical side of the work is contained in Galton's statement that statisticians are apt to be content with averages, while an average is only an isolated fact. What is wanted is a method of *calculating distribution*, and a graphic scheme for reading the distribution. For example, compared with the knowledge of the average income of an English family, a knowledge of how the total income of England was distributed would be much more important. This would tell us the proportion which had incomes of every grade from the lowest to the highest, and would enable us to rank any given family at its place in the scale.

Particularly, in dealing with problems of heredity, is a scheme of distribution necessary. The knowledge of the average stature of a kinsfolk conveys little; the knowledge of how this faculty is distributed among the members of the kindred would be valuable. Galton's first work was to invent

[*First published in the* Publications of the American Statistical Association, *N.S. I (Sept. 1889), 331–34. Not previously reprinted.*]

a scheme of distribution. The data to be dealt with, for example, are the strength of pull of 519 males as registered on a Salter's machine. The following are the figures: –

Strength of pull	*Percentage*
Under 50 pounds, ...	2
" 60 "	10
" 70 "	37
" 80 "	70
" 90 "	91
" 100 "	95
Over 100 "	100

This might be illustrated by a diagram: –

The percentages of strength are marked off on a base line, the number of pounds on the right-hand perpendicular line. Then from each per cent, 2, 10, 37, etc., is erected a perpendicular to a height equal to the corresponding number of pounds, –*i.e.*, from 37 per cent would be erected a perpendicular to a height equal to 70 pounds, since 37 per cent pulled less than 70 pounds. While a line connecting these various perpendiculars will be broken, it is evident that, if the data were numerous enough, and the strengths more closely taken, say to every pound, we would get, approximately, a curved line. The figure, bounded by a curve of this kind is a scheme of distribution. (The perpendiculars, since they serve only for scaffolding, would not apppear in an ordinary scheme.) By taking the measured strength of any individual on the side scale, say 74 pounds, carrying over a horizontal line until it meets the curve, and then dropping a perpendicular to meet the base line, the proportionate rank of the individual may be read off, – in this case 50 degrees. In other words, since 50 per cent exceed and 50 per cent fall short of his strength, he occupies a medium position, and his strength is mediocre. This position Galton always designates by M, and this M is always one of the chief constants in Galton's scheme. He notes that the M has three properties. The chance is an equal one that any previously unknown rank falls short of or exceeds M. The most probable value of any previously unknown measure is M; and, if the curve of the scheme is bilaterally symmetrical as respects M, M is identical with the ordinary average or arithmetical mean. It is evident that we have the start for an application of the theory of probability. Now, if the deviation of any grade from M is considered, that is, the error as respects the mean, we find that every measure in a scheme may be expressed by M + (±D), the + or − signifying up or down from M.

Galton's other constant he designates by Q. It is obtained as follows. Take the perpendicular at 75°, and that at 25°. Subtract the latter from the former and divide by 2, and we get a measure of the general *slope* of the curve of distribution, just as M measures the average height of the curved boundary. What it *really* gives is the deviation from the average, both in excess and in deficiency, of one half the number taken. For example, the Q of the scheme of distribution of stature is 1.7 inches. This means that one half the population differs less than 1.7 inches one way or the other from the average of the whole population.

Now, although this Q stands on its own independent basis, and can be derived from any scheme by dividing the differences of the ranks of 25° and 75° by 2, if the curve is symmetrical, it will be identical with what the mathematicians call the Probable Error. It thus becomes possible to apply the whole calculus of probability to any data capable of being expressed in a normal case of the scheme.

As matter of fact, Galton found a remarkable parallelism between results obtained by observation and those theoretically deduced from the mathematicial calculations. He took, for example, eighteen schemes of distribution, including stature, weight, breathing capacity, strength of blow, keenness of sight, for both sexes, calculated the Q in each, or the measure of deviation that half the deviations exceeded, and half fell short of, and then calculated a mean Q, as it were, for the whole eighteen. The result differs but little from that theoretically obtained by the law of frequency of error. It is evident that Galton might express his scheme in the well-known curve of error, but his curve of distribution contains all that the curve of error contains, and much besides.

For the particular results obtained, I must refer to the

book itself. One is so remarkable that it may be specified. If we call the M of the stature of the whole population P, and the mean stature of the parents P ± D, the stature of the offspring will be, on the average, P ± ⅓D. In other words, upon the average, children of parents who are exceptional, or who deviate from the mean, will themselves deviate from the mean only one third of their parents' deviation. Considering the character of his results, it is not wonderful that Galton says: "I know of scarcely anything so apt to impress the imagination as the wonderful form of cosmic order expressed by the 'law of the frequency of error.' The law would have been personified by the Greeks and deified if they had known of it. It is the supreme law of Unreason. Whenever a large sample of chaotic elements are taken in hand, and marshaled in the order of their magnitude, an unsuspected and most beautiful form of regularity proves to have been latent all along."

It is to be hoped that statisticians working in other fields, as the industrial and monetary, will acquaint themselves with Galton's development of new methods, and see how far they can be applied in their own fields. It is, of course, clear that any data dealing with the proportions of distribution of anything whatever can be diagrammatically expressed in Galton's scheme; but if it is to be anything more than a picture for the eye, it must be possible to establish an M and a Q from which the entire scheme of deviations and their relations may be, in turn, deduced, at least approximately. In other words, such a scheme, if its curve were wholly irregular, would not be likely to yield any results. Furthermore, no curve is likely to be regular unless it expresses traits which are the result of accidents, that is, of circumstances which *do* bring about certain results, though they were not intended for that purpose. For example, if we had (what we are not likely to have) accurate data regarding the accumulation of wealth in families from parents to children, there is no great reason for expecting that in two generations we would get results akin to those of Galton regarding natural heredity. The tendency of wealth to breed wealth, as illustrated by any interest table, and the tendency of extreme poverty to induce conditions which plunge children still deeper into poverty, would probably prevent the operation of the law of regression toward mediocrity. It is not likely that children of the poor would be better off, and children of the wealthier poorer in anything like the ratio of ⅔. But if we took generations enough, the operation of "accidents," such as imprudent, extravagant, and dissipated habits among the children of the rich, the growth of new industrial conditions which lessen the value of old forms of wealth, the emergence of money-makers among the poor, the development of social relations which would increase the ambition and chances of the poor, etc., we might find a similar law. That is, these accidents, or circumstances which, although in themselves irrelevant to the distribution of wealth, yet in the long run, largely determine it, would pelt down as it were the swells in the curve, and bulge out its depressions into something like a normal curve of distribution. Whether or not there is any truth in our example, it will serve to illustrate the nature of the data to which Galton's methods may be applied.

Ethics in the University of Michigan

I suppose I may best supply what is desired if I first say something about the ethical courses to be given in the collegiate year 1889–90, considered as parts of the University curriculum, and then go on to say something of their standpoint and purpose. The only required courses in philosophy in the University are those in logic and psychology, one or other of which must be taken by all candidates for degrees, excepting by the students in the various engineering courses. Psychology is required precedent to the first course in Ethics. This is a lecture course of two hours per week, given in the second semester of the year, and is taken mainly by Juniors. Following this course is a lecture course of two hours per week in Political Philosophy,—taken accordingly mainly by Seniors. In the second semester comes a seminary course in Political Philosophy, which may be taken by candidates for advanced degrees, and by undergraduates, if they are deemed suitably prepared. In recent years special courses in the Ethics of Plato, of Aristotle and of Kant have been given, but it happens that no one of them is upon the programme for this year.

The first course in Ethics is a purely general one; its aim is theoretical rather than historical or practical. The greater number of students in ethics take also the course in the History of Philosophy, three times a week through the year; and this, together with the criticism of various systems in the course in Ethics, is relied upon to give sufficient historical data. Readings and reports by the students are required; the references being to such authors as Aristotle, Plato, Hume, Kant, Mill, Spencer, Stephen, Green, Martineau, etc. For convenience the subject is discussed under three heads. The first is the theory of the Moral Ideal; the second, the objective Moral World; the third, the Concrete

[*First published in the* Ethical Record, *II (Oct. 1889), 145–48. Not previously reprinted.*]

Moral Life of the Individual. The aim of the first part is to discover the ethical ideal,—or answer the question, What is the chief end of man. The question is discussed largely on a basis of comparative criticism; the hedonistic theory, in its simplest form of individualism, and in its development in utilitarianism, and through the theory of evolution, is discussed; then is discussed the so-called theological ethics, as represented by Paley, and the theory of formal obligation, as represented by Kant; and while the attempt is made to recognize the truth in each of the previous forms, it is finally concluded that only the theory that the ideal of conduct is realization of personality answers all the demands of the problem. The same discussions that give conclusions regarding the ideal are shown to answer the problems regarding the basis and nature of obligation, and the nature of goodness. In the second part it is shown that the realization of personality both demands and occasions society, or the community of those having common interests and purposes, regulating themselves by common laws (implicit, conventional, or reflective), and recognizing common rights. This society with its substratum of expectations, institutions, laws and rights is characterized as the objective ethical world, as real in its way as the "external world" is physically. The various forms of this world in the family, the nation, the structure of industrial society, and the church, with their underlying principles, are briefly set forth. In the third part, the individual born into this world, and having to realize the ethical ideal in and through it is considered. In this connection are discussed the way in which the individual becomes aware of moral distinctions, the conditions of his freedom of action, the nature of his concrete duties and rights, and the modes of moral progress in the individual.

The second course, the one in Political Philosophy, begins by stating the various answers which have been given to the questions, first of the nature and origin of the state; secondly, of its functions; and, thirdly, of its constitution and forms. The outline of the subject being brought before the student in this comparative way, the same ground is gone over again from a different stand-point. First is taken up the general theory of society, as a natural (or biological) organism, and its gradual development into an ethical organism through the emergence of rational will is discussed. This ethical organism is shown to involve the political organization of mankind in the state. The function of the state is defined as the guaranteeing, defining, and extending of rights. This necessitates a discussion of the nature of rights, which really forms the backbone of the course. The basis of rights, the theory of "natural" and "positive" rights, the various forms of rights, are taken up. This gives occasion for consideration of questions relating to property, punishment, war, etc., which are discussed at some length. The nature and aim of law is then discussed on the basis of the results regarding rights. The lectures then take up questions relating to the actual constitution of the state, the division of its powers, its various forms as aristocracy, democracy, etc., the tendencies and limits of present legislation. The latter topic leads up to the questions of legislation as respects the family, industrial relations, etc., and in this connection are considered some of the practical problems regarding marriage and the labor question. The course closes with a brief critical discussion of current political ideals, aiming to point out the practical and morally valid aims of national life. The subject of the seminary course for 1889–90 is Special Subjects in the History of Political Philosophy. It is difficult to form the exact line which a course of this nature will take, but the intention is to make as exhaustive a study as possible of the various allied theories of the "state of nature," natural rights and the social contract theory, taking up these topics on the basis of such authors as Hobbes, Grotius, Locke, and Rousseau.

That these courses are limited in extent as well as in number is evident; with but two instructors it is impossible to do much special work in ethics without the neglect of other departments in philosophy. Another year a course will probably be offered in the Ethics of Plato, Kant or Hegel. The limited amount of the work in ethics has been less noticeable in the past because of the profound ethical spirit in which the lamented Professor Morris carried on all his work in philosophy, and which he imparted so successfully to all his instruction.

A College Course: What Should I Expect from It?

What should I expect from a college course? is, I believe, the question, my courteous editors of the *Castalian*, which you wish me to answer. It will not be out of the way, I suppose, to take the "I" who is the subject of this expectation as meaning you, me, anybody, what Walt Whitman calls "the common, that is, the divine average." There are certain things which I presume we should all pretty much agree upon. A man ought to expect a body, a physical tool, which is sound, and pliable to his purposes. He ought to have learned the rights of the body, and that these rights cannot be destroyed, nor the body cheated of them. The expectation of so many students in so many generations that the mind can be cultivated along with a systematic and continued neglect, or abuse of the physical system should be abandoned, by one and all, in the year 1890. There are certain intellectual gifts which the average student, and he below the average, should expect, while the very best student may beware lest he fall short. A certain range of information, a certain amount of learning, a mental discipline, that is, a quality of mind at once flexible and concentrated in dealing with new material, a certain attitude of mind, a mental openness and eagerness—these things should be expected almost as a matter of course. And certainly there are some moral results which should come too. One ought—whether one does or not—to expect a training of will, a cultivating and maturing of character, a reverence for truth wherever found, freedom from self-conceit and respect

[*First published in the* Castalian, *Published by the Independents of the Senior Class, University of Michigan, V* (*1890*), *26–29. Not previously reprinted.*]

for the opinions of others, sympathy for their purposes, a highness of aim in the affairs of one's life agreeable to the opportunities enjoyed, belief in whatsoever things are true and lovely and of good report. Because such expectations are so normal and so obvious, if I should attempt to enforce them I should probably run either into the Scylla of mere moralisms, or into the Charybdis of a straining for the novel. And yet in attempting to say anything upon this topic, I do not imagine that I shall, after all, do more than repeat these same things—*Nur mit ein bischen andern Worten.* Whether I shall come to my goal with less of the ballast of commonplace or of the top-sail of paradox on account of a roundabout course may perhaps be doubted.

One thing, then, that a University education should do for a man is to rid him of his provincialisms. We all—or almost all—of us come out from a sphere of life somewhat narrower than that into which we come. The question is whether in this emergence we come out of our shells, or bring them with us. Certainly the boy or girl who comes to college judging all things from the standpoint of the way they think and do "in my place," ought to have his horizon of outlook pushed out a little further, and his standard of measurement lengthened. There may be touches of provincialism in manner which nothing but actual contacts will destroy, or which will always remain as the outer tokens of a sturdy, genuine and "home-keeping" spirit. But the voyage one takes in entering college life is a voyage to a far port, and through many countries foreign in space, in time, in manner of speech and thought. If such travelling of the spirit does not remove the narrow and small cast of one's opinion and methods it is failing of its aim. The Germans call the period of youthful culture a period of "self-alienation," because in it the mind gives up its immediate interests and goes on this far journey. Let a man learn on this journey to lay aside the suit, the habit, of mental clothes woven and cut for him in his native village, and to don the foreign costumes. If he be called to wear again his old suit, he will wear it the more easily and naturally for knowing something of the fashion of other men's garments.

And when one gives up his provincialisms let him

make the renunciation complete. Partisanship, of whatever sort, or however disguised, is but provincialism of a larger growth and more imposing mien. The lesson is harder learned; the sacrifice seems greater. It is easy to take boisterousness of thought and expression for earnestness of conviction; the thoughtless assimilation of opinion from an authority already, probably, second-handed, for strength and originality of mind. To be in doubt, to suspend judgment, to await the conviction which can come only from the fact—all this seems weakness. The breadth of sympathy which feels that the world of truth is a sphere which comes into itself again, the fairness of judgment which will know both sides, and the thoroughness which will know even the inside—all this seems like needless painstaking, like unpractical theorizing, in a word, what the newspaper writers call "Mugwumpery." But all this ought a man to expect from his college course. Its name is Freedom.

And finally, a student should expect from his college course a sense of the due proportion and right values of the various interests which may claim his attention. He should find out where their centre of gravity is, and this, not as a matter of theory, but as a practical insight which may serve him instinctively in the affairs of life. He should have ingrained within him the subordination of all learning, of all the sciences and all the arts, to social relationships and sympathies. Cardinal Newman, in one of the few educational books of the world which are neither priggish nor impractical, *The Idea of a University*, says that if he were asked to choose between a university which gave degrees upon examination in all subjects to students without residence and without tutorial supervision, and a university which had no professors or examinations at all, but simply brought a number of young men together for three or four years and then sent them away again, he should "have no hesitation in giving the preference to that university which did nothing, over that which exacted of its members an acquaintance with every science under the sun." And his reason is that an education without the *human* element would produce a generation frivolous, narrow-minded and resourceless, while the contact of "a multitude of young men keen, open-hearted, sympathetic, and observant" would constantly bring out new ideas and views, fresh matter of thought and distinct principles for judging and acting. Above all it would secure a training in the relations and uses of those elements of knowledge necessary for our social being. Free contact of men and women will, at least, produce a "community constituting a whole, it will embody a specific idea, it will represent a doctrine, it will administer a code of conduct, and it will furnish principles of thought and action." In a word, it will develop an ethical atmosphere, and this will secure, as far as it goes, a real intellectual training, for it induces the recognition that "knowledge is something more than a sort of passive reception of scraps and details; it is something, and it does a something."

I have made my quotation somewhat extended, but the idea conveyed seems to me the root of all right ideas about University training. The permanent and fruitful outcome of a college education should be the training of one's *human* nature. This training alone is really practical and preparatory for life, for it alone is ethical. It is the only basis of a genuine intellectual culture, for only as all the studies of a college course find a unity in the human, in the social, do they become more than scraps and fragments. Relationship to man, to his interests and purposes, takes the dust of specialism out of its barren isolation and vitalizes it into germinant principles. With all his getting, then, the college student should require of his college course that it give him that sense of the proportions and right values which can come only of centering all studies in their human relationships.

But all this is rather intangible, you will say, to one who wishes some definite instructions as to what he should expect from his college course. Undoubtedly; but the kingdom of heaven, in learning as in other matters, cometh not with observation. The general effects, the internal results, those which give the set and fix the attitude of the spirit, are the real effects of the college education. The average graduate may have no ready answer to the inquiry five years after his graduation, what use he now makes of all his learning, of his Greek, his Mathematics, his Old High German and his knowledge of Kant's *Critiques*. If he is wise, his thoughts will take somewhat this form: "All this is a matter of no account. The thing of importance is whether I have my interests trained to alert action and ready and wide vibration. Am I avoiding stagnation, both the apparent stagnation of mental idleness, and that stagnation which simulates the form of action but is the mere vacant repetition and imitation of the thoughts of others? Above all, are my sympathies with whatever touches humanity, nearly or remotely, broad and dominant? If so, the Philistine may return to Gath; my college course has fulfilled its purpose, I have the *unum necessarium*—the one thing needful."

On Some Current Conceptions of the Term "Self"

I.

It is the aim of this paper to analyze certain conceptions involved in the terms Self and Self-consciousness as currently used. No attempt will be made to judge of the value of the ideas themselves. Indeed, there is such confusion in the use of the conceptions that an independent analysis of them would seem to be a necessary preliminary to any decision upon their validity. Whether or not philosophy is exhausted in the clearing-up of conceptions, it is certain that without an occasional clearing-up philosophy will get so entangled in the *impedimenta* of its own notions as to be hindered in its onward march. Unless this analysis is confined to ideas having or claiming to have some community of meaning, it will include ideas wholly incomparable with one another, and thus end in a mere account of the way in which various writers use the same word. A study of the terminology of philosophy is, no doubt, helpful; but, as that is not intended in this paper, I shall confine my analysis to the conception of the "transcendental self"—to the idea of self which has affiliations with the movement set going by Kant, however divergent its various developments.

For a starting-point, and to a certain extent for a basis, Professor Seth's recent work, *Hegelianism and Personality*, presents itself as convenient, occupied, as it so largely is, with just this notion of the self. In that work, three separate conceptions—used, however, interchangeably—may be dis-

[*First published in* Mind, *XV (Jan. 1890), 58–74. Not reprinted during the author's lifetime.*]

criminated. In the first place, we have it laid down that "the self *is* the world, and the world is the self. The self and the world are only two sides of the same reality: they are the same intelligible world looked at from two opposite points of view. . . . The mind and the world, subject and object, are convertible terms; we may talk indifferently of the one or the other: the content of our notion remains the same in both cases" (pp. 19–20). This result is based upon an examination of Kant's transcendental inquiry and method which is, so far as quoted above, accepted, to all appearances, by Professor Seth. The meaning of this view of the self may stand out more plainly if we call attention to another feature of it. This is that the "ultimate fact of knowledge is neither pure subject nor pure object" (p. 13). These are both abstractions: to separate them, to make independent existences of them, is to "substantiate abstractions." In truth, the self is a synthetic unity. "It binds together, as related members of one whole, what would otherwise fall apart as unrelated particulars; and, moreover, it is only through this synthesis that the unity of the Self or Ego exists. It is the unity *of* the synthesis, and, apart from its synthetic activity, would no more be real than the particulars of sense would be real without its action." It cannot be identified, in other words, with the mere act of uniting: it includes within itself what is united, just as, on the other hand, what is united has no existence outside of its being united. Because this is so—because, as Professor Seth expresses it (p. 19), "the form is the form *of* the matter, and the matter is, as it were, simply the exhibition of the form"—the self and the world are correlative, and have the same content.

This, then, is the first notion conveyed by the term self—the self is the correlative of the intelligible world. Its content is that of the intelligible world. It even *is* the intelligible world in one of its aspects. And since Professor Seth has expounded with great force the notion that the intelligible world is the only real world, that the unknowable to intelligence is "nonsense" (*Scottish Philosophy*, p. 162), we may say that, according to this notion, the self is one with the real world, when this is considered in its ultimate unity. This view is clear and self-consistent; with its truth we have nothing to do. But we find that the question as to the nature of the transcendental self has not been sufficiently answered. The question is again raised: What is the transcendental self? (*Hegelianism*, top of p. 22). And the question is answered in a way which seems to me the exact opposite of the answer just given. It now turns out that the transcendental Ego represents *merely* the *formal* unity of the universe (p. 27). Although the self was shown to be a single self, its singularity is simply that which belongs to every abstract notion—a logical identity of type (p. 29). It is the "notion of knowledge in general" (p. 30). And, finally, Kant's characterizations of it are quoted. It is "a merely logical qualitative unity of self-consciousness in thought generally." It is a "logical exposition of thought in general" (p. 35). It is, finally, the "mere form of self-consciousness in general" (p. 230).

I confess that, to me, this second position, that the self is merely the formal unity of thought, appears to be the contrary of the first position taken by Professor Seth. There the self was not formal; the form was an abstraction apart from matter. Kant was then rebuked for making the self formal. The necessity of correlating matter and form was the fundamental feature of the transcendental method. So far was the self from being merely formal that it was the world. Instead of being merely logical, the self was the unified universe; it was a synthetic unity which had no existence apart from the particulars unified in the synthesis. But in this second and revised view, Kant is praised for his superior consistency in holding that the self arrived at by his investigation is an abstract condition and not a metaphysical reality or concrete fact (p. 28). The subject which "exists only as the unity of the manifold whose central principle of connexion it is" (p. 17) becomes transformed in ten short pages into a "*focus imaginarius* into which the multiple relations which constitute the intelligible world return"—a "*principle* of unity." To cut short this comparison of contradictory statements, the language first used regarding the self conveys, as clearly as language can convey anything, that the self is objective and real, is ontological; while the second view taken is that the self is merely formal and logical. The first view is that the self and the real cannot be separated without "substantiating abstractions"; the second view is that to unite them is to "hypostatise an abstraction" (p. 30).

But, as we advance further, it appears that the outcome of the transcendental view of the self is not in reality either that the self is the real world, or that the self is a mere logical form or abstract unity of thought. The view which finally emerges is that self is the "ultimate category of thought" (p. 98). So far as the varying expressions permit us to judge, this is Professor Seth's real thought in the matter. It is, at least, the view which is unambiguously reiterated in his "Discussion" in *Mind*, XIV, 117. It is stated once in connection with passages which have been quoted as belonging to the first interpretation: "The transcendental self, as an implicate of all experience, is for a theory of knowledge simply the necessary point of view from which the universe can be unified, that is, from which it becomes a universe" (*Hegelianism*, p. 20). It is elsewhere stated that the transcendental theory of knowledge resolves itself into an immanent criticism of categories, or of the conceptions by which we express and unify our experience. This criticism shows that self-consciousness is the highest category—the most adequate to determine existence. We are thus "justified in using the conception of self-consciousness as our best key to the ultimate nature of existence as a whole" (p. 89). In fine, "self-consciousness is the ultimate category of thought—that through which we think everything else, and through which alone the universe is intelligible to us."

I cannot persuade myself that this third conception of self-consciousness is identical with either of the other two. It means less than the first, which identifies the self with the world; it means more than the second, which makes self-consciousness a merely formal or abstract unity of thought. For it must be remembered that Kant would no more have accepted self-consciousness as the ultimate category of experience, or as a category of experience at all, than he would have accepted it as identical with the real world. In fact, the various expressions which Professor Seth has quoted with approval from Kant are directed as much against making self-consciousness a category of experience as against making it a real self-existent being. How can the "poorest of all our ideas" be the richest and most comprehensive principle of philosophic explanation? The very reason for holding that the self is merely a logical unity of thought is that the self cannot be employed to determine experience at all. But perhaps it may be said that it was just the result of the Hegelian development of the Kantian method and presuppositions to demonstrate that the self, instead of being the emptiest of categories, a conception the sole use of which is to show that all our thoughts are accompanied by consciousness, is the organic system, the reality of all categories. I am not in the least concerned to deny such a contention. But this contention only shows the inadequacy of defining the self as a "merely logical qualitative unity of self-consciousness in thought generally," and not that it is consistent to unite such a view with a view that the self is our ultimate principle of verifying and explaining experience. Indeed, the purpose of Kant in calling the self merely logical was to oppose it to experience; but, when it is said from the point of view of the Hegelian development of Kant that the self is the highest logical category, the idea conveyed is that of the complete correlativity of thought in general, and this thought in particular, to experience. When Kant speaks of a logical unity of thought he means that thought is formal, not real; Hegel in speaking of a logical unity means that thought is real and not formal. The relation between thought and knowledge is not at all the same in the two cases. With Hegel, to say that self is the highest type of thought is to say that self-consciousness is the ultimate principle of knowledge. The object of Kant is to show that the self, since merely a principle of *thought*, is not a principle of *knowledge* at all. While both therefore might call the self "the logical exposition of thought in general," the phrase would have absolutely opposed meanings in the case of the two writers.

No relation of opposition exists between the transcendental self as equal to the real world and as equal to the ultimate category—between, that is, the first interpretation and the third which Professor Seth gives. But although not opposed, they are not the same. To pass directly from the one to the other *would* be to hypostatize an abstraction. The transition may be justifiable, but it cannot, of course, be assumed without justification. The transcendental self may be the highest thought of the world, but it cannot be said to be the correlative of the world, unless the content of the world can be shown to be exhausted in thinking it—or unless the transcendental self is more than a principle of thought. Because thought is objective, it does not follow that it is all there is of objectivity. The world as thought—and thus brought under the principle of self-consciousness—may be real as far as it goes, and yet not be identical with the world as known—with the whole meaning of the real world. The known world may be, for example, a world thought and felt, and not thought alone. Thus while self-consciousness—if it equalled only the ultimate category of thinking—would be an adequate determination of the world as thought, it would, after all, be only a partial determination of the whole as it really exists, and could not thus be called, as Professor Seth at first calls it, a term convertible with the world and having the same content.

These may appear distinctions so notorious that it is trifling to spend so much time upon them; but the fact that so experienced a writer as Professor Seth has presented all three interpretations as explications of the meaning of the "transcendental self" is my excuse for dwelling upon them. There is a certain kinship, indeed, between the three interpretations which would render it easy to pass unwittingly from one to another. The idea of the self as the ultimate category of philosophic explanation stands between the other two. Its content is logical, or thought; and thus when one is arguing against a writer who seems to transform this category into an existence by itself, it is easy to go to the extent of saying that it is *merely* logical, and approve an author who held to the view that it was wholly abstract, even though that author meant by that expression that self was not a category of explanation at all. But, on the other hand, having in mind the fact that self-consciousness is a notion for explaining the world in a sense in which mere "being" or "quantity" or "mechanism" is not,—that it exhausts the meaning of the universe as an object of thought, —it is easy to go to the other extreme, and hold that self-consciousness *is* the intelligible world seen from one of its sides. But none the less the conception of self as merely formal and abstract contradicts the other two conceptions; and these other two, while not mutually incompatible, are so far from being identical with each other that to pass from one to the other without more ado is to "erect an abstraction into a concrete existence."

II.

As the object of this paper is not to convict Professor Seth of either verbal or real inconsistencies, but to help to clear up certain ambiguities in the current use of the conception of "transcendental self" (these ambiguities finding an unusually clear expression, as it were, in Professor Seth's book), I wish now to pass to the historical origin of these various meanings, chiefly as found in Kant, incidentally in Hegel as related to Kant.

Kant's theory is brought out in his "Transcendental Deduction." This is so familiar that it may be given summarily. Its gist, in the second edition of the *Kritik der reinen Vernunft*, is the proof that the identity of self-consciousness involves the synthesis of the manifold of feelings through rules or principles which render this manifold objective, and that, therefore, the analytic identity of self-consciousness involves an objective synthetic unity of consciousness. That self-consciousness is identical is, in itself, a merely analytic proposition. It means nothing more than that I am I—that what *I* am conscious of is in *my* consciousness, and that what belongs to your consciousness I am not conscious of. It finds its empirical application in the fact that, unless the consciousness which has ideas to-day is identical with that which was conscious yesterday or a year ago, it can no more now be conscious of what it was conscious of then than it can now be conscious of what is in your consciousness. But this does not prove the existence of any real self or substantial mind. It is still an analytic proposition and means that the same consciousness is the same consciousness. But if we ask how we know this sameness or identity of consciousness, the barren principle becomes wonderfully fruitful. For we do not know this sameness through the various successive ideas; they are not the same, but *ex hypothesi* various. And, furthermore, instead of knowledge of the identity of self depending upon them, I should not know them even as various, unless they were already mine. The identity of self-consciousness cannot be derived from knowledge of them, for this knowledge presupposes that identity. But perhaps we may go behind the apparent variety and disparateness of our ideas, and say that one consciousness *accompanies* all these different ideas, and that knowledge of this common element is the knowledge we are in search of. This does not suffice. The mere fact that consciousness accompanies every idea gives no identity unless these ideas are already conceived as *mine*—unless identity is presupposed. Otherwise, I should "have as various and many-coloured a self as I have different ideas." If we say that the *common* element gives us that knowledge of the identity of self which we are in search for, we doubly beg the question. A common element means an identity present in the midst of difference, and thus presupposes the sameness of consciousness through different ideas; and knowledge of this common element could be attained only if it were possible to compare many and various ideas in *one* consciousness, and thus see that they had a common element. These methods of knowing the sameness of consciousness thus presuppose what they would account for.

The sole way of accounting for this analytic identity of consciousness is through the activity of consciousness in connecting or "putting together" the manifold of sense. Since this putting together occurs according to fixed rules and principles, it is an objective synthesis. Knowledge of the identity of self presupposes, therefore, a self which acts synthetically, regularly so, upon sense-material. "The original and necessary consciousness of the identity of one's self is, at the same time, a consciousness of the equally necessary unity of the synthesis of all phenomena according to conceptions. . . . The mind would never conceive the identity of itself in the manifoldness of its ideas, if it did not perceive the *identity of the action by which it subjects this manifoldness to unity.*"

The "Deduction" in the first edition, instead of beginning with the consciousness of self-identity, begins with the consciousness of objects, and asks what is involved in that. The answer is the same. Consciousness of objectivity means unity of self-consciousness, and this not a formal or analytic activity, but one which connects the manifold of sense according to rules or conceptions. Whether, then, we inquire what is involved in mere sameness of consciousness, or what is involved in an objective world, we get the same answer: a consciousness which is not formal or analytic, but which is synthetic of sense, and which acts universally (according to principles) in this synthesis.

Apparently we have here a conception of the transcendental self like the first one laid down by Professor Seth. This self, since its existence is its synthetic activity upon the particular manifold of sense, is thoroughly objective. It has precisely the same content as the real world. And the objective world, since it turns out to be the synthesis of particulars of sense through the action of self according to conceptions, is subjective; it has the same content as the transcendental self. It is the transcendental self looked at as "there," as a product, instead of as an activity or process.

The next step in the analysis is to see why Kant, after having attained to the conception of an objective self, should shift his ground. Kant, in reaching this result, or in his transcendental deduction, has proceeded as if the synthetic action of self and the manifold of sense were wholly constituted through their mutual relations to each other—as if each had no existence excepting as a factor in the self, or in the world, determined by the other. The conceptions exist only as synthetic activity upon the manifold of sense; the manifold of sense exists only as connected by these conceptions. But while Kant has chosen in the "Deduction" to consider them as mutually related to each other, they have a meaning entirely apart from this mutual qualification, which, having been abstracted from in the transcendental deduction, must now be brought in that we may see how it affects the result.

The final meaning of the manifold of sense is found, not in its relation to the synthetic notions of the understanding, but in its relation to a thing-in-itself which produces it. In order to be known by us, this manifold must, indeed, be subjected to synthesis, and enter into relation to the self. But it has its own being entirely apart from such qualification. And, on the other hand, the conceptions of the understanding are not exhaustively determined by their synthetic action upon sense. They have a nature of their own, entirely independent of this synthetic action. The transcendental deduction does not give us, therefore, an analysis of the self, or of knowledge, or of the world as such; but simply of the conditions under which a manifold of sense (having a nature outside its relations to self) is knowable by us, or of the conditions under which conceptions of the understanding become categories of experience, these conceptions having their real and essential meaning, all the while, in a purely logical character which belongs to them apart from knowledge or experience. The transcendental self is thus a name for the incident under which our knowledge occurs, instead of giving the analysis of knowledge itself. It cannot be identified, therefore, as at first it seemed it might be, with either the real object (the thing-in-itself) or with the real subject. Just as the synthetic principles of experience are in themselves logical forms of analytic thought, so the self, in its own nature, is known only as the bare unity of these logical forms, the simple "I think" that must accompany all thought. The introduction of the thing-in-itself, therefore, leads Kant to that view of the self which finally gets expression in the quotations which were made in connection with Professor Seth's second idea of the self. For it must be remembered that the introduction of the thing-in-itself into Kant's philosophy affects all the factors which enter into his account of knowledge—the nature of thought as well as the nature of sensation. It is not an excrescence which can be lopped off without reconstruction of the whole theory of knowledge. Do away with the thing-in-itself, and the conceptions, instead of being *merely* logical, are also real, for their whole existence and meaning will then be found in their synthetic relation to the sense-manifold. And the transcendental self, instead of denoting a "logical exposition of thought in general," marks the synthetic union of the logical with the manifold of sense through regular principles of activity—marks, therefore, the objective character of the self. For if we reconstruct the Kantian theory of knowledge upon its own basis and method of analysis, doing away with the thing-in-itself, the result is to show that the *merely* logical, equally with the *merely* ontological, is an impossible abstraction. The *merely* logical is not at all; the logical *is* only as the thought-factor in the entire determination of experience, requiring another factor in order to constitute the self. That Kant's position of the merely formal abstract character of the self is superior in consistency to that of some Neo-Kantians is, therefore, not so evident as is the inconsistency of the restatement of such a position by one who denies the whole notion of the thing-in-itself.

But even if we correct Kant's analysis by doing away with the thing-in-itself, retaining all features not inconsistent with it, can the result of the transcendental deduction stand without further interpretation? Admitting that the removal of the thing-in-itself would show the transcendental self not as a logical abstraction, but real as experience itself—more real, indeed, in the sense that the reality of experience is shown by analysis to involve the reality of this self, behind which we cannot go—would this removal give a self whose content was the same as the content of the known world? The answer must be in the negative. The known world is constituted by the manifold of sensation, as connected by the self through its principles of synthesis. The content of the world, as known, will not be equivalent to the whole significance of the self, therefore, unless sensation is capable of being connected by principles of synthesis which manifest the entire nature of the self. But the position of Kant (a position entirely independent of any notion of *Ding-an-sich*) is, that sensation is incapable of being so determined as to equal self-consciousness; or, if we put it from the other side, that self-consciousness, even as a real activity of synthesis, can never exhaust all its synthetic capacities upon a material of sense. Sense is, as it were, inadequate to the relations which constitute self-consciousness, and thus there must also remain a surplusage in the self, not entering into the make-up of the known world. The reason for this is, that all the manifold of sense must be determined by certain forms of perception, space and time, before being determinable by the categories of thinking. Perhaps it would be more in accordance with the Kantian spirit to say that sensation, since it is in relation to space and time, must always present itself to the synthetic action of self as a manifold of mutually external particulars. The conceptions are thus not capable of determining sensation independently, but only as sensation is already subject to time- and space-*cadres*. Every category, therefore, must receive its value from its application to sensations already a manifold of external particulars, and the result can be only the system of objects in time and space. No category of experience can be found, accordingly, higher than that which determines most exhaustively the relations of objects and events in time and space, viz., reciprocity. And, correspondingly, no object can be known which is not an object in space and time. Hence the impossibility of making the self an object, since it is the condition of all objects, through its synthetic action upon sense. Stated in more Kantian language, the result would be that self-consciousness is the unconditioned, while experience, owing to the necessary relation of the synthetic activity of self to a material already determined as externally limiting and limited, can never present an unconditioned.[1] There thus remains a distinction between self and experience, due not now to the shadow thrown on knowledge by the thing-in-itself, but by the in-

[1] I do not mean to imply that I regard Kant as teaching that objects are first given as objects in space and time, and that the action of thought follows upon the presentation of such ready-made objects; or that there can be perception without conception. On the contrary, I think that Kant teaches very distinctly that space and time (and, of course, with them everything in space and time) do not exist as perceived objects without the action of thought. But he also holds that the manifold of sense which thought synthesizes has already a formal element which determines it to relations of externality. The fact that thought never connects pure sensations as such, but only sensations partially determined by relations of perceptivity, would occupy much the same place now occupied by the notion of schematism in Kant's theory, if this theory were reconstructed merely on the basis of the elimination of the *Ding-an-sich*.

compatibility of sensation, as rendered a manifold of external particulars in space and time, to the unconditioned content of self-consciousness. Experience can never be complete enough to have a content equal to that of self-consciousness, for experience can never escape its limitation through space and time. Self-consciousness is real, and not merely logical; it is the ground of the reality of experience; it is wider than experience, and yet is unknown except so far as it is reflected through its own determinations in experience,—this is the result of our analysis of Kant, the *Ding-an-sich* being eliminated but the Kantian method and all presuppositions not involved in the notion of the *Ding-an-sich* being retained. The resulting conception of the self is, evidently, not equivalent to either of Professor Seth's two first definitions of the self. It is not a mere abstract and formal logical unity, for it involves the action of thought upon sense, and is thus synthetic and objective; and yet it is not one side of the world of experience. The world of experience is constituted by it, but the world of experience does not exhaust it.

We have next to consider the relation of this revised Kantian conception of self to the third notion of self stated in Professor Seth's book—the idea of self-consciousness as the highest category of thought and of explanation. So far we have dealt only with the general idea of thinking as synthesis of sense according to principles. The different forms of synthesis, or the categories, we have not dealt with. Kant, as is well known, had twelve of them, which he derived without further examination from certain notions which he found to be involved in the formally logical theory of judgment. It was the work of Hegel, first, to give an *independent* derivation of them, as contrasted with Kant's taking them for granted; secondly, to give an *organic* derivation of them, in placing them in relation to one another, as contrasted with the simple juxtaposition of them which is found in Kant; and, thirdly, to show the category of self-consciousness as their basis and system, instead of stopping short with reciprocity, and placing the categories in opposition to self-consciousness. Now, accepting Hegel's work so far as it thus relates to the categories, and accepting his criticisms upon the Kantian procedure in reference to them, let us again revise the Kantian results in view of Hegel's position. Will this give us the self as the supreme category of experience? The answer must be in the negative. In one way the Kantian conception will include more than the Hegelian; in another way, less. It includes more, because what Kant offers is not primarily the self as a category of explanation at all, but the self as the real ground (not, however, to be confused with cause) of experience.[2] It includes less, because, however ready Kant might be to admit the Hegelian criticism and derivation of the categories as superior to his own, he could not admit that self-consciousness may be used as a category of experience. Self-consciousness would still have the function of the Idea for Kant. It would be an ideal regulative of experience, not a category constitutive of it.

Considering first this latter point, we may say that, admitting Kant's derivation of the categories from the forms of syllogistic logic to be insufficient and artificial, granting that it is impossible to stop short with the category of reciprocity, it does not follow that the category of self-consciousness is a category of experience. The distinction between conceptions of *thought* and conceptions of *knowledge* still remains. The reason for this we have already seen. It is the peculiar relation of the categories to sense as qualified by the forms of space and time. While, therefore, we might have the thought of self-consciousness, and while as a thought it would not be empty but would be, in another sense from that in which Kant actually uses the term, the vehicle of all notions of thought—their organism, it would be impossible to use this category so as to determine sense by it. For it is impossible as long as we retain Kant's fundamental presupposition—the idea of the partial determination of sensation by relation to perception, apart from its relation to conception—to employ self-consciousness as a principle of explaining any fact of experience. Every fact of experience is capable of adequate explanation without any such category; or, conversely put, experience can never con-

2 It will be understood that we are now speaking of Kant as revised by the elimination of the *Ding-an-sich*.

vey anything adequate to the notion of self. Self-consciousness would thus be an ideal category—that is to say, it would suggest the notion of a possible experience, unlike anything that *we* can possibly experience. It would be a notion which should regulate the successive organization of our present experience by pointing to a goal that yet we never could reach, and which should also point out the limitation of our present experience.[3]

The reconstruction of the Kantian theory of categories in the light of the Hegelian logic would give the following points. First, it would derive the conceptions from a common root and place them in some organic connection with one another. Secondly, it would place the Notion of the understanding and the Idea of reason in some connection with each other. The reason, with its Ideas, would not then appear, as it does now, an accidental afterthought of Kant, or an arbitrary derivation from the theory of the syllogism. The conception included under the Idea would follow by immanent development and criticism from what are now called Notions of the understanding, and would follow as their basis in thought. The distinction between them would be between conceptions that may be used to connect sensations subject to space- and time-forms and those that may not be so used. Thirdly, the ideas of organism and teleology, which also now appear to be unconnected with the rest of the Kantian philosophy, sprung upon us without intrinsic necessity, would form part of the content of the Idea as distinguished from the Notion. And, finally, the distinction Kant now makes between theoretical and practical reason, between the fact which is and the ideal which ought to be, would get an organic connection with the rest of the philosophy. This gives the outline of a reconstruction of his ethics; for it would appear that it is just the business of moral experience to overcome that distinction between experience and self-consciousness which theoretical knowledge cannot

[3] The distinction would thus be analogous to, perhaps identical with, the distinction Kant draws between our intelligence, in which the immediate and the mediate element never wholly coincide, and an intelligence which may be described either as Intuitive Reason or a Rational Intuition.

remove. All this we can get, if we read Kant with the eyes of Hegel; but self-consciousness as an actual category of our scientific experience we cannot get unless we simply substitute Hegel for Kant.

But it is time to turn to the other point: that the transcendental self of Kant is more than self-consciousness as a supreme category of explanation. It is more, because the self of Kant (the self as it would be with the *Ding-an-sich* eliminated) is more than any category: it is a real activity or being. And it cannot be said to be more than a category only because he has hypostatized a category—that if he had understood himself he would have seen that it was just a category. There is a fundamental distinction between the Kantian critique of pure reason and the Hegelian theory of categories which makes their results disparate. Kant's object is not the examination of *thought*, but the examination of *knowledge*; and his method is not a consideration of the significance, placing, relative adequacy and inadequacy of the conceptions or aspects of thought with a view to discovering the entire meaning of thought; his method is an analysis of the *actual* factors which actually constitute knowledge. One of these factors is thought, and, therefore, the complete carrying out of the method would undoubtedly involve an examination of thought as specified into its various conceptions. But because the Hegelian *Logic* is the development of one factor in Kant, it will hardly do to say that the purpose of the Kantian *Critique* is exhausted in the purpose of Hegel's *Logic*. At least, if we do say it, it should be with the distinct consciousness that we are not completing Kant, but are abandoning the characteristic feature of his undertaking and of his method. This is, I repeat, not an immanent "criticism of categories" but an analysis of experience into its aspects and really constituent elements. And in the course of this analysis Kant comes upon a self which through various principles of synthesis puts together the manifold of sense and, thereby, constitutes experience. This, indeed, is not a theory of creation; it is not an attempt to tell how a self set to work, or by necessity would set to work, to make a universe. But because it is not a theory of creation, it does not follow that it is only a criticism of categories. The assumption that there is no middle ground between a theory of creation and a mere analysis of forms of objective thought is, to say the least, a curious one. Kant's method is the analysis of the known universe or of experience; and as a result it discovers a self acting through thought upon sensation. Thought as synthetic is action upon sense, and sense is through the synthetic action of thought. If we call them factors of experience it must be with the recognition of their intrinsic unity with each other. The self constitutes this unity; it is the activity which is the source of the correlative synthesis of thought and sense. That analysis of reality should give anything but reality would be a strange result. And the reality found by the Kantian method through analysis of reality is a self which through thought is synthetic of sense determined to be a manifold of limiting particulars by relation to space and time.

There are two strains in Kant: one is inquiry into the necessary thought or logical conditions of experience; the other is the inquiry into the actual nature of experience. The *Logic* of Hegel undoubtedly works out the former to its consistent results. The latter it does not come in contact with. The former inquiry asks what are the forms or principles by which we must think the world; or, from the other side, what the world must be, as thought. The answer is that to think the world in its completeness is to think it as self-consciousness. Now this proposition is, as I attempted to show in the earlier portion of this article, not convertible with the proposition that the world *is* self-consciousness, unless it is also shown that the world is only and just as it is for thought. But the result of Kant's inquiry into the *actual* nature of experience is to show (to his satisfaction, I mean, the *truth* of the results not being under examination) that it includes another element besides thought, namely, feeling, and that on account of this element—or at least on account of its peculiar relation to forms of perception—the world as experienced can never equal the world as thought. That is, while to *think* the world completely is to think it as self-consciousness, it is the very characteristic of experience or *knowledge* that it cannot be complete—and hence cannot give self-consciousness.

We have thus another conception of self-consciousness to put beside the three obtained from the analysis of Professor Seth. This is the conception which we reach in reconstructing Kant by means of the elimination of the *Ding-an-sich*, and by that more complete working-out of the logical side of his analysis of experience which was made by Hegel. This is the self as the activity of synthesis upon sense. Starting from this notion the other three notions may be at once placed with reference to it. The self as the *merely* logical or abstract unity of thought falls away entirely. Self-consciousness as a category of experience becomes changed into an ideal which serves at once to organize and to reveal the incompleteness of experience. Where (as in ethics) the ideal *is* the reality, self-consciousness is again a real category of experience—but of practical experience, not of theoretical. The self which could use the category of self as a category of both practical and theoretic experience would be a self whose content was the same as that of the world. "The self and the world are only two sides of the same reality" in this case. While from the standpoint of Hegel's *Logic* (I am not speaking of the rest of his philosophy) such a result could be reached only by substantiating a category, from the standpoint of Kant's *Critique* it would be reached as an analysis of the reality of experience—if it were reached at all. But it can be reached only as an ideal which serves by contrast to manifest the incompleteness of experience as it presents itself to us.

It is evident that we are now upon the verge of another difficulty. As long as sensation was regarded as given by a thing-in-itself, it was possible to form a conception of the self which did not identify it with the world. But when sense is regarded as having meaning only because it is "there" as determined by thought, just as thought is "there" only as determining sense, it would seem either that the self is just their synthetic unity (thus equalling the world) or that it must be thrust back of experience, and become a thing-in-itself. The activity of the self can hardly be a third something distinct from thought and from sense, and it cannot be their synthetic union. What, then, is it? This is, I take it, the problem which finally emerges, when Kant is made self-consistent by the elimination of the thing-in-itself, and when the logical or thought-factor of his philosophy is developed in the Hegelian manner. It is precisely, as it seems to me, the difficulty which comes to the front in Green's reconstruction of Kant. It is to meet this difficulty that he frames the idea of a completely realized self making an animal organism the vehicle of its own reproduction in time. The conditions of the problem are: a denial of the *Ding-an-sich*; the analysis of knowledge into thought, and feeling which is ἕτερον to thought; the recognition that this feeling, after all, exists only as determined by thought; and the belief that feeling enters into *our* knowledge only under conditions of space and time, although space and time, in themselves, are feeling determined by thought. No space remains to consider how far Green's conception of an eternal self communicating itself gradually through physical conditions, and thereby constituting a human self, meets the demands of the problem. But it is evident that, when the problem is conceived as just stated, the self cannot be thought of as equivalent, on the one hand, to the world, because this world, as knowable by us, is always subject to certain forms, namely, space and time, which condition sense; nor, on the other hand, as equivalent to the highest category of thought, because the self is more than thought, more than a category, namely, the activity of synthesis of sense through thought. It is, I think, this twofold character of time and space, as at once forms of knowledge conditioned by the self, and yet conditioning self as it works in us, that is the genesis of Green's notion. The truth of the conditions upon which it rests—that is, Kant read in the light of Hegel so far as is necessary to make Kant consistent—is not under examination here; but if we grant it, the theory of Green is a genuine attempt to meet a genuine problem, and not a mere hypostasis of an abstraction.

Is Logic a Dualistic Science?

The Newer Logic may be roughly described as an attempt to take account of the methods of thinking employed by science, that is, of the methods the aim of which is truth, and which deal with a material of fact. It thus contrasts with the old scholastic logic, which may be roughly described as an attempt to deal with thinking *in vacuo*, that is with methods which leave out (or abstract from) the material of fact, and which have no aim except non-contradiction of their own premises—self-consistency. We may call the latter the Logic of argument, not of truth; but the former is the Logic of science, *i.e.*, of actual knowledge.

Lotze, Sigwart, Wundt in Germany, Jevons, Bradley, and Bosanquet in England are representative names in this new logic. To it also Venn's *Empirical Logic* is a most noteworthy recent contribution. While written from a philosophical standpoint differing from that of most of the foregoing names, it has an aim common with theirs. It treats thinking as a process having relation to truth. I confess, for my part, that I could have wished Venn had chosen another philosophical standpoint; but without going into matters of ultimate interpretation, Venn raises plenty of questions well worth discussion on their own account as purely logical. Among these, as one of the most important, I would place this: Does logic imply a duality, which for logic is ultimate? Venn answers in the affirmative, calling attention however to the fact, that he means only to assert that dualism is ultimate for *logic*; the metaphysical question is not raised.

Venn's own statement is as follows: We must take for granted a duality. On the one hand, outside of us, there is

[*First published in* Open Court, *III* (*16 Jan. 1890*), *2040–43. Not previously reprinted.*]

the world of phenomena pursuing its course; and, on the other hand, within us, there is the observing and thinking mind. Logic is concerned with the judgments of the latter about the former. "The thorough-going retention of this duality is one of the leading characteristics of the whole treatment adopted in this work" (p. 22). He then goes on to show the evils resulting from a purely subjective or a purely objective treatment. The latter "would confine us to a bare statement of those laws which lie at the basis of all inductive inference," while logic must always bring in the attitude of the mind in estimating or appreciating facts. The objective view would thus exclude the whole field of inference. The purely subjective treatment, on the other hand, would reduce logic to the bare logic of self-consistency, without relation to the true or to the false. So Venn concludes (p. 26) that while there are "some sciences, like Psychology, in which the primary reference is throughout to the mental processes, there are others, like the ordinary physical sciences, in which the primary reference is throughout to the external phenomena. But a science like logic, which has to do with the processes of the human mind when judging about phenomena, occupies necessarily an intermediate position."

Now when I say that all that Mr. Venn says about the evils of a purely subjective or purely objective treatment seems to me wholly sound, and that I would agree with him in saying logic deals with the process of thought in judging about phenomena,—when I say this, I may seem to have closed the door to further discussion. But I would call attention to the fact that these phrases may have two meanings. They may mean that the mental process, the "internal thought," and the objective phenomena, the "external thing," are, for logic at least, wholly independent and separate data, and that then the logical process comes in as a third thing and brings one to bear upon the other. This is the sense in which Mr. Venn interprets the dualism and is the sense in which I should reject it. Or, again, the dualism may be interpreted as being *inside*, as it were, the logical process. That is to say, we may hold that the "mental process of the mind in judging about phenomena" is for logic, at least, ultimate and decisive. The duality between the object perceived and the thought conceived is not one with which the logical process begins, but is the result of a logical process; that is, so far as *logic* has anything to do with it.

We may illustrate the difference as follows: *There* is the physical object, the sun moving in the heavens. *Here* is my idea or concept of this object. Does logic begin with this dualism and then go on to consider how the idea may be brought into conformity with the object?

Mr. Venn would answer "Yes." To me it seems as if the judgment of the mind were, for logic, the primary fact, and as if the distinction between the idea and the fact were one which takes place within and on account of the judgment—the logical process. The question involves more than at first appears. Are there, for logic at least, two worlds, of which one has to be brought into conformity with the other, or is there but one world, and that one logical through and through?

If the question concerned a world of objects wholly unrelated to mind, it would be impossible to discuss it without raising all manner of metaphysical difficulties; but, fortunately, Mr. Venn accepts the doctrine of the "relativity of knowledge." He says (p. 16), "we postulate a world or aggregate of objects—not out of relation to human faculties in general, which would be absurd—but conditioned in relation to our representative state of faculties." And on page 28 he expressly says: "We are in no wise concerned with the question which for ages perplexed philosophers, viz., in what sense our ideas 'resemble' or are 'copies of' actual external objects. All that we compare is the impression at first hand and at second hand, the presentation and the representation." And so on page 384 he says, that it is the general aim of logical processes to secure a complete and accurate correspondence between what we think and conceive within us, and what we *observe* and *feel* without us. The question is then: How are perception and observation logically related to thinking, to conception? Does logic take up its task when these are furnished to it ready-made, thus having a dualistic basis, or do logical processes enter equally into both perception and conception, so that, from a certain standpoint, each has a logical character?

I shall attempt to sustain the latter position. In holding that logic is not dualistic, because logical processes enter into presentation as well as into scientific methods, I may, in some sense, rely upon the authority of Mr. Venn himself. One of the striking features of his logic is the way in which he attacks our "habit of regarding what we call 'objects' as being in a way marked out by nature, always and for all beings" (p. 6). This habit is so far from being justified that as he says (p. 5), "Select what object we please—the most apparently simple in itself, and the most definitely parted off from others that we can discover—yet we shall find ourselves constrained to admit that considerable mental process had been passed through before that object could be recognized as being an object, that is as possessing some degree of unity, and as requiring to be distinguished from other such unities." And Mr. Venn shows clearly and decisively, to my mind, that in the most elementary recognition of an object processes of analysis and synthesis of very considerable complexity are involved. In his forcible comparison, to expect a dog who could not exercise quite a complex analysis and synthesis to perceive a rainbow, would be hardly more reasonable than to expect him to "see" the progress of democracy in the place where he lives—although the ultimate constituent sensible events are as accessible to his observation as they are to ours (p. 7; compare pp. 143–44).

In a like manner, Mr. Venn attacks what he well calls the "alphabetic" view of nature; the idea that objects come to us, so sharply discriminated and separated that one may be represented by A, another by B, and so on. "Generally speaking what we mark out by the letters A, B, C, are more or less fictitious entities, that is, they are manifold groups, held together in a mental synthesis with the cohesive assistance of names. . . . The mere reference to individuals as the basis or starting point of our instruction presupposes that something has already been done to recognize and constitute these A, B, C as individuals" (p. 345).

Now it seems to me that as soon as we give up the view that objects are presented to the mind already distinguished from others and united into cohering wholes, we are tacitly admitting that logical processes enter into the recognition, or observation of facts. When we go further and say that the individual object becomes such to us only through a process of mental synthesis and analysis, it seems to me that the admission is more than tacit—it is express. The only ground on which the logical character of recognition of objects could be denied, would be that mental analysis and synthesis are not logical processes. I hardly think Mr. Venn would take this position; still less can I see how he or any one else would uphold it. Mr. Venn when treating more expressly of the nature of analysis and synthesis, remarks (p. 398) that "these processes are best regarded as being merely subdivisions of a much more far reaching process, viz., that of framing hypotheses or suppositions. Set this faculty to work; employ it in separating wholes into their parts and gathering up parts in order to constitute new wholes, and we have what are known as analysis and snythesis." From this view it would certainly follow that our first perceptions of objects, being due to analysis and synthesis, are, in a sense, tentative hypotheses which we form in order to account for our experiences. Of course from the standpoint of ordinary experience it sounds absurd—and is absurd for that matter—to say that "the fire burns" is a hypothesis. But from the logical standpoint, it is far from being absurd. Whence the whole chemical theory of combustion, and what is the need of it, unless the first judgment that "fire burns" is, after all, only a tentative and crude analytic-synthetic process, needing to be carried farther, to be corrected, and, finally, transformed into a hypothesis more nearly agreeing with facts? If this is not evident, substitute the judgment "the sun moves" for the one "the fire burns." The objection most likely to be made to this doctrine that presentation itself has a logical value and basis, is, I imagine, that logical processes begin only when we are aiming at truth—only when we have a definite end in view which controls the process, and that there is no such aim or end in ordinary observation. That we are not *consciously* aiming at truth and that there is no *conscious* criterion or standard which controls the mental process in pre-scientific perception, is, of course, admitted. And this unconscious functioning of logical processes in perception seems to me to be just its *differentia* (logically, I would not say psychologically or metaphysically) from scientific thinking. Ordinary perception and scientific reflection have just the same material, and follow, in the rough, the same methods. There is hypothesis, induction, and deduction, inference, generalization, classification, analysis, synthesis, whatever logical process you please to take, in the perception of the sun as shining. But for the very reason that these processes are unconsciously followed they are uneconomical, imperfect, incorrect; they contain irrelevant material and leave out what is really coherent. In a word, since the logical principles are unconscious, the result is largely illogical, that is, false. Compare such a statement as "the sun shines" with the statement which a modern astronomer would make, when speaking from the standpoint of science, about just the same experience. The latter judgment would be carefully qualified; it would be accurately quantified; the conditions, chemical and physical, of the fact would be developed. The transformation would be so great that an ordinary layman reading the scientific proposition would probably not recognize that it had any kinship to his judgment—"the sun shines." But the real subject-matter would be the same.

We do not have then two things first given—one, the facts of observation, the other the mental concepts, and then, thirdly, a logical process, starting from this dualism, and attempting to make one side of it conform to the other. Knowledge from the first, whether in the form of ordinary observation or of scientific thinking, is logical; in ordinary observation, however, the logical process is unconscious, dormant, and hence goes easily and inevitably astray. In scientific thinking, the mind knows what it is about; the logical functions are consciously used as guides and as standards. But knowledge, experience, the material of the known world are one and the same all the way; it is one and the same world which offers itself in perception and in scientific treatment; and the method of dealing with it is one and the same—logical. The only difference is in the degree of development of the logical functions present in both.

We get the same result, if we consider from a somewhat different point of view the relations of observation and inference. And here, again, Mr. Venn may furnish the starting-point. For he himself admits that we cannot find any material which is "pure" observation—that is observation without any element of inference. "Really ultimate data can no more be reached than can a first point or absolute limit in time or space." "The starting point is a merely conventional one, assumed for convenience. Everywhere, wherever we look or find ourselves, we seem to be in possession of data which are familiar to us and are justified by experience. This is our starting point, and not any really primitive data" (pp. 115 and 116). The ground for this position will occur to anyone familiar with Mill's analysis of the proposition, "I saw my brother at a certain hour this morning," where he points out that everything is inferential excepting some data of color. Venn chooses a somewhat more complex case. Some one proposes to join a walking party and it is said of him: "I can see plainly enough that he will not be fit for our excursion." The least analysis would resolve this into: "I see the man is ill, and therefore conclude he cannot take a long walk." But do we *see* that the man is ill? Obviously, we only see that he is pale, has a lax gait, etc., and hence *infer* he is ill. And each one of these apparent observations may be analyzed into an inference. Even our estimate of paleness, a color pure and simple, psychological analysis shows to be no ultimate datum, but in great part an inference.

Now if it be admitted that observation involves inference indefinitely continued, what becomes of the duality which logic had to assume as its starting-point? If there is no *pure* presentation, no fact of sense-perception not already qualified by logical processes, how can it be said that logic has to do with a comparison of the concept with the datum of presentation? Logic seems somehow to be concerned with the observation itself. Instead of having a dual material supplied to it, it is present wherever there is any known material. There is but one world, the world of knowledge, not two, an inner and outer, a world of observation and a world of conception; and this one world is everywhere logical. As the world of ordinary perception it is logical, but its logical character is undeveloped, is latent, and hence is utilized at random, that is to say, extravagantly and erroneously. As the world of scientific reflection, it is more completely logical, because its logical character is brought to consciousness, is rendered explicit, and is thus used as a criterion, or a standard, in a word, as the truth by which the false and the irrelevant may be excluded. The result is that logic has no dualistic basis.

The Logic of Verification

In a recent article in the *Open Court* having the title "Is Logic a Dualistic Science?" I attempted to show as against Mr. Venn's recent work that logical processes do not deal with the comparison of ideas, on the one hand, with perceptions on the other; the reason, in general, being that logical processes enter into the structure of perceptions as well as of ideas, and that, therefore, such processes could not be considered as beginning with the comparison of ready-made perceptions and conceptions. The opinion was then advanced that there is but one world of knowledge, whether in the form of perceptions or of ideas, and that this world is logical all the way through.

To this doctrine an objection somewhat after this fashion might be raised: Such a conception makes the process of verification impossible. If there is but one realm of knowledge, what is the standard of truth? with what shall we compare our *ideas* in order to verify them? If logic has a dualistic basis, the question is easily answered; on one hand, there is the world of conceptions, of ideas, on the other, the world of perceptions, of facts. And we test our ideas by comparing them with facts. But upon the theory of a single realm of knowledge, logical throughout, no such comparison and testing is possible. It seems upon this theory that the only criterion of truth is the consistency of ideas with themselves, and every one knows that ideas may be self-consistent, and yet untrue, or even highly absurd.

Undoubtedly the objection points to a serious difficulty, one which must be reckoned with. I shall not attempt to evade it by denying that there is a relative distinction at

[*First published in the* Open Court, *IV (24 Apr. 1890), 2225–28. Not previously reprinted.*]

least, between idea and fact. I shall rather ask what does this distinction of idea and fact (speaking always from the logical point of view) mean and how does it arise? If an objection lies against the unitary theory advanced, a still stronger objection lies against the dualistic theory. This objection I may state as follows: What is this world of facts by comparison with which we test our ideas? Is it the real, the true world? This supposes that this real world, the actual facts, are known. But if they are known, so that they can afford the standard of verification, why do we go to the trouble of forming a theory, of making a hypothesis? If we already know the facts, it certainly seems a waste of energy and of time to frame guesses, to elaborate ideas simply for the sake of going through the meaningless process of seeing whether or not they agree with a truth already perfectly known. It is evident that we only form a theory, or entertain ideas, as distinguished from facts, when we are not in possession of the truth, when we are in search of it. *Per contra*, if the facts by which we are to test our theory are not the real facts but the facts as they *seem* to be, the facts as *previously* known, there is another difficulty. It is just because we suspected these apparent facts of not being real, that we framed a theory which should get nearer to the reality of the case. It would certainly be a curious operation to test our theory by a standard whose discrediting had led to the formation of the theory. This then is the dilemma with which I would confront the dualistic notion. If the standard by which we are to test our ideas is the real fact, the actual truth, then, by the necessity of the case, the standard is unknown; if the standard is facts as they seem to be, as already apprehended, it is worthless. The only standard of value is out of reach; the attainable standard is no standard at all. In either case, verification would seem to be an impossible process.

I hope this result may at least induce us to consider the other point of view; the notion that we do not have ideas separate from facts, which we proceed to compare one with the other, but that the (undoubted) distinction between idea and fact is itself logical, brought about by and within logical processes.

Let me begin with a well-known psychological fact—that which Bain calls "primitive credulity." So far as we can judge, early childhood makes no difference between ideas and facts. It does not recognize its ideas *as* ideas, but it at once projects them into the outer realm. Suggest an idea to a baby, by saying some word which he recognizes, the name of a known object or person, and the baby looks around him to see that object. A child's mind is like an animal's; it is intensely practical. Ideas, as such, do not appeal to it. The thing, the action, is what the child is after. A baby's inability to entertain a question, or even after it can answer questions relating directly to fact, its inability to consider questions involving a "whether this or that," testify to its incapacity to hold an idea in its ideal aspect. What is it that breaks up this primitive intellectual innocency; this immediate transformation of idea into fact? Apparently, it is the disappointment of expectation, at first, and then as a further development of this, the dim perception of contradictions. The baby, when he hears the word "Papa," looks about him and does not see his father; probably, at first, the new idea, what he actually sees, simply expels the other idea. The idea of father is not retained before the mind long enough for the contradiction to be perceived. But there is at least the shock of unrealized expectation, and the feeling of the necessary adjustment to the new idea. As the mind's power of holding its ideas fixed becomes greater, the new idea will not simply drive out the other, substituting itself for it, but will struggle with it for possession of the mind. Now the actual idea contradicts the idea which the mind is endeavoring to project into actuality; it prevents this projection. It is, as it seems to me, this two-fold process: on one hand, the retaining of an idea before the mind, on the other, its repulsion from actual fact through a stronger contradictory idea, which leads the mind to the hitherto unentertained recognition of an idea as only ideal, as a *mere* idea.

This analysis seems to me to be verified by the phenomena of illiterate and savage life, of dreams, and of hypnotism, so far as we can appeal to that unsettled sphere. The difficulty savages have of discriminating ideas from facts is a commonplace of ethnology. The absence of contradictory facts retained in the mind leads us to take everything we dream as real, while we dream it. The savage continues to think of it as real when he awakes; it is only something that happened in another region of experience, when the soul sallied forth from the body. And while I would not speak dogmatically regarding hypnotism, Janet and others seem to have made it probable that its essential phenomenon is *dissociation*, the severing of the connections between groups of ideas united in ordinary sense-perception and thought. These connections being broken down, the mind experiences no contradiction on being told while in a room of a house that it is in a boat upon the ocean. The idea, having no other body of ideas over against which it is set, is taken, as in childhood, for a fact.

But to return to the argument. The mind learns through the contradictions existing between its ideas that not all can be projected as facts; some must be dismissed as false, or, at least, retained only tentatively as *possible* facts. It is this tentative holding of an idea which constitutes the logical distinction of idea and fact. The fact is the idea which nothing contradicts, which harmonizes with other ideas, which allows the mind free play and economical movement. The idea is at first the fact about which difficulties are felt, which opposes a barrier to the mind's movement, and which, if not in opposition to other facts, is, at least, in opposition to *apparent* facts. In a word, the distinction between "idea" and "fact" arises along with the distinction between real and apparent fact.

Let us test this result by considering scientific hypothesis. The mind frames a hypothesis or theory, because it is dissatisfied with its present (or rather former) judgments. The ideas which it has formerly taken to be facts, it has come to look upon with suspicion. The hypothesis is an idea which is supposed to be fact, or at least, to be nearer fact than previous ideas. But, till it can be verified, it is held only tentatively, and this holding may be of all degrees of comparative assurance, from a mere suggestion or question to a well-defined theory. The process of transforming the hypothesis, or idea entertained tentatively, into a fact, or idea held definitely, is verification. We saw at the outset the difficulties which beset the ordinary crude notion of verification, that which considers it as a process of comparing ready-made ideas with ready-made facts; let us see how our present notion meets these difficulties.

In the first place, what are the facts in contrast with which the hypothesis is regarded as merely an idea? They are not a *fixed* something; fixed either in amount, or in quality. If the idea, the hypothesis needs extension, transformation and verification, the "facts" in their turn, are in need of enlargement, alteration and significance. Take, for example, the hypothesis of evolution. The facts by which this theory is to be verified or disproved are not a fixed, unchangeable body; if the theory gets its verification through the facts, the facts get a transformed and enlarged meaning through the theory. I do not mean simply that the theory leads to the discovery of new facts, though this is noteworthy, and, I think, inexplicable on the dualistic assumption. But suppose there is some animal of which absolutely no new observation has been made since the formation of the theory of evolution; our knowledge of that animal, the *facts* of the animal have been, none the less, transformed, even revolutionized. Let this instance illustrate the relation of the facts to the idea; if the idea, the theory, is tentative, if it is pliable and must be bent to fit the facts, it should not be forgotten that the "facts" are not rigid, but are elastic to the touch of the theory.

In other words, the distinction between the idea and the facts is not between a mere mental state, on one side, and a hard and rigid body on the other. Both idea and "facts" are flexible, and verification is the process of mutual adjustment, of organic interaction. It is just because the "facts" are not final, settled facts that the mind frames its hypothesis or idea; the idea is the tentative transformation of these seeming facts into more real facts.

More in detail, we may consider the process as follows: The mind attacks the mass of facts which it suspects not to be facts piece-meal. It picks out some one aspect or relation of these "facts," isolates it (technically the process of abstraction), and of this isolated relation it forms a hypothesis, which it then sets over against the facts from which this relation has been isolated. The isolated relation constitutes, technically, the universal; the background of mass of facts is the particular. The verification is the bringing together of this universal and particular: if the universal confronted with the particulars succeeds in filling out its own abstract or empty character by absorbing the particulars into itself as its own details, it is verified. And there is no other test of a theory than this, its ability to *work*, to organize "facts" into itself as specifications of its own nature. But on the other side, the particulars attacked by the universal do not remain indifferent; through it they are placed in a new light, and as facts gain a new quality. Organized into the theory, they become more significant; what had previously been oppositions and even contradictions among them is removed, and we get a harmonious system. The important point then is to see that verification is a two-edged sword. It does not test and transform the "idea," the theory, any more than it tries and moulds the "facts." In other words, if the idea is tentative, needing to be brought before the court of the facts, so also the "facts" are inadequate and more or less contradictory—that is, they are only apparently facts. They need therefore to be harmonized and rendered significant through the idea, the hypothesis. We may indifferently describe the process as a movement of the theory upon the facts whereby the latter are rendered more rational, *i.e.*, more significant and harmonious, or as a confronting of the theory by the facts, whereby it is verified. The actual result is the same in either case: we simply describe it from two points of view.

To recapitulate the whole matter: the distinction between idea and fact is a relative one, not an absolute separation; it is made for the sake of what we may term either a more real and more complete fact, or a more adequate and certain idea. There is a period, not only in childhood, but in every science, and as to every subject-matter in every science, when idea and fact are at one. But contradictions arise; the mind therefore holds idea and fact apart, regarding the idea as tentative and the fact as apparent. To this stage, there supervenes a period in which the mind attempts to get a definitive idea—or, from the other side, a real fact. It therefore by observation, experiment, and all other means at its disposal, makes its idea as definite and coherent as possible, and thus frames a hypothesis or theory. This theory it brings to the apparent facts, in order to organize them, to give them new and additional significance. So far as this is accomplished, idea and fact again become one, to remain one until further contradictions are discovered when the process must again be gone through with. And this is the description of the actual process of knowledge, of science. We have first an unconscious identification of idea and fact, and on this basis the universe, the realm of experience, is built up. But this universe lays itself open somewhere to suspicion; this suspected aspect is held apart from the rest, as an idea, the remainder being left undisturbed as "fact." The idea is wrought over as an idea into a scientific hypothesis, and is then projected again into the facts. As verified it becomes an essential part of the facts, changing to some degree or other the character of these facts. But this new universe again behaves suspiciously: the suspicious "fact" is again arrested and condemned as a *mere* idea, but passing through the reformatory of thought issues as an hypothesis, and is turned out again into the free world of fact.

This continued process of breaking up and recombination by which knowledge detects, condemns, and transforms itself is verification. Thus the analysis of this process confirms the former contention that the logical sphere is integral and unitary.

Philosophy in American Universities: The University of Michigan

The Philosophical Courses of the University of Michigan may be conveniently classified under three heads: –

I. Beginning

1. ELEMENTARY LOGIC, in which there are two courses, one general covering the rudiments of syllogistic and deductive logic in which Jevons is used as the basis, the other in inductive logic, intended especially for scientific students, in which Fowler is used.

2. ELEMENTARY PSYCHOLOGY. The main facts regarding modern scientific researches and methods, and the various attempts at their philosophic interpretation. Dewey's *Psychology* is the book used in connection with this course.

3. INTRODUCTION TO PHILOSOPHY. A course of lectures on the main problems and principles of the theory of knowledge and reality. Each of the foregoing courses is for one semester.

II. Intermediate Courses

1. HISTORY OF PHILOSOPHY. Ancient and Modern. Lectures and readings designed to give information regarding both the historical development of thought, and the main problems developed in its course. The department of philosophy owns a large number of copies of the chief thinkers in

[*First published in the* Monist, *I* (*Oct.* 1890), 150–51. *Not previously reprinted.*]

modern philosophy, Locke, Descartes, etc., etc., and these are assigned to members of the class for readings and reports. Each student thus becomes acquainted with at least half-a-dozen of the leading writers at first-hand.

The course runs through the year.

2. ETHICS, THEORETICAL (one-half year) AND SOCIAL (Political Philosophy, one-half year also). The theoretical course attempts to arrive at an account of the ethical ideal by means of a critical consideration of the principal modern ethical theories, especial attention being paid to Utilitarianism, Evolutionary Ethics, and Kantianism. The second division of the course discusses the ethical basis and value of society and the state, law and rights, in connection with an account of the political theories of Plato, Aristotle, Grotius, Hobbes, Locke, Kant, Rousseau, Hegel, etc.

3. ÆSTHETICS. This course, like the previous one, unites the historical and theoretical treatment of æsthetic doctrines and results. It is designed largely to aid students in the interpretation and criticism of literature. It is a half-year course, and is followed by a half-year course (given in the English Department) on the Principles and Methods of Literary Criticism.

4. PHYSIOLOGICAL PSYCHOLOGY. Lectures, assigned readings and elementary experiments, and demonstrations. There is established, as yet, no separate psycho-physical laboratory, but the new-equipped physiological laboratory of the University is, through the courtesy of the Professor of Physiology, at the disposal of students in this line. Half-year course.

5. SCIENCE AND PHILOSOPHY OF RELIGION. Lectures, readings, etc., designed to give an account of the chief methods employed and results achieved in the modern historical and comparative study of religions. And also an account of the principal theoretical interpretations of religion. Half-year course.

III. Advanced Courses

1. KANT'S *Critique of Pure Reason.* A study of Kant's masterpiece at first-hand. This is accompanied by a shorter subsidiary course, treating of the development of the Kantian system, and criticisms upon it. Caird's *Critical Philosophy of Kant*, is read and discussed in connection with the latter course. Half-year course.

2. HEGEL'S *Logic.* A study of Wallace's translation of the lesser *Logic* of Hegel. Half-year course.

3. THE LOGIC OF SCIENTIFIC METHODS. A lecture course taking up the study of the Logic of Science, and intended to make the hearers acquainted with the standpoint and spirit of such authors as Lotze, Sigwart, Wundt, Mill, Jevons, Bradley, Bosanquet, and the modern movement in logic generally. Half-year course.

4. PROBLEMS IN HIGHER ÆSTHETICS. A brief course for graduate students in Æsthetics.

5. SEMINARY IN ETHICS. Discussion of the treatment of some main ethical problems by the chief modern ethical writers.

The Elementary courses are conducted mainly by text-books and recitations; the Intermediate courses by lectures and assigned readings, reports and essay-writings. The Advanced courses are pursued by class discussions, conversations, etc., on basis of work done independently by the student.

The teaching is carried on by John Dewey, J. H. Tufts, and F. N. Scott.

Moral Theory and Practice

In the first number of this journal four writers touch upon the same question,—the relation of moral theory to moral practice.* Professor Sidgwick touches it incidentally in raising the query whether what is wanted is not moral insight as much as reinforcement of moral motives; Mr. Adler touches it in discussing the relation of the organization and work of ethical societies to ethical theory; Mr. Bosanquet has one of its aspects for his subject in discussing the functions of such societies in promulgating moral ideas; and, finally, Mr. Salter is led to conceive that a great service to moral philosophy has been the fact that it has separated the "ought" from judgment as to what is, and thus kept open a region beyond science.

If any one of these writers had happened to find it within his scope directly to discuss the question of the relation of moral theory and practice, it is not likely that this article would ever have been written, but finding the subject touched upon, without direct analysis, in so many ways, I was led to attempt to clear up my own ideas. The very presence of four such articles seems to indicate that the question is in the air, and that, therefore, any moderately rational effort to clear it up for one's self may not be without interest. If Mr. Adler and Mr. Salter seem to be made the objects of my remarks in this clearing-up process, I hope it will not be attribted to a polemic spirit. Rather than seek some more impersonal, and therefore more remote, form of statement, it seems good to let the tensions discharge as they

* [Felix Adler, "The Freedom of Ethical Fellowship"; Bernard Bosanquet, "The Communication of Moral Ideas as a Function of an Ethical Society"; William M. Salter, "A Service of Ethics to Philosophy"; Henry Sidgwick, "The Morality of Strife."]

[*First published in the* International Journal of Ethics, *I* (*Jan. 1891*), *186–203. Not previously reprinted.*]

first arose; and it is through these articles of my friends that they arose.

It seems to me that I can detect in much of current ethical discussion a lurking idea that moral conduct is something other than, or over and above, conduct itself,—understanding by conduct distinctively human action, that based upon and realizing ideas. Because the notion lurks it is difficult to dislodge,—all the more when the lurking is so evanescent that one feels, in attacking it, as if the holder of its fortress might himself disown its presence. But there is an ally of this idea which is not indeed marshalled in open array upon the battle-field, but about whose presence there can be no doubt,—the idea that moral theory is something other than, or something beyond, an analysis of conduct,—the idea that it is not simply and wholly "the theory of practice." Moral theory, for example, is often regarded as an attempt to find a philosophic "basis" or foundation for moral activity in something beyond that activity itself. Now, then, when the question comes up as to the relation of moral theory and moral conduct, the man who denies any intrinsic connection is without doubt in possession. One will hardly have the hardihood to stand and assert that until the Platonic, or the Kantian, or the Spencerian system of philosophy has been "proved," moral activity is impossible. Again, moral theory is not seldom conceived as, in Mill's phrase, a nautical almanac, or an ethical prescription or cook-book,—a collection of "rules" for conduct. When this view of moral theory is held, I, for one, shall not say nay to the man who states that there is no intrinsic connection between theory and practice. The hortatory pulpit and its modern congener and heir-apparent, the editorial page of the newspaper, may be left to uphold the idea that precepts are the great moral force of the world. But yet it does not go assured that there is no intrinsic relation between theory and practice. The trouble may be, after all, in an aborted conception of theory.

What, then, is moral theory? It is all one with moral *insight*, and moral insight is the recognition of the relationships in hand. This is a very tame and prosaic conception. It makes moral insight, and therefore moral theory, consist simply in the every-day workings of the same ordinary intelligence that measures dry-goods, drives nails, sells wheat, and invents the telephone. There is no more halo about the insight that determines what I should do in this catastrophe of life when the foundations are upheaving and my bent for eternity lies waiting to be fixed, than in that which determines whether commercial conditions favor heavy or light purchases. There is nothing more divine or transcendental in resolving how to save my degraded neighbor than in the resolving of a problem in algebra, or in the mastery of Mill's theory of induction. It may be well to bow with bated breath before every working of intelligence, but to baptize moral insight with any peculiar sacredness is to find a changeling in our hands,—sentimentalism.

Moral theory, then, is the analytic perception of the conditions and relations in hand in a given act,—it is the action *in idea*. It is the construction of the act in thought against its outward construction. *It is, therefore, the doing, —the act itself, in its emerging*. So far are we from any divorce of moral theory and practice that theory is the ideal act, and conduct is the executed insight. This is our thesis.

It is true a man can walk without a certain kind of knowledge of the process of locomotion; that he can eat without a certain kind of knowledge of foods and of digestive processes.[1] But if this is to prove that conduct is other than an expression of "theory," of the conceptions of intelligence, the basis of this analogy must be looked after. A man can plough without a knowledge of aeronautics, but this hardly proves that ploughing comes before a knowledge of how to plough, and that the knowledge of how to plough is gleaned from reflecting upon the various acts of ploughing already performed. A man may talk through a telephone without understanding the theory of its construction, but it would hardly be a safe inference that therefore he could talk through it without knowing what he was going to say, much less without knowing how to talk. The child who walks may not "understand the mechanism of locomotion," but he had once painfully and slowly to form a theory of walking none the less. I should hardly know where to find a better exam-

1 See in Mr. Adler's article, Vol. 1, No. 1, pp. 20, 21.

ple of the dependence of conduct upon theory than the toil of learning to interpret and connect those signs upon which the mastery of the act of locomotion rests. And if Mr. Adler thinks the dependence of practice upon theory in locomotion has ceased with adult life, the observation of some patient suffering with complete cutaneous anæsthesia will serve to test the hypothesis. What the well-worn illustrations of walking without knowledge of the theory of locomotion, of reasoning without knowledge of the syllogism, etc., prove is that a man may know some things without knowing others, —others which, in ultimate analysis, are related. Where, however, there is anything which deserves the name of conduct, there is an idea, a "theory," at least as large as the action. Because the theory is narrow in scope it is not lacking; and it is narrow only so far as the corresponding act is abstract and partial. The average man can walk without *much* theory, because walking is not an act of *great* content. The specialist in locomotor diseases, and the painter of men and animals in motion, finds in his larger activity a knowledge of the mechanism not out of place.

And I hope the reader will not miss the point in the illustrations. For any *act* (as distinct from mere impulse) there must be "theory," and the wider the act, the greater its import, the more exigent the demand for theory. It is not likely that the wheels of moral movement are to be reversed after two thousand and more years. It was Socrates who initiated the movement, when he said that "an unexamined life is not one to be led by man." Whatever may be the case with savages and babes, the beginning of every ethical advance, under conditions of civilized existence, must be in a further "examination of life." Not even customary morality, that of respectability and of convention, is freed from dependence upon theory; it simply lives off the funded results of some once-moving examination of life.[2]

2 As Mr. Adler never expressly defines what he means by moral theory, his stand-point is, of course, difficult to deal with. But it seems to be taken for granted throughout that moral theory is something apart from the practice of which it is the theory. We are told of "borrowing from the realm of ideas a sufficient reason for accepted rules of action." We are told of motives which are different from professed doctrines, and finally of ethical theory as dealing with ideas *imported* from the region of speculation and of science, etc. (pp. 21, 22). What is this "rule" of

Perhaps, however, I shall be told that I am somewhat disingenuous in identifying an idea of action with moral theory; that theory perforce means a reflective and systematic account of things, while an idea means simply a mental conception of what should be done. I hope there is some such objector, for it gives me occasion to say that I think that such a separation of theory from idea is at the root of the confusion which I am trying to clear up. My claim is precisely that an idea of what is to be done and moral theory are identical; that the sole difference between the idea of a child, that he ought to learn the multiplication-table, or be kind to his baby-sister, and the widest moral theory—the one recognized as theory by every one—is simply one of degree of analysis of what practice is, and not a difference of kind. Action to the child is narrow and partial, and his theory is limited.

To come to close quarters with what seems to me a radically false notion of moral theory, let us take the council of pundits, called into being by Mr. Bosanquet. The question is regarding the morality of breaking down the responsibility of the parent for the sake of a good to the child. Now the reason that the answer of these pundits, as recorded by Mr. Bosanquet (p. 83 of No. 1), is of no special use is not because it is theory, but because it is *not ethical* theory. It seems a truism to remark that every theory is of its own subject-matter, and must be wholly relevant to its subject-matter. And yet this truism is all we need in order to see that the pundits have not given a conclusion in terms of moral theory at all. Conduct is absolutely individualized. Abstract action, action which is not categorical through and

---

action? If it is not an idea, a theory, I should like to know why it is allowed longer to cumber the earth. The morality of external command is no morality at all. Again, men indeed *profess* doctrines which do not touch their characters, but neither do the professions touch their intellects, —*i.e.*, they are not doctrines at all, but dogmas. For a doctrine, a theory, is, I take it, a mode of intellectual activity; a dogma, a burden or load upon intellectual activity. To identify moral theory with ideas imported from outside moral practice without any attempt to justify such a conception of theory is, I submit, a most startling performance. I should have supposed antecedently that theory is theory of practice. Is it not time that, before an attempt is made to divorce practice from theory, we should have a little effort to define what is meant by theory?

through, is the one last contradiction of logic and of life. There is no such thing as conduct in general; conduct is what and where and when and how to the last inch. The pundit, then, who begins his sentence with "If" is engaged in an analysis to reach a conclusion, and not with the conclusion as such at all. If he deserves a place on the council, he will surely decline to consider an abstract case when brought before him. Or, rather, so far as he does consider the abstraction, it will be simply for the sake of the surefootedness gained in going on to consider the concrete,—to make certain that no important condition has missed due regard in the analysis. He will say, "Let me know your specific case in all its concreteness and we will spell it out together, not in order to find some abstract rule under which it may be brought, but in order that we may see what *this* case really is." And the resulting moral "theory" is the theory of the case,—a thorough-going analysis of it. The need for such analysis is simply that the needed action may be truly moral (that is, intelligent practice); that it may meet all the demands of the relationships involved, instead of being one-sided, that is, more or less sentimental.

What I am getting at, in a word, is that the ordinary idea of moral theory shears off the very factors which make it *moral* theory at all and reduces it to the plane of physical theory. Physical science does deal with abstractions, with hypothesis. It says, "If this, then that." It deals with the relations of conditions and not with facts, or individuals, at all. It says, "I have nothing to do with your concrete falling stone, but I can tell you this, that it is a law of falling bodies that, etc. You must make your own allowances in applying this universal formula to the special case, according to the peculiar circumstances of the special case." Now, the pundit who should allow his final deliverances to go out in the form of "If this, then that," (excepting as a way of saying "I do not know enough of this concrete case to have any theory about it"), would be denying the sole condition of *moral* theory; he would be mutilating the moral fact, the individualized act, till it was a mere bundle of abstractions.

Shall I be told, then, that there can be no such thing as moral theory at all? That it is impossible to get a theory which shall be concrete and individualized as the act is concrete and individualized? Ah, but my objector, there *is* such a thing. Every man, before he acts, always has such a theory unless his act is one of mere impulse. It is true enough that he may not exhaust, that he may never exhaust, all the real concreteness of the act; but none the less his idea of the act is individualized as far as it goes; it may be a smaller individual than the real act, but this does not make it an abstract universal. What he sees, in a word, is *this* act, although the "this" he sees may not be the true complete "this."

What we come to is: Moral theory cannot exist in a book. It is, I believe, a popular superstition to identify science with a lot of formulæ and statements in a book. I have my doubts whether even the physical sciences exist as a lot of general statements held apart from facts; I suspect that our physical sciences have their existence only in our neutral attitude toward the world of fact, that they get real existence only as they become part and parcel of the meaning of the world that we daily perceive. But I am very certain that moral science is *not* a collection of abstract laws, and that it is only in the mind of an agent as an agent. It is his perception of the acts that need doing,—that is, his perception of the existing world of practice in all its concrete relationships.

In last analysis, then, the value of our council of pundits will depend upon this: not whether theory helps practice, but whether the council is capable of the kind of theory demanded. Moral theory, so far as it can exist outside of the particular agent concerned with a special act, exists in the mind of him who can reproduce the condition of that agent. Just because moral practice is so individual or concrete, you can theorize for another only as you "put yourself in his place." Browning's "Martin Relph" or "Clive" is then the model for our band of pundits rather than Kant's *Critique of Practical Reason*.[3] Put in logical terms, the question is whether our judges can use, in their judgments, the "category" of self, or only that of abstract law.

3 You meet persons who want to argue about such a poem. They are parallel with those who reduce moral theory to a lot of ifs and ands.

"This is all aside from the point," I think I shall hear. The question is not whether theory must be back of action, but whether a given theory of ethics, the Kantian, the Hedonistic, the Hegelian, must be behind it. Well, if this is the point, I would it were clearly stated. It is a dangerous procedure which concludes that because moral practice can occur without this or that ethical analysis, therefore there is no intrinsic and absolutely indispensable connection of theory and conduct.

But let us take the point so raised. What shall we say of the relation of an ethical "system," that of Mill or Spencer, to moral conduct? Or, adopting the phraseology of Mr. Bosanquet, let us admit that so far we have been speaking of "moral ideas," and now go on to raise the question of the value of "ideas about morality" for action.

I must revert again to the position already taken. Moral conduct is precisely that which realizes an idea, a conception. The breadth of action (so far as moral value is concerned and not historical outcome) is measured by the insight of the agent. What are the conditions which require action, and what is the action which they demand? Just so far as this question is raised and answered, action is moral and not *merely* instinctive, or sentimental. This is evidently a work of analysis. Like every analysis, it requires that the one making it be in possession of certain working tools. I cannot resolve this practical situation which faces me by merely looking at it. I must attack it with such instruments of analysis as I have at hand. *What we call moral rules are precisely such tools of analysis.* "I ought not to lie." Very well, then, would doing so and so be telling the truth? What *is* telling the truth in this instance? "I should do as I would be done by." Very well; what would I have done to me in this case? that is to say, what are the personal relations involved here? Some, who would be the first to repudiate the practical consequences in the way of casuistry logically involved, entertain the idea that a moral law is a command: that it actually tells us what we should or should not do! The Golden Rule gives me absolutely no knowledge, of itself, of what I should do. The question of what in this case I should do in order to do as I would be done by has still to be resolved, though the Golden Rule be a thousand times my maxim. The rule is a counsel of perfection; it is a warning that in my analysis of the moral situation (that is, of the conditions of practice) I be impartial as to the effects on me and thee. Or, it is the statement of a principle,—the principle of individuality, that the activity of every man concerned has an equal claim for consideration; that though I be a great Pharisee or the high-priest himself, I am bound to consider the welfare of that miserable sinner of a publican as I would my own. About the specific act to be done it tells, I repeat, not a jot. But it is a most marvellous tool of analysis; it helps me hew straight and fine in clearing out this jungle of relations of practice.

What this rule is, that every rule is which has any use at all. This is the grain of truth in Mill's idea of a nautical almanac. The almanac, after all, does not tell the sailor where he is nor how to navigate. It is an aid in his analysis of the required conditions of right navigation. In the supreme art of life the tools must be less mechanical; more depends upon the skill of the artist in their manipulation, but they are none the less useful. Our mastery of a required case of action would be slow and wavering if we had to forge anew our weapons of attack in each instance. The temptation to fall back on the impulse or accident of the moment would be well-nigh irresistible. And so it is well we have our rules at hand, but well only if we have them for *use*.

What is the connection of this, however, with special philosophic systems? Just this: the rule as a tool of analysis is an idea. The Golden Rule is, as suggested, the idea of the value of individuality; the rule of truthfulness is the idea of the transparence of media in all human exchanges, etc. A philosophic theory of ethics is a similar idea, but one of deeper grasp, and therefore wider hold. It bears much the same relation to the particular rule as this to the special case. It is a tool for the analysis of its meaning, and thereby a tool for giving it greater affect. It is hardly necessary, I suppose, to profess the deepest respect for the Golden Rule, but this is not inconsistent with recognizing that if it were not held open to reflective criticism, to analysis of meaning and bearing, it would surely degenerate into a mere external command. That it, or any other rule, may be a workable tool, that it may really give aid in a specific case, it must have life and spirit. What can give it the life and spirit necessary to make it other than a cramped and cramping petrification except the continued free play of intelligence upon it?

The Golden Rule itself, in other words, except as an idea among ideas, would speedily become either an external command, a merely speculative abstraction (an ideal with a big I, and no r for reality at all), or that deadest of all dead things, a preacher's mere exhortation. What would this particular rule have amounted to practically if there had not been ideas back of it, which vivified it by taking it out of its isolation, and by making it one element in a vast picture of the world,—the Pauline idea, for example, of a divine spirit incarnate in all mankind, and the Stoic idea of a republic of humanity? And if the Golden Rule now seems to stand and do its work by itself, it is because these other larger ideas, and such as they, have so realized themselves; have died as mere ideas, and been buried in the common consciousness of men, now arising thence as in effect a normal part of the outlook upon life. They have become so integrated with the content of the Golden Rule that the latter itself has become a vast idea, or working tool, of practice.

Now it will be found, upon examination, that every philosophic theory of ethics performs in its degree this same service. It serves, at its time, to preserve the minor rule, the instrument of the ordinary man, from fossilizing. Let rules be conceived as formal prescripts of some outside law-giver, human or divine, and utilitarianism responds with its new criticism,—its insistence upon their relation to human welfare. Let rules slip away into sickly sentimentalism, or harden into rude militarism, and a Kant responds with his equal assertion of law and freedom.[4] And in time these ideas filter into the average consciousness, and their truth becomes, wholly unawares to the average consciousness, a part

4 I hope I shall not be understood as endeavoring to account for the genesis of these ethical systems. I am simply illustrating the part they may play in keeping alive and active moral "rules."

of the ordinary insight into life,—a part of the meaning of the world of practice in which we live. Life looks different to-day to the man to whom Bentham and Kant are not even names, because of the formulæ of the greatest good, the autonomy of will, and the categorical imperative. In conclusion, it is a piece of scholasticism to suppose that a moral rule has its own self-defining and self-applying content. What truth-telling, what honesty, what patience, what self-respect are change with every change of intelligence, with every added insight into the relations of men and things. It is only the breath of intelligence blowing through such rules that keeps them from the putrefaction which awaits all barren idealities.

There is and can be, then, no rigid line between "ideas about morals" (if only they be really ideas,—movements of intelligence) and "moral ideas." The former are the latter in the making. It is only as our moral ideas, our conceptions of this and that thing which needs doing, are reinforced and reconstructed by larger inquiries into the reality of human relationships that they are preserved. And it is only as our ideas about morals realize themselves, only as they become part of the working behavior of the mind towards its concrete duties, that they are other than curiosities for the collector of the bric-a-brac of thought. That they are other, that the history of ethical thought is a record of profound interest to him who has the eyes to read, is because this history is a history of enlarging action; because moral theories are man's first reconstruction of the moral world into a larger and freer one.

And while it lies somewhat beyond my topic, I cannot refrain from saying that no undertaking is more tedious, because more fruitless, than the attempt to pump up moral motive forces. Set as low an estimate as we please upon the place of knowledge in action, and as high a value as we can upon the emotions, how are we to get the interest, the emotion? People are somewhat tired of hearing, "You ought to do thus and so"; they are somewhat tired of hearing, "If you would only do this and somebody else would do that, and so on, how much better everything would be." This condition of fatigue may be due to the depravity of human nature; but I think it is rather due to its goodness; human nature refuses to be moved except in the one truly human way,—through intelligence. Get the fresher, more open outlook, the refined and clarified intelligence, and the emotions will take care of themselves. They *are* there, and all they need is freeing. And it is, in power and not in word, the truth that makes free. Besides intelligence, I see but two means of moral emergence: that of hortatory preaching and that of some scheme as panacea. And both of these, it seems to me, are but attempts to replace intelligence by argument. And what, after all, is argument but halved—or quartered—intelligence?[5]

But I have another and perhaps a larger wave to face. What is the relation of knowledge, of theory, to that Ought which seems to be the very essence of moral conduct? This is the question raised by Mr. Salter, and, as I understand him, he contends that no amount of science, of knowledge, can establish obligation, either in general or in a particular case. For science is of the "is," duty of the "ought," and the "ought" is separate from the "is."

I hardly know where to begin in dealing with this conception. It opens immense fields of philosophy, both historically (compare, for instance, the movement of German ethics from Kant to Hegel) and theoretically. Besides, I seem to find two minds in Mr. Salter, with one of which I am in most hearty agreement. After contrasting in the blankest manner the world of fact and of morals, he goes on to suggest that moral forces are not only rightfully supreme over the actual forces in the world at any time, but "are so interwoven with the order of things that nothing out of harmony with them can long stand" (p. 117). This would imply that moral forces *are*, and that they do not exist nobody knows where outside the actual world, but are themselves supremely actual. With this view I find myself, as I

5 As Mr. Adler discusses the relations of theory and practice, not *per se*, but in connection with the wisdom of founding an ethical society upon a philosophic system, I may avoid misunderstanding if I say that I am not discussing the latter question even by implication. It is one thing to believe that moral theory is in so chaotic and fractional a state that consciously to build an organization upon some one part of it would lead to formalism and inefficiency. It is surely another to hold that moral practice and moral theory have no essential and intrinsic unity.

remarked, in large sympathy; but (aside from the fact that I can see no way of reconciling it with Mr. Salter's other mind) it needs much analysis. If this view means that "justice" and "love" (the moral forces specified by Mr. Salter) are something in themselves, a superfine addendum to the rest of things, or a sort of tempering of the otherwise hard physical forces, I can only confess my incapacity to frame any corresponding conception. If it means that "justice" and "love" are not something in themselves which somehow rule over and sanctify the rest of reality,—morally lawless and unsanctified in itself,—but are the actual forces of reality, taken at a certain angle and scope of working, it conveys intelligibly to me.

But limiting the question as best I can, I should say (first) that the "ought" always rises from and falls back into the "is," and (secondly) that the "ought" is itself an "is,"—the "is" of action.

The "ought" is never its own justification. We ought to do so and so simply because of the existing practical situation; because of the relationships in which we find ourselves. We may, by an abstraction, which is justifiable enough as a means of analysis, distinguish between what is and what should be; but this is far from meaning that there is any such separation in reality. Let us take, then, a specific case: Here is a street-car conductor, and the question is whether he should (ought to) join in a strike which his Union has declared. I do not intend to make and resolve some hypothetical case, but simply, in order to get out of that undoubtedly adorable, yet somewhat vague, realm to which we so naturally incline when we discuss obligation, call up the kind of fact which constitutes obligation. The man thinks of his special work, with its hardships, indeed, and yet a work, an activity, and thus a form of freedom or satisfaction; he thinks of his wage, of what it buys; of his needs, his clothing, his food, his beer and pipe. He thinks of his family, and of his relations to them; his need of protecting and helping them on; his children, that he would educate, and give an evener start in the world than he had himself; he thinks of the families of his fellows; of the need that they should live decently and advance somewhat; he thinks of his bonds to his Union; he calls up the way in which the families of the corporation which employs him live; he tries to realize the actual state of business, and imagines a possible failure and its consequences, and so on. Now where in this case do we get beyond concrete facts, and what is the "ought" but the outcome of these facts, varying as the facts vary, and expressing simply and only the situation which the facts form, so far as our man has the intelligence to get at it? And how does this case differ from any case of moral action?

What has become of moral rules and laws in this case? I cannot go over the ground already gone over (pp. 100, 101 of this article), but I must repeat that a man's duty is never to obey certain rules; his duty is always to respond to the nature of the actual demands which he finds made upon him,—demands which do not proceed from abstract rules, nor from ideals, however awe-inspiring and exalted, but from the concrete relations to men and things in which he finds himself. The rule, at worst and at best, is but an aid towards discriminating what the nature of these relations and demands is. It may be true, as Mr. Salter says, that the Golden Rule does not indicate anything that happens; in the same sense, however, it is true that the law of gravitation does not indicate anything that is. Both laws, as *mere* laws, are abstractions or hypotheses; and to keep them abstractions, to keep them away from the facts, is to keep them from indicating, or pointing to, anything. Taken in any full meaning, the law of gravitation indicates an order of physical fact in which matter behaves thus and so; the Golden Rule indicates an order of social fact, in which it is true that persons act thus and so, and not simply desirable that they should act thus and so. The Golden Rule has no more meaning apart from the real constitution of a social order than the law of gravitation has apart from the real constitution of matter and force.

In a word, a man has not to do Justice and Love and Truth; he has to do justly and truly and lovingly. And this means that he has to respond to the actual relations in which he finds himself. To do truly is to regard the whole situation as far as one sees it, and to see it as far as one can; to do justly is to give a fit and impartial regard to each member of this situation, according to its place in the system; to do lovingly is to make the whole situation one's own, not dividing into parts of which one is a warm *meum* and the other a cold *tuum*.

The correctness of the exact definitions given is a matter, of course, of no importance. The point is that all definitions given must be given in the same terms,—terms, that is, not of mere "oughts," but of concrete ways of acting in reference to a situation, not unearthly, but of facts. Let, for example, our conductor be fixed upon justice. Now, just so far as he is able to resolve "justice" into specific relations between men and men, so far he will have a definite end in view, and such emotions as are aroused within him will simply quicken him in his effort to realize these relations. But just so far as he cannot translate "justice" into such actual relations, so far it becomes a sentiment,—it is justice in general, at large. And this sentiment is almost sure to turn into a bitterness of feeling which leads astray,—to a blind feeling that things should be overturned because they are not what they should be.

And every duty, every ought, so far as it is not the outcome of analysis of the situation demanding action, must come to some such mere feeling. The logical consequences of the separation of the "ought" from the "is" is worshipping blind impulses, labelled love of justice, of truth, of humanity. Its final term is the apotheosis of sentiment, of the pious sigh, "Oh, would that things were otherwise!" If the "ought" escapes this mire, it is only to run upon a rock, —the bare, brute fact of "oughtness" with no essential meaning. It stiffens into a rigid external must, imposed no one knows why or how. The attempt to keep the "ought" unrationalized undoubtedly springs from a desire to keep it pure; to free it from dependence upon some ulterior reason, in the sense of a reason behind the act itself. But to deny that the moral act, the "ought," has a meaning behind the act itself is not incompatible with recognizing that the "ought" itself has a reason, that it is a perfect nest of meanings. To evacuate the "ought" of this intrinsic rationale is to drive out all moral quality and render it the compulsion of a superior force. It is only because the "ought" rests upon and expresses the "is" that it is something more than vague, ill-directed sentiment or rigid external command.

If the "ought" and the "is" are so close to each other, where is the relative distinction? Here: the "ought" is the "is" of *action*. There seems to be an opinion that obligation, the "oughtness," is something superadded to the analysis of the act itself; that we may have examined never so thoroughly the content of a proposed act, of some suggested end, without the idea of obligation ever presenting itself, the result being some intellectual judgment regarding bare fact. Some machinery, the exact nature of which I have never found stated, is then called in to clap on the "ought," and thus give a moral aspect to a hitherto coldly intellectual matter.

The creaking, lumbering *Deus ex machina* which in nick of time projects its proper entity upon the stage of human knowledge has, however, so often been replaced by the smooth, swift workings of a single intelligence, that we may gather courage for the hope that the "ought" too is from intelligence rather than a somewhat let down from supernal flies or sprung from an unearthly trap.

It must be remembered that the material of judgment here is practical, not theoretical. The question is not concerning the given state of things, but concerning an end to be adopted; or, rather, it is concerning the bare actual fact only so far as that points to some active outcome, to some end. The difference between a practical and a theoretical consciousness is that the former is consciousness of *something to be done*. And this consciousness of something to be done is the consciousness of duty. Suppose, once more, our conductor. He has thought out, as best he may, the existing situation, and has come to the conclusion that the only act which meets the situation, as he understands it, is to join the strike. Now, does he require some new power of mind to bring in the "ought," and to tell him that this is the act that should be done? The very question he has been considering is a question of action, of practice; what is the especial line of conduct to be followed here? The outcome of his reflections has been just: *This* step is the one to be taken. The difference between saying, "This act is the one to be done, this act will meet the situation," and saying, "The act *ought* to be done," is merely verbal. The analysis of action is from the first an analysis of what is to be done; how, then, should it come out excepting with a "this should be done"? Just as the consciousness of truth is not adventitious to a judgment of fact but constitutes its content, so the consciousness of obligation is not an annex to the judgment of action. Any being who is capable of acting from ideas—that is, whose conduct is the attempted realization of proposed ends—must conceive of these ends in terms of something to be done—of obligation. And that is what is meant by saying not only that the "ought" rests upon and expresses the "is," but that it is itself the "is" of action. What we ordinarily call an "is" is simply the "is" of fact at rest. If action, or the following out of ideas, is not a fact, with just the same claims to be considered a part of the real world as a stick or a stone, a planet, or an earthworm, then, and then only, have Mr. Salter's remarks about the separation of the "is" and the "ought," the unverifiableness of moral ideas, the attractiveness and authority of moral ideas apart from facts, and the existence of a domain beyond science, any shred of meaning.

Imagine a scene of ceaseless movement; needs, relations, institutions ever moving on. In the midst of this scene appears an intelligence who identifies himself with the wonderful spectacle of action. He finds that its law is his law, because he *is* only as a member sharing in its needs, constituted by its relations and formed by its institutions. This intelligence would know this scene that he may know himself. He puts forth his grasp, his *Begriff*, and arrests the movement. Taking the movement at a certain point and holding it there, intelligence cuts a cross-section through it to see what it is like. It has now mastered the situation, the case "is" thus and so. Then intelligence removes its brake, its abstracting hold, and the scene moves on. That to which intelligence sees it moving is the "ought to be." The "ought to be" is the larger and fuller activity into which it is the destiny and glory of the present fact to pass.

This, then, is the relation of moral theory and practice. Theory is the cross-section of the given state of action in order to know the conduct that should be; practice is the realization of the idea thus gained: it is theory in action.

Poetry and Philosophy

> The future of poetry is immense, because in poetry our race, as time goes on, will find an ever surer and surer stay. There is not a creed which is not shaken; not an accredited dogma which is not shown to be questionable; not a received tradition which does not threaten to dissolve. Our religion has materialized itself in the fact, in the supposed fact; it has attached its emotion to the fact, and now the fact is failing it. But for poetry the idea is everything. . . . Poetry attaches its emotion to the idea, the idea *is* the fact. . . . More and more mankind will discover that we have to turn to poetry to interpret life for us, to console us, to sustain us. Without poetry our science will appear incomplete; and most of what now passes for religion and philosophy will be replaced by poetry.—*Matthew Arnold*

"Not a creed unshaken," "not a dogma unquestioned, every tradition threatening to dissolve,"—this is Matthew Arnold's counterphrase to Carlyle's "Our relations all an inquiry and a doubt." In a world of disintegrated intelligence and a broken authority, Arnold sees men more and more turning to poetry for consolation, for stay, for interpretation. There is absence of any coherent social faith and order; there is doubt whether any theory of life at once valuable and verifiable, true to intelligence and worthy to the emotion, is any longer possible, and yet there is also demand for authority and for instruction. We may say science is verifiable, but it lacks sympathy, consolation, humanity; it does not afford instruction where instruction is most wanted,—in the ordering of life. What once afforded all this, says Mr. Arnold, has lost its hold as truth; it no

[*Commencement address at Smith College, 18 June 1890. First published in* Andover Review, *XVI, 105–16. Reprinted in* Characters and Events, *ed. Joseph Ratner (New York: Henry Holt and Co.,* [c1929]), *I, 3–17, with the title "Matthew Arnold and Robert Browning."*]

longer appeals verifiably to us. This is the difficulty of the situation: the true does not inspire, does not aid; that which once gave stay and interpretation is no longer true. In poetry men find a wide interpretation of life, noble ideas about life, and also a kind sympathy with all its colored moods, with all phases of its movement. Keen feeling, wide sympathy, noble ideas, serious emotion, are found there. What more do we want? What more natural than, in the difficulty of our times, men turning to poetry for guidance? We may well believe that poetry is more and more becoming our religion and our philosophy. Here, let us also add, there is no need to ask if this or that be scientifically true. "For poetry the idea is everything; all else is illusion. For poetry the idea is the fact."

We have the thought of Matthew Arnold before us. What shall we say of it? Shall we make bold to criticise the position? Spite of the clear insight of this great critic, shall we venture to say that his insight was essentially limited in range? that he saw but a small part of the forces really at work in modern thought?

We need not be detained by what our critic says regarding the existing disintegration of intellectual authority in matters of belief. Making allowance for overstatement, all will admit readily that there is enough of unrest, enough of doubt in modern thought, to make it worth while to raise this question, Where shall we find authority, the instruction which our natures demand? Shall we cease to find it in philosophy, or in science, and shall we find it in poetry?

I think none desire that poetry shall not be more and more the vehicle of serious thought and ennobling emotion, that it shall not more and more convey genuine and helpful interpretation of life. *Absit omen.* We have fallen too much on days of trivial subjects, ornate treatment, cheap sentiment, and artificial imagery not to sympathize with all that Mr. Arnold says about the high calling of poetry. We cannot too often return to the idea that its purpose is to deepen the sense of what is worthy, of what is permanent in life. The question only presses the more earnestly: How is poetry to interpret valuable meanings of life, how to animate to the execution of them; how is it to be kept from the evils that threaten it, from the frivolous, the sensual, the artificial? Can it do all this, if it is not backed and sustained by something which commends itself to the intelligence? Call this something what you will, theology, philosophy, or theory of life, how can poetry preserve its genuineness and its sustaining force, if it cut loose from all verifiable account of the universe? Who shall keep the keeper? I know of but one answer. Truth, and truth alone, can do this. And I confess I do not understand how that can be true for the imagination, for the emotions, which is not also true for intelligence.

It is easy to disparage science, it is easy to laugh at philosophy, with its "reasoning about causation and finite and infinite being." Both are remote enough from our immediate spiritual and ethical interests. Face to face with the supreme question concerning the right ordering of life they seem ludicrously insufficient. But, after all, science means only knowledge,—philosophy, only love of wisdom, only the essay at reaching the meaning of this experience of ours. I cannot believe that the attempt to know truth, to grasp the meaning of experience, is remote from conduct, from the ideals and aspirations of life. In the words of Carlyle, I verify my own conviction: "Belief, indeed, is the beginning and first condition of all spiritual force whatsoever; only so far as imagination is *believed* can there be any use or even any enjoyment of it." The imagination rests upon belief; it is from belief that it gets its cue to stay, to interpret, its consolation. If there is belief in the high and serious values of the universe, with what glory shall not the imagination portray and inspire life, what consolations shall not issue from it! But let intelligence lose this belief in the meaning and worthiness of experience, and poetry is but the tricking out of illusions, the devising of artifices. I can well comprehend that poetry may deliver truth with a personal and a passionate force which is beyond the reach of theory painting in gray on gray. Indeed, it is the emotional kindling of reality which is the true province of poetry.

Astronomers tell us that meteors are cold rock, cold as the frozen emptiness of space, molten by contact with our earthly atmosphere, and thence glowing like the stars. Thus do I conceive of poetry. The graceless, rigid, dark facts of science, of philosophy, pass through the atmosphere of personality, of the hopes and fears of a human soul, and issue illumined and to illuminate. Without the basis of fact, of fact verifiable by science, our light is a will-o'-the-wisp, a wandering flame generated in the stagnant marshes of sentiment. In a word, there must be the possibility of science and philosophy to criticise, to verify. Poets are indeed seers and makers; but if what they make has matter, has weight, if what they see is more than shadow, the poets must reveal, they must round out to high completeness, the meaning of the life that is about them. Poets cannot be freed from the conditions which attach to the intelligence of man everywhere. The poet and the ploughman gaze at the same scene, only the eyes of one are holden. If the life which the poet presents to us as throbbing, as pregnant, ever new from God, is other than the genuine revelation of the ordinary day-by-day life of man, it is but dainty foolery or clumsy masquerading. If life is, indeed, dull and blank and unappealing, poetry will be depressing, mechanical, merely decorative. If life is abundant, promising, endless, poetry will be spontaneous, buoyant, passionate; it will have enjoyment. If life carries meaning with it, fulfills purpose, makes exactions which are opportunities, poetry will be high-minded, a power to stay and to console.

Nor is this all. What life is found to be depends in large measure upon the prevailing theory of life, upon the interpretation of it which commends itself to the intelligence. Life is not a raw, unworked material to which the poet may directly apply himself. As it comes to the poet, life is already a universe of meanings, of interpretations, which indeed the poet may fill out, but not dispense with. For good or for ill, centuries of reflective thought have been interpreting life, and their interpretations remain the basis and furnish the instrument for all the poet may do; he may simply use the assimilated results of the labors of scientific men and philosophers. Let the philosophy of a time be materialistic, mechanical, and the poetry of that time is artificial and unworthy. If the poet succeeds in rising above the thought that has taken possession of contemporary life, it is because by instinct or by desire he falls back on the larger and freer ideas of an earlier day. If the ideas of a time breathe the solemn atmosphere of a divine order, if they find reality surcharged with meaning, we can imagine the poetry that results. It is the poetry of Homer, of Dante, of Shakespeare. If the philosophy of a time is agnostic, if it utters a scorn of life as it seems to be, that philosophy will also sound its note in the poetry of its day.

Thus are we brought again to our starting-point. If we are correct in our judgment that a poet must draw his sustenance from the intelligence of his time, the poetry of to-day must feel the touch of what we call our agnosticism, and the poets of to-day must be somewhat moved by this trait of contemporary life.

Are they thus moved? What is their attitude toward the agnosticism, the doubt, the pessimism, of the present day?

I wish now to speak in this relation of two poets who have recently passed from us. One of them is Mr. Arnold himself, poet as well as critic; the other is Mr. Robert Browning. How do these, both serious and high-minded poets, stand affected by the popular philosophy? How do they affect us who go to them to learn of life?

Nothing in Arnold the poet strikes us more than the teaching of Arnold the critic. Translated from the impersonal narrative of prose into the warmth of poetry, it is the same lesson. Compare the passage standing as our text with this: –

Wandering between two worlds, one dead
The other powerless to be born,
With nowhere yet to lay my head,
Like them, on earth I wait forlorn.

Or with this: –

The sea of faith
Was once, too, at the full, and round earth's shore
Lay like the folds of a bright girdle furled:
But now I only hear
Its melancholy long withdrawing roar.

Indeed, Arnold's distinguishing sign among modern poets is the melancholy beauty with which he has voiced the sense of loss; his sad backward glance at the departure of old faiths and ideals; the brooding memories of joys whose spring has fallen away; the shapeless, hopeless hope for the dawn of a new joy, new faith.

I should say that the source of regret which expires from Arnold's lines is his consciousness of a twofold isolation of man—his isolation from nature, his isolation from fellow-man. No longer, he seems to say, may man believe in his oneness with the dear nature about him: the sense of a common spirit binding them together has vanished; the sense of a common purpose outworking in both has fled. Nature, in ceasing to be divine, has ceased to be human. The faith that one idea, one fulfillment, unites in cherished bonds man to nature, is no more; in its stead, the consciousness of isolation. There is still, indeed, grateful companionship with nature, but below this companionship is the knowledge of an impassable gulf: —

Thou hast been, shalt be, art alone:
Or, if not quite alone, yet they
Who touch thee are unmating things,—
Ocean and clouds, and night and day,
Lorn autumns and triumphant springs.

The companionship is not at bottom real: it is only on man's side; Nature lacks the element of purpose which alone could give joyful response to man's needs. Man solaces and strengthens his spirit by recourse to Nature, but Nature goes her own way and man must return to his; strengthened and solaced, indeed, but only that he may live self-poised like Nature, careless, unheeding of all beyond self. Companionship no longer is rooted in the heart of things; it is no longer the outcome of a single life.

Man, repulsed from the intimacy of communion with Nature, may turn to man for fellowship; but here, too, is found isolation: —

Like drift-wood spars which meet and pass
  Upon the boundless ocean plain,
So on the sea of life, alas!
  Man meets man, meets and parts again.

No reader of Arnold can fail to notice how spontaneously he takes his most characteristic metaphor from the sea and the matters of the sea. The verses I am about to quote have the same inspiration and tell the same story. As the islands of the sea are separated by that sea which is common to them all, so men are separated by that very life in which all share. Between them is

The unplumbed, salt, estranging sea.

Yes, on the sea of life enisled,
With echoing straits between us thrown,
We mortal millions live alone.

I am aware, however, of no passage of Arnold's which comes to us so laden with the gospel of the isolation of life as that poem which gives us his reading of history, "Obermann Once More." The sad tone reaches its highest note in the description of the loss of Christian faith. From the land whence once came the words of humanity's life,—

Ah, from that silent, sacred land
Of sun and arid stone,
And crumbling wall and sultry sand,
Comes now one *word alone!*
From David's lips that word did roll,
'Tis true and living yet:
No man can save his brother's soul,
Nor pay his brother's debt.
Alone, self-poised, henceforward man
Must labor.

Not from him who identified himself with the woe and the joy of all men's lives, but from David, sounds the final word of Palestine. The life of common brotherhood, struggle and destiny of Christianity has given way to the old isolated struggle of the individual.

No man can save his brother's soul
Nor pay his brother's debt.

That is, I take it, the last word of Arnold's poetic message, his last interpretation of life. Perhaps I should rather say this is the keynote of it all. To say it is the last is to say his last message is one of weakness and despair. Contrary to this, the philosophy which Mr. Arnold leaves us is one of endeavor, of strenuous, almost buoyant, endeavor, in spite of the fact that this endeavor must spring from sadness. If man is isolated, in that isolation he may find himself, and, finding himself, living his own life, lose all his misery. Although man may not commune with Nature, he may yet follow and repeat her. If the works of Nature go on,

> *Bounded by themselves, and unregardful*
> *In what state God's other works may be,*

man should emulate this self-sufficient energy. Isolation is translated into self-dependence. Separation throws man farther into himself, deepens his consciousness of his own destiny and of his own law. The verses which close the poem called "Youth of Man," while far from the most poetical of his lines, sum up, I think, his interpretation of life:—

> *Sink, O youth, in thy soul!*
> *Yearn to the greatness of nature;*
> *Rally the good in the depths of thyself.*

This is the outcome of the loneliness of life. Regret and melancholy are not the final fruit. Obey nature, go thy way, heeding nothing less than the concerns of men. As a consolation for thy loneliness, yearn to the greatness of nature. Is man helpless to save another's soul? Then all the more let him rally the good in the depths of himself!

How does this message stand related to the dictum of Arnold that poetry is to take the place of philosophy, of theology? How does it stand related to our dictum that the interpretation of life which poetry gives us must be parallel to the demonstrations of philosophy? I do not know how any one can apprehend the message uttered by Arnold and not feel its heart and substance to be that reflective and philosophic interpretation of life given by one school of the world's great moralists,—by the Stoics. As surely as Arnold's style, his deftness, his delicacy, his simplicity testify to the influence of Virgil, of Æschylus, of Homer, so surely do his ideas and their substance testify to Marcus Aurelius and to Epictetus and to Kant. I do not mean by this that Arnold has put the *Meditations* or the *Critique of Practical Reason* into verse. I do not even imagine that Arnold had much acquaintance with Kant, or was attracted by such as he had. Speaking broadly, however, the ideas of the Stoics, of Kant, and of Matthew Arnold, grow out of the same soil. There is in all three the conception of the individual as shut off from real communion with nature and with fellow-man, and yet as bearing in himself a universal principle.

And thou, thou lonely heart,
Which never yet, without remorse,
Even for a moment didst depart
From thy remote and spherēd course
To haunt the place where passions dwell,
Back to thy solitude again.

This is precisely in the sense of Epictetus, precisely in the vein of Kant. I would not, however, insist upon detailed likeness in special points. What is alike in all is the underlying spirit, the attitude towards life. The individual flung back from the world and from society upon himself, and within himself finding the secret of a new strength, the source of a new consolation,—this is the interpretation of life common to all. How can such an interpretation have use, have enjoyment, be a consolation, be a stay in poetry, and yet have no legitimacy in theory? What alembic does the poet possess that he may apply ideas to life with the assurance that in poetry the ideas are the fact, while the same ideas in the hands of the philosopher are unverifiable, discredited dogmas, shaken creeds, or failing traditions? I cannot rid myself of the conviction that the weight and the humanity of the message of the poet are proportionate to the weighty and human ideas which he develops; that these ideas must be capable of verification to the intelligence,—

must be true in that system of knowledge which is science, in that discussion of the meaning of experience which is philosophy.

But what if Mr. Arnold's interpretation of life be partial? What if a completer account of experience, a deeper and more adventurous love of wisdom, should find community below all isolation? Would not the philosophy of life which revealed this limitation of Mr. Arnold's interpretation, reveal also the limitation of his poetry? This is the question that comes to me when I put Mr. Arnold's poetry, with all its nobility, beside the poetry of Robert Browning.

What a change from a serene yet cold air of one to the genial, glowing atmosphere of the other, which envelops and embraces everything in this world of ours as if in fear that something might escape its loving touch. What a change from the pallid colors in which one paints life to the varied warmth of the other! What a change from the almost remote and academic sympathies of the one to the passionate human sympathies of the other! Where Arnold finds food for pensive regret, a rendering of triumphant hope is borne to us from Browning. When the world tells a story of softened melancholy to Arnold, Browning reads a tale of keen and delicious joy. If Arnold sings of calm, self-poised resignation and endeavor, the trumpet peal of an abounding life bursts from Browning. Arnold stands upon the sandy, barren shore of that vast ocean where is seen only "the turbid ebb and flow of human misery," whence comes only the melancholy sounds of a withdrawing faith. Browning takes his place on this homely, every-day earth of ours: –

Do I stoop? I pluck a posey.
Do I stand and stare? All's blue.

Strenuous, abounding, triumphant optimism, – that is the note of Browning: –

How good is man's life, the men living! how fit to employ
All the heart and the soul and the senses forever in joy!

Buoyant faith, that is the attitude of Browning: –

God's in his heaven!
All's right with the world!

What is the source of this note of Browning, what the authority for his attitude? It is only when we go to his ideas, the ideas which he applies to life, by which he criticises and interprets life, that we get the secret of his superior passion, of his superior joy, of his superior sympathy. An adequate rendering of Browning's conception of the meaning of life does not come within the scope of this article. The most inadequate rendering cannot fail to note that Browning knows and tells of no isolation of man from nature, of man from man. No account, however brief, can fail to record the abundance, the intensity, the vibrating fullness, the impassioned sanity of his verse, basing themselves upon Browning's realization that the world was made for man, and that man was made for man: –

This world's no blot for us,
No blank. It means intensely and means good.

This is the uniform utterance of Browning.

Such a soul,
Such a body, and then such an earth,
For ensphering the whole!

The earth's first stuff
Was neither more nor less, enough
To house man's soul, man's need fulfill.

How the world is made for each of us!
All we perceive and know in it
Tends to some moment's product thus
When the soul declares itself.

In these verses we have the epitome of Browning's interpretation of life: the subordination of earth to man, to a common self. Just that which was conspicuously absent in Arnold is conspicuously present in Browning, – the sense of a common idea, a common purpose, in nature and in man.

Thus it is man need not simply look to nature for encouragement in bearing the burden of the world, for strength to be like her, self-poised, self-dependent. Man may rejoice in her every pulse of life, having the conviction that in her life he, too, lives; knowing that her every event furthers some deed of his, knowing that her beauty is the response to some aspiration of his. Let one know, as Browning sings in "Rabbi Ben Ezra," that nature, that the earthly life, and all "this dance of plastic circumstance," are but the machinery to shape the soul, to form the spirit; are but the potter's wheel that moulds the clay to "heaven's consummate cup"; let him know that the meaning of life, the "uses of the cup," are

> *The festal board, lamp's flash, and trumpet's peal,*
> *The new wine's foaming flow,*
> *The master's lips aglow!*—

let him know all this, and he will understand why the song of Browning is one of joy and victory.

Add to this Browning's conception of the relation of man to man. Consider how he finds in the contacts of life, not isolation, but companionship, service, love,—the first and the last word.

To relate how he finds, in the minglings of life and life, the secret and the key to our experience, would be to summarize, one by one, his poems. Even a casual acquaintance with Browning suffices to show that love, as he conceives it, is no accident and no mere occurrence of the life-journey, but at once its path and its goal. Everything

> *Of power and beauty in the world*
> *The mightiness of love is curled*
> *Inextricably round about.*
> *Love lies within it and without.*

We are led again to our old question. The greater vigor and sensuousness of Browning, his wider range, his more human touch, all spring from the ideas through which he sees and interprets life. But are the ideas true? Are they verifiable? Are they sporadic outbursts of a fancy which has no root in the nature of things, or are they the revelations of an imagination which is but another name for insight? If the ideas which give both substance and shape to Browning's poetry are only artificial make-ups of his individual fancy, what claim have they even for serious attention, to say nothing of power to stay by and to uphold? If these ideas are not ideas of soberness and of truth, as well as of fancy and passion, they are no more to us (the harsh word must be said) than freaks of a madman's brain.

If Mr. Arnold's message has weight and penetration with us, it is because that message conveys something of the reality of things. If there are messages, in comparison with which Mr. Arnold's seems pallid and academic, it is only because these other messages bring us word from a more abiding, a more human world than Mr. Arnold has known. The great power of poetry to stay and to console—a power which neither Arnold nor any other critic can exaggerate one whit—is just because of the truth, the rendering of the reality of affairs, which poetry gives us. The importance and the endurance of poetry, as of all art, are in its hold upon reality. We hear much, on this side and that, of realism. Well, we may let realism go, but we cannot let go reality. Here, too, we may turn to Robert Browning himself: —

Truth, truth, that's the gold. And all the good
I find in fancy is, it serves to set
Gold's inmost glint free.

It is because, amid the conventionalities and make-believes of our ordinary life, poetry flashes home to us some of the gold which is at the very heart and core of our every-day existence, that poetry has its power to sustain us, its sympathy to enhearten us. Now science and philosophy, I repeat, however technical and remote in form and method, are the workings of the one selfsame spirit in its communing with this same world. There are, indeed, diversities of operation. And if the advantage in directness and universality of appeal, in wealth and passionateness of garb, is upon the side of poetry, let us remember that, after all, the advantage upon the side of method and standard are with the side of science and philosophy.

Indeed, this present separation of science and art, this division of life into prose and poetry, is an unnatural divorce of the spirit. It exists and endures, not because of a glow to life which philosophy cannot catch, nor because of a verifiable truth which poetry cannot detect and convey. It exists because in the last few centuries the onward movement of life, of experience, has been so rapid, its diversification of regions and methods so wide, that it has outrun the slower step of reflective thought. Philosophy has not as yet caught the rhythmic swing of this onward movement, and written it down in a score of black and white which all may read. Or if in some degree philosophy has laid hold of the secret of this movement, it has not yet been able to tell it in straightforward, simple syllables to the common consciousness. In its own theory, this common consciousness tells by rote a doctrine of an earlier and outworn world. But this movement, which has so escaped the surer yet heavier tread of critical thought, has in manifold ways danced itself into the poetic measures of our century. The deeper and wider spiritual life which makes this movement has found an expression in Wordsworth and Shelley, in Browning and in Mr. Arnold himself, which has, as yet, been denied to it in English philosophy. That which seemed to Mr. Arnold a flight from philosophy into poetry was in reality but a flight from a hard and partial philosophy to a fuller and freer one. It is not because poetry is divorced from science that it gave Mr. Arnold's nature such satisfaction, but because his philosophic instinct was so deep and real that he revolted from the professional philosophy of the day as he found it in Great Britain, and sought refuge in the unnamed, unprofessed philosophy of the great poets of England and of all time.

Here, indeed, is just our problem. We must bridge this gap of poetry from science. We must heal this unnatural wound. We must, in the cold, reflective way of critical system, justify and organize the truth which poetry, with its quick, naïve contacts, has already felt and reported. The same movement of the spirit, bringing man and man, man and nature, into wider and closer unity, which has found expression by anticipation in poetry, must find expression by retrospection in philosophy. Thus will be hastened the day in which our sons and our daughters shall prophesy, our young men shall see visions, and our old men dream dreams.

The Present Position of Logical Theory

The remarkable fact in the intellectual life of to-day is the contradiction in which it is entangled. On one hand, we have an enormous development of science, both in specialisation of method and accumulation of material; its extension and thorough-going application to all ranges of experience. What we should expect from such a movement would be confidence of intelligence in itself, and a corresponding organisation of knowledge giving some guide and support to life. The strange thing is that instead of this we have apparently the greatest disorganisation of authority as to intellectual matters that the world has ever seen; while the prevalent attitude and creed of scientific men is philosophic agnosticism, or disbelief in their own method when it comes to fundamental matters. Such a typical representative of modern science as Mr. Huxley virtually laughs to scorn the suggestion of Mr. Frederic Harrison that science should or could become so organised as to give any support, any authoritative stay, to life.

Now I do not intend to discuss this apparent contradiction. It seems to me obvious enough that the contradiction is due to the fact that science has got far enough along to make its negative attitude towards previous codes of life evident, while its own positive principle of reconstruction is not yet evident. But without urging this view upon the reader, I wish to ask how and where in the prevailing confusion logical theory, as a synopsis of the methods and typical forms of intelligence, stands. Logical theory at once reflects

[*First published in the* Monist, *II (Oct. 1891), 1–17. Not previously reprinted.*]

and transforms the existing status of matters intellectual at any period. It reflects this, for logical theory is only the express, the overt consciousness on the part of intelligence of its own attitude and prevailing spirit. It transforms the status, because this express consciousness makes intelligence know where it stands, makes it aware of its strength and of its weakness, and by defining it to itself forces it to take up a new and more adequate place.

It is obvious, then, that as the prevailing influence in the intellectual world to-day is science, so the prevailing influence in logical theory must be the endeavor to account for, to justify, or at least to reckon with this scientific spirit. And yet if there is such confusion as we have indicated, there is also some chaos in logical theory as to the true nature and method of science. Were it otherwise, were there at present a logical theory adequate to the specific and detailed practical results of science, science and scientific men would be conscious of themselves, and would be confident in their work and attitude.

The especial problem of logic, as the theory of scientific method, is the relation of fact and thought to each other, of reality and ideas. The problem is, however, differentiated from the metaphysical theory of knowledge. Logic does not inquire into the ultimate *meaning* of fact and thought, nor into their *ultimate* relations to one another. It simply takes them from the attitude of science itself; its business being, not the justification nor refutation of this attitude, but its development into explicit doctrine. Fact means to logic no more, but certainly no less, than it means to the special sciences: it is the subject-matter under investigation, under consideration; it is that which we are trying to make out. Thought means to logic what it means to science: method. It is the attitude and form which intelligence takes in reference to fact—to its subject-matter, whether in inquiry, experiment, calculation, or statement.

Logic, then, has for its essential problem the consideration of the various typical methods and guiding principles which thought assumes in its effort to detect, master, and report fact. It is presupposed here that there is some sort of fruitful and intrinsic connection of fact and thought; that thinking, in short, is nothing but the fact in its process of translation from brute impression to lucent meaning.

But the moment such a presupposition is stated, ninety-nine persons out of a hundred think that we have plunged, *ex abrupto*, from the certainty of science into the cloudland of metaphysic. And yet just this conception of the relation of thought (method) to fact (subject-matter) is taken for granted in every scientific investigation and conclusion. Here, then, we have in outline the present position of logic. Any attempt to state, in general, or to work out, in detail, the principle of the intrinsic and fruitful relation of fact and thought which science, without conscious reflection, constantly employs in practice, seems "metaphysical" or even absurd. Why is this? The answer to this question will give the filling-up of the outline just presented.

The chief cause is that superstition which still holds enthralled so much of modern thought—I mean formal logic. And if this seems like applying a hard name to what, at best and at worst, is only an intellectual gymnastic, I can only say that formal logic seems to me to be, at present, *fons et origo malorum* in philosophy. It is true enough that nobody now takes the technical subject of formal logic very seriously—unless here and there some belated "professor." It is true that it is generally relegated to the position of a subject which, for some unclear reason, is regarded as "disciplinary" in a young man's education;—just as certain other branches are regarded as elegant accomplishments in a young woman's finishing. But while the subject itself as a doctrine or science hardly ranks very high, the conception of thought which is at the bottom of formal logic still dominates the *Zeitgeist*, and regulates the theory and the method of all those who draw their inspiration from the *Zeitgeist*. Any book of formal logic will tell us what this conception of thought is: thought is a faculty or an entity existing in the mind, apart from facts, having its own fixed forms, with which facts have nothing to do—except in so far as to pass under the yoke. Jevons puts it this way: "Just as we thus familiarly recognise the difference of form and substance in common tangible things, so we may observe in logic, that the form of an argument is one thing, quite distinct from the various subjects or matter which may be treated in that form."[1]

Professor Stock varies the good old tune in this way: "In every act of thought we may distinguish two things—(1) the object thought about, (2) the way in which the mind thinks of it. The first is called the Matter; the second the Form of Thought. Now formal . . . Logic is concerned only with the way in which the mind thinks, and has nothing to do with the particular objects thought about."[2]

It is assumed, in fine, that thought has a nature of its own independent of facts or subject-matter; that this thought, *per se*, has certain forms, and that these forms are not forms which the facts themselves take, varying with the facts, but are rigid frames, into which the facts are to be set.

Now all of this conception—the notion that the mind has a faculty of thought apart from things, the notion that this faculty is constructed, in and of itself with a fixed framework, the notion that thinking is the imposing of this fixed framework on some unyielding matter called particular objects, or facts—all of this conception appears to me highly scholastic: to be, indeed, the last struggle of mediævalism to hold thought in subjection to authority. Nothing is more surprising than the fact that while it is fashionable to reject, with great scorn, all the results and special methods of scholasticism, its foundation-stone should still be accepted as the corner-stone of the edifice of modern doctrine. It is still more surprising when we reflect that the foundation-stone is coherent only with the mediæval superstructure. The scholastics were at least consistent in holding the method of thought to be a faculty pursuing its own method apart from the course of things. They did not conceive that thought was free, that intelligence had rights, nor that there was possible science independent of data authoritatively laid down. Really believing what they professed,—that thought was something *in se*,—they held that it must be supplied with a fixed body of dogmatic fact, from tradition, from revelation—from external authority. They held that

1 Jevons, *Elementary Lessons in Logic*, p. 5.
2 Stock, *Deductive Logic*, pp. 3–4.

thought in its workings is confined to extracting from this dogmatic body of fact what is already contained in it, and to rearranging the material and its implications. To examine the *material*, to test its truth; to suppose that intelligence could cut loose from this body of authority and go straight to nature, to history itself, to find the truth; to build up a free and independent science—to this point of incoherency mediæval scholasticism never attained. To proclaim the freedom of thought, the rejection of all external authority, the right and the power of thought to get at truth for itself, and yet continue to define thought as a faculty apart from fact, is reserved for modern enlightenment! And were it not somewhat out of my present scope, I should like to show that modern culture is thus a prepared victim for the skilful dialectician of the reactionary army. If the modern *Zeitgeist* does not fall a prey to the cohorts of the army of external authority, it is not because it has any recognised methods or any recognised criterion by which it can justify its raising the "banner of the free spirit." It is simply the obstinate bulwark of outer fact, built up piecemeal by science, that protects it.

The two main forces, which have been at work against the formulæ of formal logic, are "inductive" or empirical logic on one side, and the so-called "transcendental" logic, on the other. Of these two, the influence of inductive logic in sapping in practical fashion and popular results the authority of syllogistic logic has undoubtedly been much the greater. I propose, briefly, to give certain reasons for holding, however, that the inductive logic does not furnish us with the needed theory of the relation of thought and fact. To show this adequately would demand the criticism of inductive logic in the detail of its methods, in order to bring out where it comes short. As this is impossible, I shall now confine myself to a couple of general considerations.

To begin with, the empirical logic virtually continues the conception of thought as in itself empty and formal which characterises scholastic logic. It thus has really no theory which differentiates it, as regards the nature of thought itself, from formal logic. I cannot see, for example, what quarrel the most stringent upholder of formal logic can have with Mill as to the latter's theory of the syllogism. Mill's theory is virtually simply a theory regarding the formation of the major premiss—regarding the process by which we formulate the statement that All *S* is *P*. Now, if we once accept the syllogistic position, this process lies outside the scope and problem of formal logic. It is not an affair of what Jevons calls the form of argument at all, but simply of the matter, the particular facts which make the filling of the argument. I do not see that it is any part of the business of formal logic to tell where the major premiss comes from, nor how it is got. And, on the other hand, when it comes to the manipulation of the data contained in the premiss, Mill must fall back upon the syllogistic logic. Mill's theory, so far as the thought-element is concerned, presupposes the syllogistic theory. And if this theory, on its side, does not presuppose something like Mill's inductive theory, it is simply because the logician, as a *philosopher*, may prefer "intuitionalism" to "empiricism." He may hold, that is, that the content of some major premisses is given by direct "intuition" rather than gathered from experience. But in either case, the consideration of the source of the content of the premiss belongs not to formal logic, but to the theory of knowledge.

If, then, the theory of the syllogism is incorrect in its assumptions as to the relation of fact and thought, the inductive logic must be similarly in error. Its great advantage over the old scholastic logic lies not in its logic as such, but in something back of the logic—in its account of the derivation of the material of judgment. Whatever the defects of Locke's or Mill's account of experience, any theory which somehow presupposes a first-hand contact of mind and fact (though it be only in isolated, atomic sensations) is surely preferable to a theory which falls back on tradition, or on the delivery of dogma irresponsible to any intellectual criticism. However, in its account of the derivation of the material of judgment, inductive logic is still hampered by the scholastic conception of thought. Thought since confined to the rigid framework in which the material is manipulated once obtained, is excluded from all share in the gathering of material. The result is that this material, having no intrinsic thought-side, shrinks into a more or less accidental association of more or less shifting and transitory mental states.

I shall not stop to argue that, on this ground, the "inductive" logic deprives science of its most distinctive scientific features—the permanence and objectivity of its truths. I think no one can deny that there is at least an *apparent* gap between the actual results of concrete science, and these results as they stand after the touch of the inductive logic—that the necessity and generality of science seem rather to have been explained away, than explained. I think most of the inductive logicians themselves (while endeavoring to account for this apparent necessity as generated through association) would admit that something of science *seems*, at least, to have been lost, and that the great reason for putting-up with this loss is that the inductive logic is the sole alternative to a dogmatic intuitionalism and to arbitrary spinning-out of *a priori* concepts.

Certainly as long as thought is conceived after the fashion of syllogistic logic, as a scheme furnished and fixed in itself apart from reality, so long scientific men must protest against allowing thought any part or lot in scientific procedure, and so long some such *modus operandi* as that given by Mill must be resorted to in order to explain scientific methods and results. But, on the other hand, if the scholastic idea of thought as something having its character apart from fact is once given up, the force which at present cramps the logic of science into the logic of sensationalism and empiricism is also given up.

And this brings us to the other point in general regarding the inductive or empirical logic. It is not strictly a logic at all but a metaphysic. It does not begin with the datum of science, the fruitful inquiry into fact by intelligence, at all. It does not, starting from this datum analyse the various methods and types which thought must take upon itself in order to maintain this fruitful inquiry. On the contrary, it begins with sensations, and endeavors by a theory of knowledge on the basis of sensationalism to build up the structure of cognition, ordinary and scientific. I am not concerned here with the truth of sensationalism as a metaphysical theory of knowledge, nor with the adequacy of the notion of sensation advanced by Mill. It is enough from the logical point of view to point out that such a theory is not logic—that logic does not deal with something *back* of the fact of science, but with the analysis of scientific method as such. And is it forcing matters to indicate that this retreat from logic to metaphysic is also caused by the syllogistic notion of thought? Formal thought, with its formulæ for simply unfolding a given material, is of no use in science. There is, therefore, the need of some other machinery to take the place of thought. And this is found in sensation and in "experience" according to the peculiar notion of experience current in the inductive logic.

In a word, then (without attempting to show the insufficiency of inductive logic as the theory of science by reference to its treatment of specific points) inductive logic does not meet our needs because it is not a free, unprejudiced inquiry into the special forms and methods of science, starting from the actual sciences themselves. It is founded and built up with constant reference to the scholastic notion of thought. Where it is not affected positively by it, it is still affected by its reaction from it. Instead of denying once for all validity or even sense to the notion of thinking as a special, apart process, and then beginning a free, unhampered examination with an eye single to the fact of science itself, it retains the conception of thought as valid in a certain department, and then sets out to find something in another department to supply the gap. And thus we have the usual division of inductive and deductive logic, inductive being interpreted as empirical and particular, deductive as syllogistic and formal. They are counterpart and correlative theories, the two sides of the notion of the separateness of fact and thought; they stand and fall together.

"Transcendental" logic, while usually conceived as utterly opposed in spirit and in results to inductive logic, has yet been one with it in endeavoring to abolish formal logic as the sufficient method and criterion of scientific truth. I say this although well aware that inductive logic is usually conceived as specifically "scientific," while the transcendental movement is regarded as the especial foe of science—as a belated attempt to restore an *a priori* scholasticism, by finding a scheme for evolving truth out of pure thought. This is because when the "transcendental" school talks of thought, of the synthetic and objective character of thought, of the possibility of attaining truth through thought, and of the ontological value of thought, it is understood to mean thought in the old, scholastic sense, a process apart and fixed in itself, and yet somehow evolving truth out of its own inner being, out of its own enclosed ruminations. But on the contrary, the very meaning of "transcendentalism" is not only that it is impossible to get valid truth from the evolution of thought in the scholastic sense, but that there is no such thought at all. Processes of intelligence which have their nature fixed in themselves, apart from fact and having to be externally applied to fact, are pure myths to this school. Types of thought are simply the various forms which reality progressively takes as it is progressively mastered as to its meaning,—that is, understood. Methods of thought are simply the various active attitudes into which intelligence puts itself in order to detect and grasp the fact. Instead of rigid moulds, they are flexible adaptations. Methods of thought fit fact more closely and responsively than a worn glove fits the hand. They are only the ideal evolution of the fact—and by "ideal" is here meant simply the evolution of fact into meaning.

If this is a fair description of what the "transcendental" school means by thought, it is evident that it is a co-worker with the spirit and intent of "inductive" logic. Its sole attempt is to get hold of and report the presupposition and rationale of science; its practical aim is to lay bare and exhibit the method of science so that the only seat of authority—that is, the authority, the *backing*, of truth—shall be forever manifest. It has simply gone a step further than "inductive" logic, and thrown overboard once for all the scholastic idea of thought. This has enabled it to start anew, and to form its theory of thought simply by following the principles of the actual processes by which man has, thus far in history, discovered and possessed fact.

I shall not attempt here any defence of the "transcendental" logic; I shall not even attempt to show that the interpretation of it which I have given above is correct. It must go, for the present, simply as my individual understanding of the matter. Taking this view of "transcendental" logic for granted, I wish, in order to complete our notion of the present position of logic, to consider the reasons which have thus far prevented, say, the Hegelian logic from getting any popular hold—from getting recognition from scientific men as, at least in principle, a fair statement of their own basic position and method.

The first of these reasons is that the popular comprehension of the "transcendental" movement is arrested at Kant and has never gone on to Hegel. Hegel, it is true, overshadowed Kant entirely for a considerable period. But the Hegelian régime was partly pyrotechnical rather than scientific in character; and, partly, so far as it was scientific, it exhausted itself in stimulating various detailed scientific movements—as in the history of politics, religion, art, etc. In these lines, if we trust even to those who have no faith in the Hegelian method or principles, the movement found some practical excuse for being. But the result of the case was—and its present status is—that the principle of Hegel being, for the time, lost either in display of dialectical fireworks, or in application to specific subjects, the principle itself has never met with any *general* investigation. The immense amount of labor spent on Kant during the past twenty years has made the Kantian method and principle familiar, if not acceptable, to the body of men calling themselves educated. And thus, so far as its outcome is concerned, the transcendental movement still halts with Kant.

Now, at the expense of seeming to plunge deeper in absurdity, I must say that the Kantian principle is far more "transcendental" in the usual interpretation of that term—more *a priori*, more given to emphasising some special function of some special thought-power—than the Hegelian. As against the usual opinion of the possibility of some compromise between science and Kant, while the scientific spirit and Hegel are at antipodes, it appears to me it is Kant who does violence to science, while Hegel (I speak of his essential method and not of any particular result) is the quintessence of the scientific spirit. Let me endeavor to give some reasons for this belief. Kant starts from the accepted scholastic conception of thought. Kant never dreams, for a moment, of questioning the existence of a special faculty of thought with its own peculiar and fixed forms. He states and restates that thought in itself exists apart from fact and occupies itself with fact given to it from without. Kant, it is true, gives the death-blow to scholasticism by pointing out that such a faculty of thought is purely analytic—that it simply unfolds the material given, whether that material be true or false, having no method of arriving at truth, and no test for determining truth. This fact once clearly recognised, dogmatic rationalism, or the attempt to get truth from the "logical" analysis of concepts was forever destroyed. The way was opened for an independent examination of the actual method of science.

But while Kant revealed once for all the impossibility of getting truth, of laying hold of reality, by the scholastic method, he still retained that conception of thought. He denied not its existence, but its worth as relates to truth. What was the result? Just this: when he came to his examination (criticism) of knowledge, it fell apart at once into two separate factors, an *a priori* and *a posteriori*. For if Kant finds, as against the dogmatic rationalist, that formal thought cannot give knowledge, he also finds, as against the sceptical empiricist, that unrelated sensation cannot give knowledge. Here, instead of denying, *in toto*, the existence of unrelated sensation, he contented himself with denying its functional value for knowledge. Unrelated sensation and formal thought are simply the complementary halves of each other. Admit the one, and the other is its necessary counterpart.

Kant must now piece together his two separated factors. Sensation, unrelated manifold of sensation, is *there*; thought, isolated, analytic thought, is *here*. Neither is knowledge in itself. What more natural than to put them together, and hold that knowledge is the union of a matter or stuff, of sensations, atomic in themselves, on one hand, and a form, or regulating principle of thought, empty in itself, on the other? We have two elements, both existing in isolation, and yet both useless for all purposes of knowledge. Combine them, and presto, there is science.

Such a "transcendentalism" as this may well stick in the crop of scientific men. For consider what is involved in it: an *a priori* factor, on one side, and an *a posteriori*, on the other. Kant, from one point of view, seems thus to have simply combined the weaknesses of empiricism and rationalism. He still continues to talk of experience itself as particular and contingent, and denies that it gives a basis for any universal laws. Aside from his effort in the *Kritik der Urtheilskraft* to overcome his original separation, special scientific laws are to him only more or less extensive "generalisations from experience"—as much so to him as to Locke, or Mill. Scientific men, indeed, have accustomed themselves to this derogation of their own methods and results, and, as "inductive" logicians, indulge in it quite freely themselves. But an *a priori* element, supplied by a thought fixed and separate, scientific men cannot do away with. Nor do I know any reason why they should.

It is coming short, in my opinion, of the full stature of science to treat it as a quantitative and varying generalisation of contingent particulars, but this, at least, leaves what science there is free and unhindered. But *a priori* elements supplied from outside the fact itself, *a priori* elements somehow entering into the fact from without and controlling it—this is to give up the very spirit of science. For if science means anything, it is that our ideas, our judgments may in some degree reflect and report the fact itself. Science means, on one hand, that thought is free to attack and get hold of its subject-matter, and, on the other, that fact is free to break through into thought; free to impress itself—or rather to express itself—in intelligence without vitiation or deflection. Scientific men are true to the instinct of the scientific spirit in fighting shy of a distinct *a priori* factor supplied to fact from the mind. Apriorism of this sort must seem like an effort to cramp the freedom both of intelligence and of fact, to bring them under the yoke of fixed, external forms.

Now in Hegel there is no such conception of thought and of *a priori*, as is found in Kant. Kant formulated the conception of thought as objective, but he interpreted this as meaning that thought subjective in itself *becomes* objective when synthetic of a given sense-manifold. When Hegel calls thought objective he means just what he says: that there is no special, apart faculty of thought belonging to and operated by a mind existing separate from the outer world. What Hegel means by objective thought is the meaning, the significance of the fact itself; and by methods of thought he understands simply the processes in which this meaning of fact is evolved.

There has been, of late, considerable discussion of the place and function of "relations" in knowledge. This discussion in English speculation, at least, tends to turn largely about Thomas Hill Green's reconstruction of Kantianism. I consider it unfortunate that this discussion has taken the form of a debate between empiricism and Kantianism. The question of knowledge has thus come to be whether or not certain relations are supplied by thought to sensations in order to make an orderly whole out of the latter, chaotic in themselves. Now when Hegel talks of relations of thought (not that he makes much use of just this term) he means no such separate forms. Relations of thought are, to Hegel, the typical forms of meaning which the subject-matter takes in its various progressive stages of being understood. And this is what *a priori* means from a Hegelian standpoint. It is not some element *in* knowledge; some addition of thought to experience. It is experience itself in its skeleton, in the main features of its framework.

"Refutations" of Hegel, then, which attempt to show that "thought" in itself is empty, that it waits for content from experience, that it cannot by any manipulation evolve truth out of itself are, if taken as having relevance to Hegel, simply meaningless. Hegel begins where these arguers leave off. Accepting all that they can say, he goes one step further and denies that there is any such "thought" at all anywhere in existence. The question of the relations or "categories of thought" is just the question of the broad and main aspects of fact as that fact comes to be understood.

For example, Kant would prove the *a priori* character and validity of the principle of causation by showing that without it science is impossible, that it helps "make experience." Now, in terms, Hegel's justification of this relation would be the same; he too would show that the fabric of experience implies and demands the causal relation. But in Kant's case, the justification of the principle of causality by reference to the possibility of experience means that thought must continually inject this principle *into* experience to keep experience from disappearing: that experience must be constantly braced and reinforced by the synthetic action of thought or it will collapse. In short, the need of experience for this principle of causation means its need for a certain support outside itself. But Hegel's demonstration of the validity of the causal principle is simply pointing out that the whole supports the part, while the part helps make the whole. That is to say, Hegel's reference is not to some outside action of thought in maintaining fact as an object of knowledge; it is to the entire structure of fact itself. His contention is simply that the structure of fact itself, of the subject-matter of knowledge, is such that in one of its phases it presents necessarily the aspect of causality. And if this word "necessarily" gives pause, it must be remembered what the source of necessity is. It does *not* lie in the principle of causation *per se*; it lies in the whole fact, the whole subject-matter of knowledge. It is the same sort of necessity as when we say that a complete man *must* have an eye; *i.e.*, it is the nature of the human organism to develop and sustain this organ, while the organ, in turn, contributes to and thus helps constitute the organism.

The question upon which the "refutation" of Hegel turns is not in showing that formal "thought" cannot give birth to truth except through the fructifying touch of "experience." The question is simply whether fact—the subject-matter of knowledge—is such as Hegel presents it. Is it, in general, the connected system he holds it to be? And, if a system, does it, in particular, present such phases (such relations, categories) as Hegel shows forth? These are objective questions pure and simple; questions identical, in kind, with the question whether the constitution of glucose is what some chemist claims to have found it.

This, then, is why I conceive Hegel—entirely apart from the value of any special results—to represent the quintessence of the scientific spirit. He denies not only the possibility of getting truth out of a formal, apart thought, but he denies the existence of any faculty of thought which is other than the expression of fact itself. His contention is not that "thought," in the scholastic sense, has ontological validity, but that fact, reality is significant. Even, then, were it shown that Hegel is pretty much all wrong as to the special meanings which he finds to make up the significance of reality, his main principle would be unimpeached until it is shown that fact has not a systematic, or interconnected, meaning, but is a mere hodgepodge of fragments. Whether the scientific spirit would have any interest in such a hodgepodge may, at least, be questioned.

Having dealt at such length with the first reason why as yet the "transcendental" movement has found no overt coalescence with the scientific, we may deal briefly with the remaining reason.[3] In the second place, then, the rationality of fact had not been sufficiently realised in detail in the early decades of the century to admit of the principle of the "transcendental" movement being other than misunderstood. That is to say, the development of science and, more particularly, its application to the specific facts of the world was comparatively rudimentary. On account of this lack of scientific discovery and application, the world presented itself to man's consciousness as a blank, or at least as only stuff *for* meaning, and not as itself significant. The result was that Hegel had to be interpreted subjectively. The difficulties in the way of conceiving a world upon which science had not yet expended its energies in detail, as an organism of significant relations and bearings were so great that Hegel's attempt to point out these significant types and functions as immanent in reality was inevitably misconstrued as an attempt, on Hegel's part, to prove that a system of purely "subjective" thoughts could somehow be manipulated to give objectively valid results.

3 It should be understood that in the previous discussion so far as it relates to Kant, I have taken him at his lowest terms—those of logical self-consistency. So far as Kant does not succeed in freeing himself from his original position—the existence of a formal, or apart, faculty of thought—so far his emphasis of the *a priori* in the sense already attributed to him is inevitable. But that the *tendency* of Kant is to make the thought-relations *a priori* simply in the sense of being fact's own physiognomy I should not deny.

Hegel, in other words, anticipated somewhat the actual outcome of the scientific movement. However significant fact may be, however true it may be that an apart faculty of thought is an absurdity, however certain it may be that there are no real types or methods of thought excepting those of the object-matter itself as it comes to be understood, yet to man this objective significance cannot be real till he has made it *out* in the details of scientific processes, and *made* it in applied science, in invention. Hegel's standpoint was, therefore, of necessity obscure. When the significant character of fact was not yet opened up in detail, a method working upon the basis that the only possible thought is the reflection of the significance of fact, had no chance of fair interpretation. And thus it was (and largely is) when Hegel speaks of objective thought and its relations, he is understood as having the ordinary conception of thought (that is, of thought as a purely separate, and subjective faculty), and yet as trying to prove that this apart faculty has some mysterious power of evolving truth.

The question which now confronts us as to the present place of logic is just this: Has the application of scientific thought to the world of fact gone far enough so that we can speak, without seeming strained, of the rationality of fact? When we speak of the rationality, of the intrinsic meaning of fact, can these terms be understood in their direct and obvious sense, and not in any remote, or *merely* metaphysical sense? Has the theoretical consideration of fact in its detailed study, has practical invention, as the manifestation of the rationality of fact, gone far enough so that this significance has become, or could become with some effort, as real and objective a material of study as are molecules and vibrations?

It seems to me that we are already at this stage, or are at the point of getting to it. Without arguing this question, however, (which, indeed, can be proved only by acting upon it, only *ambulando*), I would point out that the constant detailed work of science upon the world in theory and in invention, must in time give that world an evident meaning in human consciousness. What prevents scientific men from now realising this fact, is that they are still afraid of certain "transcendent" entities and forces; afraid that if they relax their hostility to metaphysic, some one will spring upon them the old scholastic scheme of external, supernatural Unrealities. To those who take the prevailing agnosticism not as a thing, but as a symptom, this agnosticism means just this: The whole set of external, or non-immanent entities, is now on the point of falling away, of dissolving. We have got just so far, popularly, as holding that they are unknowable. In other words, they are crowded to the extreme verge. One push more, and off they go. The popular consciousness will hold them not only to be unknowable, but not to be.

What then? Science freed from its fear of an external and dogmatic metaphysic, will lose its fear of metaphysic. Having unquestioned and free possession of its own domain, that of knowledge and of fact, it will also be free to build up the intrinsic metaphysic of this domain. It will be free to ask after that structure of meanings making up the skeleton of the world of knowledge. The moment this point is reached, the speculative critical logic worked out in the development of Kantian ideas, and the positive, specific work of the scientific spirit will be at one. It will be seen that logic is no revived, redecked scholasticism, but a complete abandonment of scholasticism; that it deals simply with the inner anatomy of the realm of scientific reality, and has simply endeavored, with however much of anticipation, to dissect and lay bare, at large and in general, the features of the subject-matter with which the positive sciences have been occupying themselves in particular and in detail.

That we are almost at the point of such conflux, a point where the general, and therefore somewhat abstract lines of critical logic will run into the particular, and therefore somewhat isolated, lines of positive science, is, in my opinion, the present position of logical theory.

How Do Concepts Arise from Percepts?

Failure to make some fundamental distinction may be the source of a confusion which makes all subsequent discussion mere blind thrashing in the air. The discussion of the nature of the concept has often suffered from failure to discriminate between a mental *state* and the *function* of that state. It is as if, in physiology, writers were to discuss the heart without having first decided whether they were writing of the *thing*, or of the *work* done by that thing and its *value* for the organism. Were such the case, it would not be surprising if one school of physiologists held the heart to be a definite, isolated thing, of a certain shape and size, composed of certain fibres, while another school held the heart to be a factor or member in an inter-connected unity; not a thing but an activity; and its special structure a matter of indifference compared with the general purpose subserved by this structure.

Carrying out the needed discrimination in the case of the concept, it may be said that the concept is not a term denoting a mental state or existence, but an intellectual *function* or *value*. Every mental state is, as a bare existence (taken, that is, statically) an image. As such, it is a particular, numerically and qualitatively different from every other existence and enduring only for a limited time. The nominalist is, therefore, quite right when he asserts that there is no such thing as a general idea—provided he is speaking of mental existences. But so speaking, he does not touch the question at all. The concept is the *power* which a particular

[*First published in the* Public-School Journal, *XI* (*Nov. 1891*), *128–30. Not reprinted during the author's lifetime.*]

image has of standing for or conveying a certain meaning or intellectual value. Let me borrow an illustration from, I think, Mr. Bosanquet. It is a matter of indifference what kind of a flag be used as a danger signal on the railway. It may be eight inches square, or ten, or not square at all. It may be new or old, fresh or dirty, tattered or whole. *Prior* to its adoption as a signal, it may be of any color whatever. In other words, the main thing is not what the flag *is* as an existence. The main thing is what the flag *does*. So, when we are considering the structure of a particular mental image, we have not entered the domain of concepts, or universals, at all. The concept is something which the image does; some meaning which it conveys.

What meaning? The raising of this question brings us specifically to the question of the origin of the concept from the percept. My answer to the question is: the concept arises from the percept *through realizing the full meaning implied*, but not *ex*-plicit in the percept. For example, take the percept of a triangle. So far as this is a mere percept, it is regarded wholly as a particular thing. Knowledge of it from this point of view would be exhausted in getting its exact shape, size, length of sides, degree of angles, stuff made of, color, etc. The mind would nowhere be led beyond the consideration of the bare thing present. Even if it were found that the sum of its three interior angles was equal to two right angles, this would be a trait of the particular triangle, a bare item of information, of no more general value than that the length of one side was 1 2/17 inches. But suppose the mind advances beyond the particular triangle to the thought that there is a principle involved in the triangle; that the triangle, like everything in the world, is made upon a certain principle which is embodied in it; that this principle furnishes the plans and specifications according to which anything must exist in order to be a triangle at all; a principle which, if exceeded or come short of, there is no triangle at all. What shall we call this principle? Is it not evident that, since it is this principle which constitutes the particular thing a triangle, rather than a pumpkin or a stove-pipe, it is this principle we really mean by triangle, and are attempting to know? Well, it is this principle which forms the concept, "triangle." The concept, "triangle," in other words, is the *way in which three lines are put together*; it is a *mode* or form of construction. Except as we know this mode of formation our idea of a triangle is exceedingly imperfect.

Hence, the characteristics of a concept. It is (1) "ideal" not sensuous. That is, as a mode or *way of mental action*, it cannot be felt or seen or heard. *It can be grasped only in and through the activity which constitutes it.* The only way to know the concept triangle is to make it—to go through the act of putting together the lines in the way called for. (I may remark, incidentally, that this reveals the impossibility of external or mechanical instruction. If a concept is the true meaning of a thing, and this true meaning is a mode of mental action, a process of intellectual construction, how possibly can true information be externally conveyed from one to another?) The concept is (2) general, not particular. Its generality lies in the very fact that it is a mode of action, a way of putting things or elements together. A cotton loom is particular in all its parts; every yard of cloth produced is particular, yet the way in which the parts go together and work together, the function of the loom is not particular.

So any given triangle, actual or as a mental existence, is particular. But the way of constructing triangles is not particular. It has no more to do with one triangle than with another. It is a principle in accordance with which any number of triangles may be brought into existence. *Anything* constituted in this way is a triangle.

It should be reasonably evident from what I have said that the concept of triangle contains not less but more than the percept. It is got, not by dropping traits, but by finding out what the real traits are.

It is true that certain features are excluded. But this dropping out of certain features is not what gives rise to the concept. On the contrary, *it is on the basis of the concept*, the principle of construction, *that certain features are omitted*. Nay, they are more than omitted. They are positively eliminated. They are declared to be irrelevant, to have nothing to do with the *real* triangle whatever.

The concept, in short, is knowledge of what the real object is—the object taken with reference to its principle of construction; while the percept, so called, is knowledge of the object in a more or less accidental or limited way. As to their intellectual value, concept means complete knowledge of an object—knowledge of it in its mode of genesis, and in its relations and bearings; while percept means incomplete (that is, "abstract," in the true sense of abstract) knowledge of an object,—knowledge of the object in its qualitative, spatial, and temporal limitations.

It must, however, be added that the concept always returns into and enriches the percept, so that the distinction between them is not fixed but movable. Let me once get the concept triangle; let me, that is, once see into the process by which a triangle is made a triangle, and I carry the knowledge thus gained into every particular triangle I see. The concept becomes an enriching of the meaning of the percept.

In ideal, in completed development, the percept and concept would have the same content. It would exceed my limits here to show this to be the case; but let me suggest that complete knowledge of a particular object, say a given maple tree (the percept) would involve knowledge not merely of every detail of that tree, but of *how it came to be so*. On the other hand, complete knowledge of tree-life (the concept) would involve not merely highly general ideas, but also knowledge of the particular circumstances and conditions under which tree-life became deciduous or non-deciduous; of the conditions under which the deciduous differentiated into maple, oak, beech, etc.; of the still more particular circumstances under which maple-life differentiated into this particular form of life, *this* maple tree.

Such a systematic knowledge, whether starting from an individual (when we call it percept) or starting from the principle (when we call it concept), is the ideal of every science. Our knowledge of the individual is limited until we have got at the principle involved in it. Our knowledge of the principle is imperfect (abstract) until we see how this principle acts under the multitude of different circumstances. As either is completed, it tends to approach the other.

I do not know that I am called upon to point any pedagogical morals, but I cannot resist the temptation. If what has been said is true, it is evident that there is but one genuine way to lead the mind of the pupil on from percept to concept: to present, from the first, the percept in its genesis, in its origin and growth, in its proper relations. It is *not* necessary that the rationale of the process should be explicitly pointed out, or the child made to give reasons for everything. On the contrary, prematurely fixing conscious attention upon the relations may be the very means of preventing their being grasped. But let the object be, as it were, *done* over and over again; let the relations in it be used; let the mind act in accordance with the principle involved; and sure ground is laid for the conscious apprehension of the concept later. The teacher's work is here largely confined in getting the idea to be known to the child's mind in such purified form that the child's mind must go through that constructive process which is involved in the concept. Later this process itself will become an object of reflection. First the process *used* by the mind; then the process *consciously thought* is always the normal psychological method.

Lectures VS. *Recitations: A Symposium*

As to the question regarding the best method of lecturing, I can only say that I have been wrestling with the problem for some years, and have been regretfully forced to the conclusion that the best way a man can, is the best way for him to lecture. As to your other question, I have no doubt that the introduction of the lecture system has more than justified itself. It has, wherever introduced, destroyed, once for all, the superstition that the text-book is the sum and end of learning; it has helped dispel those vicious methods of *rote* study which that superstition fostered; it has compelled the instructor himself to broaden and freshen his knowledge; and, I doubt not, has increased the use of the Library a thousandfold. That there ever will be a return from it to old-fashioned text-book work I do not believe. Where it has not displaced the text-book, it has changed the mode of handling it.

That, in its present form, it is itself the final method of instruction I am not convinced. I am inclined to think that finally its chief value will be found to have consisted in destroying the text-book fetich. With an increasing use of the printing press in preparing outlines, syllabuses, selections from authorities etc., it is possible that the set lecture will, upon the whole, be displaced by readings, reports, discussions, etc., the teacher guiding the study by questions, references, printed helps, etc. This would give us a cross between the seminary and the recitation methods. The personal equation, however, may enter largely into this forecast.

[*First published in the* Castalian, *Published by the Independents of the Senior Class, University of Michigan, VI* (1891), 65. *Not previously reprinted.*]

The Scholastic and the Speculator

1. The Scholastic

Strange stories gain credence. 'Tis currently reported the Scholastic departed this life along with the Middle Ages, driven hence by the great glare of light suddenly shed into his cobwebbed retreat. It is more likely there was no flight, only transformation. The evolutionist tells us that nothing disappears; that apparent passing away is only transition into something else. So the Scholastic changed his outward garb, the eternal traits by which he had been identified, but not his inner habit and tendency.

The character of the old Scholastic stands forth in his treatment of Aristotle. First he transferred Aristotle from the pellucid atmosphere of living Greece to his own stuffy cell. He subtracted Aristotle from life; from the circumstance of time, of place, of social and intellectual life which gave him his meaning, and regarded him *in abstracto*; in the air, that is to say. Instead of a figure in the onmoving of human intelligence, he became a philosophical pope, abstracted from all conditions, and issuing deliverances at large. He was changed from a co-efficient, from an energy contributing to the progress of mankind, to an "authority." Instead of an exponent, an indication of the place of Greek thought in the thought of humanity, he was a formula. Instead of mobility, life, in a word, there was rigidity. And all because of the abstraction, the sequestration of Aristotle from his place in the moving procession of human thought. We talk a great deal in philosophy of abstraction. It is well to remember that abstraction means in philosophy just what

[*First published in the* Inlander (*University of Michigan*), *II* (*Dec.* 1891), 145–48; *II* (*Jan.* 1892), 186–88. *Not previously reprinted.*]

it means anywhere else—carrying something off. Now a man may carry something off for two reasons. One reason is to get a good look at it, to isolate it from the crowd of things which hide and confuse it, so that its own nature may stand out. Abstraction, here, is simply raising a thing up, distinguishing it, placing it, that is to say, where it belongs. It is the normal process of the human mind in getting hold of any fact. But there is another abstraction. When a newspaper says that a cashier abstracted the contents of a safe and made his way to Canada—this is a metaphysical terminology understood of all men. This is the false abstraction philosophy talks about. It is taking a thing not out of its apparent relations in order to get it into its real relations, but taking a thing out of relations and keeping it out. Not to put too fine a point upon it, the Scholastic was an embezzler. He attempted to take Aristotle away from humanity, away from his position in the advancing column of human thought and action; he wanted to keep him for himself, for the use of his own private system, his own class-interest. The Scholastic was not commercial; he did not give and take, take in order to give, and give in order to take; he took all he could get, and gave only under compulsion—the compulsion being what we call the Renaissance. The Scholastic was "abstract"; he was the miser of philosophy; the man who wanted to save truth lest it should get away. The strong box in which he kept his riches was called "system."

Is the Scholastic dead? Has Aristotle, for example, got wholly back to earth, back, that is to say, to the concrete conditions of human life? Does he belong to the crowd, to the mass, or is he still owned, as the politicians say, by philosophers who have appropriated him to themselves? Or, to generalize the question, what are philosophy and science as conceived to-day: means of understanding and facilitating human action, or separate bodies of theories and facts supposed to have value on their own account? If the latter, then the abstraction from life is still going on. The human mind is still engaged in the process of saving and storing. *It is this saving process of mind*, and not any special act or particular portion of history, which constitutes Scholasticism.

But I have dwelt so long upon this phase of the Scholastic that I must hurry on to his other main trait. The Scholastic, when he had suffocated Aristotle by removing him from the conditions of life, proceeded to dismember the remains. Even the miser, I suppose, has to do something with his gold, or else he wouldn't know he had it . He must count it over, he must jingle it together, he must bury his fingers in it and roll the coin about. So the Scholastic had to use his learning in some way. He pulled it this way and pulled it that until he pulled it all to pieces. When anything is abstracted, when it is taken off by itself, having lost its connections, all that remains is to go over and over the same thing, dissecting, dividing, analyzing, and then sorting out and piling up the fragments. Distinction-making and collecting always accompany the scholastic habit. In every phase of life the Scholastic sees only another fly which irritates him with its restless movement; a fly to be caught and carried off—and then to be arranged and re-arranged without end, stuck in a cardboard case along with other such facts. For this same fly-sticking of the amateur scientist is an allegory. All science, all philosophy that abstracts facts and ideas from their place in the movement of life, from what it is fashionable to call evolution, is so much fly-sticking. Life departs when the thing is removed from its place in the movement, and with life goes unity. Only *disjecta membra* remain for the show-case of science.

The dawn of modern science, of experimental and historical methods, did not then destroy the Scholastic. It only compelled another alteration of outward form. Indeed by as pretty a stratagem as history records, the Scholastic in seeming to surrender to the scientific man took him captive. The Scholastic got a wider range of action. He was no longer confined to Aristotle and the Scriptures, but new fields for pillage were open. Nature and history presented vast stores from which he could abstract. The wealth to be saved up had increased indefinitely. Even the outward change is less than it often seems. The monastic cell has become a professional lecture hall; an endless mass of "authorities" have taken the place of Aristotle. *Jahresberichte*, monographs, journals without end occupy the void left by the commentators upon Aristotle. If the older Scholastic spent his laborious time in erasing the writing from old manuscripts in order to indite thereon something of his own, the new Scholastic has also his palimpsest. He criticises the criticisms with which some other Scholastic has criticised other criticisms, and the writing upon writings goes on till the substructure of reality is long obscured.

But, after all, let us be fair to the Scholastic. Abstraction is justified when it is done on a large enough scale. Man must have something to live by, and how shall he get it if he does not take it off by itself away from the maddening crowd? The crowding, the confusion in life is so great that if a man did not isolate the truth which he grasped, the truth would be at once pulled away from him. Saving is necessary. What shall a man have to work with unless he has already saved? The commerce of mind with the world requires its fund, its capitalized store, as surely as the commerce in material products. Only through the Scholastic who has continually embezzled the facts from pressure of outward things and then stored them away in safe-keeping has mankind been secured from barbarism, from mental bankruptcy, that is to say from inability on the part of intelligence to meet the demands made upon it by the necessities of action. And yet this abstraction, this saving cannot be all there is to the matter; these must have some end, some use. What is it?

II. The Speculator

The comparison of thinking with commerce is no forced analogy. There is but one commerce: The meeting of Mind and Reality. Sometimes the meeting is of one kind and we call it Thought; sometimes it is of another and we call it Language; sometimes another and we call it Art; sometimes another and we call it Justice, Rightness; sometimes another and we call it Trade. Only because we are such materialists, fixing our attention upon the rigid thing instead of upon the moving act, do we identify the last exchange especially as commerce. There is only one economy in the universe; and of this, logic, political economy, and the movements of molecules are equally phases. All contact involves two parties; all contact means exchange, and all exchange is governed by the law of reciprocity, is commercial, whether it be exchange of thought with fact, or of cotton with shoes. As in every true bargain each side gives and each gets in proportion to its giving, so in thinking. The mind must give meaning, ideas to the world that confronts it, and in return for its investment the world gives back truth and power. The due proportion of outgo and income is the problem of intelligence as of business life.

To think is to balance an idea against a fact, and every project of manufacture or of trade is a similar balancing. Nature keeps her books by the double entry system, and every venture completed must in time be referred for accounting to the original capital of truth. The law of gravitation when it emerged from the mind of Newton was the attempted equating of the credit of thought with the debit of experience. The Standard Oil Company is as much, an attempted balancing of intelligence with existing social conditions. The metaphysician says truth consists in relations; the political economist says there is no value save in exchange; the physicist that action and reaction are equal; the chemist talks of the law of equivalency; the great Teacher of Mankind says that a man finds his life only as he loses it: everywhere the same great transaction—the same cross-action.

As man saves in order to produce, so he spends in order to receive. Human intelligence has always been gathering in wealth from the wreckage of time and hugging the salvage to itself to set out its full meaning: the *scholastic*. But intelligence must throw its fund out again into the stress of life; it must venture its savings against the pressure of facts: the *speculator*.

The Yankee is the great speculator. Undisturbed by the Anglo-purist he continues his great "guess" upon life. If he ceases in any measure to say "I guess" it is only because he has gone a step farther and learned to say "I bet" so and so. If the grammar which represents old conceptions of life is against such phrases the logic of moving truth is with them. Every thought, every judgment involves a leap forward, a jump, a venture. The formal logician may attempt to derive conclusions from premises; every practical man knows that premises are only the spring-board, the point of vantage where to jump into the flood of moving fact. Some may think to dignify this phase of thought by calling it hypothesis, or tentative induction, or what-not, but the largest term that can be invented can do no more than express the jump into the unknown ocean off the spring-board of the known. No rules have ever been devised for informing one who has not "sense" or "good judgment," as the plain man calls it, how to make this jump. It always is, and always must remain the individual venture: the stake of self or some part of self against the ongoing stream of life. Every judgment a man passes on life is perforce, his "I bet," his speculation. So much of his saved capital of truth he invests in the judgment: "The state of things is thus and so." The current of fact sweeps in this judgment and returns it to him with interest. His guess, his venture has won: the logicians call it verification. Or the stream of fact carries away his investment and he never sees it again. His speculation was against the set of the market and he has lost.

Immanuel Kant wrote a treatise on the subject: "How are synthetic judgments *a priori* possible?" The question sounds technical, and yet at bottom it means only this: How does it happen that the mind can bet upon truth and win? What sort of a world must it be that welcomes the ventures of the mind and returns them with added riches? What sort of a mind can it be that dare speculate upon that vast current outside it, which can stake its pile of truth upon the moving game and receive its own with usury?

But there are scholastics and scholastics: men who save in order to get a new purchase in action, and men who save for very sake of saving. So there are speculators and speculators. The business man saves, but the ideal saving is not to have a reserve which is never touched, but to have all so used that there is no waste. There is a saving which means withdrawal, separation; there is a saving which means use parallel with the realities of the situation. The cotton merchant saves best when he invests all his funds in accordance with the movement of the cotton market. The talent hid in a napkin wasn't saved after all; the other man got it at last. There is a speculation which exists just for the sake of the speculation. Wall street is, if you please, the symbol of this speculation, just as every large business represents the speculation which occurs for the sake of getting a larger action under way. One speculation is for the profit, the pot, the other is for the game. So in the history of human intelligence there have been two kinds of thought-speculators. There have been those who have hazarded, so far as in them lay, all the store of truth for the profit of their own private venture, their system. They have laid hands on all the riches of the human race and staked them upon their theory, their personal bet. All the great philosophers have had something of this ruthless adventure of thought, this reckless throwing of the accumulated store of truth. Although the prodigal is always a more attractive figure than the miser, there must still be some better way. Only because thinking has been separated from action, the theorist from the economist in life, has speculation assumed this private form. The speculation of the merchant is business, and not gambling, just in the degree that it is itself action and action in the light. The speculation of the broker is gambling and not business just in the degree that it is not action itself, but the attempt to take advantage of the action of others, and in the degree that it is in the dark and not in the light. Action upon truth marks the merchant of thought, who, though he both saves and spends, yet neither embezzles nor gambles.

Green's Theory of the Moral Motive

A somewhat peculiar difficulty seems to attend the discussion of ethical theory, on account of its characteristic relation to action. This relation gives rise, on one side, to the belief that ethics is primarily an "art." Ethics is so much the theory of practice that it seems as if its main business were to aid in the direction of conduct. This being premised, the next step is to make out of ethics a collection of rules and precepts. A body of rigid rules is erected with the object of having always some precept which will tell just what to do. But, on the other side, it is seen to be impossible that any body of rules should be sufficiently extensive to cover the whole range of action; it is seen that to make such a body results inevitably in a casuistry which is so demoralizing as to defeat the very end desired; and that, at the best, the effect is to destroy the grace and play of life by making conduct mechanical. So the pendulum swings to the other extreme; it is denied that ethics has to deal primarily or directly with the guidance of action. Limited in this way, all there is left is a metaphysic of ethic: —an attempt to analyze the general conditions under which morality is possible; to determine, in other words, the nature of that universe or system of things which permits or requires moral action. The difficulty, then, is to find the place intermediate between a theory general to the point of abstractness, a theory which provides no help to action, and a theory which attempts to further action but does so at the expense of its spontaneity and breadth. I do not know of any theory, however, which is quite consistent to either point of view. The theory which makes the most of being practical generally shrinks, as matter of fact, from the attempt to carry out into detail its rules for living; and the most metaphysical

[*First published in the* Philosophical Review, *I* (*Nov. 1892*), *593–612. Not previously reprinted.*]

doctrine commonly tries to show that at least the main rules for morality follow from it. The difficulty is imbedded in the very nature of the science; so much so that it is far easier for the school which prides itself upon its practicality (generally the utilitarian) to accuse the other (generally the "transcendental") of vagueness than to work out any definitely concrete guidance itself; and easier for the metaphysical school to show the impossibility of deducing any detailed scheme of action from a notion like that of seeking the greatest quantity of pleasures than for it to show how its own general ideal is to be translated out of the region of the general into the specific; and, of course, all action is specific.

The difficulty is intrinsic, I say, and not the result of any mere accident of statement. Ethics is the theory of action and all action is concrete, individualized to the last ell. Ethical theory must have, then, a similar concreteness and particularity. And yet no body of rules and precepts, however extensive and however developed its casuistic, can reach out to take in the wealth of concrete action. No theory, it is safe to say, can begin to cover the action of a single individual for a single day. Is not, then, the very conception of ethical theory a misconception, a striving for something impossible? Is there not an antinomy in its very definition?

The difficulty, it may be noticed, is no other and therefore no more impossible to solve than that involved in all application of theory to practice. When, for example, a man is to build a tunnel, he has to do something quite specific, having its own concrete conditions. It is not a tunnel in general which he has to make, but a tunnel having its own special end and called for by its own set of circumstances—a set of circumstances not capable of being precisely duplicated anywhere else in the world. The work has to be done under conditions imposed by the given environment, character of soil, facility of access to machinery, and so on. It is true that so many tunnels have now been built for similar ends and under *substantially* like circumstances, that the example errs on the side of excessive mechanicalness; but we have only to imagine the tunnel building under untried special conditions, as, say, the recent engineering below the St. Clair River, to get a fair case. Now in such a case it is requisite that science, that theory, be available at every step of the undertaking, and this in the most detailed way. Every stage of the proceeding must, indeed, be absolutely controlled by scientific method. There is here the same apparent contradiction as in the moral case; and yet the solution in the case of the engineering feat is obvious. Theory is used, not as a set of fixed rules to lay down certain things to be done, but as a tool of analysis to help determine what the nature of the special case is; it is used to uncover the reality, the conditions of the matter, and thus to lay bare the circumstances which action has to meet, to synthesize. The mathematical, the mechanical, the geological theories do not say "Do this or that"; but in effect they do say, use me and you will reduce the complex conditions of which you have only some slight idea to an ordered group of relations to which action may easily adjust itself in the desired fashion. Now these conceptions of mechanics, of geology, which aid in determining the special facts at hand, are themselves, it is to be noticed, simply the *generic* statement of these same facts; the mathematics are the most general statement of any group of circumstances to be met anywhere in experience; the geology is a general statement of the conditions to be met with wherever it is an affair of the soil and so on. The theory, in other words, is not a something or other belonging to an entirely different realm from the special facts to be mastered. It is an outline statement of these same facts wrought out from previous like experiences and existing ready at hand to anticipate, and thus help solve, any particular experience. What we have then in this application of theory to the special case, with all its wealth of concrete detail, is the attack and reduction of a specific reality through the use of a general precedent idea of this same reality. Or what we have, putting it from the side of the theory, is a general conception which is so true to reality that it lends itself easily and almost inevitably to more specific and concrete statement, the moment circumstances demand such particularization. So far as the theory is "false," so far, that is, as it is not a statement, however general, of the facts of the case, so far, instead of lending itself to more specific statement, instead of fertilizing itself whenever occasion requires, it resists such specification and stands aloof as a bare generality. It neither renders individual experiences luminous, nor is fructified by them, gathering something from them which makes its own statement of reality somewhat more definite and thus more ready for use another time.

Now let us return to our moral case. The same law holds here. Ethical theory must be a general statement of the reality involved in every moral situation. It must be action stated in its more generic terms, terms so generic that every individual action will fall within the outlines it sets forth. If the theory agrees with these requirements, then we have for use in any special case a tool for analyzing that case; a method for attacking and reducing it, for laying it open so that the action called for in order to meet, to satisfy it, may readily appear. The theory must not, on one hand, stand aloof from the special thing to be done, saying, "What have I to do with thee? Thou art empirical and I am the metaphysics of conduct," nor must it, on the other hand, attempt to lay down fixed rules in advance exhausting all possible cases. It must wait upon the instruction that every new case, because of its individuality, its uniqueness, carries with it; but it must also bring to this special case such knowledge of the reality of all action, such knowledge of the end and process involved in all deeds, that it translates naturally into the concrete terms of this special case. If, for example, I object to the categorical imperative of Kant, or the pleasure of the Hedonist, that it does not assist practice, I do not mean that it does not prescribe a rigid body of fixed rules telling just what to do in every contingency of action; I mean that the theory so far comes short as a statement of the character of all moral action that it does not lend itself to uncovering, to getting at the reality of specific cases as they arise; and that, on the other hand, these special cases, not being the detailed exhibition of the same reality that is stated generally in the theory, do not react upon the theory and fructify it for further use.[1]

1 In the *International Journal of Ethics*, for January, 1891, I have developed this thought at greater length in an article upon "Moral Theory and Practice." [*Early Works*, III, 93–101.]

These remarks are introductory to a critical consideration of the theory of Thomas Hill Green regarding the moral motive or ideal. His theory would, I think, be commonly regarded as the best of the modern attempts to form a metaphysic of ethic. I wish, using this as type, to point out the inadequacy of such metaphysical theories, on the ground that they fail to meet the demand just made of truly ethical theory, that it lend itself to translation into concrete terms, and thereby to the guidance, the direction of actual conduct. I shall endeavor to show that Green's theory is not metaphysical in the only possible sense of metaphysic, such general statement of the nature of the facts to be dealt with as enables us to anticipate the actual happening, and thereby deal with it intelligently and freely, but metaphysical in the false sense, that of a general idea which remains remote from contact with actual experience. Green himself is better than his theory, and engages us in much fruitful analysis of specific moral experience, but, as I shall attempt to show, his theory, taken in logical strictness, admits of no reduction into terms of individual deeds.

Kant's separation of the self as reason from the self as want or desire, is so well known as not to require detailed statement. That this separation compels the moral motive to be purely formal, having no content except regard for law just as law needs no exposition. So far as I know it has not been pointed out that Green, while arguing against such separation of sense and reason, on the ground that we cannot know sense or desire at all except as determined by reason, yet practically repeats the dualism of Kant in slightly altered form. For the conception of action determined by the pure form of self, Green simply substitutes action determined by the self in its unity; for conduct determined by mere appetite, he substitutes conduct determined by the self in some particular aspect. The dualism between reason and sense is given up, indeed, but only to be replaced by a dualism between the end which would satisfy the self as a unity or whole, and that which satisfies it in the particular circumstances of actual conduct. The end which would satisfy the self as unity is just as far from the end which satisfies the self in any special instance of action, as, in

Kant's system, the satisfaction of pure reason is remote from the satisfaction of mere appetite. Indeed, we may go a step further, and say that the opposition is even more decided and intrinsic in Green than in Kant. It is at least conceivable, according to Kant, that in some happy moment action should take place from the motive of reason shorn of all sensuous content and thus be truly moral. But in no possible circumstance, according to Green, can action satisfy the whole self and thus be truly moral. In Kant the discrepancy between the force which appetite exercises, and the controlling force at the command of pure reason, is so great as to make very extraordinary the occurrence of a purely moral action; but at least there is no intrinsic impossibility in the conception, however heavy the odds against its actual happening. In Green, however, the thing is impossible by the very definition of morality. No thorough-going theory of total depravity ever made righteousness more impossible to the natural man than Green makes it to a human being by the very constitution of his being, and, needless to say, Green does not allow the supernatural recourse available to the Calvinist in the struggle for justification.

Let me now justify, by reference to Green, this statement that according to him the very conditions under which moral action is carried on make it impossible for a satisfactory moral action to occur. Green's analysis of the moral procedure is as follows: The difference between animal and moral action is that the animal deed simply expresses a want which impels the animal blindly forward to its own satisfaction. The want is not elevated into consciousness; that is, there is no conception of the end sought. The impulse which makes good the want is not brought into the focus of consciousness; that is, there is no conception of the nature of the means to be used in satisfying the want. Moral action arises, not through the intervention of any new kind of "nature" or want, but through the intervention of a self which reflects upon the existing wants, and through the reflection transforms them into ends or ideals conceived as satisfying the self. The self in seeing the want, in becoming conscious of it, objectifies the want, making out of it an ideal condition of itself in which it expects to find satisfaction. It is an animal thing to be simply moved by the appetite for food; it is a moral thing to become conscious of this appetite, and thereby transform the bare appetite into the conception of some end or object in which the self thinks to find its own satisfaction.[2]

The process of moral experience involves, therefore, a process in which the self, in becoming conscious of its want, objectifies that want by setting it over against itself; distinguishing the want from self and self from want. As thus distinguished, it becomes an end or ideal of the self. Now this theory so far might be developed in either of two directions. The self-distinguishing process may mean the method by which the self specifies or defines its own activity, its own satisfaction; all particular desires and their respective ends would be, in this case, simply the systematic content into which the self differentiated itself in its progressive expression. The particular desires and ends would be the modes in which the self relieved itself of its abstractness, its undeveloped character, and assumed concrete existence. The ends would not be *merely* particular, because each would be one member in the self's activity, and, as such member, universalized. The unity of the self would stand in no opposition to the particularity of the special desire; on the contrary, the unity of the self and the manifold of definite desires would be the synthetic and analytic aspects of one and the same reality, neither having any advantage metaphysical or ethical over the other. Such is *not* the interpretation Green gives. The self does not, according to him, define itself *in* the special desire; but the self distinguishes itself *from* the desire. The objectification is not of the self *in* the special end; but the self remains behind setting the special object over against itself as not adequate to itself. The self-distinction gives rise, not to a progressive realization of the self in a system of definite members or organs, but to an irreconcilable antithesis. The self as unity, as whole, falls over on one side; as unity, it is something not to be realized in any special end or activity, and therefore not in any

2 See, for example, Green, *Prolegomena to Ethics*, pp. 92, 118, 126, 134, and 160.

possible series of ends, not even a *progressus ad infinitum.* The special desire with its individual end falls over on the other side; by its contrast with the unity of the self it is condemned as a forever inadequate mode of satisfaction. The unity of the self sets up an ideal of satisfaction for itself as it withdraws from the special want, and *this* ideal set up through negation of the particular desire and its satisfaction constitutes the moral ideal. It is forever unrealizable, because it forever negates the special activities through which alone it might, after all, realize itself. The moral life is, by constitution, a self-contradiction. Says Green: "As the reflecting subject traverses the series of wants, which it distinguishes from itself while it presents their filling as its object, there arises the idea of a satisfaction on the whole—an idea never realizable, but forever striving to realize itself in the attainment of a greater command over means to the satisfaction of particular wants."[3] Green shows that the process of our active experience demands that the self, in becoming conscious of a want, set that want before itself as an object, thus distinguishing itself from the want; but he shows us no road back from the want thus objectified to the self. The unity of self has efficiency only in a negative way, to set itself up as an ideal condemning to insufficiency every concrete step towards reaching the ideal. The self becomes, not a systematic reality which is (or which may be) realizing itself in every special deed, but a far-away ideal which can be realized only through an absolute exhaustion of all its capacities. "Of a life of complete development, of activity with the end attained, we can only speak or think in negatives, and thus only can we speak or think of that state of being in which, according to our theory, the ultimate moral good must consist."[4]

Consider, then, how much worse off we are than the animals; they can get at least the satisfaction of their particular wants, while the supervention of the self in us makes us conscious of an ideal which sets itself negatively over against every attempt to realize itself, thus condemning us

3 *Prolegomena*, p. 91; see also p. 233.

4 *Prolegomena*, p. 180; and see also pp. 189, 204, 244.

to continued dissatisfaction. Speaking more accurately, the self supervenes, not completely or as an adequately compelling reality, but only as the thought of an ideal. It supervenes, not as a power active in its own satisfaction, but to make us realize the unsatisfactoriness of such seeming satisfactions as we may happen to get, and to keep us striving for something which we can never get! Surely, if Green is correct, he has revealed the illusion which has kept men striving for something which they cannot get, and, the illusion detected, men will give up the strife which leads only to dissatisfaction. Whatever may be said for an ascetic ethics, naked and professed, surely there is something at fault in the analysis which sets up satisfaction as the end, and *then* relapses into a thorough-going asceticism.

I have dwelt upon this contradiction at length, not for its own sake, but in order to emphasize the helplessness of such a theory with regard to action. It is not, I repeat, that a fixed body of precepts cannot be deduced from this conception of the moral ideal; it is that the idea cannot be *used*. Instead of being a tool which can be brought into fruitful relations to special circumstances so as to help determine what should be done, it remains the bare thought of an ideal of perfection, having nothing in common with the special set of conditions or with the special desire of the moment. Indeed, instead of helping determine the right, the satisfactory, it stands off one side and says, "No matter what you do, you will be dissatisfied. I am complete; you are partial. I am a unity; you are a fragment, and a fragment of such a kind that no amount of you and such as you can ever afford satisfaction." In a word, the ideal not only does not lend itself to specification, but it negates specification in such way that its necessary outcome, were it ever seriously adopted as a controlling theory of morals, would be to paralyze action.

The ideal of Green is thus the bare form of unity in conduct; the form devoid of all content, and essentially excluding all proposed content as inadequate to the form. The only positive significance which it has is: whatever the moral ideal, it must at least have the form of unity. Now it seems mere tautology to urge that the mere idea of unity, no matter how much you bring it in juxtaposition with concrete circumstances, does not tell *what* the unity of the situation is, or give any aid in determining that unity; at most it but sets the problem, saying, "Whatever the situation, seek for its unity." But Green's ideal cannot be made to go as far as this in the direction of concreteness; his unity is so thoroughly abstract that, instead of urging us to seek for the deed that would unify the situation, it rather says that *no* unity can be found in the situation because the situation is particular, and therefore set over against the unity.

But while it seems certain to me that any attempt to make the ideal definite must, by the very nature of the case, be at the expense of logical consistency, it will be fairer to describe briefly the various ways in which Green indicates an approach to concreteness of action. These ways may be reduced to three. In the first place, the setting of the self as ideal unity with its own unrealized satisfaction over against the particular desire with its particular satisfaction, gives rise to the notion of an unconditional good,—a good absolutely, to which, therefore, every special and relative good must conform. Hence the idea of obligation, the unquestioned ought or categorical imperative. Secondly, this same contrast keeps alive in the mind, in the face of every seeming good, the conception of a better, thus preventing the mind from sinking into any ignoble acquiescence with the present and keeping it alert for improvement. Hence the idea of moral progress. And, thirdly, this absolute good with its unqualified demands for regard upon humanity has secured in the past some degree of observance, however defective; it has compelled man to give it some shape and body. Hence the existence of permanent institutions which hold forth the eternal good not in its abstract shape but in some concrete embodiment.

The first of these modes for giving definiteness to the ideal, and thus making it available for actual conduct, may be soon dismissed. It is, over again, only the thought of *an* ideal, except it now takes the form of a law instead of that of a good or satisfaction. It is at most the consciousness *that* there is something to do and that this something has unconditioned claims upon us. We are as far as ever from any method of translating this something in general into the special thing which has to be done in a given case. And here, as before, this unconditioned law not simply fails to carry with itself any way of getting concrete, but it stands in negative relation to any transfer into particular action. It declares: "Whatever you do, you will come short of the law which demands a complete realization; and you can give only inadequate obedience, since your action is limited through your want at the moment of action." Given the general acceptance of the theory, the result would be, on account of the impossibility of conforming to the demands of the law, either a complete recklessness of conduct (since we cannot in any way satisfy this hard task-master, let us at least get what pleasure we can out of the passing moments) or a pessimism transcending anything of which Schopenhauer has dreamed.

I cannot see that the case stands any different with the idea of a Better. Granted that the thought of a better would arise from the opposition of a Good upon the whole to every special good, as depicted by Green, how are we to advance from this thought of *a* better to any notion of *what* that better is, either as to the prevailing tendency of life, the direction in which we are to look for improvement upon the whole, or in any special situation? The notion that there is a better, if a *mere* idea, that is, an idea not tending to define itself in this or that specific better, would be, it appears to me, hardly more than a mockery for all the guidance it would give conduct. How is the general consciousness of a better to be brought into such relation with the existing lines of action that it will serve as an organ of criticism, pointing out their defects and the direction in which advance is to be looked for? And I think it could be shown through a logical analysis that the conception of a good which cannot be realized "in any life that can be lived by man as we know him"[5] is so far from being a safe basis for a theory of moral progress, that it negates the very notion of progress. Progress would seem to imply a principle immanent in the process and securing continual revelation and expression there. I

5 *Prolegomena*, p. 189.

am aware of the logical difficulties bound up in the idea of progress, but these difficulties are increased rather than met by a theory which makes it consist in advance *towards* an end which is outside the process, especially when it is added that, so far as we can know, this end cannot be reached; that indeed the nature of the process towards it is such as to make the ideal always withdraw further. The only question on such a theory is whether the thought of advance *towards* the goal has any meaning, and whether we have any criterion at all by which to place ourselves; to tell where we are in the movement, and whither we are going—backward or forward.

We come, then, to the embodiment which the ideal has found for itself in the past as the sole reliance for getting self-definition into the empty form of unity of self. In their effort towards this full realization men have produced certain institutions, codes, and recognized forms of duty. In loyalty to these, taken not merely in themselves, but as expressions of the attempt to realize the ideal, man may find his primary concrete duties. Says Green: "However meagrely the perfection, the vocation, the law, may be conceived, the consciousness that there is such a thing, so far as it directs the will, must at least keep the man to the path in which human progress has so far been made. It must keep him loyal in the spirit to established morality, industrious in some work of recognized utility."[6] The criticism here may take several roads. We may point out that the question is not whether as matter of fact the ideal *has* embodied itself in institution and code with sufficient fulness so that loyalty to the institution and code is a means in which our duty and satisfaction comes specifically home to us: that the question is whether, *if* the ideal were the abstract unity—the unity negative to every special end—which Green makes it, any such embodiment would be possible. We may ask, in other words, whether Green, in order to help out the undefinable character of his ideal, its inability to assume concrete form, has not unconsciously availed himself of a fact incompatible with his theory, a fact whose very existence refutes his

6 *Prolegomena*, p. 184; see also p. 207.

theory. Or, we might approach the matter from the other side and inquire whether the relation of the absolute ideal to the special institutions in which it has found expression is of such a kind (according to the terms of Green's theory of moral experience) that loyalty to "established morality" is a safe ethical procedure. On the contrary, must not, according to the fundamental premise which Green has laid down, the relation of the ideal to *any* expression which it may have secured, be essentially—radically—negative? That is, does not the ideal in its remote and unrealizable nature stand off and condemn the past attempts to realize it as vain, as unworthy? Does not the ideal say, in substance, I am not in you; you are but nugatory attempts to shadow forth my unity? Such being the case, the path of morality would lie in turning *against* established morality rather than in following it. The moral command would be, "Be *not* loyal to existing institutions, if you would be loyal to me, the only true moral ideal." But this very negation, since it is a negation in general, since it negates not this or that feature of the established morality, but that morality *per se*, gives no aid in determining in what respect to act differently. It just says: "Do not do as you have been doing; act differently." And it is an old story in logic that an undetermined "infinite" negative conveys no intelligence. It may be true that a virtue is not an elephant, but this throws no light on the nature of either the virtue or the elephant. The negation must be with respect to an identity involved in both the compared terms before it assists judgment; that is, the ideal must be *in* the actual which it condemns, if it is to really criticise; an external standard, just because it is external, is no standard at all. There is no common ground, and hence no basis for comparison. And thus when Green goes on to say[7] that the same ideal which has embodied itself in institutions also embodies itself in the critical judgment of individuals, who are thereby enabled to look back upon the institutions and cross-examine them, thus raising up higher standards, he says something which it is highly desirable to have true, but which cannot be true, if his theory of the

7 *Prolegomena*, pp. 270 *et seq.*

purely negative relation of the unity of self-consciousness to every particular act is correct.

But we need not indulge, at length, in these various hypothetical criticisms. Green himself, with his usual candor in recognizing and stating all difficulties, no matter how hardly they bear upon his own doctrine, has clearly stated the fundamental opposition here; an opposition making it impossible that the ideal should concretely express itself in any institutional form in such way as to lend itself to the concrete determination of further conduct. The contradiction, as Green himself states it, is that while the absolute unity of self must, in order to translate into an ideal for man, find an embodiment in social forms, all such forms are, by their very nature and definition, so limited that no amount of loyalty to the institution can be regarded as an adequate satisfaction of the ideal. Or as Green puts it: "Only through society is any one enabled to give that effect to the idea of man as the object of his actions, to the idea of a possible better state of himself, without which the idea would remain like that of space to a man who had not the senses either of sight or of touch,"—that is, a merely ideal possibility, without actual meaning. And yet society necessarily puts such limits upon the individual that he cannot by his life in society give effect to the idea. "Any life which the individual can possibly live is at best so limited by the necessities of his position that it seems impossible, on supposition that a definite self-realizing principle is at work in it, that it should be an adequate expression of such a principle." "It is only so far as we are members of the society, by means of which we can conceive of the common good as our own, that the idea has any practical hold on us at all; and this very membership implies confinement in our individual realization of the idea. Each has primarily to perform the duties of his station; his capacity for action beyond the range of this duty is definitely bounded, and with it is definitely bounded also his sphere of personal interest, his character, his realized possibility."[8]

Here is the contradiction. If man were to withdraw

8 *Prolegomena*, p. 192.

from his social environment, he would lose at once the idea of the moral end, the stimulus to its realization, and the concrete means for carrying it out. The social medium is to the moral ideal what language is to thought—and more. And yet if man stays in the social environment, he is by that very residence so limited in interest and power that he cannot realize the ideal. It is the old difficulty over again.

Just as the unity of the self, taken psychologically, sets itself, in a negative way, over against every special desire, so this same unity of self, taken socially, removes itself from every special institution in which it is sought to embody it—removes itself, be it noticed, not because the embodiment *succeeds* and through the very thoroughness of the embodiment creates a new situation, requiring *its* special unification, but because of the essential futility of the attempt at embodiment. The antithesis between form and content, ideal and actual, is an undoubted fact of our experience; the question, however, is as to the meaning, the interpretation, of this fact. Is it an antithesis which arises *within* the process of moral experience, this experience bearing in its own womb both ideal and actual, both form and content, and also the rhythmic separation and redintegration of the two sides? Or, is the antithesis between the process of moral experience, *as such*, and an ideal outside of this experience and negative to it, so that experience can never embody it? It is because Green interprets the fact in the latter sense that he shuts himself up to an abstract ideal which unqualifiedly resists all specification, and which is therefore useless as an organ for our moral activity.

I have now attempted to show that Green takes the bare fact that there is unity in moral experience, abstracts that unity from experience (although its sole function is to be the unity of experience) and then, setting this unity over against the experience robbed of its significance, makes of the unity an unrealized and unrealizable ideal and condemns the experience, shorn of its unity, to continual dissatisfaction. I have tried to show this, both in general, from the nature of Green's analysis, and, more in particular, from a consideration of the three special modes in which the ideal endeavors to get relatively concrete form. Since I have treated the theory as reduced to its naked logical consistency, I may have appeared to some to have dealt with it rather harshly, though not, I hope, unjustly. But aside from the fact that the truest reverence we can render any of the heroes of thought is to use his thinking to forward our own struggle for truth, philosophy seems, at present, to be suffering from a refusal to subject certain ideas to unswerving analysis because of sympathy with the moral atmosphere which bathes those ideas, and because of the apparent service of those ideas in reclothing in philosophic form ideas endeared to the human mind through centuries of practical usefulness in forms traditional and symbolic.

In closing, I wish to point out that the abstract theories of morals, of which we have just been considering the best modern type, are not aberrations of an individual thinker; that, on the contrary, they are the inevitable outcome of a certain stage of social development, recurring at each of those nodal points in progress when humanity, becoming conscious of the principle which has hitherto unconsciously underlain its activity, abstracts that principle from the institutions through which it has previously acted preparatory to securing better organs for it—institutions, that is, through which it shall flow more freely and more fully. The error consists in transforming this purely historical opposition, an opposition which has meaning only with reference to the movement of a single process, into a rigid or absolute separation. That is to say, at the moment in which a given cycle of history has so far succeeded that it can express its principle free from the mass of incident with which it had been bound up (and so hidden from consciousness) at that moment this principle appears in purely negative form. It is the negation of the preceding movement because in it that movement has succeeded—has summed itself up. Success always negates the process which leads up to it, because it renders that process unnecessary; it takes away from it all function and thus all excuse for being. Just so, for example, Hellenic life transcended itself in Socrates; in him it became conscious of the principle (the universality of the self, to express it roughly) which had been striving to realize itself. The movement having come to consciousness, having generalized itself, its principle at once assumed a negative relation to the forms in which this principle had been only partially embodied. Just because Socrates was, in his consciousness, a complete Greek, he wrote the epitaph of Greece. So, to take another obvious example, Jesus, in fulfilling the law, transcended it, so that those who were "in Christ Jesus, were no longer under the law." Now just because the principle in its completion, its generalization is negative to its own partial realizations or embodiments, just because it negates its own immediate historic antecedents, it is easy to conceive of it as negative to *all* embodiment. At a certain stage of the movement, this transformation of a historic into an absolute negative is not only easy, but, as it would seem, inevitable. This stage is the moment when the principle which sums up one movement is seen to be the law for the next movement and has not as yet got organized into further outward or institutional forms. For the moment (the moment may last a century) the principle having transcended one institutional expression, and not having succeeded in getting another, seems to be wholly in the air—essentially negative to all possible realization. The very completeness with which the principle sums up and states the reality of life seems, by the one great paradox, to put it in opposition to that reality—to make of it something essentially transcending experience. The great example of this is the fortune of the Christian idea. As it was originally stated, it was not put forth as a specially religious truth; religious, that is, in a sense which marked off religion as a sphere by itself; it was propounded as the realization of the meaning of experience, as the working truth which all experience bases itself upon and carries with itself. This truth was that man is an expression or an organ of the Reality of the universe. That, as such organ, he participates in truth and, through the completeness of his access to ultimate truth, is free, there being no essential barriers to his action either in his relation to the world or in his relations to his fellow-men. Stated more in the language of the time, man was an incarnation of God and in virtue of this incarnation redeemed from evil. Now this principle, if we regard it as having historical relations and not something intruded into the world from outside, without continuity with previous experience, this principle, I say, must have been the generalization of previous life; such a generalization as plucking its principle from that experience negated it. And yet this principle, at the outset, only quickened men's consciousness of their slaveries—this idea of participation in the Absolute only made men feel more deeply the limitations of their activity and hence their "finitude." Thus the principle seemed negative not only to preceding institutions but to all contemporaneous institutions; indeed, these contemporaneous institutions were, of course, only the survivals of the preceding institutions. Until such time, then, as the new principle should succeed in getting itself organized into forms more adequate to itself (the development of science, the conquest of nature through the application of this science in invention and industry, and its application to the activities of men in determining their relations to one another and the resulting forms of social organization) this principle must have seemed remote from, negative to, all possible normal life. Thus, in being forced apart from actual life, the principle was conceived, not any longer as a working method of life, but as something wholly supernatural. So absolutely was a negation which was only historic in its meaning frozen into an absolute negative.

Now the ethical theory which Green represents appears under similar historic conditions. Physical science in its advance has got to the thought of a continuous unity embodied in all natural process. In the theory of evolution this unity of process has ceased to be either a supernatural datum or a merely philosophic speculation. It has assumed the proportions of fact. So social organization has gone far enough in the direction of democracy that the principle of movement towards unity comes to consciousness in that direction. In every direction there is coming to consciousness the power of an organizing activity underlying and rendering tributary to itself the apparently rigid dualisms holding over from the mediæval structure. This unity, just because it is the manifestation of the reality realizing itself in the institutions characteristic of the past, is negative to those institutions; it is the reality of which they are the phenomena. That is, these institutions have their meaning as pointing to or indicating the organizing unity; they are the *attempts* to express it. Succeeding in their attempt at expression, they are superseded. They have realized their purpose, their function. The principle in which they have summed themselves up, in which they have executed themselves, has the floor; it has command of the scene of action. When that which is whole is come, that which is in part shall be done away. Now this principle of a single, comprehensive, and organizing unity being historically negative to its concrete conditions, to former institutions, is easily conceived as negative to all embodiment. While, in reality, we are conscious of this organizing principle only because it *is* getting concrete manifestation, only because, indeed, it *has* secured such embodiment as to appear as the directing principle or method of life, the first realization of the principle is negative; we become conscious, in the light of this organizing unity, of its *non-being*, of its still partial embodiment, of the resistances which it still has to overcome—this is, of its divided character. Translate this negation, which is a phase in every individualized movement, into a hard and fast thing, and you get an ideal set over against the actual (and the possible) experience as such. So it was with Green: only because the single organizing unity had got expression for itself could he conceive it at all; only because it had emerged so thoroughly as the reality of all experience could he contrast it, as he did, with the particular experiences of which it was the meaning. Only because the institutions of life had through centuries of conception finally given birth to this idea as their own idea and reality, could Green use this idea to condemn those institutions. Such is the irony of all history; it so thoroughly realizes and embodies ideas that these very ideas are turned against it as its own condemnation. But the life which is going on in history, instead of accusing its children of their ungratefulness, makes use of the very ideas by which it is condemned to secure still wider revelation of its own meaning.

Two Phases of Renan's Life: The Faith of 1850 and the Doubt of 1890

I have been much interested in the recent articles upon Renan in the *Open Court*, and hope that the discussion may not end at once. Particularly do I hope that the discussion of his *Future of Science* may continue, as I think that book is far from having received the attention, or exercised the influence, it deserves. Many things in it tend to arouse interest. The way in which the great philosophic formulations of Germany, just then losing currency as official doctrine, were continued by passing over into the attitude and atmosphere of science, especially of historic science, is a point fastening attention. That which in Hegel had been an attempt at a comprehensive philosophising of the universe has become, in Renan, the conception and method of the science of philology. The conception of philology is a science of the human intellect as a single whole developing throughout all history, and having its record in language, in a sense which understands by language all records which the human race has left of itself, whether in the *form* of language, or in its substance—in literature. The method (and this is 1848) is fixed by the idea of evolution. "The science of man will only then be placed in its true light when students realise that consciousness is evolved—that it only attains its plenitude after having gone through diverse phases. . . . The great progress of modern thought has been the substitution of the category of *evolution* for that of

[*First published in the* Open Court, *VI* (29 *Dec.* 1892), 3505–6. *Reprinted in* Characters and Events, *I*, 18–23, *under the title* "*Ernest Renan.*"]

being; . . . formerly everything was conceived as 'being,' as an accomplished fact; people spoke of law, of religion, of politics, of poetry in an absolute fashion. At present everything is conceived as in process of *formation*" (p. 169. I refer to the American translation). And when we go on to consider the law of evolution: from the undifferentiated homogeneous, the syncrete, through the multiplicity which results from analysis, to a synthesis which comprehends, while it never destroys, the multiplicity: when we consider this, the transference of the Hegelian doctrine becomes even more marked. It is the same law, only considered now as the law of historic growth, not as the dialectic unfolding of the absolute.

Remembering the date, Renan's protest against the psychology of the time and his sketch of its true course attain importance. His protest is directed against the static and purely individual character of the current psychology. Psychology has confined itself to a study of the human intellect in its mature state. The necessity for the future is a form of psychology which Renan, significantly enough, terms an *embryogeny* of the human soul, a psychology which shall study the first appearance and gradual development of those powers which we now have ready-made. Not less striking, in its prevision, is the idea that this genetic science is to deal equally with the race and with the individual in their growth from infancy. Surely there is something more than a chance anticipation of the modern conception of the relation of ontogeny and phylogeny when Renan says, "Each individual travels in his turn along the line which the whole of mankind has followed, and the series of the development of human reason is parallel to the progress of individual reason." Aside, then, from the study of childhood, Renan suggests as a method of reproducing the mind of the past, the products, the monuments in which the mind has recorded itself. Chief of these records is language. "The deep study of its mechanism and history will always prove the most efficacious means of mastering primeval psychology." Through this study we should get, Renan goes on to say, "the facts which interested the mind at its first awakening, the influences that affected it, the laws that governed it." Beyond this, psychology is to give less emphasis, less absoluteness, to the manifestations of psychical life in the individual and more to those of humanity. History itself, in final definition is to be conceived as the psychology of humanity (pp. 152–68).

Of interest again is Renan's grasp of the conflict which is always going on between specialisation and generalisation in science, and his idea of the way to direct the conflict, so as to sustain the minimum of loss. The discussion is of special interest in connection with the present reaction against Renan's work as too viewy, too given to broad generalisation, lacking in the detailed element of technical research. The balance is difficult to keep, but certainly Renan's theory cannot be charged with erring in this direction, and if his practice errs the next generation may count the error no more heinous than that of a devotion to detail which carefully ignores all larger meaning. On one side, Renan demands an ever increasing amount of specialistic work, of monographs, of technical research, on every point however minute. Although the "grand" histories have already been attempted, yet without more numerous and extensive monographs, their real history cannot be written short of a century. He even goes to the point of saying that the "true heroes of science are they, who, capable of the loftiest views have been able to resign themselves to the rôle of humble monographers." And again, "the specialist-savant, instead of deserting the true arena of humanity, is the one who labors most efficaciously to the progress of the intellect, seeing that he alone can provide us with the materials for constructions." But all this is no excuse for the isolation and dispersion which exists at present. "The great present obstacle is the dispersion of work, the self-isolation among special studies which renders the labors of the philologist available only to himself and a small number engaged in the same subject." The defect is not in the multiplicity or minuteness of investigations, but in the fact that there is no machinery for distributing them, no apparatus for condensing and concentrating the results of the special research of one so as to put them at the disposal of all others. It is a form of egotism which insists that one's monograph shall always remain in just the state in which one wrote it; which resists all reduction of it to its gist so as to make it available, in its net outcome, for any and all investigators. The real need is for organisation, for control not of the liberty of individual specialisation, but of the results so reached. Our ideal must be to reproduce on a large scale the ideal attained, in small, in certain monastic orders—a grand scientific workshop (pp. 212–40).

Suggestive as are all these and many other special discussions of Renan, the most important thing to my mind is, after all, the conception which Renan had, in 1850, of the universal—the social, the religious significance of science and his partial retraction of this faith in 1890. The book in question, *The Future of Science*, was written, it may be of interest to recall, in 1848 and 1849. It was the outcome of the conflux of two movements—the growth of the scientific spirit in Renan in his progress out of Catholicism and of the political movement which found its expression in the various revolutions of '48. The volume breathes a constant and bracing tone of optimism: the *Future of Science* is not the future of erudition nor yet of knowledge as such. It is a social future, a development of humanity, which Renan has in mind. This was the origin of the book—"the need I felt of summing up in a volume the new [*i.e.*, social] faith which had replaced the shattered Catholicism." But just as he was ready to publish he went to Italy in connection with certain researches in the literary history of France and in Averroism. The artistic side of life, till then, as he says, closed to him, opened; it unbent him. Nearly all his ideals of 1848 vanished as impossible of realisation. He became, as he puts it, reconciled to reality—a world in which "a great deal of evil is the necessary condition to any good, in which an imperceptible amount of aroma requires for its extraction an enormous *caput mortuum* of dead matter." Was he reconciled to reality? or was it that the æsthetic spell passed over him, that he went to Italy a democrat—a believer in the universal function of science—and returned an aristocrat—sceptical of the intellectual and artistic life as one capable of being shared in by any beyond the select few? However it was, when he came back to his volume it no longer satisfied him, either in substance or in style. The *coup d'état*, happening soon after, added the finishing touch. The result was the Renan with whom we are most familiar: the man quite disillusioned, quite conscious of the impossibility of deciding among the multitude of ends which life presents, something of a dilettante, but always sympathetic and always conscientiously bent on the faithful culture of that spot of ground which belonged to him to till. The contrast between the enthusiast of 1848, apparently most interested in science because of the social mission of science, and the Renan of 1890, purposely ignoring its social function, is one of the most interesting things that I know of in literary history. I cannot do better than to close these remarks with a quotation from the *Moderne Geister* of Brandes. After quoting the later creed of Renan as summed up in the saying, "The scholar is a spectator in the universe; he knows the universe belongs to him only as an object of study," he goes on: "it is difficult to measure the demoralising effect upon French scholars exercised by the Second Empire; how their life became accommodated to the *fait accompli*. Everywhere under Napoleon III the higher French culture is characterised by an inclination to quietism and fatalism. Traces of this influence are to be seen everywhere. Complete freedom from enthusiasm was quite synonymous with culture and ripeness of judgment." Brandes quotes what Renan said to him in disparagement of universal education: in contrast read the enthusiastic plea for universal culture in the *Future of Science* and the transition is before you.

The Renan of 1848 wrote: "The most sublime works are those which humanity has made collectively and to which no name can be attached. . . . What do I care for the man that stands between humanity and me? What do I care for the insignificant syllables of his name? That name itself is a lie; it is not he; it is the nation; it is humanity toiling at a point of space and time that is the real author." In 1871, in his *Intellectual and Moral Reform* Renan writes: "At its outset, civilisation was an aristocratic accomplishment: it was the work of a very few—nobles and priests—who made it obtain through what the democrats call the imposition of force. The continued preservation of civilisation is also the work of the aristocratic class." In 1848 he wrote: "Only one course remains and that is to broaden the basis of the family and to find room for all at the banqueting table of light. . . . The aristocracy constitutes an odious monopoly if it does not set before it for its aim the tutelage of the masses—their gradual elevation." In 1871, his tone is: "The people properly so-called and the peasantry, to-day the absolute masters of the house, are in reality only intruders, wasps who have usurped possession of a hive they did not build."

Book Reviews

The Critical Philosophy of Immanuel Kant, by Edward Caird, LL.D., Professor of Moral Philosophy in the University of Glasgow. Two volumes. Glasgow: James Maclehose and Sons (Macmillan and Co., N. Y.), 1889.

Dr. Caird's former book on Kant has been out of print for some years, and it was understood that its author was preparing a more extended work. The first treatise, it will be recalled, covered only the *Critique of Pure Reason*. The implied promise has been most amply redeemed. We have now a report upon all of Kant's work, the minor writings as well as the three main *Critiques*, even the former exposition being entirely rewritten. The reviewer who would undertake to give anything approaching a fair account of these thirteen hundred compact although clear octavo pages must be either wiser than the present reviewer is, or more ignorant than he would be willing to confess himself. Yet there are some things which at least may be said *about* these volumes,—some things upon which there would be no difference of opinion among those competent to judge. All would admit that Professor Caird has written *the* book upon Kant in the English language,—most would add, in any language. About the thoroughness, the accuracy, the clearness of the exposition, there could hardly be two opinions. Concerning the maturity, the lucidity, the deftness, the firm-handling of the critical portion, I do not see how judgments could vary. That Dr. Caird has made what is, as to substance, a contribution to the history of thought of the very first order, and that in form his volumes have a unity, a massiveness, and a simplicity of treatment which marks them as a work of art, must be the verdict. All this, whatever philosophic stand-

[*First published in the* Andover Review, *XIII (Mar. 1890), 325–27. Not previously reprinted.*]

point the critic may himself occupy. The opinion of the absolute philosophic value of the work will of course depend upon the extent to which the critic shares the view of philosophic method and results embodied in it. To pretend in a short notice upon such a point to do more than express one's own conviction is sheer dogmatism. I can only say, then, that for myself I believe these volumes to be the richest and wisest outcome yet published of the philosophic Renascence now in progress in Great Britain. And I do not know who will transcend them until Professor Caird himself shall do it. Were I asked not only for the best English account of the Kantian philosophy, but for the best account of philosophy itself in the English language, I should point without hesitation to Caird's *Critical Philosophy of Kant*. But this judgment depends, as I said before, upon the critic's own philosophic position. That the work marks an epoch in the English treatment of the history of philosophy depends upon no position.

Only a few words may be said, to give the reader an idea of the method of Professor Caird in these volumes. After an extremely suggestive chapter upon "The Idea of Criticism," we have almost two hundred pages given to an account of Kant's life and relation to his times; his connection with his precursors from Descartes (this part is not quite so full as in Professor Caird's former book); and then what the Germans call an *Entwicklungsgeschichte* of Kant up to the point of his undertaking of the *Kritik der reinen Vernunft*. In this portion, the author has not only utilized the very numerous and detailed researches of German writers, but has materially added to them. Then follows an exposition of all Kant's critical writings, following approximately a chronological order. The account of the *Critique of Pure Reason* opens with a condensed and clear outline of the whole,—of its problem and the solution. From this point on, Dr. Caird's method is uniform. He first sets forth, in a way at once so accurate and so clear as to be the despair of the average reader who has struggled with Kant's tortuosities, Kant's own doctrine. Kant becomes fairly transparent in the lucidity of Caird's treatment, not, however, at the expense of any minimizing of difficulties.

Then follows the criticism. If the exposition is so admirable, what words remain with which to characterize the criticism? It is wholly an immanent criticism. We are shown whence Kant started; we are shown the nature and requirements of Kant's own method in dealing with the subject-matter; we are shown how far Kant goes in the reconstruction of the views from which he sets out; and we are shown how much further he should have gone in order to be true to his own principle. The great, the permanent value of Caird's work is to me the fact that he sets up no external standard by which to try Kant, but that he so develops Kant as to make him pass judgment upon himself. Here we have the Kant held back and hampered by prepossessions inherited from previous dualisms, set over against the Kant freed from his bonds and developed into consistency and integrity. In this way the book becomes, in effect, a summary of the entire Kanto-Hegelian movement, and, in addition, a statement of constructive philosophic results.

To summarize this re-creation of Kant is an impossibility,—the summary is the book itself. Professor Caird's philosophic position may, perhaps, be indicated, if I say that he has absorbed all the results of such criticism as that of Thomas Hill Green, but that he has a positive, constructive touch which in final seems to have been denied Green. The great Oxford thinker seems never to have quite freed himself from the negative element in Kant,—the idea that the regress from the world to self is an abstracting process, resulting in the notion of a spirit, *for* which indeed reality exists, but of which in itself nothing may be said. It may be roughly laid down as the purpose of Caird's work to show that, according to Kant's own principles, the movement from the world to mind, and from both to God, is a movement from the partial to the complete, from the abstract to the concrete, in which the lower becomes a factor in the spiritual process of the higher. The carrying-out of the purpose, not merely as a general principle, but in the treatment of all specific philosophic questions, is the heart of these two volumes. Dr. Caird shows that Kant reconstructed the previous dualism, that of mind set over against the world, so far as to show that all existence is existence *for* a self, for mind, but that, still in the toils of the very dualism which he was overthrowing, he denied that anything could be known of this self as such. Since, too, the known world is known only in relation to a self which is only logical, not real, that world was to Kant only phenomenal. The world of reality is shut off from intelligence. But Caird shows that the inevitable outcome of Kant is that existence is not only a phenomenon *for* self, but a phenomenon *of* self,—an element in the spiritual process of God. The result on the side of knowledge is to show that, since nature is only a factor in the self-determination of spirit, a solution of the most pressing of contemporary problems is possible. The categories of physical science can be reconciled with the principles of the moral and religious life by being taken up into them. Nature must, in Caird's words, take a new aspect, if it be conceived as standing in a necessary relation to spirit; "not only must we deny that the explanation which seems to be sufficient for matter is sufficient for life and mind, but, since matter is necessarily related to mind, we must deny that the explanation in question is sufficient even for matter. We must 'level up' and not 'level down'; we must not only deny that matter can explain spirit, but we must say that even matter itself cannot be fully understood except as an element in a spiritual world."

The same imperfect overcoming of the dualism between mind and the world, which is at the basis of Kant's unsatisfactory position as regards knowledge, affects also Kant's æsthetic, ethical, and religious position. In respect to the latter question, Caird shows clearly how the separation of the self from reality leads to Kant's conception of the moral law and of freedom as merely formal; to his conception of the moral ideal as something which merely *ought* to be, but is not; to his separation, in the name of freedom, of one individual from another; to his conception of society as essentially only an external collection of individuals; and to his denial of the possibility of any objective moral mediation. As a summary of Caird's idea of the relation of the moral will to nature, to humanity, and to God, the following quotation must serve: "Nature can be a means to the realization of our life, only in so far as in spirit nature comes to *a* self and to *its* self; that is, in so far as spirit reveals what nature implicitly contained. And other spiritual beings can be a means to the realization of our individual life, only in so far as our individual life itself becomes a means to the realization of a principle which is identical in them and in us. We cannot live except as we die to live; and the culmination of the effort after the realization of our own Will and our own Good must be the consciousness that *Deo parere libertas est*, and that all things 'can be ours' only as 'we are God's.' " So far, then, is freedom from being, as Kant conceives it, an assertion of the individual's will in his isolation, that "the *truth* of freedom lies in the unity of the self with the principle that is realizing itself in all nature and history. Behind the freedom that breaks the bonds of nature and necessity, we find a divine necessity in union with which alone man can be truly free. But, just because it is a divine necessity, it cannot really be an external necessity." With the impression derived from these words, we may fairly leave these volumes, hoping that we may have said enough of them to induce every philosophic-minded reader to turn to them himself.

Kant's Critical Philosophy for English Readers, by Mahaffy and Bernard. Vol. I, *The Kritik of the Pure Reason* explained and defended; Vol. II, *The Prolegomena*, translated with Notes and Appendices. London and New York: Macmillan and Co., 1889.

In connection with Caird's book, it is worth while to direct attention to Mahaffy and Bernard's edition of the *Critique of Pure Reason* and of the *Prolegomena*. Mahaffy's books, almost a score of years ago, were practically the first to direct the attention of the English-speaking public to Kant as he really was. Mansel and Hamilton had indeed presented a Kant of whom the less said the better. Mahaffy, however, left his work in an incomplete form; with the aid

[*First published in the* Andover Review, *XIII* (*Mar. 1890*), *328. Not previously reprinted.*]

of Mr. Bernard it has now been happily completed, and reprinted in a more convenient and accessible form. The *Prolegomena* does not appear to have been much changed from the first edition; the *Critique*, with its omissions and additions, is practically a new work. The *Prolegomena* is a translation; the *Critique* a paraphrase and condensation, with occasional explanatory and critical remarks, which are, however, carefully distinguished from the exposition. The plan of the work is such and its carrying-out so careful and accurate that it fills a position not occupied by any other of the numerous Kant expositions. The writer speaks from personal experience in saying that it is a most admirable book with which to introduce advanced under-graduates in our colleges to Kant. The exposition of the "Transcendental Deduction" is hardly up to the level of the rest of the book. And one feels occasionally as if the authors, in their condensations, had omitted the nub of the matter; but, on the whole, the book is a judicious and accurate rendering of Kant's thought into a form more valuable for the ordinary student than that supplied by a translation. One who has been through this book will be admirably prepared to take up his Caird.

A History of Philosophy, by J. E. Erdmann, Professor of Philosophy in the University of Halle. English translation, edited by N. S. Hough, of the University of Minnesota. In three volumes. New York: Macmillan and Co., 1890.

The philosophic public has had of late its interest aroused by the prospectus of a "Library of Philosophy," promising to cover the field of philosophy in a wholly adequate way. The promise is large and taking. It includes three series of volumes, one containing works upon the development of particular schools; the second, the history of theory in particular departments; the third, original and independent contributions. The names of the writers are an

[*First published in the* Andover Review, *XIII* (*Apr. 1890*), *453–54. Not previously reprinted.*]

assurance that the execution will be as thorough and critical as the plan is comprehensive. They comprise, in the first series, such well-known authors as Professors Wallace, Seth, Sorley, and Watson; in the second, Adamson, Bosanquet, and Pfleiderer, of Berlin; in the third, Edward Caird, and Ward (the author of the article upon "Psychology" in the *Encyclopædia Britannica*). When the series is completed, the English reader of philosophy will not cast such longing and envious eyes upon Germany as at present.

The introductory and "inaugural" volume of the series is the one before us. It was, we think, a happy thought to open the series with a general history of philosophy, one giving in a summary and yet comprehensive and reasoned way an outlook over the entire field. Some writer of English might perhaps have been found who would have produced an original treatise as good as the one of Erdmann's. But to have attempted it would have involved taking a great risk. Authors who are competent for such work are apt to fly at higher game. The combination of qualities necessary to produce a work of the scope and grade of Erdmann's is rare. Industry, accuracy, and a fair degree of philosophic understanding may give us a work like Ueberweg's, but Erdmann's history, while in no way superseding Ueberweg's as a handbook for general use, yet occupies a different position. Erdmann wrote his book, not as a reference-book, to give in brief compass a digest of the writings of various authors, but as a genuine history of philosophy, tracing, in a genetic way, the development of thought in its treatment of philosophic problems. Its purpose is to develop a philosophic intelligence rather than to furnish information. When we add that, to the successful execution of this intention, Erdmann unites a minute and exhaustive knowledge of philosophic sources at first hand, equaled over the entire field of philosophy probably by no other one man (Teller, Benno, Erdmann, and others may excel in periods), we are in a condition to form some idea of the value of the book. To the student who wishes, not simply a general idea of the course of philosophy, nor a summary of what this and that man has said, but a somewhat detailed knowledge of the evolution of thought and of what this and the other writer have contributed to it, Erdmann is indispensable; there is no substitute. Were it not that the book has hitherto been shut up within the confines of a German style, often crabbed and almost always complex, I should feel myself guilty of impertinent condescension in even appearing to commend the book. To those who know the history, it stands for itself in no more need of a word of praise than Ueberweg in his line, Kuno Fischer in his, or Teller in his. Comparisons with the original German of portions of the text selected at random reveal, with one exception, a successful outcome of what must have been a difficult and often tedious task. The editor is to be congratulated that he has reduced to such uniformity of style and rendering the work of the six different hands (two of them, by the way, besides the editor, Americans) from whom the translation proceeded. The exception to the successful result is to be found in the work of the translator of the portion "Since Hegel." This is probably, from a translator's standpoint, the most difficult part of the whole history. It is the more to be regretted that it was not executed by a hand as competent as the other portions of the text found. It is a pity that Professor Hough did not exercise his editorial prerogatives more vigorously upon this part. Examination of pages 72–77 of Volume III shows nine renderings either incorrect or decidedly unhappy. It is only fair to add that other selections showed nothing like this proportion of error. The editor's own translations are, upon the whole, the most spirited and idiomatic of any. It is to be hoped that the book will find its way rapidly, and that a second edition will soon be called for.

Studies in Hegel's Philosophy of Religion, by J. MacBride Sterrett, D.D., Professor of Ethics and Apologetics in the Seabury Divinity School. New York: D. Appleton and Co., 1890.

There is a prevailing impression that Hegel is synonymous with the "mystical," that is, misty, and that his very

[*First published in the* Andover Review, *XIII (June 1890), 684–85. Not previously reprinted.*]

touch upon a commentator leaves confusion of thought and speech behind it. Dr. Sterrett has not so suffered. A more vigorous and straightforward piece of writing as well as of thinking it has not often been my fortune to meet with. The book before us is fairly buoyant in its vigor; fairly aggressive in its straightforwardness. The purpose of the book is, as Dr. Sterrett frankly informs us, in his Preface, apologetic. But he has a worthy conception of Apologetics. To show forth religion as a necessary and genuine factor in the conscious life of man, to show forth Christianity as the fruition of religion—this is what Dr. Sterrett understands by Apologetics. Early in the book he tells us that his "own interest in the study began and continues as a purely theological one—the intellectual search for God as the self-conscious Reason of all that really is" (p. 14). More particularly Dr. Sterrett considers Hegel's Philosophy of Religion in the assistance which it may give in the *present* needs of Apologetics—in the attempt to conceive God and religion under the conditions imposed by the changed state of modern science and culture. This is not, Dr. Sterrett remarks, the highest vindication that thought can make of religion; the highest is to show the authority of the absolute *idea* of Religion. Both in this higher work and in the translating of the ever-valid religious ideas out of outworn and inadequate forms and language into more adequate and convincing modern forms theology has much to learn from Hegel. This is the spirit in which Dr. Sterrett has undertaken his task.

His basis is, therefore, a broad one. It is nothing more nor less than that a Philosophy of Religion is the only final Apologetics for Christianity. "Either this Philosophy of Religion must be attained, or we must rest on the external evidences of miracle and councils. The only other alternative is to refuse to examine, to ask for no evidences, to keep the simple faith of childhood in mature years by arbitrary repression of thought" (p. 96). "The Bible, Reason, and the Church, one after another, are made the standing ground of Apologetics, and yet not one of them is infallible. Each one needs a larger apologetic to vindicate its authority. They are all relatively sufficient grounds when *themselves* grounded upon the authority of the absolute idea of Religion" (p. 97).

I emphasize this conception of the Philosophy of Religion as the basis of any Apologetics, because it seems to me the key-note of Dr. Sterrett's whole book. Discussion of this position is out of the question within the limits of my space, but I find myself in heartiest sympathy with it. A few words regarding the method of the book may be useful. The first two chapters are a running sketch, wholly informal and yet as accurate as their purpose requires, of Hegelianism and of the development of the philosophic treatment of religions. The third, fourth, seventh, and eighth chapters follow Hegel in the main, giving expositions of his "Introduction," of his chapters on the "Vital Idea of Religion," the "Classification of the Pre-Christian Religions," and "Christianity as the Absolute Religion." Chapters Five and Six do not claim any direct relation to Hegel, but are expositions from an independent, yet sympathetic, standpoint of the matters treated in the other chapters. As Dr. Sterrett, even when expounding Hegel, keeps in view not students desirous of making themselves specialists in the Hegelian technique, but those interested in the broader movement of the Hegelian ideas, it should be evident that he has produced a work of great value to all interested in the fundamental questions of modern theology. I cannot but think it a happy omen in the present juncture of our theology, when the attempt to find God immanent in the world and in history is becoming so manifest, that Dr. Sterrett should give us a book whose whole trend is so forcibly and consciously in that direction.

I cannot close without briefly calling attention to three further features of the book—and first, the notable appendix upon Church Union. For one, I am thoroughly convinced that when the happy day of church union comes, it will come not upon the lines laid down by Dr. Sterrett, for he refuses to lay down hard lines, but in the spirit which breathes through all his words. Another is the spirit of honesty, of fairness, of love for straightforward intellectual dealing which animates what Dr. Sterrett writes. It is sometimes reported that our Theological Seminaries are not favorable to intellectual light and honesty. There will hardly be a question about the Seminary from which issues this book and the one of Dr. Kedney's recently noticed in this *Review*. The third feature is that rare thing in philosophical writing—the happy and really illustrative use of the dangerous metaphor. I had a number of passages marked for quotation, but one or two must suffice. Speaking of agnosticism and mysticism, Dr. Sterrett says: "The one utterly saps the vitality of thought, the other only floods it with more sap than it has channels prepared to receive." And speaking of the way in which spirit finds itself in that which seems at first to limit it, he says: "Thus it was that old Rome realized herself. Her god *Terminus* was elastic enough to include and transform all *hostes* into *cives sui*, and she became the imperial mistress of the world."

Elementary Psychology, with Practical Applications to Education and Conduct of Life, including an Outline of Logic, by J. H. Baker, A.M. New York: Effingham Maynard and Co., 1890. 232 pp.

Mr. Baker has written a succinct and, as far as possible, clear condensation of the current Scotch psychology, enriching it, upon occasion, with material from the empiricist writers, especially Bain. The book shows no trace of the influence of German thought, whether from the schools of Kant, of Herbart, or of the modern experimentalists like Fechner and Wundt.

We are informed in the Preface that "the importance of physiological psychology is duly regarded," and near the beginning of the book there are six or eight pages devoted to a highly technical description of the nervous system, going into such points as a nerve-fiber "consists of three parts, an extremely thin outer membrane, a white, semi-liquid sheath, and a translucent axis cylinder." The description, however, is not always quite accurate; the account, *e.g.*, of the sympathetic system belongs to the realm of "popular" science rather than to science proper. We are told that the cerebrum is the seat of mind, and that lower centers constitute the

[*First published in the* Educational Review, *I* (*May 1891*), *495–96. Not previously reprinted.*]

"reflex apparatus," by which, among other things, sensation is occasioned. Later on, sensation is taken out of this precarious position and restored to the mind. In spite of this account of nerve physiology, it cannot be said that the modern movement in physiological psychology has affected the standpoint or method of the book. Isolated items from the realm of cerebral physiology are scattered through the book, but are not assimilated in any organic way. They produce the effect of pieces of grit in a Scotch porridge.

When it is said that the book is not influenced in its inner spirit or practical outcome, either by German thought or modern experimental methods, but that it is a simple, well-condensed, and well-arranged exposition of the formulæ, which descend in the line of succession from Reid and Hamilton, vivified somewhat by Bain, the reader is in a fair position to judge the book. The term "faculty" is hardly used in the work, and we are told (p. 45) that the mind "is to be regarded as a unit." But as no attempt is made anywhere to find any fundamental mental function or process, and as perception, memory, phantasy, imagination, and thinking are all strung along one after the other, with no attempt to trace any unity, whether by way of underlying activity or by way of growth, the mind seems "to be regarded as a unit" for metaphysical rather than for psychological or practical purposes. We are informed, also, at large, that the mind is self-activity, but no attempt to connect the various details of physical life with this principle appears.

The educational applications are judicious and safe summaries of the usual "pedagogy" of teachers' institutes. Some are suggested more directly by the psychological theories themselves, and some have originated rather in the school-room, and then been attached to the psychology. Those who do not regard the Scotch psychology as very true, profound, or suggestive, will naturally prefer the latter to the former. Speaking from within the standpoint of the book itself, I see but one objection likely to arise—perhaps the attempt is made to cover too much ground within the compass of 232 pages. A summary of formal logic is introduced into the chapter on thinking, and there is the usual pocket of the Scotch school, labeled Intuitions, into which are stowed away, as self-evident, all the chief problems which have vexed the world's great reflective philosophers for two thousand years—problems like substance, personality, space, and time. Upon the whole, the book is, in form and in substance, an admirable reflection of the ideas and methods of the vast bulk of our teachers who are earnestly striving, along the lines of the ordinary pedagogy of our normal schools and teachers' institutes, to elevate education. To discuss, therefore, its substance would be to go beyond the limits of a review of this book into the question of the value, scientific and educational, of the current psychology.

What Is Reality? by Francis Howe Johnson. Boston and New York: Houghton, Mifflin and Co.

The question, "What is Reality?" is a comprehensive question, and it is not to be expected that the answer should be a wholly conclusive one. It lies not much against Mr. Johnson, then, that he has been more successful in his inquiry than in his reply. In the course of his reflections he has at least gone over much of modern philosophy and presented it to the reader in a clear, straightforward style. As Mr. Johnson has obvious gifts of exposition, it is a pity his information is not always derived at first hand. His account of Hegel, for example, clearly comes not from Hegel himself but from Seth's refutation of him in his *Hegelianism and Personality*. This would not be of much account, if the "refutation" were other than a simple misunderstanding. As it is, the result is more than a mere misstatement of Hegel's position. It is a failure on the part of Mr. Johnson to grasp the meaning of the whole modern "idealistic" movement in thought, and the failure affects the constructive as well as the critical portion of the book before us. It rests on the assumption of the old dualism between the thought world and the thing world, and takes it for granted that the problem of philosophy is how to get the bridge that

[*First published in the* Inlander (*University of Michigan*), *II* (*Mar.* 1892), 282–83. *Not previously reprinted.*]

takes us across the chasm. Thus he divides modern methods into subjective and objective analyses, ranking the method of German philosophy as subjective, and the method of science as objective, and contrasts both with the appeal to life, his own position being that that proposition expresses reality whose affirmation it is necessary to *live*. Had Mr. Johnson seen that this was precisely the result which German philosophy from Kant to Hegel was driving at, had he seen, for example, that Hegel's logic is neither subjective nor objective analysis, but analysis of the life which underlies and overlies all division into objective and subjective, his own theory would have been more coherent than it is, especially as relates to the relation of revelation to knowledge. As it is, Mr. Johnson is left with a gap between the ordinary process of experience and the method of revelation. Mr. Johnson does his best to cover the gap by various connecting links, but the very fact that the links are required testifies to the gap.

Too much cannot be said in praise of the candor and honest purport of Mr. Johnson's work. It is a good omen for the future of American thought when a book having, in a sense an apologetic intent, is so fair (and so fair without effort) to opponents and so open to light as is the work of Mr. Johnson.

The Story of the Odyssey, by the Rev. A. J. Church. New York: Macmillan and Co.

If, as Mr. Howells says, the stories are all told, the *Odyssey* of Homer is more responsible for this result than any other one writing. As the *Iliad* is the heroic epic of humanity, the *Odyssey* is the story-book. The comparative philologist finds in it, by type or incident, the whole mythological repertory of the ancient world; the psychologist finds in it all the representative scenes and contacts of which the mind is possessed. That this story-book of the romantic childhood of the world should be retold for the childhood of

[*First published in the* Inlander (*University of Michigan*), *II* (*Mar.* 1892), 286–87. *Not previously reprinted.*]

to-day is fitting. Professor Church has already demonstrated his capacity in this direction by his stories from the Bible, the *Iliad*, and from Lucian, and his telling of the *Odyssey* bears out his reputation. The educationalists of Germany use the *Odyssey* as one of the strongholds of children's training. It is a way as effective as charming for introducing the child into the inheritance of the race.

The Angle of Reflection

1

The principle of universal suffrage has been making great strides of late. We have been accustomed, for some years, to its extension from the field of politics to those of social life and business. The determining of the most popular young lady in the Sandemenian parish by ballot at the church fair, or of the most gentlemanly clerk at Thread, Ribands and Co., by majority vote, are familiar enough. The principle was introduced into literature a number of years ago, by several so-called literary journals, in the matter of voting for the most popular or best novel, poem, etc., published within a given time. From this, it was an easy stage to voting for the "best" authors.

The *Critic* of New York—a journal which would probably object to the prefix of so-called to literary—took the last step. If we have a republic of letters, why not have universal suffrage there also? So several years ago the *Critic* opened the boxes to receive votes for an Academy—to consist of forty members like the institution of similar name in France. These immortals once banded together, what more natural than that the *Critic* should wish to weave a garland of immortelles? And a short time ago the *Critic* declared the polls open for receiving votes for an Academy of poetesses, fictionistes and authoresses in general. By what seems an ungallant discrimination, the number was limited to twenty. Not so the votes, however. Every one that voted seems to

[*First published in the* Inlander (*University of Michigan*), *I* (*Mar.* 1891), 35–37. *Not previously reprinted. Each of the six unsigned articles entitled "The Angle of Reflection" has been numbered in chronological order. See A Note on the Texts for details concerning Dewey's authorship of the articles.*]

have had a "lady friend," of a literary turn of mind; and the number of persons voted for must have surprised everybody except the increasing number of persons who hunt through the newspapers compiling selections of American literature. The particular incident ray, however, which has impinged so as to call out these reflections is the fact that no Michigan poetess or authoress seems to have received votes. Not even the whilom sweet singer of Michigan, whose refrain

That game they call croquet, croquet,
That game they call croquet,

must have haunted the head of many a distracted man, received any votes.

Many theories may, of course, be advanced to account for this state of things. It may be contended that Michigan people are not yet in favor of applying the principle of majority-rule to literature. Others may prefer to argue that Michiganders do not draw their literary sustenance from the *Critic*, and hence were not alive to the great campaign going on in the literary world. Something possibly might be made out for the assertion that the campaign was too languid to arouse a people habituated to warm political strife. We are too firm believers in the democratic principle to take interest in a vote taken without stump-speaking, torch-light processions, and inducements to "blocks of five." Where were the orators urging the claims of Blanche Willis Howard, and free trade with Germany, or the transparencies suggesting a vote for Gail Hamilton and the old flag?

But, after all, the dearth of candidates from this region may indicate that the star of literary empire does not westward take its way. It perhaps has transferred its central light from Boston to New York; but it does not seem to have the strength required to climb the Alleganies. The fixing of the Columbian Fair at Chicago rather than at New York marks a distinct shifting in matters industrial and social; signs are not wanting that the centre of political gravity is now in the Mississippi Valley. Western methods and styles of journalism have taken possession of Boston and New York. But where is the literature of the west? There has been, indeed, some western flora, but the plants are rather sporadic, local and tender. Mr. Howells—a westerner whose western spirit only in his last work has broken through its coat of Boston varnish—from his observatory in *Harper's Monthly* scours the prairies for literary comets, but reports with regret only an occasional flash-light.

Perhaps this failure of the west to produce as much literary crop to the acre as the territory about Boston and New York is more closely connected with the failure of the country to produce as yet a distinctively American literature than we think. We may flatter ourselves with the belief that the real life of America germinates in western soil, and its spirit broods over western plains. For the west then there can be no literature until this germinating life flowers, until this brooding spirit comes to consciousness of itself. The western literature must tarry until the American idea has come to know and to feel itself. The east with its more cramped position, more rigid traditions and more self-conscious attitude can do the partial thing, because it lacks the whole. It can follow English lines and take the British outlook, and thus bring forth what passes as literature until the vast, inchoate, turbid spirit of America shall find her own articulate voice. This view may express only the provincial pride of the woolly west—or there may be something in it.

At all events, to come from general speculation to actual business, if there is any of the *Ethos* of the west latent in or about this University, the *Inlander* is here for the purpose of helping it take form. By title and by position of the University, the *Inlander* stands in this middle western country which does not seem as yet to count (either by work or voting in the *Critic*) in the literary world. It desires both to express and to encourage the articulate voicing of that part of the vast dumb Inland to which it belongs. The reflector, who is occupying this angle at present, has a friend who says that the only literary sense is the ability to discriminate between hot and cold. And it is this literary sense which the *Inlander* would cultivate. That conception which regards literature as a sort of technical process or extra polish apart from the ordinary run of life it is not concerned with. But that literary sense which consists in the free perception and natural reporting of the currents of life which are actually in movement, it would desire to have expressed in its pages and to stimulate in its audience.

2

President Eliot, of Harvard, recently visited as is well known, the colleges of the West. It may not be as well known that on his return he gave in a public talk some account of the educational outlook in the West, with special reference to Harvard and its work. He found that the West is indebted to Harvard for three great educational gifts. The first is the elective system, which he finds to have been introduced more extensively throughout the West than in any New England college, save Harvard. Even the University of Minnesota, with comparatively small resources, offers a wider degree of election than Yale. The second gift of Harvard is the idea that increase of power is to be aimed at, rather than acquisition of knowledge. It is this idea that has led to modifications in the traditional curriculum, and to "the changes that were made here *first* (*sic*) in the conditions of entrance—the dropping of Greek and Latin from the requirements." The third contribution of Harvard to the West is individualization of instruction—the introduction of laboratory work, of conferences and seminaries, and other methods where the instructor must give personal attention to the student.

Without doubt, these principles will all pass as thoroughly sound in this locality, however it may be elsewhere. And we are all glad to join in President Eliot's congratulations at Cambridge that these principles, introduced by Harvard, have found such ready and ample welcome in the West. Nor is our pleasure to be marred by possible objections to President Eliot's facts, notably his assertions that seminary work and the dropping of Greek and Latin from

[*First published in the* Inlander (*University of Michigan*), *I* (*Apr. 1891*), *82–84. Not previously reprinted.*]

entrance requirements are the original accomplishments of Harvard. We shall simply regret that with all the store of information that President Eliot gathered in his western trip, he could not have added the real facts in these directions. But the educational debt of the country to Harvard is, in all conscience, large enough when all corrections are made.

Give and take is the law of nature and of life; and it is not surprising to find that President Eliot, like a wise man, wishes to know what return Harvard is to have. His answer is that the West should send Harvard an increasing number of students. Here, too, we shall rejoice in the rejoicings of our sister University. But is it not possible that some exchange has already taken place? Is it not possible that the West has already made some educational gifts to Harvard and to the East, gifts greatly more important than any number of students would be? We of the University of Michigan, at least, are not accustomed to think of ourselves entirely as recipients, however tardy the colleges of the East may be in receiving our generous gifts.

Let us see whether we cannot parallel the three presents that we have received with three gifts that the West has made. First and foremost, there is the conception of the democratic idea in higher education. It is not too much to say that higher education in the East was built up and fostered upon the *class* idea. Even after the notion that the University was a training school for clergymen passed away, the idea lingered in the East that it was for special classes rather than for the people themselves. The conception that the University is only the culmination of the *common* school education belongs to the West;—may we not add, with proper modesty (since it was the doing of our forefathers and not of ourselves) to the University of Michigan? And the readjustment of the studies of the course, the readjustment of entrance requirements, the putting of all departments on the level of a free and generous competition belongs (*pace* President Eliot) to the working out of no pedagogical abstraction such as that power and not knowledge is the end of education. It is the easy and natural outcome of the democratic idea in education; the idea that higher education, as well as the three R's, is of and for the people, and not for some cultivated classes. Third, the earnest and systematic attempt to make an organic connection between the University and the preparatory schools is the affair of the West. Of course large preparatory schools with very intimate connections with the University are much older than the West; but the connection of the University with high schools, with the public schools as found in every village of any size, is the accomplishment of the West. To those who conceive of University education as a sort of sacred scholarship to be preserved, at all hazards, from the contaminating touch of the masses, all this must seem very grievous; but to those who believe in the democratic idea, it presents large and commanding features—features which need not fear to be set side by side with the contributions of any University. Meantime it is interesting to note the gradual shifting of the eastern colleges to this basis, and to hear the acclaim with which they greet as a new educational discovery every approach to what is now axiomatic in the West.

3

The Reflector in the last issue of the *Inlander*, made remark to the effect that one of the main functions of the typical Eastern educationalist is to raise a great noise, *pro* and *con*, about methods that have been quietly adopted for a greater or less period in the State Universities of the West. The remark has been twice underscored by events of the last month. One of these events was the rejection by the highest governing board of Harvard University of the plan of shortening the course formulated by the Faculty of Harvard. The other is the adoption (as reported in the newspapers) by Cornell of the so-called Columbia plan by which Law work may be combined with Senior Literary work so that a student may take both degrees in five years.

[*First published in the* Inlander *(University of Michigan), I (May 1891), 119–20. Not previously reprinted.*]

The Harvard plan was heralded through the newspapers as a sweeping reduction of the collegiate course to three years. Stated in this broad way, the plan is misreported. As matter of fact the plan looked towards the substitution of a certain number of courses or of hours for a certain number of years, making it possible for the better class of students to graduate in three or in three and a half years. This plan, it is hardly necessary to say to those acquainted with the University of Michigan, has been in operation here for a considerable number of years, without arousing one-fiftieth of the tempestuous agitation that the mere suggestion of it at Harvard awakened. And in the fashion of the East usual when discussing the matter of electives, co-education, the relation of the classics to the collegiate curriculum, etc., the proposal has been discussed wholly on *a priori* grounds, with no reference to experience. The bare fact that such a plan has been carried out, with relative, if not absolute, success in a western University, was too brutely empirical for the tender mental systems of our Eastern friends. Long may they be preserved from too close contact with the rude realities of experience! How could that refined discussion and argumentation which is so dear to every true Lover of Culture be carried on, if we were obliged to take heed of facts?

The Columbia plan, which so far has met a happier fate than the Harvard, has also been in practical, although not in nominal, operation in the University of Michigan for some time. The *modus operandi* is different, the actual outcome the same. In Cornell and Columbia, if I rightly understand it, the student is able to substitute the entire first year's work of the Law School for the fourth year's work of the Literary Department. Here a student who has only a certain number of hours to "get off" is able to carry part or all of the law work simultaneously with the literary work. Which of these two means of reaching the same end is the better remains to be decided by comparison of their actual workings. But taking such things as these into account, a BUREAU FOR THE DISTRIBUTION OF WESTERN COLLEGIATE METHODS AMONG EASTERN UNIVERSITIES might be a paying scheme.

The adoption of such methods in the West and their discussion in the East, are both, however, only symptoms of a larger movement—of the tendency to do what the politicians call "getting close to the hearts of the people." Pretty much all recent educational change falls into one or other of two lines, these two lines marking simply a growing division of labor. On one side, there is the tendency towards specialization, towards minute personal research, towards everything which the present educational predominance of Germany identifies with scholarship. The other tendency is towards the distribution of the resulting ideas. (I should call it the popularization of ideas were it not for the cold chill which runs down the spine of the aforesaid Lover of Culture whenever he hears the word "popular.") University extension, the forcing of technical instruction into institutions once priding themselves on being wholly literary, the tendency towards a closer union of academic and professional work, the shortening of the course, the broadening of the literary curriculum, are all only evidences of this movement. And democracy, popularization, as has been more than once remarked, is like the grave; it takes, but it never surrenders what it takes. We should cultivate the Lover of Culture carefully, for the time may be coming when he shall be a rare specimen—the prospect of his total extinction we veil our faces from.

4

A clever young Englishman—one of the literary Socialists who cluster about William Morris, who look upon Socialism as a religious rather than an economic movement, and who are bringing a distinctly new spirit into the critical treatment of literature through the press of Walter Scott—well, a clever young Englishman, to get back to my beginning, remarked to me that in many respects the social question

[*First published in the* Inlander (*University of Michigan*), *I* (*June 1891*), *153–56. Not previously reprinted.*]

seemed to him more promising in England than in America. As one evidence he noted that it was much easier to get together the working people and the men learned in economics in England than here. There the educated University men look upon it as almost a religious duty, certainly a privilege, to go to the workingmen's clubs and unions and to discuss social questions with them. The laboring class eagerly hang on the lips of these their teachers. It seemed to my friend that, while this country was nominally more democratic, there was no such willing commingling of classes here. The workingmen, here, think they know just as much as any college professor, and would be suspicious of the advances of the educated class. The University men, he thought, rather looked down, from their side, upon Knights of Labor and such like organizations, and hardly think it worth while to display their treasures before them.

As an American and a supposed democrat, I was led to think about this matter. As I thought, it occurred to me that my English socialistic friend was probably right in his facts but wrong in his inferences. The very fact in England, of which he was speaking, was based upon the idea of a separation of classes, and of a benevolent desire on the part of some of the "upper" class to aid the "lower." It implied that the democratic movement was not the life-blood flowing in the very veins of the social structure, but something to be passed about from hand to hand. The American laborer draws his sustenance from the same great currents of political and commercial life at which the professor or doctor of philosophy must drink. Often he feels that while he may not know as much of some abstract principles or as many statistical details as the University man, he is, in truth, nearer to the real sources of knowledge. In a word, if there is such a thing as democracy in the very life movements of the state, it is highly absurd to propose a "mingling of classes." This may mark a step *toward* democracy, but, democracy attained, it is not necessary to peddle it around from one individual to another.

The attempt to transfer the University Extension movement from England to America has led me to follow this line of thought somewhat further. There can be no doubt that in England this movement has assumed large social, and even, in the true sense, political proportions. It has not been merely a diffusion of learning, or a widening of information. It has not been simply an educational affair, in the limited sense of the term. It has marked the growth of common interests and actions between the educated young men of England and the laboring men. It has been a great step in the breaking down of class barriers. It has been one large phase and one large instrument in the democratic advance.

Is it reasonable to expect that University Extension will assume any such important social function in this country? Some of the managers of the Extension in this country seem to anticipate that it will. They are making a great stir, great claims, and are even proposing to raise a large sum of money, something like a hundred thousand dollars, as a permanent endowment fund. Now there need be no doubt of the *educational* importance of this movement. To extend learning, to diffuse the results of scholarly research, to give University men a closer contact with other phases of life than their own, is a useful thing. So regarded, the University Extension movement may be looked at as superimposing a higher layer and more advanced methods upon the Chautauqua substratum. Multitudes of literary clubs, clubs for study of social questions, now exist about the country in all stages of organization and disintegration. The University Extension movement affords these clubs and societies a centre. They may crystallize, so far as they have serious aims, about the Extension. Thus they will get better instruction, more definite and less floating ends, and some systematic supervision. But does this University Extension, after all, represent in principle anything more organic, more important socially, than these literary clubs, however much more effectively the University Extension may realize the principle?

Take the conditions, physical and social, under which the Extension must be carried on in this country. England is a compact country with dense population. All the University professors and fellows in Great Britain could be conveyed in carriages over the whole of England in a few days. Under such circumstances, University Extension is only a matter of extending professors; a matter of hiring a few carryalls or railway coaches, more or less, to deposit University men here and there. In other words, it becomes essentially an individual matter—a matter of getting certain men of one class face to face with men of another. The very increase of distance in the United States, those physical conditions which have compelled the development of the railway and the telegraph, and which have forced the substitution of large social tendencies for merely individual efforts, changed all this in our country. University Extension, in the ordinarily accepted sense, becomes a locality affair instead of an organized social affair as in England. The University of Michigan might, for example, lend its professors, and extend its courses to local audiences in Detroit, Grand Rapids, Saginaw, etc., but it is difficult to see how it, or any combination of American Universities, can do for this country, in any large sense, what the Universities of Oxford and Cambridge have done for England in this movement. This country is too big, its currents of life too organic.

On the other hand, what is University Extension? It must be the extension of the inner spirit of the University. Certainly no one would claim to-day that the lectures are the highest development of the University spirit. And yet the movement so far as already organized seems to propose nothing beyond an extension of lecturers and lectures, with assigned readings and examinations. Now this as an educational matter is well and good; as a social matter it is quite another affair. The vast mass of our population is already pretty well occupied; books, magazines and newspapers, to say nothing of theatres and lecture courses, fill up leisure moments. As a scheme for the diffusion of knowledge, in other words, the University Extension would seem to be somewhat anticipated by the wide-spread reading habits of the population. The Extension may direct and supplement somewhat this reading. How much more can it do? I cannot help thinking about this extension matter (on its social, as distinct from its merely educational, side) as I did about the remark of my Socialist friend. There can no large social importance attach to it, because democracy has already gone so much farther in this country than in England; it is so much in the atmosphere we breathe, in the currents in which we live that the merely individual phases of it are reduced to a minimum.

5

It is striking that some of the most poetic features of our American life, centering in our politics, are just those which are popularly esteemed, not only non-poetic, but highly objectionable—even as blots upon our character and repute. The "intelligent foreigner," visiting our shores and seeing a certain easy expression of some large good nature of democracy which is to him inexplicable, "finds much to admire in the American civilization, but notes with regret one feature, which if not taken earnestly in hand by the American people—must in time"—etc., etc. The native editorial writer does not wish to rank in culture and refinement below the aristocratic visitor from abroad, and so takes up the cry, assuring the distinguished visitor that the "better classes" of America share his sentiments, his regrets and his fears, and beg of him that they may not be held responsible for the doings of the "lower classes"—in a word, of the bhoys. The Ward Association, the band which runs "wid de machine," its captain, the local boss, his lieutenant the heeler—this band, in reality one of the most picturesque features of American life, is the recipient of the largest amount of this condescending abuse.

In truth, only a Homer could do justice to the free and vivid experiences of one of the modern clans, with its Agamemnon, the local king of men, its Odysseus, skilled in wiles, its Nestor who narrates to the boys tales of the bygone days when he too went to Albany. Who but Homer could describe the gathering of the Cohorts in "de fift" or "de ate" ward as they pour forth to a campaign picnic? The

[*First published in the* Inlander (*University of Michigan*), *II* (*Oct. 1891*), *50–52. Not previously reprinted.*]

generosity of the great-souled Boss, who bears the entire expense of transporting the whole ward to the picnic grounds of a neighboring island; the orderly disorder of the tribe as to the martial music of "Comrades" or the soothing strains of "Annie Rooney" it marches to the dock; the plenteous breakfast feast, with its varied libations, its abundant larder; then the manly games, the foot race, the boxing-match, the tug of war, with the great-souled Boss encouraging and giving forth medals? Is there any one so lost to a sense of the unity of human nature as not to know that the ever fresh and naïve scenes depicted by the Greek bard had the same spirit and motives? Suppose that a picnic does sometimes threaten to end in a row, as in a recent one near New York City, because the chicken is kept till the third course—a time when the hearts of brave men are already so satisfied that they cannot do justice to the daintiest viand of the feast. Does any one believe that in the assemblies celebrated by Homer there were no heartburnings, because of unequal distributions of the swing-paced, crook-horned oxen? Are games less ideal, less manly now because the prizes are won by O'Flahertys and Weissenbrodts instead of by Laodamases and Euryaluses? Do you really think that Ajax or Agamemnon was entirely unmindful of the necessity of strengthening his "holt on the boys" when he furnished a great gala day? The facts are the same. Only the idealizing eye of the poet now fails.

No, let us be ashamed of our attempt to load the faults of the whole people upon a given class, especially when these faults are by no means the meanest or the most sordid of our deficiencies, when indeed they have a certain large heartedness and good faith all their own. Nothing is more ill-considered, nothing in worse taste than the denunciations of the "machine" and of the "boys" now so freely dispensed from the self-styled "better class" of journals. How comes it that the "boys" are in such full possession of the machine? Are politics an exception to the law that no result is attained save by the expenditure of energy, and will the ideal politics of the superior editorial writer do themselves? Who is to attend to the practical management of the details of party manœuvering and government? If the business class which in the *New York Times* and *Evening Post* arrogates to itself the possession of sound sense as to the state needs, and the scholarly class which through the mouth of the *Nation* assumes a monopoly of high ideals, if these classes are so busy making money and acquiring culture that they have no time or thought to give to political details, the "boys" may well put in the claim to be occupying an otherwise unowned and unworked field. Let us, at least, have the good taste not to complain too loudly of the unsavory way in which one class does a necessary work to which we refuse to put our hands. Let us at least have the grace to permit the boys to continue their parades, their picnics and their local sovereignties untroubled by our unmeaning scoldings. In a word, let us no longer, in the plentitude of our wealth and wisdom, blame one class when the whole organism is responsible. If it is true that "we" are so superior in culture and business ability, it is possible there may come a day when this superiority will be deemed a reason for holding us, the "better classes," chiefly responsible.

6

The Volapük fad seems to have suffered the fate of all fads. All faddists are cannibals, save that they reverse the order. The Sandwich Islander killed his victim and then ate him. The faddist devours his fad, and the devoured fad expires. The fad lasts only while acquiring, and once acquired but whets the appetite for a new one. However, the natural history of fads is not my topic. What an absurdity—to create a language without an atmosphere, without a setting in human thought, without an abyss of human emotions! Only Jonathan Swift could do justice to the massive stupidity, to the imbecility, lacking all the poetry of the genuine lunatic, which conceived of a language meant to express "things," instead of ideas and feelings.

[*First published in the* Inlander (*University of Michigan*), *II* (*Nov.* 1891), 96–97. *Not previously reprinted.*]

For language is the unexpugnable home, the reservoir that cannot be drawn dry, of poetry. M. Jourdain talked prose without knowing it, but a greater miracle than that enacts itself daily. The stiffnecked Prosaist, who is incarnate Philistinism, becomes a poet when he uses language. The generous mother of us all, foreseeing the narrow straits, the heavy ruts into which life was to come, bore us into an atmosphere where we cannot enter save by enduring it with ourselves, save by poetizing it. And this is the medium into which we must enter whenever we approach our fellows' language. The Volapükist was an enemy of the entire human race: he sought to sterilize with his noxious vapors the one unescapable, ever pregnant medium of imagination; to get the mind out of itself into bare contact with "things."

Any one who has occasion to read much in other languages, and especially to go abruptly from one tongue to another, must always notice how the entire atmosphere, intellectual and emotional, changes also. To *read* a language is to drink in, to absorb the whole *Gemüth* of a nationality: to *translate*—what is it but another way of thinking your own already sufficiently wearisome thoughts?

I do not suppose that any two minds get just the same atmospheric effect, the same over-tones, the same "physical fringe," the same coloring of accompanying mental images from a language. But as for myself, the French language produces upon me the effect of out-of-doors—not indeed the exhilaration of the open air, the brisk and driving wind, but the simple out-of-doors effect. There is expansion, but a bounded expansion, the definite horizon, the clearest perspective; the rounded dome is over all, a common air washes all. It is a sunlit out of doors; there are clouds and shadows, but clouds and shadows which, after all, only serve to mark out the light, to give solidity to the perspective. One walks easily, securely in such a world; he knows where he started from, where he is going; east and west, north and south are as distinct as in the world of nature. The eye is the guiding sense.

What a change when I go to a German book!—the change from *joli* to *schön*. I find my eye upon which I had been relying, gradually growing dim and blear. Tone takes the place of light. How different the shadings! In French they were shadings of color, which, with all their graduations and continuities yet define, each having its own characteristic value. In German the shading blends, mixes, runs all into one. It is the modulation of music. I leave out of doors, or if I remain without, it is no longer the landscape, half in sun, half in shade which I see; it is the murmuring of leaves, the rustling in the trees I hear. Everywhere a vague mysterious stirring which with some secret tie makes all things one. But generally I find myself taken within doors—the concert chamber, the lecture hall, the domestic fire place, these are the loved abodes of sound. Closeness has taken the place of openness; sometimes the closeness of suffocation, of an unaired room, sometimes the closeness of concentrated depth and power; but closeness always. In French I look on and the meaning unfolds. It is there—*Voilà*. In German the general meaning oozes in and fills me, I know not how, but the details, the particulars I have to struggle to catch. I have to listen hard for them. I do not know if you, my reader, have the same experience. I know, however, this is no general theory concocted by me, but an attempt to convey the kind of actual sensuous images which surrounds and bathes what I read.

Introduction to Philosophy: Syllabus of Course 5

Philosophical Department

UNIVERSITY OF MICHIGAN

February, 1892

SECTION 1.—Philosophy (science) is the conscious inquiry into experience. It is the attempt of experience to attain to its own validity and fullness; the realization of the meaning of experience.

Science and philosophy can only report the actual condition of life, or experience. Their business is to reveal experience in its truth, its reality. They state what *is*.

The only distinction between science and philosophy is that the latter reports the more generic (the wider) features of life; the former the more detailed and specific.

SECTION 2.—The separation of science and philosophy has reference to the incompleteness of knowledge. Although our experience goes on within the whole, the whole is the last thing of which we become conscious *as* a whole of included factors. Thus the trouble with philosophy is the difficulty of getting the whole, the generic, before consciousness in such a way that it may be naturally reported. The partial thing may be broken off from the whole and then described with comparative ease. But this process of multiplying pieces seems to leave the generic, the whole beyond and out of sight. It makes the whole remote, and capable of description only in unnatural ("metaphysical," "transcendental") terms. Thus science, as relating to the part, and philosophy as referring to the whole, fall apart. Philosophy suffers by being made vague and unreal; science in becoming partial and thus rigid.

The search for philosophy is not a peculiar or technical

[*Preserved in the University of Michigan Historical Collections. Not previously reprinted.*]

search; it is objective and general; it is the search for the real whole. Just so far as this whole is really attained in experience, it becomes possible to treat it in a direct, natural way, *but only in so far*. In two directions, the whole is now more definitely realized than ever before, so that we get a language for reporting it. These two directions are the two phases of action. On one hand, science has revealed to us, in outline, at least, the type action of the individual organism, the process involved in every complete act. On the other hand, as life has become freer, social action has revealed the principle involved in it. The action of the psycho-physical and of the political body, in other words, give us such perception of the whole that we may report the latter, thus translating philosophical truth into common terms.

Chapter First—the Psycho-Physical Act

SECTION 3.—The unit of nervous action is called the reflex-arc. (See Spencer, *Psychology*, Vol. I, first three chapters, especially pp. 27 ff.; James, *Psychology*, Vol. I, p. 12, pp. 20–21; Von Hartmann, *Philosophy of Unconscious*, Vol. I, pp. 127 ff.) This term covers not simply the narrower "reflex" of physiology (the winking of an eye, for example) but every unified action, or completed portion of conduct. *Illustrations*: the movement of an amœba, the impulse of a child for food, the perception of color, a word like "civilization," with its whole meaning, a virtuous act, a philosophic theory. Each is a unified action; and in this unity of action various conditions are brought to a head or focussed. Each is a co-ordination of certain experiences; each is an *expression*, more or less direct, more or less explicit, of the whole of life; it is the manifold circumstance of the Universe attaining a unity in action.

Such an activity as finds expression then in an entire reflex-arc is a whole, a concrete, an individual. It is the *Self* in more or less developed form.

SECTION 4.—There are, evidently, two sides in the reflex-arc. These sides have no separation in fact, but may be distinguished by us. One side is the *diversity of conditions* involved; the other side is the *unity of action*.

To the unity corresponds the Self as *Will*; to the diversity, the Self as *Intelligence*. *Illustrations*: instinctive taking of food; hearing an enemy's footstep; hearing a bell; the scientific analysis of sound, and so on. *Problem.*—If Intelligence and Will are so closely connected, how do you account for their apparent disconnection in such an example as the last?

SECTION 5.—Taking up the reflex-arc on the side of its diversity, we may further distinguish two phases: There is the simple *diversity as such*; the multiple conditions involved in an act. This is the *sensory* side of knowledge. Any one of the diverse conditions taken *per se* constitutes *a* sensation or *stimulus*. Each of these in itself may be itself an act containing its conditions or factors. For example, within the action of taking food there is contained hunger as a condition. This hunger is itself, in turn, an activity, involving various factors of muscular change, and conditions of respiration, circulation, etc. The visual perception of the food is another element contained in the act. This, in turn, is itself an act unifying its conditions, etc. Either of these acts considered *per se* is a *stimulus* to the act of eating. In reality, it is simply one phase of, one process *within*, the act. *The sensory elements in experience are simply the various more or less distinct minor activities contained within an act of larger range.*

SECTION 6.—The diverse conditions, or minor acts, involved within a unified action, have also their adjustments to each other. Each holds in check the others, and in turn is held by them. No one of them discharges *by itself* but only in the whole of which it is one member. This mutual checking and re-inforcing of the various contained minor actions is the *co-ordination* of the sensory elements.

This co-ordination, co-operation, mutual adjustment, etc., is the *relation* of the sensory element. *It is thus the ideal side of knowledge*. For example, in an act, whether of taking food or of looking at a picture, what gives the activity of the optical apparatus—the sensation of color—its ideal value (its meaning) is the other similar minor activities or reflexes going on together with it, all within the larger reflex.

Illustrations may be found in cases of psychical blindness, deafness, aphasia, etc. See James' *Psychology*, Vol. 1, pp. 48–52 and references there.

SECTION 7.—The sensation, the stimulus (the contained minor reflex) is evidently an abstraction taken *per se*. It acts only in its adjustment or co-ordination with other reflexes. This co-ordination or mutual re-inforcement and limitation, is equally an abstraction taken *per se*.

Problem: Consider how the old question of sensationalism *vs.* rationalism stands when each element is considered from the standpoint of the whole action, or reflex-arc; when, that is, sensation is considered as itself an act, and the ideal element, or relation, as the active adjustment of that act.

SECTION 8.—The reflex-arc, in its unity, is thus a co-ordination of distinct but adjusted minor reflexes, or acts. It is a moving equilibrium of actions.

In other words, *will*, the action or whole self, is the ordered unity of action; this unity being constituted by the relationships of subordinate activities.

Will is evidently the more developed according (1) as there is a wider number of distinct activities (minor reflexes) contained within an act, and (2) as these minor activities are more thoroughly adjusted to one another—unified.

The stages and process of development will be described later. So far we have been dealing simply with the *accomplished* (objective) action.

Chapter Second—the Philosophical Reading: the Objective Categories

SECTION 9.—In the type-action, we have the universe expressed, and from its structure, therefore, we may read the main philosophic ideas. Every such action is representative of the whole because it *is* the whole in concentrated form, *not* because it is part of the whole.

THE UNIT OR REPRESENTATIVE WHOLE IN EXPERIENCE IS A CENTRALIZED, AND THEREFORE, ORDERED MOVEMENT. (1) It is a movement in its every phase and moment and (2) this movement is centred; it comes to a head or unity in a certain doing.

SECTION 10.—Looking at any human experience, it is evident (1) that whatever occurs outside the body is motion; (2) that what goes on within, say the eye, is motion; (3) that this motion is continued along what we call the sensory nerve; (4) that it is further propagated in the brain, entering there into the existing moving tensions and discharges; (5) that this movement continues out through what we call the motor nerve; (6) and effects some further movement in muscle or gland—what we call an "outward act."

All this is one continuous movement without breach, or insertion of any extraneous element. Viewed from the standpoint of the actual fact, the distinctions into external stimulus, receiving, conveying, registering, executing, organs are wholly subordinate. They exist within the one movement and are phases of its development. They are distinctions referring to the *specific office* performed in each phase of movement.

SECTION 11.—The centralized movement is *what is*. It is the reality, the concrete fact, the individual (*i.e.*, the undivided, the total).

Every such unity, no matter how apparently limited in scope, *is*, and that absolutely or without qualification. It is an end in itself; *i.e.*, an object. This is none the less true, although, as we shall see, in reference to other similar individuals or unified acts, it may be a contribution or function.

SECTION 12.—Within the unity, or centred movement, certain distinctions occur. The first main distinction is that of function and material. That is, the movement may be looked at on either of two sides; as *proceeds*, the net outcome, and as *process*. We have *what* is done or effected, and also *how* it is done. The what, the proceeds, is the function side; the how, the process, is the material side of a movement.

I. The *function* is the office performed in a unified act, the service rendered; the contribution made.

The idea of function evidently comes in when we consider the reference of a given centred movement to other similar unities, or to a wider movement into which all enter. While the hearing of a bell is itself an end, or object, it may also be a factor in a larger movement—the operation of a factory. So considered, it is functional. *a*] The inclusive whole is the *standard* which measures the included unity. *b*] The contribution of the included movement, as measured by the larger whole, is the *value*. Function, value, standard are correlative categories.

Note: "Category" is a term used to denote any typical aspect or distinction of reality.

II. We may drop out of attention, for a time, the unity (the end or proceeds) of a given movement, and consider the elements entering into the movement as such. These elements are the material of the unity. The material is the *diverse* or *manifold* side of action, as the function is the *unity* side.

We may carry the abstraction further. (1) A given unity of action, as the movement of the eye, may in time largely lose its independent character, and become almost entirely a factor of a more inclusive end or object. This end or object may vary from time to time, and yet the special action (the eye movement) remains *pretty much* identical with what it was before. Thus we get to thinking of the movement, apart from any special function, simply as material at large for *some* function or other. Thus reduced in meaning, the material constitutes what we call *possibility* or *potentiality*. (2) We may now restore the function by thinking of the potential in some concrete movement, and then we get the category of *actuality—force*. The actual is thus, the material taken in specific operation; the possible is the material taken without reference to its specific operation.

SECTION 13.—The categories of "*condition*," and "*end*" refer to the same distinctions as material and function. The end is the movement taken *as centred—i.e.*, as to its unity. The conditions are the actions constituent of or included in the unity. Just as by abstraction—leaving out of account certain integral phases—we reduce the category of material to potential, so we reduce conditions to *means*. Then we think of the "means" as somehow leading up to an end outside of, or beyond, themselves, although, in reality, the means are simply the diverse phases or conditions *of* the end. The ideas of means and end fall apart because of the delay which may intervene between a given minor action and its operation in a further function.

SECTION 14.—The categories of *cause* and *effect* have the same reference; the effect is the proceeds; the cause, the process. We do not have first causes, and then an effect. The effect *is* always, and is the existing unity of movement—the aspect, again, of centralization. The "causes" are the diverse activities entering into, constituting the effect.

The mental separation of cause and effect has the same origin as the separation of potential and actual; conditions and end. A given action may be remote from a *specific* function upon which attention is concentrated, and may then through intermediate movements finally pass into a movement having the function under consideration. Here, that is as remote from one another, cause and effect do not refer directly to the same object.

SECTION 15.—A given movement considered as a centralization of diverse conditions, or included movements, is relatively *organic*. Each of the manifold included activities is relatively *mechanical*; that is, when taken out of the whole of which it is a constituent factor. The term *organism* refers equally to the whole and to the constituent factors. Each of these factors or conditions may be considered either as *member* or *organ*. It is organ when looked at as expressing the whole; it is member when regarded as contributing to the whole. The eye, for example, as active function, helps constitute the integral movement of the organism; it is a member, it *serves*. But the activity of the eye is, in reality, nothing but one differentiation of the action of the entire organism. The organism resides (dynamically) in the eye. So considered, the eye is organ.

SECTION 16.—Taken as material, or conditions, the various included movements are *static*. Taken in their operation (that is, their co-operation in constituting the unity) they are *dynamic*.

Static does not mean dead or at rest. It is movement taken as *position*. The static phase of an individual is the *distribution* of force involved in its operation. The dynamic is the individual considered not as distribution of force but as co-ordinated force. They are related as the divisions of labor and the working together of these divisions. Compare energy of position and kinetic energy.

SECTION 17.—The *particulars* are the differentiated or minor activities, the divisions of labor, involved in an individual, or unified movement. The *universals* are the *ways* in which these various subordinate activities *work*. They are the lines or modes of activity of the individual. The various minor activities (particulars) co-ordinate or unify, thus constituting, maintaining, the individual. The ways in which they link *together* are the universals. We may sum up as follows:

Individual; System; Organic; Standard; Unified Movement = The Real.

Particular,	Universal,
Static,	Dynamic,
Mechanical,	Organic {Member, Organ,
Causes,	Effect,
Conditions,	End,
Material,	Function,
[Possibility],	[Actuality],
Manifold,	Unity,
Sensory,	Ideal.

SECTION 18.—The objective categories are the categories of the unified movement; *i.e.*, of the integral, complete or ordered action. The *object* is this unified action; anything is objective as far as it is such ordered action or a part of it.

What is called in psychology the percept (the individual or concrete object) is, in other words, a unified movement or expression of conditions. It is an action, a unity of construction, a doing, or performing. Perceiving an orange is experiencing and the complete percept is the full experience.

The *subjective* is this unified action in process of development. It is the unity in process of forming. It is the process of *working out* the action, of working out the proper divisions and co-operations of labor. Take the movement at any stage short of its attained unity and it is, relatively, subjective. The objective is the end at which the subjective is aiming. The subjective is complete in the objective. The categories of development (the subjective categories) will be taken up later.

Chapter Third—Social Action

We have now to see how the universe is expressed in social action, and how the examination of any complete social action reveals the same processes and categories as the psycho-physical act.

SECTION 19.—Any social organization is a concrete unity, or true individual, for example, a family, a school or class, a business corporation, a political district. It is a unity; its unity is co-ordinated movement. In the co-ordinated movement we have, on one side, the divisions of labor; the various services or functions performed by the various members of the family. These are the *specific* directions of movement. On the other hand, we have the working together, the co-operation of these divisions. Each member of the family is (simply as member of the family) *what he does in constituting the family*. His *individuality* is found in his specific membership and organship. His *universality* is found in the fact that this individuality does not exist in isolation, but in action, that is in connection, in co-operation.

SECTION 20.—The particular member evidently has, then, two sides. He is an expression, or unification, of certain forces, forces of heredity manifested in bodily make up, and of environment, climate, occupation, etc. So taken, (leaving out of account, for the moment, the function which he performs in constituting a whole) the individual is a *natural* being. (Compare the sensory side of an object, or experience.) This is, relatively, the given, the material side. It is natural capacity. But so taken, the individual is pure abstraction. He is not simply an outcome of various currents, but, since a centralization, he performs, he *acts*. In this action, he becomes a factor in constituting the larger movement, the family, the business corporation, the class in college, etc. He *functions*. The natural individual by entering as member into the larger individual and sharing its action is *spiritualized*. His function, (*i.e.*, his natural capacities in *action*) is his spirit. (Compare the ideal side of an object.)

Problem 1. Consider from this point of view, a member of a nomadic tribe; a member of a village community; the citizen of Athens in the time of Pericles; a citizen of the U. S. to-day.

Problem 2. Work out here the categories of standard, value, static, organic, universal and particular.

SECTION 21.—The ways in which the social unity (movement) maintains itself are *laws*. The laws are not something imposed from without: they are not forces which "govern" something different submitted to these laws: they are the typical forms in which the one movement displays itself. (Compare with category.) The whole society, taken as movement, and not in cross-section or in arrest, is the standard; it is the system. To understand a given fact is to place it with reference to this system—just as to understand an astronomical fact is to place it with reference to the solar system. The possibility of a science of society consists in getting hold of the whole in its movement and then using that as standard to decide particular facts by.

Problems: Discover and state the meaning of government, of rights, in the light of the one co-ordinating movement. What is the meaning of the railroad, of the telephone? What is the meaning of hieroglyphics, of a book?

Chapter Fourth—the Subjective Categories

We have been dealing with movement as centred or co-ordinated action. This is the *objective* (the end). We may leave out of account, however, the unity as attained and consider simply the process as working towards, as developing a unity. This is the *subjective*. In its *completeness*, the subjective is thus one with the objective; the subjective attains its meaning, its point, in its unity and is then objective. But taking it *short* of its attained unity, the process is subjective in a sense which *relatively* distinguishes it from the objective.

SECTION 22.—There are three types of objective categories, as we have seen; the Whole or System; the Particular as Specific mode or operation of the system; the Universal as co-operation of the particulars of the system. There are three stages which may be distinguished in the process *towards* the centre, and thus three types of subjective categories. The first of these is the starting point, the *undeveloped* or *implicit* material. This, *in itself*, is a unity of co-ordinated movements; but considered with reference to what is to come after, to come out of it, it is an undeveloped unity; its content is all bound up in it, and has yet to be freed (expressed or revealed), made explicit or brought to consciousness. Thus the amœba, with reference to itself, is an expression of the universe, being a co-ordination of its movement. But this unity taken as a starting point, is highly implicit; the universal is somehow *bound up* in the amœba, but it is not brought out. This stage may also be called the *syncrete*. It is the unity with the differences unrealized; they are somehow suppressed, covered up. (Man at first, for example, did not *consciously* distinguish himself from his environment. A child does not break up the world into a multiplicity of objects consciously distinct from one another. Knowledge begins with the "sensation continuum." A people's religion is in the beginning of history one with their art, science, politics. The historian of the universe begins with it as a nebulous gas, etc. In each case, we have at the outset, a unity in which differences are so fused as to be confused.)

SECTION 23.—This unity is, so far as differences are unexpressed, a passive or natural unity. As the differences emerge (through the continued movement) the unity seems to be lost, and we have instead a multitude of separate units. Thus the homogeneous nebulous gas is divided into an indefinite multitude of centres of force; the "sensation continuum" breaks up into a large number of apparently separate feelings, etc. This is the analytic (in the sense of divided, segregated) stage. The differences become explicit at the expense of unity. It may also be called *discrete*.

SECTION 24.—Third, is the period in which these various diverse units come together and are adjusted to one another. There is a putting together of the isolated units. This process has two sides, according as we look at either what we are emerging from or what we are going towards, the negative and the positive sides. As respects the old isolated units their first coming together appears as opposition and friction, and even as disintegration. The positive side is the new and wider unity emerging, which comprehends within itself all the old units, no longer isolated but so adjusted to one another that each now serves as a member of the new unity. This third phase of the subjective categories, in other words, is the working out of units hitherto isolated into distinct factors of a co-ordinated or centralized unity of movement. Compare, historically, the disintegration of old local centres when another community is coming into existence. Looked at from the standpoint of the old narrower unities, this is a process of disintegration. So the old Greek cities in the Macedonian supremacy; the house and guild industries through factory industry, etc. That is, the first of the categories of development is syncrete, or *internally* one, without divisions of labor. The second is discrete or *externally* separate. When these move into relations to one another, the first effect is to break up the syncrete internally, introducing diversities into it, and it is only at a later period that the co-ordination of the discrete effecting a new organization, is brought about.

SECTION 25.—It is obvious that there is a certain parallelism between the subjective and the objective categories. We may sum them up as follows:

1. Syncrete—internal unity.
2. Discrete—external diversity.
3. Process of Adjusting—negative, or disintegrating, as regards old unities; positive or integrating as regards new unity.
4. The Particular—an adjusted division of labor, or distribution of force—Static, etc.
5. The Universal—the correlation or active co-operation of the particulars—Dynamic, etc.
6. The Adjusted Individual—the organism, having, on one side, its distributions of force, on the other, its co-operations. Standard, etc.

In this catalogue, four is the same as one, but having become adjusted, so that it is no longer homogeneous or characterless in itself, but having become a definite member, with a definite function in a larger system. Five is the polar to two; while in two we have simply *external* relation between the particular unities, in five we have this relationship internal and organic. It is the *way* the particulars operate together. So six is the same as three; only in three the whole is simply in *process* of adjustment, the struggle is going on. In six, the adjustment is effected; the process of re-organization has completed itself in the new organization. These relations may be expressed as follows:

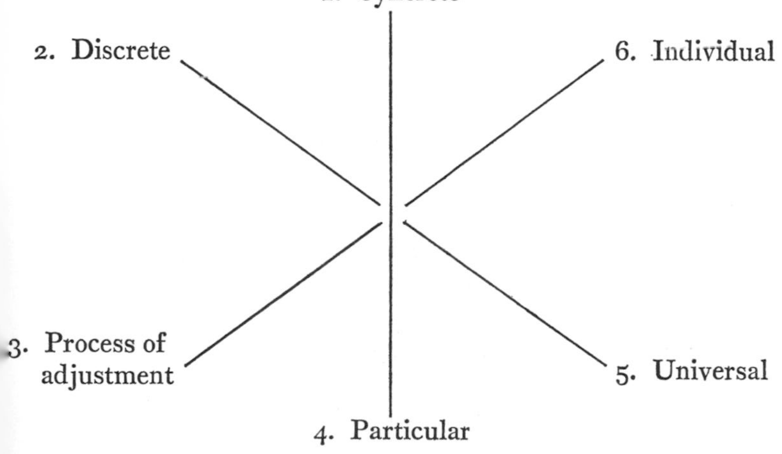

Number six or the completed (organized) action may be simply the beginning of another activity—*i.e.*, it may be number one with reference to a further organization of action.[1]

Chapter Fifth—the Historical Development

SECTION 26.—The general course of the development of thought has been from an *immediate* objective through a subjective back to an objective mediated by the subjective. That is from action without conscious principle through separation of the principle back to action controlled by it. The Greeks began by setting up some purely objective principle, as water, air, fire, number, reason (reason, *nous*, to the Greek was a principle of objective order or proportion, not a process of reasoning), and by attempting to refer all things *directly* to this principle. The difficulties, the contradictions arising made men conscious that the principle itself must be examined and criticised before it could be *used*. The process of explaining the universe by reference to the principle was checked, and the principle was turned back upon itself in reflection. In other words, it was recognized that principles of explanation are ideas, not bare things; that they are *tools* and, as tools, need perfecting if they are to be used properly. Thus there followed the *subjective* period, in which attention was seemingly withdrawn from the "objective" world, and riveted upon concepts or ideas. The development and systematizing of these was made an end in itself. But only *seemingly* withdrawn. These concepts were themselves abstractions, or reductions, of the original "objective"; and they were, in turn, only tools for getting at and handling a freer and fuller objective. While attention was concentrated on the concepts they seemed to be not tools but ends in themselves; this very concentration, however, served to bring the tools to a working point. Hence the transfer to the third period was made. In this period, attention is again directed to the objective, but the necessity of obtaining the objective through a certain *method*, in a certain *way*, instead of immediately, is recog-

[1] This method of showing the relations of the categories is borrowed from Mr. Lloyd.

nized. The subjective, the concepts, of the second period become instruments for inquiring into fact and thus become modes of action.

SECTION 27.—The first period, which was at its height before the time of the Sophists and Socrates may be called the exclusively "scientific." That is, it assumed that reality surrendered its meaning directly; that method (an idea) was not required to get at the significance of reality. The second period, which was at its height in the Scholastic period of the Middle Ages, was the exclusively "philosophic." That is, it neglected the domain of particular fact, and devoted itself almost entirely to the consideration of generalities or concepts, without attempting to use these ideas. The third period, which has not yet reached its height, is the philosophic-scientific period. That is to say, it is recognized, on one hand, that fact does not give up its meaning of itself or directly, but only as apprehended through the medium of method or general ideas. On the other hand, it is recognized that general ideas are not ends in themselves, that they have no value by themselves, but only as the instruments with which to approach and test apparent fact and secure its real meaning. This reciprocal attitude sums up in the word *experiment*. Experiment is not a matter of physical manipulation, but of the method of applying "ideas" to "fact" (the isolated subjective to the isolated objective) in such way that they unite into a fact having meaning, or idea having body, that is, a concrete action. The whole process may be otherwise stated as the progress from *a*] the percept, as the universal concealed in the individual, through *b*] the concept, or universal abstracted from the individual back to *c*] a conceptualized percept, or intuition, that is, an individual transparent with genuine meaning, or relationships.

SECTION 28.—In more detail, the process has been as follows: Science began when men first conceived a distinction between appearance and reality; saw that the given experience, just as it happened, was not real of itself, but that there was some principle to which it must be referred. Then began the search for the principle, air, fire, water, logos, as the case might be. Thus there arose the primary distinctions of thought, as these were worked out in early Greek science.

1. The principle was the whole or unity—the "one," while the given events were the "many."

2. It was the "universal," while the special events were the "particulars."

3. It was the eternal and full ("Being"), while the events were the transitory and seeming ("Non-Being").

These two sides, however, were not separated; the universal and eternal was the unity of the particular and the many—not something existing side by side with them. As science proceeded, these objective distinctions came to be identified more and more with distinctions of knowledge. The universal and one was identified with "reason"; the changing and many was identified with the senses or "opinion." The source of truth—reality was placed in reason. Socrates logically declared that to "know self" was the root of all wisdom, and the universals were concepts—Platonic "Ideas"—as modes of operation of the self. Thus reality came to be conceived as an "Idea" or spiritual world abstracted from and even remote from the actual. Two worlds are now in process of development, each having its own sphere and character. This is well illustrated in Plato; the key to Plato being that, in his *intention*, the "Ideas" or universals are simply the reality of the sensible and phenomenal world, while in *practice*, he cannot succeed in thus interconnecting them.

SECTION 29.—The introduction of Christianity emphasized: the tendency commenced by Socrates to find reality in self, holding that the self is incarnate God, and hence, an absolute end superior to all its surroundings and merely particular experiences. It made the theoretical truth of Greek philosophy a practical or moral truth—one to be worked out in life. The same two opposed tendencies were now transferred over into Christianity. On one hand, the tendency was to regard the self as the reality, the embodied truth of the world, the free spirit for which all particular experience exists. Such was the doctrine at its beginning. But *practically* this conception seemed to be contradicted on all sides;

the self was not practically free, was not practically one with its surroundings. The institutions of life (industrial and political) did not lend themselves to the freedom of the self, but hemmed it in; they were not spiritual, but "evil," needing to be overcome and transformed. Thus the outcome was a translation of the dualistic tendency of Greek thought into a fixed and rigid separation. This as typified in the mediæval church involved:

1. A separation of the spiritual from the natural, the former being regarded as wholly supernatural—separation of God from the world.

2. A separation of theory from practice, of the subjective from the objective,—*i.e.*, separation of the *church* from the *state*. Man's relation to God having been abstracted from his relation to the world, two institutions grew up, each dealing with its own sphere. The former (church) was realized especially in the contemplative life—in consciousness as such; the state standing for practice has only finite or limited ends. (Hence the ease with which mediæval theology formulated itself in the philosophical ideas of Aristotle.)

3. A separation of the organ of knowledge by which man knew the "spiritual," or God, from that by which he knew the natural or secular—the separation of philosophy (theology) and science.

The contradiction here in every case is that the "natural" side, the state, the senses, the ordinary course of experience is no longer regarded as mere appearance, or non-being; but as *a* reality, side by side with the higher reality—two parallel realities, each real in its own sphere.

SECTION 30.—As the spiritual kept realizing itself more and more *in* the natural (that is, as the self instead of finding itself set over against a hostile nature and institutions, succeeded in subjugating nature and transforming institutions) the latter got additional meaning until each of the two sides come to have *equal* value. Thus modern times begin with the assertion of:

1. Mind *and* matter—as correlate realities.
2. Infinite *and* finite.
3. Reason *and* sense.

Nor, indeed, was it long before the tendency arose to give the latter of the two correlates superior practical value, and while still allowing the former superior theoretical value, to treat it virtually as an empty and powerless abstraction. (Compare the course of the old discussion of primary and secondary causes.) This complete dualism, however, was only a starting point for a movement towards a reconciliation towards making the spiritual the unity and law *of* the natural, and the natural simply the *embodied* or *expressed* spiritual.

SECTION 31.—The tendency toward integration grew up from each side separately. Each of the two phases separated in the mediæval period, the physical and the ideal, claimed to be the whole and strove to absorb the other. Modern times present not a passive parallelism, but an opposition of materialism and idealism. With the growth of physical science the whole world was conceived capable of adequate explanation in terms of matter and motion. The existence of the spiritual or ideal realm was denied; or, it was said, if there is any such world it cannot be known. But, upon the other side, analysis of the conditions of knowing seemed to reveal that "matter" or the "world" could not be known *per se* at all, but only in relation to the knower. Parallel with the development of physical science was a development of psychological science. While physical science went to make the "external" primary and the "internal" a derivative from it, psychological science reversed the process. The history of philosophy for the last four centuries is a record of this conflict within science itself. Upon the whole, philosophy, technically so-called, has tended to identify itself with the psychological side, but the tendency in this direction has been met and checked in the other direction by the rapid popular acceptance of the results of physical science.

SECTION 32.—It will be noticed that both of these tendencies, however opposed in conclusion, agree in their fundamental premise. *Both start from the standpoint of knowledge*, and attempt to read the world in terms of knowledge, that is, of contemplation or intellectual formulation. Just because both sides occupy the same fundamental standpoint the quarrel between them cannot be reconciled. The key to the reconciliation consists in shifting the point of view. *Reality is not to be read in terms of knowledge as such, but in terms of action.* So read, the opposition between the internal and the external, the physical and the psychical, ceases to be ultimate and becomes instrumental. We have in this distinction a *means* to the end of action. The physical and the psychical are recognized as the primary distributions of power requisite to the highest (freest) action. All action whatever is carried on through divisions of labor (distributions of power), and in order to get the most efficient action this division must go to the point of extreme tension or antagonism; the distribution of force must be polar. So in this case; the physical and the psychical represent the tension necessary to the exercise of force. Distinguished from each other as much as possible, the maximum of utilizable energy is developed.

SECTION 33.—Upon both sides (the physical and psychical) the tendency, at present, is (1) to pass over from the standpoint of knowledge to that of action, and (2) as passing over to demand the other side as the conplementary division of labor, instead of standing over against it in irreconcilable opposition.

The development of industry and commerce in the modern world has gone to show that the "physical" as such is not an end in itself, but is material for human action. Iron, coal, cotton and water are seen not to have their reality by themselves, but in the developed action of man up to which they lead and of which they become factors. They are seen to be real not when isolated, *and thus fixed*, but only in their unification (their co-ordination) *and thus in movement.* Iron, coal and water, for example, get their fuller reality (unity of relations) in the locomotive when that functions as a part of man's action. Furthermore, taken as material *of action* they demand the other side, the psychical. The *relationship* into which coal, iron and water enter, *the way they move together*, is worked out through "mind"; the "mind" in discovering the relationships of the iron gives it its full reality, its free and complete movement. (I quote the word "mind" because mind is not some *thing which* does this relating; it *is* the unifying or relating as abstracted from that unified or related. The "mind," in other words, is simply the universal, the co-ordinating of the particulars in a given case.) On the other side, the more knowledge, understanding of things, we get, the less that knowledge is an end in itself, and the more it is simply a *way to act*, a tool or method of construction. Just as the physical turns out to be the *material or content of action* and not a something *per se*, so the psychical turns out to be the *form or method of action*. Each side involves the other; they are only the primary distinctions of action itself. Thus what the present period of science points to is a return to the earliest category of man, that of action, except that the earlier action was unconscious of itself, and therefore uncontrolled; while the later is thoroughly conscious (through science) of its two phases, (1) the *material* involved in action, the real possibilities of action, and (2) the *way* in which to handle this material in order to get out of it all there is in it.

Chapter Sixth—the Divisions of Philosophy

SECTION 34.—There are three philosophic sciences, corresponding to three ways in which the individual, or organized action may be regarded. These are Logic, Æsthetic and Ethic. Logic is the general theory of science; the theory, that is, of the standard and method of knowledge. It deals with action on its mental side, setting forth the road by which action is reduced to its reality; set in order or subjected. It deals with truth as *method*. Æsthetic deals with truth as *expressed* or *embodied*—*i.e.*, with reference to its expression, the manner of uttering it so as to realize it in its fullness. It deals primarily with the outward side of action. Ethic treats action as action, analyzing it into its factors and relationships—it deals with the constitution of action. Internal and external are both alike to it—simply constituting elements.

Chapter Seventh—Logic

SECTION 35.—Knowledge is *statement* of action. This statement is judgment. Action is stated through being arrested or checked, that is, viewed as if arrested. The checking breaks the action into two phases; the "what has been done" and the "what is to do." That is, the checking arrests action and makes a cross-section of it—this cross-section stands for the *factum* or thing done. But on the other hand, this very checking only makes the *direction* of action more prominent; it separates or abstracts the general direction or principle of action from the special thing done or doing. In becoming abstracted, the principle appears as that which is to be done with the fact; the way of handling it. It is an idea. In the technical terms of logic, the "fact" is the subject of the judgment; the "idea" is the predicate. That is, the action in arrest, the thing done, becomes the subject-matter or material. The subject of the judgment is thus always "sensuous," the predicate "ideal"—*i.e.*, what we call sense is the activity taken as arrested or "past," what we call ideal is the projection of the activity. So, also, a judgment read from the side of its subject is extensive, from the side of its predicate intensive. The subject-matter is the manifold particular conditions; the predicate is the meaning which unifies. Again, the subject is percept, the predicate concept. The point in each case is to see that we do not have two independent sides, but the differentiation, the main division of labor, of action. That is, it is again (see Sec. 29), a case of producing a tension or opposition of forces in order to realize the maximum energy. The connection of the two, the actual bringing of the method upon the material constitutes the *copula.* The reality or force of the judgment is the value effected; it is neither subject nor predicate nor a union of the two, but the action resulting from the handling of the "fact" by "idea"; the action resulting from reflecting a given mode of operating back into a given material. Every complete judgment, in other words, transcends itself, passing, when complete, over into action, and this action is the reality of the judgment.

SECTION 36.—A judgment thus involves differentiation and identification; the differences being the statement of the factors of the action, the identity being the uniting or coming together of these factors in the act itself; *i.e.*, the unity of a judgment is always the act which connects the various conditions stated in a judgment. Hence, also, the analytic and synthetic factors of every judgment. The analysis states the conditions of an action; the synthesis is the function which, on one side, is constituted by these conditions, and which, on the other side, realizes them.

SECTION 37.—Judgments are classified according to the extent to which they state (make explicit) the action involved. In the naïve or dogmatic judgment (the assertion of common sense), the action is almost all implicit or unrealized; *i.e.*, the judgment is an impression. Examples: "How hot it is!" "it rains"; "my tooth aches," etc. Such judgments are sometimes called sense judgments. These uncritical judgments develop in two directions, the categorical, and the hypothetical. *The categorical proceeds to develop the subject-matter of the judgment*; to tell *what* it is that is hot; to give all the particulars of the tooth ache, etc. That is, the categorical judgment isolates or abstracts the particular conditions, defining them just as far as possible. The judgment regarding the heat, for example, would tell the exact temperature in degrees; the exact latitude and longitude of the place; the exact humidity, state of the wind and sky and so on; it would attempt to register all the particular conditions involved in the state of the temperature. The result is to transform the vague subject-matter into a definite one. The categorical judgment is thus *descriptive*; and the descriptive side of every science (astronomy, geology, botany, etc.) is the categorical development of some subject-matter. At the same time, the hypothetical judgment takes up the connection or unity of the particulars. *It develops the predicate* of the judgment. The hypothetical judgment is thus at the other pole from the categorical. While the latter states only particulars, describing the "actual fact" as it is called, the hypothetical states only the universal, the *connection* of conditions. It does not pretend to state any existing thing, or historical event, but simply a relation or law; *if* or *where* one condition or circumstance is found there some other circumstance will also be found, leaving it an open question whether the conditions actually occur or not. While the categorical judgment by itself would only give us a mass or aggregate of brute facts, the hypothetical by itself would give us only an abstract idea. One is all on the ground without general meaning; the other is all in the air without specific existence. But neither the categorical nor the hypothetical judgment has any such separate existence; they are not so much *two* judgments, as they are developments of the two phases, subject and predicate, "fact" and "idea," of judgment.

SECTION 38.—This very separation creates the tension which compels the two phases back into their unity. The original action which was being stated has now been stretched to its utmost point (Analysis) and now must re-unite in further (freer) action (Synthesis). The process of uniting is experiment, or "verification." The "idea" (the predicate or hypothetical judgment) has to be tested, by being carried over into the particular conditions or "facts"; while these have to be connected together or given meaning, instead of remaining so many blank, separate particulars. The "idea" is tested, or verified; the "facts" are harmonized, explained, rationalized. The result is a new judgment, in which the idea is wholly embodied in facts, or in which the facts are self-luminous; the fact, the reality, in which there is no segregation whatever of the two factors. This is, in other words, a concrete action. The action which has had its various phases distinguished and then re-united is the *disjunctive* judgment—the statement of the individual or organic system. It should be noted here that what we call the "facts" (as distinct from the idea—the particular conditions into which an action is disintegrated when it is arrested) are not the test or standard by which the idea or hypothesis is measured. Both "facts" and "idea" are measured by the action in which they unite; *it* only is the test or standard, the truth. The standard of truth is not something arrested or fixed; it is the ongoing movement, the continued doing.

Chapter Eighth—Art

SECTION 39.—Logic deals with the statement of action; the resolution of action into its constituent factors. Science deals with the manner or mode of action,—its *Law*. Even in experiment, where the idea or universal is, through action, carried out into the particulars, the look of logic is backward; how does the experiment affect the idea, what new light does it throw upon the facts? Art looks forward; how shall the action be brought into being and maintained? It is the expression or manifestation side it is concerned with; not the resolution or statement side.

SECTION 40.—The aim of art is to discover the method of expression which shall secure the best organization of action; the fullest or freest movement. It aims at seeing to it that the ideal side gets a complete embodiment in the fact side; or, what is the same thing, that the facts become completely permeated with their idea so as to move harmoniously and thus freely.

SECTION 41.—The historical classification of the arts depends upon the degree to which this complete interpenetration is attained. Certain special or limited regions of material will, *in their limitation*, first secure the desired end. Thus we have the "fine arts," technically so-called; *i.e.*, freedom of action is reached as to coloring or form or sound, and we have the special fine art of painting, sculpture, music, etc. Then the other and wider regions which have not as yet realized their unity (*i.e.*, been freed through attaining their idea or purpose) are regarded as "material," or "sensuous." The separation is even carried so far that people come to regard this distinction which is purely historical (showing how far at a given time action has realized itself or become free) as indicating two kinds of action in life, two spheres of existence, one beautiful, ideal, artistic, etc., the other merely useful and material. On the contrary, however, the distinction has only a *negative* value, showing the limit to free action at a given time. That is, if a statue at a given date is regarded as essentially artistic, and a locomotive as merely useful, it is because owing to the narrow relations of the former the whole has attained expression in it, while the whole (the function in the service of the organized action of man) has only partially subdued the latter. The limitation in the artistic character of the locomotive, in other words, is the extent to which it functions in the interest of a part or class, instead of in the interest of the whole, so that its full meaning and energy are not freed or realized in consciousness. The development of the arts is thus a political phenomenon, since the whole which is seeking to embody itself in every particular is nothing less than the organized action of man. So far as the whole moves freely through any part, that part is artistic.

Chapter Ninth–Ethic

SECTION 42.–Ethic unites the two sides distinguished in logic and æsthetic. It deals with the practical situation; the organized action.

OUTLINES

OF A

Critical Theory of Ethics

BY

JOHN DEWEY

PROFESSOR OF PHILOSOPHY IN THE UNIVERSITY OF MICHIGAN

ANN ARBOR, MICHIGAN

REGISTER PUBLISHING COMPANY

The Inland Press

1891

Preface

Although the following pages have taken shape in connection with class-room work, they are intended as an independent contribution to ethical science. It is commonly demanded of such a work that its readers shall have some prefatory hint of its sources and deviations. In accordance with this custom, I may state that for the backbone of the theory here presented—the conception of the will as the expression of ideas, and of social ideas; the notion of an objective ethical world realized in institutions which afford moral ideals, theatre and impetus to the individual; the notion of the moral life as growth in freedom, as the individual finds and conforms to the law of his social placing—for this backbone I am especially indebted to Green's *Prolegomena to Ethics*, to Mr. Bradley's *Ethical Studies*, to Professor Caird's *Social Philosophy of Comte* and *Critical Philosophy of Kant* (to this latter book in particular my indebtedness is fundamental), and to Alexander's *Moral Order and Progress*. Although I have not been able to adopt the standpoint or the method of Mr. Spencer, or of Mr. Leslie Stephen, my obligation to the *Data of Ethics* and to the *Science of Ethics* (especially to the latter) is large.

As to the specific forms which give a flesh and blood of its own to this backbone, I may call attention to the idea of desire as the ideal activity in contrast with actual possession; to the analysis of individuality into function including capacity and environment; to the treatment of the social bearings of science and art (a point concerning which I am indebted to my friend, Mr. Franklin Ford); to the statement of an ethical postulate; to the accounts of obligation, of moral rules, and of moral badness.

While the book is an analysis, in outline, of the main elements of the theory of ethics rather than a discussion of all possible detailed questions, it will not be found the less fitted, I hope, to give a student an idea of the main methods and problems of contemporary ethics. Other teachers, indeed, may agree that a general outline is better than a blanket-mortgage spread over and forestalling all the activity of the student's mind.

I have not been unmindful of the advisability of avoiding in presentation both undue polemic, and undue dogmatism without sufficient reference to the statements of others. I hope the method hit upon, of comparing opposite one-sided views with the aim of discovering a theory apparently more adequate, will help keep the balance. I have quoted freely from the chief modern authorities, hoping that the tastes here given will tempt the reader to the banquet waiting in the authors themselves. The occasional references introduced are not bibliographical, nor intended as exhaustive statements of authorities consulted; they are meant as aids to an intelligent reading on the part of the general student. For this reason they are confined mainly to modern English writings.

Introduction

I. Definition of Ethics

The term ethics is derived from a Greek word meaning manners, customs, habits, just as the term morals is derived from a Latin word with a similar meaning. This suggests the character of the science as an account of human action. Anthropology, ethnology, psychology, are also, in their way, accounts of human action. But these latter branches of knowledge simply *describe*, while the business of ethics is to *judge*.

This does not mean that it belongs to ethics to prescribe what man ought to do; but that its business is to detect the element of obligation in conduct, to examine conduct to see what gives it its *worth*. Anthropology, etc., do not take into account the *whole* of action, but simply some of its aspects—either external or internal. Ethics deals with conduct in its entirety, with reference, that is, to what makes it conduct, its *end*, its real meaning. Ethics is the science of conduct, understanding by conduct man's activity in its whole reach.

Three of the branches of philosophy may be called *normative*, implying that they deal with some *norm*, *standard* or *end*, estimating the value of their respective subject-matters as tested by this end. These are Logic, dealing with the end Truth, and the value of intellectual processes with respect to it; Æsthetics, dealing with Beauty and the value of emotional conditions as referred to it; and Ethics, as defined above. But this norm in no case comes from outside the subject-matter; it is the subject-matter considered in its totality.

II. Meaning of Moral

In its widest sense, the term moral or ethical means nothing more than relating to conduct; having to do with practice, when we look at conduct or practice from the point of view not of its occurrence, but of its value. Action is something which takes place, and as such it may be described like any objective fact. But action has also relation to an end, and so considered it is *moral*. The first step in ethics is to fix firmly in mind the idea that the term moral does not mean any special or peculiar kind of conduct, but simply means practice and action, conduct viewed not partially, but in connection with the end which it realizes.

It should be noted that the term moral has a wider and a narrower sense. In the wider sense it means action in the moral sphere, as opposed to *non*-moral, and thus includes both good and bad conduct. In the narrower sense it means moral, as opposed to *im*-moral. See Bradley, *Ethical Studies*, p. 53 n., for a further meaning.

III. Meaning of Conduct

Ethics then has to do with conduct or action viewed completely, or in relation to its end. But what is conduct? It must be distinguished from action in general; for any process of change, the working of a pump, the growth of a plant, the barking of a dog, may be called action. Conduct implies more than something taking place; it implies purpose, motive, intention; that the agent knows what he is about, that he has something which he is aiming at. All action accomplishes something or brings about results, but conduct has the result *in view*. It occurs for the sake of producing this result. Conduct does not simply, like action in general, have a cause, but also a reason, and the reason is present to the mind of the agent. There can be conduct only when there is a being who can propose to himself, as an end to be reached by himself, something which he regards as worth while. Such a being is a moral agent, and his action, when conscious, is conduct.

IV. Division of Ethics

The main ethical problem is just this: What is the conduct that really deserves the name of conduct, the conduct of which all other kinds of action can be only a perverted or deflected form? Or, since it is the end which gives action its moral value, what is the true end, *summum bonum* of man? Knowing this, we have a standard by which we judge particular acts. Those which embody this end are *right*, others wrong. The question of the rightness of conduct is simply a special form of the question concerning the nature of the end or good. But the end bears another relation to specific acts. They are not only marked off by it as right or wrong, but they have to fulfill it. The end or good decides what should be or *ought* to be. Any act necessary to fulfill the end is a *duty*. Our second inquiry will be as to the nature of obligation or duty. Then we have to discuss the nature of a being who is capable of action, of manifesting and realizing the end; capable of right (or wrong), of obligatory and good action. This will lead us to discuss the question of *Freedom*, or *Moral Capacity and its Realization*. The discussion of these three abstract questions will constitute Part One of our theory; Part Two will take up the various forms and institutions in which the good is objectively realized, the family, state, etc.; while Part Three will be devoted to an account of the moral experience of the individual.

V. The Motive in Conduct

Before taking up the first problem presented, the nature of the good or the end of conduct, it is necessary to analyze somewhat further the various sides and factors of conduct in order to see where the distinctly ethical element is to be found. The elements particularly deserving consideration are (1) the Motive; (2) the Feelings or Sentiments; (3) Consequences of the Act; (4) Character of Agent. We shall begin with

1. *The Motive.*

The motive of the act is the end aimed at by the agent in performing the act. Thus the motive of Julius Cæsar in crossing the Rubicon was the whole series of results which he intended to reach by that act of his. The motive of a person in coming to college is to gain knowledge, to prepare himself for a certain profession. The motive is thus identical with the ideal element of the action, the purpose in view.

2. The Feelings or Disposition.

Some writers speak of the feelings under which the agent acts as his motive. Thus we may suppose Julius Cæsar "moved" by the feelings of ambition, of revenge, etc., in crossing the Rubicon. The student may be "moved" by curiosity, by vainglory, by emulation, by conscience, in coming to college. It is better, however, to regard the motive as the reason for which the act is performed, and to use the term moving or impelling cause for the feelings in their relation to action. Thus we may imagine a parent asking a child why he struck a playmate, meaning what was the motive of the action. If the child should reply that he struck his playmate because he was angry, this answer would give the moving cause or impelling force of the action, but not its motive. The motive would be the idea of punishing this playmate, of getting even with him, of taking something away from him. The motive is the end which he desired to reach by striking and on account of which he struck. This is implied by the fact that the parent would ask, "What *made* you *angry*?"

VI. Moral Bearing of These Distinctions

It is the feelings which supply the impelling force to action. They may be termed, collectively, the *natural disposition*. The natural disposition in itself has no *moral* value. This has been well illustrated by Bentham.

Works, I, *Principles of Morals and Legislation*, pp. 49–55. Bentham here uses the term "motive" to designate what we have called the moving cause.

We may select of the many examples which he gives that of curiosity. We may imagine a boy spinning a top, reading a useful book and letting a wild ox loose in a road. Now curiosity may be the "motive" of each of these acts, yet the first act would generally be called morally indifferent, the second good, the third abominable.

What we mean by the "natural" feelings, then, is the feelings considered in abstraction from activity. Benevolence, as a *mere* feeling, has no higher moral value than malevolence. But if it is directed upon action it gets a value at once; let the end, the act, be right, and benevolence becomes a name for a *moral* disposition—a tendency to *act* in the due way. Nothing is more important than to distinguish between mere sentiments, and feeling as an element in conduct.

VII. Relation of Consequences and Conduct

Do the consequences of an act have anything to do with its morality? We may say no, pointing to the fact that a man who does his best we call good, although the consequences of his act may be far from good. We say his purpose in acting was right, and using as he did all the knowledge that he had, he is not to be blamed for its bad consequences. On the other hand, it is evident that we do take into account consequences in estimating the moral value of an act. Suppose, to use one of Bentham's examples, a person were about to shoot an animal but foresaw that in doing so there was a strong probability that he would also wound some bystander. If he shot and the spectator were wounded, should we not hold the agent morally responsible? Are there not multitudes of intended acts of which we say that we cannot tell whether they are good or bad until we know how they are likely to turn out?

The solution of the difficulty is in recognizing the ambiguity of the term "consequences." It may mean the whole outcome of the act. When I speak, I set in motion the air, and its vibrations have, in turn, long chains of effects. Whatever I do must have an endless succession of "consequences" of which I can know but very little; just so far as, in any act, I am ignorant of the conditions under which it is performed, so far I am ignorant of its consequences. *Such* consequences are wholly irrelevant morally. They have no more to do with the morality of the act than has the fact that the earth is revolving while the act is taking place.

But we may mean by consequences the *foreseen* consequences of an act. Just in the degree that any consequence is considered likely to result from an act, just in that degree it gets moral value, for it becomes *part of the act* itself. The reason that in many cases we cannot judge of the morality of an intended act until we can judge its probable results, is that until we know of these results the action is a mere abstraction, having no content at all. *The conceived results constitute the content of the act to be performed.* They are not merely relevant to its morality, but *are* its moral quality. The question is whether any consequence is foreseen, conceived, or not. The foreseen, the *ideal* consequences are the end of the act, and as such form the *motive.*

See on Secs. VI and VII, Alexander, *Moral Order and Progress*, pp. 36–46; on Sec. VII, Green, *Prolegomena to Ethics*, pp. 317–23.

VIII. Character and Conduct

We have seen that the moral sentiments, or the moral disposition (distinguished from the feelings as passing emotions), on one side, and the consequences as ideal or conceived (distinguished from the consequences that, *de facto*, result), on the other, both have moral value. If we take the moral feelings, not one by one, but as a whole, as an *attitude* of the agent toward conduct, as expressing the kind of motives which upon the whole moves him to action, we have *character*. And just so, if we take the consequences willed, not one by one, but as a whole, as the kind of end which the agent endeavors to realize, we have *conduct*. Character and conduct are, morally, the same thing, looked at first inwardly and then outwardly. Character, except as manifest in conduct, is a barren ideality. Our moral judgments are always severe upon a man who has nothing to show but "good intentions" never executed. This is what character comes to, apart from conduct. Our only way of telling the nature of character is the conduct that issues from it. But, on the other hand, conduct is mere outward formalism, excepting as it manifests character. To say that a man's conduct is good, unless it is the manifestation of a good character, is to pass a judgment which is self-contradictory.

See Alexander, *Moral Order*, pp. 48–50 and p. 39.

From this point of view we are enabled to identify the two senses of motive already discussed—the ideal of action and the moving feelings. Apart from each other they are abstractions. Cæsar's motive in crossing the Rubicon may have been "ambition," but this was not some bare feeling. It was a feeling of ambition produced in view of the contemplation of a certain end which he wished to reach. So a boy's motive in striking a playmate may be anger, but this means (if the act is anything more than one of blind physical reaction) an anger having its conscious cause and aim, and not some abstract feeling of anger in general. The feeling which has its nature made what it is by the conceived end, and the end which has ceased to be a bare abstract conception and become an interest, are all one with each other.

Morality is then a matter pertaining to character—to the feelings and inclinations as transformed by ends of action; and to conduct—to conceived ends transformed into act under the influence of emotions. But what *kind* of character, of conduct, is right or realizes its true end? This brings us to our first problem.

PART ONE

FUNDAMENTAL ETHICAL NOTIONS

1

The Good

IX. Subdivision of Theories

We may recognize three main types of theories regarding the good, of which the first two represent (we shall attempt to show) each respectively one side of the truth, while the third combines the one-sided truths of the other two. Of the first two theories one is abstract, because it tends to find the good in the mere consequences of conduct aside from character. This is the hedonistic theory, which finds the good to be pleasure. This is either individualistic or universalistic according as it takes individual or general pleasure to be the good. The second type of theories attempts to find the good in the motive of conduct apart from consequences even as willed; it reduces the good to conformity to abstract moral law. The best type of this theory is the Kantian. We shall criticise these theories with a view to developing the factors necessary to a true moral theory.

X. Hedonism

According to the strict hedonistic position, the pleasure resulting to the agent from his act is the end of conduct and is therefore the criterion of its morality. The position as usually taken involves, first, that pleasure is psychologically the sole motive to action; and, secondly, that the results of an act in the way of the pain or pleasure it produces are the only tests we have of the rightness of the act.

It is said above that these two points are involved in the hedonistic position as *usually* taken. They are not *necessarily* involved.

Sidgwick (*Methods of Ethics*, Bk. I, Ch. 4 and Bk. IV, Ch. 1) holds that pleasure is not the object of desire or motive of action, but that happiness is the moral end and criterion. On the other hand Hodgson (*Theory of Practice*, Vol. II, Ch. 2) holds that pleasure may be the motive (in the sense of impelling force) but it is never the criterion of conduct. Kant adopts the psychology of hedonism regarding pleasure as the object of desire, but holds that on that very account no object of desire can be the standard of moral conduct.

A good statement of strict individualistic hedonism is the following from Barratt, *Physical Ethics*, p. 71: "If man aims at pleasure merely by the physical law of action, that pleasure must evidently be ultimately his own, and whether it be or not preceded by phenomena which he calls the pain and pleasure of others, is a question not of principle but of detail, just as the force of a pound weight is unaltered whether it be composed of lead or of feathers, or whether it act directly or through pulleys."

XI. The Hedonistic Position Supported

Hedonism holds that pleasure is both the natural end and the proper criterion of action:

The following quotation from Bentham (*Principles of Morals*, p. 1) gives a statement of both these elements. "Nature has placed man under the governance of two sovereign masters, pain and pleasure. It is for them alone to point out what we ought to do, [*i.e.*, they are criteria] as well as to determine what we shall do [motives]. On the one hand, the standard of right or wrong [criterion]; on the other the chain of causes and effects [motives], are fastened to their throne."

1. *Pleasure as Criterion*

That the tendency of an action to produce pleasure is the standard for judging its moral value is generally held by the hedonists to be so axiomatic as to be beyond argument.

See Bain, *Moral Science*, p. 27. "The ultimate data must be accepted as self-evident: they have no higher authority than that mankind generally are disposed to accept them. . . . Now there can be no proof offered for the position that happiness is the proper end of all human pursuits, the criterion of all right conduct. It is an ultimate or final assumption to be tested by reference to the individual judgment of mankind." So Bentham, *Principles of Morals*, p. 2, "The principle is not susceptible of direct proofs for that which is used to prove everything else can not itself be proved; a chain of proofs must have their commencement somewhere." Mill, *Utilitarianism* (*Dissertations and Discussions*, Vol. III), pp. 348–49. "The only proof capable of being given that an object is visible is that people actually see it. In like manner the sole evidence it is possible to produce that anything is desirable is that people do actually desire it." See Stephen, *Science of Ethics*, p. 42; Spencer, *Data of Ethics*, pp. 30–32 and p. 46; Lotze, *Practical Philosophy*, pp. 18–19; Sidgwick, *Methods of Ethics*, pp. 368–69.

Hedonism, then, represents the good or the desirable and pleasure to be two names for the same fact. What indeed can be worth while unless it be either enjoyable in itself or at least a means to enjoyment? Would theft be considered bad if it resulted in pleasure or truth itself good if its universal effect were pain?

2. *Pleasure as Object of Desire*

It is also urged that psychological analysis shows that pleasure is not only the desirable, but also always the *desired*. Desire for an object is only a short way of saying desire for the pleasure which that object may bring. To want food is to want the pleasure it brings; to want scientific ability is to desire to find satisfaction, or attain happiness. Thus it is laid down as a general principle that the invariable object of desire, and motive of action is some pleasure to be attained; the action itself and the direct end of action being simply means to pleasure.

For a strong statement of this doctrine see Mill, *Utilitarianism*, pp. 354–55. "Desiring a thing and finding it pleasant, aversion to it and thinking of it as painful, are phenomena entirely inseparable, or rather two parts of the same phenomenon,—in strictness of language, two different modes of naming the same psychological fact; to think of an object as desirable and to think of it as pleasant are one and the same thing." See also, Bain, *Emotions and Will*, p. 436, *Senses and Intellect*, pp. 338–44; Sully, *Outlines of Psychology*, p. 575, "The inclination or tendency of the active mind towards what is pleasurable and away from what is painful is the essential fact in willing." Also pp. 576–77.

XII. Criticism: Pleasure Not the End of Impulse

Taking up the points in reverse order, we shall endeavor to show first, that the motive of action, in the sense of end aimed at, is not pleasure. This point in itself, is, of course, rather psychological than ethical. Taking up then the psychology of pleasure in its connection with will, we shall discuss its relation to impulse, to desire and to motive.

It is generally agreed that the raw material of volition is found in some form or other of the impulsive or instinctive actions. Such tendencies (*e.g.*, the impulse for food, for drink, for unimpeded motion) clearly precede the reaching of an end, and hence the experience of any pleasure in the end. Our first actions, at least, are not for pleasure; on the contrary, there is an activity for some independent end, and this end being reached there is pleasure in an act which has succeeded. This suggests as a possible principle that pleasure is not so much the end of action, as an element in the activity which reaches an end. What Aristotle says of another matter is certainly true of instinctive action. "It is not true of every characteristic function that its action is attended with pleasure, *except indeed the pleasure of attaining its end.*"

See Martineau, *Types of Ethical Theory*, Vol. II, pp. 299–300; Sidgwick, *Methods of Ethics*, pp. 38–45.

XIII. Criticism: Pleasure Not the End of Desire

It may, however, be said that, while our instinctive actions have another end than pleasure, this is not true of conscious desires—that, indeed, just the difference between instinct and desire is that the former goes blindly to its end, while the latter superimposes the thought of the pleasure to be reached upon the mere instinct. So we have to analyze the nature of desire.

A child, led by impulse, has put a piece of sugar into his mouth, just as, under the same circumstances, he would put a piece of stone into his mouth. But his action results in a state of pleasure wholly unforeseen by him. Now the next time the child sees the sugar he will not merely have the impulse to put it in his mouth. There will also be the remembrance of the pleasure enjoyed from sugar previously. There is consciousness of sugar as satisfying impulse and hence desire for it.

1. This is a description of an instance of desire. Does it bear us out in the doctrine that pleasure is the object of desire? It is possible that, in an irrational animal, the experience of eating food reinforces the original instinct for it with associated images of pleasure. But even this is very different from a desire for pleasure. It is simply the primordial instinct intensified and rendered more acute by new sensational factors joined to it. In the strict sense, there is still no desire, but only *stronger* impulse. Wherever there is desire there is not only a feeling of pleasure associated with other feelings (*e.g.*, those of hunger, thirst), but there is the *consciousness of an object in which satisfaction is found.* The error of the hedonistic psychology is in omitting one's consciousness of an *object* which satisfies. The hedonists are quite right in holding that the end of desire is not any object external to consciousness, but a condition of consciousness itself. The error begins in eliminating all objective (that is, active) elements from consciousness, and declaring it to be a mere state of feeling or sensation. The practical consciousness, or will, cannot be reduced to mere feeling, any more than the theoretical consciousness, or knowledge, can be so reduced.

Even Mill, in his statement of the hedonistic psychology, does not succeed in making the object of desire mere pleasure as a state of feeling. It is the "pleasant *thing*" and not pleasure alone which he finds equivalent to the desire. It is true enough that sugar as an external fact does not awaken desire, but it is equally true that a child does not want a passive pleasure. What he wants is his own activity in which he makes the sugar his own. And it should be remembered that the case of sugar is at once a trivial and an exceptional one. Not even children want simply sweetmeats; and the larger the character which finds expression in wants, the more does the direct object of want, the bread, the meat, become a mere element in a larger system of activity. What a man wants is to live, and he wants sweetmeats, amusements, etc., just as he wants substantials—on account of their value in life.

Professor James compares the idea that pleasure is the end of desire to saying that "because no steamer can go to sea without incidentally consuming coal, . . . therefore no steamer can go to sea for any other motive than that of coal-consumption." *Psychology*, Vol. II, p. 558. See the entire passage, pp. 549–59.

2. But granting that an "object" and a "pleasure" are both necessary to desire, it may be argued that the "object" is ultimately a means to "pleasure." This expressly raises a question already incidentally touched upon: What is the controlling element in desire? Why is the object thought of as pleasant? Simply because it is thought of as satisfying want. The hedonists, says Green (*Prolegomena to Ethics*, p. 168), make the "mistake of supposing that a desire can be excited by the anticipation of its own satisfaction." This is to say, of course, that it exists before it exists, and thus brings itself into being.

Green, *Prolegomena*, p. 167, states the matter thus: "Ordinary motives are interests in the attainment of objects, without which it seems to the man that he cannot satisfy himself, and in the attainment of which, *because he has desired them*, he will find a certain pleasure, but only because he has previously desired them, not because pleasures are the objects desired." Bradley says on this same point (*Ethical Studies*, p. 230): "The difference is between my finding my pleasure in an end, and my finding means for the end of my pleasure, and the difference is enormous." Consult the entire passage, pp. 226–35. See also Caird, *Critical Philosophy of Kant*, Vol. II, p. 229.

It is the object, then, which controls, and the pleasure is on account of the attaining of the desired object. But even this statement makes more division in desire than actually exists; for

3. The real object of desire is activity itself. The will takes its rise, as we have seen, in impulse; in the reaching for something to satisfy some felt lack. Now, in reality,

desire adds nothing to impulse excepting *consciousness* of the impulse. Volitional action does not differ from impulsive or instinctive, *except in bringing to consciousness the nature of the want and of the activity necessary to satisfy it.* But this makes just the difference between "natural" or animal activity, and "moral" or human activity. To be conscious of the impulse is to elevate it from a blind impelling force to an intended or proposed end; and thus, by bringing it *before* consciousness, both to extend its range and to idealize it, spiritualize it. To be conscious of an impulse for food means to give up the unreasoned and momentary seizing of it; to consider the relation of things to this want, what will satisfy it best, most easily, etc. The *object* of desire is not something outside the action; it is an element in the enlarged action. And as we become more and more conscious of impulse for food, we analyze our action into more and more "objects" of desire, but these objects never become anything apart from the action itself. They are simply its analyzed and defined content. Man wants activity still, but he knows better what activity means and includes.

Thus, when we learn what the activity means, it changes its character. To the animal the activity wanted is simply that of eating the food, of realizing the momentary impulse. To man the activity becomes enlarged to include the satisfaction of a whole life, and not of one life singly, but of the family, etc., connected with the single life. The material well-being of the family becomes one of the objects of desire into which the original impulse has grown. But we misinterpret, when we conceive of this well-being as an external object lying outside the action. It means simply one aspect of the fuller action. By like growing consciousness of the meaning of the impulse, production and exchange of commodities are organized. The impulse for food is extended to include a whole range of commercial activities.

It is evident that this growing consciousness of the nature of an impulse, whereby we resolve it into manifold and comprehensive activities, also takes the impulse out of its isolation and brings it into connection with other impulses. We come to have not a series of disconnected impulses, but one all-inclusive activity in which various subordinate activities (or conscious impulses) are included. Thus, in the previous example, the impulse for food is united with the family impulse, and with the impulse for communication and intercourse with society generally. It is this growing unity with the whole range of man's action that is the "spiritualizing" of the impulse—the natural and brutal impulse being just that which insists upon itself irrespective of all other wants. The spiritualizing of the impulse is organizing it so that it becomes one factor in action. Thus we literally come to "eat to live," meaning by life not mere physical existence, but the whole possible sphere of active human relations.

4. Relation of activity to pleasure. We have seen that the "object" of desire in itself is a mere abstraction; that the real object is full activity itself. We are always after larger scope of movement, fuller income in order to get larger outgo. The "thing" is always for the sake of doing; is a part of the doing. The idea that anything less or other than life (movement, action, and doing), can satisfy man is as ridiculous when compared with the actual course of things in history, as it is false psychologically. Freedom is what we want, and freedom means full unimpeded play of interests, that is, of conscious impulses (see Secs. XXXIV and LI). If the object is a mere abstraction apart from activity, much more is pleasure. Mere pleasure as an object is simply the extreme of passivity, of mere having, as against action or doing. It is *possible* to make pleasure to some degree the object of desire; this is just what the voluptuary does. But it is a commonplace that the voluptuary always defeats himself. He never gets satisfaction who identifies satisfaction with having pleasures. The reason is evident enough. Activity is what we want, and since pleasure comes from getting what we want, pleasure comes only with activity. To give up the activity, and attempt to get the pleasure is a contradiction in effect. Hence also the "hedonistic paradox" —that in order to get pleasure we must aim at something else.

There is an interesting recognition of this in Mill himself, (see his *Autobiography*, p. 142). And in his *Utilitarianism*, in discussing the feasibility of getting happiness, he shows (pp. 318–19) that the sources of happiness are an intelligent interest in surrounding things —objects of nature, achievements of art, incidents of history—and especially an unselfish devotion to others. Which is to say that man does not find satisfaction in pleasure as such at all, but only in objective affairs—that is, in complete interpretation, in activity with a wide and full content. Further consideration of the end of desire and its relation to pleasure may be found in Green, *Prolegomena*, pp. 123–32, 163–67; Bradley, *Mind*, Vol. XIII, p. 1; and Dewey, *Psychology*, pp. 360–65 [*Early Works*, II, 310–14].

XIV. Criticism: Character and Pleasure

It now being admitted that the end of desire is activity itself in which the "object" and "pleasure" are simply factors, what is the moving spring to action? What is it that arouses the mind to the larger activity? Most of the hedonists have confounded the two senses of motive already spoken of, and have held that *because* pleasure is the end of desire, therefore it is the moving spring of conduct (or more often that because it is the moving spring of conduct it *therefore* is the end of desire).

Mr. Stephen (*Science of Ethics*, pp. 46–58), although classing himself as a hedonist, has brought out this confusion very clearly. Ordinary hedonism confounds, as he shows, the judgment of what is pleasant—the supposed end —with the pleasant judgment—the moving spring. (See also Bradley, *Ethical Studies*, pp. 232–36.) It may be admitted that it is feeling which moves to action, but it is the *present* feeling which moves. If the feeling aimed at moves, it is only as through anticipation it becomes the present feeling. Now is this present feeling which moves (1) mere pleasure and (2) mere feeling at all? This introduces us to the question of the relation of pleasure (and of feeling in general) to character.

1. If the existing state of consciousness—that which moves—were pure pleasure, why should there be any movement, any act at all? The feeling which moves must be in so far complex: over against the pleasure felt in the anticipation of an end as satisfying, there must be pain felt in the contrasting unsatisfactory present condition. There must be tension between the anticipated or ideal action, and the actual or present (relative) non-action. And it is this tension, in which pain is just as normal an element as pleasure, which moves. Desire is just this tension of an action which satisfies, and yet is only ideal, against an actual possession which, in contrast with the ideal action, is felt as incomplete action, or lack, and hence as unsatisfactory.

2. The question now comes as to the nature of this tension. We may call it "feeling," if we will, and say that feeling is the sole motive power to action. But there is no such thing as feeling at large, and the important thing, morally, is what *kind* of feeling moves. To take a mere abstraction like "feeling" for the source of action is, at root, the fallacy of hedonism. To raise the question, What is it that makes the feeling what it is, is to recognize that the feeling, taken concretely, is *character* in a certain attitude.

Stephen, who has insisted with great force that feeling is the sole "motive" to action, has yet shown with equal cogency the moral uselessness of such a doctrine, when feeling is left undefined (*Science of Ethics*, p. 44). "The love of happiness must express the sole possible motive of Judas Iscariot and his master; it must explain the conduct of Stylites on his column, of Tiberius at Capreæ, of A Kempis in his cell, and of Nelson in the cockpit of the Victory. It must be equally good for saints, martyrs, heroes, cowards, debauchees, ascetics, mystics, cynics, misers, prodigals, men, women, and babes in arms." Surely, this is only to say, in effect, that "love of happiness" is a pure bit of scholasticism, an undefined entity.

In a hedonistic argument (by Stanton Coit, *Mind*, Vol. XI, p. 349), the fallacy is seen in the following discussion. The story is told of Abraham Lincoln that he once passed an animal in distress by the side of the road, and that, after going by, he finally went back and got him out of the ditch. On being praised for his act, he replied that he did it on his own account, since he kept getting more uncomfortable as he thought of the animal in distress. From this, it cannot be inferred that love of pleasure is at the basis of moral acts. The mere lumping off of feeling as the spring of conduct overlooks the only important thing morally—the fact that Lincoln felt pain at the thought of the animal unrelieved, and pleasure at the idea of its relief, just because he was a man of compassionate *character*. It was not the feeling, but the character revealed in, and creative of, the feeling that was the real source of the act.

To connect this with our previous account of desire (p. 257): the important thing morally is that the nature of the tension between fact and idea—the actual state and the ideal activity—is an expression of character. What kind of activity does it take to satisfy a man? Does riding in a comfortable carriage, and following the course of his own reflections exhaust his need of action? or does his full activity require that note be taken of a suffering animal? It is the kind of character one is (that is, the kind of activity which satisfies and expresses one) which decides what pleasure shall be taken in an anticipated end, what feeling of lack or hindrance (what pain) there shall be in the given state, and hence what the resulting tension, or desire, shall be. It is, therefore, character which moves to conduct.

Mere wishing, the mere floating fancy of this or that thing as desirable, is not desire. To *want* is an active projection of character; really and deeply to want is no surface and passing feeling; it is the stirring of character to its depths. There may be repressed activity; that is not, of itself, desire. There may be an image of larger activity; that is not, of itself, desire. But given the *consciousness* of a repressed activity in view of the perception of a possible larger action, and a man strives within himself to break his bonds and reach the new satisfaction. This striving within one's self, before the activity becomes overt, is the emotional antecedent of action. But this inward striving or tension, which constitutes desire, is so far from being *mere* emotion that it is character itself—character as it turns an inward or ideal advance into an outward, or real progress, into action.

We may fall back on Aristotle's statement (p. 38, of Peters' translation of his *Ethics*): "The pleasure or pain that accompanies an act must be regarded as a *test* of *character*. He who abstains from the pleasures of the body and rejoices in his abstinence is temperate, while he who is vexed at having to abstain is still profligate. As Plato tells us, man needs to be so trained from youth up as to take pleasure and pain *in the right objects*."

XV. Summary

The truth in hedonism is its conviction that the good, the end of man, is not to be found in any outward object, but only in what comes home to man in his own conscious experience. The error is in reducing this experience to mere having, to bare feelings or affections, eliminating the element of doing. It is this doing which satisfies man, and it is this which involves as its content (as knowledge of impulse, instead of blind impulse) objective and permanent ends. When Mill speaks of the end of desire as a "satisfied life," (p. 317 of *Utilitarianism*) he carries our assent; but to reduce this satisfied life to feelings of pleasure, and absence of pains, is to destroy the life and hence the satisfaction. As Mill recognizes, a life bounded by the agent's own feelings would be, as of course, a life "centred in his own miserable individuality" (Mill, *Utilitarianism*, p. 319). Such words have meaning only because they suggest the contrast with activity in which are comprehended, as "ends" or "objects" (that is, as part of its defined content) things—art, science and industry—and persons (see Secs. XXXIV and XXXV).

Here too we must "back to Aristotle." According to him the end of conduct is *eudaimonia*, success, welfare, satisfied life. But *eudaimonia* is found not in pleasure, but in the fulfillment of human powers and functions, in which fulfillment, since it is fulfillment, pleasure is had (*Ethics*, Bk. I, Chs. 4–8).

We now take up the question whether pleasure is a standard of right action, having finished the discussion concerning it as an end of desire.

XVI. Pleasure as the Standard of Conduct

The line of criticism on this point may be stated as follows: Pleasure fails as a standard for the very reason that it fails as a motive. Pleasure, *as conceived by the hedonist*, is passive, merely agreeable sensations, without any objective and qualitative (active) character. This being so, there is no permanent, fixed basis to which we may refer *acts* and by which we may judge them. A standard implies a single comprehensive end which unifies all acts and through connection with which each gets its moral value fixed. Only action can be a standard for acts. To reduce all acts to means to getting a mere state of feeling is the inevitable consequence of hedonism. So reducing them is to deprive them of any standard of value.

An end to serve as standard must be (1) a comprehensive end for all the acts of an individual, and (2) an end comprehending the activities of various individuals—a common good.

1. The moral end must be that for the sake of which all conduct occurs—the *organizing principle* of conduct—a totality, a system. If pleasure is the end it is because each detail of conduct gets its placing, its moral value through relation to pleasure, through the contribution it makes to pleasure.

2. The moral end must also include the ends of the various agents who make up society. It must be capable of constituting a social system out of the acts of various agents, as well as an individual system out of the various acts of one agent; or, more simply, the moral end must be not only the good for all the particular acts of an individual, but must be a *common good*—a good which in satisfying one, satisfies others.

All ethical theories would claim that the end proposed by them served these two purposes. We shall endeavor to show that the hedonistic theory, the doctrine that the pleasure is the good, is not capable of serving either of them.

XVII. Pleasure Not a Standard

1. It does not unify character. In the first place, the hedonistic theory makes an unreal and impossible separation between conduct and character. The psychology of hedonism comes into conflict with its ethics. According to the former the motive of all action is to secure pleasure or avoid pain. So far as the motive is concerned, on this theory there can be no immoral action at all. That the agent should not be moved by pleasure, and by what, at the time of acting, is the greatest pleasure possible, would be a psychological impossibility. Every motive would be good, or rather there would be no distinction of good or bad pertaining to the motive. The character of the agent, as measured by his

motives, could never, under such circumstances, have any moral quality.

To the consequences of action, or the conduct proper, however, the terms good and bad might be applied. Although the agent is moved by pleasurable feelings, the result of his action may be painful and thus bad. In a word, on the hedonistic theory, it is only the external consequences of conduct, or conduct divorced from character, to which moral adjectives have any application. Such a separation not only contradicts our experience (see Sec. VIII), but inverts the true order of moral judgment. Consequences do not enter into the moral estimate at all, except so far as, being foreseen, they are the act in idea. That is, it is only as the consequences are taken up into the motive, and thus related to character, that they are subject to moral judgment. Indeed, except so far as action expresses character, it is not conduct, but mere physical sequence, as irrelevant to morality as the change in blood distribution, which also is the "result" of an action. Hedonism has to rule out at the start the only thing that gives totality to action—the character of the agent, or conduct as the outcome of motives. Furthermore, the ordinary judgment of men, instead of saying that the sole moral motive is to get pleasure, would say that to reduce everything to means for getting pleasure is the very essence of immorality.

On the point above, compare Bentham, *Principles of Morals*, p. 48. "A motive is substantially nothing more than pleasure or pain operating in a certain manner. Now pleasure is in itself a good: nay, even, setting aside immunity from pain, the only good; pain is in itself an evil, and, indeed, without exception, the only evil; or else the words good and evil have no meaning. And this is alike true of every sort of pain and of every sort of pleasure. It follows, therefore, immediately and incontestably, that there is no such thing as any sort of motive that is in itself a bad one. If motives are good or bad, it is only on account of their effects; good on account of their tendency to produce pleasure or avert pain; bad on account of their tendency to produce pain or avert pleasure. Now the case is, that from one and the same motive, and from every kind of motive, may proceed actions that are good, others that are bad and others that are indifferent." Further, on p. 60, Bentham asks: "Is there nothing, then, about a man that can properly be termed good or bad, when on such or such an occasion he suffers himself to be governed by such or such a motive? Yes, certainly, his *disposition*. Now disposition is a kind of fictitious entity, feigned for the convenience of discourse, in order to express what there is supposed to be *permanent* in a man's frame of mind. It is with disposition as with everything else; it will be good or bad according to its effects." The first quotation, it will be noticed, simply states that the motive is in itself always good, while conduct (*i.e.*, consequences) may be good, bad or indifferent. The second quotation seems, however, to pass moral judgment upon character under the name of disposition. But disposition is judged according to the tendency of a person's actions. A good or bad disposition, here, can mean nothing intrinsic to the person, but only that the person has been observed to act in ways that usually produce pain or pleasure, as the case may be. The term is a "fiction," and is a backhanded way of expressing a somewhat habitual *result* of a given person's conduct his motive remaining good (or for pleasure) all the time. The agent would never pronounce any such judgment upon his own disposition, unless as a sort of surprise that, his motive being "good," his actions turn out so "bad" all the time. At most, the judgment regarding disposition is a sort of label put upon a man by others, a label of "Look out for him, he is dangerous," or, "Behold, a helpful man."

The moral standard of hedonism does not, then, bear any relation to the character of the agent, does not enable us to judge it, either as a whole or in any specific manifestation.

XVIII. It Does Not Give a Criterion for Concrete Acts

Pleasure, as the end, fails also to throw light on the moral value of any specific acts. Its failure in this respect is, indeed, only the other side of that just spoken of. There is no organizing principle, no "universal" on the basis of which various acts fall into a system or order. The moral life is left a series of shreds and patches, where each act is torn off, as to its moral value, from every other. Each act is right or wrong, according as *it* gives pleasure or pain, and independently of any whole of life. There is, indeed, no whole of moral life at all, but only a series of isolated, disconnected acts. Possession, passivity, *mere* feeling, by its very nature cannot unite—each feeling is itself and that is the end of it. It is action which reduces multiplicity to unity. We cannot say, in the hedonistic theory, that pleasure is the end, but *pleasures*.

Each act stands by itself—the only question is: What pleasure will *it* give? The settling of this question is the "hedonistic calculus." We must discover the intensity, duration, certainty, degree of nearness of the pleasure likely to arise from the given act, and also its purity, or likelihood of being accompanied by secondary pains and pleasures. Then we are to strike the balance between the respective sums on the pleasure and pain sides, and, according as this balance is one of pleasure or pain, the act is good or evil.

Bentham, *Principles of Morals*, p. 16, was the first to go into detail as to this method. He has also given certain memoriter verses stating "the points on which the whole fabric of morals and legislation may be seen to rest.

Intense, long, certain, speedy, fruitful, pure
Such marks in pleasures and in pains endure,
Such pleasures seek, if private be thy end.
If it be public, wide let them extend.
Such pains avoid whichever be thy view,
If pains must come, let them extend to few."

This, however, in its reference to others, states the utilitarian as well as the hedonistic view.

Now, it must be remembered that, if pleasure is the end, there is no intrinsic connection between the motive of the act, and its result. It is not claimed that there is anything belonging intrinsically to the motive of the act which makes it result in pleasure or pain. To make such a claim would be to declare the moral quality of the act the criterion of the pleasure, instead of pleasure the criterion of the act. The pleasures are external to the act; they are irrelevant and accidental to its quality. There is no "universal," no intrinsic bond of connection between the act and its consequences. The consequence is a mere particular state of feeling, which, in this instance, the act has happened to bring about.

More concretely, this act of truth-telling has in this instance, brought about pleasure. Shall we call it right? Right in *this* instance, of course; but is it right generally? Is truth-telling, as such, right, or is it merely that this instance of it happens to be right? Evidently, on the hedonistic basis, we cannot get beyond the latter judgment. *Prior* to any act, there will be plenty of difficulties in telling whether it, as *particular*, is right or wrong. The consequences depend not merely on the result intended, but upon a multitude of circumstances outside of the foresight and control of the agent. And there can be only a precarious calculation of possibilities and probabilities—a method which would always favor laxity of conduct in all but the most conscientious of men, and which would throw the conscientious into uncertainty and perplexity in the degree of their conscientiousness.

"If once the pleas of instinct are to be abolished and replaced by a hedonistic arithmetic, the whole realm of animated nature has to be reckoned with in weaving the tissue of moral relations, and the problem becomes infinite and insoluble."—Martineau, *Types of Ethical Theory*, Vol. II, p. 334.

But waive this; let the particular case be settled. There is still no law, no principle, indeed no presumption as to future conduct. The act is not right *because* it is *truth-telling*, but because, in this instance, circumstances were such as to throw a balance of pleasure in its favor. This establishes no certainty, no probability as to its next outcome. The result *then* will depend wholly upon circumstances existing *then*—circumstances which have no intrinsic relation to the act and which must change from time to time.

The hedonist would escape this abolition of all principle, or even rule, by falling back upon a number of cases—"past experience" it is called. We have found in a number of cases that a certain procedure has resulted in pleasure, and this result is sufficient to guide us in a vast number of cases which come up.

Says Mill (*Utilitarianism*, pp. 332–34): "During the whole past duration of the species, mankind have been learning by experience the tendencies of actions, on which experience all the prudence as well as all the morality of life are dependent. . . . Mankind must by this time have acquired positive belief as to the effects of some actions on their happiness; and the beliefs which have thus come down are the rules of morality for the multitude, and for the philosopher, until he has succeeded in finding better. . . . Nobody argues that the art of navigation is not founded on astronomy, because sailors cannot wait to calculate the 'Nautical Almanac.' Being rational creatures, they go to sea with it ready calculated; and all rational creatures go out upon the sea of life with their minds made up on the common questions of right and wrong, as well as on many of the far more difficult questions of wise and foolish."

That we do learn from experience the moral nature of actions is undoubted. The only question is: *if* hedonism were true, *could* we so learn? Suppose that I were convinced that the results of murder in the past had been generally, or even without exception (though this could not be proved), painful; as long as the act and the result in the way of feeling (pain or pleasure) are conceived as having no intrinsic connection, this would not prove that in the present instance murder will give a surplus of pain. I am not thinking of committing murder in general, but of murder under certain specific present circumstances. These circumstances may, and, to some extent, *must* vary from all previous instances of murder. How then can I reason from them to it? Or, rather, let me use the previous cases as much as I may, the moral quality of the act I am now to perform must still be judged not from them, but from the circumstances of the present case. To judge otherwise, is, on hedonistic principles, to be careless, perhaps criminally careless as to one's conduct. The more convinced a man is of the truth of hedonism and the more conscientious he is, the more he is bound *not* to be guided by previous circumstances, but to form his judgment anew concerning the new case. This result flows out of the very nature of the hedonistic ideal. Pleasure is not an activity, but simply a particular feeling, enduring only while it is felt. Moreover, there is in it no principle which connects it intrinsically with any *kind* of action. To suppose then that, because ninety-nine cases of murder have resulted in pain, the hundredth will, is on a par with reasoning that because ninety-nine days have been frosty, the hundreth will be. Each case, taken as particular, must be decided wholly by itself. There is no continuous moral life, and no system of conduct. There is only a succession of unlike acts.

Mill, in his examination of Whewell, (*Dissertations*, Vol. III, pp. 158–59), tries to establish a general principle, if not a universal law, by arguing that, even in exceptional cases, the agent is bound to respect the rule, because to act otherwise would weaken the rule, and thus lead to its being disregarded in other cases, in which its observance results in pleasure. There are, he says, persons so wicked that their removal from the earth would undoubtedly increase the sum total of happiness. But if persons were to violate the general rule in these cases, it would tend to destroy the rule. "If it were thought allowable for any one to put to death at pleasure any human being whom he believes that the world would be well rid of,—nobody's life would be safe." That is to say, if every one were really to act upon and carry out the hedonistic principle, no rule of life would exist. This does very well as a *reductio ad absurdum* of hedonism, or as an argument against adopting hedonism, but it is difficult to see how Mill thought that it established a "rule" on a hedonistic basis. Mill's argument comes to saying that if hedonism were uniformly acted upon, it would defeat itself—that is, pleasure would not result. Therefore, in order to get pleasure, we must not act upon the principle of hedonism at all, but follow a general rule. Otherwise put: hedonism gives no general rule, but we must have a general rule to make hedonism work and therefore there is a general rule! This begging of the question comes out even more plainly as Mill goes on: "If one person may break through the rule on his own judgment, the same liberty cannot be refused to others; and, since no one could rely on the rule's being observed, the rule would cease to exist." All of this is obviously true, but it amounts to saying: "We *must* have a rule, and this we would not have if we carried out the hedonistic principle in each case; therefore, we must not carry it out." A principle, that carried out destroys all rules which pretend to rest upon it, lays itself open to suspicion. Mill assumes the entire question in assuming that there is a rule. Grant this, and the necessity of not "making exceptions," that is, of not applying the hedonistic standard to each case, on its own merits, follows. But the argument which Mill needs to meet is that hedonism *requires* us to apply the standard to each case in itself, and that, therefore, there *is* no rule. Mill simply says—*assume* the rule, and it follows, etc.

See Bradley, *Ethical Studies*, pp. 96–101; Green, *Prolegomena*, Bk. IV, Ch. 3; Martineau, *Types of Ethical Theory*, Vol. II, pp. 329–34.

XIX. The Sum and Quality of Pleasure as the Standard

We have been dealing with hedonism in its strict form —that which makes *a* pleasure, considered as to its intensity, certainty, etc., the end of an act. Hedonism in this form fails to unify life, and fails, therefore, to supply any standard. But the end of conduct is often stated to be the greatest possible sum of pleasures, thus introducing a certain element of generality. Mill goes further and brings in the idea of quality of pleasure.

Regarding the sum of pleasures the following from Sidgwick (*Methods of Ethics*, p. 382; see also p. 114) gives the hedonistic statement. "The assumption is involved that all pleasures are capable of being compared qualitatively with one another and with all pains; that every feeling has a certain intensive quality, positive or negative (or perhaps zero) in respect to its desirableness and that the quantity may be known, so that each may be weighed in ethical scales against any other. This assumption is involved in the very notion of maximum happiness," as the attempt to make "as great as possible a sum of elements not quantitatively commensurable would be a mathematical absurdity."

1. *Sum of Pleasures as the Moral End*

This first, taken as criterion, comes into conflict with the hedonistic psychology of pleasure as the motive of acts; and, secondly, it requires some objective standard by means of which pleasure is to be summed, and is, in so far, a surrender of the whole hedonistic position.

a] If the object of desire is pleasure or a state of feeling which exists only as it is felt, it is impossible that we should desire a greatest sum of pleasures. We can desire a pleasure and that only. It is not even possible that we should ever desire a continuous series of pleasures. We can desire one pleasure and when that is gone, another, but we cannot unify our desires enough to aim at even a sum of pleasures.

This is well put by Green (*Prolegomena*, p. 236). "For the feeling of a pleased person, or in relation to his sense of enjoyment, pleasure cannot form a sum. However numerous the sources of a state of pleasant feeling, it is one and is over before another can be enjoyed. It and its successors can be added together in thought, but not in enjoyment or in imagination of an enjoyment. If the desire is only for pleasure, *i.e.*, for an enjoyment or feeling of pleasure, we are simply victims of words when we talk of desire for a sum of pleasures, much more when we take the greatest imaginable sum to be the most desirable." See the whole passage, pp. 235–46.

b] But the phrase "sum of pleasures" undoubtedly has a meaning—though the fact that it has a meaning shows the untruth of the hedonistic psychology. Surrendering this psychology, what shall we say of the maximum possibility of pleasure as the criterion of the morality of acts? It must be conceded that this conception does afford some basis—although a rather slippery one—for the unification of conduct. Each act is considered now not in its isolation merely, but in its connection with other acts, according as its relation to them may increase or decrease the possible sum of future happiness. But this very fact that some universal, or element of relation, albeit a quantitative one, has been introduced, arouses this inquiry: Whence do we derive it? How do we get the thought of a sum of pleasure, and of a maximum sum? *Only by taking into account the objective conditions upon which pleasures depend, and by judging the pleasures from the standpoint of these objective conditions.* When we imagine we are thinking of a sum of pleasures, we are really thinking of that totality of conditions which will come nearest affording us self-satisfaction—we are thinking of a comprehensive and continuous activity whose various parts are adjusted to one another. Because it is complete activity, it is necessarily conceived as giving the greatest possible pleasure, but apart from reference to complete activity and apart from the objects in which this is realized, the phrase "greatest sum of happiness" is a mere phrase. Pleasures must be measured by a standard, by a yard stick, before they can be summed in thought, and the yard stick we use is the activity in which the pleasure comes. We do not measure conduct by pleasure, but we compare and sum up pleasures on the basis of the objects which occasion them. To add feelings, mere transitory consequences, without first reducing those feelings to a common denominator by their relation to one objective standard, is an impossibility. Pleasure is a sort of sign or symbol of the object which satisfies, and we may carry on our judgment, if we will, in terms of the sign, without reference to the standard, but to argue as if the sign were the thing, as if the sum of pleasure were the activity, is suicidal.

Thus Green says (*Prolegomena*, p. 244): "In truth a man's reference to his own true happiness is a reference to the objects which chiefly interest him, and has its controlling power on that account. More strictly, it is a reference to an ideal state of well-being, a state in which he shall be satisfied; *but the objects of the man's chief interests supply the filling of that ideal state.*" See the argument as put by Alexander (*Moral Order and Progress*, pp. 199–200). Alexander has also brought out (*Moral Order*, pp. 207–10) that even if we are going to use a quantitative standard, the idea of a sum is not a very happy one. It is not so much a sum of pleasures we want, as a certain proportionate distribution and combination of pleasures. "To regard the greatest sum of pleasures as the test of conduct, supposing that we could express it in units of pleasure, would be like declaring that when you had an atomic weight of 98 you had sulphuric acid. The numerical test would be useless unless we knew what elements were to be combined, and in what proportion. Similarly till we know what kinds of activities (and therefore what kinds of pleasures) go with one another to form the end, the greatest sum of pleasures will give us only the equivalent of the end, but will not tell us what the composition of the end is, still less how to get at it; or, to put the matter more simply, when we know what the characters of persons are, and how they are combined in morality, we then estimate the corresponding sum of pleasures" (p. 209).

2. *A Certain Quality of Pleasure the End*

Some moralists, notably John Stuart Mill, introduce considerations regarding the quality of pleasure into the conception of the end. "It is quite compatible," says Mill, "with the principle of utility to recognize the fact that some kinds of pleasure are more desirable and more valuable than others" (*Utilitarianism*, p. 310). Is it compatible? Is kind of pleasure the same thing as pleasure? Does not strict hedonism demand that all kinds of pleasure equally present as to intensity in consciousness shall be of the same value? To say otherwise is to give up pleasure as such as the standard and to hold that we have means for discriminating the respective values of pleasures which simply, *as feelings*, are the same. It is to hold, that is to say, that there is some standard of value external to the pleasures as such, by means of which their moral quality may be judged. In this case, this independent standard is the real moral criterion which we are employing. Hedonism is surrendered.

Kant's position on this point seems impregnable. "It is surprising," he says, "that men otherwise astute can think it possible to distinguish between higher and lower desires, according as the ideas which are connected with the feeling of pleasure have their origin in the senses or in the understanding; for when we inquire what are the determining grounds of desire, and place them in some expected pleasantness, it is of no consequence whence the *idea* of this pleasing object is derived, but only how much it *pleases*. . . . The only thing that concerns one, in order to decide choice, is how great, how long continued, how easily obtained and how often repeated, this agreeableness is. For as to the man who wants money to spend, it is all the same whether the gold was dug out of the mountain or washed out of the sand, provided it is everywhere accepted at the same value; so the man who cares only for the enjoyment of life does not ask whether the ideas are of the understanding or the senses, but only *how much* and *how great pleasure* they will give for the longest time."

See also Bradley, *Ethical Studies*, pp. 105–10.

When we ask how the differences in quality are established and how we translate this qualitative difference into moral difference, the surrender of pleasure as the standard becomes even more evident. We must know not only the fact of different qualities, but how to decide which is "higher" than any other. We must bring the qualities before a tribunal of judgment which applies to them some standard of measurement. In themselves qualities may be different, but they are not higher and lower. What is the tribunal and what is the law of judgment? According to Mill the tribunal is the preference of those who are acquainted with both kinds of pleasure.

"Of two pleasures, if there be one to which all, or almost all who have experience of both, give a decided preference, irrespective of any feeling of moral obligation to prefer it, that is the more desirable pleasure." It is an unquestionable fact that such differences exist. "Few human creatures would consent to be changed into any of the lower animals for a promise of the fullest allowance of a beast's pleasures. No intelligent person would consent to be a fool; no instructed person would be an ignoramus; no person of feeling and conscience would be selfish and base, even though they should be persuaded that the fool, the dunce or the rascal is better satisfied with his lot than they are with theirs. . . . It is better to be a human being dissatisfied, than a pig satisfied; better to be a Socrates dissatisfied, than a fool satisfied. And if the fool or the pig are of a different opinion, it is because they only know their own side of the question. The other party to the comparison knows both sides."—Mill, *Utilitarianism*, pp. 311–13. And in an omitted portion Mill says the reason that one of the higher faculty would prefer a suffering which goes along with that higher capacity, to more pleasure on a lower plane, is something of which "the most appropriate appellation is a sense of dignity, which all human beings possess in one form or another."

A question immediately arises regarding this standard of preferability. Is it the mere historical fact that some man, who has experienced both, prefers A to B that makes A more desirable? Surely I might say that if that person prefers A, A is more desirable to him, but that I for my part prefer B, and that I do not intend to give up my preference. And why should I, even though thousands of other men happened to prefer A? B is the greater pleasure, none the less, to me, and as a hedonist I must cling to the only standard that I have. The hedonists, in a word, have appealed to feeling, and to feeling they must go for judgment. And feeling exists only as it is felt and only to him who feels it.

On the other hand, perhaps it is not the bare fact that some men prefer one pleasure to another that makes it more desirable, but something in the character of the men who prefer. And this is what Mill implies. It is a "sense of dignity" belonging to man which makes his judgment of pleasure better than that of animals; it is the human being against the pig, Socrates against the fool, the good man against the rascal. This is the complete surrender of hedonism, and the all but explicit assertion that human character, goodness, wisdom, are the criteria of pleasure, instead of pleasure the criterion of character and goodness. Mill's "sense of dignity," which is to be considered in all estimates of pleasures, is just the sense of a moral (or active) capacity and destiny belonging to man. To refer pleasures to *this* is to make it the standard, and with this standard the anti-hedonist may well be content, while asking, however, for its further analysis.

To sum up our long discussion of pleasure as a criterion of conduct in respect of its unity, we may say: Pleasure, *as it actually exists in man*, may be taken as *a* criterion, although not the really primary one, of action. But this is not hedonism; for pleasure as it *exists* is something more than pleasurable feeling; it is qualified through and through by the kind of action which it accompanies, by the kind of objects which the activity comprehends. And thus it is always a secondary criterion. The moment we begin to analyze we must ask what *kind of activity*, what kind of object it is which the pleasure accompanies and of which it is a symbol. We may, if we will, calculate a man's wealth in terms of dollars and cents; but this is only because we can translate the money, the symbol, into goods, the reality. To desire pleasure instead of an activity of self, is to substitute symbol for fact, and a symbol cut off from fact ceases to be a symbol. Pleasure, as the hedonist treats it, mere agreeable feeling without active and thus objective relationships, is wholly an abstraction. Since an abstraction, to make it the end of desire results in self-contradiction; while to make it the standard of conduct is to deprive life of all unity, all system, in a word—of all standard.

XX. The Failure of Pleasure as a Standard to Unify Conduct Socially

Thus far our examination of the hedonistic criterion has been devoted to showing that it will not make a system out of individual conduct. We have now to recognize the fact that pleasure is not a common good, and therefore fails to give a social unity to conduct—that is, it does not offer an end for which men may co-operate, or a good which reached by one must be shared by another. No argument is needed to show, theoretically, that any proposed moral criterion must, in order to be valid, harmonize the interests and activities of different men, or to show, practically, that the whole tendency of the modern democratic and philanthropic movement has been to discover and realize a good in which men shall share on the basis of an equal principle. It is contended that hedonism fails to satisfy these needs. According to it, the end for each man is his own pleasure. Pleasure is nothing objective in which men may equally participate. It is purely individual in the most exclusive sense of that term. It is a state of feeling and can be enjoyed only while felt, and only by the one who feels it. To set it up for the ideal of conduct is to turn life into an exclusive and excluding struggle for possession of the means of personal enjoyment; it is to erect into a principle the idea of the war of all against all. No end more thoroughly disintegrating than individual agreeable sensation could well be imagined.

Says Kant, (p. 116 of Abbott's trans., entitled *Kant's Theory of Ethics*), on the basis of the desire of happiness "there results a harmony like that which a certain satirical poem depicts as existing between a married couple bent on going to ruin: O, marvellous harmony, what he wishes, she wishes also; or like what is said of the pledge of Francis I to the emperor Charles V, what my brother Charles wishes that I wish also (viz., Milan)."

Almost all modern moralists who take pleasure as the end conceive it to be not individual pleasure, but the happiness of all men or even of all sentient creatures. Thus we are brought to the consideration of Utilitarianism.

Says Mill, (*Utilitarianism*, p. 323), "The happiness which forms the Utilitarian standard of what is right in conduct is not the agent's own happiness, but that of all concerned; as between his own happiness and that of others, Utilitarianism requires him to be as strictly impartial as a disinterested and benevolent spectator." And (p. 315) the Utilitarian standard is "not the agent's own greatest happiness, but the greatest amount of happiness altogether." See also Sidgwick (*Methods of Ethics*, p. 379), "By Utilitarianism is here meant the ethical theory, first distinctly formulated by Bentham, that the conduct which, under any given circumstances is externally or objectively right is that which will produce the greatest amount of happiness *on the whole*; that is, taking into account all whose happiness is affected by the conduct. It would tend to clearness if we might call this principle, and the method based upon it, by some such name as Universalistic hedonism." As popularly put, the utilitarian standard is the "greatest happiness of the greatest number." While in its calculation "each is to count for one and only one" (Bentham). And finally Bain (*Emotions and Will*, p. 303), "Utility is opposed to the selfish theory, for, as propounded, it always implies the good of society generally, and the subordination of individual interests to the general good."

XXI. Criticism of Utilitarianism

The utilitarian theory certainly does away entirely with one of the two main objections to hedonism—its failure to provide a general, as distinct from a private end. The question which we have to meet, however, is whether this extension of the end from the individual to society is consistent with the fundamental principles of hedonism. *How* do we get from individual pleasure to the happiness of all?

An intuitional utilitarian, like Sidgwick, has ready an answer which is not open to the empirical utilitarians, like Bentham, Mill and Bain. *Methods of Ethics*, Bk. III, Chs. 13–14, p. 355. "We may obtain the *self-evident principle* that the good of any one individual is of no more importance, as a part of universal good, than the good of any other. The abstract principle of the duty of benevolence, *so far as it is cognizable by direct intuition*" is, "that one is morally bound to regard the good of any other individual as much as one's own"—and p. 364, "*the principles, so far as they are immediately known by abstract intuition*, can only be stated as precepts to seek (1) one's own good on the whole, and (2) the good of any other no less than one's own, in so far as it is no less an element of universal good." Sidgwick, that is, differs in two important points from most utilitarians. He holds that pleasure is not the sole, or even the usual object of desire. And he holds that we have an immediate faculty of rational intuition which informs us that the good of others is as desirable an end of our conduct as is our own happiness. Our former arguments against pleasure as the *end*, bear, of course, equally against this theory, but not the following arguments. Criticisms of this position of Sidgwick's will be found in Green (*Prolegomena*, pp. 406–15); Bradley (*Ethical Studies*, pp. 114–17).

The popular answer to the question how we get from individual to general happiness, misses the entire point of the question. This answer simply says that happiness is "*intrinsically* desirable." Let it be so; but "happiness" in this general way is a mere abstraction. Happiness is always a particular condition of one particular person. Whose happiness is desirable and *to whom*? Because my happiness is intrinsically desirable to me, does it follow that your happiness is intrinsically desirable to me? Indeed, in the hedonistic psychology, is it not nonsense to say that a state of your feeling is desirable to me? Mill's amplified version of the popular answer brings out the ambiguity all the more plainly. He says (*Utilitarianism*, p. 349), "No reason can be given why the general happiness is desirable, except that each person, so far as he believes it to be obtainable, desires his own happiness. This, however, being a fact, we have not only all the proof which the case admits of, but all which it is possible to require, that happiness is a good; that each person's happiness is a good to that person; and the general happiness, therefore, a good to the aggregate of all persons." But does it follow that because the happiness of A is an end to A, the happiness of B an end to B, and the happiness of C an end to C, that, therefore, the happiness of B and C is an end to A? There is obviously no connection between the premises and the supposed conclusion. And there appears to be, as Mill puts it, only an account of the ambiguity of his last clause, "the general happiness a good to the aggregate of all persons." The good of A and B and C may be a good to the aggregate (A + B + C), but what universalistic hedonism requires is that the aggregate good of A + B + C, be a good to A and to B and to C taken separately—a very different proposition. Mill is guilty of the fallacy known logically as the fallacy of division—arguing from a collective whole to the distributed units. Because all men want to be happy, it hardly follows that every man wants all to be happy. There is, accordingly, no *direct* road from individualistic hedonism—private pleasure—to universalistic—general pleasure. Moreover, if we adopt the usual psychology of hedonism and say that pleasure is the motive of acting, it is absolutely absurd to say that general pleasure can be a motive. How can I be moved by the happiness which exists in some one else? I may feel a pleasure resembling his, and be moved by it, but that is quite a different matter.

XXII. Indirect Means of Identifying Private and General Pleasure

Is there any *indirect* method of going from the pleasure of one to the pleasure of all? Upon the whole, the utilitarians do not claim that there is any natural and immediate connection between the desire for private and for general happiness, but suppose that there are certain means which are instrumental in bringing about an identity. Of these means the sympathetic emotions and the influence of law and of education are the chief. Each of these, moreover, co-operates with the other.

1. Sympathetic and Social Emotions

We are so constituted by nature that we take pleasure in the happiness of others and feel pain in their misery. A proper regard for our own welfare must lead us, therefore, to take an interest in the pleasure of others. Our own feelings, moreover, are largely influenced by the feelings of others toward us. If we act in a certain way we shall incur the disapprobation of others, and this, independently of any overt punishment it may lead them to inflict upon us, arouses feelings of shame, of inferiority, of being under the displeasure of others, feelings all of which are decidedly painful. The more enlightened our judgment, the more we see how our pleasures are bound up in those of others.

"The Dictates of Utility" (Bentham, *Principles of Morals*, p. 56), "are neither more nor less than the dictates of the most extensive and enlightened (that is, well advised) benevolence," and (p. 18), "The pleasures of benevolence are the pleasures resulting from the view of any pleasures supposed to be possessed by the beings who may be the objects of benevolence. . . . These may also be called the pleasures of good will, the pleasures of sympathy, or the pleasures of the benevolent or social affections"; and (pp. 143–44), "What motives (independent of such as legislation and religion may choose to furnish) can one man have to consult the happiness of another? . . . In answer to this, it cannot but be admitted that the only interests which a man at all times and upon all occasions is sure to find *adequate* motives for consulting, are his own. Notwithstanding this, there are no occasions in which a man has not some motives for consulting the happiness of other men. In the first place he has, on all occasions, the purely social motive of sympathy and benevolence; in the next place he has, on most occasions, the semi-social motives of love of amity and love of reputation." And so in the *Deontology*, which, however, was not published by Bentham himself, p. 203, "The more enlightened one is, the more one forms the habit of general benevolence, because it is seen that the interests of men combine with each other in more points than they conflict in."

2. Education and Law

Education, working directly and internally upon the feelings, and government, appealing to them from without through commands and penalties, are constantly effecting an increasing identity of self-interest and regard for others.

These means supplement the action of sympathy and the more instinctive emotions. They stimulate and even induce a proper interest in the pleasures of others. In governmental law, with its punishments, we have an express instrument for making the pleasures of one harmonize with (or at least not conflict with) the pleasures of others.

Thus Bentham, after stating that an enlightened mind perceives the identity of self-interest and that of others (or of *egoism* and *altruism*, as these interests are now commonly called), goes on (*Deontology*, p. 201): "The majority do not have sufficient enlightenment, nor enough moral feeling so that their character goes beyond the aid of laws, and so the legislator should supplement the frailty of this natural interest, in adding to it an artificial interest more appreciable and more continuous. Thus the government augments and extends the connexion which exists between prudence and benevolence." Mill says (*Utilitarianism*, p. 323): "To do as you would be done by, and to love your neighbor as yourself, constitute the ideal perfection of utilitarian morality. As the means of making the nearest approach to this ideal, utility would enjoin, first, that laws and social arrangements should place the happiness or the interest of every individual as nearly as possible in harmony with the interest of the whole; and, secondly, that education and opinion, which have so vast a power over human character, should so use that power as to establish in the mind of every individual an indissoluble association between his own happiness and the good of the whole."

XXIII. Private Pleasures and General Welfare

In criticism of these indirect methods of establishing the identity of "egoism" and "altruism," it may be said:

1. That the supposed relation between the private and the general happiness is extrinsic, and hence always accidental and open to exception.

It is not contended that there is any order which *morally* demands that there be an identity of interests. It is simply argued that there are certain physical and psychological forces which operate, *as matter of fact*, to bring about such a result. Now we may admit, if we like, that such forces exist and that they are capable of accomplishing all that Bentham and Mill claim for them. But all that is established is, at most, a certain state of facts which is interesting as a state of facts, but which has no especial moral bearing. It is not pretended that there is in the very order of things any necessary and intrinsic connection between the happiness of one and of another. Such identity as exists, therefore, must be a mere external result of the action of certain forces. It is accidental. This being the case, how can it constitute the universal ideal of action? Why is it not open for an agent, under exceptional circumstances, to act for his own pleasure, to the exclusion of that of others? We may admit that, upon the whole (or that always, though this is wholly impossible to prove) in past experience, personal pleasure has been best attained by a certain regard for the pleasures of others; but the connection being wholly empirical (that is, of past instances and not of an intrinsic law), we may ask how it can be claimed that the same connection is *certain* to hold in this new case? Nor is it probable that any one would claim that the connection between individual pleasure and general pleasure had been so universal and invariable in past experience.

Intrinsic moral considerations (that is, those based on the very nature of human action) being put aside, a pretty strong case could be made out for the statement that individual happiness is best attained by ignoring the happiness of others. Probably the most that can be established on the other side is that a due prudence dictates that *some* attention be paid to the pleasures of others, in calculating one's own pleasures.

And this suggests:

2. That the end is still private pleasure, general pleasure being simply a means. Granting all that the hedonists urge, what their arguments prove is not that the general pleasure is the end of action, but that, private pleasure being the end, regard for the pleasures of others is one of the most efficient means of reaching it. If private pleasure is a selfish end, the end is not less selfish because the road to it happens to bring pleasure to others also.

See Royce, *Religious Aspect of Philosophy*, pp. 61–74.

3. The use of education and law to bring about this identity, presupposes that we already have the *ideal* of the

identity as something desirable to realize—it takes for granted the very thing to be proved. Why should it occur to men to use the private influence of opinion and education, and the public influences of law and penalty to identify private welfare with public, unless they were already convinced that general welfare was the end of conduct, the one desirable thing? What the hedonist has to do is to show how, from the end of private happiness, we may get to the end of general happiness. What Bentham and Mill do show is, that if we take general happiness as the end, we may and do use education and law to bring about an identity of personal and general pleasures. This may go undoubted, but the question how we get the general happiness as the end, the good, remains unanswered.

Nor is this all. The conception of general happiness, taken by itself, has all the abstractness, vagueness and uncertainty of that of personal happiness, multiplied indefinitely by the greater number of persons introduced. To calculate the effects of actions upon the general happiness—when happiness is interpreted as a state of feeling—is an impossibility. And thus it is that when one is speaking of pleasures one is really thinking of welfare, or well-being, or satisfied and progressive human lives. Happiness is considered as it would be, if determined by certain active and well defined interests, and thus the hedonistic theory, while contradicting itself, gets apparently all the support of an opposed theory. Universalistic hedonism thus, more or less expressly, takes for granted a social order, or community of persons, of which the agent is simply one member like any other. This is the ideal which it proposes to realize. In this way—although at the cost of logical suicide—the ideal gets a content and a definiteness upon which it is possible to base judgments.

That this social organization of persons is the ideal which Mill is actually thinking of, rather than any succession of states of agreeable sensation, is evident by his treatment of the whole subject. Mill is quite clear that education and opinion may produce *any* sort of feeling, as well as truly benevolent motives to actions. For example, in his critique of Whewell, he says, (*Dissertations*, Vol. III, p. 154): "All experience shows that the moral feelings are preëminently artificial, and the products of culture; that even when reasonable, they are no more spontaneous than the growth of corn and wine (which are quite as natural), and that the most senseless and pernicious feeling can as easily be raised to the utmost intensity by inculcation, as hemlock and thistles could be reared to luxuriant growth by sowing them instead of wheat." It is certainly implied here that legislation, education and public opinion must have as a presupposed standard the identity of general and private interests or else they may produce anything whatever. That is to say, Mill instead of arriving at his result of general happiness simply takes it for granted.

This fact and the further fact that he virtually defines happiness through certain objective interests and ends (thus reversing the true hedonistic position) is obvious from the following, (Mill, *Utilitarianism*, pp. 343–47): After again stating that the moral feelings are capable of cultivation in almost any direction, and stating that moral associations that are of artificial construction dissolve through the force of intellectual analysis (*cf.* his *Autobiography*, p. 136), and that the association of pleasure with the feeling of duty would similarly dissolve unless it had a *natural* basis of sentiment, he goes on: "But there is this basis of powerful *natural* sentiment. This firm foundation is that of the social feelings of mankind; the desire to be in unity with our fellow-creatures. *The social state is at once so natural, so necessary, and so habitual to man that except in some unusual circumstances, or by an effort of voluntary abstraction he never conceives of himself otherwise than as a member of a body.* Any condition, therefore, which is essential to a state of society becomes more and more an inseparable part of every person's conception of the state of things which he is born into, and which is the destiny of a human being." Mill then goes on to describe some of the ways in which the social unity manifests itself and influences the individual's conduct. Then the latter "comes, as though instinctively, to be conscious of himself as a being who *of course* pays regard to others. The good of others becomes to him a thing naturally and necessarily to be attended to, like any of the physical conditions of our existence. *The deeply-rooted conception which every individual even now has of himself as a social being tends to make him feel it as one of his natural wants, that there should be harmony between his feelings and aims and those of his fellow-creatures.* This conviction is the ultimate sanction of the greatest happiness morality."

It is to be noticed that there are involved in this account three ideas, any one of which involves such a reconstruction of the pleasure theory as to be a surrender of hedonism.

1. There is, in one instance, a *natural* (or intrinsic) connection between the end of conduct and the feelings, and not simply an external or artificial bond. This is in the case

of the social feelings. In other words, in one case the ideal, that is, happiness, is intrinsically, or necessarily connected with a certain kind of conduct, that flowing from the social impulses. This, of course, reverses hedonism for it makes happiness dependent upon a certain kind of conduct, instead of determining the nature of conduct according as it happens to result in pleasure or pain.

2. Man conceives of himself, of his end or of his destiny as a member of a social body, and this conception determines the nature of his wants and aims. That is to say, it is not mere happiness that a man wants, but a certain *kind* of happiness, that which would satisfy a man who conceived of himself as social, or having ends and interests in common with others.

3. Finally, it is not mere general "happiness" which is the end, at all. It is social unity; "harmony of feelings and aims," a beneficial condition for one's self in which the benefits of all are included. Instead of the essentially vague idea of states of pleasurable sensation we have the conception of a community of interests and ends, in securing which alone is true happiness to be found. This conception of the moral ideal we regard as essentially true, but it is not hedonism. It gives up wholly the notion that pleasure is the *desired*, and, since it sets up a standard by which it determines pleasure, it gives up equally the notion that pleasure as such is the *desirable*.

In addition to the works already referred to, the following will give fuller ideas of hedonism and utilitarianism: For historical treatment see Sidgwick, *History of Ethics*; Jodl, *Geschichte der Ethik*, Vol. II, pp. 432–68; Bain, *Moral Science*, [Historical Mention]; Guyau, *La Morale Anglaise Contemporaine*; Wallace, *Epicureanism*; Pater, *Marius, the Epicurean*; Paley, *Moral and Political Philosophy*; Grote, *Examination of the Utilitarian Philosophy* (especially fair and valuable criticism); Lecky, *History of European Morals*, Vol. I, Ch. 1; Birks, *Utilitarianism* (hostile); Blackie, *Four Phases of Morals*, essay on "Utilitarianism" (hostile); Gizycki, *Students' Manual of Ethical Philosophy* (Coit's trans., favorable); Calderwood, *Handbook of Moral Philosophy* (opposed); Laurie, *Ethica* (*e.g.*, p. 37). "The object of will is not pleasure, not yet happiness, but reason-given law—the law of harmony; but this necessarily ascertained through feeling, and, therefore, through happiness."

Wilson and Fowler, *Principles of Morals*, Vol. I, pp. 98–112; Vol. II, pp. 262–73; Paulsen, *System der Ethik*, pp. 195–210.

XXIV. The Utilitarian Theory Combined With the Doctrine of Evolution

There has lately been an attempt to combine utilitarian morality with the theory of evolution. This position, chiefly as occupied by Herbert Spencer and Leslie Stephen, we shall now examine.

Alexander, also, *Moral Order and Progress*, makes large use of the theory of evolution, but does not attempt to unite it with any form of hedonism.

For the combination, at least three decided advantages are claimed over ordinary utilitarianism.

1. It transforms "empirical rules" into "rational laws." The evolutionary hedonists regard pleasure as the good, but hold that the theory of evolution enables them to judge *of the relation of acts to pleasure* much better than the ordinary theory. As Mr. Spencer puts it, the ordinary theory is not scientific, because it does not fully recognize the principle of causation as existing between certain acts as causes, and pleasures (or pains) as effects. It undoubtedly recognizes that some acts *do* result in pain or pleasure, but does not show *how* or *why* they so result. By the aid of the theory of evolution we can demonstrate that certain acts *must* be beneficial because furthering evolution, and others painful because retarding it.

Spencer, *Data of Ethics*, pp. 57–58. "Morality properly so-called—the science of right conduct—has for its object to determine *how* and *why* certain rules of conduct are detrimental, and certain other rules beneficial. Those good and bad results cannot be accidental, but must be necessary consequences of the constitution of things; and I conceive it to be the business of moral science to *deduce*, *from the laws of life and the conditions of existence*, what kinds of action *necessarily* tend to produce happiness, and what kinds to produce unhappiness. Having done this, its deductions are to be recognized as laws of conduct; and are to be conformed to irrespective of a direct estimation of happiness or misery. . . . The objection which I have to the current utilitarianism is, that it recognizes no more developed form of utility—does not see that it has reached but the initial stage of moral science. . . . It is supposed that in future, as now, utility is to be determined only by observation of results; and that there is no possibility of knowing by deduction from fundamental principles what conduct *must* be detrimental and what conduct *must* be beneficial." *Cf.* also Ch. 9, and Stephen, *Science of Ethics*, Ch. 9.

It is contended, then, that by the use of the evolutionary theory, we may substitute certain conditions, which in the very nature of things tend to produce happiness, for a calculation, based upon observation of more or less varying cases in the past, of the probable results of the specific action. Thus we get a fixed objective standard and do away with all the objections based upon the uncertainty, vagueness and liability to exceptions, of the ordinary utilitarian morality.

Spencer, *Data of Ethics*, p. 162: "When alleging that empirical utilitarianism is but introductory to rational utilitarianism I pointed out that the last does not take welfare for its *immediate* object of pursuit, but takes for its immediate object of pursuit conformity to certain principles which, in the nature of things, causally determine welfare."

2. It reconciles "intuitionalism" with "empiricism." The theory of evolution not only gives us an objective standard on which happiness necessarily depends, and from which we may derive our laws of conduct, instead of deriving them from observation of particular cases, but it enables us to recognize that there are certain moral ideas now innate or intuitive. The whole human race, the whole animal race, has for an indefinite time been undergoing experiences of what leads to pleasure and of what leads to pain, until finally the results of these experiences have become organized into our very physical and mental make-up. The first point was that we could substitute for consideration of results consideration of the causes which determine these results; the present point is that so far as we have to use results, we can use those of the race, instead of the short span of the individual's life.

Spencer, *Data of Ethics*, pp. 123–24. "The experiences of utility organized and consolidated through all past generations of the human race have been producing corresponding nervous modifications, which, by continued transmission and accumulation, have become in us certain faculties of moral intuition—certain emotions corresponding to right and wrong conduct, which have no apparent basis in the individual experiences of utility. . . . The evolution hypothesis thus enables us to reconcile opposed moral theories. . . . The doctrine of innate powers of moral perception become congruous with the utilitarian doctrine, when it is seen that preferences and aversions are rendered organic by inheritance of the effects of pleasurable and painful experiences in progenitors."

3. It reconciles "egoism" with "altruism." As we have seen, the relation of personal pleasure to general happiness presents very serious difficulties to hedonism. It is claimed, however, that the very process of evolution necessitates a certain identity. The being which survives must be the being which has properly adapted himself to his environment, which is largely social, and there is assurance that the conduct will be adapted to the environment just in the degree in which pleasure is taken in acts which concern the welfare of others. If an agent has no pleasure in such acts he will either not perform them, or perform them only occasionally, and thus will not meet the conditions of surviving. If surrounding conditions demand constantly certain actions, those actions in time must come to be pleasurable. The conditions of survival demand altruistic action, and hence such action must become pleasurable to the agent (and in that sense egotistic).

"From the laws of life (Spencer, *Data of Ethics*, p. 250) it must be concluded that unceasing social discipline will so mould human action, that eventually sympathetic pleasures will be pursued to the fullest extent advantageous to each and all. . . . Though pleasure may be gained by giving pleasure, yet the thought of the sympathetic pleasure to be gained will not occupy consciousness, but only the thought of the pleasure given."

XXV. Criticism of Evolutionary Utilitarianism

Regarding the whole foregoing scheme, it may be said so far as it is true, or suggestive of truth, it is not hedonistic. It does not judge actions from their effects in the way of pleasure or pain, but it judges pleasures from the basis of an independent standard "in the nature of things." It is expressly declared that happiness is not to be so much the end, as the *test* of conduct, and it is not happiness in general, of every sort and kind, but a certain kind of happiness, happiness conditioned by certain modes of activity, that is the test. Spencer's hedonism in its final result hardly comes to more than saying that in the case of a perfect individual in a perfect society, every action whatever would be accompanied by pleasure, and that, therefore, *in such a society*, pleasure would be an infallible sign and test of the morality of action—a position which is not denied by any ethical writer whatever, unless a few extreme ascetics. Such a position simply determines the value of pleasure by an independent criterion, and then goes on to say *of pleasure so determined*, that it is the test of the morality of action. This may be true, but, true or not, it is not hedonistic.

Furthermore, this standard by which the nature of pleasure is determined is itself an ethical (that is, active) standard. We have already seen that Spencer conceives that the modes of producing happiness are to be deduced from the "laws of life and the conditions of existence." This might be, of course, a deduction from *physical* laws and conditions. But when we find that the laws and conditions which Spencer employs are mainly those of *social* life, it is difficult to see why he is not employing a strictly ethical standard. To deduce not right actions directly from happiness, but the kinds of actions which will produce happiness from a consideration of a certain ideal of social relationships seems like a reversal of hedonism; but this is what Mr. Spencer does.

XXVI. The Real Criterion of Evolutionary Ethics

Mr. Spencer expressly recognizes that there exists

1. An ideal code of conduct, formulating the conduct of the completely adapted man in the completely evolved society. Such a code is called absolute ethics as distinguished from relative ethics—a code the injunctions of which are alone to be considered "as absolutely right, in contrast with those that are relatively right or least wrong, and which, as a system of ideal conduct, is to serve as a standard for our guidance in solving, as well as we can, the problems of real conduct" (p. 275 of the *Data of Ethics*). "The ideal code deals, it will be observed, with the behavior of the completely adapted man in a completely evolved society." This ideal as elsewhere stated, is "an ideal social being so constituted that his spontaneous activities are congruous with the conditions imposed by the social environment formed by other such beings. . . . The ultimate man is one in whom there is a correspondence between all the promptings of his nature and all the requirements of his life as carried on in society" (p. 275). Furthermore, "to make the ideal man serve as a standard, he has to be defined *in terms of the conditions which his nature fulfill*—in terms of the objective requisites which must be met before conduct can be right" (p. 279). "Hence it is manifest that we must consider the ideal man as existing in the ideal social state" (p. 280).

Here we have in the most express terms the recognition of a final and permanent standard with reference to which the nature of happiness is determined, and the standard is one of social relationships. To be sure it is claimed that the standard is one which results in greatest happiness, but every ethical theory has always claimed that the ideal moral condition would be accompanied by the maximum possible happiness.

2. The ideal state is defined with reference to the end of evolution. That is, Spencer defines pleasure from an independent standard instead of using pleasure as the standard. This standard is to be got at by considering that idea of "fully evolved conduct" given by the theory of evolution. This fully evolved conduct implies: (*i.*) Greatest possible quantity of life, both in length and breadth; (*ii.*) Similar maintenance of life in progeny; and (*iii.*) Life in which there is no interference of actions by one with those of another, and, indeed, life in which the "members of a society give material help in the achievement of ends," thus rendering the "lives of all more complete." (See Ch. 2 of *Data of Ethics*.) Furthermore, the "complete life here identified with the ideally moral life" may be otherwise defined as a life of perfect equilibrium (p. 74), or balance of func-

tions (p. 90), and this considered not simply with reference to the individual, but also with reference to the relation of the individual to society. "Complete life in a complete society is but another name for complete equilibrium between the co-ordinated activities of each social unit and those of the aggregate of units" (*Data of Ethics*, p. 74, and the whole of Ch. 5. See also pp. 169–70 for the position that the end is a society in which each individual has full functions freely exercised in due harmony, and is, p. 100, "the spontaneous exercise of duly proportioned faculties").

3. Not only is pleasure thus determined by an objective standard of "complete living in a complete society" but it is expressly recognized that *as things are now, pleasure is not a perfect guide to, or even test of action.* And this difficulty is thought to be removed by reference to the ideal state in which right action and happiness will fully coincide.

The failure of pleasure as a perfect test and guide of right conduct, comes out in at least three cases: –

1. There is the conflict of one set of pleasures with another, or of present happiness with future, one lot having to be surrendered for the sake of another. This is wrong, since pleasure as such is good, and, although a fact at present, exists only on account of the incomplete development of society. When there is "complete adjustment of humanity to the social state there will be recognition of the truth that actions are completely right only when, besides being conducive to future happiness, special and general, they are immediately pleasurable, and that painfulness, not only ultimate but proximate, is the concomitant of actions which are wrong" (*Data of Ethics*, p. 99. See for various cases in which "pleasures are not connected with actions which must be performed" and for the statement that this difficulty will be removed in an ideal state of society, p. 77; pp. 85–87; pp. 98–99).

2. There is also, at present, a conflict of individual happiness with social welfare. In the first place, as long as there exist antagonistic societies, the individual is called upon to sacrifice his own happiness to that of others, but "such moralities are, by their definition, shown to belong to incomplete conduct; not to conduct that is fully evolved"

(see *Data of Ethics*, pp. 133–37). Furthermore, there will be conflict of claims, and consequent compromises between one's own pleasure and that of others (p. 148), until there is a society in which there is "complete living through voluntary co-operation," this implying negatively that one shall not interfere with another and shall fulfill contracts, and positively that men shall spontaneously help to aid one another lives beyond any specified agreement (pp. 146–49).

3. There is, at present, a conflict of obligation with pleasure. Needed activities, in other words, have often to be performed under a pressure, which either lessens the pleasure of the action, or brings pain, the act being performed, however, to avoid a greater pain (so that this point really comes under the first head). But "the remoulding of human nature into fitness for the requirements of social life, must eventually make all needful activities pleasurable, while it makes displeasurable all activities at variance with these requirements" (*Data of Ethics*, p. 183). "The things now done with dislike, through sense of obligation, will be done then with immediate liking" (p. 184, and p. 186; and pp. 255–56). All the quotations on these various points are simply so many recognitions that pleasure and pain as such are not tests of morality, but that they become so when morality is independently realized. Pleasure is *not* now a test of conduct, but becomes such a test as fast as activity becomes full and complete! What is this but to admit (what was claimed in Sec. XIII) that activity itself is what man wants; not *mere* activity, but the activity which belongs to man as man, and which therefore has for its realized content all man's practical relationships.

Of Spencer's conception of the ideal as something not now realized, but to be some time or other realized once for all, we have said nothing. But see below, Sec. LXIV, and also Alexander, *Moral Order*, pp. 264–77, and also James, *Unitarian Review*, Vol. XXII, pp. 212–13.

We have attempted, above, to deal with evolutionary ethics only in the one point of its supposed connection with pleasure as a standard. Accounts and criticisms of a broader scope will be found in Darwin, *Descent of Man*; Martineau, *Types of Ethical Theory*, Vol. II, pp. 335–93; Schurman, *Ethical Import of Darwinism*; Sorley, *Ethics of Naturalism*, Chs. 5, and 6; Stephen, *Science of Ethics*, particularly pp. 31–34, 78–89, 359–79; Royce, *Religious Aspect of Philosophy*, pp. 74–85; Everett, *Poetry, Comedy and Duty*, essay on the "New Ethics"; Seth in *Mind*, Jan. 1889, on "Evolution of Morality"; Dewey, *Andover Review*, Vol. VII, p. 573 [*Early Works* I, 205]; Hyslop, *Andover Review*, Vol. IX, p. 348.

XXVII. Formal Ethics

We come now to the ethical theories which attempt to find the good not only in the will itself, but in the will irrespective of any end to be reached by the will. The typical instance of such theories is the Kantian, and we shall, therefore, make that the basis of our examination. Kant's theory, however, is primarily a theory not of the good, but of the nature of duty, and that makes a statement of his doctrine somewhat more difficult.

"The concept of good and evil must not be determined before the moral law (of which it seems as if it must be the foundation), but only after it and by means of it" (Kant's *Theory of Ethics*, Abbott's trans., p. 154).

Separating, as far as we can, his theory of the good from that of duty, we get the following results:

1. Goodness belongs to the will, and to that alone. "Nothing can possibly be conceived, in the world or out of it, which can be called good without qualification except a good will." The will is not good because of what it brings about, or what it is fitted to bring about; that is, it is not good on account of its adaptation to any end outside of itself. It is good in itself. "It is like a jewel which shines by its own light, having its whole value in itself."

2. The good, then, is not to be found in any *object* of will or of desire, nor in the will *so far as it is directed towards an end outside itself*. For the will to be moved by inclination or by desire is for it to be moved for the sake of some external end, which, moreover, is always pleasure (Kant, *i.e.*, agrees with the hedonists regarding the object of desire, but on that very ground denies that pleasure is the good or the desirable). If, then, no object of desire can be the motive of a good will, what is its motive? Evidently only some principle derived from the will itself. The good will is the will which acts from regard to its own law.

3. What is the nature of this law? All objects of desire (*i.e.*, all material) have been excluded from it. It must, therefore, be purely formal. The only content of the law of the good will is the *idea of law itself*. The good will acts from reverences for law *as law*. It not only acts *in conformity with law*, but has the conception of law as its directing spring.

4. There must, however, be some application of this motive of law in general to particular motives or acts. This is secured as follows: The idea of law carries with it the idea of universality or self-identity. To act from the idea of law is then so to act that the motive of action can be generalized—made a motive for all conduct. The good will is the *legislative* will; the will whose motive can be made a law for conduct universally. The question in a specific case is then: Can your motive here be made universal, *i.e.*, a law? If the action is bad, determined by an object of desire, it will be contingent and variable, since pleasures are different to different persons and to the same person from moment to moment. The will is good, then, when its motive (or maxim) is to be found solely in the *legislative form* of the action, or in its fitness to be generalized into a universal principle of conduct, and the law of the good will is: "Act so that the maxim of thy will can always at the same time hold good as a principle of universal legislation" (*Kant's Theory of Ethics*, Abbott's trans., p. 119; also p. 55).

5. The application may be illustrated by the following cases:

a] Some one, wearied by what he conceives to be the entire misery of life proposes to commit suicide, but he asks himself whether this maxim based on the principle of self-love could become a universal law of nature; and "we see at once that a system of nature in which the very feeling, whose office is to compel men to the preservation of life, should lead men by a universal law to death, cannot be conceived without contradiction." That is to say, the principle of the motive which would lead a man to suicide cannot be generalized without becoming contradictory—it cannot be made a law universal.

b] An individual wishes to borrow money which he

knows that he cannot repay. Can the maxim of this act be universalized? Evidently not: "a system of nature in which it should be a universal law to promise without performing, for the sake of private good, would contradict itself, for then no one would believe the promise—the promise itself would become impossible as well as the end it had in view."

c] A man finds that he has certain powers, but is disinclined to develop them. Can he make the maxim of such conduct a universal law? He cannot *will* that it should become universal. "As a rational being, he must will that his faculties be developed."

d] A prosperous individual is disinclined to relieve the misery of others. Can his maxim be generalized? "It is impossible to *will* that such a principle should have the universal validity of a law of nature. For a will which resolved this would contradict itself, in as much as many cases might occur in which one would have need of the love and sympathy of others, and in which, by such a law of nature, sprung from his own will, he would deprive himself of all hope of the aid he desires."

In conclusion, then, the good is the good will itself, and the will is good in virtue of the bare form of its action, independently of all special material willed.

See *Kant's Theory of Ethics*, Abbott's trans., pp. 9–46, 105–20. Caird's *Critical Philosophy of Kant*, Vol. II, pp. 171–81, 209–12.

XXVIII. Relation of This Theory to Hedonism

The Kantian theory, as already noticed, agrees in its psychology with hedonism. It holds that pleasures are the objects of desire. But it reverses the conclusion which hedonism draws from this fact *as to the desirable*. Since pleasures are the object of desire, and pleasures can give no law, no universality to action, the end of action must be found wholly *outside* the pleasures, and wholly outside the desires. It can be found only in the bare law of the will itself.

1. Hedonism finds the end of conduct, or the desirable, wholly determined by the various particular desires which a man happens to have; Kantianism holds that to discover the end of conduct, we must wholly exclude the desires.

2. Hedonism holds that the rightness of conduct is determined wholly by its consequences; Kantianism holds that the consequences have nothing to do with the rightness of an act, but that it is decided wholly by the motive of the act.

From this contrast, we may anticipate both our criticism of the Kantian theory and our conception of the true end of action. The fundamental error of hedonism and Kantianism is the same—the supposition that desires are for pleasure only. Let it be recognized that desires are for objects conceived as satisfying or developing the self, and that pleasure is incidental to this fulfillment of the capacities of self, and we have the means of escaping the one-sidedness of Kantianism as well as of hedonism. We can see that the end is neither the procuring of particular pleasures through the various desires, nor action from the mere idea of abstract law in general, but that it is the *satisfaction of desires according to law*. The desire in its particular character does not give the law; this, as we saw in our criticism of hedonism, is to take away all law from conduct and to leave us at the mercy of our chance desires as they come and go. On the other hand the law is not something wholly apart from the desires. This, as we shall see, is equally to deprive us of a law capable of governing conduct. The law is the law of the desires themselves—the harmony and adjustment of desires necessary to make them instruments in fulfilling the special destiny or business of the agent.

From the same point of view we can see that the criterion is found neither in the consequences of our acts as *pleasures*, nor *apart from consequences*. It is found indeed in the consequences of acts, *but in their complete consequences*:—those upon the agent and society, as helping or hindering them in fulfillment of their respective functions.

XXIX. Criticism of Kantian Criterion of Conduct

1. *With reference to the unification of the conduct of the individual.* Of pleasure as the object of desire, we need

now say nothing further, but may proceed at once to the criticism of the theory that the will, acting according to the mere idea of law in general, is the end of man and hence that it is the criterion of the rightness or wrongness of his acts. We shall attempt to show that such an end is wholly empty, and that it fails (as much as hedonism) to unify conduct or to place any specific act as to its morality.

The difficulty of the end proposed by Kant is that it is an abstraction; that it is remote. The hedonist leaves out one element from conduct, and takes into account the merely particular or individualistic side; the Kantian abstracts the opposite element—the merely universal. The formal universal, or universal stripped of all particular content, has, considered as an end of action, at least three defects.

a] It is an end which would make impossible that very conduct of which it is taken to be the end—that is, moral conduct. In denying that pleasure is the end of action, we took pains to show that it (or rather the feeling due to the tension between pleasure of a state considered better and the pain of the experienced worse state) is a necessary element in the force impelling to action. The mere conception of an end is purely intellectual; there is nothing in it to move to action. It must be *felt* as valuable, as worth having, and as more valuable than the present condition before it can induce to action. It must *interest*, in a word, and thus excite desire. But if feeling is, as Kant declares, to be excluded from the motive to action, because it is pathological or related to pleasure as the object of desire, how can there be any force moving to action? The mind seems to be set over against a purely theoretical idea of an end, with nothing to connect the mind with the end. Unless the end interests, unless it arouses emotion, why should the agent ever aim at it? And if the law does excite feeling or desire, must not this, on Kant's theory, be desire for pleasure and thus vitiate the morality of the act? We seem to be in a dilemma, one side of which makes moral action impossible by taking away all inducing force, while the other makes it impossible by introducing an immoral factor into the motive.

Kant attempts to escape from this difficulty by claiming that there is one feeling which is rational, and not sensuous in quality, being excited not by the conception of pleasure or pain, but by that of the moral law itself. This is the feeling of reverence, and through this feeling we can be moved to moral action. Waiving the question whether the mere idea of law in general would be capable of arousing any moral sentiment—or, putting the matter from the other side, whether Kant gives us a true account of the feeling of reverence—it is clear that this admission is fatal to Kant's theory. If desire or feeling as such is sensuous (or *pathological*, as Kant terms it), what right have we to make this one exception? And if we can make this one exception, why not others? If it is possible in the case of reverence, why not in the case, say, of patriotism, or of friendship, or of philanthropy, or of love—or even of curiosity, or of indignation, or of desire for approbation? Kant's separation of reverence, as the one moral sentiment from all others as pathological, is wholly arbitrary. The only distinction we can draw is of the feelings as they well up naturally in reaction upon stimuli, sentiments not conceived and thus neither moral nor immoral, and sentiments as transformed by ends of action, in which case all without exception may be moral or immoral, according to the character of the end. The Kantian separation is not only arbitrary psychologically, but is false historically. So far is it from true that the only moral sentiment is reverence for law, that men must have been moved toward action for centuries by motives of love and hate and social regard, before they became capable of such an abstract feeling as reverence. And it may be questioned whether this feeling, as Kant treats it, is even the highest or ultimate form of moral sentiment—whether it is not transitional to love, in which there is complete union of the individual interest on one hand, and the objective end on the other.

For these criticisms at greater length, see Caird, *Critical Philosophy of Kant*, Vol. II, Bk. II, Ch. 4.

b] The Kantian end would not bring about any system in conduct—on the contrary, it would tend to differences and collisions. What is required to give unity to the sphere of conduct is, as we have seen, a principle which shall comprehend all the motives to action, giving each its due place in contributing to the whole—a universal which shall organize the various particular acts into a harmonious system. Now Kant's conception of the good does not lead to such result. We may even say that it makes it impossible. According to Kant each act must be considered independently of every other, and must be capable of generalization on its own account. Each motive of action must be capable of being *itself* a universal law of nature. Each particular rule of action is thus made absolute, and we are left not with one universal which comprehends all particulars in their relations to one another, but literally with a lot of universals. These not only fail to have a unity, but each, as absolute, must contradict some other. If the principles always to tell the truth and always to preserve life are universal *in themselves*, and not universal simply *through their relation to some total and controlling principle of life*, it must be impossible to reconcile them when they come into conflict.

See Caird, *Critical Philosophy of Kant*, Vol. II, pp. 187–90, and p. 215. *Cf.* "Treated as universal and without exception, even two such commands, as *e.g.*, 'Thou shalt not steal,' and 'Thou shalt not kill,' must ultimately come into conflict with each other; for, if all other interests are to be postponed to the maintenance of the rights of property, it is impossible that all other interests should also be postponed to the preservation of human life—and to make either property or life an absolute end is to raise a particular into a universal, to treat a part as if it were a whole. But the true moral vindication of each particular interest cannot be found in elevating it into something universal and absolute, but only in determining its place in relation to the others in a complete system of morality."

c] The principle is so empty of all content that it does not enable us to judge of any specific act.

A caution should be noticed here, which is equally applicable to the criticism of hedonism: When it is said that the end does not enable us to judge of specific acts, the objection is not that the *theory* (Kantianism or hedonism, as the case may be) does not give us rules for moral conduct. It is not the business of any theory, however correct as a theory, to lay down rules for conduct. The theory has simply to discover what the *end* is, and it is the end in view which determines specific acts. It is no more the business of ethics to tell what in particular a man ought to do, than it is of trigonometry to survey land. But trigonometry must state the principles by which land *is* surveyed, and so ethics must state the end by which conduct *is* governed. The objection to hedonism and Kantianism is that the end they give does not *itself* stand in any practical relation to conduct. We do not object to Kantianism because the *theory* does not help us as to specific acts, but because the *end*, formal law, does not help us, while the real moral end must determine the whole of conduct.

Suppose a man thrown into the complex surroundings of life with an intelligence fully developed, but with no previous knowledge of right or wrong, or of the prevailing moral code. He is to know, however, that goodness is to be found in the good will, and that the good will is the will moved by the mere idea of the universality of law. Can we imagine such an one deriving from his knowledge any idea of what concrete ends he ought to pursue and what to avoid? He is surrounded by special circumstances calling for special acts, and all he knows is that *whatever* he does is to be done from respect for its universal or legislative quality. What community is there between this principle and *what* he is to do? There is no bridge from the mere thought of universal law to any concrete end coming under the law. There is no common principle out of which grows the conception of law on one hand, and of the various special ends of action, on the other.

Suppose, however, that ends are independently suggested or proposed, will the Kantian conception serve to *test* their moral fitness? Will the conception that the end must be capable of being generalized tell us whether this or that end is one to be followed? The fact is, that there is no end whatever that *in* or *by itself*, cannot be considered as self-identical, or as universal. If we presuppose a certain rule, or if we presuppose a certain moral order, it may be true that a given motive cannot be universalized without coming into conflict with this presupposed rule or order. But aside from some moral system into connection with which a proposed end may be brought, for purposes of comparison, lying is just as capable as truth-telling of generalization. There is no more contradiction in the motive of universal stealing than there is in that of universal honesty—unless there is as standard some order or system of things into which the proposed action is to fit as a member. And this makes not the bare universality of the act, but the system, the real criterion for determining the morality of the act.

Thus Mill remarks, regarding Kant's four illustrations (*ante*, pp. 291–92), that Kant really has to employ utilitarian considerations to decide whether the act is moral or not.

For the foregoing criticisms, see Bradley, *Ethical Studies*, Essay IV; Caird, *Critical Philosophy of Kant*, Vol. II, pp. 185–86, and 212–14, and, indeed, the whole of Ch. 2 of Bk. II.

XXX. Criticism of Kantian Criterion of Conduct

2. *With reference to the furnishing of a common good or end.* If the Kantian end is so formal and empty as not to enable us to bring into relation with one another the various acts of one individual, we may agree, without argument, that it does not provide us with an end which shall unify the acts of different men into a connected order of conduct. The moral end, the acting from regard for law as law, is presented to each individual by himself, entirely apart from his relations to others. That he has such relations may, indeed, furnish additional material to which the law must be applied, but is something to which the character of the law is wholly indifferent. The end is not in itself a social end, and it is a mere accident if in any case social considerations have to be taken into account. It is of the very quality of the end that it appeals to the individual as an isolated individual.

It is interesting to note the way in which Kant, without expressly giving up the purely formal character of the moral end, gives it more and more content, and that content social. The moral law is not imposed by any external authority, but by the rational will itself. To be conscious of a universal self-imposed law is to be conscious of one's self as having a universal aspect. The source of the law and its end are both in the will—in the rational self. Thus man is an end to himself, for the rational self is man. Such a being is a person—"Rational beings are *persons*, because their nature marks them out as ends in themselves, *i.e.*, as beings who should never be used merely as means. . . . Such beings are not ends simply *for us*, whose existence as brought about by our action has value, but *objective ends*, *i.e.*, beings whose existence is an end in itself, an end for which no other end can be substituted so as to reduce it to a mere means." Thus, we get a second formula. "Always treat humanity, both in your own person and in the person of others, as an end and never merely as a means" (*Kant's Theory of Ethics*, Abbott's trans., pp. 46–47; Caird, *Critical Philosophy of Kant*, Vol. II, p. 219). Here the criterion of action is no longer the bare self-consistency of its motive, but its consistency with the rational nature of the agent, that which constitutes him a person. And, too, "the will of every rational being is likewise a universally law-giving will" (*Kant's Theory of Ethics*, Abbott, p. 49). The conception of humanity embodied in others as well as in one's self is introduced, and thus our criterion is socialized. Even now, however, we have a lot of persons, each of whom has to be considered as an end in himself, rather than a social unity as to which every individual has an equal and common reference. Kant advances to this latter idea in his notion of a "Kingdom of ends." "We get the idea of a complete and systematically connected totality of all ends—a whole system of rational beings as ends in themselves as well as of the special ends which each of them may set up for himself—*i.e.*, a kingdom of ends. . . . Morality is the reference of all deeds to the legislation which alone can make such a kingdom possible." (See *Kant's Theory of Ethics*, Abbott's trans., pp. 51–52.) This transformation of a mere formal universal into a society or kingdom of persons—while not sufficiently analyzed as Kant states it (see Caird, *Critical Philosophy of Kant*, Vol. II, pp. 225–26)—gives us truly a social criterion, and we shall hereafter meet something resembling it as the true ideal. As finally stated, it does not differ in essential content from Mill's individual who "conceives of himself only as a member of a body," or from Spencer's free man in a free society.

XXXI. Value of Kantian Theory

We must not leave the Kantian theory with the impression that it is simply the caprice of a philosopher's brain. In two respects, at least, it presents us, as we shall see, with elements that must be adopted; and even where false it is highly instructive.

Kant's fundamental error is in his conception that all desires or inclinations are for private pleasure, and are, therefore, to be excluded from the conception of the moral end. Kant's conclusion, accordingly, that the good will is purely formal follows inevitably if ever it is granted that there is any intrinsic opposition between inclination as such, and reason or moral law as such. If there is such an opposition, *all* desire must be excluded from relation to the end. We cannot make a compromise by distinguishing between higher and lower desires. On the contrary, if the end is to have content, it must include all desires, leaving out none as in itself base or unworthy. Kant's great negative service was showing that the ascetic principle logically results in pure formalism—meaning by ascetic principle that which disconnects inclinations from moral action.

Kant's positive service was, first, his clear insight into the fact that the good is to be found only in activity; that the will itself, and nothing beyond itself, is the end; and that to adopt any other doctrine, is to adopt an immoral principle, since it is to subordinate the will (character, self and personality), to some outside end. His second great service was in showing the necessity of putting in abeyance the immediate satisfaction of each desire as it happens to arise, and of subordinating it to some law not to be found in the particular desire. He showed that not the particular desire, but only the desire as controlled by the idea of law could be the motive of moral action. And if he fell into the error of holding that this meant that the desire must be excluded from the moral motive, this error does not make it less true that every particular desire must be controlled by a universal law. The truth of asceticism is that the desire must be checked until subordinated to the activity of the whole man. See Caird, *Critical Philosophy of Kant*, Vol. II, p. 200; pp. 203–7, 226–27.

XXXII. The Problem and Its Solution

If we gather together the results of our observations of hedonism and of Kantianism we get something like the following problem and solution in outline. The end of action, or the good, is the realized will, the developed or satisfied self. This satisfied self is found neither in the getting of a lot of pleasures through the satisfaction of desires just as they happen to arise, nor in obedience to law simply because it is law. It is found in *satisfaction of desires according to law*. This law, however, is not something external to the desires, but is their own law. Each desire is only one striving of character for larger action, and the only way in which it can really find satisfaction (that is, pass from inward striving into outward action) is *as* a manifestation of character. A desire, taken as a desire for its own apparent or direct end *only*, is an abstraction. It is a desire for an entire and continuous activity, and its satisfaction requires that it be fitted into this entire and continuous activity; that it be made conformable to the conditions which will bring the whole man into action. It is this fitting-in which is the law of the desire—the "universal" controlling its particular nature. This "fitting-in" is no mechanical shearing off, nor stretching out, but a reconstruction of the natural desire till it becomes an expression of the whole man. The problem then is to find that special form of character, of self, which includes and transforms all special desires. This form of character is at once the Good and the Law of man.

We cannot be content with the notion that the end is the satisfaction of the self, a satisfaction at once including and subordinating the ends of the particular desire. This tells us nothing positive—however valuable it may be negatively in warning us against one-sided notions—until we know *what* that whole self is, and *in what* concretely its satisfaction consists. As the first step towards such a more concrete formula, we may say:

XXXIII. The Moral End or the Good Is the Realization by a Person and as a Person of Individuality

In saying that this realization is *by a person* and *as a person* we are saying nothing new. We are simply repeating what we have already learned about moral conduct (Sec. III). Conduct is not that which simply reaches certain consequences—a bullet shot from a rifle does that; there is conduct only when the consequences are foreseen; made the reason of action. A person is a being capable of conduct—a being capable of proposing to himself ends and of attempting to realize them.

But what is the meaning of the rest of the formula? What do we mean by individuality? We may distinguish two factors—or better two aspects, two sides—in individuality. On one side, it means special disposition, temperament, gifts, bent, or inclination; on the other side, it means special station, situation, limitations, surroundings, opportunities, etc. Or, let us say, it means *specific capacity* and *specific environment*. Each of these elements, apart from the other, is a bare abstraction and without reality. Nor is it strictly correct to say that individuality is constituted by these two factors *together*. It is rather, as intimated above, that each is individuality looked at from a certain point of view, from within or from without.

If we are apt to identify individuality with the inner side alone, with capacity apart from its surroundings, a little reflection will show the error. Even the most devoted adherent of "self-culture" would not hold that a gift could be developed, or a disposition manifested, in isolation from all exterior circumstances. Let the disposition, the gift be what it may (amiable or irascible, a talent for music or for abstract science, or for engineering), its existence, to say nothing of its culture, apart from some surroundings is bare nonsense. If a person shuts himself up in a closet or goes out into the desert the better to cultivate his capacities, there is still the desert or the closet there; and it is as conditioned by them, and with reference to them that he must cultivate himself. For more is true than that, as a matter of fact, no man can wholly withdraw himself from surroundings; the important point is that the manner and the purpose of exercising his capacity is always *relative* to and *dependent* upon the surroundings. Apart from the environment the capacity is mere emptiness; the exercise of capacity is always establishing a relation to something exterior to itself. All we can say of capacity apart from environment is that *if* certain circumstances were supplied, there would be something there. We call a capacity *capability*, possibility, as if for the very purpose of emphasizing the necessity of external supplementing.

We get the same fact, on the other side, by calling to mind that circumstances, environment are not indifferent or irrelevant to individuality. The difference between one individual and another lies as much in the station in which each is placed as in the capacity of each. That is to say, environment enters into individuality as a constituent factor, helping make it what it is.

On the other hand, it is capacity which makes the environment really an environment *to* the individual.

The environment is not simply the facts which happen

objectively to lie about an agent; it is such part of the facts as may be *related* to the capacity and the disposition and gifts of the agent. Two members of the same family may have what, to the outward eye, are exactly the same surroundings, and yet each may draw from these surroundings wholly unlike stimulus, material and motives. Each has a different environment, made different by his own mode of selection; by the different way in which his interests and desires play upon the plastic material about him. It is not, then, the environment as physical of which we are speaking, but as it appeals to consciousness, as it is affected by the make-up of the agent. This is the *practical* or *moral* environment. The environment is not, then, what is then and there present in space. To the Christian martyr the sufferings of his master, and the rewards of faithfulness to come to himself were more real parts of his environment than the stake and fire. A Darwin or a Wallace may find his environment in South America or the Philippine Islands—or, indeed, in every fact of a certain sort wherever found upon the earth or in whatever geological era. A man of philanthropic instincts may find *his* environment among Indians or Congo negroes. Whatever, however near or remote in time and space, an individual's capacities and needs relate him to, is his environment. The moment we realize that only what one conceives as proper material for calling out and expressing some internal capacity is a part of his surroundings, we see not only that capacity depends upon environment, but that environment depends upon capacity. In other words, we see that each in itself is an abstraction, and that the real thing is the individual who is constituted by capacity and environment in their relation to one another.

Function is a term which we may use to express union of the two sides of individuality. The idea of function is that of an active relation established between power of doing, on one side, and something to be done on the other. To exercise a function as a student is not to cultivate tastes and possibilities internally; it is also to meet external demands, the demands of fact, of teachers, of others needing knowledge. The citizen exercises his function not simply in cultivating sentiments of patriotism within; one has to meet the needs of the city, the country in which one lives. The realization of an artistic function is not poring over emotions of beauty pumped up within one's self; it is the exercise of some calling. On the other hand, it hardly needs saying that the function of a student, a citizen, an artist, is not exercised in bare conformity to certain external requirements. Without the inner disposition and inclination, we call conduct dead, perfunctory, hypocritical. An activity is not functional, unless it is organic, expressing the life of the agent.

A function thus includes two sides—the external and the internal—and reduces them to elements in one activity. We get an analogy in any animal function. The digestive function includes the material appropriated, just as much as it does the organ appropriating. It is the service, the work which the organ does *in* appropriating material. So, morally, function is capacity *in action*; environment transformed into an element in personal service.

Thus we get another formula for the moral end:

The performance by a person of his specific function, this function consisting in an activity which realizes wants and powers with reference to their peculiar surroundings.

XXXIV. Moral Functions as Interests

If morality consists in the exercise of one's *specific* functions, it follows that no *detailed* account of the content of the moral end can possibly be given. This content is thoroughly individual or infinite. It is concrete to the core, including every detail of conduct, and this not in a rigid formula, but in the movement of life. All we can do is, by abstraction, to select some of the main features of the end, such as the more common and the more permanent. While each individual has his own particular functions, which can no more be exhausted by definition or description than the qualities of any other individual object, it is also true that we can recognize certain typical functions to be found permanently and in all. These make, as it were, the skeleton of the moral end which each clothes with his own flesh and blood.

Functions are *interests*—objective interests were not

the term tautological. Interests have three traits worth special mention.

1. They are *active*. An interest is not an emotion produced from without. It is the reaction of the emotion to the object. Interest is identified, in ordinary speech, with attention; we *take* an interest, or, if we say simply "interested," that involves some excitation, some action just beginning. We talk of a man's interests, meaning his occupations or range of activities.

2. They are *objective*. The emotion aroused goes out to some object, and is fixed upon that; we are always interested *in something*. The active element of interest is precisely that which takes it out of the inner mood itself and gives it a terminus, an end in an object.

3. An interest is *satisfaction*. It is its own reward. It is not a striving for something unrealized, or a mere condition of tension. It is the satisfaction in some object which the mind already has. This object may be possessed in some greater or less degree, in full realization or in faint grasp, but interest attaches to it as possessed. This differentiates it from desire, even where otherwise the states are the same. Desire refers to the lack, to what is not present to the mind. One state of mind may be called both interest in, and desire for, knowledge, but desire emphasizes the unknown, while interest is on account of the finding of self, of intelligence, in the object. Interest is the union in feeling, through action, of self and an object. An interest in life is had when a man can practically identify himself with some object lying beyond his immediate or already acquired self and thus be led to further expression of himself.

To have an interest, then, is to be alert, to have an object, and to find satisfaction in an activity which brings this object home to self.

Not every interest carries with it *complete* satisfaction. But no interest can be wholly thwarted. The purer the interest, the more the interest is in the object for its own sake, and not for that of some ulterior consequence, the more the interest fulfills itself. "It is better to have loved and lost than never to have loved at all," and love is simply the highest power of interest—interest freed from all extrinsic stuff.

Of the interests, two abstract forms may be recognized, interest in persons and interest in things. And these may be subdivided: Interest in persons: interest in *self* and *others*. Interest in things—into their contemplation (*knowledge*) and into their production (*art*). And art again may be either productive of things to be contemplated (fine art), or useful—manufactures, industry, etc. The moral end, then, or the Good will consist in the exercise of these interests, varied as they may be in each individual by the special turn which his capacities and opportunities take.

XXXV. The Exercise of Interests as the Moral End

Let us now, as a means of rendering our conception of the moral end more concrete, consider briefly each of the forms of interest.

1. *Interest in Self*

We must free ourselves from any notion that an interest in self is non-moral, if not actually immoral. The latter position is seldom consciously assumed, but it is not uncommon to have interest in self, under the name of prudence, marked off from the moral sphere. Interest in self, if the interest is pure, is just as much an interest in the moral end as interest in anything or anybody else. Interest in self may take the form of selfishness, or of sentimentalism; but this is only an *impure* interest, an interest not in self, but in some consequences to which the self may be directed. Interest in self may take many forms, according to the side of self which is the object of attention, and according to the range of the self taken into account. A *rudimentary* form is prudence, but even this, instead of being non-moral, is, in proper place and degree, moral, as moral as benevolence; and, if not in its proper place, immoral. From such an interest there are all stages up to the interest in self as it most deeply and broadly is, the sense of honor, moral dignity, self-respect, conscientiousness, that attempt to be and to make the most of one's self, which is at the very root of moral endeavor.

The ground that is usually given for making the distinction between Prudence, Self-Regard, Self-Love as non-moral, and Benevolence, Altruism, etc., as moral, is that in the former case a mere regard for one's own advantage dictates proper conduct, while in the latter case there must be a positive virtuous intent. We may, for example, be pointed to some cool calculating man who takes care of his health and his property, who indeed is generally "prudent," because he sees that it is for his advantage, and be told that while such an end is not immoral it is certainly not moral. But in return it must be asked what is meant here by advantage? If by it is meant private pleasure, or advantage over somebody else, then this conduct does not spring from interest in self at all, but from interest in some exterior consequence, and as springing from such an impure interest is not simply non-moral, but positively immoral. On the other hand, if "advantage" means regard for one's whole function, one's place in the moral order, then such interest in self is moral. Care for bodily health in the interest of efficiency in conduct is supremely moral beside reckless disregard of it in the interest of some supposed higher or more spiritual function.

If it is meant that conduct is immoral because it springs from some interest on the part of the agent, the reply is that all conduct must so arise, and that any other supposition leads us immediately into asceticism and into formalism.

2. *Interest in Others*

The generic form of interest in others is sympathy, this being specified by the various forms of social organization of which the individual is a member. A person is, we have seen, one who can conceive of ends and can act to realize these ends. Only a person, therefore, can conceive of others as ends, and so have true sympathy.

It is not meant, of course, that animals do not perform acts which, *de facto*, are altruistic or even self-sacrificing. What is meant is that the animal does not act from the *idea* of others of his kind as ends in themselves. If the animal does so act, it cannot be denied the name of person.

True interest in others is pure, or disinterested, in the sense of having no reference to some further and external consequence to one's self. Interest in others need not be moral (or pure) any more than interest in self is necessarily immoral (or impure). It is a mistake to distinguish interest in self as *egoistic* and interest in others as *altruistic*. Genuine interests, whatever their object, are both egoistic and altruistic. They are egoistic simply because they *are inter-*

ests—imply satisfaction in a realized end. If man is truly a social being, constituted by his relationships to others, then social action must inevitably realize himself, and be, in that sense, egoistic. And on the other hand, if the individual's interest in himself is in himself *as* a member of society, then such interest is thoroughly altruistic. In fact, the very idea of altruism is likely to carry a false impression when it is so much insisted upon, as it is nowadays in popular literature, as the essence of morality. The term as used seems to imply that the mere giving up of one's self to others, as others, is somehow moral. Just as there may be an immoral interest in self, so there may be an immoral "altruism." It is immoral in any case to sacrifice the actual relationships in the case, those which demand action, to some feeling outside themselves—as immoral when the feeling to which the sacrifice is offered up is labelled "benevolence," as when it is termed "greediness." It is no excuse when a man gives unwisely to a beggar that he feels benevolent. *Moral* benevolence is the feeling directed toward a certain end which is known to be the fit or right end, the end which expresses the situation. The question is as to the *aim* in giving. Apart from this aim, the act is simply relieving the agent's own feelings and has no moral quality. Rather it is immoral; for feelings do have a moral *capacity*, that is, a relation to ends of action, and hence to satisfy them on their account, to deprive them of their practical reference, is bad. Aside from what this illustrates, there is a tendency in the present emphasis of altruism to erect the principle of charity, in a sense which implies continued social inequality, and social slavery, or undue dependence of one upon another, into a fundamental moral principle. It is well to "do good" to others, but it is much better to do this by securing for them the freedom which makes it possible for them to get along in the future without such "altruism" from others. There is what has been well termed an "egotism of renunciation"; a desire to do for others which, at bottom, is simply an attempt to regulate their conduct. Much of altruism is an egoism of a larger radius, and its tendency is to "manufacture a gigantic self," as in the case where a father sacrifices everything for his children or a wife for her husband.

See Caird, *Critical Philosophy of Kant*, Vol. II, p. 402. See also Hinton, *The Law-Breaker*, pp. 287–88: "The real meaning of the difficulty about a word for 'regard for others' is that we do not want it. It would mislead us if we had it. It is not a regard for *others* that we need, but simply a *true* regard, a regard to the facts, to nature; it is only a truth to facts in our regard, and its nature is obscured by a reference to 'others,' as if that were the essential point. . . . It is not as being for others, but as being *true*, that the regard for others is demanded."

Some ethical writers have gone to the other extreme and held that all benevolence is a disguised or an enlightened selfishness, since having a necessary reference to self. The reference to self must be admitted; unless the action springs from an interest of the agent himself the act may be outwardly useful, but cannot be moral. But the argument alluded to inverts the true relation involved. If a man's interests are such that he can find satisfaction only in the satisfaction of others, what an absurdity to say that his acting from these interests is selfish! The very fact of such identity of self with others in his interest is the proof of his unselfishness.

See Leslie Stephen, *Science of Ethics*, p. 241, for an admirable discussion of this difficulty. When it is said that your pain is painful to me, he says, the inference is often "insinuated that I dislike your pain because it is painful to me in some special relation. I do not dislike it *as* your pain, but in virtue of some particular consequence, such, for example, as its making you less able to render me a service. In that case *I do not really object to your pain as your pain at all*, but only to some removable and accidental consequences." (And see his whole treatment of sympathy, pp. 230–45.) The whole question is shown to come to this: Is my interest in, my sympathy with, your joy and sorrow as such, or in your joy and sorrow as contributing to mine? If the latter, of course the interest is selfish, not being an interest in others at all. But if the former, then the fact that such sympathy involves one's own satisfaction is the best proof that man is not selfishly constructed. When Stephen goes on to say that such sympathy does not involve the existence of a real unity larger than the individual, he seems to me to misread his own facts, probably because he conceives of this unity as some abstract or external thing.

Discussion regarding self-love and benevolence, or, in modern phrase, egoism and altruism, has been rife in English ethics since the time of Hobbes, and especially of Shaftesbury and Butler. See, in particular, the *Sermons* of the latter, which gave the central point of discussion for almost a century. With reference to the special weakness of this point of view, with its co-ordination of two independent principles, see Green, *Philosophical Works*, Vol. III, pp. 99–104. The essential lack (the lack which we have tried to make good in the definition of individuality as the union of capacity and surroundings in function), was the failure to analyze the idea of the individual. Individuality being defined as an exclusive principle, the inevitable result was either (*i.*) the "disguised selfishness" theory; or (*ii.*) the assumption of two fundamentally different principles in man. The ordinary distinction between prudence and virtue is an echo of the latter theory. Then, finally, (*iii.*) a third principle, generally called conscience by Butler, was brought in as umpire in the conflict of prudence and virtue.

Suggestive modern treatment of the matter, from a variety of points of view, will be found in Spencer, *Data of Ethics*, Chs. 11–13; Stephen, *Science of Ethics*, Ch. 6; Sidgwick, *Methods of Ethics*, Bk. V, Ch. 7; Royce, *Religious Aspect of Philosophy*, Ch. 4; Sorley, *Ethics of Naturalism*, pp. 134–50; Alexander, *Moral Order*, pp. 172–80; Caird, *Critical Philosophy of Kant*, Vol. II, pp. 400–405; Paulsen, *System der Ethik*, pp. 295–311.

3. *Interest in Science and Art*

Man is interested in the world about him; the knowledge of the nature and relations of this world become one of his most absorbing pursuits. Man identifies himself with the meaning of this world to the point that he can be satisfied only as he spells out and reads its meaning. (See, for example, Browning's "Grammarian's Funeral.") The scientific interest is no less a controlling motive of man than the personal interest. This knowledge is not a means for having agreeable sensations; it is not dilettanteism or "love of culture"; it is interest in the large and goodly frame of things. And so it is with art; man has interests which can be satisfied only in the reconstruction of nature in the way of the useful and the beautiful.

I have made no distinction between "fine" and "useful" art. The discussion of this question does not belong here, but the rigid separation of them in æsthetic theory seems to me to have no justification. Both are products of intelligence in the service of interests, and the only difference is in the range of intelligence and interests concerned. "Use" is a *limited* service and hence implies an external end; beauty is complete use or service, and hence not mere use at all, but self-expression. Historically, all art which has not been merely sentimental and "literary" has sprung from interest in good workmanship in the realizing of an idea.

It seems as if here interests violated their general law, and, in the case of use at least, were an interest in some ulterior end. But it may be questioned whether a carpenter whose aim was consciously beyond the work he was doing, would be a good workman—and this whether the further end is his own private advantage, or social benefit at large. The thought of the further benefit to self and of the utility to accrue to some one else, will, if it becomes a *part* of what he is doing, undoubtedly intensify his interest—it must do so, for it enlarges its content. But to *identify* one's own or another's well-being with work, and to make the work a mere *means* to this welfare, are two quite different things. The good artisan "has his heart in his work." His self-respect makes it necessary for him to respect this technical or artistic capacity, and to do the best by it that he can without scrimping or lowering. To a good business man business is not the mere means to money-making; and it is sentimentalism (and hence immoral) to demand that it be a mere means to the good of society. The business, if it is a moral one (and *any* business, *so far* as it is thus carried on, is moral), is carried on for the sake of the activity itself, as a realizing of capacity in a specific situation.

XXXVI. The Moral Quality of Science

We seem, however, to meet here, in relation to science and art, a difficulty which threatens our whole theory. Can it be claimed, it may be asked, that devotion to science or art constitutes goodness in the same sense that devotion to the interests of one's family or state constitutes it? No one doubts that a good father or a good citizen is a good man, in so far forth. Are we ready to say that a good chemist or good carpenter, or good musician is, in so far, a good man? In a word, is there not a reference to the good of persons present in one case and absent in another, and does not its absence preclude the scientific and artistic activities from any share, *as such*, in the moral end?

It must be remembered that the moral end does not refer to some consequence which happens, *de facto*, to be reached. It refers to an end *willed*; *i.e.*, to an idea held to and realized as an idea. And this fact shows us the way to meet the query, in part at least. If, when we say good carpenter, or good merchant, we are speaking from the standpoint of results, independently of the idea conceived as end in the mind of the agent; if we mean simply, "we like what that man does," then the term good has no moral value. A man may paint "good" pictures and not be, in so far, a good man, but in this sense a man may *do* a great deal of "good," and yet not be a good man. It was agreed at the outset that moral goodness pertains to the kind of idea or end which a man clings to, and not to what he happens to effect visibly to others.

If a scientific man pursues truth as a mere means to reputation, to wealth, etc., we do not (or should not) hesitate to call him immoral.

This does not mean that if he *thinks* of the reputation, or of wealth, he is immoral, for he may foresee wealth and the reputation as necessarily bound up in what he is doing; it may become a part of the end. It means that if knowledge of truth is a *mere means* to an end beyond it, the man is immoral.

What reason is there why we should not call him moral if he does his work for its own sake, from interest in this cause which takes him outside his "own miserable individuality," in Mill's phrase? After all, the phrase a "good father" means but a character manifesting itself in certain relations, as is right according to these relations; the phrase has moral significance not in itself, but with reference to the end aimed at by character. And so it is with the phrase "a good carpenter." That also means devotion of character to certain outer relations for their own sake. These relations may not be so important, but that is not lack of moral meaning.

XXXVII. Adjustment to Environment

So far we have been discussing the moral ideal in terms of its inner side—capacity, interest. We shall now discuss it on its outer or objective side—as "adjustment to environment" in the phrase made familiar by the evolutionists. Certain cautions, however, must be noted in the use of the phrase. We must keep clearly in mind the relativity of environment to inner capacity; that it exists only as one element of function. Even a plant must do something more than adjust itself *to* a fixed environment; it must assert itself *against* its surroundings, subordinating them and transforming them into material and nutriment; and, on the surface of things, it is evident that *transformation* of existing circumstances is moral duty rather than mere reproduction of them. The environment must be plastic to the ends of the agent.

But admitting that environment is made what it is by the powers and aims of the agent, what sense shall we attribute to the term adjustment? Not bare conformity to circumstances, nor bare external reproduction of them, even when circumstances are taken in their proper moral meaning. The child in the family who simply adjusts himself *to* his relationships in the family, may be living a moral life only in outward seeming. The citizen of the state may transgress no laws of the state, he may punctiliously fulfill every contract, and yet be a selfish man. True adjustment must consist in *willing* the maintenance and development of moral surroundings as *one's own end.* The child must take the spirit of the family into himself and live out this spirit according to his special membership in the family. So a soldier in the army, a friend in a mutual association, etc. Adjustment to intellectual environment is not mere conformity of ideas to facts. It is the living assimilation of these facts into one's own intellectual life, and maintaining and asserting them as *truth.*

There are environments existing prior to the activities of any individual agent; the family, for example, is prior to the moral activity of a child born into it, but the point is to see that "adjustment," to have a moral sense, means *making the environment a reality for one's self.* A true description of the case would say that the child takes for his own end, ends already existing for the wills of others. And, in making them his own, he creates and supports for himself an environment that already exists for others. In such cases there is no special transformation of the existing environment; there is simply the process of making it the environment for one's self. So in learning, the child simply appropriates to himself the intellectual environment already in existence for others. But in the activity of the man of science there is more than such personal reproduction and creation; there is increase, or even reconstruction of the prior environment. While the ordinary citizen hardly does more than make his own the environment of ends and interests already sustained in the wills of others, the moral reformer may remake the whole. But whether one case or the other, adjustment is not outer conformity; it is living realization of certain relations in and through the will of the agent.

XXXVIII. The Moral End Is the Realization of a Community of Wills

Since the perfomance of function is, on the other side, the creation, perpetuation, and further development of an environment, of relations to the wills of others, its performance *is a common good.* It satisfies others who participate in the environment. The member of the family, of the state, etc., in exercising his function, contributes to the whole of which he is a member by realizing its spirit in himself. But the question discussed in Section XXXVI recurs under another aspect. Granting that the satisfying of personal interests realizes a common good, what shall we say of the impersonal interests—interests in science and art. Is the good carpenter or chemist not only in so far a good man, but also a good social member? In other words, does every form of moral activity realize a common good, or is the moral end partly social, partly non-social?

One objection sometimes brought to the doctrine that the moral end is entirely social, may be now briefly dismissed. This is the objection that a man has moral duties toward *himself*. Certainly, but what of *himself*? If he is essentially a social member, his duties toward himself have a social basis and bearing. The only relevant question is whether one is wholly a social member—whether scientific and artistic activities may not be non-social.

The ground here taken is that the moral end is wholly social. This does not mean that science and art are means to some social welfare beyond themselves. We have already stated that even the production of utilities must, as moral, be its own end. The position then is that intellectual and artistic interests *are themselves* social, when considered in the completeness of their relations—that interest in the development of intelligence is, in and of itself, interest in the well-being of society.

Unless this be true there is no moral end at all, but only moral ends. There is no comprehensive unity in life, but a number of ends which, being irreducible to a common principle, must be combined on the best principle of compromise available. We have no "The Good," but an aggregate of fragmentary ends.

It helps nothing to say that this necessary unity is found in the *self* to be realized, unless we are pointed to something in the self that unites the social and non-social functions. Our objection is that the separation of intellectual interests from social makes a chasm in the self.

For the same reason it follows that in the case of a collision of social with intellectual ends—say the conflict of a man's interests as a member of a family with his interests in new scientific discovery—no reconciliation is possible. If the interests are forms of social interest, there is a common end in both, on the basis of which the conflict can be resolved. While such considerations do not prove that there is but one end, and that social, they may well make us hesitate about carelessly taking a position of which they are the logical consequence.

Of course, every one recognizes that a certain amount of scientific and artistic interest is social in character. A certain amount of interest in truth, or in intelligence, a certain amount of susceptibility to beauty, a certain amount of devotion to utility, are universally recognized to be necessary to make judicious, agreeable and efficient social members. The whole system of modern education has meaning only on this supposition.

More than this: A certain amount of intelligence, and

a certain amount of susceptibility to embodied ideals, *must* exist to give moral conduct. A moral end is, as we have seen, always a *conception*, an idea. The very act of bringing conduct out of the impulsive into the moral sphere, depends upon the development of intelligence so as to transform a feeling into the perception of a situation. And, as we watch moral development from childhood to maturity, is it not evident that progress consists in power to conceive of larger and better defined ends? to analyze the situation which demands active response, the function which needs exercise, into specific relations, instead of taking it partially or even upon some one else's say so? Conduct, so far as not based upon an intelligent recognition and realization of the relationships involved, is either sentimental, or *merely* habitual —in the former case immoral, and in the latter failing of the complete morality possible.

If the necessary part played in conduct by artistic cultivation is not so plain, it is largely because "Art" has been made such an unreal Fetich—a sort of superfine and extraneous polish to be acquired only by specially cultivated people. In reality, living is itself the supreme art; it requires fineness of touch; skill and thoroughness of workmanship; susceptible response and delicate adjustment to a situation apart from reflective analysis; instinctive perception of the proper harmonies of act and act, of man and man. Active art is the embodiment of ideals; the clothing of ideas otherwise abstract in their peculiar and fit garb of concrete outward detail; passive art is the quick and accurate response to such embodiments as are already made. What were human conduct without the one and the other?

Granting the necessity of knowledge and of its artistic application in conduct, the question arises as to where the line is to be drawn. Evidently, if anywhere, at specialisms, remote philosophic or mathematical endeavors; life-times spent in inventive attempts without appreciable outcome. But to draw the line is not easy. The remote of one generation is the social tool of the next; the abstract mathematics and physics of the sixteenth and seventeenth centuries are the great social forces of the nineteenth—the locomotive, the telegraph, the telephone, etc. And how, in any case, can we tell a scientific investigator that up to a certain experiment or calculation his work may be social, beyond that, not? All that we can say is that beyond a certain point its social character is not obvious to sense and that the work must be carried on by faith.

Thus it is that we dispose of objections like Bradley's (*Ethical Studies*, p. 202): "Nothing is easier than to suppose a life of art or speculation which, as far as we can see, though true to itself, has, so far as others are concerned, been sheer waste or even loss, and which knew that it was so." That we cannot *see* any social *result* in such cases has nothing to do with the question whether or not the interests themselves are social. We may imagine a life of philanthropic activity, say of devotion to emancipation of slaves in a country wholly given over to slavery, or of a teacher in an unenlightened country, which, as far as we can see, (though, in this case, as in the one referred to by Mr. Bradley, everything depends upon how far we *can* see) has been sheer waste, so far as influence on others is concerned. The point is whether in such cases the life lived is not one of devotion to the interests of humanity as such.

We have been trying to show that every one admits that science and art, up to a certain point, are social, and that to draw a line where they cease to be so, is in reality to draw a line where we cease to *see* their social character. That we should cease to *see* it, is necessary in the case of almost every advance. Just because the new scientific movement is new, we can realize its social effects only afterwards. But it may be questioned whether the motive which actuates the man of science is not, when fully realized, a *faith* in the social bearing of what he is doing. If we were to go into a metaphysical analysis, the question would have to be raised whether a barely intellectual fact or theory be not a pure abstraction—an unreality if kept apart entirely from the activities of men in relation to one another.

XXXIX. Science and Art as Necessary Factors of Social Welfare

Let us consider the problem on its other side. What kind of an interest is our interest in persons, our distinctively social interest? Suppose we attempt to separate our interests in truth, beauty, and use from our interest in persons: *What remains in the persons to be interested in?* Is not a necessary part of our interest in persons, an interest in them as beings fulfilling their respective intellectual and artistic capacities; and if we cut this out of our social interest, have we not maimed and stunted our interest in persons? We wish the fullest life possible to ourselves and to others. And the fullest life means largely a complete and free development of capacities in knowledge and production —production of beauty and use. Our interest in others is not satisfied as long as their intelligence is cramped, their appreciation of truth feeble, their emotions hard and uncomprehensive, their powers of production compressed. To will their true good is to will the freeing of all such gifts to the highest degree. Shall we say that their true good requires that they shall go to the point of understanding algebra, but not quaternions, of understanding ordinary mechanics, but not to working out an electro-magnetic theory of light? to ability to appreciate ordinary chords and tunes, but not to the attempt to make further developments in music?

And this throws light upon the case referred to by Mr. Bradley. *Social* welfare demands that the individual be permitted to devote himself to the fulfilling of *any* scientific or artistic capacity that he finds within himself—provided, of course, it does not conflict with some more important capacity—irrespective of results. To say to a man: You may devote yourself to this gift, provided you demonstrate beforehand its social bearing, would be to talk nonsense. The new discovery is not yet made. It is absolutely required by the interests of a progressive society that it allow freedom to the individual to develop such functions as he finds in himself, irrespective of any *proved* social effect. Here, as elsewhere, morality works by faith, not by sight.

Indeed the ordinary conception of social interests, of benevolence, needs a large over-hauling. It is practically equivalent to doing something directly for others—to one form or another of charity. But this is only negative morality. A true social interest is that which wills for others freedom from dependence on our *direct* help, which wills to them the self-directed power of exercising, in and by themselves, their own functions. Any will short of this is not social but selfish, willing the dependence of others that we may continue benignly altruistic. The idea of "giving pleasure" to others, "making others happy," if it means anything else than securing conditions so that they may act freely in their own satisfaction, means slavery.

As society advances, social interest must consist more and more in free devotion to intelligence for its own sake, to science, art and industry, and in rejoicing in the exercise of such freedom by others. Meantime, it is truth which makes free.

See Spencer, *Data of Ethics*, pp. 249–57, where this doctrine is stated with great force.

Where, finally, does the social character of science and art come in? Just here: they are elements in the perfection of individuality, and they are elements whose very nature is to be moving, not rigid; distributed from one to another and not monopolistic possessions. If there are forms of science and art which, at present, are static, being merely owned collections of facts, as one may have a collection of butterflies in a frame, or of etchings in a closed portfolio, this is not because they are science and art, but imperfect science and art. To complete their scientific and artistic character is to set these facts in motion; to hurl them against the world of physical forces till new instruments of man's activity are formed, and to set them in circulation so that others may also participate in their truth and rejoice in their beauty. So far as scientific or artistic attainments are treasured as individual possessions, so far it *is* true that they are not social—but so far it is *also* true that they are immoral: indeed that they are not fully scientific or artistic, being subordinated to having certain sensations.

The intellectual movement of the last four or five centuries has resulted in an infinite specialization in methods, and in an immense accumulation of fact. It is quite true, since the diversity of fact and of method has not yet been brought to an organic unity, that their social bearing is not yet realized. But when the unity is attained (as attained it must be if there is unity in the object of knowledge), it will pass into a corresponding unity of practice. And then the question as to the social character of even the most specialized knowledge will seem absurd. It will be to ask whether men can co-operate better when they do not know than when they do know what they want. Meantime the intellectual confusion, and the resulting divorce of knowledge from practice, exists. But this constitutes a part of the environment of which action must take heed. It makes it one of the pressing duties that every man of intelligence should do his part in bringing out the public and common aspects of knowledge. *The* duty of the present is the socializing of intelligence—the realizing of its bearing upon social practice.

XL. The Ethical Postulate

We have attempted to show that the various interests are social in their very nature. We have not attempted to show that this can be seen or proved in any given case. On the contrary, in most, if not all cases, the agent acts from a faith that, in realizing his own capacity, he will satisfy the needs of society. If he were asked to *prove* that his devotion to his function were right because certain to promote social good, he might well reply: "That is none of my affair. I have only to work myself out as strength and opportunity are given me, and let the results take care of themselves. I did not make the world, and if it turns out that devotion to the capacity which was given me, and loyalty to the surroundings in which I find myself do not result in good, I do not hold myself responsible. But, after all, I cannot believe that it will so turn out. What is really good for me *must* turn out good for all, or else there is no good in the world at all." The basis, in a word, of moral conduct, with respect to the exercise of function, is a faith that moral self-satisfaction (that is, satisfaction in accordance with the performance of function as already defined) means social satisfaction—or the faith that self and others make a true community. Now such faith or conviction is at the basis of all moral conduct—not simply of the scientific or artistic. Interest in self must mean belief in one's business, conviction of its legitimacy and worth, even prior to any sensible demonstration. Under any circumstances, such demonstration can extend only to past action; the social efficiency of any new end must be a matter of faith. Where such faith is wanting, action becomes halting and character weak. Forcible action fails, and its place is taken by a feeble idealism, of vague longing for that which is not, or by a pessimistic and fruitless discontent with things as they are—leading, in either case, to neglect of actual and pressing duty. The basis of moral strength is *limitation*, the resolve to be one's self only, and to be loyal to the actual powers and surroundings of that self. The saying of Carlyle's about doing the "duty that lies nearest," and of Goethe's that "America is here or nowhere," both imply that faith in the existing moral capacity and environment is the basis of conduct. All fruitful and sound human endeavor roots in the conviction that there is something absolutely worth while, something "divine" in the demands imposed by one's actual situation and powers. In the great moral heroes of the world the conviction of the worth of their destiny, and of what they were meant to do, has amounted to a kind of fatalism. They have done not simply what they *could* do, but what they *must* do.

On the other hand, effective social interest is based upon what is vaguely called "faith in humanity," or, more specifically, belief in the value of each man's individuality, belief in some particular function which he might exercise, given appropriate conditions and stimuli. Moral interest in others must be an interest in their possibilities, rather than in their accomplishments; or, better, in their accomplishments so far as these testify to a fulfilling of function—to a working out of capacity. Sympathy and work for men which do not grow out of faith in them are a perfunctory and unfertile sort of thing.

This faith is generally analyzed no further; it is left as faith in one's "calling" or in "humanity." But what is meant is just this: in the performing of such special service as each is capable of, there is to be found not only the satisfaction of self, but also the satisfaction of the entire moral order, the furthering of the community in which one lives. All moral conduct is based upon such a faith; and *moral theory must recognize this as the postulate upon which it rests.* In calling it a postulate, we do not mean that it is a postulate which our theory makes or must make in order to be a theory; but that, through analysis, theory *finds that moral practice makes this postulate*, and that with its reality the reality and value of conduct are bound up.

In calling it a postulate we do not mean to call it unprovable, much less unverifiable, for moral experience is itself, so far as it goes, its verification. But we mean that the further consideration of this postulate, its demonstration or (if the case so be) its refutation, do not belong to the realm of ethics as such. Each branch of human experience rests upon some presupposition which, *for that branch*, is ultimate. The further inquiry into such presuppositions belongs not to mathematics, or physics, or ethics, but to metaphysics.

Unless, then, we are to extend our ethical theory to inquire into the possibility and value of moral experience, unless, that is, we are to make an excursion into the metaphysics of ethics, we have here reached our foundation. The ethical postulate, the presupposition involved in conduct, is this:

IN THE REALIZATION OF INDIVIDUALITY THERE IS FOUND ALSO THE NEEDED REALIZATION OF SOME COMMUNITY OF PERSONS OF WHICH THE INDIVIDUAL IS A MEMBER; AND, CONVERSELY, THE AGENT WHO DULY SATISFIES THE COMMUNITY IN WHICH HE SHARES, BY THAT SAME CONDUCT SATISFIES HIMSELF.

Otherwise put, the postulate is that there is a community of persons; a good which realized by the will of one is made not private but public. It is this unity of individuals as respects the end of action, this existence of a practical common good, that makes what we call the moral order of the world.

Shakespeare has stated the postulate—

To thine own self be true;
And it must follow, as the night the day,
Thou can'st not then be false to any man.

Its significance may be further developed by comparing it with the scientific postulate.

All science rests upon the conviction of the thoroughgoing and permanent unity of the world of objects known—a unity which is sometimes termed the "uniformity of nature" or the "reign of law"; without this conviction that objects are not mere isolated and transitory appearances, but are connected together in a system by laws or relations, science would be an impossibility. Moral experience *makes for the world of practice* an assumption analogous in kind to that which intellectual experience makes for the world of knowledge. And just as it is not the affair of science, as such, or even of logic (the theory of science) to justify this presupposition of science, or to do more than show its presence in intellectual experience, so it is not the business of conduct, or even of ethics (the theory of conduct) to justify what we have termed the "ethical postulate." In each case the further inquiry belongs to metaphysics.

XLI. Does the End Proposed Serve as a Criterion of Conduct?

We have now concluded that an end which may be termed indifferently "The Realization of Individuality," "The Performance of Specific Functions," "The Satisfaction of Interests," "The Realization of a Community of Individuals" is the moral end. Will this end serve the two aims (see Sec. XVI) required of a criterion, or standard: (1) Will it unify individual conduct? (2) Will it afford a common good? We have just been endeavoring to show that it does both of these things; that as the realization of one's specific capacity, it unifies individual conduct, and that, as the performance of function, it serves to satisfy the entire community. To take up just these points, accordingly, would involve a repetition of what has been said, and we shall therefore take up instead some aspects of the individual and social unity of conduct, not already considered.

1. *The System of Individual Conduct*

We must be careful not to interpret the idea of specific function too rigidly or abstractly. It does not mean that each one has some supreme mission in life to which everything else must be sacrificed—that a man is to be an artist, or a soldier, or a student, or a day-laborer and nothing else. On the contrary, the idea of function is that which comprehends all the various sides of life, and it cannot be narrowed below the meaning we have already given: the due adjustment of capacity and surroundings. Whenever there is any capacity or any circumstance, no matter how trivial, there is something included in the exercise of function, and, therefore to be satisfied—according to its place, of course, in the whole of life. Amusements and all the minor details of life are included within the scope of morality. They are elements in the exercise of function, and their insignificance and triviality does not exclude them from the grasp of duty and of the good. It is a mistake to suppose that because it is optional or indifferent—as it constantly is—what acts among the minor details of life are to be done or left undone, or unimportant whether they are done or left undone at all, therefore such acts have no moral value. Morality consists in treating them just as they are—if they are slight or trivial they are to be performed as slight and trivial. Morality does not simply permit the performance of such acts, but demands it. To try to make, in the interests of duty, a serious matter out of every detail of life would be immoral—as much so, in kind, as to make light of momentous matters.

See Alexander, *Moral Order*, pp. 53–54; Bradley, *Ethical Studies*, pp. 194–97.

Consider, also, how this conception of the end stands in definite relation to concrete acts; how it explains the possibility of decision as to whether this or that proposed act is right. We do not have to trace the connection of the act with some end beyond, as pleasure, or abstract law. We have only to analyze the *act itself*. We have certain definite and wholly concrete facts; the given capacity of the person at the given moment, and his given surroundings. The judgment as to the nature of these facts is, in and of itself, a judgment as to the act to be done. The question is not: What is the probability that this act will result in the balance of maximum pleasure; it is not what general rule can we hunt up under which to bring this case. It is simply: *What is this case?* The moral act is not that which satisfies some far-away principle, hedonistic or transcendental. It is that which meets the present, actual situation. Difficulties indeed, arise, but they are simply the difficulty of resolving a complex case; they are intellectual, not moral. The case made out, the moral end stands forth. No extraneous manipulation, to bring the case under some foreign end, is required.

And this suggests the elasticity of the criterion. In fact moral conduct is entirely individualized. It is where, when, how and of whom. There has been much useless discussion as to the absolute or relative character of morals—useless because the terms absolute and relative are not defined. If absolute is taken to mean immobile and rigid, it is anything but desirable that morals should be absolute. If the physical world is a scene of movement, in which there is no rest, it is a poor compliment to pay the moral world to conceive of it as static and lifeless. A rigid criterion in a world of developing social relations would speedily prove no criterion at all. It would be an abstract rule, taking no account of the individualized character of each act; its individuality of capacity and of surroundings, of time, place and relationships involved. A truly absolute criterion is one which adjusts itself to each case according to the specific nature of the case; one which moves with the moving world. On the other hand, if relative means uncertain in application, changing in time and place without reason for change in the facts themselves, then certainly the criterion is not relative. If it means taking note of all concrete relations involved, it *is* relative. The absoluteness, in fine, of the standard of action consists not in some rigid statement, but in never-failing application. Universality here, as elsewhere, resides not in a thing, but in a way, a method of action. The absolute standard is the one applicable to all deeds, and the conception of the exercise of function is thus absolute, covering all conduct from the mainly impulsive action of the savage to the most complex reaches of modern life.

Aristotle's well known theory of the "mean" seems to have its bearing here. "It is possible," he says (Peters' trans. of *Ethics*, p.

46), "to feel fear, confidence, desire, anger, pity, and generally to be affected pleasantly and painfully, either too much or too little—in either case wrongfully; but to be affected thus at the right *times*, and on the right *occasions*, and toward the right *persons*, and with the right *object* and in the right *fashions*, is the mean course and the best course, and these are characteristics of virtue." The right time, occasion, person, purpose and fashion—what is it but the complete individualization of conduct in order to meet the whole demands of the whole situation, instead of some abstraction? And what else do we mean by fit, due, proper, right action, but that which just hits the mark, without falling short or deflecting, and, to mix the metaphor, without slopping over?

2. *The System of Social Conduct, or Common Good*

Moral conduct springs from the faith that all right action is social and its purpose is to justify this faith by working out the social values involved. The term "moral community" can mean only a unity of action, made what it is by the co-operating activities of diverse individuals. There is unity in the work of a factory, not in spite of, but *because of* the division of labor. Each workman forms the unity not by doing the same that everybody else does, or by trying to do the whole, but by doing his specific part. The unity is the one activity which their varied activities make. And so it is with the moral activity of society and the activities of individuals. The more individualized the functions, the more perfect the unity. (See Sec. LII.)

The exercise of function by an agent serves, then, both to define and to unite him. It makes him a *distinct* social member at the same time that it makes him a *member*. Possession of peculiar capacities, and special surroundings mark one person off from another and make him an individual; and the due adjustment of capacities to surroundings (in the exercise of function) effects, therefore, the realization of individuality—the realization of what we specifically are as distinct from others. At the same time, this distinction is not isolation; the exercise of function is the performing of a special *service* without which the social whole is defective. Individuality means not separation, but defined position in a whole; special aptitude in constituting the whole.

We are now in a position to take up the consideration

of the two other fundamental ethical conceptions—obligation and freedom. These ideas answer respectively to the two sides of the exercise of function. On the one hand, the performing of a function realizes the social whole. Man is thus "bound" by the relations necessary to constitute this whole. He is subject to the conditions which the existence and growth of the social unity impose. He is, in a word, under *obligation*; the performance of his function is duty owed to the community of which he is a member.

But on the other hand, activity in the way of function realizes the individual; it is what makes him an individual, or distinct person. In the performance of his own function the agent satisfies his own interests and gains power. In it is found his *freedom*.

Obligation thus corresponds to the *social* satisfaction, freedom to the *self*-satisfaction, involved in the exercise of function; and they can no more be separated from each other than the correlative satisfaction can be. One has to realize himself as a member of a community. In this fact are found both freedom and duty.

2

The Idea of Obligation

XLII. Theories Regarding Moral Authority

The idea of obligation or duty has two sides. There is the idea of law, of something which controls conduct, and there is the *consciousness* of the necessity of conforming to this law. There is, of course, no separation between the two sides, but the consideration of the latter side—the recognition of obligation—may be best dealt with in discussing conscience. Here we shall deal simply with the fact that there is such a thing in conduct as law controlling action, and constituting obligation. Theories regarding obligation may, for our purposes, be subdivided into those which make its exercise restraint or coercion (and which therefore hold that in perfect moral conduct, duty as such disappears); and those which hold that obligation is a normal element in conduct as such, and that it is not, essentially, but only under certain circumstances, coercive. Of the former type, some theories (mainly the hedonistic) regard the restraint as originally imposed from without upon the desires of the individual, while others (as the Kantian) regard it as imposed by man's reason upon his desires and inclinations.

XLIII. Bain's Theory of Obligation

It is obvious that the question of obligation presents considerable difficulty to the hedonistic school. If the end of conduct is pleasure, as the satisfaction of desire, why should not each desire be satisfied, if possible, as it arises, and thus pleasure secured? What meaning is there in the term "duty" or "obligation" if the moral end or good coincides wholly with the natural end of the inclinations themselves? It is evident, at all events, that the term can have significance only if there is some cause preventing the desires as they arise from natural satisfaction. The problem of obligation in hedonism thus becomes the problem of discovering that outside force which restrains, or, at least, constrains, the desire from immediate gratification. According to Bain, this outside force is social disapprobation manifested through the form of punishment.

"I consider that the proper meaning, or import of the terms [duty, obligation] refers to that class of action which is enforced by the sanction of punishment. . . . The powers that impose the obligatory sanction are Law and Society, or the community acting through the Government by public judicial acts, and apart from the Government by the unofficial expressions of disapprobation and the exclusion from social good offices" *Emotions and Will*, p. 286. See also pp. 321–23 and p. 527.

Through this "actual and ideal avoidance of certain acts and dread of punishment" the individual learns to forego the gratification of some of his natural impulses, and learns also to cultivate and even to originate desires not at first spontaneous. "The child is open from the first to the blame and praise of others, and thus is led to do or avoid certain acts."

On the model, however, of the action of this external authority there grows up, in time an internal authority—"an ideal resemblance of public authority" (p. 287), or "a *fac simile* of the system of government around us" (p. 313).

"The sentiment, at first formed and cultivated by the relations of actual command and obedience, may come at last to stand upon an independent foundation. . . . When the young mind, accustomed at the outset to implicitly obeying any set of rules is sufficiently advanced to appreciate the motive—the utilities or the sentiment that led to their imposition—the character of the conscience is entirely changed. . . . Regard is now had to the intent and meaning of the law, and not to the mere fact of its being prescribed by some power" (*Emotions and Will*, p. 318).

But when the sense of obligation becomes entirely detached from the social sanction, "even then the notion, sentiment or form of duty is derived from what society imposes, although the particular matter is quite different. Social obligation develops in the mind originally the feeling and habit of obligation, and this remains although the particular articles are changed" (p. 319n.). *Cf.* also Bain, *Moral Science*, pp. 20–21 and 41–43.

XLIV. Spencer's Theory of Obligation

Spencer's theory is, in substance, an enlarged and better analyzed restatement of Bain's theory. Bain nowhere clearly states in what the essence of obligation consists, when it becomes independent, when the internal *fac simile* is formed. *Why* should I not gratify my desires as I please in case social pressure is absent or lets up? Spencer supplies the missing element. According to him, "the essential trait in the moral consciousness is the control of some feeling or feelings by some other feeling or feelings" (*Data of Ethics*, p. 113). The kind of feeling which controls is that which is more complex and which relates to more remote ends; or, we are "obliged" to give up more immediate, special and direct pleasures for the sake of securing more general, remote and indirect ones. Obligation, in its essence, is the surrender or subordination of present to future satisfaction. This control, restraint, or suppression may be "independent" or, self-imposed, but is not so at first, either in the man or in the child. Prior to self-restraint are the restraints imposed by the "visible ruler, the invisible ruler and society at large"—the policeman, the priest and public opinion. The man is induced to postpone immediate gratification through his fear of others, especially of the chief, of the dead and of social displeasure—"legal penalty, supernatural punishment and social reprobation." Thus there grows up the sense of obligation. This refers at first only to the above-mentioned extrinsic effects of action. But finally the mind learns to consider the intrinsic effect of the action itself—the evil inflicted by the evil deed, and then the sense of duty, or coercion, evolved through the aforesaid external agencies, becomes transferred to this new mode of controlling action. Desires are now controlled through considerations of what their *own* effects would be, were the desires acted upon.

It follows "that the sense of duty or moral obligation is transitory, and will diminish as fast as moralization increases" (*Data of Ethics*, p. 127). Even when compulsion is self-imposed, there is still compulsion, coercion, and this must be done away with. It *is* done away with as far as an act which is at first done only for the sake of its own remoter consequences comes to be done for its own sake. And this will ultimately occur, if the act is continued, since "persistence in performing a duty ends in making it a pleasure."

See Guyau, *La Morale Anglaise Contemporaine*, besides the works of Bain and Spencer. In addition to objections which will forthwith be made, we may here note a false abstraction of Spencer's. He makes the act and its consequences *two* things, while the act and its consequences (provided they are known as such) are the same thing, no matter whether consequences are near or remote. The only distinction is that consequences once not known as such at all are seen in time to be really consequences, and thus to be part of the content of the act. The transfer from the "external consequences" imposed by the ruler, priest and public-opinion to the intrinsic consequences of the act itself, is thus a transfer from an immoral to a moral basis. This is very different from a change of the form of obligation itself.

XLV. Criticism of these Theories

Putting aside the consideration of the relation of desire to duty, (the question whether duty is essentially coercive), until after we have taken up the Kantian idea of obligation, we may note the following objections to the theories just stated. Their great defect is that they do not give us any method of differentiating moral coercion (or obligation) from the action of mere superior physical force. Taking it (first) upon the side of the individual: Is there any reason *why* the individual submits to the external authority of government except that he *has* to do so? He may argue that, since others possess superior force, he will avoid certain pains by conforming to their demands, but such yielding, whether temporary or permanent, to superior force is very far from being a recognition that one *ought* to act as the superior force dictates. The theories must logically commit us to the doctrine that "might makes right" in its baldest form. Every one knows that, when the individual surrenders the natural gratifications of his desires to the command of others, if his sole reason is the superior force of the commanding party, he does not forego in the surrender his right to such gratification the moment he has the chance to get it.

Actual slavery would be the model school of duties, if these theories were true.

The facts adduced by Bain and Spencer—the growth of the recognition of duties in the child through the authority of the parents, and in the savage through the use of authority by the chief—are real enough, but what they prove is that obligation may be brought home to one by force, not that force creates obligation. The child and the man yield to force in such a way that their sense of duty is developed only in case they recognize, implicitly, the force or the authority as already *right*. Let it be recognized that *rightful* force (as distinct from mere brute strength) resides in certain social authorities, and these social authorities may do much, beyond the shadow of doubt, to give effect to the special deeds and relations which are to be considered obligatory. These theories, in fine, take the fact of obligation for granted, and, at most, only show the historical process by which its fuller recognition is brought about. Force in the service of right is one thing; force as constituting and creating right is another.

And this is to say (secondly), considering the matter from the side of society, that the theories of Bain and Spencer do not explain why or how social authority should exercise coercive force over the individual. If it is implied that they do so in the moral interests of the individual or of the community, this takes it for granted that there already is in existence a moral ideal obligatory upon the individual. If it is implied that they exercise coercive force in the interests of their own private pleasure, this might establish a despotism, or lead to a political revolt, but it is difficult to see how it could create the fact of duty. When we consider any concrete case, we see that society, in its compelling of the individual, is possessed of moral ideals; and that it conceives itself not merely as having the *power* to make the individual conform to them, nor as having the *right* merely; but as under the bounden *duty* of bringing home to the individual *his* duties. The social authorities do not, perforce, create morality, but they embody and make effective the existing morality. It is only just because the actions which they impose are thought of as *good*, good for others as for themselves, that this imposition is taken out of the realm of tyranny into that of duty (see Sec. XXXVIII).

XLVI. The Kantian Theory of Obligation

As we have seen, Kant takes the conception of duty as the primary ethical notion, superior to that of the good, and places it in the most abrupt opposition to desire. The relation of duty to desire is not control of some feelings by others, but rather suppression of all desire (not in itself, but as a *motive* of action) in favor of the consciousness of law universal. We have, on one side, according to Kant, the desire and inclination, which are sensuous and pathological. These constitute man's "lower nature." On the other side there is Reason, which is essentially universal, above all caprice and all prostitution to private pleasure. This Reason, or "higher nature," imposes a law upon the sentient being of man, a law which takes the form of a command (the "Categorical Imperative"). This relation of a higher rational nature issuing commands to a lower sensuous nature (both within man himself), is the very essence of duty. If man were wholly a sentient being, he would have only to follow his natural impulses, like the animals. If he were only a rational being, he would necessarily obey his reason, and there would still be no talk of obligation. But because of the dualism, because of the absolute opposition between Reason and Desire, man is a being subject to obligation. Reason says to the desires "Thou shalt" or "Thou shalt not." Yet this obligation is not externally imposed; the man as rational imposes it upon himself as sensuous. Thus Kant says that, in the realm of morality, man is both sovereign and subject.

The reflex influence of Rousseau's social theories upon Kant's moral doctrines in this respect is worthy of more attention than it usually receives. Kant's moral theory is hardly more than a translation of Rousseau's politics into ethical terms, through its union with Kant's previously established dualism of reason and sense.

XLVII. Criticism of the Kantian Theory

1. No one can deny that a genuine opposition exists between the "natural" desires and moral activity. The being that satisfies each desire or appetite as it arises, without reference of it to, or control of it by, some principle, has not had the horizon of conduct lift before him. But Kant makes the satisfaction of desire *as such* (not of this or that desire) antagonistic to action from duty. Kant was forced into this position by his fundamental division of sense from reason, but it carries with it its own condemnation and thus that of the premises from which it is derived. It comes to saying that the actual desires and appetites are not what they ought to be. This, in itself, is true enough. But when Kant goes on to say, as he virtually does, that what ought to be *cannot* be, that the desires as such cannot be brought into harmony with principle, he has made the moral life not only a riddle, but a riddle with no answer. If mankind were once convinced that the moral ideal were something which ought to be but which could not be, we may easily imagine how much longer moral endeavor would continue. The first or immediate stimulus to moral effort is the conviction that the desires and appetites are not what they should be; the underlying and continuing stimulus is the conviction that the expression of desires in harmony with law is the sole abiding good of man. To reconcile the two is the very meaning of the moral struggle (see Sec. LXIV). Strictly, according to Kant, morality would either leave the appetites untouched or would abolish them—in either case destroying morality.

See Caird, *Critical Philosophy of Kant*, Vol. II, pp. 226–28.

2. Kant again seems to be on the right track in declaring that obligation is not anything externally imposed, but is the law of man's being, self-imposed. This principle of "autonomy" is the only escape from a theory of obligation which would make obligation external, and regard for it slavish fear, or servile hope of reward. To regard even a Divine Being as the author of obligation is to make it a form of external constraint, appealing only to hope or fear, unless this Divine Being is shown to be organically connected with self.

But this abstract universal reason which somehow dwells, without mediation or reason, in each individual, seems to be somewhat scholastic, a trifle mythological. There is undoubtedly in man's experience a function which corresponds to what Kant is aiming, thus mythologically, to describe. But it is one thing to recognize an opposition of a desire, in its isolation, to desire as organic to the function of the whole man; it is another to split man into a blank dualism of an abstract reason, on one side, having no antecedents or bearings, and of a mess of appetites, having only animal relationship, on the other. The truth that Kant is aiming to preserve seems to be fairly stated as two-fold: first, that duty is self-imposed, and thus the dutiful will autonomous or free; and, second, the presence of struggle in man between a "lower" and a "higher." The first point seems to be sufficiently met by the idea already advanced that self, or individuality, is essentially social, being constituted not by isolated capacity, but by capacity acting in response to the needs of an environment—an environment which, when taken in its fullness, is a community of persons. Any law imposed by such a self would be "universal," but this universality would not be an isolated possession of the individual; it would be another name for the concrete social relationships which make the individual what he is, as a social member or organ. Furthermore, such a universal law would not be formal, but would have a content—these same relationships.

The second point seems to be met by recognizing that in the realization of the law of social function, conflict must occur between the desire as an immediate and direct expression of the individual—the desire in its isolation—and desire as an expression of the whole man; desire, that is, as wholly conformable to the needs of the surroundings. Such a conflict is real enough, as every one's experience will testify, but it is a conflict which may be solved—which must be solved so far as morality is attained. And since it is a conflict within desire itself, its solution or morality, does not require any impossible obliteration of desire, nor any acting from an "ought" which has no relation to what "is." This, indeed, is *the* failure of the Kantian Ethics: in separating what should be from what is, it deprives the latter, the existing social world as well as the desires of the individual, of all moral value; while, by the same separation, it condemns that which should be to a barren abstraction. An "ought" which does not root in and flower from the "is," which is not the fuller realization of the actual state of social relationships, is a mere pious wish that things should be better. And morality, that is, right action, is not so feeble as this would come to.

XLVIII. The Source and Nature of Obligation

The basis of a correct theory of obligation lies, as already stated, in holding fast to its concrete relations to the moral end, or good. This end consists in an activity in which capacity is exercised in accordance with surroundings, with the social needs which affect the individual. It is implied in this very idea, that the end is not something which the individual may set up at his own arbitrary will. The social needs give control, law, authority. The individual may not manifest his capacity, satisfy his desires, apart from their specific relation to the environment in which they exist. The general fact of obligation which is constituted through this control of capacity by the wider function is, of course, differentiated into specific "laws" or duties by the various forms which the one function takes, as capacity and circumstances vary.

In other words, obligation or duty is simply the aspect which the good or the moral end assumes, as the individual conceives of it. From the very fact that the end is the good, and yet is not realized by the individual, it presents itself to him as that which *should be realized*—as the ideal of action. It requires no further argument to show that obligation is at once self-imposed, and social in its content. It is self-imposed because it flows from the good, from the idea of the full activity of the individual's own will. It is no law imposed from without; but is his own law, the law of his own function, of his individuality. Its social content flows from the fact that this individuality is not mere capacity, but is this capacity *acting*, and acting so as to comprehend social relationships.

Suppose that man's good and his conviction of duty were divorced from one another—that man's duty were other than to fulfill his own specific function. Such a thing would make duty purely formal; the moral law would have no intrinsic relation to daily conduct, to the expression of man's powers and wants. There have, indeed, been moralists who think they do the Lord service, who think they add to the dignity and sacredness of Duty by making it other than the idea of the activity of man, regulated indeed, but regulated only by its own principle of activity. But such moralists in their desire to consecrate the idea of duty remove from it all content, and leave it an empty abstraction. On the other hand, their eagerness to give absoluteness and imperativeness to duty by making it a law other than that of the normal expression of man, casts discredit upon the one moral reality—the full, free play of human life. In denying that duty is simply the *intrinsic* law, the *self*-manifestation of this life, they make this life immoral, or at least non-moral. They degrade it to a bundle of appetites and powers having no moral value until the outside moral law is applied to them. In reality, the dignity and imperativeness of duty are simply the manifest dignity and unconditioned worth of human life as exhibited in its free activity. The whole idea of the separateness of duty from the concrete flow of human action is a virulent example of the fallacy mentioned in an early section—the fallacy that moral action means something more than action itself (see Sec. II).

The attempt to act upon a theory of the divorce of satisfaction and duty, to carry it out in practice, means the maiming of desire through distrust of its moral significance, and thus, by withdrawing the impetus of action, the reduction of life to mere passivity. So far as this does not happen, it means the erection of the struggle itself, the erection of the opposition of law to desire, into the very principle of the moral life. The essential principle of the moral life, that good consists in the freeing of impulse, of appetite, of desire, of power, by enabling them to flow in the channel of a unified and full end is lost sight of, and the free service of the spirit is reduced to the slavish fear of a bond-man under a hard taskmaster.

The essential point in the analysis of moral law, or obligation, having been found, we may briefly discuss some subsidiary points.

1. *The Relation of Duty to a Given Desire*

As any desire arises, it will be, except so far as character has already been moralized, a demand for its own satisfaction; the desire, in a word, will be isolated. In so far, duty will be in a negative attitude towards the desire; it will insist first upon its limitation, and then upon its transformation. So far as it is merely limitative, it demands the denying of the desire, and so far assumes a coercive form. But this limitation is not for its own sake, but for that of the transformation of desire into a freer and more adequate form—into a form, that is, where it will carry with it, when it passes into action, *more of activity*, than the original desire would have done.

Does duty itself disappear when its constraint disappears? On the contrary, so far as an act is done unwillingly, under constraint, so far the act is impure, and *undutiful.* The very fact that there is need of constraint shows that the self is divided; that there is a two-fold interest and purpose—one in the law of the activity according to function, the other in the special end of the particular desire. Let the act be done *wholly as duty*, and it is done wholly for its own sake; love, passion take the place of constraint. This suggests:

2. *Duty for Duty's Sake*

It is clear that such an expression states a real moral fact; unless a duty is done *as* duty it is not done morally. An act may be outwardly just what morality demands, and yet if done for the sake of some private advantage it is not counted moral. As Kant expresses it, an act must be done not only in accordance with duty, but *from duty.* This truth, however, is misinterpreted when it is taken to mean that the act is to be done for the sake of duty, and duty is conceived as a third thing outside the act itself. Such a theory contradicts the true sense of the phrase "duty for duty's sake," for it makes the act done not for its own sake, but as a mere means to an abstract law beyond itself. "Do the right because it is the right" means do the right *thing* because it *is* the right thing; that is, do the act disinterestedly from interest in the act itself. A duty is always some act or line of action, not a third thing outside the act to which it is to conform. In short, duty means *the act which is to be done*, and "duty for duty's sake" means do the required act as it really is; do not degrade it into a means for some ulterior end. This is as true in practice as in theory. A man who does his duty not for the sake of the acts themselves, but for the sake of some abstract "ideal" which he christens duty in general, will have a morality at once hard and barren, and weak and sentimental.

3. *The Agency of Moral Authority in Prescribing Moral Law and Stimulating to Moral Conduct*

The facts, relied upon by Bain and Spencer, as to the part played by social influences in imposing duties, are undeniable. The facts, however, are unaccountable upon the theory of these writers, as that theory would, as we have seen, explain only the influence of society in producing acts done from fear or for hope of reward. But if the individual and others are equally members of one society, if the performance by each man of his own function constitutes a good common to all, it is inevitable that social authorities should be an influence in constituting and teaching duties. The community, in imposing its own needs and demands upon the individual, is simply arousing him to a knowledge of his relationships in life, to a knowledge of the moral environment in which he lives, and of the acts which he must perform if he is to realize his individuality. The community in awakening moral consciousness in the morally immature may appeal to motives of hope and fear. But even this fact does not mean that to the child, duty is necessarily constituted by fear of punishment or hope of reward. It means simply that his capacity and his surroundings are both so undeveloped that the exercise of his function takes mainly the form of pleasing others. He may still do his duty *as* his duty, but his duty now consists in pleasing others.

On Obligation see Green, *Prolegomena*, pp. 352–56; Alexander, *Moral Order*, pp. 142–47. For different views, Martineau, *Types of Ethical Theory*, Vol. II, pp. 92–119; Calderwood, *Handbook of Moral Philosophy*, pp. 131–38; and see also, Grote, *Treatise on Moral Ideals*, Ch. 7.

3

The Idea of Freedom

XLIX. The Forms of Freedom

We may now deal, more briefly, with the problem of moral capacity. It is, in principle, the ability to conceive of an end and to be governed in action by this conceived end. We may consider this capacity in three aspects, as negative, as potential and as positive.

1. *Negative Aspect of Freedom*

The power to be governed in action by the thought of some end to be reached is freedom *from* the appetites and desires. An animal which does not have the power of proposing ends to itself is impelled to action by its wants and appetites just as they come into consciousness. It is *irritated* into acting. Each impulse demands its own satisfaction, and the animal is helpless to rise above the particular want. But a *person*, one who can direct his action by conscious ends, is emancipated from subjection to the particular appetites. He can consider their relation to the end which he has set before himself, and can reject, modify or use them as best agrees with the purposed end. This capacity to control and subjugate impulses by reflection upon their relationship to a rational end is the power of self-government, and the more distinct and the more comprehensive in scope the end is, the more real the self-government.

2. *Potential Freedom*

The power to conceive of ends involves the possibility of thinking of many and various ends, and even of ends which are contrary to one another. If an agent could conceive of but one end in some case, it would always seem to him afterwards that he had been necessitated to act in the direction of that end; but the power to put various ends before self constitutes "freedom of choice," or potential freedom. After action, the agent calls to mind that there was another end open to him, and that if he did not choose the other end, it was because of something in his character which made him prefer the one he actually chose.

L. Moral Responsibility

Here we have the basis of moral *responsibility* or *accountability*. There is no responsibility for any result which is not intended or foreseen. Such a consequence is only physical, not moral. (Sec. VII.) But when any result has been foreseen, and adopted as foreseen, such result is the outcome not of any external circumstances, nor of mere desires and impulses, but of the agent's conception of his own end. Now, because the result thus flows from the agent's own conception of an end, he feels himself responsible for it.

It must be remembered that the end adopted is that which is conceived *as satisfying self*—that, indeed, when we say end of action, we mean only some proposed form of self-satisfaction. The adopted end always indicates, therefore, that sort of condition which the agent considers to be good, or self-satisfactory. It is because a result flows from the agent's *ideal of himself*, the thought of himself which he considers desirable or worth realizing, that the agent feels himself responsible. The result is simply an expression of himself; a manifestation of what he would have himself be. Responsibility is thus one aspect of the identity of character and conduct. (Sec. VII.) We are responsible for our conduct because that conduct is ourselves objectified in actions.

The idea of responsibility is intensified whenever there have been two contrary lines of conduct conceived, of which one has been chosen. If the end adopted turns out not to be satisfactory, but, rather, unworthy and degrading, the agent feels that he *might* have chosen the other end, and that if he did not, it was because his character was such, his ideal of himself was such, that this other end did not appeal to him. The actual result is felt to be the outcome of an unworthy character manifested in the adoption of a low form of satisfaction; and the evident contrast of this low form with a higher form, present to consciousness but rejected, makes the sense of responsibility more acute. As such, it is the judgment of disapprobation passed upon conduct; the feeling of remorse and of the desert of punishment. Freedom as the power of conceiving ends and of realizing the ideal end in action, is thus the basis both of responsibility and of approbation (or disapprobation).

The Freedom of Indifference. It is this potential freedom, arising from the power of proposing various ends of action, which, misinterpreted, gives rise to the theory of a liberty of indifferent choice—the theory that the agent can choose this or that without any ground or motive. The real experience is the knowledge, after the choice of one end, that since another end was also present to consciousness that other end might have been chosen, *if only the character had been such as to find its satisfaction in that other end.* The theory of indifference misconstrues this fact to mean that the agent might just as well have chosen that other end, without any if or qualification whatever. The theory of indifference, moreover, defeats its own end. The point which it is anxious to save is responsibility. It sees that if only one course of action were ever open to an agent, without the possibility of any *conception* of another course, an agent, so acting, could not be held responsible for not having adopted that other course. And so it argues that there must always be the possibility of indifferent or alternate choice; the possibility of adopting this or that line of action without any motive. But if such were the case responsibility would be destroyed. If the end chosen is not an expression of character, if it does not manifest the agent's ideal of himself, if its choice is a matter of indifference, it does not signify morally, but is mere accident or caprice. It is because choice is *not* a matter of indifference, but an outcome of character that the agent feels responsibility, and approves or disapproves. He virtually says: "I am responsible for this outcome, not because I could have chosen another end just as well *without any reason*, but because I thought of another end and rejected it; because my character was such that that end did not seem good, and was such that this end did seem good. My character is myself, and in this unworthy end I stand self-condemned."

LI. Moral Reformation

Freedom considered as potential, depending upon the power of the agent to frame diverse ends, is the basis not only of responsibility, but also of the possibility of reformation, or of change in character and conduct. All moral action is the expression of self, but the self is not something fixed or rigid. It includes as a necessary part of itself the possibility of framing conceptions of what it would be, and there is, therefore, at any time the possibility of acting upon some ideal hitherto unrealized. If conduct were the expression of character, in a sense which identified character wholly with past attainments, then reformation would be impossible. What a man once was he must always continue to be. But past attainments do not exhaust all the possibilities of character. Since conduct necessarily implies a continuous adjustment of developing capacity to new conditions, there is the ability to frame a changed ideal of self-satisfaction—that is, ability to lead a new life. That the new ideal is adopted from experience of the unworthy nature of former deeds is what we should expect. The chosen end having proved itself unsatisfactory, the alternative end, previously rejected, recurs to consciousness with added claims. To sum up: The doctrine that choice depends upon character is correct, but the doctrine is misused when taken to mean that a man's outward conduct will always be in the same direction that it has been. Character involves all the ideas of different and of better things which have been present to the agent, although he has never attempted to carry them out. And there is always the possibility that, if the proper influences are brought to bear, some one of these latent ideals may be made vital, and wholly change the bent of character and of conduct.

LII. Positive Freedom

The *capacity* of freedom lies in the power to form an ideal or conception of an end. *Actual* freedom lies in the realization of that end which actually satisfies. An end may be freely adopted, and yet its actual working-out may result not in freedom, but in slavery. It may result in rendering the agent more subject to his passions, less able to direct his own conduct, and more cramped and feeble in powers. Only that end which executed really effects greater energy and comprehensiveness of character makes for actual freedom. In a word, only the good man, the man who is truly realizing his individuality, is free, in the positive sense of that word.

Every action which is not in the line of performance of functions must necessarily result in self-enslavement. The end of desire is activity; and it is only in fullness and unity of activity that freedom is found. When desires are not unified—when, that is, the idea of the exercise of function does not control conduct—one desire must conflict with another. Action is directed now this way, now that, and there is friction, loss of power. On account of this same lack of control of desires by the comprehensive law of social activity, one member of society is brought into conflict with another, with waste of energy, and with impeded and divided activity and satisfaction of desire. Exercise of function, on the other hand, unifies the desires, giving each its relative, although subordinate, place. It fits each into the others, and, through the harmonious adjustment of one to another, effects that complete and unhindered action which is freedom. The performance of specific function falls also into free relations with the activities of other persons, co-operating with them, giving and receiving what is needed, and thus constituting full liberty. Other aspects of freedom, as the negative and the potential, are simply means instrumental to the realization of individuality, and when not employed toward this, their true end, they become methods of enslaving the agent.

On the subject of moral freedom, as, upon the whole, in agreement with the view presented here: See Green, *Prolegomena to Ethics*, pp. 90–117, 142–58; Bradley, *Ethical Studies*, Ch. 1; Caird, *Philosophy of Kant*, Vol. II, Bk. II, Ch. 3; Alexander, *Moral Order*, pp. 336–41.

And, for a view agreeing in part, Stephen, *Science of Ethics*, pp. 278–93.

For presentations of the freedom of indifference, see Lotze, *Practical Philosophy*, Ch. 3; Martineau, *Types of Ethical Theory*, Vol. II, pp. 34–40; Calderwood, *Handbook of Moral Philosophy*.

PART TWO

THE ETHICAL WORLD

LIII. The Reality of Moral Relations

The habit of conceiving moral action as a certain *kind* of action, instead of all action so far as it really is action, leads us to conceive of morality as a highly desirable something which somehow ought to be brought into our lives, but which upon the whole is not. It gives rise to the habit of conceiving morality as a vague ideal which it is praiseworthy for the individual to strive for, but which depends wholly for its existence upon the individual's wish in the matter. Morality, that is, is considered as a relation existing between something which merely *ought to be*, on one hand, and the individual's choice, or his conscience on the other. This point of view has found typical expression in Bishop Butler's saying: "If conscience had might as it has right, it would rule the world."

But right is not such a helpless creature. It exists not in word but in power. The moral world is, here and now; it is a reality apart from the wishes, or failures to wish, of any given individual. It bears the same relation to the individual's activity that the "physical world" does to his knowledge. Not till the individual has to spin the physical world out of his consciousness in order to know it, will it be necessary for him to create morality by his choice, before it can exist. As knowledge is mastery in one's self of the real world, the reproduction of it in self-consciousness, so moral action is the appropriation and vital self-expression of the values contained in the existing practical world.

The existence of this moral world is not anything vaguely mysterious. Imagine a well organized factory, in which there is some comprehensive industry carried on—say the production of cotton cloth. This is the end; it is a common end—that for which each individual labors. Not all individuals, however, are doing the same thing. The more perfect the activity, the better organized the work, the more differentiated their respective labors. This is the side of individual activity or freedom. To make the analogy with moral activity complete we have to suppose that each individual is doing the work because of itself, and not merely as drudgery for the sake of some further end, as pay. Now these various individuals are bound together by their various acts; some more nearly because doing closely allied things, all somewhat, because contributing to a common activity. This is the side of laws and duties.

This group of the differentiated and yet related activities is the analogue of the moral world. There are certain wants which have constantly to be fulfilled; certain ends which demand co-operating activities, and which establish fixed relations between men. There is a world of ends, a realm of definite activities in existence, as concrete as the ends and activities in our imagined factory. The child finds, then, ends and actions in existence when he is born. More than this: he is not born as a mere spectator of the world; he is born *into* it. He finds himself encompassed by such relations, and he finds his own being and activity intermeshed with them. If he takes away from himself, as an agent, what he has, as sharing in these ends and actions, nothing remains.

LIV. Moral Institutions

This world of purposes and activities is differentiated into various institutions. The child is born as a member of a *family*; as he grows up he finds that others have possessions which he must respect, that is, he runs upon the institution of *property*. As he grows still older, he finds persons outside of the family of whose actions he must take account as respects his own: *society*, in the limited sense as meaning relations of special intimacy or acquaintanceship. Then he finds the political institutions; the city, state and nation. He finds an educational institution, the school, the college; religious institutions, the church, etc., etc. Everywhere he finds men having common wants and thus proposing common ends and using co-operative modes of action. To these organized modes of action, with their reference to common interests and purposes, he must adjust his activities; he must take his part therein, if he acts at all, though it be only negatively or hostilely, as in evil conduct. These institutions *are* morality real and objective; the individual becomes moral as he shares in this moral world, and takes his due place in it.

Institutions, then, are organized modes of action, on the basis of the wants and interests which unite men. They differ as the family from the town, the church from the state, according to the scope and character of the wants from which they spring. They are not bare *facts* like objects of knowledge; they are *practical*, existing for the sake of, and by means of the will—as execution of ideas which have interest. Because they are expressions of common purposes and ideas, they are not merely private will and intelligence, but, in the literal sense, *public* will and reason.

The moral endeavor of man thus takes the form not of isolated fancies about right and wrong, not of attempts to frame a morality for himself, not of efforts to bring into being some praiseworthy ideal never realized; but the form of sustaining and furthering the moral world of which he is a member. Since the world is one of action, and not of contemplation like the world of knowledge, it can be sustained and furthered only as he makes its ends his own, and identifies himself and his satisfaction with the activities in which other wills find their fulfillment.

This is simply a more concrete rendering of what has already been said about the moral environment (see Sec. XXXIII).

LV. The Aspects of a Moral Institution

An institution is, as we have seen, the expression of unity of desires and ideas; it is general intelligence in action, or common will. As such common will, it is, as respects the merely private or exclusive wants and aims of its members, absolutely *sovereign*. It must aim to control them. It must set before them the common end or ideal and insist upon this as the only real end of individual conduct. The ends so imposed by the public reason are *laws*. But these laws are for the sake of realizing the *common* end, of securing that organized unity of action in which alone the individual can find freedom and fullness of action, or his own satisfaction. Thus the activity of the common will gives freedom, or *rights*, to the various members of the institution.

Every institution, then, has its sovereignty, or authority, and its laws and rights. It is only a false abstraction which makes us conceive of sovereignty, or authority, and of law and of rights as inhering only in some supreme organization, as the national state. The family, the school, the neighborhood group, has its authority as respects its members, imposes its ideals of action, or laws, and confers its respective satisfactions in way of enlarged freedom, or rights. It is true that no one of these institutions is isolated; that each stands in relation with other like and unlike institutions. Each minor institution is a member of some more comprehensive whole, to which it bears the same relation that the individual bears to it. That is to say, *its* sovereignty gives way to the authority of the more comprehensive organization; its laws must be in harmony with the laws which flow from the larger activity; its rights must become aspects of a fuller satisfaction. Only humanity or the organized activity of all the wants, powers and interests common to men, can have absolute sovereignty, law and rights.

But the narrower group has its relations, none the less, although, in ultimate analysis, they flow from and manifest the wider good, which, as wider, must be controlling. Without such minor local authorities, rights and laws, humanity would be a meaningless abstraction, and its activity wholly empty. There is an authority in the family, and the moral growth of the child consists in identifying the law of his own conduct with the ends aimed at by the institution, and in growing into maturity and freedom of manhood through the rights which are bestowed upon him as such a member. Within its own range this institution is ultimate. But its range is not ultimate; the family, valuable and sacred as it is, does not exist for itself. It is not a larger selfishness. It exists as one mode of realizing that comprehensive common good to which all institutions must contribute, if they are not to decay. It is the same with property, the school, the local church, and with the national state.

We can now translate into more concrete terms what was said, in Part One, regarding the good, obligation and freedom. That performance of function which is "the good," is now seen to consist in vital union with, and reproduction of, the practical institutions of which one is a member. The maintenance of such institutions by the free participation therein of individual wills, is, of itself, the common good. Freedom also gets concreteness; it is the assured rights, or powers of action which one gets as such a member: —powers which are not mere claims, nor simply claims recognized as valid by others, but claims reinforced by the will of the whole community. Freedom becomes real in the ethical world; it becomes force and efficiency of action, because it does not mean some private possession of the individual, but means the whole co-operating and organized action of an institution in securing to an individual some power of self-expression.

LVI. Moral Law and the Ethical World

Without the idea of the ethical world, as the unified activity of diverse functions exercised by different individuals, the idea of the good, and of freedom, would be undefined. But probably no one has ever attempted to conceive of the good and of freedom in total abstraction from the normal activity of man. Such has not been the lot of duty, or of the element of law. Often by implication, sometimes in so many words, it is stated that while a physical law may be accounted for, since it is simply an abstract from observed facts, a moral law stands wholly above and apart from actual facts; it expresses solely what "ought to be" and not what is; that, indeed, whether anything in accordance with it ever has existed or not, is a matter of no essential moral importance theoretically, however it may be practically. Now it is evident that a law of something which has not existed, does not and perhaps never will exist, is essentially inexplicable and mysterious. It is as against such a notion of moral law that the idea of a real ethical world has perhaps its greatest service.

A moral law, *e.g.*, the law of justice, is no more *merely* a law of what ought to be than is the law of gravitation. As the latter states a certain relation of moving masses to one another, so the law of justice states a certain relation of active wills to one another. For a given individual, at a given time and circumstances, the law of justice may appear as the law of something which ought to be, but is not: —is not *for him in this respect*, that is to say. But the very fact that it ought to be for him implies that it already is for others. It *is* a law of the society of which he is a member. And it is because he *is* a member of a society having this law, that is a law of what *should* be for him.

Would then justice cease to be a law for him if it were not observed at all in the society of which he is a member? Such a question is as contradictory as asking what would happen to a planet if the solar system went out of existence. It is the law of justice (with other such laws) that *makes* society; that is, it is those active relations which find expression in these laws that unify individuals so that they have a common end, and thus mutual duties. To imagine the abolition of these laws is to imagine the abolition of society; and to ask for the law of individual conduct apart from all relationship, actual or ideal, to society, is to ask in what morality consists when moral conditions are destroyed. A society in which the social bond we call justice does not obtain to some degree in the relations of man to man, is *not* society; and, on the other hand, wherever some law of justice actually obtains, there the law *is* for every individual who is a member of the society.

This does not mean that the "is," the actual status of the moral world, is identical with the "ought," or the ideal relations of man to man. But it does mean that there is no obligation, either in general or as any specific duty, which does not *grow* out of the "is," the actual relations now obtaining.[1] The ethical world at any given time is undoubt-

[1] See Secs. LIX, LX and LXIII for discussion of other aspects of this question.

edly imperfect, and, *therefore*, it demands a certain act to meet the situation. The very imperfection, the very badness in the present condition of things, is a part of the environment with reference to which we must act; it is, thus, an element in the *law* of future action that it shall not exactly repeat the existing condition. In other words, the "is" gives the law of the "ought," but it is a part of this law that the "ought" shall not be as the "is." It is because the relation of justice does hold in members of a stratum of society, having a certain position, power or wealth, but does not hold between this section and another class, that the law of what should be is equal justice for all. In holding that actual social relations afford the law of what should be, we must not forget that these actual relations have a negative as well as a positive side, and that the new law must be framed in view of the negatives, the deficiencies, the wrongs, the contradictions, as well as of the positive attainments. A moral law, to sum up, is the principle of action, which, acted upon, will meet the needs of the existing situation as respects the wants, powers, and circumstances of the individuals concerned. It is no far-away abstraction, but expresses the *movement* of the ethical world.

One example will help define the discussion. Take the case of a street railway conductor, whose union has ordered a strike. What determines the law of his conduct under the circumstances? Evidently the existing ethical institutions of which he is a member, so far as he is conscious of their needs. To determine what he should do, he does not hunt up some law of an "ought" apart from what is; if he should hunt for and should find such a law he would not know what to do with it. Just because it is apart from his concrete circumstances it is no guide, no law for his conduct at all. He has to act not in view of some abstract principle, but in view of a concrete situation. He considers his present wage, its relation to his needs and abilities; his capacity and taste for this and for that work; the reasons for the strike; the conditions of labor at present with reference to winning the strike, and as to the chance of getting other work. He considers his family, their needs and developing powers; the demand that they should live decently; that his children should be fairly educated and get a fair start in the world; he considers his relationships to his fellow members in the union, etc. These considerations, and such as these, give the law to his decision in so far as he acts morally and not instinctively. Where in this law-giving is there any separation from facts? On the contrary, the more right the act (the nearer it comes to its proper law), the more it will simply express and reflect the actual concrete facts. The law, in other words, of action, is the law of actual social forces in their onward movement, in so far as these demand some response in the way of conduct from the individual.

We may restate from this point of view, what we have already learned: A moral law is thoroughly individualized. It cannot be duplicated; it cannot be for one act just what it is for another. The ethical world is too rich in capacity and circumstance to permit of monotony; it is too swift in its movement to allow of bare repetition. It will not hold still; it moves on, and moral law is the law of action required from individuals by this movement.

The consideration of specific institutions, as the family, industrial society, civil society, the nation, etc., with their respective rights and laws, belongs rather to political philosophy than to the general theory of ethics.

PART THREE

THE MORAL LIFE OF THE INDIVIDUAL

LVII. Division of Subject

We have now analyzed the fundamental moral notions—the good, duty and freedom; we have considered their objective realization, and seen that they are outwardly expressed in social relations, the more typical and abiding of which we call institutions; that abstract duties are realized in the laws created and imposed by such institutions, and that abstract freedom is realized in the rights possessed by members in them. We have now to consider the concrete moral life of an individual born into this existing ethical world and finding himself confronted with institutions in which he must execute his part, and in which he obtains his satisfaction and free activity. We have to consider how these institutions appeal to the individual, awakening in him a distinct *moral* consciousness, or the consciousness of active relations to persons, in antithesis to the theoretical consciousness of relations which exist in contemplation; how the individual behaves towards these institutions, realizing them by assuming his proper position in them, or attempting to thwart them by living in isolation from them; and how a moral character is thus called into being. More shortly, we have to deal (1) with the practical consciousness, or the formation and growth of ideals of conduct; (2) with the moral struggle, or the process of realizing ideals, and (3) with moral character, or the virtues.

1

The Formation and Growth of Ideals

LVIII. Analysis of Conscience

The practical consciousness, or the recognition of ends and relations of action, is what is usually termed *conscience*. The analysis of conscience shows that it involves three elements, which may be distinguished in theory, although they have no separate existence in the actual fact of conscience itself. These three elements are (1) the knowledge of certain specific forms of conduct, (2) the recognition of the authority or obligatoriness of the forms, and (3) the emotional factors which cluster about this recognition. That is to say, we often speak (1) of conscience telling or informing us of duties; we speak of an enlightened or unenlightened conscience; of savage, or mediæval, or modern conscience. Here we are evidently thinking of the kind and range of particular acts considered right or wrong. But we also speak (2) of the authority and majesty of conscience; of the commands of conscience, etc. Here we are thinking of the consciousness of *obligation in general*. The savage and the civilized man may vary greatly in their estimate of what particular acts are right or wrong, and yet agree in the recognition that such acts as are right are absolutely obligatory. Finally we speak of an approving or disapproving, or remorseful conscience, of a tender or a hardened conscience, of the pangs, the pricks of conscience, etc. Here (3) we are evidently dealing with the responsiveness of the disposition to moral distinctions, either in particular acts, or in the recognition of moral law in general.

LIX. Conscience as the Recognition of Special Acts as Right or Wrong

Conscience in this sense is no peculiar, separate faculty of mind. It is simply intelligence dealing with a certain subject-matter. That is, conscience is distinguished not by the kind of mental activity at work, but by the kind of material the mind works upon. Intelligence deals with the nature and relations of things, and we call it understanding; intelligence deals with the relations of persons and deeds, and it is termed conscience.

We may, with advantage, recognize these stages in the development of intelligence as dealing with moral relationships:

1. *The Customary or Conventional Conscience*

The existing moral world, with the types and varieties of institutions peculiar to it, is constantly impressing itself upon the immature mind; it makes certain demands of moral agents and enforces them with all the means in its power—punishment, reward, blame, public-opinion, and the bestowal of social leadership. These demands and expectations naturally give rise to certain convictions in the individual as to what he should or should not do. Such convictions are not the outcome of independent reflection, but of the moulding influence of social institutions. Moreover the morality of a time becomes consolidated into proverbs, maxims and law-codes. It takes shape in certain habitual ways of looking at and judging matters. All these are instilled into the growing mind through language, literature, association and legal custom, until they leave in the mind a corresponding habit and attitude toward things to be done. This process may be compared to the process by which knowledge of the world of things is first attained. Certain of the more permanent features of this world, especially those whose observance is important in relation to continued physical existence and well-being, impress themselves upon the mind. Consciousness, with no reflective activity of its own, comes to mirror some of the main outlines of the world. The more important distinctions are fixed in language, and they find their way into the individual mind, giving it unconsciously a certain bent and coloring.

2. *The Loyal Conscience*

But just as the mind, which seems at first to have the facts and features of the world poured into itself as a passive vessel, comes in time through its own experience to appreciate something of their meaning, and, to some extent, to verify them for itself; so the mind in its moral relations. Without forming any critical theory of the institutions and codes which are forming character, without even considering whether they are what they should be, the individual yet comes at least to a practical recognition that it is in these institutions that he gets his satisfactions, and through these codes that he is protected. He identifies himself, his own life, with the social forms and ideals in which he lives, and repels any attack upon them as he would an attack upon himself. The demands which the existing institutions make upon him are not felt as the coercions of a despot, but as expressions of his own will, and requiring loyalty as such. The conventional conscience, if it does not grow into this, tends to become slavish, while an intelligence which practically realizes, although without continual reflection, the *significance* of conventional morality is *free* in its convictions and service.

3. *The Independent or Reflective Conscience*

The intelligence may not simply appropriate, as its own, conventions embodied in current institutions and codes, but may *reflect* upon them. It may ask: What is this institution of family, property for? Does the institution in its present form work as it should work, or is some modification required? Does this rule which is now current embody the true needs of the situation, or is it an antiquated expression of by-gone relations? What is the true spirit of existing institutions, and what sort of conduct does this spirit demand?

Here, in a word, we have the same relation to the ethical world, that we have in physical science to the external world. Intelligence is not content, on its theoretical side, with having facts impressed upon it by direct contact or through language; it is not content with coming to feel for itself the value of the truths so impressed. It assumes an independent attitude, putting itself over against nature and cross-questioning her. It proposes its own ideas, its own theories and hypotheses, and manipulates facts to see if this rational meaning can be verified. It criticises what passes as truth, and pushes on to more adequate statement.

The correlative attempt, on the part of intelligence on its practical side, may have a larger or a smaller scope. In its wider course it aims to criticise and to re-form prevailing social ideals and institutions—even those apparently most fixed. This is the work of the great moral teachers of the world. But in order that conscience be critical, it is not necessary that its range be so wide. The average member of a civilized community is nowadays called upon to reflect upon his immediate relationships in life, to see if they are what they should be; to regulate his own conduct by rules which he follows not simply because they are customary, but the result of his own examination of the situation. There is no difference in kind between the grander and the minuter work. And it is only the constant exercise of reflective examination on the smaller scale which makes possible, and which gives efficiency to, the deeper criticism and transformation.

LX. Reflective Conscience and the Ethical World

This conception of conscience as critical and reflective is one of the chief fruits of the Socratic ethics, fructified by the new meaning given life through the Christian spirit. It involves the "right of free conscience"—the right of the individual to know the good, to know the end of action, for himself, rather than to have some good, however imposing and however beneficent, enjoined from without. It is this principle of subjective freedom, says Hegel, which marks the turning-point in the distinction of modern from ancient times (Sec. 124, *Grundlinien der Philosophie des Rechts*, Vol. VIII of Hegel's *Works*).[2]

2 I hardly need say how largely I am indebted in the treatment of this topic, and indeed, in the whole matter of the "ethical world," to Hegel.

But this notion of conscience is misinterpreted when the content as well as the form of conscience is thought to be individual. There is no right of private judgment, in the sense that there is not a public source and standard of judgment. What is meant by this right is that the standard, the source, is not the opinion of some other person, or group of persons. It is a common, objective standard. It is that embodied in social relationships themselves.

The conception of conscience as a private possession, to be exercised by each one in independence of historical forms and contemporary ideals, is thoroughly misleading. The saying "I had to follow my own notion of what is right" has been made thc excuse for all sorts of capricious, obstinate and sentimental performance. It is of such notions that Hegel further says: "The striving for a morality of one's own is futile, and by its very nature impossible of attainment; in respect of morality the saying of the wisest men of antiquity is the only true one: To be moral is to live in accordance with the moral tradition of one's country" (Hegel, *Works*, Vol. 1, p. 389). And in discussing the same question, Bradley has said that the wish to have a morality of one's own better than that of the world is to be on the threshold of morality (*Ethical Studies*, p. 180).

Yet, on the other hand, conscience should not simply repeat the burden of existing usages and opinions. No one can claim that the existing morality embodies the highest possible conception of personal relations. A morality which does not recognize both the possibility and the necessity of advance is immorality. Where then is the way out from a capricious self-conceit, on one hand, and a dead conformity on the other? Reflective conscience must be *based* on the moral consciousness expressed in existing institutions, manners and beliefs. Otherwise it is empty and arbitrary. But the existing moral status is never wholly self-consistent. It realizes ideals in one relation which it does not in another; it gives rights to "aristocrats" which it denies to low-born; to men, which it refuses to women; it exempts the rich from obligations which it imposes upon the poor. Its institutions embody a common good which turns out to be good only to a privileged few, and thus existing in self-contradiction. They suggest ends which they execute only feebly or intermittently. Reflective intelligence cross-questions the existing morality; and extracts from it the ideal which it pretends to embody, and thus is able to criticise the existing morality in the light of its *own* ideal. It points out the inconsistencies, the incoherencies, the compromises, the failures, between the actual practice and the theory at the basis of this practice. And thus the new ideal proposed by the individual is not a product of his private opinions, but is the outcome of the ideal embodied in existing customs, ideas and institutions.

LXI. The Sense of Obligation

There has been much discussion regarding the nature of the act of mind by which obligation is recognized. A not uncommon view has been that the sense of duty as such must be the work of a peculiar faculty of the mind. Admitting that the recognition of this or that particular thing as right or wrong, is the work of ordinary intelligence, it is held that the additional recognition of the absolute obligatoriness of the right cannot be the work of this intelligence. For our intellect is confined to judging what is or has been; the conception of obligation, of something which should be, wholly transcends its scope. There is, therefore, some special faculty called conscience which affixes to the ordinary judgments the stamp of the categorical imperative "You ought."

See for example Maurice on *The Conscience*. The view is traceable historically to Kant's conception of Practical Reason, but as the view is ordinarily advanced the function of Practical Reason in Kant's philosophy is overlooked. The Practical Reason is no special faculty of man's being; it is his consciousness of himself as an acting being; that is, as a being capable of acting from ideas. Kant never separates the consciousness of duty from the very nature of will as the realization of conceptions. In the average modern presentation, this intrinsic connection of duty with activity is absent. Conscience becomes a faculty whose function it is to clap the idea of duty upon the existent conception of an act; and this existent conception is regarded as morally indifferent.

It is true that Kant's Practical Reason has a certain separateness or isolation. But this is because of his general separation of the rational from the sensuous factor, and not because of any separation of the consciousness of action from the consciousness of duty. If Kant erred in his divorce of desire and duty, then even the relative apartness of the Practical Reason must be given up. The consciousness of obligation is involved in the recognition of *any* end of conduct, and not simply in the end of abstract law.

Such a conception of conscience, however, is open to serious objections. Aside from the fact that large numbers of men declare that no amount of introspection reveals any such machinery within themselves, this separate faculty seems quite superfluous. The real distinction is not between the consciousness of an action with, and without, the recognition of duty, but between a consciousness which is and one which is not capable of conduct. Any being who is capable of putting before himself ideas as motives of conduct, who is capable of forming a conception of something which he would realize, is, by that very fact, capable of a sense of obligation. The consciousness of an end to be realized, the idea of something to be done, is, in and of itself, the consciousness of duty.

Let us consider again the horse-car conductor (see Sec. LVI). After he has analyzed the situation which faces him and decided that a given course of conduct is the one which fits the situation, does he require some additional faculty to inform him that this course is the one which should be followed? The analysis of practical ideas, that is, of proposed ends of conduct, is from the first an analysis of what should be done. Such being the case, it is no marvel that the conclusion of the reflection is: "This should (ought to) be done."

Indeed, just as every judgment about existent fact naturally takes the form "S *is* P," so every judgment regarding an activity which executes an idea takes the form, "S ought (or ought not) to be P." It requires no additional faculty of mind, after intelligence has been studying the motions of the moon, to insert itself, and affirm some objective relation or truth—as that the moon's motions are explainable by the law of gravitation. It is the very essence of theoretical judgment, judgment regarding fact, to state truth—what is. And it is the very essence of practical judgment, judgment regarding deeds, to state that active relation which we call obligation, what *ought to be*.

The judgment as to what a practical situation *is*, is an untrue or abstract judgment.

The practical situation is itself an *activity*; the needs, powers, and circumstances which make it are moving on. At no instant in time is the scene quiescent. But the agent, in order to determine his course of action in view of this situation, has to *fix* it; he has to arrest its onward movement in order to tell what it is. So his abstracting intellect cuts a cross-section through its on-going, and says "This *is* the situation." Now the judgment "This ought to be the situation," or "in view of the situation, my conduct ought to be thus and so," is simply restoring the movement which the mind has temporarily put out of sight. By means of its cross-section, intelligence has detected the principle, or law of movement, of the situation, and it is on the basis of this movement that conscience declares what ought to be.

Just as the fact of moral law, or of authority, of the incumbency of duty, needs for its explanation no separation of the "is" from the "ought" (see Sec. LVI), but only recognition of the law of the "is" which is, perforce, a law of movement, and of change;—so the consciousness of law, "the sense of obligation" requires no special mental faculty which may declare what ought to be. The intelligence that is capable of declaring truth, or what is, is capable also of making known obligation. For obligation is only *practical* truth, the "is" of doing.

See upon this point, as well as upon the relation of laws and rules to action, my article in Vol. I, No. 2, of the *International Journal of Ethics*, entitled "Moral Theory and Practice." [*Early Works*, III, 93–109.]

LXII. Conscience as Emotional Disposition

Probably no judgment is entirely free from emotional coloring and accompaniments. It is doubtful whether the most indifferent judgment is not based upon, and does not appeal to, some interest. Certainly all the more important judgments awaken some response from the self, and excite its interests to their depths. Some of them may be excited by the intrinsic nature of the subject-matter under judgment, while others are the results of associations more or less accidental. The former will necessarily be aroused in every being, who has any emotional nature at all, whenever the judgment is made, while the latter will vary from time to time, and may entirely pass away. That moral judgments, judgments of what should be (or should have been) done, arouse emotional response, is therefore no cause for surprise. It may help clear up difficulties if we distinguish three kinds of such emotional accompaniment.

1. There are, first, the interests belonging to the sense of obligation as such. We have just seen that this sense of obligation is nothing separate from the consciousness of the particular act which is to be performed. Nevertheless the consciousness of obligation, of an authority and law, recurs with every act, while the special content of the act constantly varies. Thus an idea of law, or of duty in general, is formed, distinct from any special duty. Being formed, it arouses the special emotional excitation appropriate to it. The formation of this general idea of duty, and the growth of feeling of duty as such, is helped on through the fact that children (and adults so far as their moral life is immature) need to have their moral judgments constantly reinforced by recurrence to the thought of law. That is to say, a child, who is not capable of seeing the true moral bearings and claims of an act, is yet continually required to perform such an act on the ground that it *is* obligatory. The feeling, therefore, is natural and legitimate. It must, however, go hand in hand with the feelings aroused by the special moral relations under consideration. Disconnected from such union, it necessarily leads to slavish and arbitrary forms of conduct. A child, for example, who is constantly taught to perform acts simply because he *ought* to do so, without having at the same time his intelligence directed to the nature of the act which is obligatory (without, that is, being led to see how or why it is obligatory), may have a strongly developed sense of obligation. As he grows up, however, this sense of duty will be largely one of dread and apprehension; a feeling of constraint, rather than of free service.

Besides this, it will be largely a matter of accident to what act this feeling attaches itself. Anything that comes to the mind with the force of associations of past education, any ideal that forces itself persistently into consciousness from any source may awaken this sense of obligation, wholly irrespective of the true nature of the act. This is the explanation of strongly "conscientious" persons, whose morality is yet unintelligent and blundering. It is of such persons that it has been said that a thoroughly *good* man can do more harm than a number of bad men.

When, however, the feeling of obligation in general is developed along with particular moral judgments (that is, along with the habit of considering the special nature of acts performed), it is one of the strongest supports to morality. Acts constantly need to be performed which are recognized as right and as obligatory, and yet with reference to which there is no fixed habit of conduct. In these cases, the more direct, or spontaneous, stimulus to action is wanting.

If, however, there is a strong sense of obligation in general, this may attach itself to the particular act and thus afford the needed impetus. In unusual experiences, and in cases where the ordinary motive-forces are lacking, such a feeling of regard for law may be the only sure stay of right conduct.

2. There is the emotional accompaniment appropriate to the special content of the act. If, for example, the required act has to do with some person, there arise in consciousness the feelings of interest, of love and friendship, or of dislike, which belong to that person. If it relate to some piece of work to be done, the sweeping of a room, the taking of a journey, the painting of a picture, there are the interests natural to such subjects. These feelings when aroused necessarily form part of the emotional attitude as respects the act. It is the strength and normal welling-up of such specific interests which afford the best assurance of healthy and progressive moral conduct, as distinct from mere sentimental dwelling upon ideals. Only interests prevent the divorce of feelings and ideas from habits of action. Such interests are the union of the subjective element, the self, and the objective, the special relations to be realized (Sec. xxxiv),

and thus necessarily produce a right and healthy attitude towards moral ends. It is obvious that in a normal moral life, the law of obligation in general, and the specific interests in particular cases, should more and more fuse. The interests, at their strongest, take the form of *love*. And thus there is realized the ideal of an effective character; the union of law and inclination in its pure form—love for the action in and of itself.

3. Emotions due to accidental associations. It is matter of common notice that the moral feelings are rarely wholly pure; that all sorts of sentiments, due to associations of time and place and person not strictly belonging to the acts themselves, cluster about them. While this is true, we should not forget the great difficulty there is in marking off any associations as *wholly* external to the nature of the act. We may say that mere fear of punishment is such a wholly external feeling, having no place in moral emotion. Yet it may be doubted whether there is any feeling that may be called mere fear of punishment. It is, perhaps, fear of punishment by a parent, for whom one has love and respect, and thus the fear has partially a genuinely moral aspect. Some writers would call the æsthetic feelings, the feelings of beauty, of harmony, which gather about moral ends adventitious. Yet the fact that other moralists have made all moral feelings essentially æsthetic, as due to the perception of the fitness and proportion of the acts, should warn us from regarding æsthetic feelings as wholly external. About all that can be said is that feelings which do not spring from *some* aspect of the content of the act itself should be extruded, with growing maturity of character, from influence upon conduct.

LXIII. Conscientiousness

Conscientiousness is primarily the virtue of intelligence in regard to conduct. That is to say, it is the formed habit of bringing intelligence to bear upon the analysis of moral relations—the habit of considering what ought to be done. It is based upon the recognition of the idea first distinctly formulated by Socrates—that "an unexamined life is not one that should be led by man." It is the outgrowth of the customary morality embodied in usages, codes and social institutions, but it is an advance upon custom, because it requires a meaning and a reason. It is the mark of a "character which will not be satisfied without understanding the law that it obeys; without knowing what the good is, for which the demand has hitherto been blindly at work" (Green, *Prolegomena*, p. 270). Conscientiousness, then, is reflective intelligence grown into character. It involves a greater and wider recognition of obligation in general, and a larger and more stable emotional response to everything that presents itself as duty; as well as the habit of deliberate consideration of the moral situation and of the acts demanded by it.

Conscientiousness is an analysis of the conditions under which conduct takes place, and of the action that will meet these conditions; it is a thoroughly *objective* analysis. What is sometimes termed conscientiousness is merely the habit of analyzing internal moods and sentiments; of prying into "motives" in that sense of motive which identifies it not with the end of action, but with some subjective state of emotion. Thus considered, conscientiousness is morbid. We are sometimes warned against *over*-conscientiousness. But such conscientiousness means simply over-regard of one's private self; keeping an eye upon the effect of conduct on one's internal state, rather than upon conduct itself. Over-conscientiousness is as impossible as over-intelligence, since it is simply the application of intelligence to conduct. It is as little morbid and introspective as is the analysis of any fact in nature. Another notion which is sometimes thought to be bound up with that of conscience, also has nothing to do with it; namely, the notion of a precision and coldness opposed to all large spontaneity and broad sympathy in conduct. The reflective man of narrow insight and cramped conduct is often called the conscientious man and opposed to the man of generous impulses. This comes from identifying conscience with a ready-made code of rules, and its action with the application of some such fixed code to all acts as they come up. It is evident, on the contrary, that such a habit is opposed to conscience. Conscience means the consideration of each case *in itself*; measuring it not by any outside code, but in the existing moral situation.

On conscientiousness, see Green, *Prolegomena*, pp. 269–71 and 323–27; and Alexander, *Moral Order*, pp. 156–60. These writers, however, seem to identify it too much with internal scrutiny. Green, for example, expressly identifies conscientiousness with a man's "questioning about himself, whether he has been as good as he should have been, whether a better man would not have acted otherwise than he has done" (*Prolegomena*, p. 323). He again speaks of it as "comparison of our own practice, as we know it on the inner side in relation to the motives and character which it expresses, with an ideal of virtue." The first definition seems to be misleading. Questioning as to whether the end adopted was what it should have been, *i.e.*, whether the analysis of the situation was correctly performed, may be of great service in aiding future decisions, but questioning regarding the purity of one's own "motive" does not seem of much avail. In a man upon the whole good, such questioning is apt to be paralyzing. The energy that should go to conduct goes to anxiety about one's conduct. It is the view of goodness as directed mainly towards one's own private motives, which has led such writers as Henry James, Sr., and Mr. Hinton, to conceive of "morality," the struggle for goodness, to be in essence bad. They conceived of the struggle for "private goodness" as no different from the struggle for private pleasure, although likely, of course, to lead to better things. Nor in a bad man is such scrutiny of "motive," as apart from objective end, of much value. The bad man is generally aware of the badness of his motive without much close examination. The truth aimed at by Green is, I think, amply covered by recognizing that conscientiousness as a constant will to know what should be, and to re-adjust conduct to meet the new insight, is the spring of the moral life.

LXIV. Moral Commands, Rules and Systems

What is the part played by specific commands and by general rules in the examination of conduct by conscience? We should note, in the first place, that commands are not rules, and rules are not commands. A command, to be a command, must be specific and individual. It must refer to time, place and circumstance. "Thou shalt do no murder" is not strictly speaking a command, for it allows questioning as to what is murder. Is killing in war murder? Is the hanging of criminals murder? Is taking life in self-defense murder? Regarded simply as a command, this command would be "void for uncertainty." A true command is a specific injunction of one person to another to do or not to do a stated thing or things. Under what conditions do commands play a part in moral conduct? In cases where the intelligence of the agent is so undeveloped that he cannot realize for himself the situation and see the act required, and when a part of the agent's environment is constituted by others who have such required knowledge, there *is* a moral element in command and in obedience.

This explains the moral responsibility of parents to children and of children to parents. The soldier, too, in recognizing a general's command, is recognizing the situation as it exists for him. Were there simply superior force on one side, and fear on the other, the relation would be an immoral one. It is implied, of course, in such an instance as the parents' command, that it be so directed as to enable the child more and more to dispense with it—that is, that it be of such a character as to give the child insight into the situation for himself. Here is the transition from a command to a rule.

A rule does not tell what to do or what to leave undone. The Golden Rule, for example, does not tell me how to act in any specific case. *A rule is a tool of analysis*. The moral situation, or capacity in its relation to environment, is often an extremely complicated affair. How shall the individual resolve it? How shall he pick it to pieces, so as to see its real nature and the act demanded by it? It is evident that the analysis will be the more truly and speedily performed if the agent has a method by which to attack it, certain principles in the light of which he may view it, instruments for cross-questioning it and making it render up its meaning. Moral rules perform this service. While the Golden Rule does not of itself give one jot of information as to what I should do in a given case, it does, if accepted, immensely simplify the situation. Without it I should perhaps have to act blindly; with it the question comes to this: What should I, under the given circumstances, like to have done to me? This settled, the whole question of what should be done is settled.

It is obvious, then, that the value of a moral rule depends upon its potency in revealing the inner spirit and reality of individual deeds. Rules in the negative form, rules whose application is limited in scope because of an attempt to be specific, are midway between commands proper and rules. The Golden Rule, on the other hand, is positive, and not attempting to define any specific act, covers in its range all relations of man to man. It is indeed only a concrete and forcible statement of the ethical principle itself, the idea of a common good, or of a community of persons. This is also a convenient place for considering the practical value of ethical systems. We have already seen that no system can attempt to tell what in particular should be done. The principle of a system, however, may be of some aid in analyzing a specific case. In this way, a system may be regarded as a highly generalized rule. It attempts to state some fundamental principle which lies at the basis of moral conduct. So far as it succeeds in doing this, there is the possibility of its practical application in particular cases, although, of course, the mediate rules must continue to be the working tools of mankind—on account of their decided concrete character, and because they have themselves taken shape under the pressure of practice rather than of more theoretical needs.

LXV. Development of Moral Ideals

Thus far we have been speaking of conscience mainly as to its method of working. We have now to speak more definitely of its content, or of the development of ideals of action.

It is of the very nature of moral conduct to be progressive. Permanence of *specific* ideals means moral death. We say that truth-telling, charity, loyalty, temperance, have always been moral ends and while this is true, the statement as ordinarily made is apt to hide from us the fact that the content of the various ideals (what is *meant* by temperance, etc.) has been constantly changing, and this of necessity. The realization of moral ends must bring about a changed situation, so that the repetition of the same ends would no longer satisfy. This progress has two sides: the satisfaction of wants leads to a larger view of what satisfaction really is, *i.e.*, to the creation of new capacities and wants; while adjustment to the environment creates wider and more complex social relationships.

Let the act be one of intelligence. Some new fact or law is discovered. On one hand, this discovery may arouse a hitherto comparatively dormant mind; it may suggest the possession of capacities previously latent; it may stimulate mental activity and create a thirst for expanding knowledge. This readjustment of intellectual needs and powers may be comparatively slight, or it may amount, as it has with many a young person, to a revolution. On the other hand, the new fact changes the intellectual outlook, the mental horizon, and, by transforming somewhat the relations of things, demands new conduct. All this, even when the growth of knowledge concerns only the physical world. But development of insight into social needs and affairs has a larger and more direct progressive influence. The social world exists spiritually, as conceived, and a new conception of it, new perception of its scope and bearings, is, perforce, a change of that world. And thus it is with the satisfaction of the human want of knowledge, that patience, courage, self-respect, humility, benevolence, all change character. When, for example, psychology has given an increase of knowledge regarding men's motives, political economy an increase of knowledge regarding men's wants, when historical knowledge has added its testimony regarding the effects of indiscriminate giving, charity must change its content. While once, the mere supplying of food or money by one to another may have been right as meeting the recognized relations, charity now comes to mean large responsibility in knowledge of antecedents and circumstances, need of organization, careful tracing of consequences, and, above all, effort to remove the conditions which made the want possible. The activity involved has infinitely widened.

Let the act be in the region of industrial life—a new invention. The invention of the telephone does not simply satisfy an old want—it creates new. It brings about the possibility of closer social relations, extends the distribution of intelligence, facilitates commerce. It is a common saying that the luxury of one generation is the necessity of the next;

that is to say, what once satisfied a somewhat remote need becomes in time the basis upon which new needs grow up. Energy previously pent up is set free, new power and ideals are evoked. Consider again a person assuming a family relation. This seems, at first, to consist mainly in the satisfaction of certain common and obvious human wants. But this satisfaction, if moral, turns out rather to be the creation of new insight into life, of new relationships, and thus of new energies and ideals. We may generalize these instances. The secret of the moral life is not getting or having, it is doing and thus being. The getting and the possessing side of life has a moral value only when it is made the stimulus and nutriment of new and wider acting. To solve the equation between getting and doing is the moral problem of life. Let the possession be acquiesced in for its own sake, and not as the way to freer (and thus more moral) action, and the selfish life has set in (see Sec. LXVII). It is essential to moral activity that it feed itself into larger appetites and thus into larger life.

This must not be taken to deny that there is a mechanical side even to the moral life. A merchant, for example, may do the same thing over and over again, like going to his business every morning at the same hour. This is a moral act and yet it does not seem to lead to a change in moral wants or surroundings. Yet even in such cases it should be noted that it is only outwardly that the act is the *same*. In itself, that is, in its relation to the will of the agent, it is simply one element in the whole of character; and as character opens up, the act must change somewhat also. It is performed somehow in a new spirit. If this is not to some extent true, if such acts become wholly mechanical, the moral life is hardening into the rigidity of death.

This progressive development consists on one side in a richer and subtler individual activity, in increased individualization, in wider and freer functions of life; on the other it consists in increase in number of those persons whose ideal is a "common good," or who have membership in the same moral community; and, further, it consists in more complex relations between them. It is both intensive and extensive.

History is one record of growth in the sense of specific powers. Its track is marked by the appearance of more and more internal and distinguishing traits; of new divisions of labor and corresponding freedom in functioning. It begins with groups in which everything is massed, and the good is common only in the sense of being undifferentiated for all. It progresses with the evolution of individuality, of the peculiar gifts entrusted to each, and hence of the specific service demanded of each.

The other side, the enlargement of the community of ends, has been termed growth in "comprehensiveness." History is again a record of the widening of the social consciousness—of the range of persons whose interests have to be taken into account in action. There has been a period in which the community was nothing more than a man's own immediate family group, this enlarging to the clan, the city, the social class, the nation; until now, in theory, the community of interests and ends is humanity itself.

This growth in comprehensiveness is not simply a growth in the number of persons having a common end. The quantitative growth reacts upon the *nature* of the ends themselves. For example, when the conceived community is small, bravery may consist mainly in willingness to fight for the recognized community against other hostile groups. As these groups become themselves included in the moral community, courage must change its form, and become resoluteness and integrity of purpose in defending manhood and humanity as such. That is to say, as long as the community is based largely upon physical facts, like oneness of blood, of territory, etc., the ideal of courage will have a somewhat external and physical manifestation. Let the community be truly spiritual, consisting in recognition of unity of destiny and function in co-operation toward an all-inclusive life, and the ideal of courage becomes more internal and spiritual, consisting in loyalty to the possibilities of humanity, whenever and wherever found.

On this development of moral ideals, and especially of the growth in "comprehensiveness" as reacting upon the intrinsic form which the ideal itself takes, see Green, *Prolegomena*, pp. 264–308, followed by Alexander, *Moral Order*, pp. 384–98. For the process of change of ideals in general, see Alexander, pp. 271–92, and 369–71.

2

The Moral Struggle or the Realizing of Ideals

LXVI. Goodness as a Struggle

We have already seen that the bare repetition of identically the same acts does not consist with morality. To aim at securing a satisfaction precisely like the one already experienced, is to fail to recognize the altered capacity and environment, and the altered duty. Moral satisfaction prior to an act is *ideal*; ideal not simply in the sense of being conceived, or present to thought, but ideal in the sense that it has not been already enjoyed. Some satisfaction has been enjoyed in a previous activity, but that very satisfaction has so enlarged and complicated the situation, that its mere repetition would not afford moral or active satisfaction, but only what Kant terms "pathological" satisfaction. Morality thus assumes the form of a struggle. The past satisfaction speaks for itself; it has been verified in experience, it has conveyed its worth to our very senses. We have tried and tasted it, and know that it is good. If morality lay in the repetition of similar satisfactions, it would not be a struggle. We should know experimentally beforehand that the chosen end would bring us satisfaction, and should be at rest in that knowledge. But when morality lies in striving for satisfactions which have not verified themselves to our sense, it always requires an effort. We have to surrender the enjoyed good, and stake ourselves upon that of which we cannot say: We *know* it is good. To surrender the actual experienced good for a possible ideal good is the struggle.

We arrive, in what is termed the opposition of desire and duty, at the heart of the moral struggle. Of course, taken strictly, there can be no opposition here. The duty which did not awaken *any* desire would not appeal to the mind even as a duty. But we may distinguish between a desire which is based on past satisfaction actually experienced, and desire based simply upon the idea that the end is *desirable*—that it ought to be desired. It may seem strange to speak of a desire based simply upon the recognition that an end *should* be desired, but the possibility of awakening such a desire and the degree of its strength are the test of a moral character. How far does this end awaken response in me because I see that it is the end which is fit and due? How far does it awaken this response although it does not fall into line with past satisfactions, or although it actually thwarts some habitual satisfaction? Here is the opposition of duty and desire. It lies in the contrast of a good which has demonstrated itself as such in experience, and a good whose claim to be good rests only on the fact that it is the act which meets the situation. It is the contrast between a good of possession, and one of action.

From this point of view morality is a life of *aspiration*, and of *faith*; there is required constant willingness to give up past goods as the good, and to press on to new ends; not because past achievements are bad, but because, being good, they have created a situation which demands larger and more intricately related achievements. This willingness is aspiration and it implies *faith*. Only the old good is of sight, has verified itself to sense. The new ideal, the end which meets the situation, is felt as good only in so far as the character has formed the conviction that to meet obligation is itself a good, whether bringing sensible satisfaction or not. You can prove to a man that he ought to act so and so (that is to say, that such an act is the one which fits the present occasion), but you cannot *prove* to him that the performance of that duty will be good. Only faith in the moral order, in the identity of duty and the good, can assert this. Every time an agent takes as his end (that is, chooses as good) an activity which he has not already tried, he asserts his belief in the goodness of right action as such. This faith is not a mere intellectual thing, but it is practical—the staking of self upon activity as against passive possession.

LXVII. Moral Badness

Badness originates in the contrast which thus comes about between *having* the repetition of former action, and *doing*—pressing forward to the new right action. Goodness is the choice of doing; the refusal to be content with past good as exhausting the entire content of goodness. It is, says Green, "in the continued effort to be better that goodness consists." The man, however bad his past and however limited his range of intellectual, æsthetic and social activity, who is dissatisfied with his past, and whose dissatisfaction manifests itself in act, is accounted better than the man of a respectable past and higher plane of life who has lapsed into contented acquiescence with past deeds. For past deeds are not *deeds*, they are passive enjoyments. The bad man, on the other hand, is not the man who loves badness *in and for itself*. Such a man would be a mad man or a devil. All conduct, bad as well as good, is for the sake of *some* satisfaction, that is, some good. In the bad man, the satisfaction which is aimed at is *simply* the one congruent with existing inclinations, irrespective of the sufficiency of those inclinations in view of the changed capacity and environment: it is a good of *having*. The bad man, that is to say, does not recognize any *ideal* or *active* good; any good which has not already commended itself to him as such. This good may be good in *itself*; but, as distinguished from the good which requires action, that which would fulfill the present capacity or meet the present situation, it is bad.

Thus Alexander terms badness *a survival*, in part at least, of former goodness. Hinton says (*Philosophy and Religion*, p. 146), "That a thing is wrong does not mean that it ought never to have been done or thought, but that it ought to be left off." It will be noted that we are not dealing with the metaphysical or the religious problem of the nature and origin of evil, but simply with an account of bad action as it appears in individual conduct.

Badness has four traits, all derivable from this basal fact. They are: (1) Lawlessness, (2) Selfishness, (3) Baseness, (4) Demoralization.

1. Lawlessness

When desire and duty, that is, when desires based on past having and on future acting, conflict, the bad man lets duty go. He virtually denies that it is a good at all—it may be a good in the abstract but not a good for him. He denies that obligation as such has any value; that any end is to be consulted save his own state of mind. He denies that there is law for conduct—at least any law beyond the inclination which he happens to have at the time of action. Keeping himself within that which has verified itself to his feeling in the past, he abrogates all authority excepting that of his own immediate feelings.

2. Selfishness

It has already been shown that the self is not necessarily immoral, and hence that action for self is not necessarily bad—indeed, that the true self is social and interest in it right (see Sec. XXXV). But when a satisfaction based on past experience is set against one proceeding from an act as meeting obligation, there grows up a divorce in the self. The actual self, the self recognizing only past and sensible satisfaction, is set over against the self which recognizes the necessity of expansion and a wider environment. Since the former self confines its action to benefits demonstrably accruing to itself, while the latter, in meeting the demands of the situation, necessarily contributes to the satisfaction of others, one takes the form of a *private* self, a self whose good is set over against and exclusive of that of others, while the self recognizing obligation becomes a social self—the self which performs its due function in society. It is, again, the contrast between getting and doing.

All moral action is based upon the presupposition of the identity of good (Sec. XL), but it by no means follows that this identity of good can be demonstrated to the agent at the time of action. On the contrary, it is matter of the commonest experience that the sensible good, the demonstrable good (that is, the one visible on the line of past satisfaction) may be contradictory to the act which would satisfy the interests of others. The identity of interests can be proved *only by acting upon it*; to the agent, prior to action, it is a matter of faith. Choice presents itself then in these cases as a test: Do you believe that the Good is simply your private good, or is the true Good, is *your* good, one which includes the good of others? The condemnation passed upon the "selfish" man is that he virtually declares that good is essentially exclusive and private. He shuts himself up within himself, within, that is, his past achievements, and the inclinations based upon them. The good man goes out of himself in new action. Bad action is thus essentially narrowing, it confines the self; good action is expansive and vital, it moves on to a larger self.

In fine, all conduct, good and bad, satisfies the self; bad conduct, however, aims at a self which, keeping its eye upon its private and assured satisfaction, refuses to recognize the increasing function with its larger social range,—the "selfish" self.

Light is thrown upon this point by referring to what was said about interest (Sec. XXXIV). Interest is *active* feeling, feeling turned upon an object, and going out toward it so as to identify it with self. In this active and objective interest there is satisfaction, but the satisfaction is *in* the activity which has the object for its content. This is the satisfaction of the good self. In the bad self, interest is reduced to mere feeling; for the aim of life in such a self is simply to have certain feelings as its own possession; activity and its object are degraded into mere means for getting these sensations.

Activity has two sides; as activity, as projection or expression of one's powers, it satisfies self; as activity, also, it has some end, some object, for its content. The activity as such, therefore, the activity for its own sake, must involve the realization of this object for its own sake. But in having, in getting, there is no such creation or maintenance of an object for itself. Objects cease to be "ends in themselves" when they cease to be the content of action; and are degraded into means of private satisfaction, that is, of sensation.

3. *Baseness*

For, when we say that bad action takes account of ideals only on the basis of possession, we say, in effect, that it takes account only of *sensible* satisfaction. As it is in the progressive movement of morality that there arises the distinction of the law-abiding and the lawless self, of the social and the selfish self, so in the same aspect there comes into existence the distinction of the low, degraded, sensual self, as against the higher or spiritual self. In themselves, or naturally, there is no desire high, none low. But when an inclination for an end which consists in possession comes into conflict with one which includes an active satisfaction—one not previously enjoyed—the contrast arises. It is wrong to say, with Kant, that the bad act is simply for pleasure; for the bad act, the choice of a past satisfaction as against the aspiration for a wider good, may have a large content—it may be the good of one's family; it may be scientific or æsthetic culture. Yet the moment a man begins to live on the plane of past satisfaction as such, he has begun to live on the plane of "sense," or for pleasure. The refusal to recognize the ideal good, to acknowledge activity as good, throws the agent back into a life of dwelling upon his own sensible good, and thus he falls more and more into a life of dwelling upon mere sensations. What made the past good a good at all was the spirit, the activity, in it, and when it is no longer an activity, but a mere keeping, the life is gone out of it. The selfish life must degenerate into mere sensuality—although when sensuality is "refined" we call it sentimentality.

4. Demoralization

Morality is activity; exercise of function. To cease this activity is not to remain on the attained level, for that, *when attained*, was active. It is to relapse, to slip down into badness. The moral end is always an activity. To fail in this activity is, therefore, to involve character in disintegration. It can be kept together only by constant organizing activity; only by acting upon new wants and moving toward new situations. Let this activity cease, and disorganization ensues, as surely as the body decays when life goes, instead of simply remaining inert as it was. Bad conduct is thus *unprincipled*; it has no centre, no movement. The good man is "organic"; he uses his attainments to discover new needs, and to assimilate new material. He lives from within outwards, his character is compact, coherent; he has *integrity*. The bad man, having no controlling unity, has no consistent line of action; his motives of conduct contradict one another; he follows this maxim in relation to this person, that in relation to another; character is *demoralized*.

The bad man is unstable and double-minded. He is not one person, but a group of conflicting wills. So far as he is really bad he becomes as many persons as he has desires. His conduct cannot be made universal. He always makes exceptions in favor of himself. He does not want moral relations abolished, but relaxed or deflected in his own case, while they still hold for other men.

This is the truth at the basis of Kant's contention regarding goodness as conduct whose maxim is capable of generalization. See also Bradley, *Ethical Studies*, pp. 261–71. And Alexander, *Moral Order*, pp. 309–12.

LXVIII. Goodness in its Relation to the Struggle

1. Two aspects of this we have already noted; one, that of conscientiousness, or habitual alertness and responsiveness of intelligence to the nature of obligation, both in general and as to the specific acts which are obligatory. The other is that goodness, in this relation, consists in *progressive* adjustment, involving aspiration as to future conduct, and correlative humility as to present achievements of character.

2. We may state what has already been suggested, that goodness as self-sacrifice or self-renunciation has also its place here. The moral attitude is one of renunciation, because, on account of the constantly growing wants and circumstances, the satisfactions which belong to the actually realized self must be given up for active goods. That the self-sacrifice takes largely the form of the surrender of private interests to the welfare of the whole, is explained by what has just been said regarding selfishness. Self-sacrifice is not in any way the moral end or the last word. Life is lost that it may be found. The smaller local life of the private self is given up in order that the richer and fuller life of the social or active self may be realized. But none the less the self-sacrifice at the time that it is made is genuine and real.

While it is involved in the very nature of morality that moral conduct shall bring greater activity, larger life, the motive of the agent in self-sacrifice is not to give up the lesser satisfaction for the sake of getting a greater. It is only so far as he is already moral that he is convinced that the new duty will bring satisfaction, and his conviction is not one of sense, but of faith. To the agent at the time of action, it is a real satisfaction which is given up for one that is only ideal, and given up because the ideal satisfaction is ethical, active—one congruent to duty, while the actual satisfaction is only pathological; that is, congruent to the actualized self—to the having, instead of the doing self.

3. Goodness is not remoteness from badness. In one sense, goodness is based upon badness; that is, good action is always based upon action good once, but bad if persisted in under changing circumstances. The moral struggle thus presents itself as the conflict between this "bad" and the good which would duly meet the existing situation. This good, of course, does not involve the annihilation of the previously attained good—the present bad—but its subordination; its use in the new function. This is the explanation of the apparently paradoxical statement that badness is the material of good action—a statement literally correct when badness is understood as it is here. Evil is simply that which goodness has to *overcome*—has to make an element of itself.

Badness, as just spoken of, is only potential—the end is bad as contrasted with the better. Badness may also, of course, be actual; the bad end may be chosen, and adopted into character. Even in this sense, goodness is not the absence of evil, or entire freedom from it. Badness even on this basis is the material of goodness; it is to be put under foot and made an element in good action. But how can actual evil be made a factor of right conduct? In this way; the good man learns from his own bad acts; he does not continue to repeat such acts, nor does he, while recognizing their badness, simply endeavor to do right without regard to the previous bad conduct. Perceiving the effect of his own wrong acts, the change produced in his own capacities, and his altered relations to other people, he acts so as to meet the situation which his own bad act has helped to create. Conduct is then right, although made what it is, to some degree, by previous wrong conduct.

In this connection, the introduction of Christianity made one of its largest ethical contributions. It showed how it was possible for a man to put his badness behind him and even make it an element in goodness. Teaching that the world of social relations was itself an ethical reality and a good (a redeemed world), it taught that the individual, by identifying himself with the spirit of this ethical world, might be freed from slavery to his past evil; that by recognizing and taking for his own the evil in the world, instead of engaging in an isolated struggle to become good by himself, he might make the evil a factor in his own right action.

Moreover, by placing morality in activity and not in some thing, or in conformity to an external law, Christianity changed the nature of the struggle. While the old struggle had been an effort to get away from evil to a good beyond, Christianity made the struggle itself a good. It, then, was no longer the effort to escape to some fixed, unchanging state; the constant onward movement was itself the goal. Virtue, as Hegel says, is the battle, the struggle, carried to its full.

4. The conception of merit. This is, essentially, the idea of social desert—the idea that an agent deserves well of others on account of his act or his character. An action evokes two kinds of judgments: first, that the act is right or virtuous, that it fulfills duty. This judgment may be passed by any one; as well by the agent as by any one else. It is simply the recognition of the moral character of the act. But a right act may also awaken a conviction of desert; that the act is one which furthers the needs of society, and thus is meritorious.

This is *not* a judgment which the agent can pass upon his own act. Virtue and duty are strictly coextensive; no act can be so virtuous, so right, as to go beyond meeting the demands of the situation. Everything is a duty which needs to be done in a given situation; the doing of what needs to be done is right or virtuous. While the agent may and must approve of right action in himself, he cannot claim desert or reward because of its virtuousness; he simply does what he should.

Others, however, may see that the act has been done in the face of great temptation; after a hard struggle; that it denotes some unusual qualification or executes some remarkable service. It is not only right, but obligatory, for others to take due notice of these qualities, of these deeds. Such notice is as requisite as it is to show gratitude for generosity, or forgiveness to a repentant man.

Two errors are to be avoided here; both arising from the identification of merit with virtue. One view holds that the virtue and merit consist in doing something over and above duty. There is a minimum of action which is obligatory; to perform this, since it is obligatory, is no virtue. Anything above this is virtuous. The other view reverses this and holds that since no man can do more than he ought, there is no such thing as merit. Great excellence or heroism in one man is no more meritorious than ordinary conduct in another; since the one man is naturally more gifted than the other. But while one act is no more right or virtuous than another, it may be more meritorious, because contributing more to moral welfare or progress. To depreciate the meritorious deed is a sign of a carping, a grudging or a mean spirit.

The respective relations of duty, virtue and merit have been variously discussed. Different views will be found in Sidgwick, *Methods of Ethics*, Bk. III, Ch. 4; Alexander, *Moral Order*, pp. 187–95 and 242–47; Stephen, *Science of Ethics*, pp. 293–303; Martineau, *Types of Ethical Theory*, Vol. II, pp. 78–81; Laurie, *Ethica*, pp. 145–48.

3

Realized Morality or the Virtues

LXIX. Goodness as Found in Character

We have treated of the forming of moral ideals, and of the attempt to realize them against the counter attractions of sensible desire. We have now to treat these ideals as actual ends of conduct and thus reacting upon the agent. The good character, considered in relation to the moral *struggle*, is the one which chooses the right end, which endeavors to be better. The good character *in itself* is that made by this choice. It is good for the self to choose a due end in an effort caused by contrary allurements. But the very fact of the struggle witnesses that morality is not yet the natural and spontaneous manifestation of character. A *wholly* good man would feel such satisfaction in the contemplation of the ideal good that contrary desires would not affect him. He would take pleasure only in the right. Every accomplished moral deed tends to bring this about. Moral realization brings satisfaction. The satisfaction becomes one with the right act. Duty and desire grow into harmony. Interest and virtue tend toward unity.

This is the truth aimed at, but not attained, by the hedonistic school. In complete moral action, happiness and rightness know no divorce. And this is true, even though the act, in some of its aspects, involves pain. The act, so far as its quality of rightness is concerned, calls forth unalloyed satisfaction, however bound up with pain to self and to others in some respects. The error of hedonism is not in insisting that right action is pleasurable, but in its failure to supply content to the idea of happiness, in its failure to define what happiness is. In the failure to show those active relations of man to nature and to man involved in human satisfaction, it reduces happiness to the abstraction of agreeable sensation.

A virtue then, in the full sense, that is as the expression of virtuous character, and not of the struggle of character to be virtuous against the allurements of passive goods, is an *interest.* The system of virtues includes the various forms which interest assumes. Truthfulness, for example, is interest in the media of human exchange; generosity is interest in sharing any form of superior endowment with others less rich by nature or training, etc. It is distinguished from natural generosity, which may be mere impulse, by its being an interest in the activity or social relation itself, instead of in some accidental accompaniment of the relation.

Another way of getting at the nature of the virtues is to consider them as forms of freedom. Positive freedom is the good, it is realized activity, the full and unhindered performance of function. A virtue is any one aspect which the free performance of function may take. Meekness is one form of the adjustment of capacity to surroundings; honesty another; indignation another; scientific excellence another, and so on. In each of these virtues, the agent realizes his freedom: Freedom from subjection to caprice and blind appetite, freedom in the full play of activity.

LXX. Two Kinds of Virtues

We may recognize two types of virtuous action. These are:

1. *The Special Virtues*

These arise from special capacities or special opportunities. The Greek sense of virtue was almost that of "excellence," some special fitness or power of an agent. There is the virtue of a painter, of a scientific investigator, of a philanthropist, of a comedian, of a statesman, and so on. The special act may be manifested in view of some special occasion, some special demand of the environment—charity, thankfulness, patriotism, chastity, etc. Goodness, as the realization of the moral end, is a system, and the special virtues are the particular members of the system.

2. *Cardinal Virtues*

Besides these special members of a system, however, the whole system itself may present various aspects. That is to say, even in a special act the whole spirit of the man may be called out, and this expression of the whole character is a cardinal virtue. While the special virtues differ in content, as humility from bravery, earnestness from compassion, the cardinal virtues have the same content, showing only different sides of it. Conscientiousness, for example, is a cardinal virtue. It does not have to do with an act belonging to some particular capacity, or evoked by some special circumstance, but with the spirit of the whole self as manifested in the will to recognize duty—both its obligatoriness in general and the concrete forms which it takes. Truthfulness as a special virtue would be the desire to make word correspond to fact in some instance of speech. As a cardinal virtue, it is the constant will to clarify and render true to their ideal all human relations—those of man to man, and man to nature.

LXXI. The Cardinal Virtues

The cardinal virtues are marked by

1. *Wholeness*

This or that virtue, not calling the whole character into play, but only some special power, is partial. But a cardinal virtue is not *a* virtue, but the spirit in which all acts are performed. It lies in the attitude which the agent takes towards duty; his obedience to recognized forms, his readiness to respond to new duties, his enthusiasm in moving forward to new relations. It is a common remark that moral codes change from "Do not" to "Do," and from this to "Be." A Mosaic code may attempt to regulate the specific acts of life. Christianity says, "Be ye perfect." The effort to exhaust the various special right acts is futile. They are not the same for any two men, and they change constantly with the same man. The very words which denote virtues come less and less to mean specific acts, and more the spirit in which conduct occurs. Purity, for example, does not mean freedom from certain limited outward forms of defilement; but comes to signify rightness of natures as a whole, their freedom from all self-seeking or exclusive desire for private pleasure, etc. Thus purity of heart comes to mean perfect goodness.

2. *Disinterestedness*

Any act, to be virtuous, must of course be disinterested, but we may now connect this disinterestedness with the integral nature of moral action just spoken of. Immoral action never takes account of the whole nature of an end; it deflects the end to some ulterior purpose; it bends it to the private satisfaction of the agent; it takes a part of it by making exceptions in favor of self. Bad action is never "objective." It is "abstract"; it takes into account only such portion of the act as satisfies some existing need of the private self. The immoral man shows his partial character again by being full of casuistries, devices by which he can get the act removed from its natural placing and considered in some other light: —this act, for example, *would* be dishonest, of course, if done under certain circumstances, but since I have certain praiseworthy feelings, certain remote intentions, it may now be considered otherwise. It is a large part of the badness of "good" people that instead of taking the whole act just as it is, they endeavor to make the natural feelings in their own mind—feelings of charity, or benevolence—do substitute duty for the end aimed at; they excuse wrong acts on the ground that their "intentions" were good, meaning by intentions the prevailing mood of their mind. It is in this sense that "hell is paved with good intentions."

Now it is against this deflection, perversion and mutilating of the act that disinterestedness takes its stand. Disinterested does not mean without interest, but without interest in anything except *the act itself*. The interest is not in the wonderful moods or sentiments with which we do the act; it is not in some ulterior end to be gained by it, or in some private advantage which it will bring, but in the act itself—in the real and concrete relations involved. There is a vague French saying that "morality is the nature of things." If this phrase has a meaning it is that moral conduct is not a manifestation of private feelings nor a search for some unattainable ideal, but observance and reproduction of actual relations. And this is the mark of a disinterested character.

Conclusion

LXXII. The Practical End of Morality

Virtues, then, are cardinal, and character is integral, just in the degree in which every want is a want of the whole man. So far as this occurs, the burden of the moral struggle is transformed into freedom of movement. There is no longer effort to bring the particular desire into conformity with a law, or a universal, outside itself. The fitting-in of each special desire, as it arises, to the organism of character takes place without friction; as a natural re-adjustment. There is not constraint, but growth. On the other side, the attained character does not tend to petrify into a fixed possession which resists the response to needs that grow out of the enlarged environment. It is plastic to new wants and demands; it does not require to be wrenched and wracked into agreement with the required act, but moves into it, of itself. The law is not an external ideal, but the principle of the movement. There is the identity of freedom and law in the good.

This union of inclination and duty in act is the practical end. All the world's great reformers have set as their goal this ideal, which may be termed either the freeing of wants, or the humanizing of the moral law. It will help summarize our whole discussion, if we see how the theories of hedonism and of Kant have endeavored to express this same goal. Hedonism, indeed, has this identity for its fundamental principle. It holds strongly to the idea of moral law immanent in human wants themselves. But its error lies in taking this identity of desire and the good, as a direct or immediate unity, while, in reality, it exists only in and through activity; it is a unity which can be attained only as the result of a process. It mistakes an ideal which is realized only in action for bare fact which exists of itself.

Hedonism, as represented by Spencer, recognizes, it is true, that the unity of desire and duty is not an immediate or natural one; but only to fall into the error of holding that the separation is due to some external causes, and that when these are removed we shall have a fixed millennium. As against this doctrine, we must recognize that the difference between want and duty is always removed so far as conduct is moral; that it is not an ideal in the sense of something to be attained at some remote period, but an ideal in the sense of being the very meaning of moral activity whenever and wherever it occurs. The realizing of this ideal is not something to be sometime reached once for all, but progress is itself the ideal. Wants are ever growing larger, and thus freedom ever comes to have a wider scope (Sec. LXV).

Kant recognizes that the identity of duty and inclination is not a natural fact, but is the ideal. However, he understands by ideal something which ought to be, but is not. Morality is ever a struggle to get desire into unity with law, but a struggle doomed, by its very conditions, not to succeed. The law is the straight line of duty, which the asymptotic curve of desire may approximate, but never touch. An earthly taint of pleasure-seeking always clings to our wants, and makes of morality a striving which defeats itself.

The theory that morality lies in the realization of individuality recognizes that there is no direct, or natural, identity of desire and law, but also recognizes that their identification is not an impossible task. The problem is solved in the exercise of function, where the desires, however, are not unclothed, but clothed upon. Flowing in the channel of response to the demands of the moral environment, they unite, at once, social service and individual freedom.

LXXIII. The Means of Moralization

This practical end of the unification of desire and duty, in the play of moral interests, is reached, therefore, so far as the desires are socialized. A want is socialized when it is not a want for its own isolated and fixed satisfaction, but reflects the needs of the environment. This implies, of course, that it is bound by countless ties to the whole body of desires and capacities. The eye, in seeing for itself, sees for the whole body, because it is not isolated but, through its connections, an organ of a system. In this same way, the satisfaction of a want for food, or for commercial activity, may necessitate a satisfaction of the whole social system.

But how shall this socialization of wants be secured? It is in answering this question that we are brought again to a point already discussed at length: the moral bearings of intelligence. It is intelligence that is the sole sure means of taking a want out of the isolation of merely impulsive action. It is the passing of the desire through the alembic of ideas that, in rationalizing and spiritualizing it, makes it an expression of the want of the whole man, and thus of social needs.

To know one's self was declared by Socrates, who first brought to conscious birth the spirit of the moral life, to be the very core of moral endeavor. This knowledge of self has taken, indeed, a more circuitous and a more painful path, than Socrates anticipated. Man has had, during two thousand years of science, to go around through nature to find himself, and as yet he has not wholly come back to himself —he oftentimes seems still lost in the wilderness of an outer world. But when man does get back to himself it will be as a victor laden with the spoils of subdued nature. Having secured, in theory and invention, his unity with nature, his knowledge of himself will rest on a wide and certain basis.

This is the final justification of the moral value of science and art. It is because through them wants are interconnected, unified and socialized, that they are, when all is said and done, the preëminent moral means. And if we do not readily recognize them in this garb, it is because we have made of them such fixed things, that is, such abstractions, by placing them outside the movement of human life.

List of symbols

A. Designation of sources

A1 The Angle of Reflection [1]
A2 The Angle of Reflection [2]
A3 The Angle of Reflection [3]
A4 The Angle of Reflection [4]
A5 The Angle of Reflection [5]
A6 The Angle of Reflection [6]
BP Review of *Elementary Psychology* by James Hutchins Baker
C A College Course: What Should I Expect From It?
CK Review of *The Critical Philosophy of Immanuel Kant* by Edward Caird
CP How Do Concepts Arise from Percepts?
CR Review of *The Story of the Odyssey* by Alfred John Church
CS On Some Current Conceptions of the Term "Self"
E Ethics in the University of Michigan
EH Review of *A History of Philosophy* by Johann Eduard Erdmann
F The Lesson of Contemporary French Literature
G The Philosophy of Thomas Hill Green
GS Galton's Statistical Methods
GT Green's Theory of the Moral Motive
J Review of *What Is Reality?* by Francis Howe Johnson
L Is Logic a Dualistic Science?
LR Lectures *vs.* Recitations: A Symposium
LT The Present Position of Logical Theory
LV The Logic of Verification
M The Late Professor Morris
MK Review of *Kant's Critical Philosophy for English Readers* by Mahaffy and Bernard
MT Moral Theory and Practice
OE *Outlines of a Critical Theory of Ethics*
P1 Poetry and Philosophy (*Andover Review*)
P2 Poetry and Philosophy (*Characters and Events*)
PM Philosophy in American Universities: The University of Michigan

PS Introduction to Philosophy: Syllabus of Course 5
R Two Phases of Renan's Life
SH Review of *Studies in Hegel's Philosophy of Religion* by James Sterrett
SS The Scholastic and the Speculator

B. Other designations

Page-line number at left is from present edition. All lines of print except running heads and chapter titles are counted.

Reading preceding bracket is from present edition.

Square bracket signals end of reading from present edition, followed by the symbol identifying first appearance of reading.

W means "Works"—the present edition—and is used for emendations made here for the first time.

D means "Dewey" and is used for his changes.

The abbreviation *om.* means the reading before the bracket was omitted in the editions and printings identified after the abbreviation.

The abbreviation *rom.* means roman type and is used to signal the omission of italics.

The asterisk indicates that a textual note on that emendation follows the tabulation of emendations.

For emendations restricted to punctuation, the wavy dash ~ means the same word(s) as before the bracket, and the inferior caret ‸ indicates the absence of a punctuation mark.

Checklist of references

In Dewey's references, corrections and expansions in titles, authors' names, etc., have been made silently and conform to those in the original works. Corresponding corrections which became necessary in the texts appear in the List of Emendations in the Copy-Texts.

Following each Checklist entry are the symbol references to the work in which Dewey mentions or quotes from that entry in the present volume. When Dewey's reference included page numbers, it was possible to identify the edition he used. In other references, among the various editions possibly available to him, the one listed is the most likely source by reason of place or date of publication, or on the evidence from correspondence and other materials, and its general accessibility during the period.

Adler, Felix. "The Freedom of Ethical Fellowship," *International Journal of Ethics*, I (Oct. 1890), 16–30. (MT)

Alexander, Samuel. *Moral Order and Progress: An Analysis of Ethical Conceptions*. London: Trübner and Co., 1889. (OE)

Aristotle. *The Nicomachean Ethics of Aristotle*. 2d ed. Trans. F. H. Peters. London: Kegan Paul, Trench and Co., 1884. (OE)

Arnold, Matthew. *Poems*. II. London: Macmillan and Co., 1869. [The Dewey quotations appear in the following poems: "Switzerland," pp. 78–101; "Dover Beach," pp. 108–9; "Youth of Man," pp. 162–67; "Self-Dependence," pp. 198–99; "Stanzas From the Grand Chartreuse," pp. 215–25; and "Obermann Once More," pp. 239–56.] (P1)

———. "Introduction," in *The English Poets*, I, xvii–xlvii. Ed. Thomas Humphry Ward. London, New York: Macmillan and Co., 1881. (P1)

Bain, Alexander. *The Emotions and the Will*. London: John W. Parker and Son, 1859. (OE)

———. *Moral Science: A Compendium of Ethics*. New York: D. Appleton and Co., 1882. (OE)

Baker, James Hutchins. *Elementary Psychology, With Practical Applications to Education and Conduct of Life*. New York: Effingham Maynard and Co., 1890. (BP)

Barrett, Alfred. *Physical Ethics; or, the Science of Action.* London: Williams and Norgate, 1869. (OE)

Bentham, Jeremy. *Deontology; or the Science of Morality.* Ed. John Bowring. 2 vols. London: Longman, Rees, Orme, Browne, Green, and Longman, 1834. (OE)

———. *The Works of Jeremy Bentham.* Ed. John Bowring. 11 vols. Edinburgh: William Tait, 1838–43. (OE)

Bernard, John H., and Mahaffy, John P. *Kant's Critical Philosophy for English Readers.* 2 vols. London: Macmillan and Co., 1889. (MK)

Birks, Thomas Rawson. *Modern Utilitarianism; or, the Systems of Paley, Bentham, and Mill Examined and Compared.* London: Macmillan and Co., 1874. (OE)

Blackie, John Stuart. *Four Phases of Morals: Socrates, Aristotle, Christianity, Utilitarianism.* Edinburgh: Edmonston and Douglas, 1871; *ibid.*, New York: Scribner, Armstrong and Co., 1872. (OE)

Bosanquet, Bernard. "The Communication of Moral Ideas as a Function of an Ethical Society," *International Journal of Ethics*, I (Oct. 1890), 79–97. (MT)

Bourget, Paul. *Essais de psychologie contemporaine.* Paris: A. Lemerre, [1883]. (F)

———. *Nouveaux essais de psychologie contemporaine.* Paris: Alphonse Lemerre, 1886. (F)

Bradley, Francis Herbert. *Ethical Studies.* London: H. S. King and Co., 1876. (OE)

———. "On Pleasure, Pain, Desire and Volition," *Mind*, XIII (Jan. 1888), 1–36. (OE)

Brandes, Georg Morris Cohen. *Moderne Geister.* Frankfurt: Rütten and Loening, 1887. (R)

Browning, Robert. *The Poetical Works of Robert Browning.* III–VII, XIV–XV. London: Smith, Elder, and Co., 1888, 1889. [The poems Dewey quotes from or mentions are: "Pippa Passes," III, 5–79; "Fra Lippo Lippi," IV, 205–20; "A Grammarian's Funeral," V, 154–60; "Christmas Eve and Easter Day," V, 209–307; "Saul," VI, 98–124; "By the Fireside," VI, 126–41; "Rabbi Ben Ezra," VII, 109–19; "At the 'Mermaid,'" XIV, 31–38; "The Two Poets of Croisic," XIV, 205–79; "Martin Relph," XV, 3–16; and "Clive," XV, 88–107.] (MT, P1, OE)

Butler, Joseph. *Fifteen Sermons.* London: Longman, Brown, Green, and Longmans, 1856. (OE)

Caird, Edward. *The Critical Philosophy of Immanuel Kant.* 2 vols. Glasgow: James Maclehose and Sons, 1889. (PM, CK, OE)

———. *The Social Philosophy and Religion of Comte.* New York: Macmillan and Co., 1885. (OE)

———. "Preface," in *Essays in Philosophical Criticism*, eds. Andrew Seth and R. B. Haldane, pp. 1–7. London: Longmans, Green, and Co., 1883. (G)

Calderwood, Henry. *Handbook of Moral Philosophy.* London: Macmillan and Co., 1872. (OE)

Carlyle, Thomas. *Critical and Miscellaneous Essays.* IV. London: Chapman and Hall, 1872. (P1)

Church, Alfred John. *The Story of the Odyssey.* New York: Macmillan and Co., 1891. (CR)

Coit, Stanton. "The Final Aim of Moral Action," *Mind*, XI (July 1886), 324–52. (OE)

Darwin, Charles Robert. *The Descent of Man, and Selection in Relation to Sex.* 2 vols. London: J. Murray, 1871. (OE)

Dewey, John. *Early Essays and LEIBNIZ'S NEW ESSAYS CONCERNING THE HUMAN UNDERSTANDING* (*The Early Works of John Dewey, 1882–1898*, I). Carbondale: Southern Illinois University Press, 1969.

———. *Psychology* (*The Early Works of John Dewey, 1882–1898*, II). Carbondale: Southern Illinois University Press, 1967. (PM, OE)

———. "Ethics and Physical Science," in *Early Works*, I, 205–26. (OE)

———. "Is Logic a Dualistic Science?" in *Early Works*, III, 75–82. (LV)

———. "Moral Theory and Practice," in *Early Works*, III, 93–109. (GT, OE)

Erdmann, J. E. *A History of Philosophy.* English trans., ed. N. S. Hough. 3 vols. New York: Macmillan and Co., 1890. (EH)

Everett, Charles Carroll. *Poetry, Comedy, and Duty.* Boston, New York: Houghton, Mifflin and Co., 1888. (OE)

Fowler, Thomas. *The Elements of Inductive Logic.* 3d ed. cor. and rev. Oxford: Clarendon Press, 1876. (PM)

———, and Wilson, John Matthias. *The Principles of Morals.* 2 vols. Oxford: Clarendon Press, 1886–87. (OE)

Galton, Francis. *Natural Inheritance.* London, New York: Macmillan and Co., 1889. (GS)

Gizycki, Georg von. *A Students' Manual of Ethical Philosophy.* Trans. S. Coit. London: Sonnenschein and Co., 1889. (OE)

Green, Thomas Hill. *Prolegomena to Ethics.* Ed. A. C. Bradley. Oxford: Clarendon Press, 1883. (G, GT, OE)

———. *Works of Thomas Hill Green.* Ed. R. L. Nettleship. 3 vols. London, New York: Longmans, Green, and Co., 1885–88. [Vol. I contains the "Introductions" to *A Treatise of Human Nature* by David Hume; Green's *Lectures on the Principles of Political Obligation* are printed in Vol. II.] (G, OE)

———. "Mr. Herbert Spencer and Mr. G. H. Lewes," Pt. 1, *Contemporary Review*, XXXI (Dec.–Mar. 1878), 25–53; Pt. 2, *ibid.*, XXXI (Dec.–Mar. 1878), 745–69; Pt. 3, *ibid.*, XXXII (Apr.–July 1878), 751–72. (G)

———. "Mr. Hodgson's Article 'Professor Green as a Critic,'" *Contemporary Review*, XXXIX (Jan.–June 1881), 109–24. (G)

Grote, John. *An Examination of the Utilitarian Philosophy*. Cambridge, England: Deighton, Bell, and Co., 1870. (OE)

———. *A Treatise on the Moral Ideals*. Cambridge, England: Deighton, Bell and Co., 1876. (OE)

Guyau, Jean-Marie. *La morale anglaise contemporaine, morale de l'utilité et de l'évolution*. Paris: G. Baillière, 1879. (OE)

Hamilton, D. H. "The Kantian Philosophy," *New Englander*, XV (Feb. 1857), 16–101. (MK)

Hartmann, Eduard von. *Philosophy of the Unconscious*. Trans. William Chatterton Coupland. 3 vols. London: Trübner and Co., 1884. (PS)

Hegel, Georg Wilhelm Friedrich. *Die Logik*. Pt. 1 of *Encyclopædie der philosophischen Wissenschaften*. 2d ed. Heidelberg: A. Oswald, 1827. English translation by W. Wallace. Oxford: Clarendon Press, 1874. (CS, PM)

———. *Werke*. Eds. Philipp Marheineke *et al.* 19 vols. Berlin: Duncker and Humblot, 1832–45, 1887. (CS, OE)

Hinton, James. *The Law-Breaker and the Coming of the Law*. Ed. M. Hinton, with introd. by H. H. Ellis. London: Kegan Paul and Co., 1884. (OE)

———. *Philosophy and Religion*. 2d ed. Selections from the late J. H. Ed. Caroline Haddon. London: Kegan Paul, Trench and Co., 1884. (OE)

Hodgson, Shadworth Holloway. *The Theory of Practice, an Ethical Enquiry*. 2 vols. London: Longmans, Green, Reader and Dyer, 1870. (OE)

Homer. *Homer*. Trans. Alexander Pope. 3 vols. New York: Harper and Bros., 1848. (CR)

Hyslop, James Hervey. "Evolution and Ethical Problems," *Andover Review*, IX (Apr. 1888), 348–66. (OE)

James, William. *The Principles of Psychology*. 2 vols. New York: Henry Holt and Co., 1890. (PS, OE)

———. "The Dilemma of Determinism," *Unitarian Review*, XXII (Sept. 1884), 193–224. (OE)

Jevons, William Stanley. *Elementary Lessons in Logic: Deductive and Inductive*. New ed. London, New York: Macmillan and Co., 1881. (PM, LT)

———. *Studies in Deductive Logic: A Manual for Students.* New York: Macmillan and Co., 1880. (PM)

Jodl, Friedrich. *Geschichte der Ethik, in der neueren Philosophie.* 2 vols. Stuttgart: J. G. Cotta, 1882–89. (OE)

Johnson, Francis Howe. *What Is Reality? An Inquiry as to the Reasonableness of Natural Religion, and the Naturalness of Revealed Religion.* New York: Houghton, Mifflin and Co., 1891. (J)

Kant, Immanuel. *Immanuel Kants sämmtliche Werke.* Eds. Karl Rosenkranz and Friedrich Wilhelm Schubert. 14 vols. Leipzig: L. Voss, 1838–42. (MT, LT, SS)

———. *Kant's Critique of Practical Reason and Other Works on the Theory of Ethics.* 3rd ed. Trans. Thomas Kingsmill Abbott. London: Longmans, Green, and Co., 1883. (OE)

———. *Kritik der reinen Vernunft.* Riga: Johann Friedrich Hartknoch, 1781; 2d ed., *ibid.*, 1787. (CS, CK)

Laurie, Simon Somerville (Scotus Novanticus). *Ethica: or, the Ethics of Reason.* London: Williams and Norgate, 1885. (OE)

Lecky, William Edward Hartpole. *History of European Morals from Augustus to Charlemagne.* 3d ed. rev. 2 vols. New York: D. Appleton and Co., 1879. (OE)

Lotze, Hermann. *Outlines of Practical Philosophy.* Trans. George T. Ladd. Boston: Ginn and Co., 1885. (OE)

Mahaffy, John P., and Bernard, John H. *Kant's Critical Philosophy for English Readers.* 2 vols. London: Macmillan and Co., 1889. (MK)

Mansel, Henry Longueville. *A Lecture on the Philosophy of Kant.* Oxford: John Henry and James Parker, 1856. (MK)

Martineau, James. *Types of Ethical Theory.* 2 vols. Oxford: Clarendon Press, 1885. (OE)

Maurice, John Frederick Denison. *The Conscience.* London: Macmillan and Co., 1868. (OE)

Mill, John Stuart. *Autobiography.* London: Longmans, Green, Reader and Dyer, 1873. (OE)

———. *Dissertations and Discussions, Political, Philosophical and Historical.* 4 vols. New York: Henry Holt and Co., 1874. [*Utilitarianism* is printed in Vol. III.] (OE)

Morris, George Sylvester. *British Thought and Thinkers: Introductory Studies, Critical, Biographical and Philosophical.* Chicago: S. C. Griggs and Co., 1880. (M)

———. *The Final Cause as Principle of Cognition and Principle in Nature.* London: Robert Hardwicke, 1875. (M)

———. *Hegel's Philosophy of the State and of History* (German Philosophical Classics for English Readers and Students, ed.

George S. Morris). Chicago: S. C. Griggs and Co., 1887. (M)

———. *Kant's Critique of Pure Reason* (German Philosophical Classics for English Readers and Students, ed. George S. Morris). Chicago: S. C. Griggs and Co., 1882. (M)

———. *Philosophy and Christianity.* New York: Robert Carter and Bros., 1883. (M)

———. *The Theory of Unconscious Intelligence as Opposed to Theism.* London: Hardwicke and Bogue, [n.d.]. (M)

———. *University Education* (University of Michigan Philosophical Papers, First Series, No. 1). Ann Arbor: Andrews and Witherby, 1886. (M)

———. "Friedrich Adolph Trendelenburg," *New Englander*, XXXIII (Apr. 1874), 287–336. (M)

———. "Philosophy and Its Specific Problems," *Princeton Review*, N.S. IX (Mar. 1882), 203–32. (M)

———. "The Philosophy of Art," *Journal of Speculative Philosophy*, X (Jan. 1876), 1–16. (M)

Newman, John Henry (Cardinal). *The Idea of a University Defined and Illustrated.* 4th ed. London: Basil Montagu Pickering, 1875. (C)

Paley, William. *Moral and Political Philosophy.* New York: S. King, 1824. (OE)

Pater, Walter Horatio. *Marius the Epicurean: His Sensations and Ideas.* 2d ed. London: Macmillan and Co., 1885. (OE)

Paulsen, Friedrich. *System der Ethik.* 2 Pts. Berlin: Besser, 1889. (OE)

Plato. *The Dialogues of Plato.* Trans. B. Jowett. I. New York: Charles Scribner and Co., 1871. (M, MT, OE)

Pringle-Pattison. [See Seth Pringle-Pattison, Andrew.]

Renan, Ernest. *The Future of Science.* Trans. [?]. Boston: Roberts Bros., 1891. (R)

———. *La réforme intellectuelle et morale.* Paris: Michel-Lévy frères, 1871. (R)

Royce, Josiah. *The Religious Aspect of Philosophy: A Critique of the Bases of Conduct and of Faith.* Boston, New York: Houghton, Mifflin and Co., 1885. (OE)

Salter, William M. "A Service of Ethics to Philosophy," *International Journal of Ethics*, I (Oct. 1890), 114–19. (MT)

Schurman, Jacob Gould. *The Ethical Import of Darwinism.* New York: C. Scribner's Sons, 1887. (OE)

Seth, James. "The Evolution of Morality," *Mind*, XIV (Jan. 1889), 27–49. (OE)

Seth Pringle-Pattison, Andrew. *Hegelianism and Personality.* Edinburgh, London: William Blackwood and Sons, 1887. (CS, J)

———. *Scottish Philosophy: A Comparison of the Scottish and German Answers to Hume.* Edinburgh, London: William Blackwood and Sons, 1885. (CS)

———. "Hegel and His Recent Critics," *Mind*, XIV (Jan. 1889), 116–19. [One of several essays in the section in *Mind* entitled "Discussions."] (CS)

Sidgwick, Henry. *The Methods of Ethics.* 2d ed. London: Macmillan and Co., 1877. (OE)

———. *Outlines of the History of Ethics, for English Readers.* London, Edinburgh: Macmillan and Co., 1886. (OE)

———. "The Morality of Strife," *International Journal of Ethics*, I (Oct. 1890), 1–15. (MT)

Sorley, William Richie. *On the Ethics of Naturalism.* London, Edinburgh: William Blackwood and Sons, 1885. (OE)

Spencer, Herbert. *The Data of Ethics.* 2d ed. New York: D. Appleton and Co., 1880. (OE)

———. *The Principles of Psychology.* New York: D. Appleton and Co., 1878. (PS)

Stephen, Leslie. *The Science of Ethics.* London: Smith, Elder, and Co., 1882. (OE)

Sterrett, James MacBride. *Studies in Hegel's Philosophy of Religion.* New York: D. Appleton and Co., 1890. (SH)

Stock, St. George. *Deductive Logic.* Oxford, London: Longmans, Green and Co., 1888. (LT)

Sully, James. *Outlines of Psychology, with Special Reference to the Theory of Education.* London: Longmans, Green, and Co., 1884. (OE)

Ueberweg, Friedrich. *A History of Philosophy from Thales to the Present Time.* Trans. George Sylvester Morris. 2 vols. New York: Charles Scribner and Co., 1871–73. (M, EH)

Venn, John. *The Principles of Empirical or Inductive Logic.* London, New York: Macmillan and Co., 1889. (L, LV)

Wallace, William. *Epicureanism.* New York: Pott, Young, and Co., 1880. (OE)

Ward, Mrs. Humphry. *Robert Elsmere.* London, New York: Macmillan and Co., 1888. (G)

Ward, James. "Psychology," *Encyclopædia Britannica* (9th ed.), XX, 37–85. (EH)

Wilson, John Matthias, and Fowler, Thomas. *The Principles of Morals.* 2 vols. Oxford: Clarendon Press, 1886–87. (OE)

Textual principles and procedures

These volumes of *The Early Works of John Dewey, 1882–1898*, offer a definitive critical text of his published writings arranged in a generally chronological order.

A text may be called "definitive," or "established," (a) when an editor has exhaustively determined the authority, in whole and in part, of all preserved documents containing the work under examination; (b) when the text is then based on the most authoritative documents produced in the work's publishing history; and (c) when the complete textual data of all appropriate documents are recorded, together with a full account of all divergences from the edition chosen as copy-text (the basis for the edited text) so that the student may recover the meaningful (substantive) readings of any document used in the preparation of the edited text.

A text may be called "critical" when an editor does not content himself with faithfully reprinting any single document without modification but instead intervenes to correct the faults or aberrations of the copy-text on his own authority or to alter it by reference to the corrections and revisions of some authoritative edition later than the edition or manuscript chosen as copy-text.[1]

The first step in the establishment of a critical text is the determination of the exact forms of the texts in the early editions and of the facts about their relationship one to another. An important distinction must be made immediately between an "edition" and a "printing" or "impression." Technically, an edition comprises a particular typesetting, without regard for the number of printings made at different times from this typesetting or its plates.[2]

1 Various terms used here to describe textual principles and operations are discussed at length in Fredson Bowers, "Established Texts and Definitive Editions," *Philological Quarterly*, XLI (1962), 1–17; and in "Textual Criticism," *The Aims and Methods of Scholarship in Modern Languages and Literatures*, ed. James Thorpe (New York: The Modern Language Association of America, 1963), pp. 23–42.

2 In the present edition the use of the bibliographical terms "edition," "impression" (or "printing"), "issue," and "state" follows that recommended in Fredson Bowers, *Principles of Bibliographical Description* (Princeton: Princeton University Press, 1949; offset by Russell and Russell, New York, 1962), pp. 379–426.

Textual variation is most commonly found when for one reason or another a publisher decides to make a new typesetting, since changes are inevitable in the mechanical process of transmitting the words from the copy to the new form. Some of these changes may have authority if the writer himself took the opportunity presented by the new edition to correct or to revise his work; the remaining changes can have no authority since they emanate from publishers' readers or the compositors and may run the gamut from normal house-styling to positive though inadvertent error.

To establish texts for the present edition, all true editions up to Dewey's death in 1952 have been collated, their substantive variants recorded, and a decision made whether on the whole the new editions seem to contain authorial revision, or whether on the whole they represent no more variation than is normally to be anticipated in a series of unattended reprints. When new editions do give every evidence that they were revised by the author, an attempt is thereupon made to distinguish his corrections and revisions from the normal variation of publisher and printer that can have no authority.

Ordinarily, Dewey did not revise his work merely for stylistic felicity but instead to clarify, amplify, and sometimes even to alter his meaning. For this reason, the nature of the changes usually provides sufficient evidence to determine whether or not Dewey had himself revised a new edition.

On the other hand, alterations of various kinds can be made in the plates in preparation for running off more copies to form a new impression, or printing. Often these changes originate with the publisher, whose readers have seen misprints or other actual or fancied errors in the earlier printing and now take the opportunity to correct the plates. Although these corrections may prove to be so necessary or desirable that an editor will wish to accept them, they can have no basic authority, of course, when they were not ordered by Dewey himself. Moreover, it may happen that in the course of resetting a line to conform to the publisher's requested correction the printer may inadvertently make a different error that was not caught by the casual proofreading usually adopted for plate-changes. In addition, similar errors may be found when for purely mechanical reasons, such as damage to plates in storage between printings, or an attempt to refurbish excessive wear attacking a plate, the printer without the knowledge of the publisher or author may reset a page in whole or in part to make a new plate or extensively to modify an old one.

Corrections, as distinguished from revisions, made by a publisher's reader are almost impossible to separate from the corrections of an author unless they seem to bring variants into conformity with house-style, in which case their non-authoritative origin is manifest. On the other hand, meaningful revisions such as Dewey ordered made in the plates of both the 1889 and 1891 reprintings of *Psychology* are always recognizable owing to their particular nature or extent.

Not only every new edition but even every printing during an author's lifetime carries within itself the possibility for authorial correction or revision that an editor must take into account. Hence the first step in the establishment of the present text has been the collection of all known editions and impressions of each work, followed by the determination of their order and relationship from the examination of internal as well as external evidence. That is, publishers' markings may indicate the order of separate impressions, as found in the American Book Company's reprints of *Psychology*; but sometimes no external evidence is available, or else (like a failure to change the date on a title page) it is untrustworthy, and then internal evidence based on the wear and deterioration of the plates, combined with their repair, must be utilized to separate one otherwise indistinguishable impression from another and to determine its order in the printing history of the plates.

Such evidence has been gathered by the scrupulous examination of available copies of every known edition on the Hinman Collating Machine, which has enabled the editors to discover the alterations made from time to time in the plates during their printing history, all of which have been recorded so that the evidence may be made available of the total body of facts from which the editors worked. This full stemma, then, of the total number of editions and impressions of any Dewey work, and their order, establishes the necessary physical base for proceeding to the investigation of the complete body of evidence about textual variation and its order of development, a matter that has a crucial bearing upon the determination of the authority of the variants in any given edition or impression.

Modern critics have come to a general agreement about the following propositions for the determination of authority in the process of editing a definitive edition that attempts to establish an author's text, in every respect. For overall authority, nothing can take the place of the manuscript that was used by the printer, because it stands in the closest relation to the author's intentions. In only one respect can the printed edition manufactured from this manuscript exceed the manuscript in authority, and that is in the specific alterations made in proof by the author, which give us his final revised intentions. It is the editor's task to isolate these from other variants such as errors made by the compositor that were overlooked in the proofreading. The distinction between authorial revision in proof and compositorial sophistication of a text is not always easy to make, but informed critical and bibliographical investigation of the corpus of substantive variants between manuscript and printed text will ordinarily yield satisfactory results.

That is, when meaning is involved distinctions can be made. But when meaning is not involved, as in the hundreds and sometimes thousands of variations between manuscript and print in respect to spelling, punctuation, capitalization, and word-division, the inevitable assumption holds that the author has not engaged himself to vast sums of overcharges for proof-corrections, and that the ordinarily expected house-styling has taken place, sometimes initiated by a publisher's reader, but always concluded by the compositors.

A distinction develops, hence, between the words of a text —the "substantives"—and the forms that these words take in respect to their spelling, punctuation, capitalization, or division, what are known as the "accidentals" of a text.[3] Editorial criticism may attempt to assess the authority of the substantives, but one must take it that, as against a printer's-copy manuscript, no printed edition can have full authority in respect to the accidentals.

On the other hand, some authors—and Dewey was often among these—are extremely careless in the typing of the accidentals in their manuscripts since they are relatively indifferent to anomalies and expect the printer to set all right for publication. Thus in some respects it is not uncommon to find that the printed edition's accidentals may be superior to those of the manuscript in matters of consistency and even of correctness. Yet every author whether consciously or unconsciously, and often whether consistently or inconsistently, does use the forms of the accidentals of his text as a method for conveying meaning. For example, Dewey frequently capitalized words he expected to be taken as concepts, thus distinguishing them in meaning from non-capital-

3 The use of these terms, and the application to editorial principles of the divided authority between both parts of an author's text, was initiated by Sir Walter Greg in "The Rationale of Copy-Text," *Studies in Bibliography*, III (1950–51), 19–36. For an extension and added demonstration, see Fredson Bowers, "Current Theories of Copy-Text," *Modern Philology*, LXVIII (1950), 12–20.

ized forms of the same words. That he was not consistent does not alter the fact that he used such a device, which an editor must respect.

It follows that the words of the printed first edition have in general a superior, although not a unique, authority over those of the manuscript form of the text in view of the ever-present possibility that substantive variants in the print can represent authorial revision in proof. On the other hand, the author's accidentals, insofar as they are viable in correctness or consistency, have a superior authority in manuscript from that in the printed form that has undergone the ministrations of copyreaders and compositors.

In these circumstances, a critical text—which is to say an eclectic text—will endeavor to join both authorities by printing each of the two major elements in the text from the form that is uniquely superior in its closeness to the author's own habits or intentions, although either element may be altered as necessary by editorial intervention to restore true authority, or purity.

This editorial principle can be extended logically to the situation when an author's manuscript has not been preserved, or is not available for use. In this circumstance the first edition, which is the only edition set directly from the author's manuscript, must necessarily take the place of the manuscript as the prime authority. If the author has not intervened to alter matters in any subsequent impression or edition, this first edition remains the single authority for both parts of the text and must therefore become the copy-text or basis for the definitive edition, although subject to editorial correction. Later impressions or editions may unauthoritatively alter, and even correct the text, but unless the author has himself ordered such alterations the changes have no authority and may only suggest possible necessary or advisable corrections to an editor. Indeed, the usual history of a text in these circumstances is one of chronological degeneration into ever more corrupt readings.

On the other hand, when in a later impression or edition the author does indeed make his own revisions and corrections, these represent his altered intentions which must be accepted by an editor. The earlier readings should be recorded, because they have a historical importance in the development of the author's thought, but they obviously must be superseded by the author's final intentions. The substantive readings of a revised impression or edition, then, have a general authority superior to those in a preceding form.

Early editors were inclined to take as copy-text the last edition of a work published in the author's lifetime, on the supposition that if he had corrected or revised it this edition would contain the maximum authority. This procedure is no longer current, for in relieving the editor of the necessity to demonstrate that any authorial revision had indeed taken place it usually resulted (in cases when no authoritative intervention had occurred) in an editorial reprint of the most corrupt edition of all. And even when somewhere in the publishing history authoritative revision had appeared, the naïve editorial acceptance of *all* substantive variants in the last edition as necessarily authorial produced an unscholarly mixture of true revisions side by side with the inevitable corruptions of a reprint.

No uncritical acceptance of *all* substantive readings in any edition, whether or not revised, therefore, meets modern standards of scholarly textual criticism. It is the duty of an editor to assess all the variants that have accumulated in a text during its history and to choose on critical and bibliographical evidence those that appear to be authorial while rejecting those that appear to be printers' corruptions.[4]

As suggested above, however, in cases when the manuscript is not available the accidentals of a first edition must necessarily be more authoritative, as a whole, than those of any later reprint. House-styled as in part these first-edition accidentals may be, the fact that they were set directly from the author's manuscript will often have influenced the compositors to adopt the manuscript forms; and in any event, they must necessarily represent a closer approximation of the manuscript accidentals than can any reprint, which is only one printed edition further house-styled and set from another printed edition. What changes in the accidentals may take place in a revised edition at the order of an author are often impossible to isolate, but they must necessarily be fewer than the substantive alterations that were the chief reason for his intervention, especially with an author like Dewey.

On the modern textual principle of divided authority, therefore, the copy-text for this edition of Dewey remains stable as the earliest authority closest to the author, usually the first edition;[5] and hence the accidentals for Dewey's texts are estab-

4 As a case-history the first edition of Nathaniel Hawthorne's *House of the Seven Gables* may be cited. In this, scrupulous editorial investigation established that two-thirds of the substantive variants between the manuscript and first edition were unauthoritative in the print and were to be rejected. See the Centenary Edition of Hawthorne, Vol. II (Columbus: Ohio State University Press, 1965), pp. xlvii–lviii.

5 Most Dewey manuscripts were not preserved, and among those extant some are in private hands and not available for re-editing. Those that have been studied or utilized suggest that the copy given to the

lished as those of the first editions printed from his manuscripts, when the manuscripts are not available. Whenever it is ascertained that no authorial revision or correction took place in any subsequent impression or edition, the first edition remains the final authority for the substantives as well. On the other hand, when substantive revisions were made in later impressions or editions, those that the editors believe are authorial are adopted in preference to the readings of the first edition, and thus an eclectic text is established that combines the highest authority in respect to the substantives drawn from revised forms of the text with the highest authority of the accidentals drawn from the edition closest to the manuscript source. In short, the copy-text remains the first edition, but into the texture of its accidentals are inserted the revised readings that have been selectively ascertained to represent Dewey's altered intentions.

In the process of editing, the principle has been adopted that each separate work is to be treated as an independent unit in respect to its accidentals. That is, each unit has its own problems of copy-text, with inevitable variation in the nature of the printer's copy and the house-styling given it, ranging from that found in all sorts of journals to that required by different book-publishers. Thus although an attempt has been made to secure uniformity of editorial result within each unit, certain features may vary between independent works within the present edition. For example, if the spelling or some other important feature of the accidentals differs within a given work, the editors attempt to reduce the variation to uniformity according to Dewey's own style as ascertained from his manuscripts. On

---

printer might vary widely in legibility and in styling. According to his associates, Dewey usually composed on the typewriter with a margin-stop set at the left but seldom at the right, with the result that some words might be typed on the platen instead of on the paper. Customarily the machine was set for triple-spacing; revisions and additions were then typed in so that the final page might look as if it had been single-spaced. Handwritten comments might also be added, as well as handwritten revisions of the typed material.

Dewey was characteristically indifferent about his spelling; punctuation could be sporadic or altogether lacking. Colleagues have told of being asked by Dewey to work over a manuscript and put it into shape for the printer. One of Dewey's long-time editors in Henry Holt and Co. has stated ". . . I tried a number of times to 'improve' his style, but whenever I made a substantial change I found that I also had changed the sense and therefore had to reinstate the original. I did go over many passages with him and he improved them. He permitted us to use our house style, but I kept as close to the original as I could." (Letter from Charles A. Madison, 25 June 1964, preserved in Dewey Project Offices, Southern Illinois University, Carbondale, Illinois.)

the other hand, if no variation is present in some such feature within an editorial unit, the copy-text form is retained even though it is known to be contrary to Dewey's own practice. That is, the editors have taken a narrow view of what constitutes authority and have declined to alter the copy-text in such respects except when variation itself is present that can be reduced to authoritative normality or when presumptive error requires correction.

Except for the small amount of silent alteration listed below, every editorial change in the chosen copy-text has been recorded, with its immediate source, and the original copy-text reading has been provided, whether in the substantives or the accidentals. The complete account will be found in the lists of emendations.

In most texts that have a reprinting history a certain number of variants will be positive errors or else unnecessary changes that are unauthoritative and have not been adopted by the present editors. All substantives of this kind have been recorded whether occurring in new impressions or in new editions. Likewise, all accidentals that in the history of the plates have been changed from the copy-text plating are also recorded so that the maximum information will be available to the student of the material on which the editors drew in making their estimates of the authority or non-authority of variants.[6] However, when in a new edition the text is reset throughout, the number of accidentals changes would be too large to list. In addition, since the editors will have adopted as emendations of the copy-text all such accidentals variants that seem to be either authoritative or advisable changes, no useful purpose would be served by listing the hundreds and hundreds of publishers' or printers' unauthoritative normalizings of the text on which they worked.

Since the number of rejected variants of the kind noted above that qualify for recording[7] is comparatively limited, no separate list has been made and this group of variants has been incorporated with the appropriate emendations lists.

In the emendations lists an asterisk prefixed to the page-line number indicates that the emendation, or the refusal to emend, recorded in this item is discussed in the Textual Notes that follow each list.

6 Changes made in the plates that correct errors that would otherwise have been silently made in the copy-text by editorial intervention (see below) are nevertheless recorded for the sake of completeness.

7 Such rejected readings from editions later than the copy-text are to be distinguished from copy-text readings rejected in favor of subsequent revision or correction. These are recorded as emendations, of course.

In special cases separate lists within the textual material may substitute for part of the Emendations in the Copy-Texts. For example, in the early articles as represented in Volume I the importance of capitalization to indicate concept meanings as distinct from non-concepts called for a certain amount of editorial emendation to correct the required sense from the inconsistent copy-text usage. The importance for meaning of these key words that have been emended is best called to the attention of the student in a separate list, whereas they might be overlooked if buried among a mass of material of other import in the general list of emendations. Similarly, some alterations or revisions in the system of headings in certain texts have seemed to warrant separate lists, as in the reworked headings system of *Psychology*. In several volumes, a list of full and correct quotations has also been provided as a supplement to the Checklist of References, as described below.

The editors have made a number of silent alterations in the copy-text. These concern chiefly the mechanical presentation of the text and have nothing whatever to do with meaning, else they would have been recorded.

The most general class of these silent alterations has to do with Dewey's system of references whether within the text, in footnotes, or in lists of authorities that he might append. These references have been checked for accuracy, and the details of capitalization, punctuation, and of bibliographical reference have been normalized for the reader's convenience. When a reference is within the text, its form may be condensed following Dewey's own pattern when the expanded information required by the reader to check the reference will be found in an appended list of authorities. Except for the silent emendations mentioned and changes which appear in the emendations lists, Dewey's footnotes are kept in their original form and position, since their references are completed in the appended Checklist of References.

In Dewey's texts, all quotations have been retained just as he wrote them even though not always strictly accurate, since that was the form on which he was founding his ideas. The section entitled Correction of Quotations gives the correct quotation and will be helpful to the reader in determining from the form of the quotation—whether accurate or sketchy—whether Dewey had the source open before him or was relying on his memory.

All references in footnotes or within the text (and also in the rejected readings of the copy-text) that relate to points taken up within the work in question (whether by backward or by forward reference) have had the appropriate pages of the present edition substituted for their original page numbers applying to the copy-text itself.

A second large class of silent alterations concerns itself with the articles that Dewey published in England, wherein the English printer had styled in his own manner the American spellings, punctuation system, and other forms of the accidentals or presentation. Logically, on the principle of treating each separate text as an independent unit, the editors might have retained the English styling of these works; but for the convenience of American readers, and in some part as a means of automatically returning to certain undoubted features of the manuscripts that served as printer's copy, they have chosen instead silently to Americanize the elements in such copy-texts that were styled in the English manner when these run contrary to what can be established as Dewey's own usage. Thus words like "emphasise" have been altered silently to "emphasize," "colour" to "color"; and the position of punctuation in relation to quotation marks has been altered to American usage.

For the rest, the silent changes are mechanical and concern themselves with correcting typographical errors that could not be mistaken as true readings, making regular some anomalous typographical conventions or use of fonts, expanding most abbreviations, and so on. Typical examples are the removal of periods and dashes after headings, the expansion of "&c" to "etc.," changing syntactical punctuation after roman or italic words (or in italic passages) to follow a logical system, expanding titles such as "Professor" or "Governor," supplying accent marks in foreign words, and normalizing German "ue" to "ü" whether in lower case or capitals. Roman numbers in chapter headings are silently altered to Arabic, as are all references to them.

These remarks concern the general treatment of most texts in the present edition. When unusual features call for unusual treatment, special notice in the respective notes on the texts will be given of modifications or of additions. The intent of the editorial treatment both in large and in small matters, and in the recording of the textual information, has been to provide a clean reading text for the general user, with all the specialized material isolated for the convenience of the student who wishes to consult it.

The result has been to establish in the wording Dewey's final intentions in their most authoritative form divorced from verbal corruption whether in the copy-text or in subsequent printings or editions. To this crucial aim has been added the further attempt to present Dewey's final verbal intentions within a logically contrived system of accidentals that in their texture are as close as controlled editorial theory can establish to their most authoritative form according to the documentary evidence that has been preserved for each work.

Fredson Bowers

10 March 1969

A note on the texts

1 *Early Essays*

During the years 1889–1892 John Dewey first engaged in the varied and strenuous activity characteristic of his professional career. In 1889 he revised his *Psychology*, published only two years earlier. In 1891 he revised the book again, even more extensively than in 1889. Also in 1891 his *Outlines of a Critical Theory of Ethics* appeared. Between 1889 and 1892 he published twenty-five articles in fourteen journals and this does not include his six brief "Angle of Reflection" contributions to the *Inlander* or any of the material which might be attributed to him as "a regular contributor to the editorial columns of *The Christian Union*."[1]

Although his publications of the period are the chief concern of this discussion, Dewey's other activities must be noted as they relate to his published works. In the fall of 1888 he took the chair of philosophy at the University of Minnesota, where he was a one-man department. After only six months he received word that his former professor, department chairman, colleague and friend, George Sylvester Morris, had died. Morris' death left the Philosophy Department at the University of Michigan without a chairman; John Dewey, twenty-nine years old, was elected to succeed him. The essays in the present volume appropriately start with Dewey's tribute to George S. Morris, published in the spring of 1889, before Dewey returned to the University of Michigan campus for the fall semester.

In addition to his regular duties as Chairman and as Professor on full schedule, he served as President of the Philosophical Society, was active in the Michigan Schoolmasters' Club, was one of two advisers to the student literary monthly, *Inlander*, planned with Franklin Ford a philosophical newspaper, "Thought News," which was never published, taught a regular Bible class on "Church History" at the Congregational Church,

1 *Teste* Fred Newton Scott, "John Dewey," *Castalian*, VI (1891), 26. None of these contributions is signed by Dewey; it has not been possible to identify any as his.

and appeared as platform speaker before Bible Institutes, meetings of the Philosophical Society, and discussions and debates of the Michigan Schoolmasters' Club.

Most of these activities entailed preparation of written materials. Among those not published and apparently not extant are addresses to the Philosophical Society entitled "What Is the Cause of Materialistic Ideas and What Truths Do They Contain?" "Hegel and Recent Thought," "Sir Henry Maine's Conception of Democracy," "The Philosophical Catharsis," and "The Interpretation of Literature";[2] a debate on "Mental Powers" with Burke A. Hinsdale at an 1891 meeting of the Michigan Schoolmasters' Club; a paper on "The Relation of the Present Philosophical Movement to Religious Thought" before the Congregational Convention in Ann Arbor, 1891; a special discussion series, "Philosophic Study of Paul's Epistles," sponsored by the Students' Christian Association for advanced students in philosophy; and "The Significance of Parables," a talk "by many considered to be the best"[3] at a Bible Institute sponsored by the Students' Christian Association, 1892.

Dewey's projected newspaper, "Thought News,"[4] is important because Dewey's aims for it indicate his concerns in 1892, which bear on other works published and unpublished. The *Detroit Tribune* of 13 April 1892 quotes what seems to have been a written statement from Dewey about the paper's approach: "When philosophic ideas are not inculcated by themselves but used as tools to point out the meaning of phases of social life they begin to have some life and value. . . . When it can be seen for example, that Walt Whitman's poetry, the great development of short stories at present, the centralizing tendency in the railroads and the introduction of business methods into charity organizations are all parts of one organic social movement, then the philosophic ideas about organism begin to look like something definite."

In this four-year period Dewey published articles in the following journals: (1) University of Michigan publications (*Palladium*, *Castalian*, *Inlander*), (2) *Christian Union*, (3) *Andover Review*, (4) *Publications of the American Statistical Association*, (5) *Ethical Record* and *International Journal of Ethics*, (6) *Mind*, (7) *Monist* and *Open Court*, (8) *Educa-*

2 "The Interpretation of Literature" was summarized in the *University* [*of Michigan*] *Record*, I (Feb. 1892), 88.

3 *Monthly Bulletin*, XIV (Nov. 1892), 45.

4 The detailed story of the proposed publication appears in Willinda Savage, "John Dewey and 'Thought News' at the University of Michigan," *Michigan Alumnus Quarterly Review*, LVI (May 1950), 204–9.

tional Review and *Public-School Journal*, and (9) *Philosophical Review*.

The *Palladium*, which carried "The Late Professor Morris" in 1889, was then in its thirtieth year of publication, an annual published by the fraternities and eventually consolidated into the *Michiganensian* in 1897. In addition to the lists of secret society members with which it had started, the *Palladium* had gradually come to include cuts and drawings and literary material. Years later, with hundreds of articles to his credit, Dewey remembered his only contribution to that journal very well and pointed out that his article on Professor Morris for the Students Annual was not listed in the bibliography of his writings [Columbia University Press, 1929].[5]

To counterbalance *Palladium*, a group of anti-secret society independents had started *University Castalia* in 1866; after publishing only five volumes the magazine disappeared, to be revived in 1890 under the name *Castalian*. Dewey helped the "new" publication with his article in 1890, "A College Course: What Should I Expect From It?" and with his contribution in 1891 to a symposium on "Lectures *vs.* Recitations." Typically, Dewey went even further to help the student editors of *Castalian*; in 1891 he wrote to Dr. Herbert B. Adams, Professor at Johns Hopkins, that the editors of *Castalian* intended to have a symposium on college life in different universities and wanted to have Johns Hopkins represented. The editors were responsible young men, he said, and he would appreciate any help that Adams could give.[6]

The third University of Michigan publication in which Dewey published was *Inlander*, the student monthly literary magazine which he helped found with F. N. Scott in 1891. From the time of its founding until he left the University in 1894, Dewey continued to serve as one of the two advisers, meeting regularly with the editors. In 1891 *Inlander* published six Dewey contributions under the heading "The Angle of Reflection." Although he did not sign these articles, Dewey later unequivocally claimed authorship of them to Lewis Vander Velde (see note 5).

In its first number, March 1891, the editors stated *Inlander*'s goals: "Although *The Inlander* endeavors to represent

5 Letter to Lewis Vander Velde, 14 Dec. 1939. Preserved in the University of Michigan Historical Collections. Lewis Vander Velde was Professor of History and the first Director of the Michigan Historical Collections, a post to which he was appointed in 1938. Dewey's letter to him was apparently in answer to a request for materials for the Collections.

6 Letter of 20 June 1891, in Manuscripts Division, Johns Hopkins University.

the University, yet it does not confine its field to subjects having only local color, nor limit the range of its contributions to University life. Its aim is to present the best literature of the Institution in a manner acceptable to the general reader." Dewey's "Angle of Reflection" articles illustrate the approach he advocated for "Thought News"—the use of philosophy to interpret literary and social questions. Three signed articles by Dewey also appeared in *Inlander*: a two-part article, "The Scholastic and the Speculator," in 1891, and two reviews in 1892.

Christian Union, to which Dewey may also have contributed unsigned pieces, published a signed article, "The Lesson of Contemporary French Literature." This journal was later known as *Outlook* and subsequently as *Outlook and Independent*. At the time of Dewey's closest relation with *Christian Union*, it described itself editorially as "a novelty—this newspaper which [was] religious without being ecclesiastical, earnest without being polemic, and broad without being indifferent."

Another journal for which Dewey wrote at this time, *Andover Review*, described itself quite simply as "A Religious and Theological Monthly," and was edited by professors in the Andover Theological Seminary. In the period 1889–1891 Dewey wrote two articles and four book reviews for this magazine; as was so often true, the reviews show the main directions Dewey's thought was taking at the time.

In 1889, in the first volume of a new journal entitled *Publications of the American Statistical Association*, Dewey reviewed Francis Galton's *Natural Inheritance* under the title "Galton's Statistical Methods." This was Dewey's only contribution to the periodical; his article addresses itself rather closely to the subject of Galton's statistical methods with little speculation on broader topics.

Looking forward to his return to Michigan in the late summer of 1889, Dewey had prepared outlines for his own courses and had clearly in mind the general structure of other departmental offerings. An insight into both appears in an article in *Ethical Record* for October 1889, "Ethics in the University of Michigan," describing courses to be given in this area of philosophy in 1889–1890. In Dewey's description of the basic course in Ethics, the general structure of his *Outlines of a Critical Theory of Ethics* is presented two years before publication of the book.

Ethical Record, which claimed to be "devoted to the advancement of ethical knowledge and practice," was published by the Society for Ethical Culture of Philadelphia and ran for three years. In October 1890 it became *International Journal of Ethics*, where Dewey's "Moral Theory and Practice" appeared in 1891.

In 1886 and 1887 Dewey published three articles in *Mind* (part of a well-known exchange with Shadworth Hodgson),[7] and in 1888 the journal ran George Croom Robertson's favorable review of his book on Leibniz.[8] Dewey's fourth contribution to *Mind*, "On Some Current Conceptions of the Term 'Self,'" appeared in 1890. This magazine, designed "to bring philosophical inquiries, as far as possible to their psychological base," was a natural outlet for Dewey's early work in psychology. The parallel between his point of view and that of the editors can be found in his second *Mind* article, where he had stated that "[psychology] is . . . in short, *philosophic method*."[9]

The Open Court Publishing Company, with which Dewey's long association was to culminate in the publication of *Experience and Nature* (1925), grew out of two journals where Dewey published articles in 1890–1892. The first, founded in February 1887 by the German immigrant E. C. Hegeler and edited by Paul Carus, was *Open Court*, "devoted to the science of religion, the religion of science, and the extension of the religious parliament idea." In April 1887, *Publishers' Weekly* announced that the new fortnightly publication "inclines to philosophic discussion of social problems and will no doubt appeal strongly to the mass of sober and dispassionate freethinkers."[10] The other journal was *Monist*, founded by E. C. Hegeler three years later, with Paul Carus again editor. *Publishers' Weekly* noted that "the magazine will be devoted to the establishment and illustration of the principles of Monism in Philosophy, Exact Science, Religion and Sociology. So far as the fulfilment of this aim will allow, it will bear a popular character; publishing articles of general interest as well as those of a more special character."[11] Among the prospective contributors were Professor Joseph Le Conte, William James, Charles S. Peirce, G. L. Romanes, E. D. Cope, Max Müller, Ernst Häckel, and Théodule Ribot. Carl Jackson writes that "Hegeler contributed the financial resources for the enterprise, Carus the intellectual capital

7 "The Psychological Standpoint," 122–43; "Psychology as Philosophic Method," 144–67; and "'Illusory Psychology,'" 168–75, *Early Essays and LEIBNIZ'S NEW ESSAYS CONCERNING THE HUMAN UNDERSTANDING* (*The Early Works of John Dewey, 1882–1898*, I [Carbondale: Southern Illinois University Press, 1969]).

8 XIII (1888), 612.

9 *Early Works*, I, 144.

10 2 Apr. 1887, p. 491.

11 27 Sept. 1890, p. 345.

and editorial direction. . . . *The Open Court* and *Monist* provided significant outlets over the next half century for scholarship and speculation in philosophy, religion, science—and Oriental thought. . . . Meticulous scholarship was combined with popular presentation; at one time or another practically every serious question that agitated the early XXth-century American mind was dealt with. The circulation of these two journals was small but their readers included some of the most significant figures of the day."[12]

Dewey's two articles in *Open Court* for 1890, "Is Logic a Dualistic Science?" and "The Logic of Verification," along with "The Present Position of Logical Theory," an article in *Monist* the following year, provide a full statement of his logical position at the time. The first, which contained his original use of the word "logic" in a full-length article, was a review of John Venn's *Principles of Empirical or Inductive Logic.* In *Open Court* for 1892 Dewey published the first of his two articles on Ernest Renan, "Two Phases of Renan's Life," a piece described by Morton White as exhibiting at a very early stage "Dewey's long crusade for the application of intelligence in social affairs."[13]

In the first number of *Monist* Dewey supplied information for "Philosophy in American Universities," listing courses at the University of Michigan on three levels of work. A year later *Monist* issued his "The Present Position of Logical Theory." A copy of the galley proof for this article, marked with Dewey's corrections and changes, is among the papers of the Open Court Publishing Company[14] and provides valuable insight into Dewey's methods of working at the time. Since *Monist* did not incorporate Dewey's changes,[15] the form of the text here given represents the author's final intentions for the first time. (All variants are noted in a special appendix giving the findings of the historical collation. As it is the only presently known document of its kind, a sample from the marked galleys is reproduced in this volume just before the article.) Dewey's manner of preparing manuscript (see Textual Principles and

12 "The Meeting of East and West: The Case of Paul Carus," *Journal of the History of Ideas*, XXIX (Jan.–Mar. 1968), 75.

13 *The Origin of Dewey's Instrumentalism* (New York: Columbia University Press, 1943), p. 102. Dewey's credo was first formulated in a letter of 3 June 1891 to William James concerning Franklin Ford. See Ralph Barton Perry, *The Thought and Character of William James*, II (Boston: Little, Brown, and Co., 1935), 518–19.

14 University Archives, Morris Library, Southern Illinois University.

15 Possibly because the corrected proof was not returned in time. *Cf.* the initialed handwritten note for the Open Court Publishing Co. on the galley proof facsimile preceding the article in this volume.

Procedures) during most of his writing career involved habits developing from his use of typewriters. In this early period, however, he still wrote out his manuscripts.[16] The galley corrections show an attention to detail not characteristic of his typewritten copy, such as the change from roman to italic type of the abbreviation "*i.e.*," the insertion and deletion of commas, the careful marking of capital letters, and, indeed, a more than usual care in the correction of typographical errors.

In 1891 Dewey also contributed two articles to journals chiefly concerned with pedagogical matters. *Educational Review* had begun in January 1891 under the editorship of Nicholas Murray Butler; Dewey's review of James Hutchins Baker's *Elementary Psychology* appeared in May of that year. Dewey's reputation as an authority in the area of psychology made him a natural choice to review the book. At the same time, he could hardly take issue with the magazine's statement in its first number: "The REVIEW has no policy that is not consistent with the scientific study and discussion of education."[17] This piece was the first of ten articles that Dewey in time contributed to the journal, which merged with *School and Society* in 1928. *Public-School Journal*, where "How Do Concepts Arise from Percepts?" appeared in 1891, had succeeded *Illinois School Journal* in 1889, announcing: "The *Public-School Journal* is a school magazine for the Mississippi Valley, which, as we interpret it, means a school journal for the United States. There is no sort of question, in the minds of well informed persons, of the fact that the Mississippi Valley is leading the educational thought of the present, as well as our political affairs."[18]

The *Monist* article discussed earlier, "The Present Position of Logical Theory," was summarized in the first number of *Philosophical Review*, January 1892, and in November of that year the journal published "Green's Theory of the Moral Motive." This article was the first of thirty-three Dewey contributed to *Philosophical Review* through the years. Its stated purpose was "the organization, the diffusion, and the increase of philosophical knowledge and activity in America. . . . The philosophical genius of the nation will, it is expected, find in the new periodical a medium of free expression, an aid to full and harmonious development, and an instrument for ministering to its needs."[19]

16 The earliest document typewritten by Dewey at present known is a letter to Thomas Davidson, 9 Oct. 1892, in the Yale University Library.

17 I (Jan. 1891), 61.

18 IX (Sept. 1889), 31.

19 I (Jan. 1892), 5–6.

Despite his heavy work load in upper-division classes, Dewey continued to teach a course entitled "Introduction to Philosophy." In the second semester of 1892, which opened in February, notes for that class were available in printed form. No publication information has been located, but it seems likely that the Inland Press, which printed *Inlander* and which also printed (for the Register Publishing Company) Dewey's *Outlines of a Critical Theory of Ethics*, also published this syllabus. The surviving printed form is apparently incomplete. The same material breaking off at the same point, survives also in a typescript prepared, with some modifications and notes, by Dewey's student H. Heath Bawden.[20] The pages of notes are easily distinguishable from the text of the syllabus and it is therefore possible to compare the printed version with the typed copy. Sight collation of the two specimens shows that they are identical except for minor differences in styling. A similar set of notes for the October 1892 Introduction to Philosophy course may have been prepared, but no copy has been located.[21]

II *Outlines of a Critical Theory of Ethics*

As noted earlier, Dewey had previewed *Outlines of a Critical Theory of Ethics* two years before it was published, when he wrote in 1889 about the basic course in Ethics in "Ethics in the University of Michigan." In the years after his return from the University of Minnesota, Dewey regularly taught the same course. The class work led to the publication of *Outlines*, and the book was in turn used as a textbook for the class.[22] Dewey's

20 H. Heath Bawden Collection, Pius XII Library, St. Louis University.

21 Willinda Savage, "The Evolution of John Dewey's Philosophy of Experimentalism as Developed at the University of Michigan" (unpublished Ed.D. dissertation, University of Michigan, 1950), lists (p. 302): "Introduction to Philosophy and General Conclusions Regarding our Experience," Syllabus (Oct. 1892), Pamphlets, Vol. I, The Philosophical Department, University of Michigan, 1–14.

M. H. Thomas, *John Dewey: A Centennial Bibliography* (Chicago: University of Chicago Press, 1962), lists (p. 7): "Introduction to Philosophy." October, 1892 [Ann Arbor, 1892]. 14 pp. cover-title. . . . May be found in the Michigan Historical Collections, University of Michigan; binder's title: *Pamphlets*, Vol. I, *The Philosophical Department, University of Michigan.*

Searches of the catalogues and holdings of the Michigan Historical Collections have failed to turn up a copy or listing of this syllabus, and there is no record of its disappearance.

22 He wrote Thomas Davidson late in 1890 that he had at that time an outline on Ethics in press for the use of his classes. Letter preserved in the Yale University Library.

first statement in the "Preface" to *Outlines* indicated, however, that he considered it more than a textbook: "Although the following pages have taken shape in connection with class-room work, they are intended as an independent contribution to ethical science."[23] His references in the "Preface" to possible uses of the book[24] showed that he wanted readers to be aware of its dual emphasis. One reviewer thought this approach the book's chief weakness, saying that "it is, therefore, neither a text-book nor a treatise on ethics. It is a sort of mixture of both, and insufficiently adapted to either of them."[25]

Eight reviews of *Outlines* appeared,[26] two of them by one reviewer and one in French. The reviews were generally unfavorable. The strongest condemnation came in J. H. Hyslop's statement that the book "is of poor paper, poor print, and poor construction, . . . thrown together in too promiscuous a form and without adequate analysis of the various problems which the student has to solve" (*Educational Review*, p. 297). The *New Englander and Yale Review* writer gently echoed Hyslop: "It suggests the wish, on the part of his friends, for more wealth and maturity of resources, for more freshness and vivacity of treatment, and for a more thorough settling of the positions to be assumed on delicate and difficult problems, before essaying the task of publication" (p. 275). Josiah Royce pointed out that the book "has precisely the office that vital and sinewy optimism always has. Herein lies also its limitation" (p. 505). At the other extreme, the British reviewer in *Mind* highly approved the book: "From its clearness of exposition, candour in statement and appreciation of opposing views, and vigour and independence of thought, the work ought to prove highly serviceable to students of Ethics, whether more or less advanced" (p. 424).

Four reviews appeared in July 1891, one in September 1891, one in October 1891, and two in January of 1892. Yet in May 1891, well before the first review was published, Dewey sensed the nature of the reaction. He wrote William James:

23 *Early Essays and OUTLINES OF A CRITICAL THEORY OF ETHICS* (*The Early Works of John Dewey, 1882–1898*, III [Carbondale: Southern Illinois University Press, 1969]), 239.

24 *Early Works*, III, 240.

25 James Hervey Hyslop, *Andover Review*, XVI (July 1891), 95.

26 In addition to Hyslop in *Andover Review*, these were: James Hervey Hyslop, *Educational Review*, II (Oct. 1891), 297–98; Josiah Royce, *International Journal of Ethics*, I (July 1891), 503–5; *Mind*, [unsigned], XVI (July 1891), 424; *Monist*, [unsigned], I (July 1891), 600–601; *New Englander and Yale Review*, [unsigned], LV (Sept. 1891), 275; Thomas Davidson, *Philosophical Review*, I (Jan. 1892), 95–99; G. Rodier, *Revue philosophique*, XXXIII (Jan.–June 1892), 97.

"The book has received a little of what is called 'favorable comment' as well as more or less of the reverse. . . . The present preceptual [sic] structure is so great, and such a weighty thing, both in theory and in practice, that I don't anticipate any success for the book."[27]

The book was in print for four years; it had appeared some time in the first quarter of 1891, and toward the end of 1894 Dewey wrote in the preface to his *The Study of Ethics: A Syllabus*, "The edition of my *Outlines of Ethics* [has] been exhausted."[28]

The exact date of the publication of *Outlines of Ethics* cannot be established because there is no record of a copyright registration, and the publisher's records are no longer extant. The notice "Copyright, 1891. Register Publishing Co., Ann Arbor, Mich." appears on the verso of the title page, but three searches of the Combined Book Indexes failed to disclose any registrations under book title, author's name, or publishing company.[29]

The Register Publishing Company was incorporated in Ann Arbor in 1890,[30] the year before Dewey's book appeared. As shown on the facsimile title page of *Outlines* in this volume, the names of both the Register Publishing Company and The Inland Press were used. The Inland Press apparently printed the *Ann Arbor Register* (the newspaper from which the publishing company had grown) and other materials issued under Register's imprint as well as under its own. The connection between Register and Inland was made explicit in *Inlander*, which read on its title page "The Inland Press, Ann Arbor, Michigan," and which ran an advertisement in the June 1891 issue: "The Register Publishing Company, The Inland Press, Ann Arbor, Michigan, prints the *Inlander*, and it does all kinds of fine book and pamphlet work." The Register Publishing Company went out of existence in 1899,[31] and the newspaper was absorbed by the *Ann Arbor Courier*.

Because of the dual listing of Register Publishing Company

27 Perry, *William James*, II, 517.

28 "Prefatory Note," p. [iii]. It should be noted, however, that the *U.S. Catalog of Books in Print*, 1899 (Minneapolis: H. W. Wilson) lists "*Critical Theory of Ethics*. $1.20. Register."

29 Final search report and covering letter from Waldo H. Moore, Chief, Reference Division, Copyright Office, Library of Congress, 24 June 1968, in Dewey Project Offices, Southern Illinois University, Carbondale, Illinois.

30 Louis W. Doll, *A History of the Newspapers of Ann Arbor, 1829–1920* (Detroit: Wayne State University Press, 1959), p. 95.

31 Doll, *Newspapers of Ann Arbor*, pp. 97–98.

and Inland Press, *Outlines* has been variously catalogued. The original spine read "Outlines of Ethics | J. Dewey | Inland Press," and Inland Press advertisements appeared on pp. [255–56] at the rear. The Inland Press was apparently the more common designation at the time the book was published: "The latest work from [Dewey's] pen is *Outlines of a Critical Theory of Ethics*, issued by the Inland Press of this city."[32] But in 1939 Dewey said that both his early books on ethics were published by the Register Publishing Company of Ann Arbor.[33]

On the evidence of letters from Dewey to William James, the date of publication of *Outlines* may be assigned to the first quarter of 1891. In the April 1891 issue of *International Journal of Ethics*, James had published an article entitled "The Moral Philosopher and the Moral Life."[34] In June 1891 Dewey wrote James: "I had read your ethical article once and recommended it to my class to read. . . . I was only sorry that the discussion of obligation, in particular, had not appeared before I wrote my *Ethics*."[35]

Twelve copies of *Outlines* were collated on the Hinman Machine. The collation indicates that, although printed in a newspaper shop at a time when several newspapers had started using linotype machines, the book was apparently hand-set and not plated. No variants were discovered by the collation and all emendations of the text have therefore been made editorially. A copy of *Outlines* owned by the Dewey Project, the first below, was used as printer's-copy for the present edition.

Jo Ann Boydston

1 April 1969

COPIES OF *Outlines of a Critical Theory of Ethics* USED IN COLLATION

1. Dewey Project. F. B. Peck, Salina, Kansas, handwritten on front paste-down.
2. Southern Illinois University, Morris Library. E575 18D handwritten on p. [v].

32 F. N. Scott, "John Dewey," *Castalian*, VI (1891), 27.
33 Letter to Vander Velde, 14 Dec. 1939.
34 I, 330–54.
35 Perry, *William James*, II, 517. See also the letter of 10 May 1891 cited in note 27.

3. University of Illinois Library. M. C. Priest handwritten on p. [iii]. 288935 stamped on p. [v]. Rebound.
4. University of Minnesota. The Library of the University of Minnesota, Accession 10669, on printed label, glued to front paste-down; same, handwritten on p. [iv]. Rebound.
5. University of Manitoba Library. 14033 stamped on front paste-down.
6. University of New Brunswick, Bonar Law-Bennett Library. 18573 handwritten on front paste-down and p. [iii]. Rebound.
7. Queen's University Library, Kingston, Ontario. 18168 stamped on p. [v].
8. Dalhousie Library, Halifax. Dalhousie College Library stamped on first binder's end-paper. 3J37/D52 handwritten on p. [vii].
9. University of California. 49976 handwritten on p. [iv]. Rebound.
10. Western Reserve University. 111010 stamped on p. [v]. Library of Adelbert College of Western Reserve University, Bequeathed by Professor George Trumbull Ladd of Yale University, on printed label glued to front paste-down.
11. Dewey Project. Gift of Herbert Schneider. J. Ratner, handwritten on front paste-down. H. W. Schneider, handwritten on front binder's paper. John Dewey, autograph signature, p. [i].
12. Princeton University. From the Library of Roger Bruce Cash Johnson, '87 / Member of the Philosophy Faculty from 1905 to 1935, printed on label glued to front binder's paste-down. Princeton University stamped on p. [iii]. 6307.297.3 and 1957–9 handwritten on p. [v].

Emendations in the copy-texts

The following kinds of emendations have been made silently throughout the volume:

1. Typographical or other kinds of errors that do not make words have been corrected: "signi-|cant."
2. Book titles and journal titles have been put in italic type; articles and sections of books have been put in quotation marks.
3. Single quotation marks have been changed to double when not inside quoted material; beginning and ending quotation marks have been supplied when necessary.
4. Superior numbers have been assigned consecutively throughout an item to Dewey's footnotes; the asterisk has been used only for editorial footnotes.
5. "Prof." has been expanded to "Professor," and capitalized when used as a title. Ampersands, as in publishers' names, have been expanded to "and."
6. The consistently British house-styling of accidentals in *Mind* articles has been Americanized. However, in *Andover Review*, *Open Court*, and *Monist*, "-ise" verb forms have been allowed to stand because no variants were present nor was there an overall pattern of British house-styling. In *Outlines*, the one occurrence of "criticize" was regularized to "criticise."
7. "I. e." has been altered to "*i.e.*" and "*viz.*" to "viz." throughout to conform to Dewey's regular usage.
8. In *Outlines*, the form of documentation has been made consistent and complete: "*op. cit.*" has been eliminated; volume and section numbers have been given in Roman, and chapter numbers in Arabic; abbreviations have been regularized; book titles have been supplied where necessary.

LIST OF EMENDATIONS

4.8 lator;] W; ~: M
*6.4 arbitrary [ ] of] W; arbitrary of M
6.19 catholic] W; Catholic M

8.10 words,] W; ∼‸ M
*10.18–20 *The Theory of Unconscious Intelligence as Opposed to Theism* and *The Final Cause as Principle of Cognition in Nature*] W; *The Theory of the Unconscious in Nature as Opposed to Theism* and *The Idea of Final Cause* M
15.7 *Lectures on the Principles of Political Obligation*] W; lectures upon "Political Obligations" G
*30.3 Stoic] W; stoic G
30.15 ones] W; one M
*33.21 Reason] W; reason G
*37.24–26 I have . . . [Stendhal]] W; *om.* F
39.36 point] W; points F
*44.10 70] W; 80 GS
*44.11 70] W; 80 GS
48.26 Ethics] W; ethics E
48.29 Stephen] W; Stephens E
*49.6 is] W; are E
54.17 training.] W; ∼‸ C
75.8 non-contradiction] W; ∼‸∼ L
*83.19 conceptions,] W; ∼‸ LV
99.n2 ands] W; ans MT
*104.20 "ought" "is"] W; ‸∼‸ ‸∼‸ MT
116.15 Once] P2; once P1
145.36 principle] W; principal CP
153.3 premises] W; premisses SS
156.23 antinomy] W; antimony GT
157.12 theories] W; theory GT
175.16 attain] W; attains R
*176.1 it."] W; ∼.‸ R
*176.5 humanity‸ ‸] W; ∼." R
189.14 Five and Six] W; five and six SH
*193.31 philologist] W; philologists CR
199.25 East] W; east A2
206.22 machine,] W; ∼‸ A5
207.32 nothing‸] W; ∼, A5
209.6 foreseeing] W; forseeing A6
209.10–11 fellows' language] W; ∼-∼ A6
210.19 reader,] W; ∼‸ A6
212.33 *Self*] W; SELF PS
*214.3 psychical] W; physical PS
214.13 reflex-arc] W; ∼‸∼ PS
214.16 act] W; arc PS
214.17 reflex-arc] W; ∼‸act PS
216.24 remains] W; remain PS
221.34 at] W; as PS

224.25 world] W; word PS
225.29 percept] W; preccpt PS
226.18 Platonic] W; platonic PS
228.5 (Compare] W; ‸~ PS
228.30 so-called] W; ~‸~ PS
230.38 through] W; though PS
233.13 Analysis] W; analysis PS
234.20 arts,] W; ~‸ PS
234.26 far] W; for PS
239.20 Stephen,] W; ~‸ OE
251.4 *Principles of Morals*, p. 2,] W; *Enquiry*, I, II, OE
253.2 unforeseen] W; unforseen OE
253.30 his] W; its OE
254.3–4 sweet-|meats] W; sweat-meats OE
267.22 work] W; works OE
268.18 the‸] W; ~, OE
270.27 Does] W; does OE
271.6 is.] W; ~‸ OE
274.32 Bentham] W; *Bentham* OE
274.32 *Will*] W; Mill OE
277.22 (pp. 143–44)] W; (p. 144) OE
281.41 are] W; is OE
282.38 *Handbook*] W; Hand-Book OE
282.39 37] W; 10 OE
285.28 250] W; 205 OE
287.15 279] W; 179 OE
289.20 184] W; 84 OE
290.4 573] W; 570 OE
293.16 as] W; of OE
301.2 be] W; *om.* OE
307.1 Altruism,] W; ~‸ OE
309.2 287–88] W; 287 OE
318.3 our] W; out OE
322.15 belongs] W; belong OE
347.32 seen,] W; ~‸ OE
351.35 his] W; its OE
359.24 faculty called conscience] W; moral in faculty called OE
361.35 entirely] W; entire-| OE
382.4 ideals] W; ideas OE

TEXTUAL NOTES

6.4 arbitrary] one or more words have apparently been omitted following "arbitrary".

10.18–20 *The Theory of Unconscious Intelligence as Opposed to Theism* and *The Final Cause as Principle of Cognition in Nature*] Dewey's memory confused the two titles and led to his erroneous versions in M.

30.3 Stoic] The specific reference to a philosophical school requires the capital letter.

33.21 Reason] Consistency with the same phrase at 27.39, and "eternal Reason" at 27.2, enforces the capital here.

37.24–26 I have . . . [Stendhal]] This clause from Bourget appears to have been omitted in Dewey's article either by Dewey or by the printer. The reference to "five" persons indicates that the omission was accidental.

44.10, 11 70] The erroneous "80" in the original printing probably stemmed from a mis-reading of the table in Galton's work.

49.6 is] The singular "theory" is clearly intended to serve as subject of the sentence; the "are" of E seems to result from the contamination of the plural modifiers as if Dewey felt that "the hedonistic theory" had been elided before "in its development" and again before "through the theory of evolution".

83.19 conceptions,] The balance of the sentence, in which "facts" are set against "ideas" and "perceptions" against "conceptions", requires "of ideas" to be marked off by a comma in opposition to "conceptions".

104.20 "ought" "is"] The numerous other references to these terms in the article uniformly use quotation marks. There appears to be no substantive reason for the omission of them here and they have therefore been supplied.

176.1, 5 it." . . . humanity‸ ‸] The page reference at 176.5, covering all quotations in the preceding paragraph, apparently led to the misplacement of the quotation marks at the end of the paragraph. The quoted material ends as signalled here; the remaining lines are Dewey's summary and have been so pointed.

193.29 philologist] Both the singular form of the verb "finds" and the parallel phrase "the psychologist" indicate that the plural subject was a misprint or an oversight.

214.3 psychical] The context makes the original "physical" clearly a typographical error.

Historical collation of "The Present Position of Logical Theory"

Dewey's marked copy of the galley proof for "The Present Position of Logical Theory" was discovered among the papers of the Open Court Publishing Company, now preserved at Southern Illinois University. The author's corrections were not incorporated into the *Monist* version of 1891. The corrected galley proof (LT *proof*) has been used as copy-text for this edition. In the list below, the readings of the original proof before alteration by Dewey have been recorded as have the variants in the printed *Monist* form from the original proofs. D stands for Dewey's written alterations and LT for the invariant readings of the galley proof and *Monist* article. When these latter two differ, the galleys are distinguished as LT *proof* from the *Monist* version, LT.

On the galley proof, Dewey's mark to delete "do" at 136.16 may have been inscribed when he thought of using another word like "make" because of the "do" in the next sentence; but he then failed to substitute a word. Hence the editors have in this instance chosen to follow LT and LT *proof*. The carets in LT *proof* at 138.6 are not editorial notations but represent original misprints in the galley proof.

125.2 hand,] D; ~‸ LT
125.6 movement‸] D; ~, LT
125.6 would be] D; would seem to be LT
125.7 itself,] D; ~; LT
125.8 knowledge‸] LT *proof*; ~, LT
125.10 apparently, the greatest] D; probably, the greatest apparent LT
125.21 to make] D; so that LT
125.22 lifc evident] D; life is evident LT
126.2 this] D; it LT
126.4 attitude‸] D; ~, LT
126.4 and] D; *om.* LT
126.4–5 the status] D; it LT
126.13 indicated,] D; ~, then‸
126.14 also some] D; also manifested some LT

126.14 theory‸] D; ~, LT
126.22 ideas] D; thought LT
126.22 The problem] D; It LT
126.26 itself;] D; ~, LT
126.32 Thought means] D; Thought too means LT
126.36 has] D; would have LT
126.36–37 considera-|tion] W; consider-|tion LT
127.10 Any] D; It is that any LT
127.26 education;—] LT *proof*; ~;‸ LT
127.31 theory] D; doctrine LT
127.34 is: thought] D; is: that thought LT
127.35 having] D; and that it has LT
127.36–37 as to pass] D; as they pass LT
128.7 Logic] LT *proof*; logic LT
128.17 itself‸] D; ~, LT
128.20–21 me highly] D; me as highly LT
128.21 scholastic: to be, indeed,] D; scholastic, as LT
128.29 were at least consistent in holding] D; when they held that LT
128.30 to be] D; was LT
128.31 things.] D; were at least consistent LT
128.n2 pp. 3–4] W; p. 3 LT
129.3 rearranging] LT; re-|arrange LT *proof*
129.12 is] D; was LT
129.32–33 bring out] D; show LT
129.35 with,] D; with, then, LT
130.21 the consideration] LT *proof*; this consideration LT
130.22–23 the theory of knowledge] D; metaphysics LT
130.31 first-hand] LT; ~‸~ LT *proof*
130.35 However,] D; But LT
130.37 Thought since] D; Thought, being LT
130.38–39 manipulated once obtained] D; manipulated. After being obtained LT *proof*; manipulated after being obtained LT
131.7 science,] LT *proof*; ~‸ LT
131.20 itself‸] D; ~, LT
131.22 procedure, and so] D; procedure. So LT
131.25 as something] D; as this something LT
131.26 force] D; cause LT
131.29 ¶ And] D; And LT
131.31 datum] D; fact LT
131.32 science, the] D; science, the fact of the LT
131.33 datum] D; fact LT
132.9 Some other machinery] LT *proof*; Some machinery LT

132.25 the conception] D; this conception LT
132.26–27 something in another department to supply the gap.] D; something to supply the gap in another department. LT
132.30 correlative] D; corelative LT *proof*; correlative LT
133.1 by finding] D; and to find LT
133.4 attaining truth] D; attaining absolute truth LT
133.6 to mean] D; as meaning LT
133.15 this school] D; his school LT
133.23 of] D; *of* LT
133.30 only] D; true LT
134.2 Taking] D; Simply taking LT
134.8 position] D; present position LT *proof*; presupposition LT
134.15 stimulating] D; stimluating LT
134.20 that the] D; that because the LT
134.20 being] D; was LT
134.25 the Kantian] D; *om.* LT
134.29 plunge deeper] D; plunge myself deeper LT
134.30 absurdity, I] D; absurdity than I have already gone, I LT
134.30 is far] D; is by far LT
134.33 thought-power] LT; ~∧~ LT *proof*
134.34 opinion of the possibility of some] D; opinion that while some LT
134.35 Kant, while the] D; Kant is possible, the LT
134.36 me it] D; me that it LT
135.18 denied∧] D; ~, LT
135.25 Here,] D; Here to, LT *proof*; Here too, LT
135.32 *there*;] D; ~, LT
136.10–11 "generalisa-|tions from experience"] D; ∧~∧ LT
136.12 men,] D; ~∧ LT
136.16 cannot do away] LT; can-|not away D
136.19 quantitative] D; quantitive LT
136.34 freedom both of] D; freedom of LT
137.31 further∧] D; ~, LT
138.5 experience] D; it LT
138.6 braced] D; ∧∧ced LT *proof*; braced LT
138.19 necessity] LT *proof*; this necessity LT
138.23 *i. e.*,] D; i. e.∧ LT
138.26 The] D; It is then evident that LT
138.28–29 "expe-|rience."] D; ∧~." LT
138.31 the] D; a LT
138.31 system he] D; system as he LT
138.32 phases∧] LT; ~, LT *proof*
139.4–5 were it shown] D; if it were shown LT

139.7 is] D; were LT

139.18 other] D; otherwise LT

139.19 of science] D; *om.* LT

139.20 its application to] D; the application of science to LT

139.21 was comparatively] D; was then comparatively LT

139.25 had to] D; must LT

139.26 world$_{\wedge}$] D; ~, LT

139.28 great$_{\wedge}$] D; ~, LT

139.32–33 manipu-|lated] D; so manipulated as LT

139.n4 apart] LT; a part LT *proof*

139.n4–5 thought—] LT; ~$_{\wedge}$ LT *proof*

139.n7 own physiognomy] D; own anatomy and physiognomy LT

140.5 thought excepting] D; thought at all excepting LT

140.9 it in applied science, in] D; it applied science$_{\wedge}$ in LT

140.11–12 method working] D; method which worked LT

140.14 when] D; that when LT

140.17 separate,] LT *proof*; ~$_{\wedge}$ LT

140.20 us as] D; us, therefore, as LT

140.27 fact] D; nature LT

140.36 *ambulando*] D; *ambulands* LT *proof*; *ambulando* LT

140.36),] LT *proof*; ,) LT

141.4 Unrealities] LT *proof*; unrealities LT

141.7–8 We have got] D; We got LT

141.11 them] D; *om.* LT

141.11 to be] D; that they are LT

141.11–12 but not to be.] D; but that they are not LT

141.18 that] D; the LT

141.18 meanings making up] D; meanings that make up LT

141.19 the world] D; this world LT

141.22 that logic] D; that this logic LT

141.25 anatomy] W; anat-|omy D; ana-|tomy LT

141.27–28 the subject-matter with which] D; the same subject-matter, which LT

141.29 themselves in] D; themselves with in LT

141.31 where] LT; when LT *proof*

141.32 into] D; in to LT

141.33 science$_{\wedge}$] LT *proof*; ~, LT

Correction of quotations

Dewey represented source material in every way, from memorial paraphrase to verbatim copy. Within this range of extremes, several classes of variations appear. In some cases Dewey cited his source fully in footnotes; in others he mentioned authors' names; in still others, he assumed the reader would identify the sources and omitted any documentation. His form of citation varies widely as well, and quotation marks do not necessarily signal a direct or precise quotation.

All material enclosed in quotation marks in this volume (except when the device is obviously used for emphasis or restatement) has been searched out, and the documentation has been verified and emended when necessary. Emendations in documentation are described in Textual Principles and Procedures (p. lviii), but the editors have considered Dewey's variations from the original quotations of sufficient importance to list them.[1] One lengthy restoration was necessary in a quotation, and it appears in the List of Emendations. Otherwise all quotations have been retained as they were first published. The variable form of quotation suggests that, like many scholars of the period, Dewey was unconcerned about precision in matters of form, but many of the changes in cited materials may have arisen in the printing process. For example, comparing Dewey's quotations with the originals reveals that some journals house-styled the quoted materials as well as Dewey's own, changing "-ize" forms to "-ise," "-ise" to "-ize," "-our" to "-or." Such variations are not listed here.

The most frequent alteration Dewey made in quoted material

1 Four editions (1873, 1879, 1883, 1889) of *Kant's Critique of Practical Reason*, translated by Thomas Kingsmill Abbott, were available during the period covered by this volume. Dewey may have used the 1873 edition, the only edition of which no copy has been located for comparison. Page references given by Dewey match pages in the 1883 and 1889 editions; they do not match those in the 1879 edition. The corrections shown here, with Dewey's typical patterns of variation, are from the 1883 edition. However, four passages (291.31–35, 292.2–6, 298.34–40, and 299.13–18) have, in the 1883 edition, numerous and more substantive differences that seem to stem from translator's revisions rather than from Dewey's usual kind of changes. As it was not possible without examining the 1873 version to determine which variations were Dewey's, these passages have been omitted from the list of corrections.

was to change or omit punctuation. He also often failed to use ellipses or separated quotations to show that material had been left out. No citation of the Dewey material or of the original appears if the changes were only of this kind—omitted or changed punctuation, including ellipses. In the case of omitted ellipses, attention is called to short phrases; if, however, a line or more has been left out, no attention has been called to the omission.

Italics have been considered accidentals, and when Dewey omitted those used in his source, the omission is not noted, though Dewey's added italics are listed. If changed or omitted accidentals have substantive implications, as in the capitalization of some concept words, the quotation is noted. Quotations from Dewey as well as from his source appear in a form designed to assist the reader in determining whether Dewey had the book open before him or was relying on his memory.

Notations in this section follow the formula: page-line numbers from the present text, followed by the text condensed to first and last words or such as make for sufficient clarity, then a square bracket, followed by the symbol identifying the Dewey item. After a semicolon comes the necessary correction, whether of one word or a longer passage, as required. Finally, in parentheses, the author's surname and shortened source-title from the Checklist of References are followed by a comma, and the page-line reference to the source.

5.20 only the empty] M; only the abstract, but otherwise empty (Morris, *British Thought*, 7.13–14)

5.20–21 and inexplicable] M; and uninstructive, and, by any law of sufficient reason, inexplicable (Morris, *British Thought*, 7.14–15)

5.23 return to the world] M; return to what is termed the literal fact of experience, or, better, to the world (Morris, *British Thought*, 8.1–3)

5.23 such as it had] M; such as, under the influence of a dawning mental activity, guided by sensitive experience and by instruction, it had (Morris, *British Thought*, 8.3–5)

5.30–31 dissolving again became] M; dissolving, recovered its relative consistency and became again (Morris, *British Thought*, 8.13–14)

5.31 world. It] M; world, or of "*the* world," as it was for me. It (Morris, *British Thought*, 8.14–15)

5.32 world that I] M; world—a conception kaleidoscopic, apparently half arbitrary, half accidental—that I (Morris, *British Thought*, 8.16–17)

5.36 not] M; hardly (Morris, *British Thought*, 8.27)
5.37 negative!] M; ~. (Morris, *British Thought*, 8.28)
8.15 Reason in him is] M; In the case of Plato reason is (Morris, *British Thought*, 54.27–28)
8.32 spot] M; place (Plato, *Dialogues*, I, 585.3)
8.33 and the inward man] M; and inward man (Plato, *Dialogues*, I, 585.4)
9.1 idealism] M; Idealism (Morris, *British Thought*, 65.24)
9.3 its] M; his (Morris, *British Thought*, 65.26)
9.4 his] M; its (Morris, *British Thought*, 65.27)
12.28–29 the institution] M; the one (Morris, *University Education*, 20.2)
12.29 the] M; this (Morris, *University Education*, 20.3)
12.30–31 freedom—knowledge of the truth.] M; freedom. It is devoted to the fullest and freest cultivation of universal intelligence, or to the quest and recognition of any and all truth, and this for the sake of truth alone, and of the freedom which is through the truth. (Morris, *University Education*, 20.4–7)
12.35 rightfully] M; rightly (Morris, *University Education*, 17.12)
12.35 until they] M; until, like the praises of the special sciences, they (Morris, *University Education*, 17.12–13)
12.39 the] M; that (Morris, *British Thought*, 61.27)
12.40 simply protest] M; simply through protest (Morris, *British Thought*, 61.28)
12.40 change, but by] M; "change of some sort," but by (Morris, *British Thought*, 61.29)
20.23 would] G; must (Green, *Works*, I, 36.26)
27.3 God] G; He (Green, *Prolegomena*, 198.3)
27.35 of development] G; of the development (Green, *Prolegomena*, 201.13–14)
27.37 thought. Human] G; thought. Language presupposes thought as a capacity, but in us the capacity of thought is only actualised in language. So human (Green, *Prolegomena*, 192.30–32)
27.37 *capacity*] G; *rom.* (Green, *Prolegomena*, 192.33)
28.5–6 his own personality and to conceive] G; his personality—his nature as an object to himself—and to conceive (Green, *Prolegomena*, 205.5–6)
28.7 others; it is] G; others, so it is (Green, *Prolegomena*, 201.7)
28.7 society, also, that] G; society that (Green, *Prolegomena*, 201.7)

31.6–7 actual condition] G; actual present condition (Green, *Prolegomena*, 291.33)

32.1–2 admit not to be slaves much] G; admit that it is wrong to use as chattels much (Green, *Prolegomena*, 263.9–10)

32.4 in] G; of (Green, *Prolegomena*, 263.14)

32.6 society is] G; society may be, and is, (Green, *Prolegomena*, 263.16–17)

32.9 is unrealized] G; is in effect unrealised (Green, *Prolegomena*, 263.19)

32.31 which is really the only ideal] G; to whom he is thus related (Green, *Prolegomena*, 329.12–13)

32.34 one] G; the act (Green, *Prolegomena*, 329.29)

58.31–32 exists only as the unity of the manifold] CS; exist only as a manifold (Seth, *Hegelianism*, 17.6)

59.27 is] CS; as (Seth, *Hegelianism*, 98.7)

76.9 those laws which] L; those objective laws or regularities which (Venn, *Principles*, 22.29–30)

77.26 would be] L; would of course be (Venn, *Principles*, 16.18)

77.27 our] L; one (Venn, *Principles*, 16.19)

78.14 that considerable] L; that a considerable (Venn, *Principles*, 5.38)

81.8 The starting point] L; any such starting point (Venn, *Principles*, 115.26–27)

110.1–2 poetry our race,] P1; poetry, where it is worthy of its high destinies, our race, (Arnold, "Introduction," xvii.1–2)

110.14 passes for religion] P1; passes with us for religion (Arnold, "Introduction," xviii.5–6)

110.18–19 Our relations all an inquiry and a doubt] P1; Our whole relations to the Universe and to our fellow-man have become an Inquiry, a Doubt (Carlyle, *Essays*, 17.27–29)

111.13 all else is] P1; the rest is a world of (Arnold, "Introduction," xvii.9)

111.13 For poetry the idea is] P1; Poetry attaches its emotion to the idea; the idea *is* (Arnold, "Introduction," xvii.10–11)

112.12 reasoning] P1; reasonings (Arnold, "Introduction," xviii.14)

112.24 imagination is *believed*‸] P1; Imagination, were it but momentarily, is *believed*, (Carlyle, *Essays*, 56.27–28)

112.24–25 or even any] P1; or meaning in it, any (Carlyle, *Essays*, 56.28)

114.30 them] P1; these (Arnold, *Poems*, II, 219.10)

114.36 melancholy‸ long‸] P1; ~, ~, (Arnold, *Poems*, II, 109.5)

115.20 Who] P1; Which (Arnold, *Poems*, II, 95.16)
115.38 meets] P1; nears (Arnold, *Poems*, II, 101.12)
115.38 parts] P1; leaves (Arnold, *Poems*, II, 101.12)
116.9 on] P1; in (Arnold, *Poems*, II, 97.2)
116.10–11 thrown, / We mortal] P1; thrown, / Dotting the shoreless watery wild, / We mortals (Arnold, *Poems*, II, 97.3–5)
116.21 *one*] P1; *rom.* (Arnold, *Poems*, II, 248.12)
116.22 that] P1; this (Arnold, *Poems*, II, 248.13)
118.19 dwell,] P1; reign— (Arnold, *Poems*, II, 95.1)
120.18 No] P1; Nor (Browning, *Works*, IV, 217.14)
120.21–22 earth, / For ensphering] P1; earth for insphering (Browning, *Works*, VI, 120.7)
120.22 whole!] P1; ~? (Browning, *Works*, VI, 120.8)
120.26 the] P1; a (Browning, *Works*, VI, 140.5)
121.12 the] P1; a (Browning, *Works*, VII, 119.3)
121.16 master's] P1; Master's (Browning, *Works*, VII, 119.6)
121.30 is] P1; was (Browning, *Works*, V, 304.10)
121.32 lies] P1; lay (Browning, *Works*, V, 304.12)
165.34 life that] GT; life that has been, or is, or (as it would seem) that (Green, *Prolegomena*, 189.13–14)
168.18 man] GT; himself (Green, *Prolegomena*, 200.24)
168.27 definite] GT; divine (Green, *Prolegomena*, 192.7)
168.29 is only] GT; is in fact only (Green, *Prolegomena*, 192.18)
168.29–30 society, by means of which] GT; society, of which (Green, *Prolegomena*, 192.18)
168.33 perform] GT; fulfil (Green, *Prolegomena*, 192.22)
168.35 this duty] GT; those duties (Green, *Prolegomena*, 192.23)
168.36 interest] GT; interests (Green, *Prolegomena*, 192.25)
174.22 realise] R; are persuaded (Renan, *Future of Science*, 169.17)
174.22 consciousness is evolved—that] R; *conscience* evolves itself, vague, feeble, non-centralized at first, in the individual as well as in aggregate humanity, that (Renan, *Future of Science*, 169.18–20)
174.25–175.1 that of *being*;] R; the category of the "*being*"; (Renan, *Future of Science*, 169.27–28)
175.1 conceived] R; considered (Renan, *Future of Science*, 169.30–31)
175.1–2 'being,' as an accomplished fact;] R; "being" (an accomplished fact); (Renan, *Future of Science*, 169.31)
175.4 conceived] R; considered (Renan, *Future of Science*, 169.34)
175.4 *formation*] R; *rom.* (Renan, *Future of Science*, 169.34)

175.31 is parallel] R; is exactly parallel (Renan, *Future of Science*, 153.5)

175.39–176.1 the facts which interested the mind at its first awakening, the influences that affected it, the laws that governed it.] R; of facts of the human intellect at its first awakening, the influences by which it was governed at first, the laws that governed its first manifestations. (Renan, *Future of Science*, 156.1–4)

176.23–24 true heroes] R; heroes (Renan, *Future of Science*, 219.30)

176.25 able to] R; able at the same time to resist all anticipated thought and to (Renan, *Future of Science*, 219.31–32)

176.26–27 instead of] R; far from (Renan, *Future of Science*, 222.25)

176.29–30 for constructions] R; for its constructions (Renan, *Future of Science*, 222.29)

176.31–35 great present obstacle is the dispersion of work, the self-isolation among special studies‸ which renders the labors of the philologist available only to himself and a small number engaged in the same subject] R; great obstacle which checks the progress of philological studies seems to me to lie in that dispersion of work, in that self-isolation among special studies, which render the labours of the philologist only available to himself and to a small number of friends who are engaged upon the same subject (Renan, *Future of Science*, 231.13–18)

177.24–25 which had] R; which with me had (Renan, *Future of Science*, v.13)

177.25 replaced the shattered] R; replaced shattered (Renan, *Future of Science*, v.13)

177.32 to any] R; of a small amount of (Renan, *Future of Science*, vi.20)

177.33 amount] R; quantity (Renan, *Future of Science*, vi.21)

177.33 requires for its extraction] R; is extracted from (Renan, *Future of Science*, vi.21)

177.34 dead] R; spoiled (Renan, *Future of Science*, vi.22)

178.32 that] R; who (Renan, *Future of Science*, 180.29)

178.34 he;] R; ~, (Renan, *Future of Science*, 180.31)

178.35 that] R; who (Renan, *Future of Science*, 180.33)

179.2 broaden] R; widen (Renan, *Future of Science*, 313.37)

179.5–6 masses—their] R; masses; that is to say their (Renan, *Future of Science*, 317.3)

184.9 all things 'can be ours'] CK; "all things can be ours," (Caird, *Critical Philosophy*, II, 628.12)

184.12 of freedom lies] CK; of the freedom or self-determining power, which we recognise in the self, lies (Caird, *Critical Philosophy*, II, 629.2–3)

184.13 self with] CK; self as such with (Caird, *Critical Philosophy*, II, 629.3–4)

188.14–15 ‸God as . . . really is.‸] SH; "God as the self-conscious Reason of all that really is." (Sterrett, *Hegel's Philosophy of Religion*, 14.6–7)

189.11 "Introduction"] SH; Hegel's Introduction to His Philosophy of Religion (Sterrett, *Hegel's Philosophy of Religion*, 38)

189.12 "Vital Idea of Religion,"] SH; The Vital Idea (Begriff) of Religion (Sterrett, *Hegel's Philosophy of Religion*, 61)

189.12–13 "Classification of the Pre-Christian Religions,"] SH; Classification of the Positive (Pre-Christian) Religions (Sterrett, *Hegel's Philosophy of Religion*, 233)

189.13–14 "Christianity as the Absolute Religion."] SH; The Absolute Religion (Sterrett, *Hegel's Philosophy of Religion*, 268)

250.18 pain and pleasure] OE; pleasures and pains (Barratt, *Physical Ethics*, 71.9)

251.2 pursuits] OE; pursuit (Bain, *Moral Science*, 27.25)

251.5 The principle is not susceptible of direct proofs for] OE; Is it susceptible of any direct proof? It should seem not: for (Bentham, *Works*, I, 2:2.24–26)

251.37 desirable and] OE; desirable (unless for the sake of its consequences), and (Mill, *Dissertations*, III, 354.30–31)

254.24 man that he] OE; man in his actual state that he (Green, *Prolegomena*, 167.23)

254.24–25 in the attainment of] OE; in attaining (Green, *Prolegomena*, 167.24)

254.25 *because he has desired them*] OE; *rom.* (Green, *Prolegomena*, 167.24)

259.32 regarded] OE; taken (Aristotle, *Ethics*, 38.19)

259.32 *test* of *character*] OE; test of the formed habit or character (Aristotle, *Ethics*, 38.19)

259.33 his] OE; the (Aristotle, *Ethics*, 38.21)

259.35 from youth] OE; from his youth (Aristotle, *Ethics*, 38.30)

259.36 *in the right objects*] OE; *rom.* (Aristotle, *Ethics*, 38.31)

265.32 During the whole] OE; namely, the whole (Mill, *Dissertations*, III, 332.10)

265.33 the species] OE; the human species (Mill, *Dissertations*, III, 332.11)

265.36 belief] OE; beliefs (Mill, *Dissertations*, III, 332.32)
268.9 qualitatively] OE; quantitatively (Sidgwick, *Methods of Ethics*, 382.12)
268.10 quality] OE; quantity (Sidgwick, *Methods of Ethics*, 382.13)
268.11 to] OE; of (Sidgwick, *Methods of Ethics*, 382.14)
268.11 the] OE; this (Sidgwick, *Methods of Ethics*, 382.15)
268.12 ethical] OE; ideal (Sidgwick, *Methods of Ethics*, 382.16)
268.35 the] OE; then (Green, *Prolegomena*, 236.19)
270.1–2 *but the objects of the man's chief interests supply the filling of that ideal state*] OE; *rom.* (Green, *Prolegomena*, 244.8–9)
270.11 unless] OE; till (Alexander, *Moral Order*, 209.18)
270.17 simply, when we] OE; simply, since acts depend on character, when we (Alexander, *Moral Order*, 209.25–26)
270.18 then] OE; can (Alexander, *Moral Order*, 209.28)
270.39 astute‸] OE; acute, (Abbott, *Kant's Critique*, 109.13)
271.4 one] OE; him (Abbott, *Kant's Critique*, 110.15)
271.6 For] OE; Just (Abbott, *Kant's Critique*, 110.17)
271.31 person] OE; human being (Mill, *Dissertations*, III, 311.15)
271.36 be a Socrates] OE; be Socrates (Mill, *Dissertations*, III, 312.31)
274.5 there] OE; In this manner, then (Abbott, *Kant's Critique*, 116.7)
274.26 *on the whole*] OE; *rom.* (Sidgwick, *Methods of Ethics*, 379.16)
274.35 interests] OE; interest (Bain, *Emotions*, 303.4)
275.7 *self-evident principle*] OE; *rom.* (Sidgwick, *Methods of Ethics*, 355.23)
275.9–10 *so far as it is cognizable by direct intuition*] OE; *rom.* (Sidgwick, *Methods of Ethics*, 355.33)
275.12–13 *the principles, so far as they are immediately known by abstract intuition*] OE; these principles themselves so far as they are immediately known by abstract intuition (Sidgwick, *Methods of Ethics*, 364.1–2)
277.23 choose] OE; chance (Bentham, *Works*, I, 143:2.57)
277.30 and] OE; or (Bentham, *Works*, I, 144:1.7)
278.20–21 or the interest] OE; or (as, speaking practically, it may be called) the interest (Mill, *Dissertations*, III, 323.24–25)
280.40–281.1 preëmi-|nently] OE; eminently (Mill, *Dissertations*, III, 154.15–16)
281.1 products] OE; product (Mill, *Dissertations*, III, 154.16)
281.4 feeling] OE; feelings (Mill, *Dissertations*, III, 154.19–20)

281.21 *natural*] OE; *rom.* (Mill, *Dissertations*, III, 343.17)

281.23–26 *The social state is at once so natural, so necessary, and so habitual to man*^ *that except in some unusual circumstances, or by an effort of voluntary abstraction*^ *he never conceives of himself otherwise than as a member of a body.*] OE; The social state is at once so natural, so necessary, and so habitual to man, that except in some unusual circumstances, or by an effort of voluntary abstraction, he never conceives himself otherwise than as a member of a body; (Mill, *Dissertations*, III, 343.26–30)

281.36–39 *The deeply-rooted conception which every individual even now has of himself as a social being tends to make him feel it as one of his natural wants, that there should be harmony between his feelings and aims and those of his fellow-creatures.*] OE; The deeply rooted conception which every individual even now has of himself as a social being tends to make him feel it one of his natural wants, that there should be harmony between his feelings and aims and those of his fellow-creatures. (Mill, *Dissertations*, III, 347.2–7)

283.29 rules] OE; modes (Spencer, *Data of Ethics*, 57.24)

283.30 rules] OE; modes (Spencer, *Data of Ethics*, 57.24)

283.32–33 *deduce, from the laws of life and the conditions of existence*] OE; *rom.* (Spencer, *Data of Ethics*, 57.27)

283.34 *necessarily*] OE; *rom.* (Spencer, *Data of Ethics*, 57.28)

284.1 utility] OE; Morality (Spencer, *Data of Ethics*, 58.4)

284.18 *immediate*] OE; *rom.* (Spencer, *Data of Ethics*, 162.23–24)

285.4 corresponding] OE; responding (Spencer, *Data of Ethics*, 123.34)

285.30 be pursued] OE; be spontaneously pursued (Spencer, *Data of Ethics*, 250.8–9)

285.32 may] OE; will (Spencer, *Data of Ethics*, 250.15)

287.4 a] OE; the (Spencer, *Data of Ethics*, 275.24)

287.6 being so] OE; being may be conceived as so (Spencer, *Data of Ethics*, 275.9)

287.9 whom there is a] OE; whom this process has gone so far as to produce a (Spencer, *Data of Ethics*, 275.18–19)

287.12–13 *in terms of the conditions which his nature fulfill*] OE; in terms of the conditions which his nature fulfils (Spencer, *Data of Ethics*, 279.22–23)

287.14 the] OE; those (Spencer, *Data of Ethics*, 279.24)

287.14 requisites] OE; requirements (Spencer, *Data of Ethics*, 279.24)

288.12 living] OE; life (Spencer, *Data of Ethics*, 74.2)
288.25 state‸ there will be recognition] OE; state, will go recognition (Spencer, *Data of Ethics*, 99.31)
288.26 truth] OE; truths (Spencer, *Data of Ethics*, 99.31)
288.39 definition] OE; definitions (Spencer, *Data of Ethics*, 137.9)
289.19 dislike, through sense] OE; dislike‸ from a sense (Spencer, *Data of Ethics*, 184.10)
290.22 or out] OE; or even out (Abbott, *Kant's Critique*, 9.1)
290.27 which shines] OE; it would still shine (Abbott, *Kant's Critique*, 10.18–19)
290.28 having] OE; as a thing which has (Abbott, *Kant's Critique*, 10.10)
292.10 must] OE; necessarily (Abbott, *Kant's Critique*, 41.6)
296.21 conflict] OE; collision (Caird, *Critical Philosophy*, II, 189.8)
296.26 a whole] OE; the whole (Caird, *Critical Philosophy*, II, 189.14)
298.41–299.1 person of] OE; persons of (Caird, *Critical Philosophy*, II, 219.32)
299.25 conceives of himself only] OE; conceives himself otherwise than (Mill, *Dissertations*, III, 343.29)
309.3 for] OE; to (Hinton, *Law-Breaker*, 287.32)
309.4–5 *others* that we need] OE; others we need (Hinton, *Law-Breaker*, 288.2–3)
326.3 wrongfully] OE; wrongly (Aristotle, *Ethics*, 46.6)
326.3 *times*] OE; *rom.* (Aristotle, *Ethics*, 46.7)
326.4 *occasions*] OE; *rom.* (Aristotle, *Ethics*, 46.7)
326.4 *persons*] OE; *rom.* (Aristotle, *Ethics*, 46.8)
326.5 *object*] OE; *rom.* (Aristotle, *Ethics*, 46.8)
326.5 *fashions*] OE; fashion (Aristotle, *Ethics*, 46.9)
329.16–17 avoidance of certain acts and dread] OE; avoidance and dread (Bain, *Emotions*, 529.1)
329.25–26 *fac simile*] OE; facsimile (Bain, *Emotions*, 313.35)
329.26 government around] OE; government as practised around (Bain, *Emotions*, 313.35–36)
329.31 motive] OE; motives (Bain, *Emotions*, 318.24)
329.33 changed] OE; transformed (Bain, *Emotions*, 318.26)
329.36 obligation] OE; obedience (Bain, *Emotions*, 319.n8)
330.26 legal penalty, supernatural punishment and social reprobation] OE; legal punishment, or divine vengeance, or public reprobation (Spencer, *Data of Ethics*, 115.1–2)
345.14–15 If conscience had might as it has right, it would rule the world] OE; Had it strength, as it has right, had it power,

as it has manifest authority, it would absolutely govern the world (Butler, *Fifteen Sermons*, 55.22–24)

365.6 that] OE; which (Green, *Prolegomena*, 270.19)

365.6 the good] OE; the true good (Green, *Prolegomena*, 270.20)

365.7 been blindly] OE; been more blindly (Green, *Prolegomena*, 270.21)

Word-division list

Word-division at the end of a line in the copy-texts may present something of a problem for editorial decision whether Dewey's own general custom (insofar as it coincides with the style of the copy-texts themselves) requires certain words to be treated as hyphenated or as unhyphenated compounds. The editors have decided the form of clear-cut cases silently. However, all doubtful examples, or examples that need emphasis, have been listed here, according to the formula

242.14 *im*-moral

The reader should observe that in the present edition (W), all end-of-the-line hyphenations are the modern printer's unless specific record is made of those hyphenated compounds within the line in the copy-texts that are ambiguously broken and hyphenated at the end of the line by W, which are recorded as in the formula

33.39 every-|day every-day G

1. Compounds, or possible compounds, broken at the end of the line in the copy-texts occurring internally in W:

5.25 world-inhabited
11.35 class-room
20.29 English-speaking
21.32 roundabout
22.36 piecemeal
36.8 standpoint
38.35 many-sided
65.23 thing-in-itself
66.7 thing-in-itself
67.12 space-*cadres*
67.29 thing-in-itself
74.1 thing-in-itself
81.30 starting-point
83.8 ready-made
87.3 ready-made
91.25 psycho-physical

92.7 Half-year
94.12 battle-field
96.34 once-moving
101.25 well-nigh
104.30 interwoven
136.40 sense-manifold
147.8 text-book
185.13 under-graduates
191.13 well-condensed
194.1 to-day
203.24 life-blood
204.22 superimpos-|ing
204.24 substratum
212.33 reflex-arc
219.18 psycho-physical
232.25 subject-matter
242.14 *im*-moral
255.40 all-inclusive
257.40 non-action
272.30 anti-he-|donist
281.39 *fellow-creatures*
301.4 fitting-in
303.12 make-up
306.17 non-moral
315.18 non-social
335.8 two-fold

II. Compounds, or possible compounds, that are broken and hyphenated at the end of the line in W but appear as hyphenated compounds within the line in the copy-texts:

33.39 every-|day] every-day G
40.28 ever-|changing] ever-changing F
67.n13 *Ding-an-|sich*] *Ding-an-sich* CS
71.8 *Ding-an-|sich*] *Ding-an-sich* CS
73.4 *Ding-an-|sich*] *Ding-an-sich* CS
88.16 two-|edged] two-edged LV
91.19 half-|year] half-year PM
97.26 subject-|matter] subject-matter MT
98.9 sure-|footedness] sure-footedness MT
113.4 will-o'-the-|wisp] will-o'-the-wisp P1
138.29 subject-|matter] subject-matter LT
139.n6 thought-|relations] thought-relations LT
143.17 *im*-|plied] *im*-plied CP

154.8 thought-|speculators] thought-speculators SS
182.5 subject-|matter] subject-matter CK
227.27 non-|being] non-being PS
253.39 sweet-|meats] sweet-meats OE
254.3 sweet-|meats] sweat-meats OE
283.27 so-|called] so-called OE
323.3 thorough-|going] thor-|ough-going OE
325.2 far-|away] far-away OE
337.15 non-|moral] non-moral OE
365.26 Over-|conscientiousness] Over-conscien-|tiousness OE
388.31 inter-|connected] inter-connected OE

III. Compounds, or possible compounds, broken at the end of the line in the copy-texts and in W:

48.4 stand-|point
128.28 super-|structure
212.16 reflex-|arc
212.35 reflex-|arc
215.16 stand-|point
367.30 cross-|questioning

Index

Index